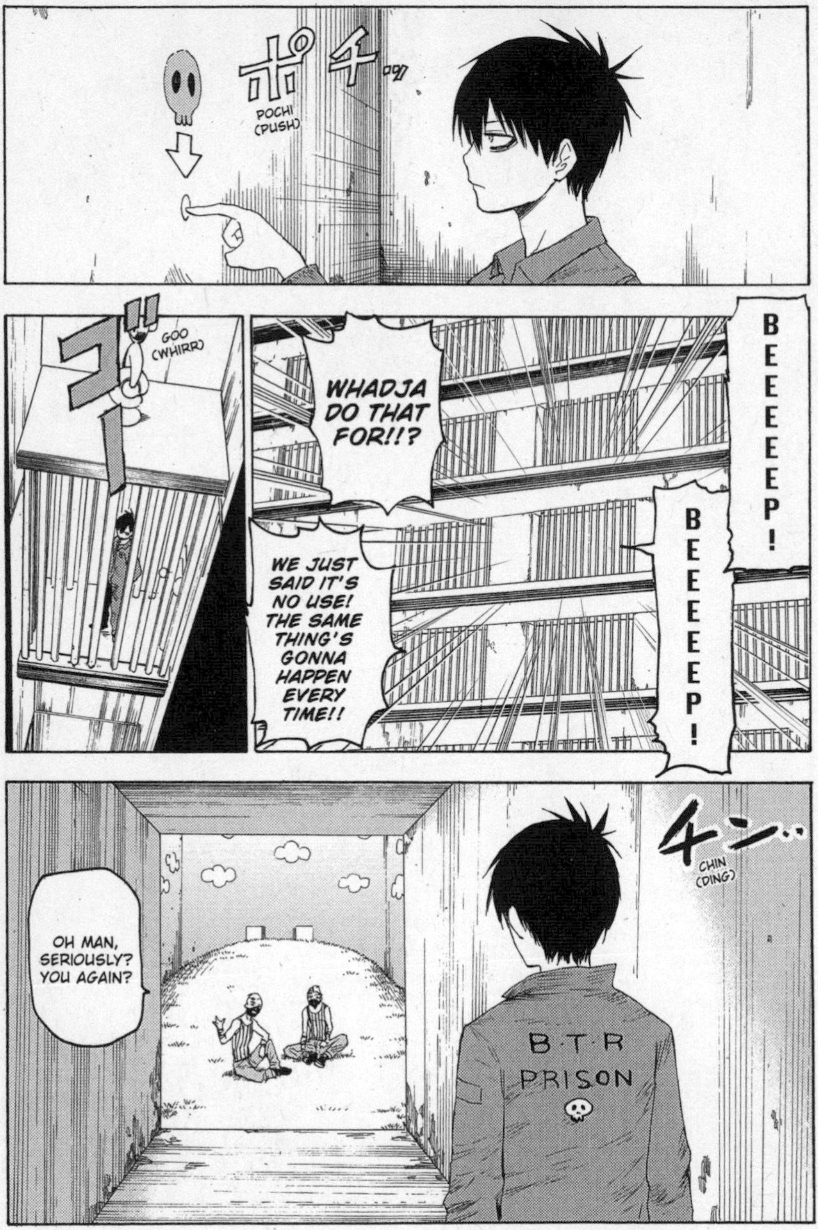
ポチッ
POCHI (PUSH)
BEEEEEEP!
BEEEEEEP!
WHADJA DO THAT FOR!!?
WE JUST SAID IT'S NO USE! THE SAME THING'S GONNA HAPPEN EVERY TIME!!
GOO (WHIRR)
チン…
CHIN (DING)
OH MAN, SERIOUSLY? YOU AGAIN?
B·T·R PRISON

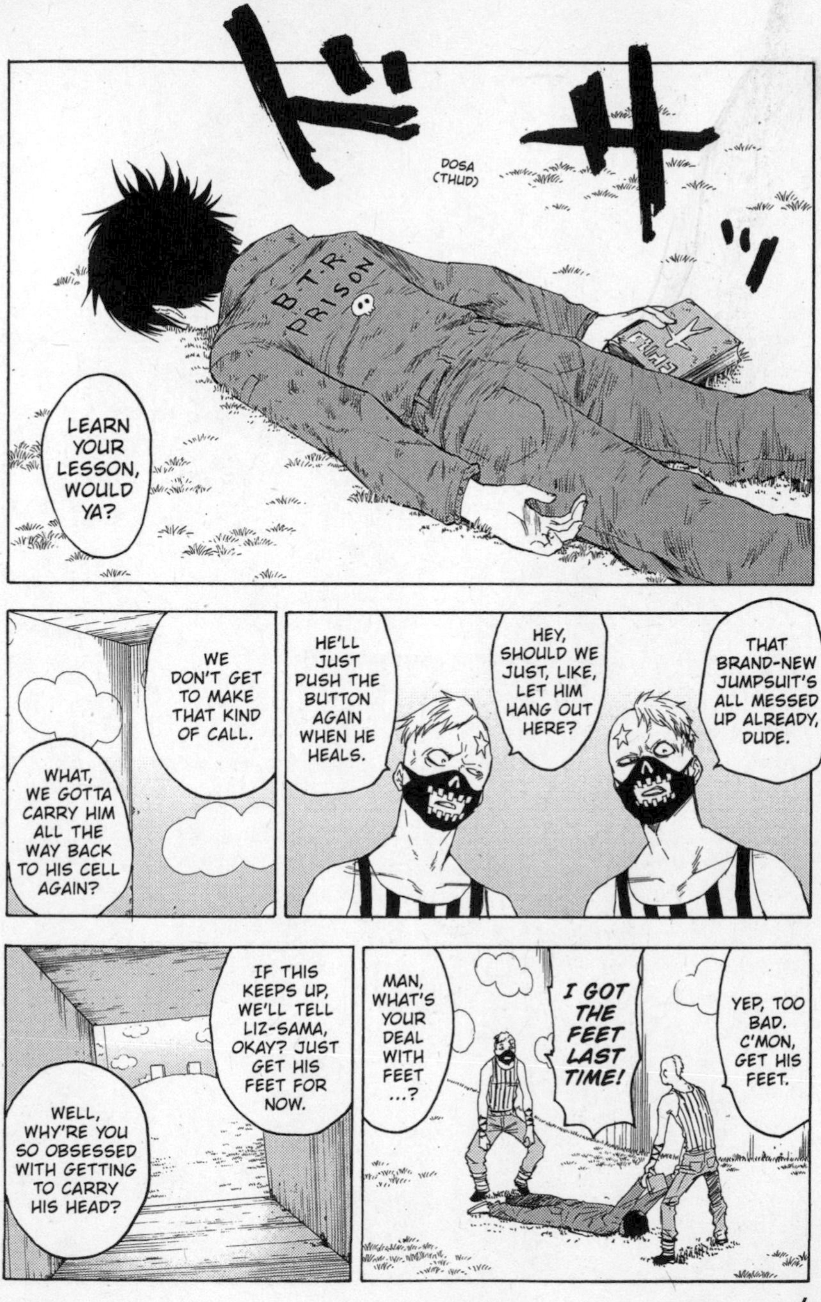
ドサッ
DOSA (THUD)
B.T.R. PRISON
LEARN YOUR LESSON, WOULD YA?
THAT BRAND-NEW JUMPSUIT'S ALL MESSED UP ALREADY, DUDE.
HEY, SHOULD WE JUST, LIKE, LET HIM HANG OUT HERE?
HE'LL JUST PUSH THE BUTTON AGAIN WHEN HE HEALS.
WE DON'T GET TO MAKE THAT KIND OF CALL.
WHAT, WE GOTTA CARRY HIM ALL THE WAY BACK TO HIS CELL AGAIN?
YEP, TOO BAD. C'MON, GET HIS FEET.
I GOT THE FEET LAST TIME!
MAN, WHAT'S YOUR DEAL WITH FEET ...?
IF THIS KEEPS UP, WE'LL TELL LIZ-SAMA, OKAY? JUST GET HIS FEET FOR NOW.
WELL, WHY'RE YOU SO OBSESSED WITH GETTING TO CARRY HIS HEAD?

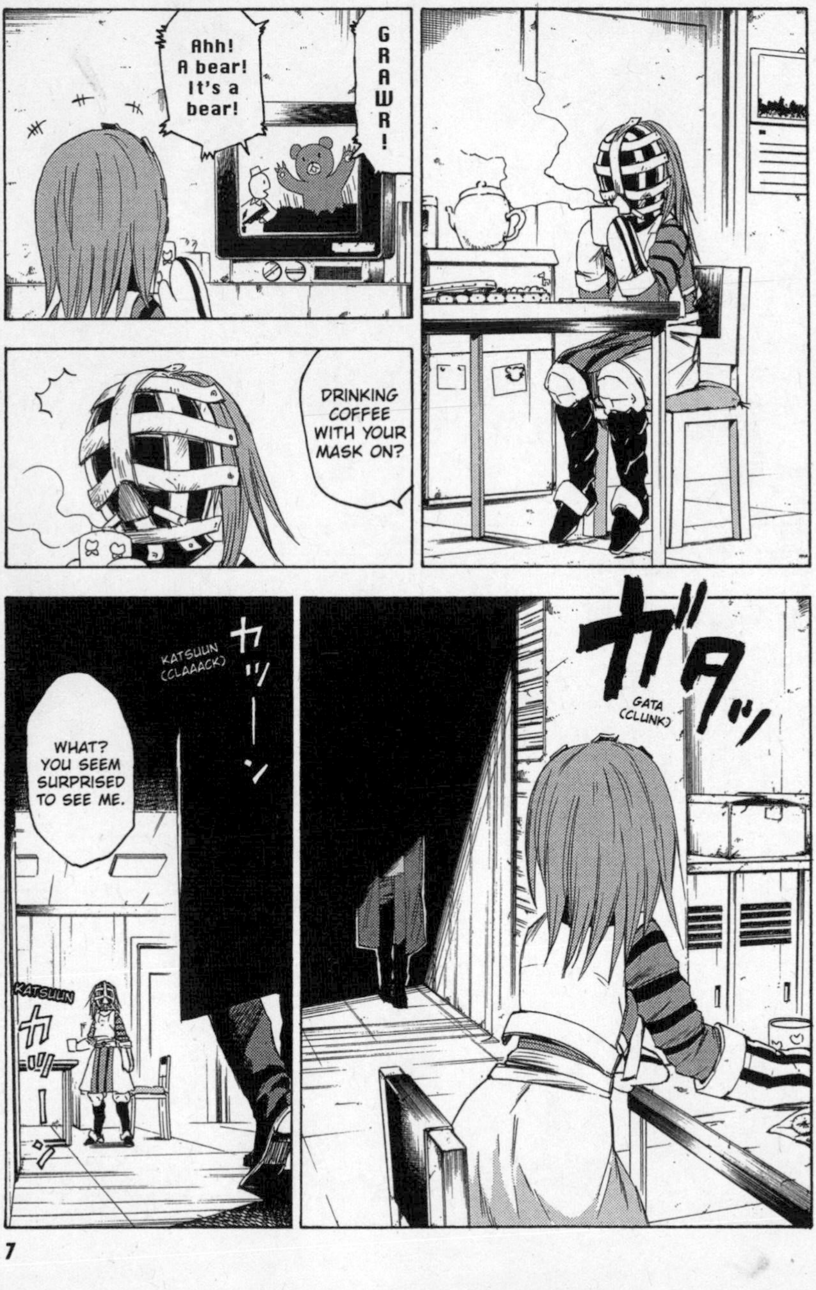

Ahh! A bear! It's a bear!
GRAWR!
DRINKING COFFEE WITH YOUR MASK ON?
ガタッ
GATA (CLUNK)
カツーン
KATSUUN (CLAAACK)
WHAT? YOU SEEM SURPRISED TO SEE ME.
KATSUUN

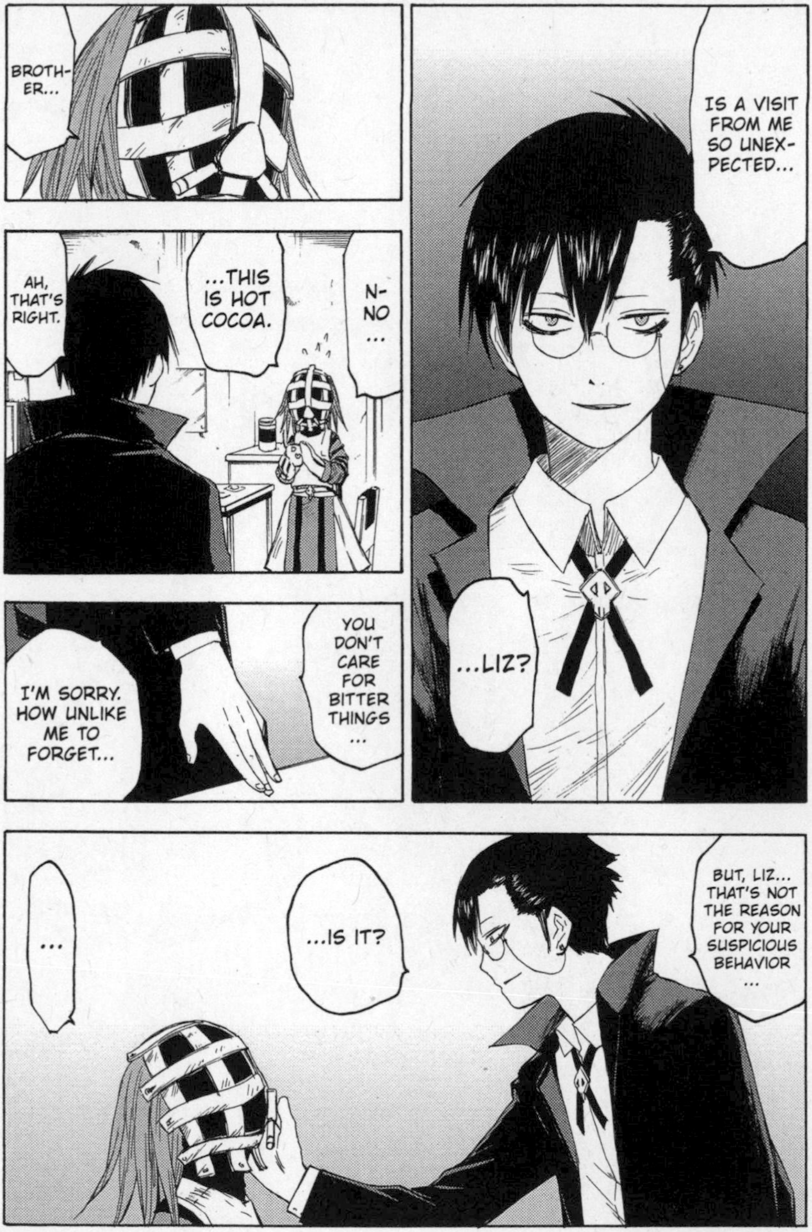
IS A VISIT FROM ME SO UNEXPECTED...
...LIZ?
BROTHER-ER...
N-NO...
...THIS IS HOT COCOA.
AH, THAT'S RIGHT.
YOU DON'T CARE FOR BITTER THINGS...
I'M SORRY. HOW UNLIKE ME TO FORGET...
BUT, LIZ... THAT'S NOT THE REASON FOR YOUR SUSPICIOUS BEHAVIOR...
...IS IT?
...

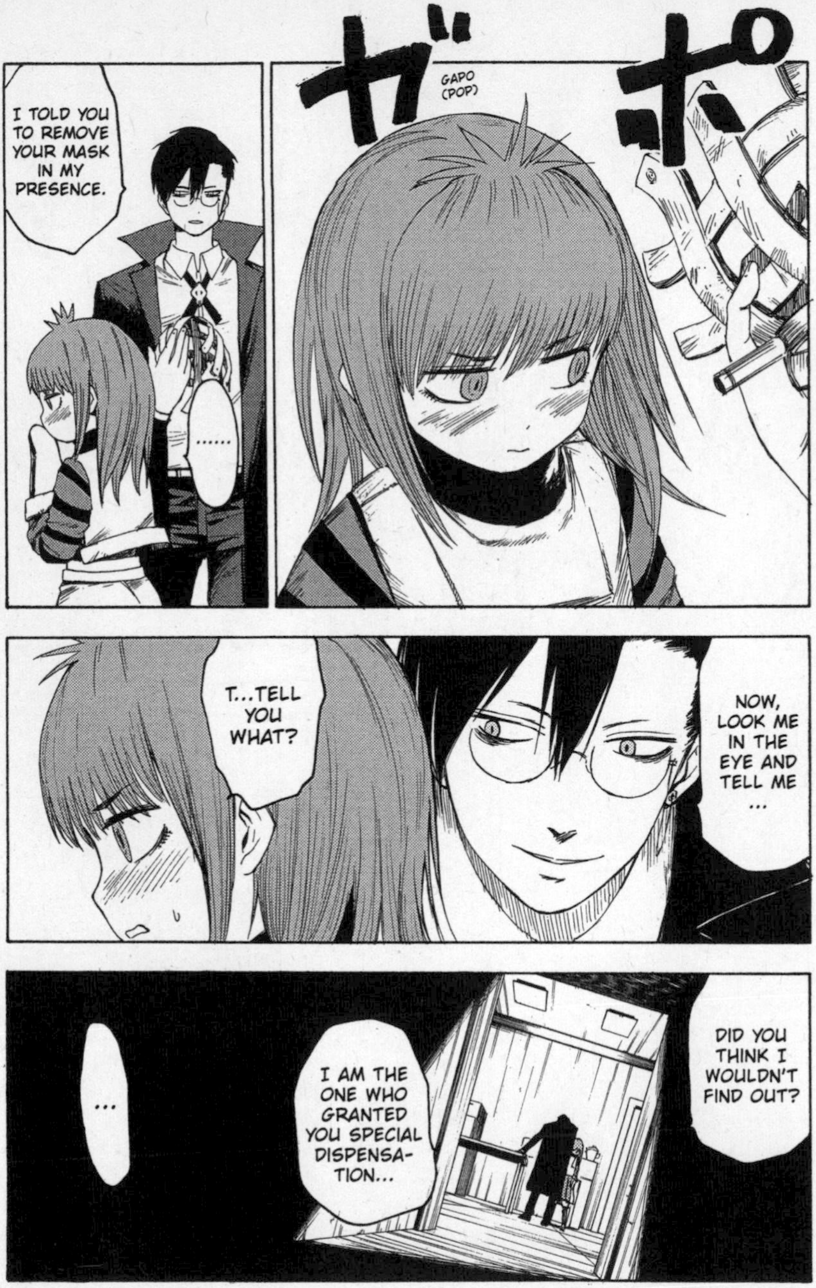
ガポ
GAPO (POP)
I TOLD YOU TO REMOVE YOUR MASK IN MY PRESENCE.
......
NOW, LOOK ME IN THE EYE AND TELL ME ...
T...TELL YOU WHAT?
DID YOU THINK I WOULDN'T FIND OUT?
I AM THE ONE WHO GRANTED YOU SPECIAL DISPENSA-TION...
...

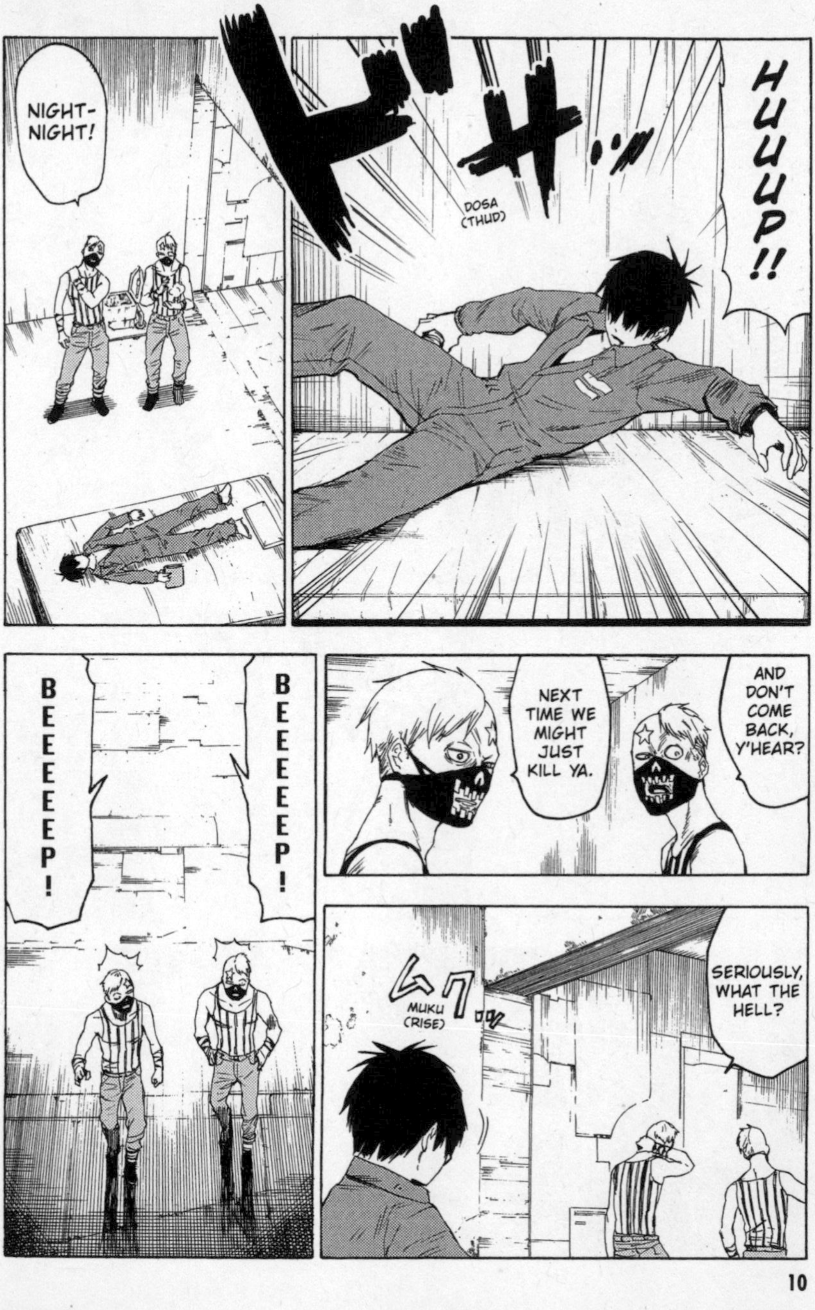
HUUUUP!!
DOSA (THUD)
NIGHT-NIGHT!
AND DON'T COME BACK, Y'HEAR?
NEXT TIME WE MIGHT JUST KILL YA.
SERIOUSLY, WHAT THE HELL?
MUKU (RISE)
BEEEEEEP!
BEEEEEEP!

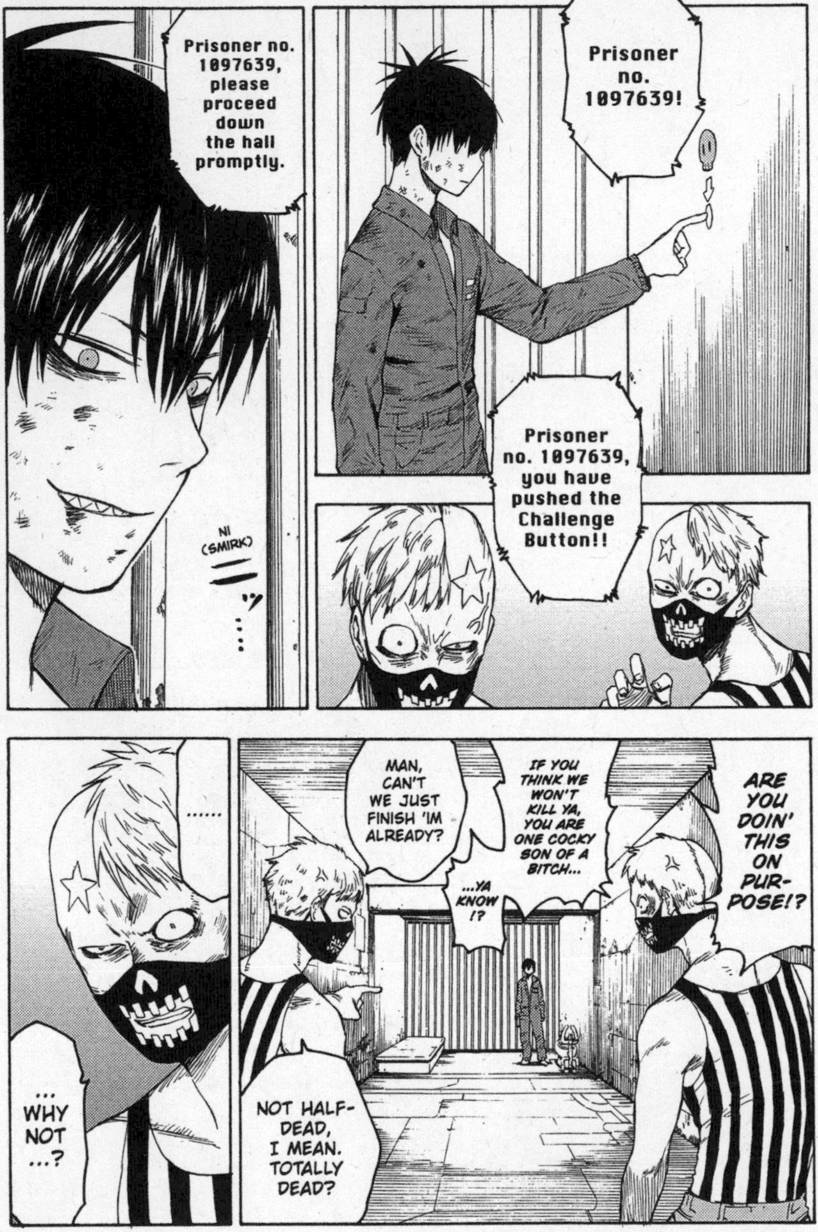

Prisoner no. 1097639!
Prisoner no. 1097639, you have pushed the Challenge Button!!
Prisoner no. 1097639, please proceed down the hall promptly.
NI (SMIRK)
....
ARE YOU DOIN' THIS ON PURPOSE!?
IF YOU THINK WE WON'T KILL YA, YOU ARE ONE COCKY SON OF A BITCH...
...YA KNOW!?
MAN, CAN'T WE JUST FINISH 'IM ALREADY?
NOT HALF-DEAD, I MEAN. TOTALLY DEAD?
......
...WHY NOT ...?

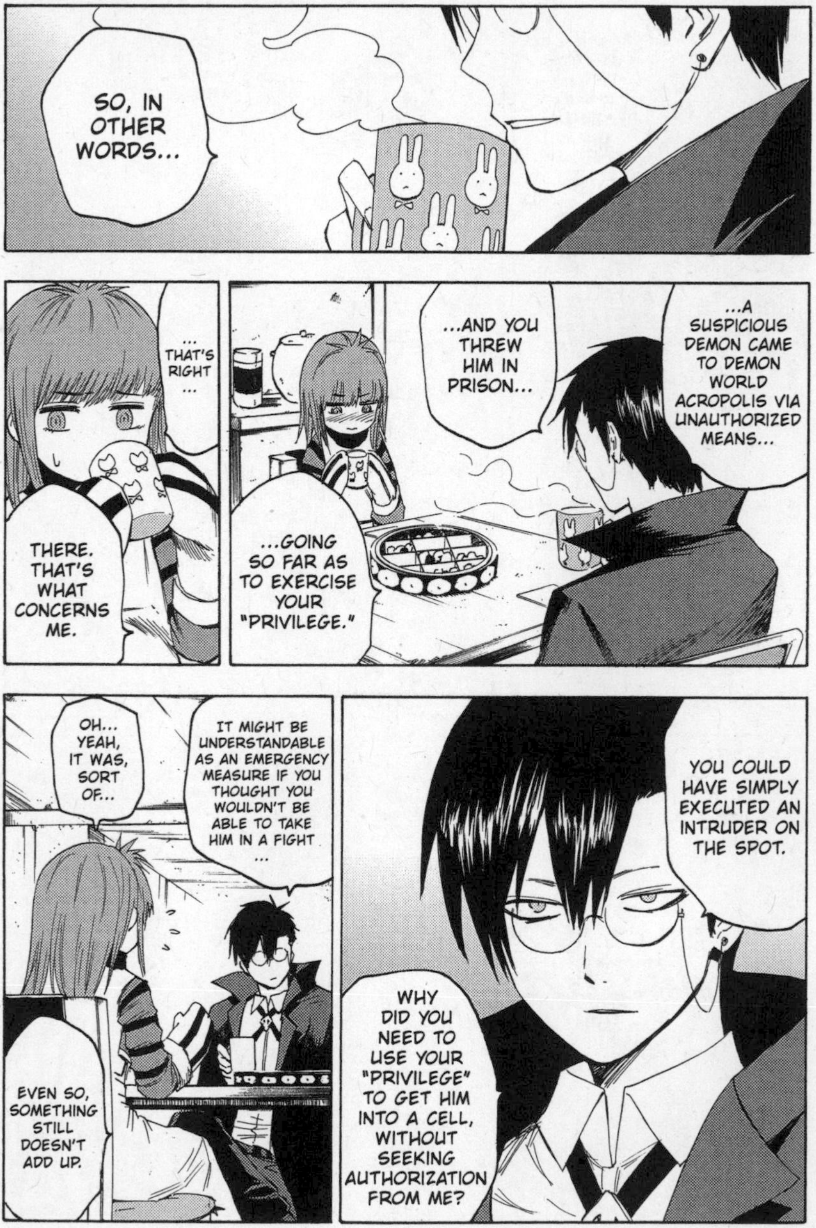
SO, IN OTHER WORDS...
...A SUSPICIOUS DEMON CAME TO DEMON WORLD ACROPOLIS VIA UNAUTHORIZED MEANS...
...AND YOU THREW HIM IN PRISON...
...GOING SO FAR AS TO EXERCISE YOUR "PRIVILEGE."
...THAT'S RIGHT...
THERE. THAT'S WHAT CONCERNS ME.
YOU COULD HAVE SIMPLY EXECUTED AN INTRUDER ON THE SPOT.
WHY DID YOU NEED TO USE YOUR "PRIVILEGE" TO GET HIM INTO A CELL, WITHOUT SEEKING AUTHORIZATION FROM ME?
IT MIGHT BE UNDERSTANDABLE AS AN EMERGENCY MEASURE IF YOU THOUGHT YOU WOULDN'T BE ABLE TO TAKE HIM IN A FIGHT...
OH... YEAH, IT WAS, SORT OF...
EVEN SO, SOMETHING STILL DOESN'T ADD UP.

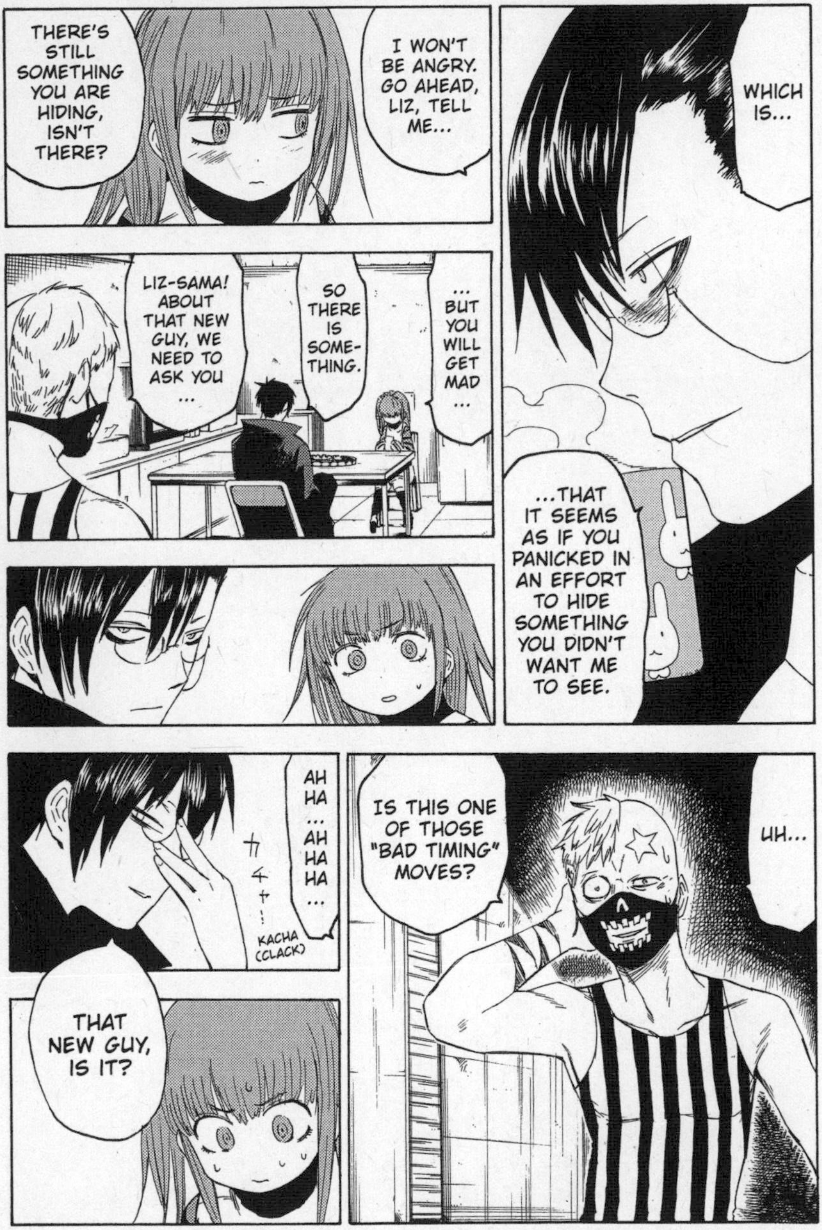
WHICH IS...
...THAT IT SEEMS AS IF YOU PANICKED IN AN EFFORT TO HIDE SOMETHING YOU DIDN'T WANT ME TO SEE.
I WON'T BE ANGRY. GO AHEAD, LIZ, TELL ME...
THERE'S STILL SOMETHING YOU ARE HIDING, ISN'T THERE?
... BUT YOU WILL GET MAD ...
SO THERE IS SOME-THING.
LIZ-SAMA! ABOUT THAT NEW GUY, WE NEED TO ASK YOU ...
UH...
IS THIS ONE OF THOSE "BAD TIMING" MOVES?
AH HA ... AH HA HA ...
カチャ!!
KACHA (CLACK)
THAT NEW GUY, IS IT?

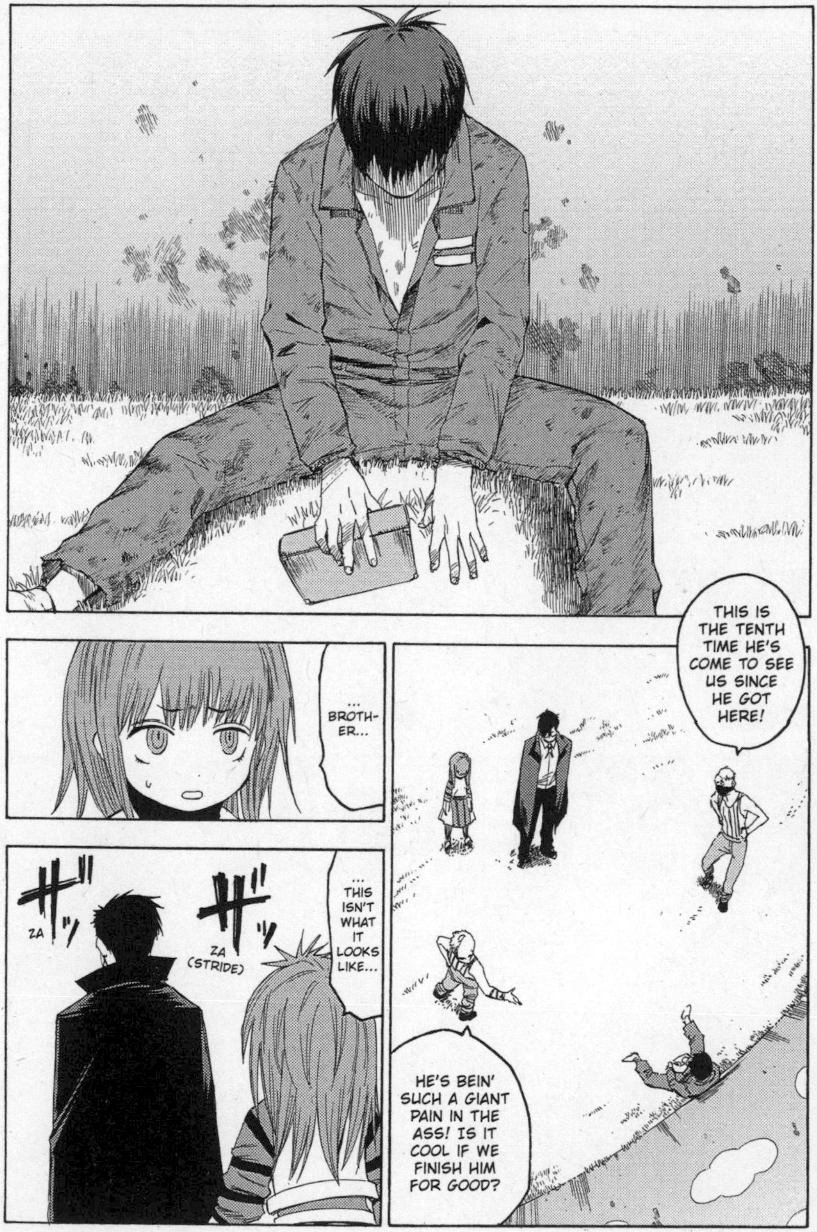
THIS IS THE TENTH TIME HE'S COME TO SEE US SINCE HE GOT HERE!
HE'S BEIN' SUCH A GIANT PAIN IN THE ASS! IS IT COOL IF WE FINISH HIM FOR GOOD?
...BROTHER-ER...
...THIS ISN'T WHAT IT LOOKS LIKE...
ザッ
ZA (STRIDE)
ザッ
ZA

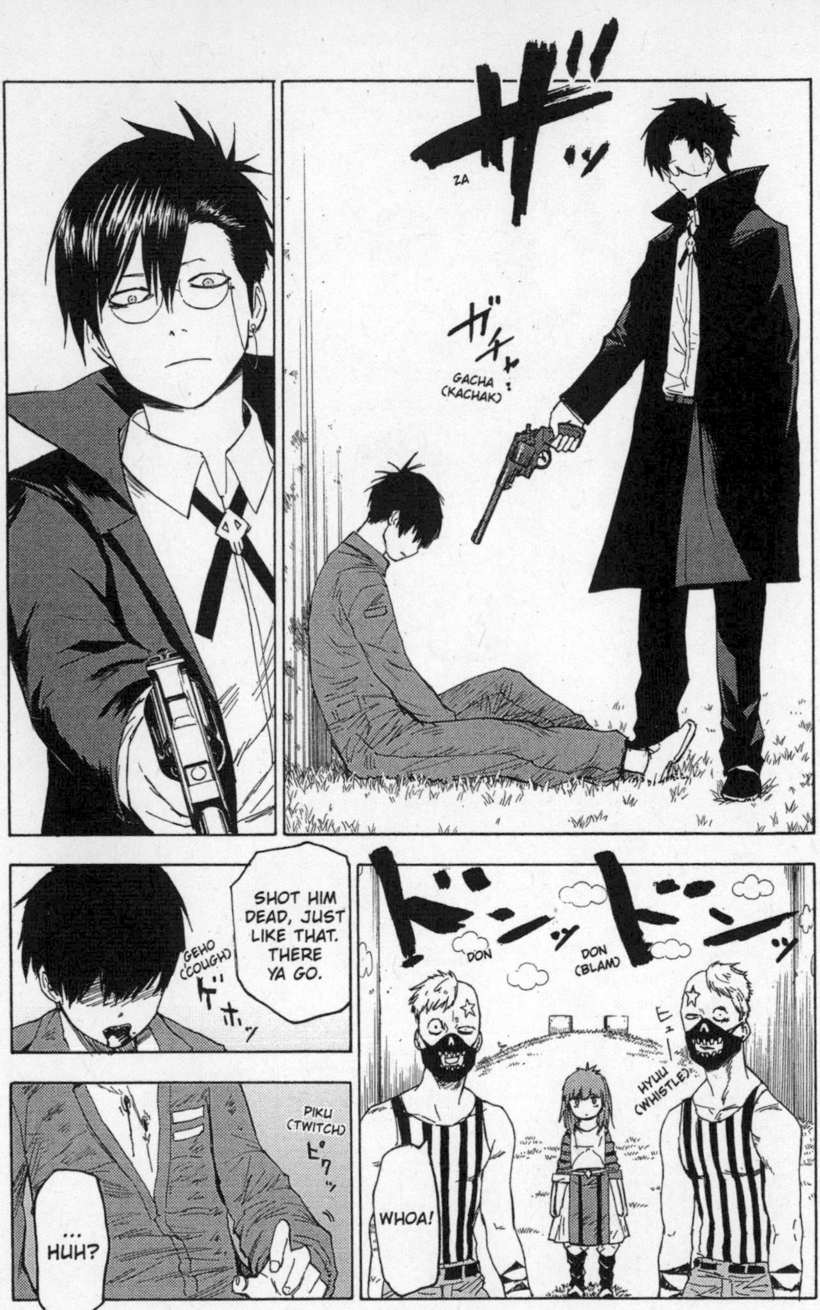

ZA
GACHA (KACHAK)
DON
DON (BLAM)
HYUU (WHISTLE)
WHOA!
SHOT HIM DEAD, JUST LIKE THAT. THERE YA GO.
GEHO (COUGH)
PIKU (TWITCH)
... HUH?

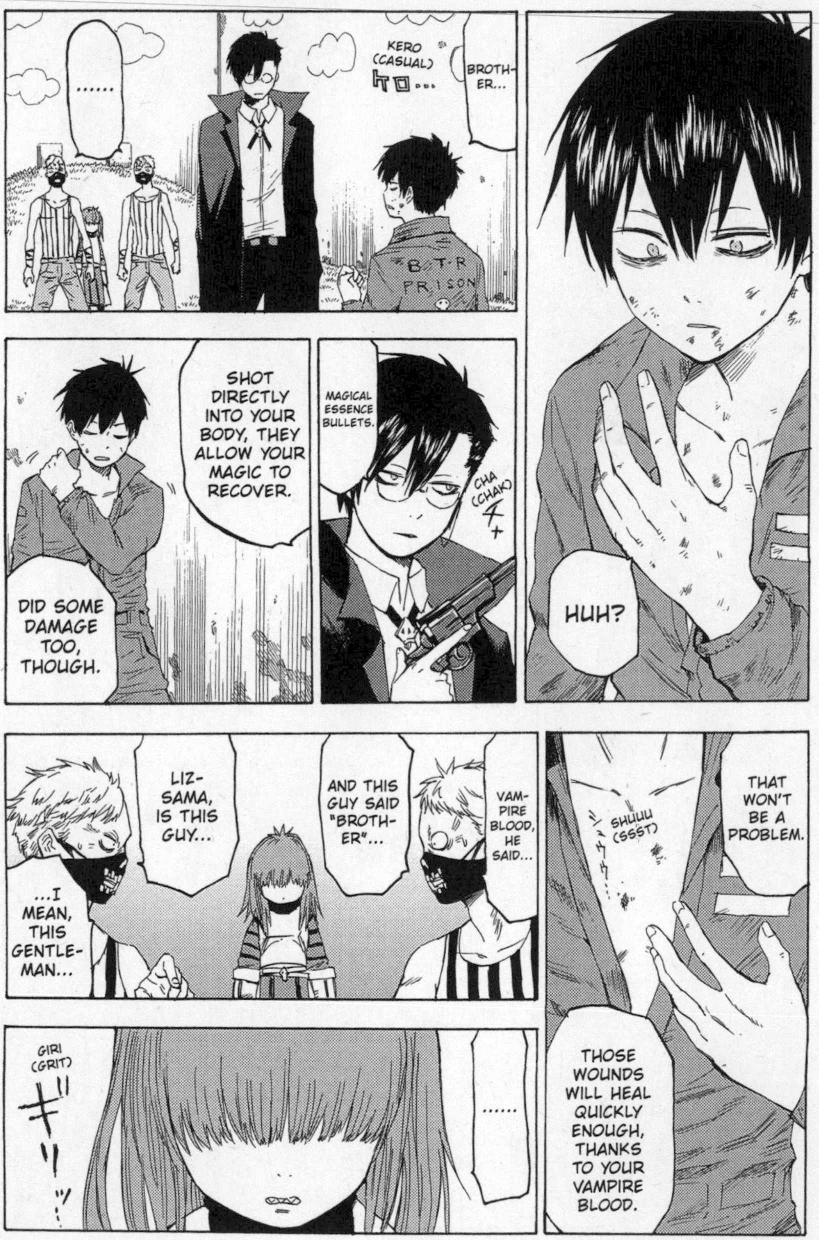
HUH?
BROTH-ER...
KERO (CASUAL)
ケロ...
......
MAGICAL ESSENCE BULLETS.
CHA (CHAK)
SHOT DIRECTLY INTO YOUR BODY, THEY ALLOW YOUR MAGIC TO RECOVER.
DID SOME DAMAGE TOO, THOUGH.
THAT WON'T BE A PROBLEM.
SHUUU (SSST)
THOSE WOUNDS WILL HEAL QUICKLY ENOUGH, THANKS TO YOUR VAMPIRE BLOOD.
VAM-PIRE BLOOD, HE SAID...
AND THIS GUY SAID "BROTH-ER"...
LIZ-SAMA, IS THIS GUY...
...I MEAN, THIS GENTLE-MAN...
......
GIRI (GRIT)

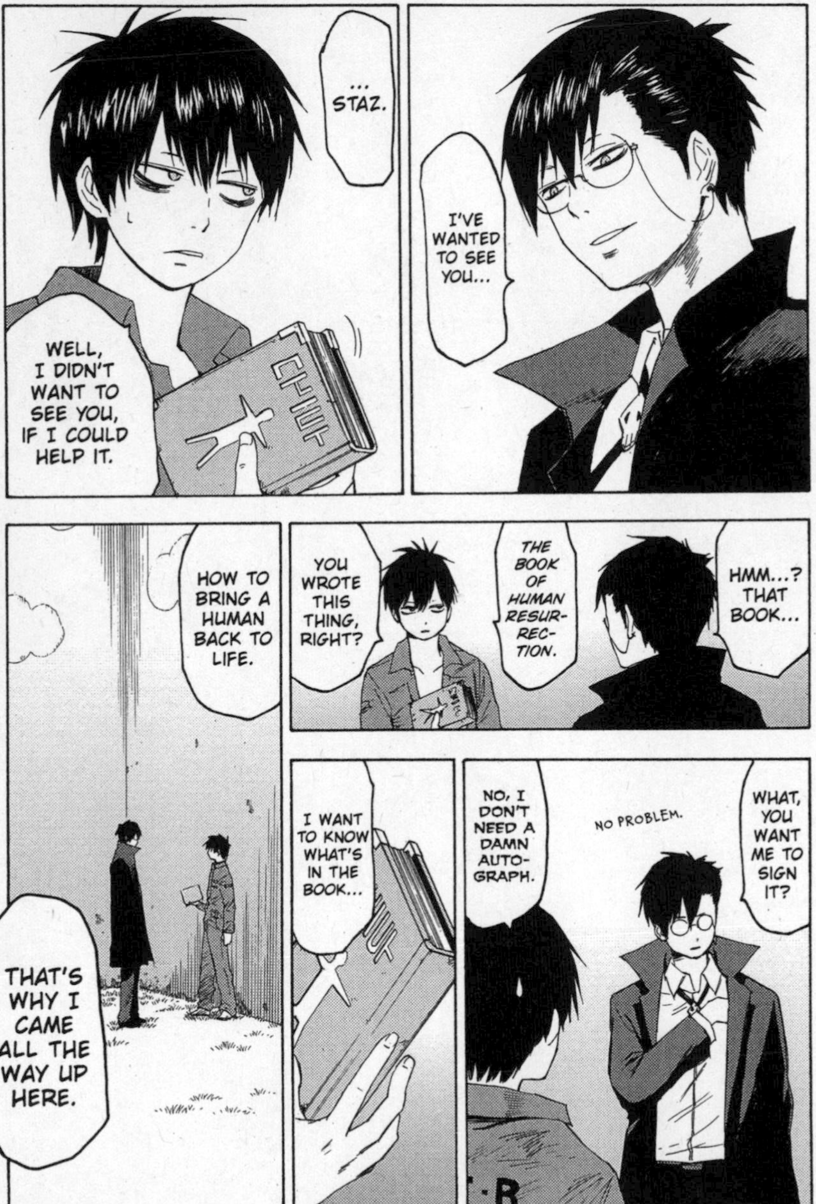
I'VE WANTED TO SEE YOU...
...STAZ.
WELL, I DIDN'T WANT TO SEE YOU, IF I COULD HELP IT.
HMM...? THAT BOOK...
THE BOOK OF HUMAN RESURRECTION.
YOU WROTE THIS THING, RIGHT?
WHAT, YOU WANT ME TO SIGN IT?
NO PROBLEM.
NO, I DON'T NEED A DAMN AUTOGRAPH.
I WANT TO KNOW WHAT'S IN THE BOOK...
HOW TO BRING A HUMAN BACK TO LIFE.
THAT'S WHY I CAME ALL THE WAY UP HERE.

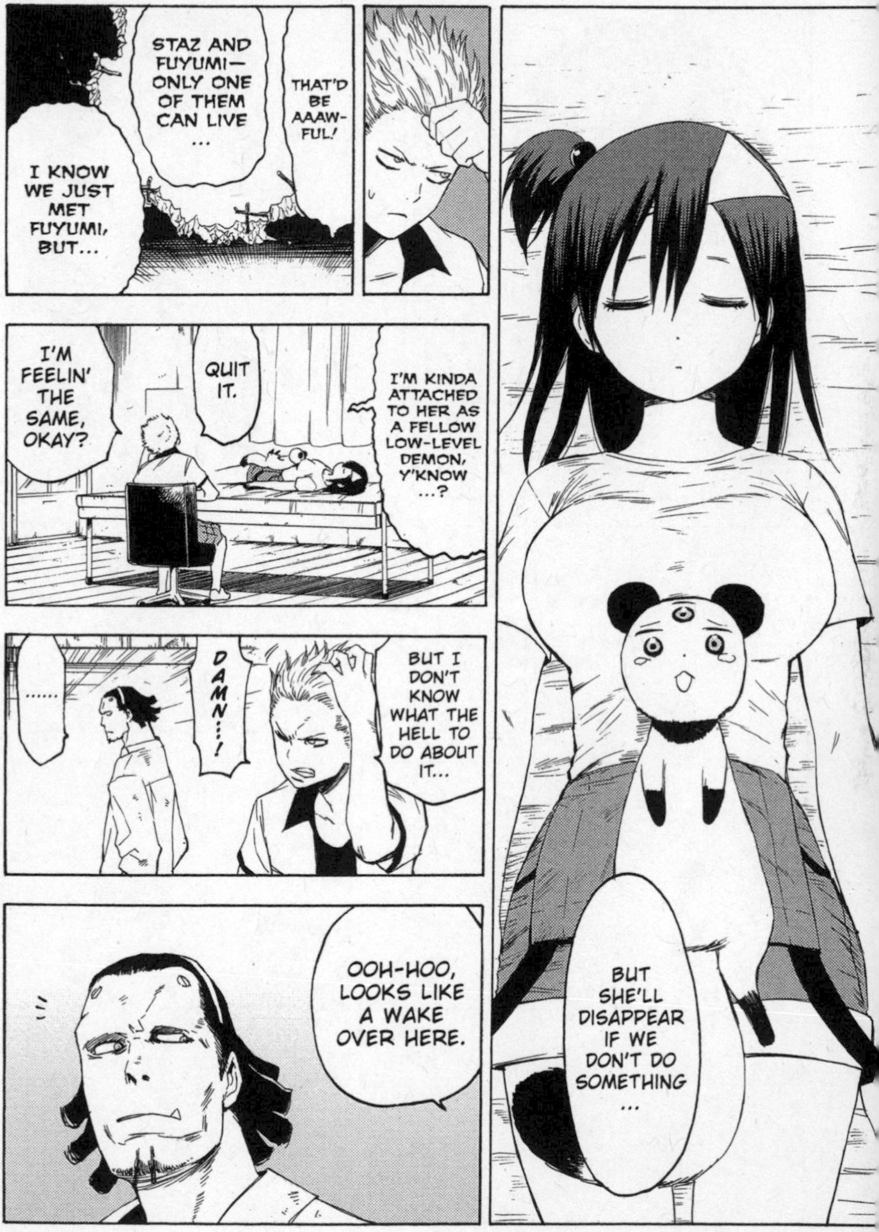
BUT SHE'LL DISAPPEAR IF WE DON'T DO SOMETHING ...
THAT'D BE AAAW-FUL!
STAZ AND FUYUMI— ONLY ONE OF THEM CAN LIVE ...
I KNOW WE JUST MET FUYUMI, BUT...
I'M KINDA ATTACHED TO HER AS A FELLOW LOW-LEVEL DEMON, Y'KNOW ...?
QUIT IT.
I'M FEELIN' THE SAME, OKAY?
BUT I DON'T KNOW WHAT THE HELL TO DO ABOUT IT...
DAMN...!
......
OOH-HOO, LOOKS LIKE A WAKE OVER HERE.

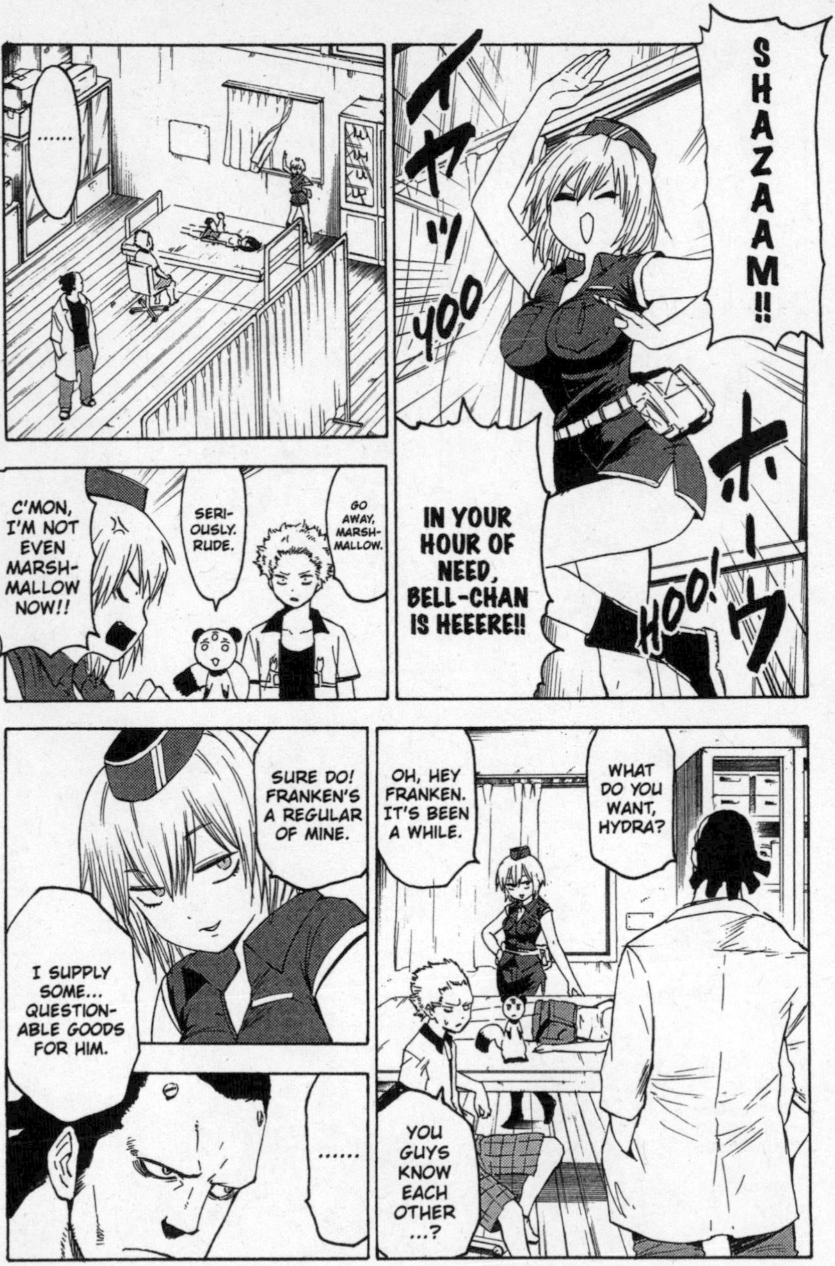
SHAZAAM!!
イヤッ
YOO
IN YOUR HOUR OF NEED, BELL-CHAN IS HEEERE!!
ホーウ
HOO!
......
GO AWAY, MARSH-MALLOW.
SERI-OUSLY. RUDE.
C'MON, I'M NOT EVEN MARSH-MALLOW NOW!!
WHAT DO YOU WANT, HYDRA?
OH, HEY FRANKEN. IT'S BEEN A WHILE.
YOU GUYS KNOW EACH OTHER ...?
SURE DO! FRANKEN'S A REGULAR OF MINE.
I SUPPLY SOME... QUESTION-ABLE GOODS FOR HIM.
......

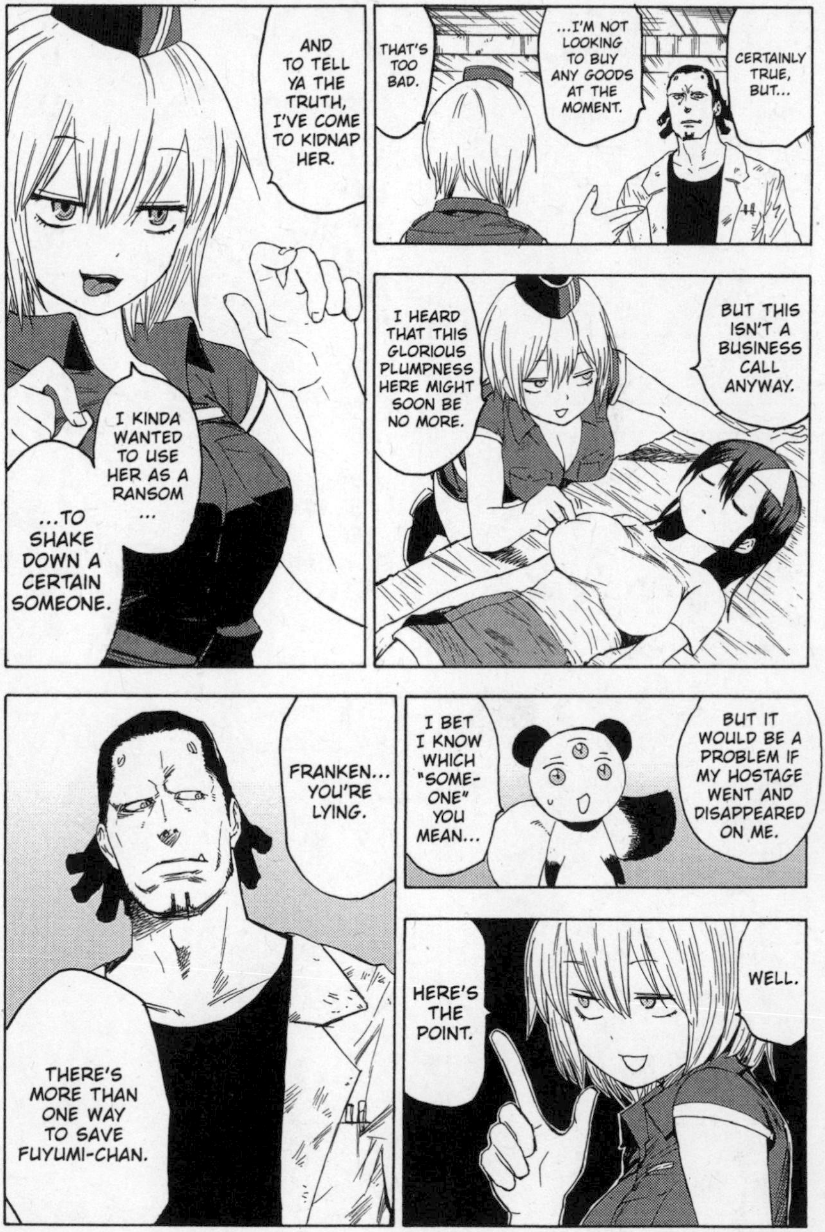
CERTAINLY TRUE, BUT...
...I'M NOT LOOKING TO BUY ANY GOODS AT THE MOMENT.
THAT'S TOO BAD.
BUT THIS ISN'T A BUSINESS CALL ANYWAY.
I HEARD THAT THIS GLORIOUS PLUMPNESS HERE MIGHT SOON BE NO MORE.
AND TO TELL YA THE TRUTH, I'VE COME TO KIDNAP HER.
I KINDA WANTED TO USE HER AS A RANSOM...
...TO SHAKE DOWN A CERTAIN SOMEONE.
BUT IT WOULD BE A PROBLEM IF MY HOSTAGE WENT AND DISAPPEARED ON ME.
I BET I KNOW WHICH "SOME-ONE" YOU MEAN...
WELL.
HERE'S THE POINT.
FRANKEN... YOU'RE LYING.
THERE'S MORE THAN ONE WAY TO SAVE FUYUMI-CHAN.

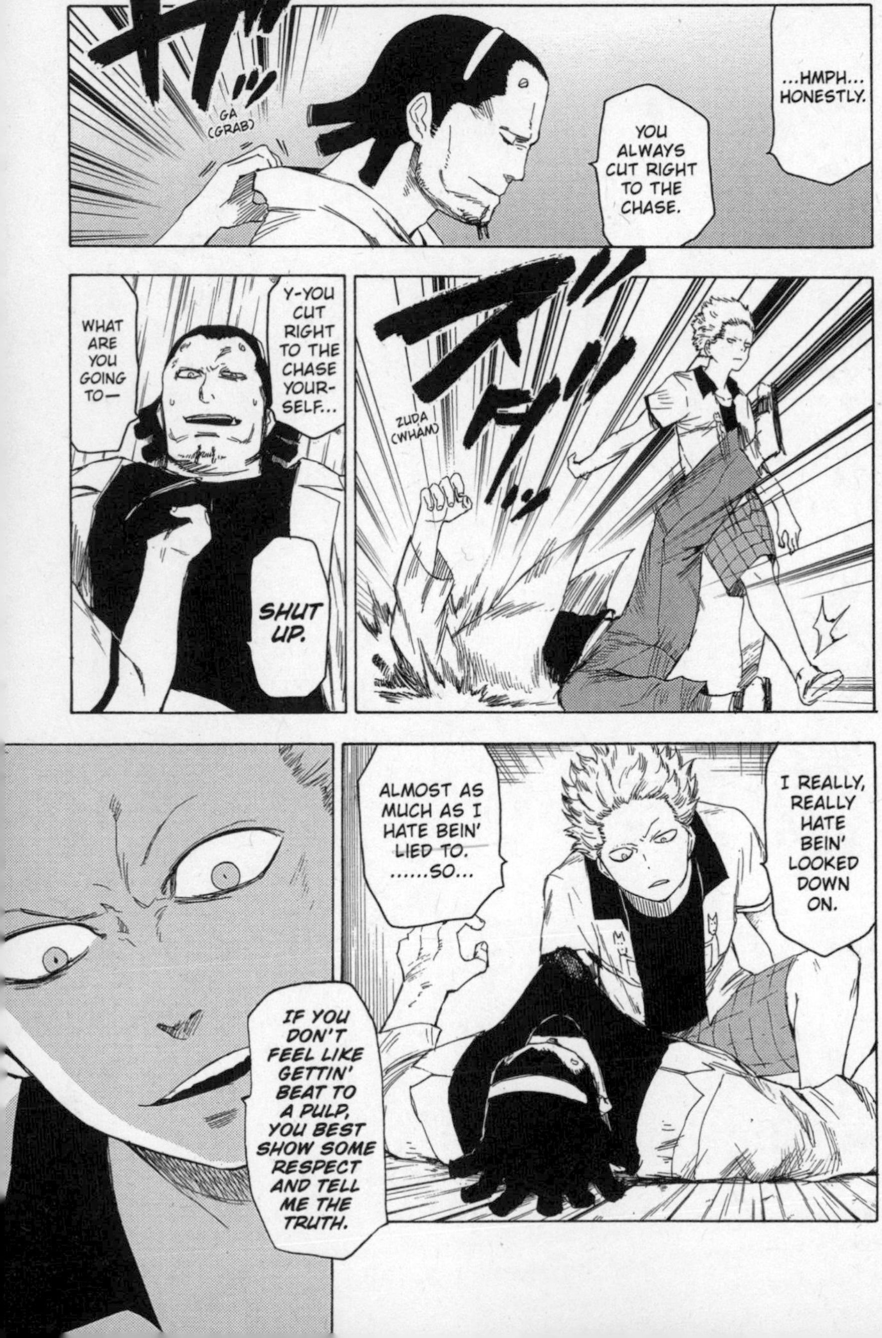
...HMPH... HONESTLY.
YOU ALWAYS CUT RIGHT TO THE CHASE.
GA (GRAB)
ZUDA (WHAM)
Y-YOU CUT RIGHT TO THE CHASE YOURSELF...
WHAT ARE YOU GOING TO—
SHUT UP.
I REALLY, REALLY HATE BEIN' LOOKED DOWN ON.
ALMOST AS MUCH AS I HATE BEIN' LIED TO. ......SO...
IF YOU DON'T FEEL LIKE GETTIN' BEAT TO A PULP, YOU BEST SHOW SOME RESPECT AND TELL ME THE TRUTH.

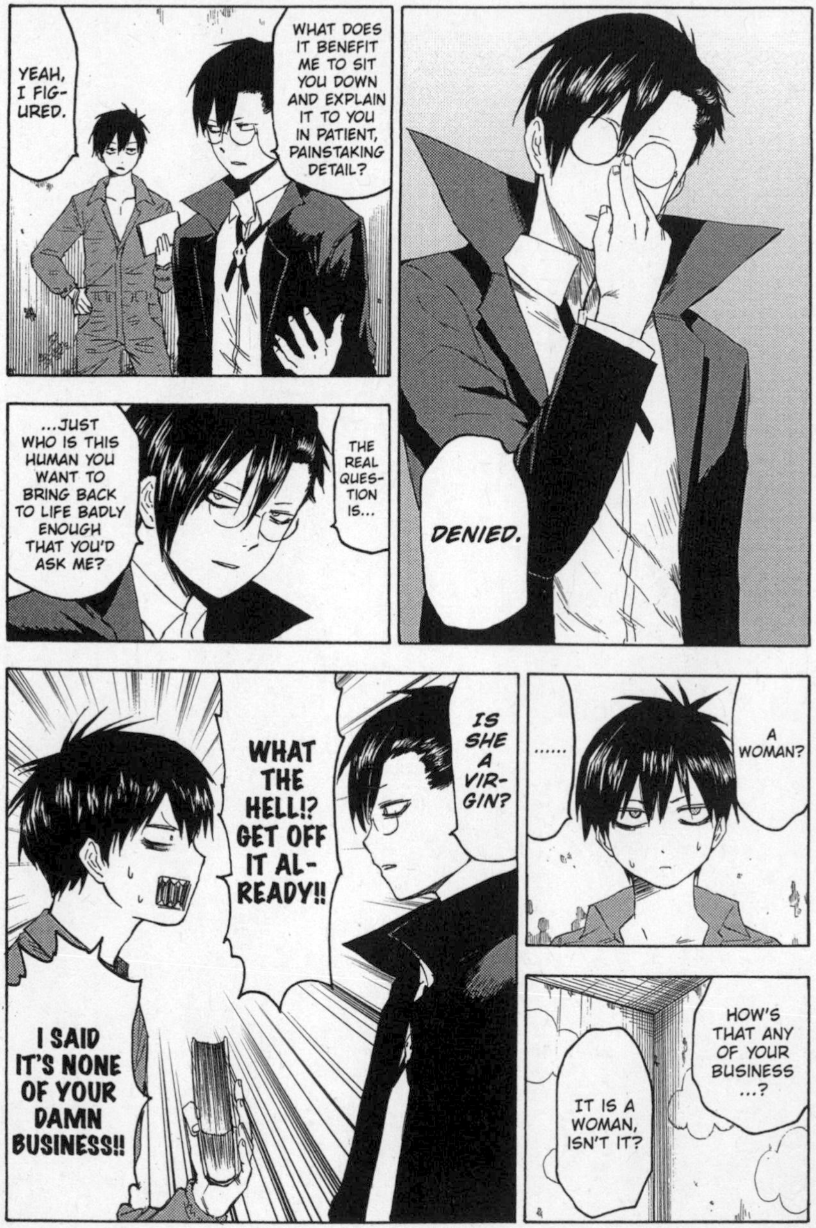
DENIED.
WHAT DOES IT BENEFIT ME TO SIT YOU DOWN AND EXPLAIN IT TO YOU IN PATIENT, PAINSTAKING DETAIL?
YEAH, I FIGURED.
THE REAL QUESTION IS...
...JUST WHO IS THIS HUMAN YOU WANT TO BRING BACK TO LIFE BADLY ENOUGH THAT YOU'D ASK ME?
A WOMAN?
......
HOW'S THAT ANY OF YOUR BUSINESS...?
IT IS A WOMAN, ISN'T IT?
IS SHE A VIRGIN?
WHAT THE HELL!? GET OFF IT ALREADY!!
I SAID IT'S NONE OF YOUR DAMN BUSINESS!!

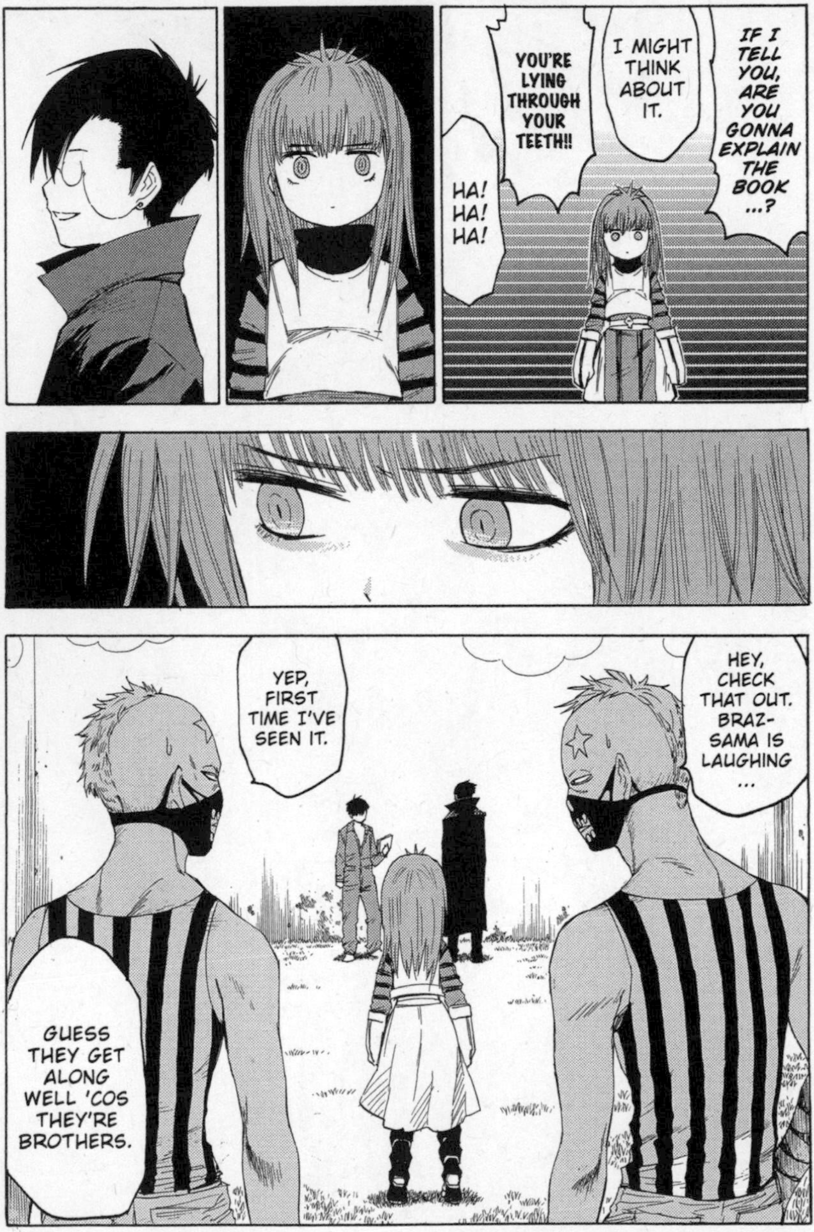
IF I TELL YOU, ARE YOU GONNA EXPLAIN THE BOOK ...?
I MIGHT THINK ABOUT IT.
YOU'RE LYING THROUGH YOUR TEETH!!
HA! HA! HA!
HEY, CHECK THAT OUT. BRAZ-SAMA IS LAUGHING ...
YEP, FIRST TIME I'VE SEEN IT.
GUESS THEY GET ALONG WELL 'COS THEY'RE BROTHERS.

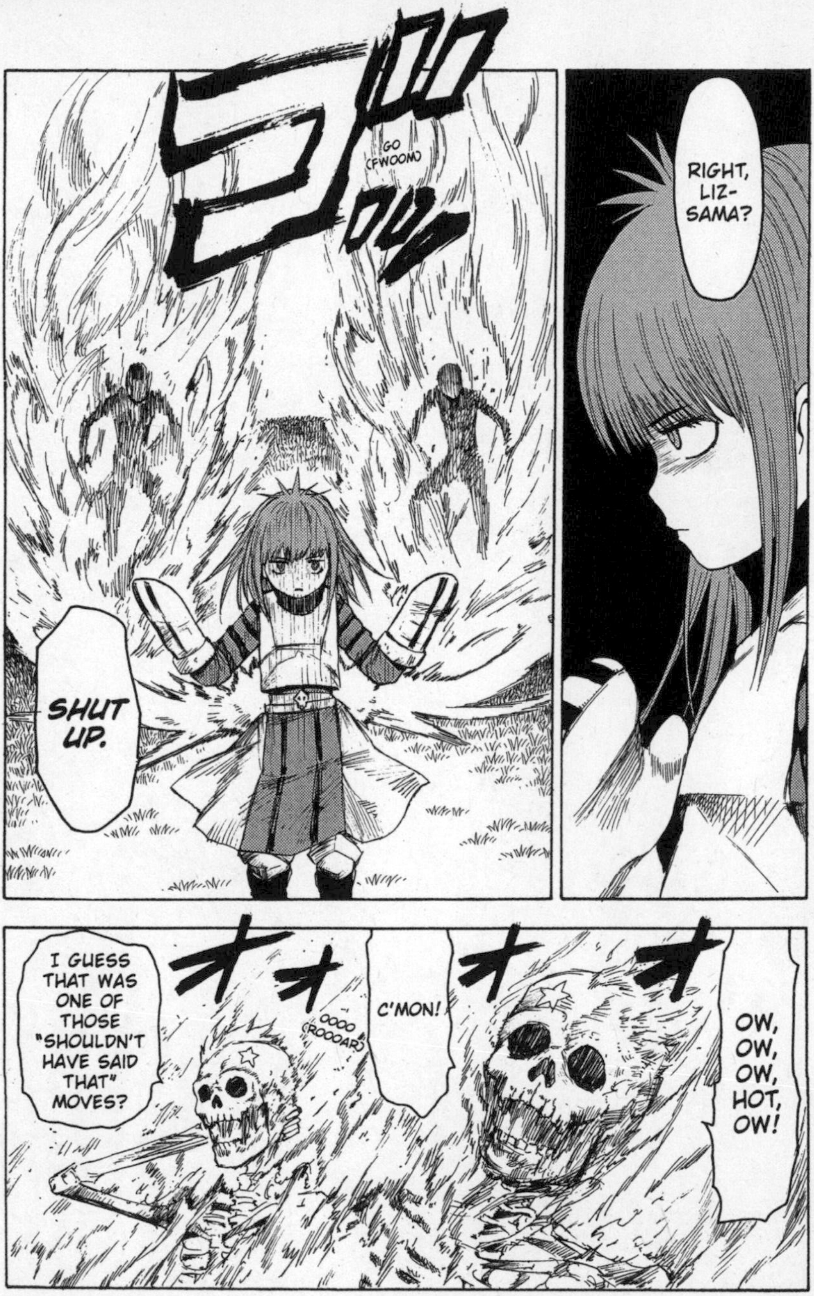
RIGHT, LIZ-SAMA?
GO (FWOOM)
SHUT UP.
OW, OW, OW, HOT, OW!
C'MON!
OOOO (ROOOAR)
I GUESS THAT WAS ONE OF THOSE "SHOULDN'T HAVE SAID THAT" MOVES?

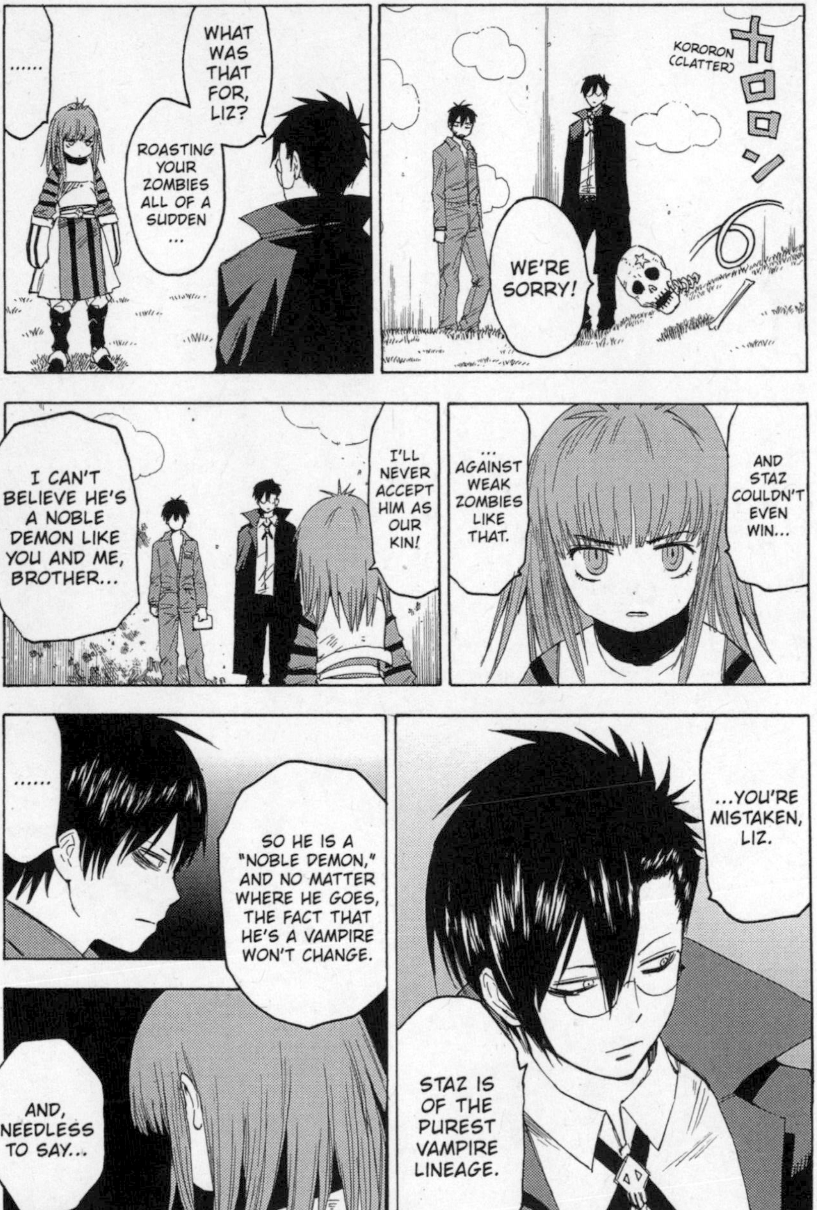
カロロン
KORORON (CLATTER)
WE'RE SORRY!
WHAT WAS THAT FOR, LIZ?
ROASTING YOUR ZOMBIES ALL OF A SUDDEN ...
......
AND STAZ COULDN'T EVEN WIN...
... AGAINST WEAK ZOMBIES LIKE THAT.
I'LL NEVER ACCEPT HIM AS OUR KIN!
I CAN'T BELIEVE HE'S A NOBLE DEMON LIKE YOU AND ME, BROTHER...
...YOU'RE MISTAKEN, LIZ.
STAZ IS OF THE PUREST VAMPIRE LINEAGE.
SO HE IS A "NOBLE DEMON," AND NO MATTER WHERE HE GOES, THE FACT THAT HE'S A VAMPIRE WON'T CHANGE.
......
AND, NEEDLESS TO SAY...

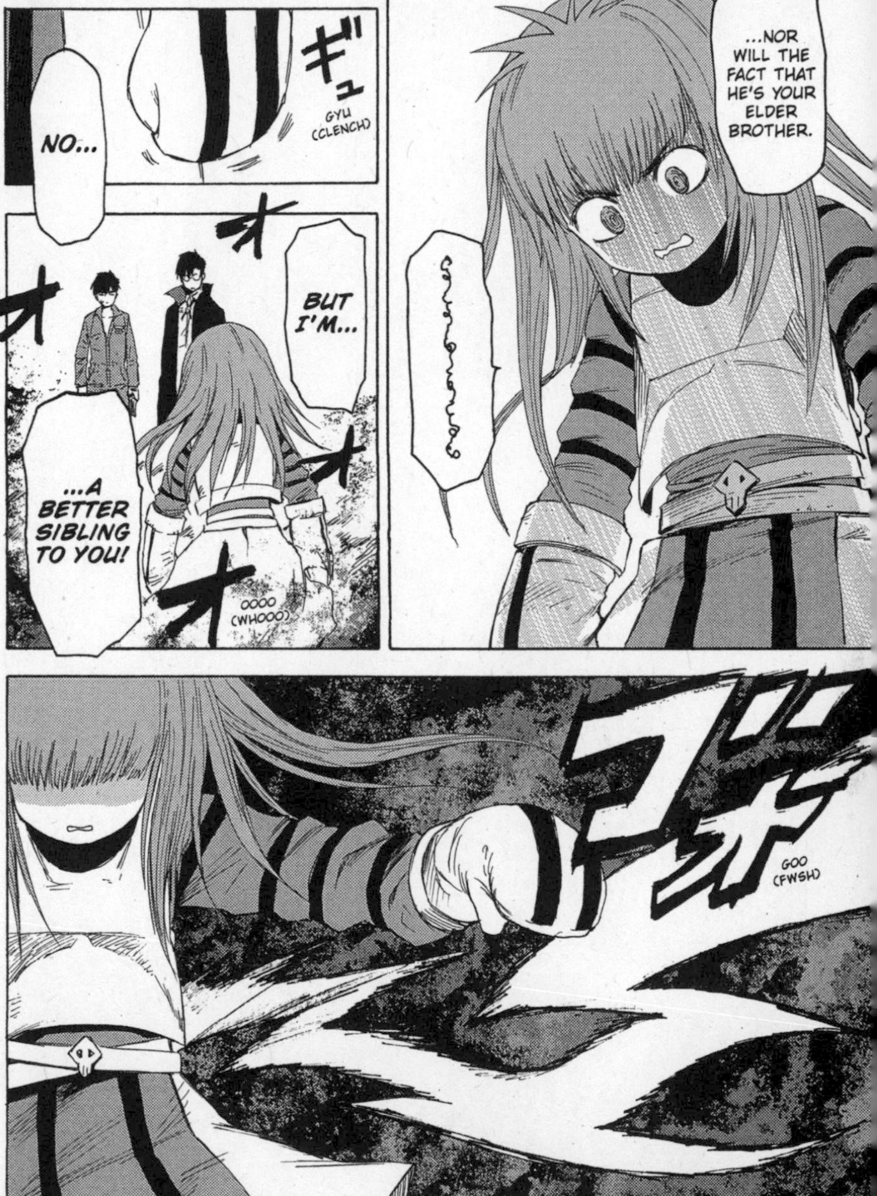

...NOR WILL THE FACT THAT HE'S YOUR ELDER BROTHER.
......
ギュ
GYU (CLENCH)
NO...
BUT I'M...
...A BETTER SIBLING TO YOU!
オ
OOOO (WHOOO)
GOO (FWSH)

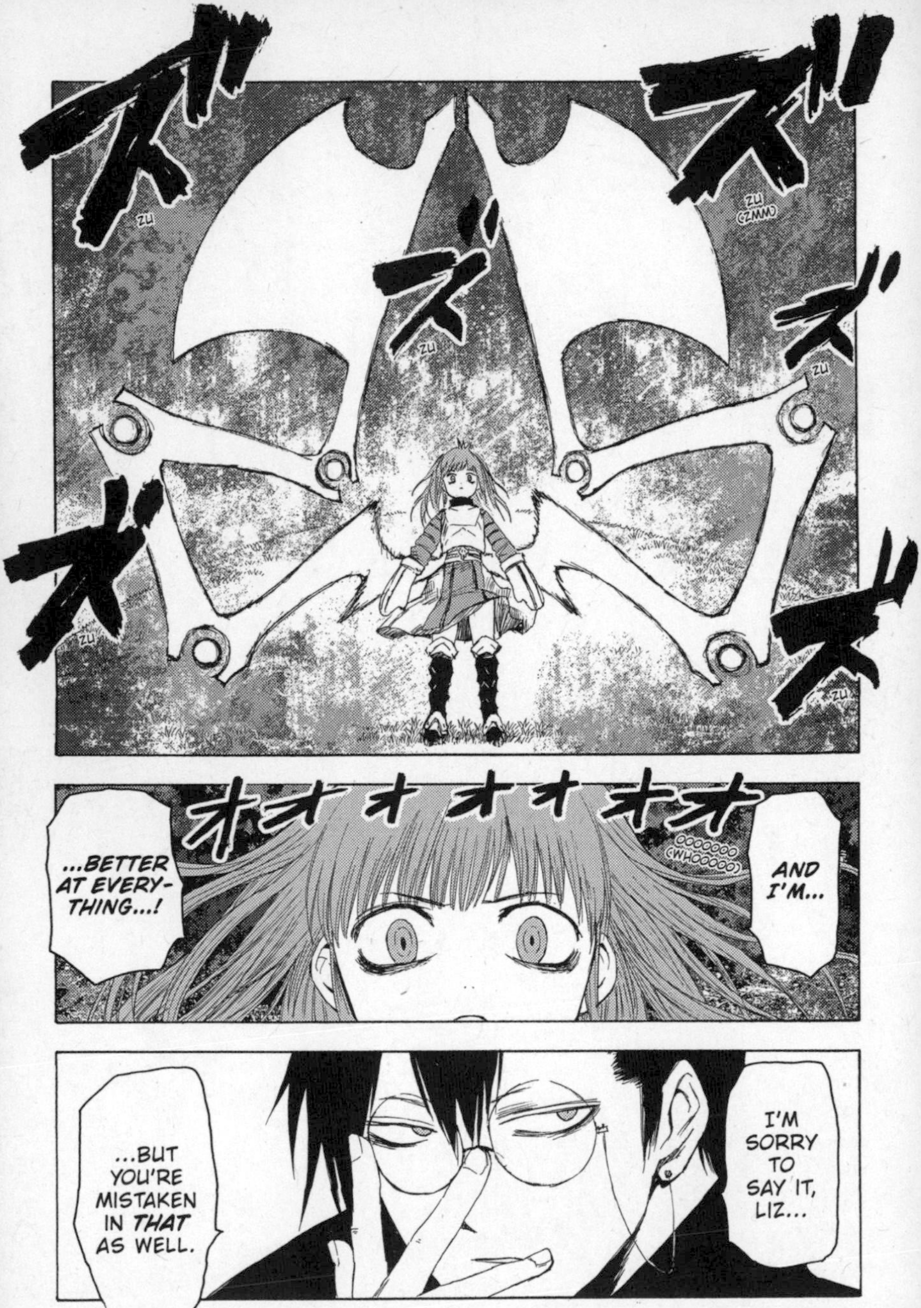
ZU (ZMM)
ZU
ZU
ZU
ZU
ZU
OOOOOOO (WHOOOOOO)
AND I'M...
...BETTER AT EVERY-THING...!
I'M SORRY TO SAY IT, LIZ...
...BUT YOU'RE MISTAKEN IN *THAT* AS WELL.

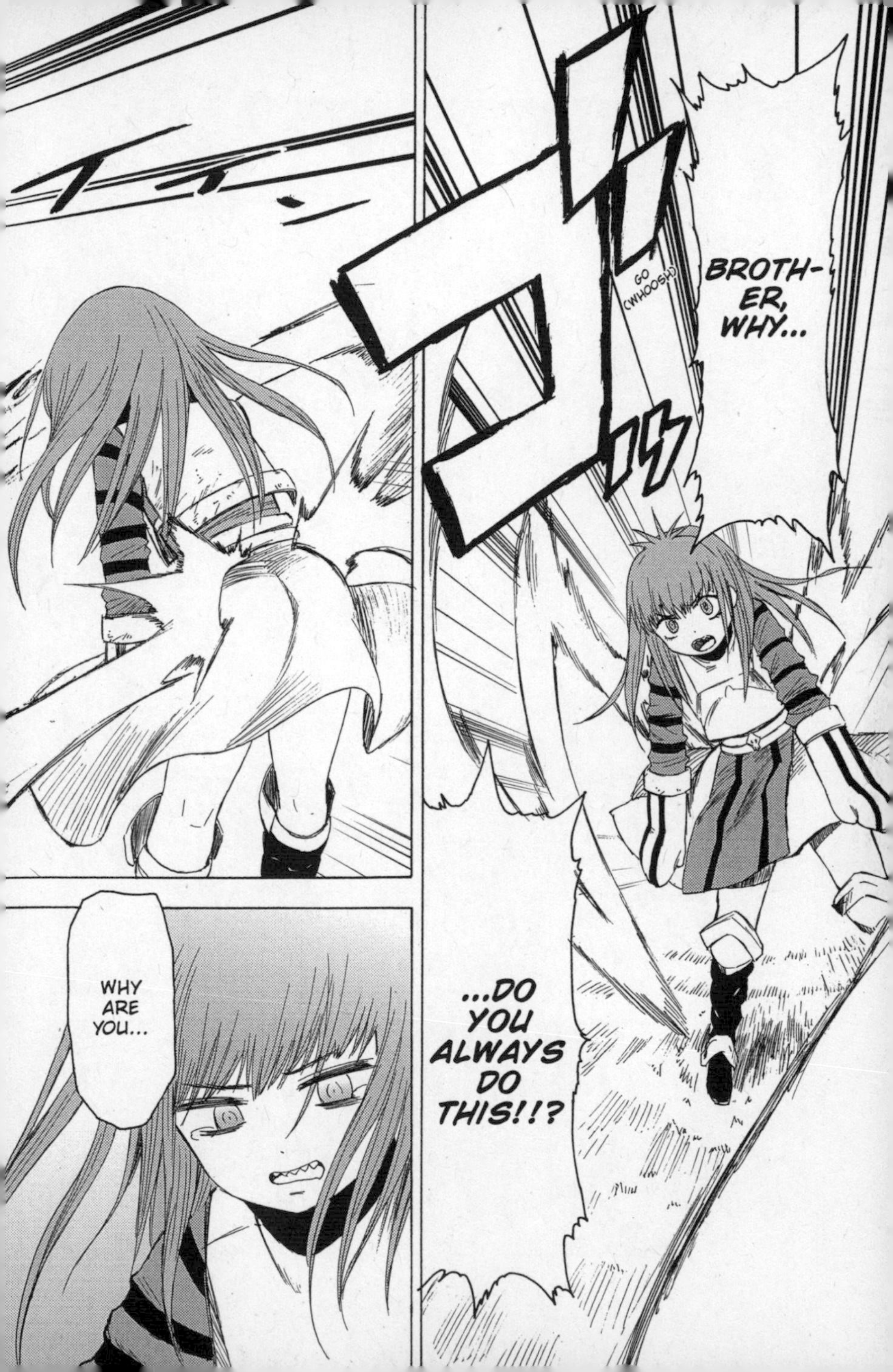
BROTHER-ER, WHY...
GO (WHOOSH)
...DO YOU ALWAYS DO THIS!!?
WHY ARE YOU...

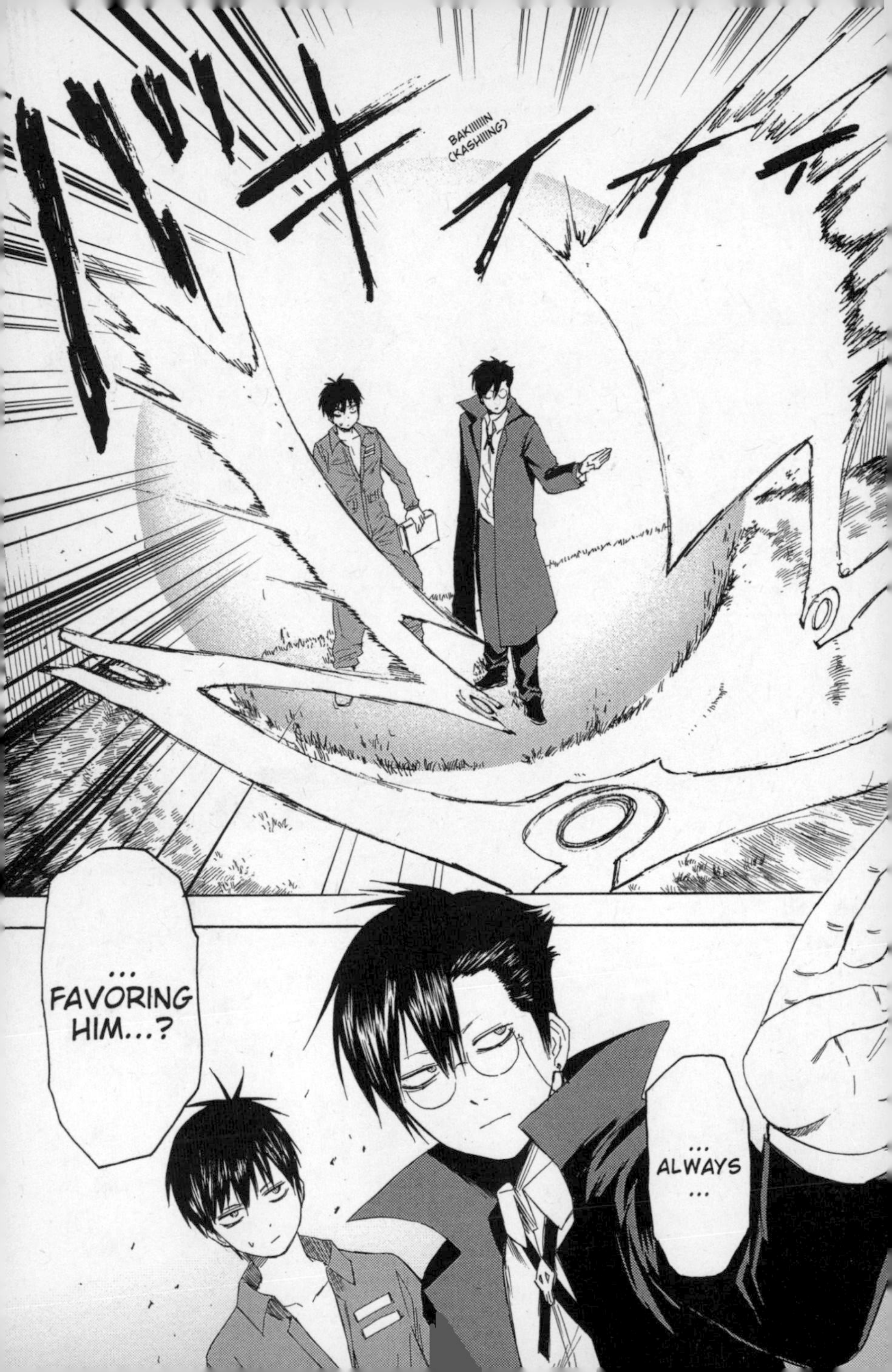
BAKIIIIIIN
(KASHIIING)
... ALWAYS ...
... FAVORING HIM...?

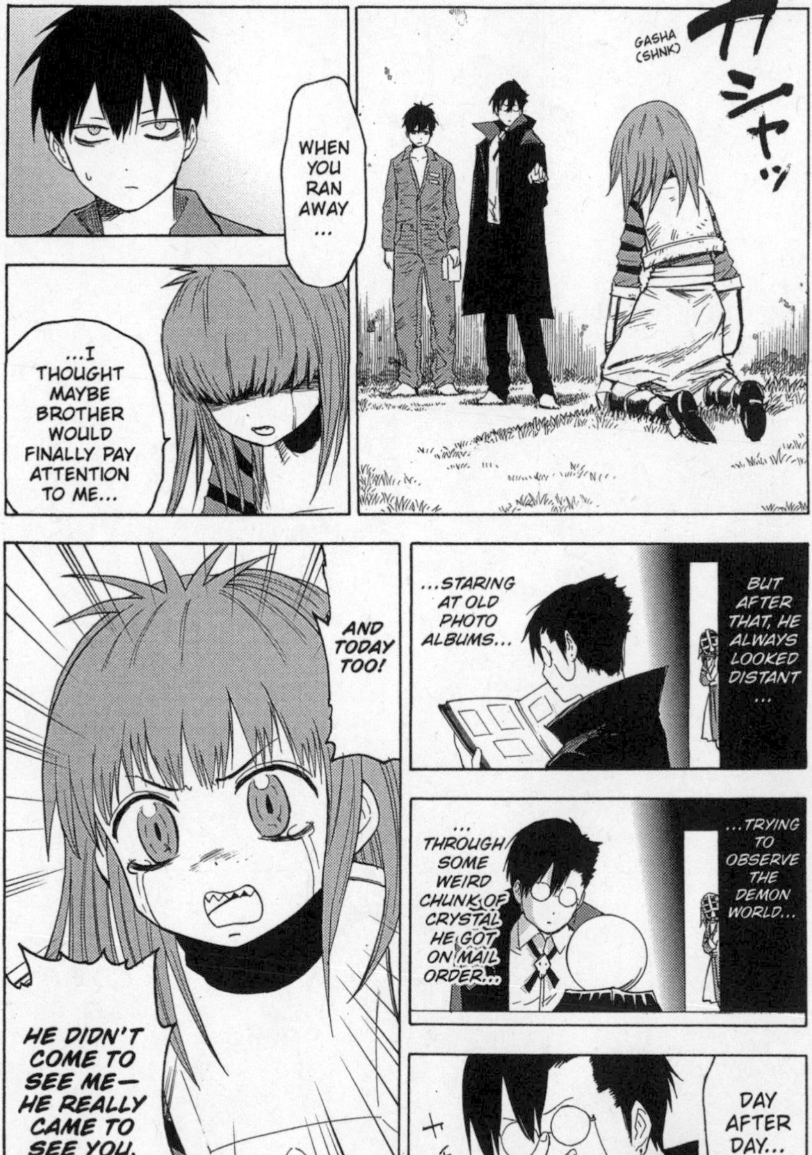

ガシャッ
GASHA (SHNK)
WHEN YOU RAN AWAY ...
...I THOUGHT MAYBE BROTHER WOULD FINALLY PAY ATTENTION TO ME...
BUT AFTER THAT, HE ALWAYS LOOKED DISTANT ...
...STARING AT OLD PHOTO ALBUMS...
...TRYING TO OBSERVE THE DEMON WORLD...
... THROUGH SOME WEIRD CHUNK OF CRYSTAL HE GOT ON MAIL ORDER...
DAY AFTER DAY...
KACHA (CLACK)
AND TODAY TOO!
HE DIDN'T COME TO SEE ME—HE REALLY CAME TO SEE YOU, STAZ!!

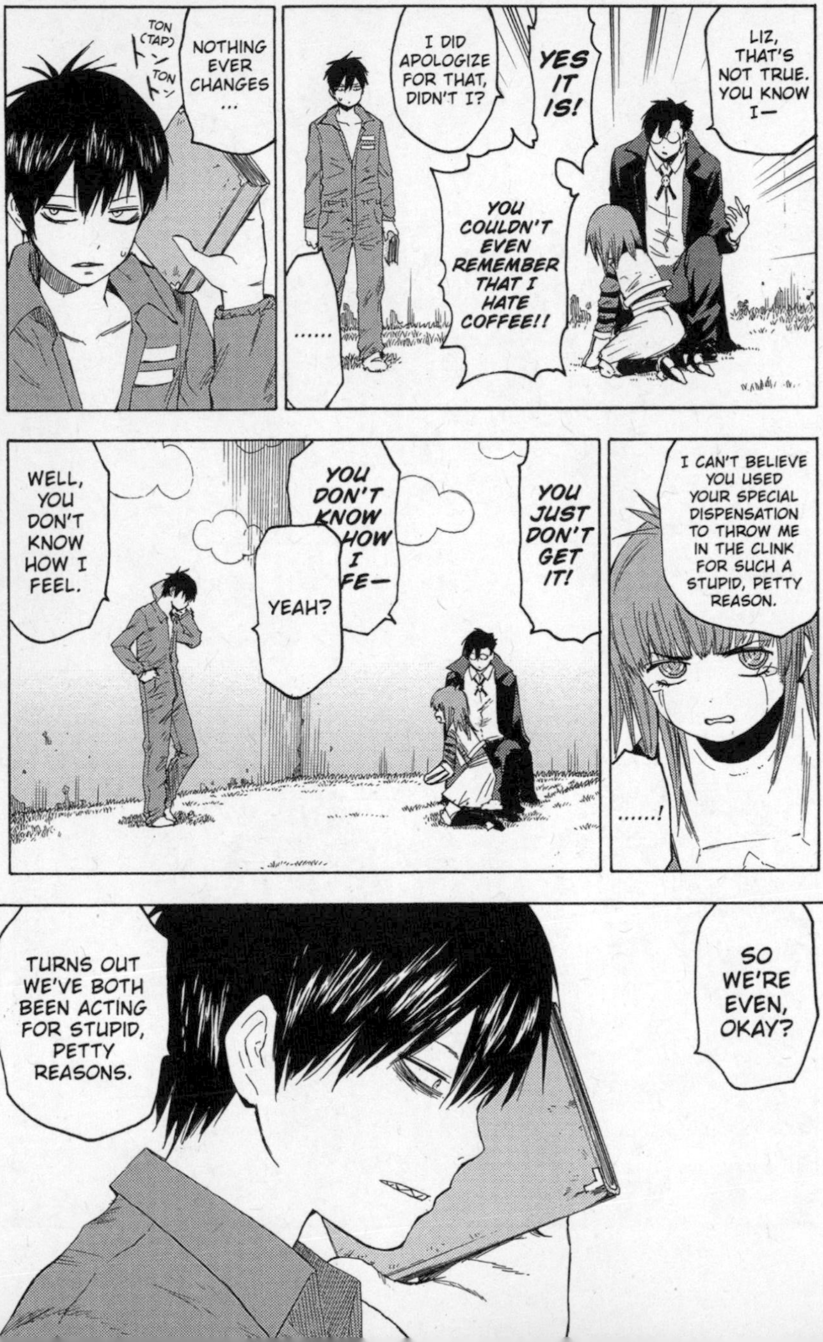
LIZ, THAT'S NOT TRUE. YOU KNOW I—
YES IT IS!
YOU COULDN'T EVEN REMEMBER THAT I HATE COFFEE!!
I DID APOLOGIZE FOR THAT, DIDN'T I?
......
TON (TAP) TON
NOTHING EVER CHANGES ...
I CAN'T BELIEVE YOU USED YOUR SPECIAL DISPENSATION TO THROW ME IN THE CLINK FOR SUCH A STUPID, PETTY REASON.
......!
YOU JUST DON'T GET IT!
YOU DON'T KNOW HOW I FE—
YEAH?
WELL, YOU DON'T KNOW HOW I FEEL.
TURNS OUT WE'VE BOTH BEEN ACTING FOR STUPID, PETTY REASONS.
SO WE'RE EVEN, OKAY?

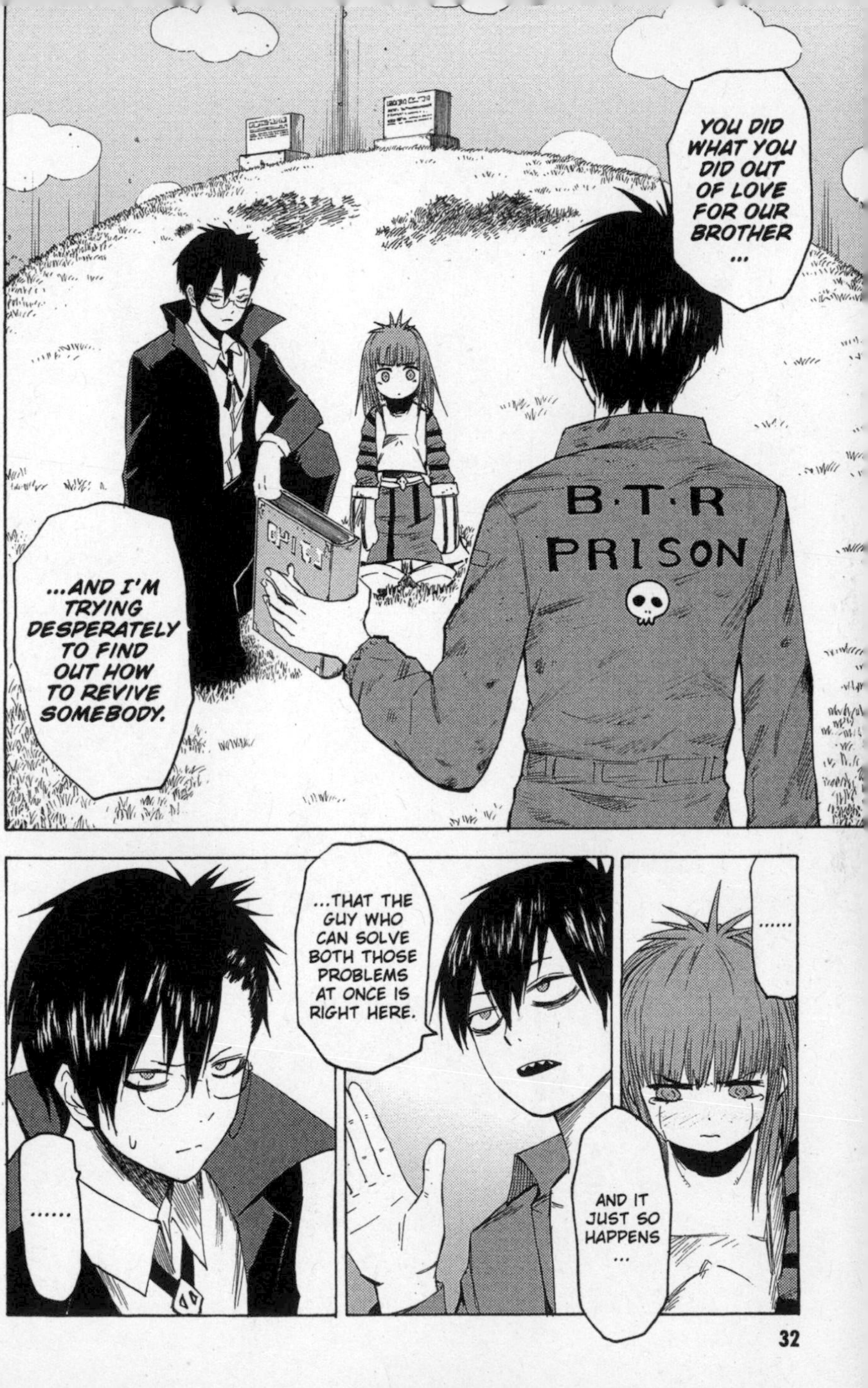
YOU DID WHAT YOU DID OUT OF LOVE FOR OUR BROTHER ...
B·T·R PRISON
...AND I'M TRYING DESPERATELY TO FIND OUT HOW TO REVIVE SOMEBODY.
......
AND IT JUST SO HAPPENS ...
...THAT THE GUY WHO CAN SOLVE BOTH THOSE PROBLEMS AT ONCE IS RIGHT HERE.
......

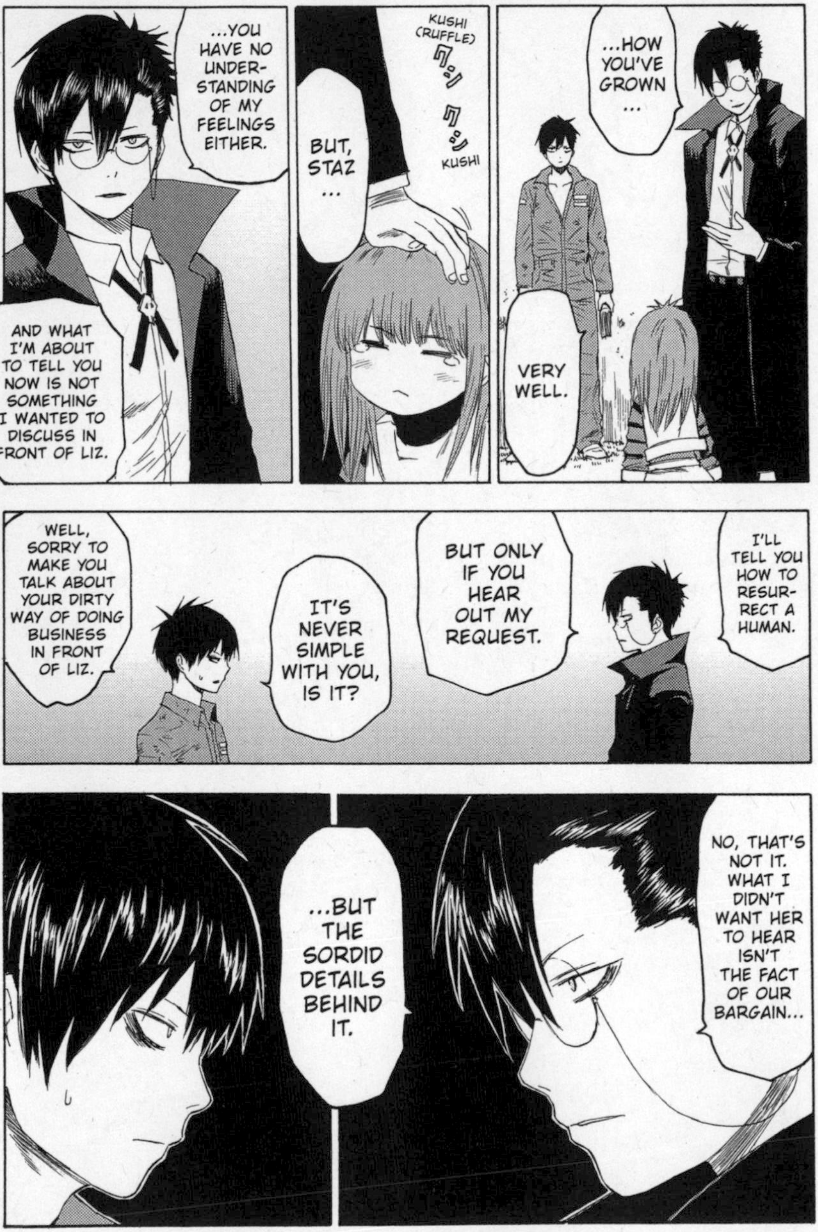
...HOW YOU'VE GROWN ...
VERY WELL.
KUSHI (RUFFLE)
クシ
クシ
KUSHI
BUT, STAZ ...
...YOU HAVE NO UNDER-STANDING OF MY FEELINGS EITHER.
AND WHAT I'M ABOUT TO TELL YOU NOW IS NOT SOMETHING I WANTED TO DISCUSS IN FRONT OF LIZ.
I'LL TELL YOU HOW TO RESUR-RECT A HUMAN.
BUT ONLY IF YOU HEAR OUT MY REQUEST.
IT'S NEVER SIMPLE WITH YOU, IS IT?
WELL, SORRY TO MAKE YOU TALK ABOUT YOUR DIRTY WAY OF DOING BUSINESS IN FRONT OF LIZ.
NO, THAT'S NOT IT. WHAT I DIDN'T WANT HER TO HEAR ISN'T THE FACT OF OUR BARGAIN...
...BUT THE SORDID DETAILS BEHIND IT.

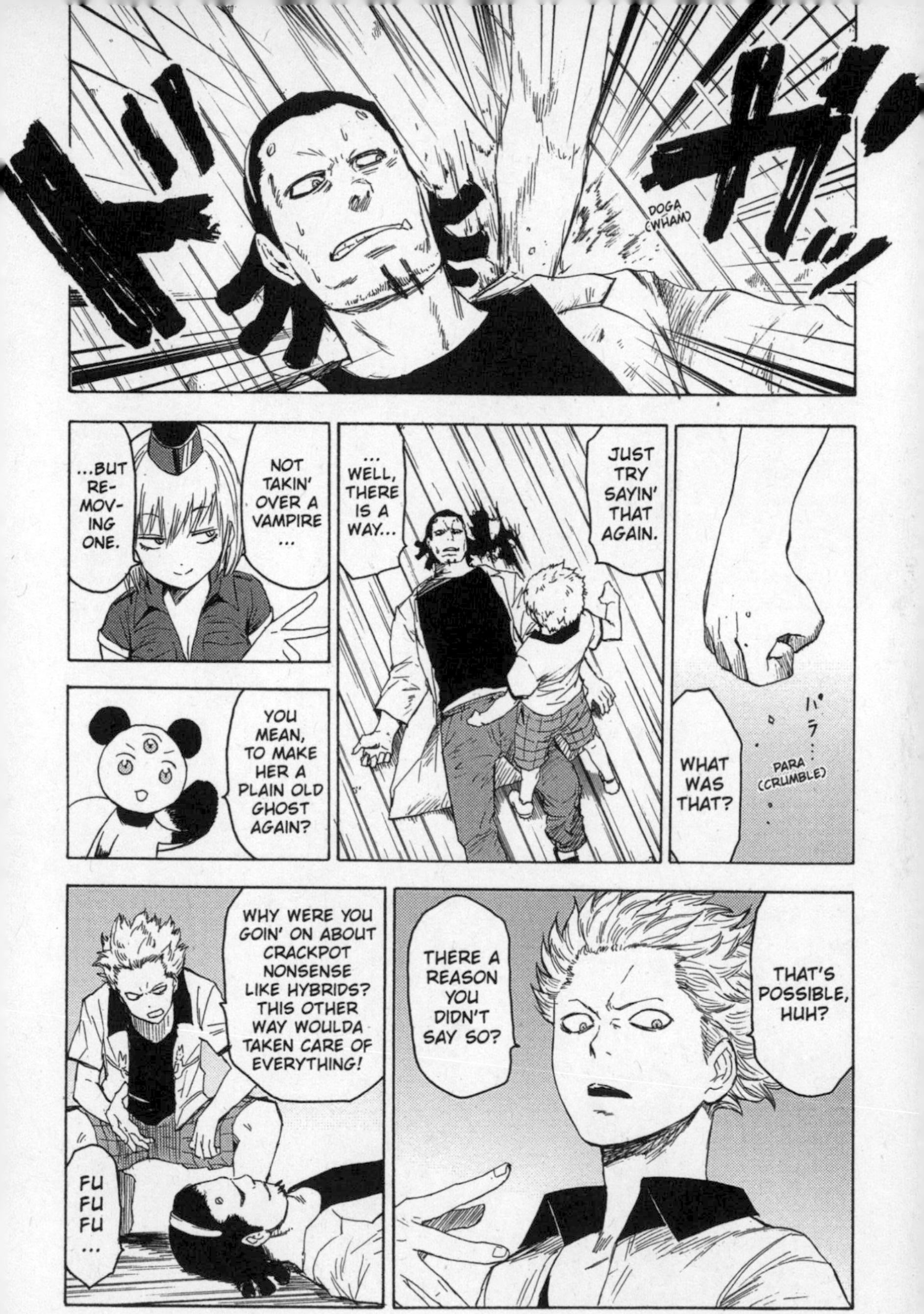
DOGA (WHAM)
WHAT WAS THAT?
PARA (CRUMBLE)
JUST TRY SAYIN' THAT AGAIN.
... WELL, THERE IS A WAY...
NOT TAKIN' OVER A VAMPIRE ...
...BUT RE-MOV-ING ONE.
YOU MEAN, TO MAKE HER A PLAIN OLD GHOST AGAIN?
THAT'S POSSIBLE, HUH?
THERE A REASON YOU DIDN'T SAY SO?
WHY WERE YOU GOIN' ON ABOUT CRACKPOT NONSENSE LIKE HYBRIDS? THIS OTHER WAY WOULDA TAKEN CARE OF EVERYTHING!
FU FU FU ...

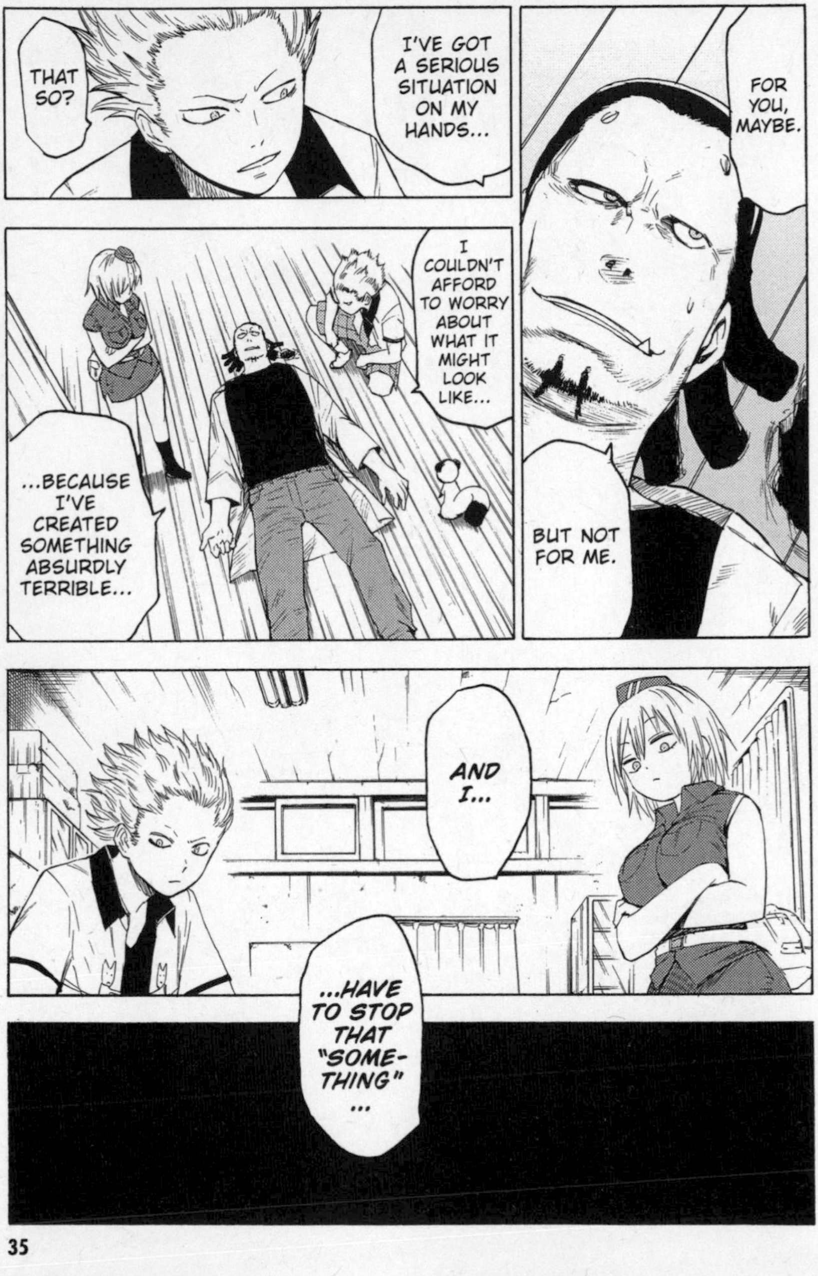
FOR YOU, MAYBE.
BUT NOT FOR ME.
I'VE GOT A SERIOUS SITUATION ON MY HANDS...
THAT SO?
I COULDN'T AFFORD TO WORRY ABOUT WHAT IT MIGHT LOOK LIKE...
...BECAUSE I'VE CREATED SOMETHING ABSURDLY TERRIBLE...
AND I...
...HAVE TO STOP THAT "SOME-THING"...

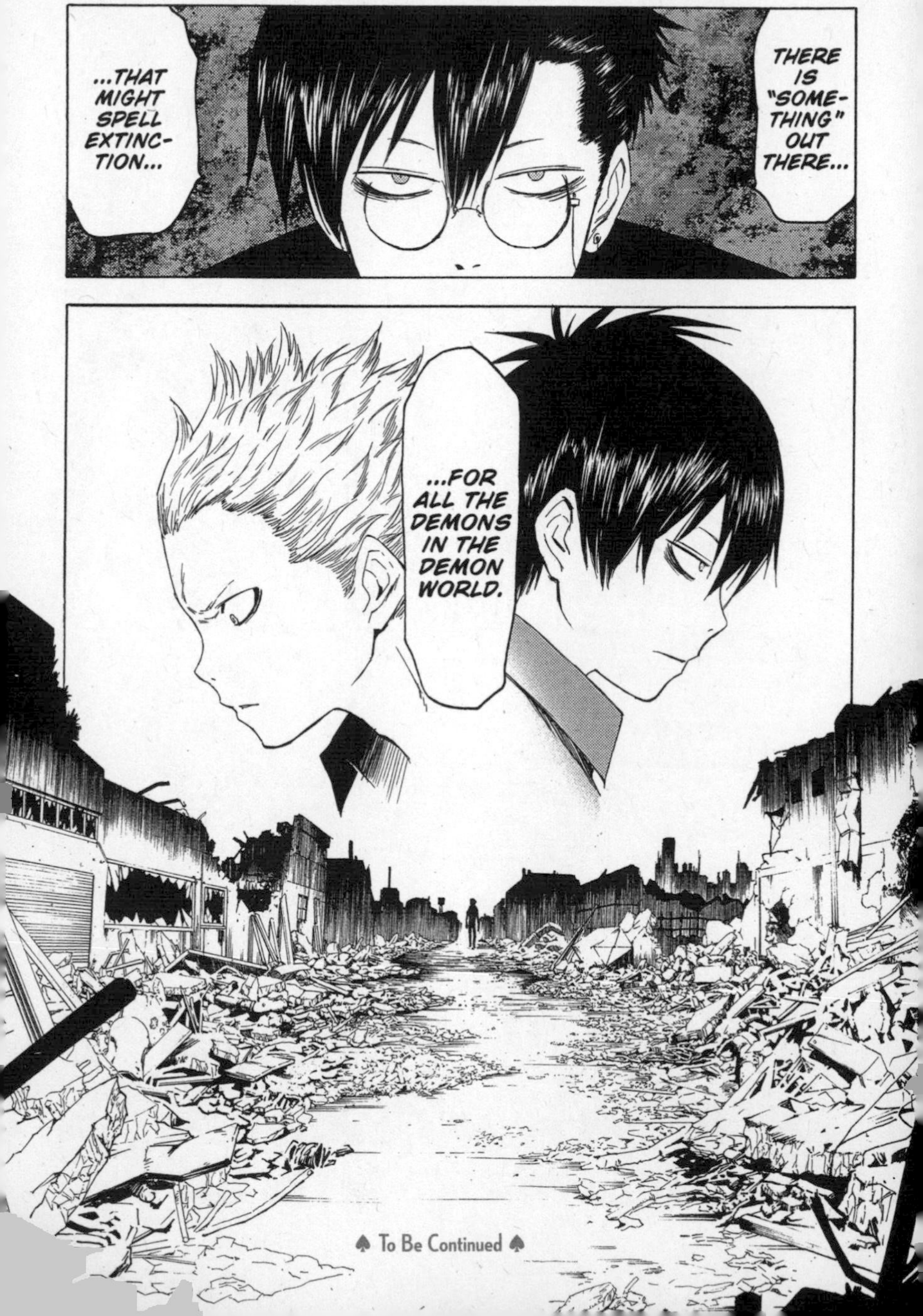
THERE IS "SOMETHING" OUT THERE...
...THAT MIGHT SPELL EXTINCTION...
...FOR ALL THE DEMONS IN THE DEMON WORLD.
♠ To Be Continued ♠

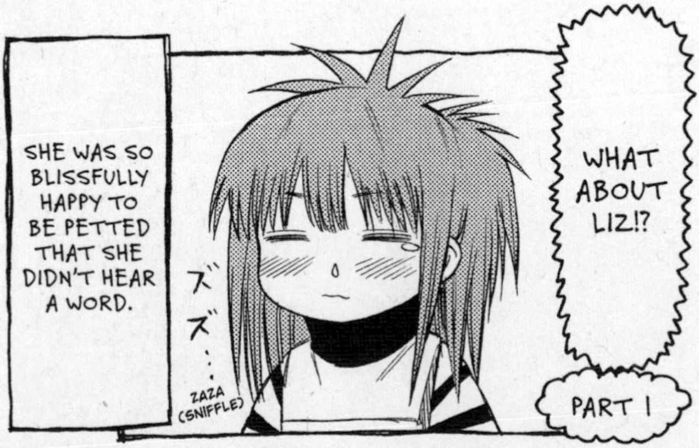
WHAT ABOUT LIZ!?
PART 1
ズズ…
ZAZA (SNIFFLE)
SHE WAS SO BLISSFULLY HAPPY TO BE PETTED THAT SHE DIDN'T HEAR A WORD.

BLOOD LAD

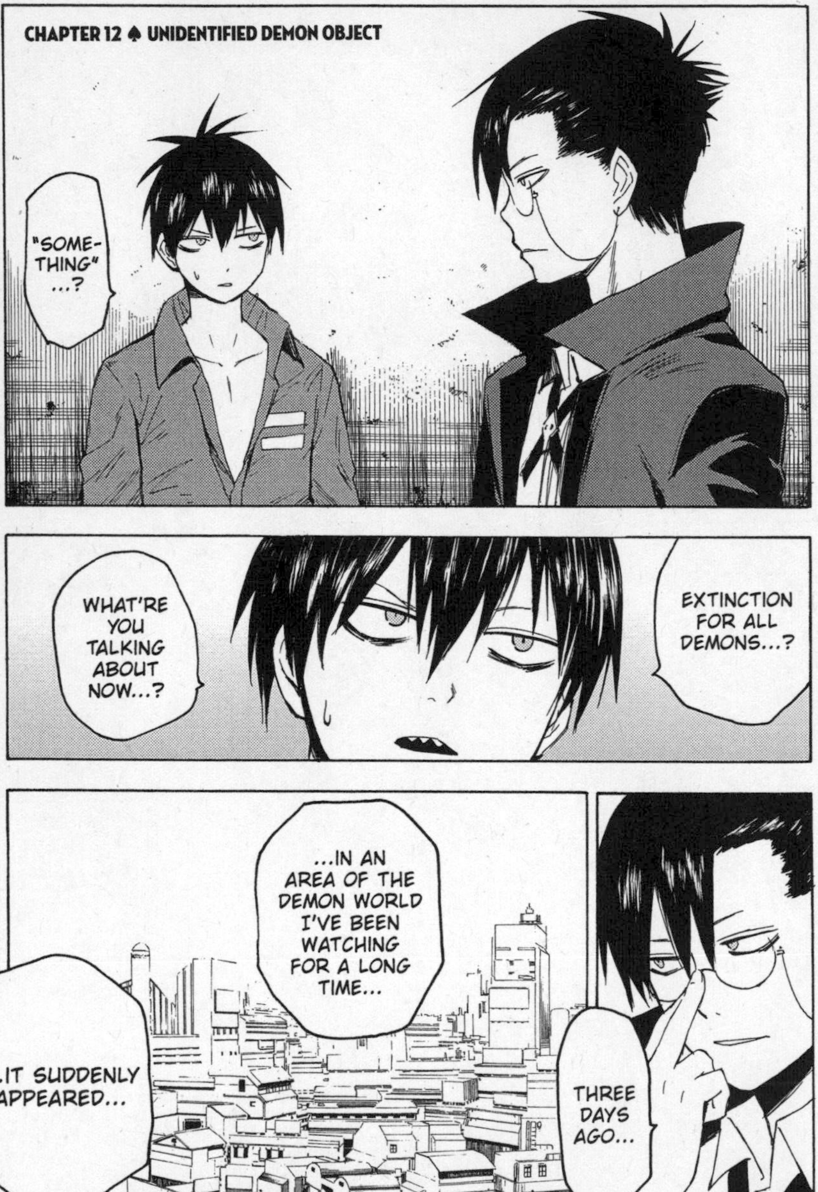
CHAPTER 12 ♠ UNIDENTIFIED DEMON OBJECT
"SOMETHING" ...?
EXTINCTION FOR ALL DEMONS...?
WHAT'RE YOU TALKING ABOUT NOW...?
THREE DAYS AGO...
...IN AN AREA OF THE DEMON WORLD I'VE BEEN WATCHING FOR A LONG TIME...
...IT SUDDENLY APPEARED...

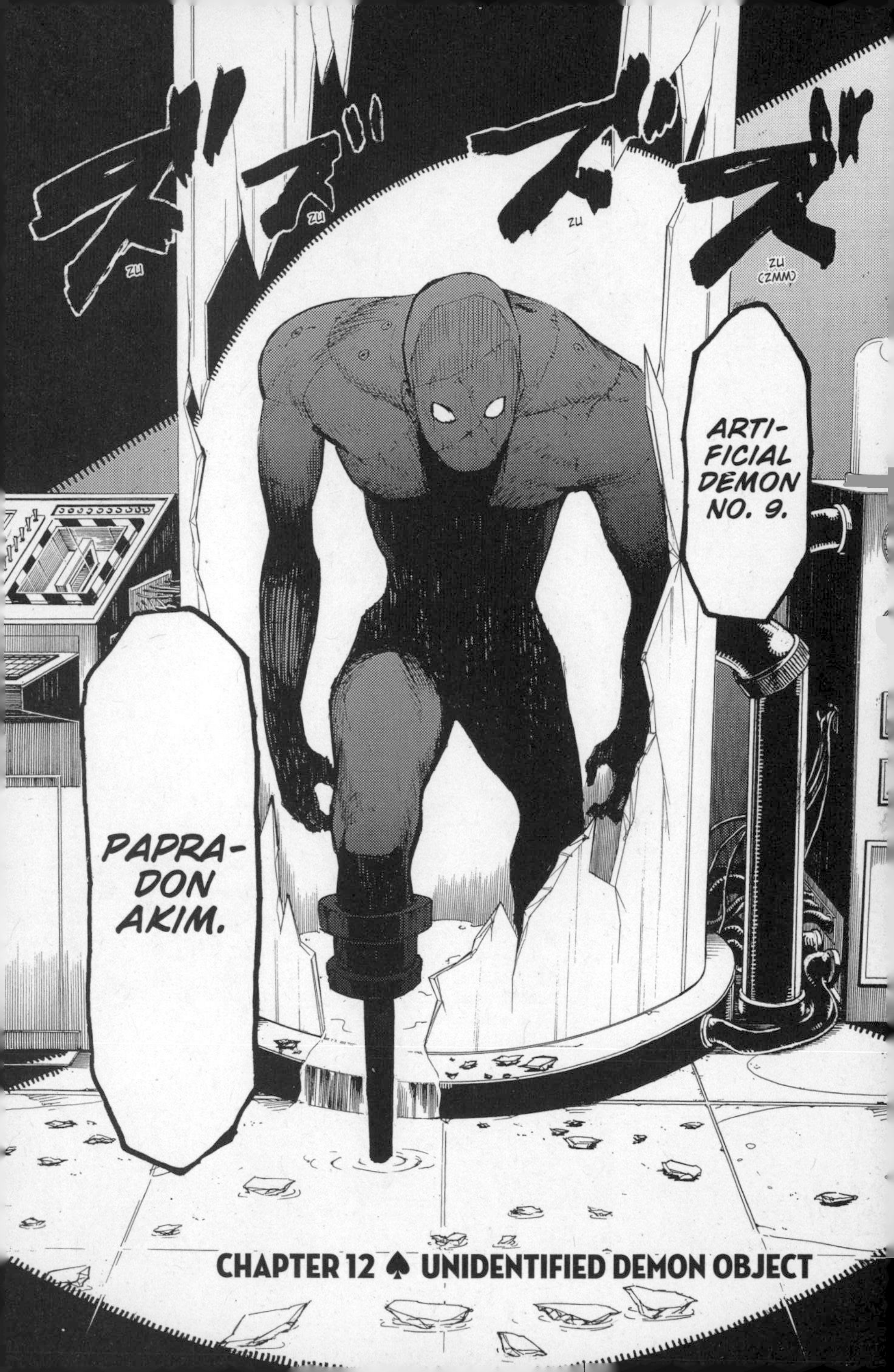
ZU (ZMM)
ZU
ZU
ZU
ARTI-FICIAL DEMON NO. 9.
PAPRA-DON AKIM.
CHAPTER 12 ♠ UNIDENTIFIED DEMON OBJECT

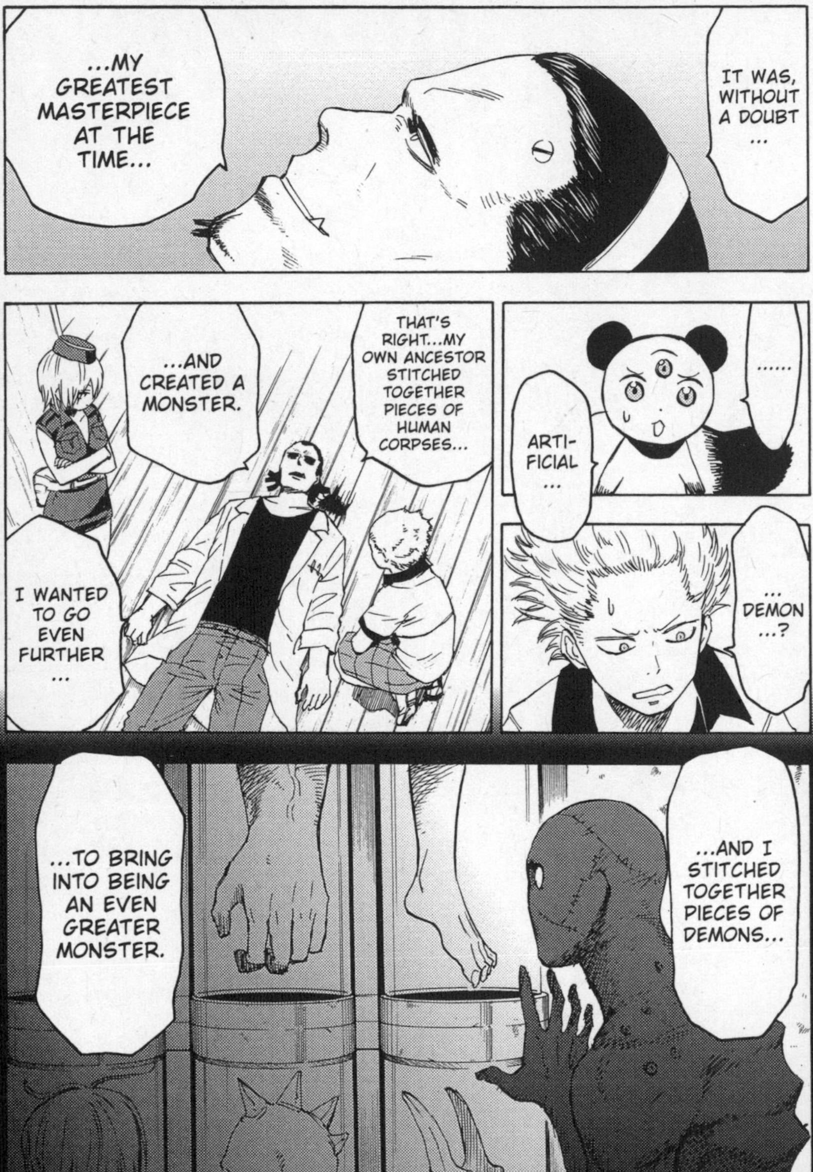
IT WAS, WITHOUT A DOUBT ...
...MY GREATEST MASTERPIECE AT THE TIME...
......
ARTI-FICIAL ...
... DEMON ...?
THAT'S RIGHT...MY OWN ANCESTOR STITCHED TOGETHER PIECES OF HUMAN CORPSES...
...AND CREATED A MONSTER.
I WANTED TO GO EVEN FURTHER ...
...AND I STITCHED TOGETHER PIECES OF DEMONS...
...TO BRING INTO BEING AN EVEN GREATER MONSTER.

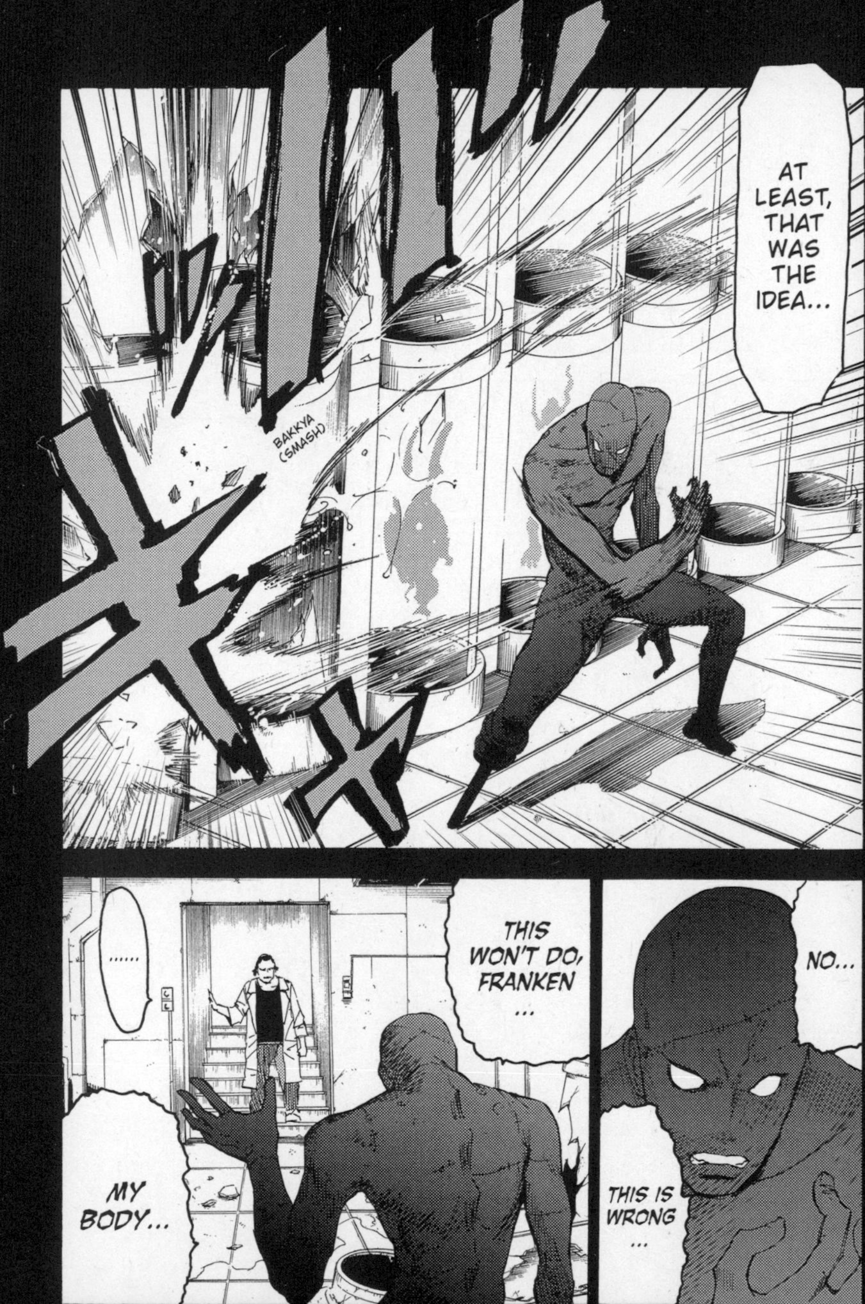
AT LEAST, THAT WAS THE IDEA...
BAKKYA (SMASH)
NO...
THIS IS WRONG ...
THIS WON'T DO, FRANKEN ...
......
MY BODY...

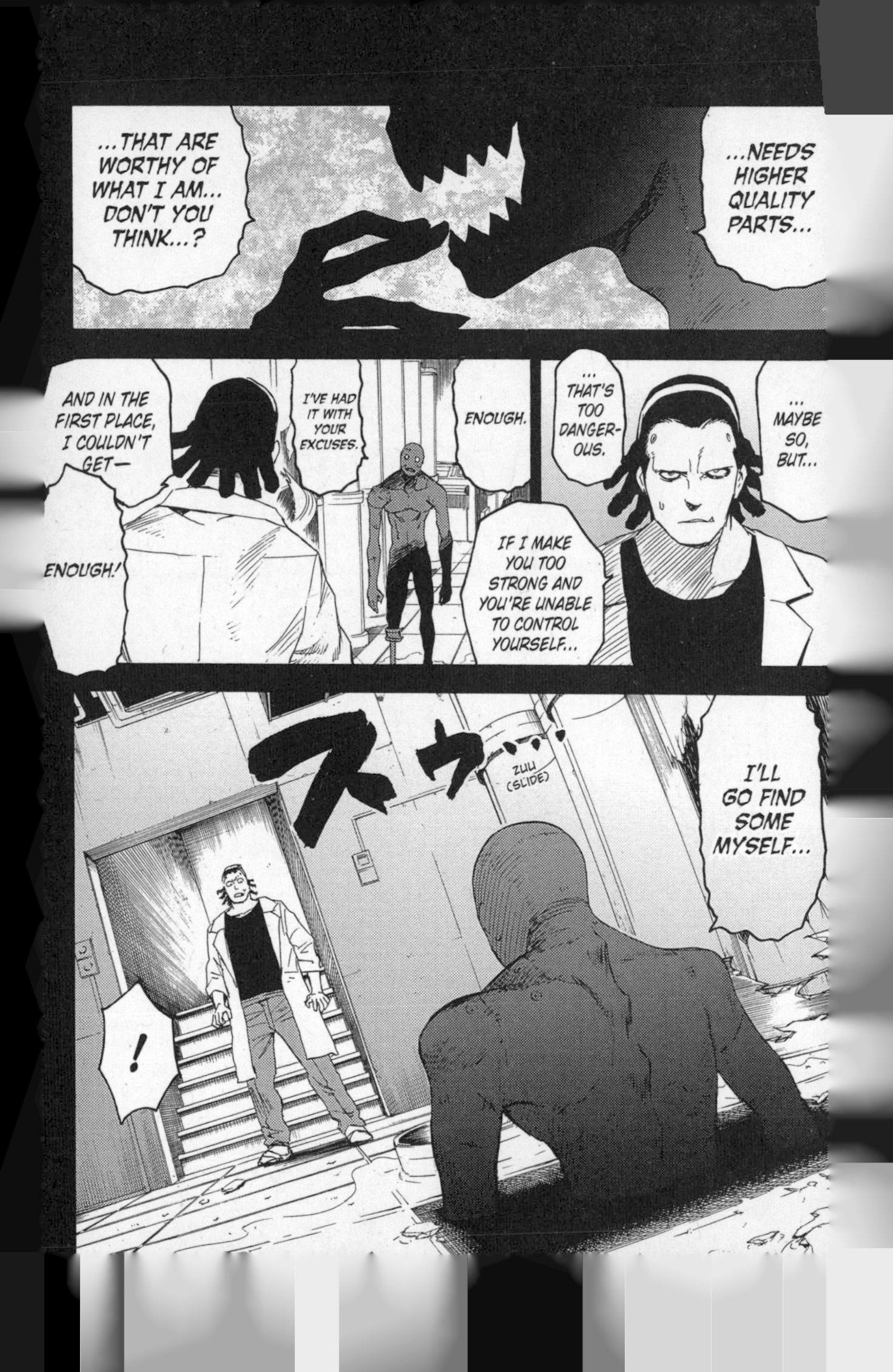
...NEEDS HIGHER QUALITY PARTS...
...THAT ARE WORTHY OF WHAT I AM... DON'T YOU THINK...?
... MAYBE SO, BUT...
... THAT'S TOO DANGER-OUS.
IF I MAKE YOU TOO STRONG AND YOU'RE UNABLE TO CONTROL YOURSELF...
ENOUGH.
I'VE HAD IT WITH YOUR EXCUSES.
AND IN THE FIRST PLACE, I COULDN'T GET—
ENOUGH!
I'LL GO FIND SOME MYSELF...
ZUU (SLIDE)
!

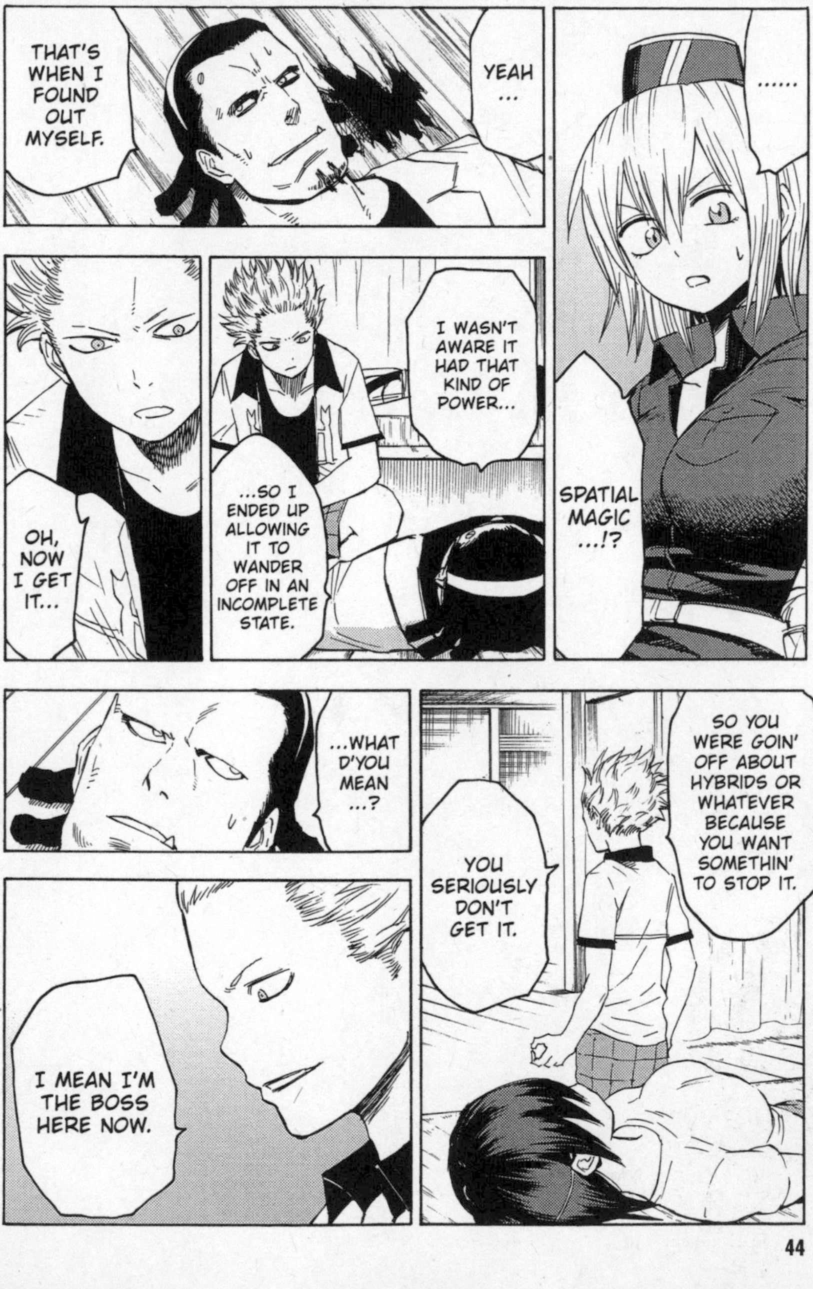
......
SPATIAL MAGIC ...!?
YEAH ...
THAT'S WHEN I FOUND OUT MYSELF.
I WASN'T AWARE IT HAD THAT KIND OF POWER...
...SO I ENDED UP ALLOWING IT TO WANDER OFF IN AN INCOMPLETE STATE.
OH, NOW I GET IT...
SO YOU WERE GOIN' OFF ABOUT HYBRIDS OR WHATEVER BECAUSE YOU WANT SOMETHIN' TO STOP IT.
YOU SERIOUSLY DON'T GET IT.
...WHAT D'YOU MEAN ...?
I MEAN I'M THE BOSS HERE NOW.

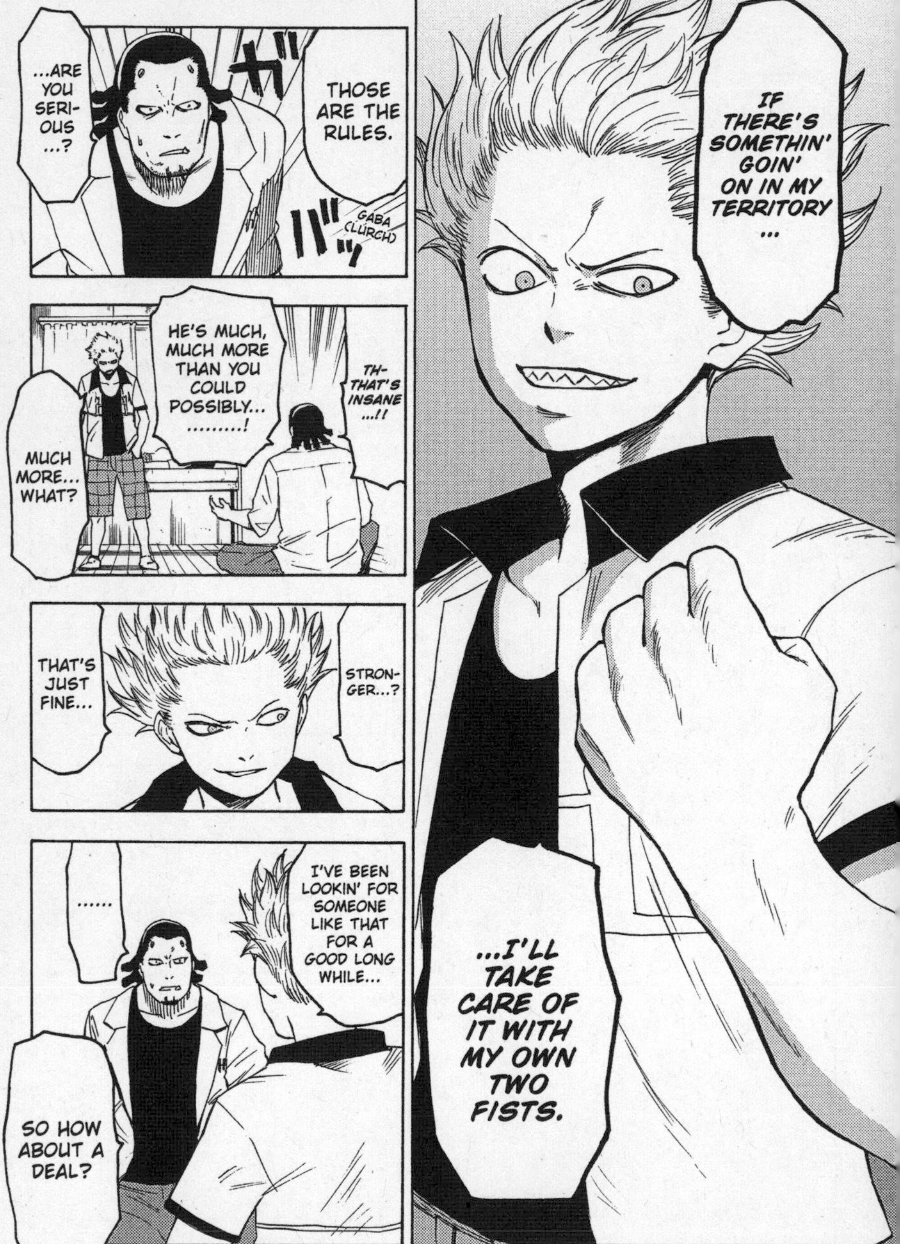
IF THERE'S SOMETHIN' GOIN' ON IN MY TERRITORY ...
...I'LL TAKE CARE OF IT WITH MY OWN TWO FISTS.
THOSE ARE THE RULES.
GABA (LURCH)
...ARE YOU SERI-OUS ...?
TH-THAT'S INSANE ...!!
HE'S MUCH, MUCH MORE THAN YOU COULD POSSIBLY... ....!
MUCH MORE... WHAT?
STRON-GER...?
THAT'S JUST FINE...
I'VE BEEN LOOKIN' FOR SOMEONE LIKE THAT FOR A GOOD LONG WHILE...
......
SO HOW ABOUT A DEAL?

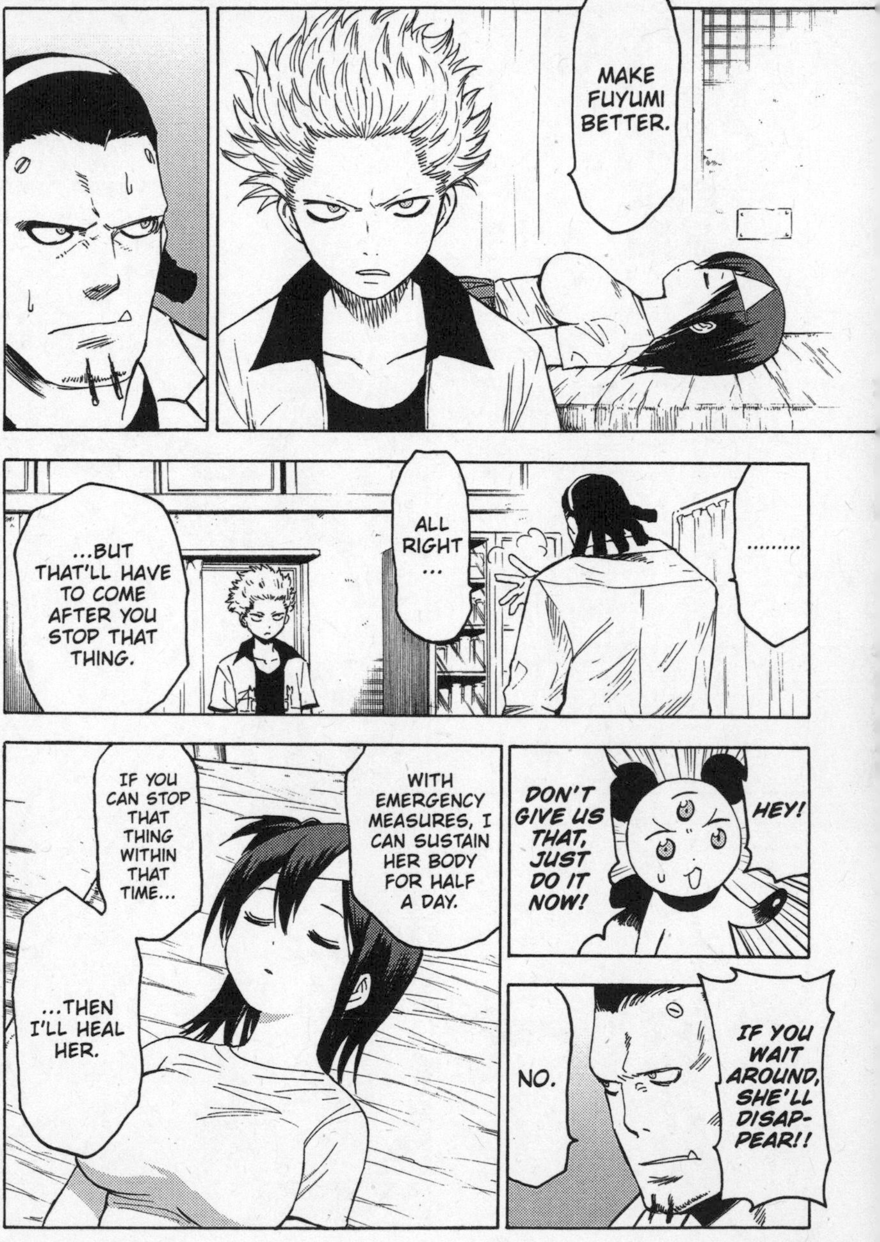
MAKE FUYUMI BETTER.
....
ALL RIGHT ...
...BUT THAT'LL HAVE TO COME AFTER YOU STOP THAT THING.
HEY!
DON'T GIVE US THAT, JUST DO IT NOW!
IF YOU WAIT AROUND, SHE'LL DISAP-PEAR!!
NO.
WITH EMERGENCY MEASURES, I CAN SUSTAIN HER BODY FOR HALF A DAY.
IF YOU CAN STOP THAT THING WITHIN THAT TIME...
...THEN I'LL HEAL HER.

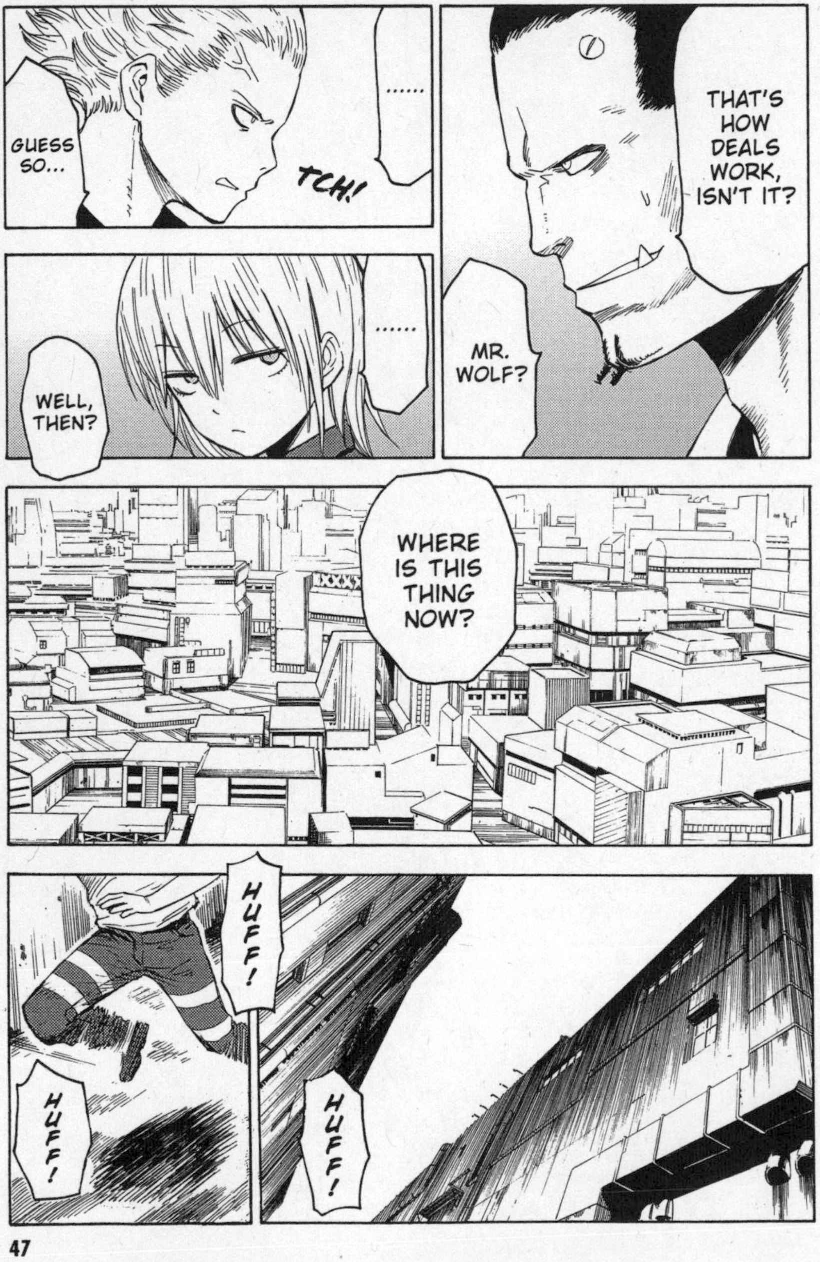
THAT'S HOW DEALS WORK, ISN'T IT?
MR. WOLF?
......
TCH!
GUESS SO...
......
WELL, THEN?
WHERE IS THIS THING NOW?
HUFF!
HUFF!
HUFF!

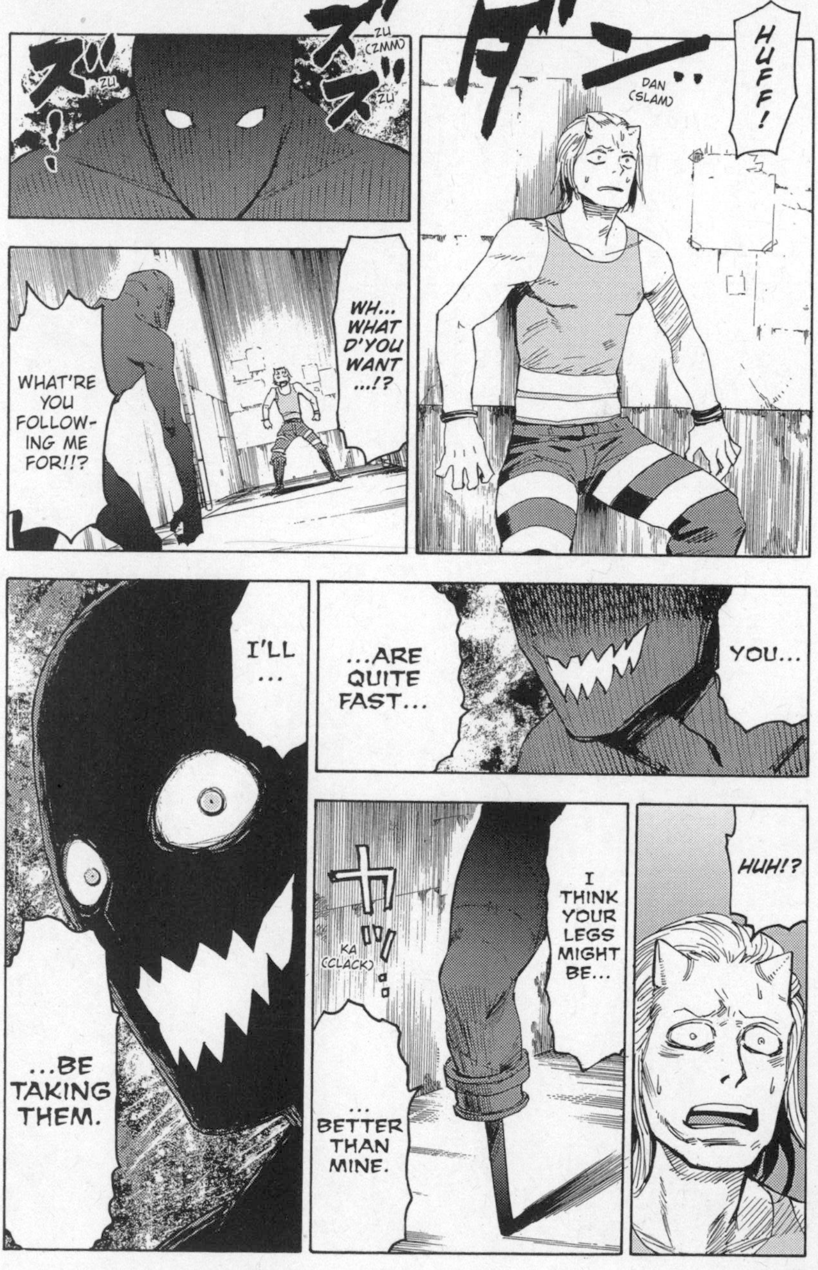

DAN (SLAM)
HUFF!
ZU (ZMM)
ZU
ZU
WH... WHAT D'YOU WANT ...!?
WHAT'RE YOU FOLLOW-ING ME FOR!!?
YOU...
...ARE QUITE FAST...
HUH!?
I THINK YOUR LEGS MIGHT BE...
KA (CLACK)
... BETTER THAN MINE.
I'LL ...
...BE TAKING THEM.

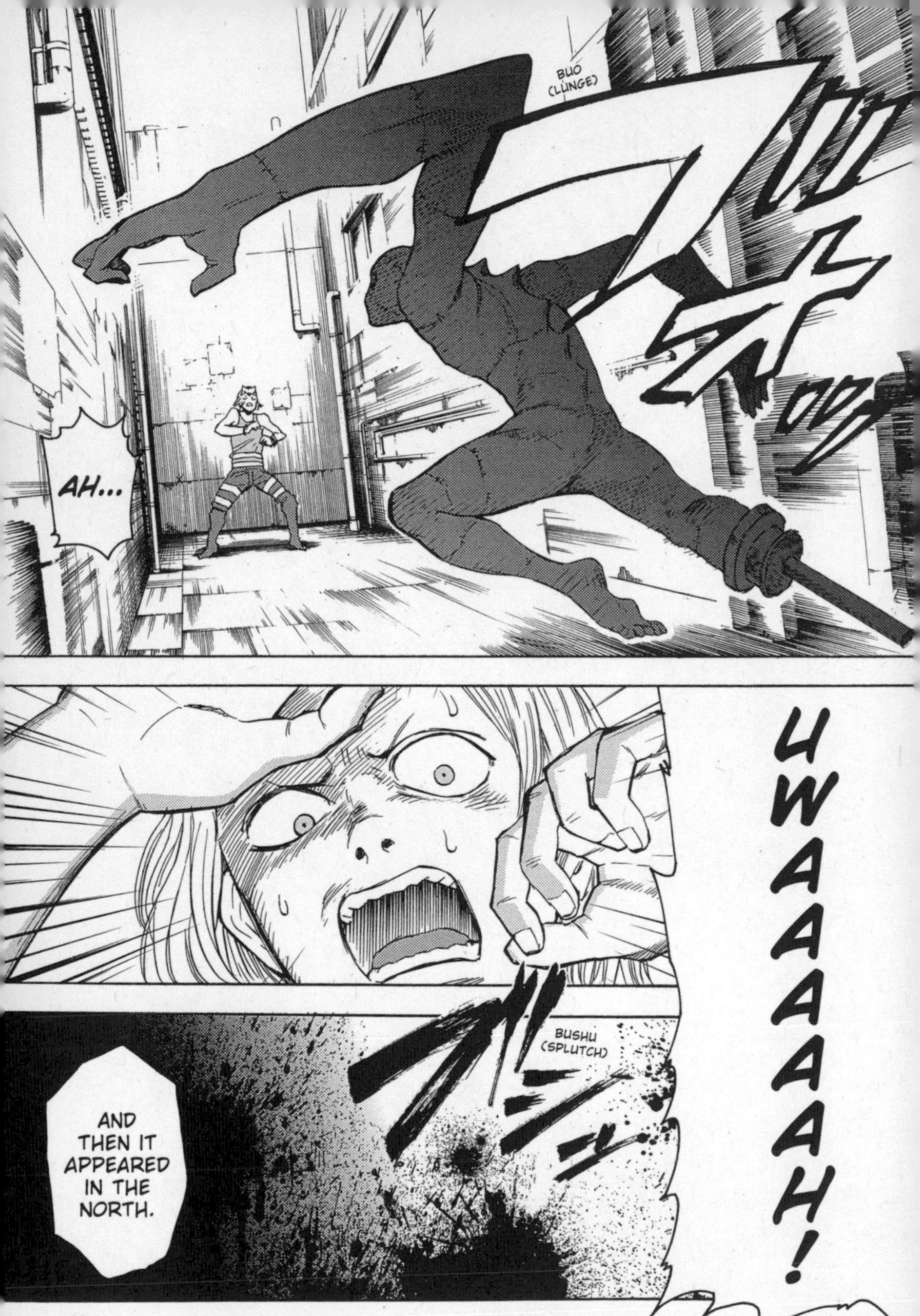
BUO (LUNGE)
AH...
UWAAAAAAAH!
BUSHU (SPLUTCH)
AND THEN IT APPEARED IN THE NORTH.

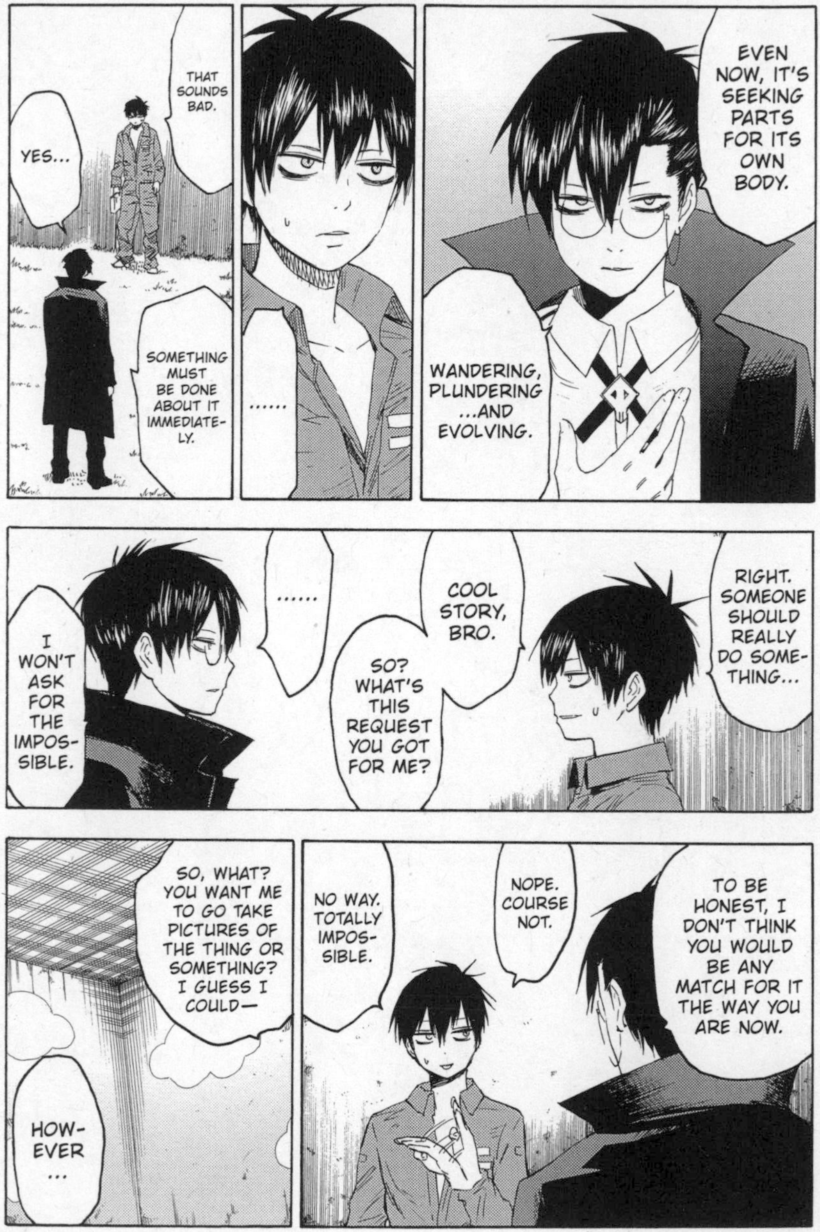
EVEN NOW, IT'S SEEKING PARTS FOR ITS OWN BODY.
WANDERING, PLUNDERING ...AND EVOLVING.
......
THAT SOUNDS BAD.
YES...
SOMETHING MUST BE DONE ABOUT IT IMMEDIATELY.
RIGHT. SOMEONE SHOULD REALLY DO SOMETHING...
COOL STORY, BRO.
SO? WHAT'S THIS REQUEST YOU GOT FOR ME?
......
I WON'T ASK FOR THE IMPOSSIBLE.
TO BE HONEST, I DON'T THINK YOU WOULD BE ANY MATCH FOR IT THE WAY YOU ARE NOW.
NOPE. COURSE NOT.
NO WAY. TOTALLY IMPOSSIBLE.
SO, WHAT? YOU WANT ME TO GO TAKE PICTURES OF THE THING OR SOMETHING? I GUESS I COULD—
HOWEVER...

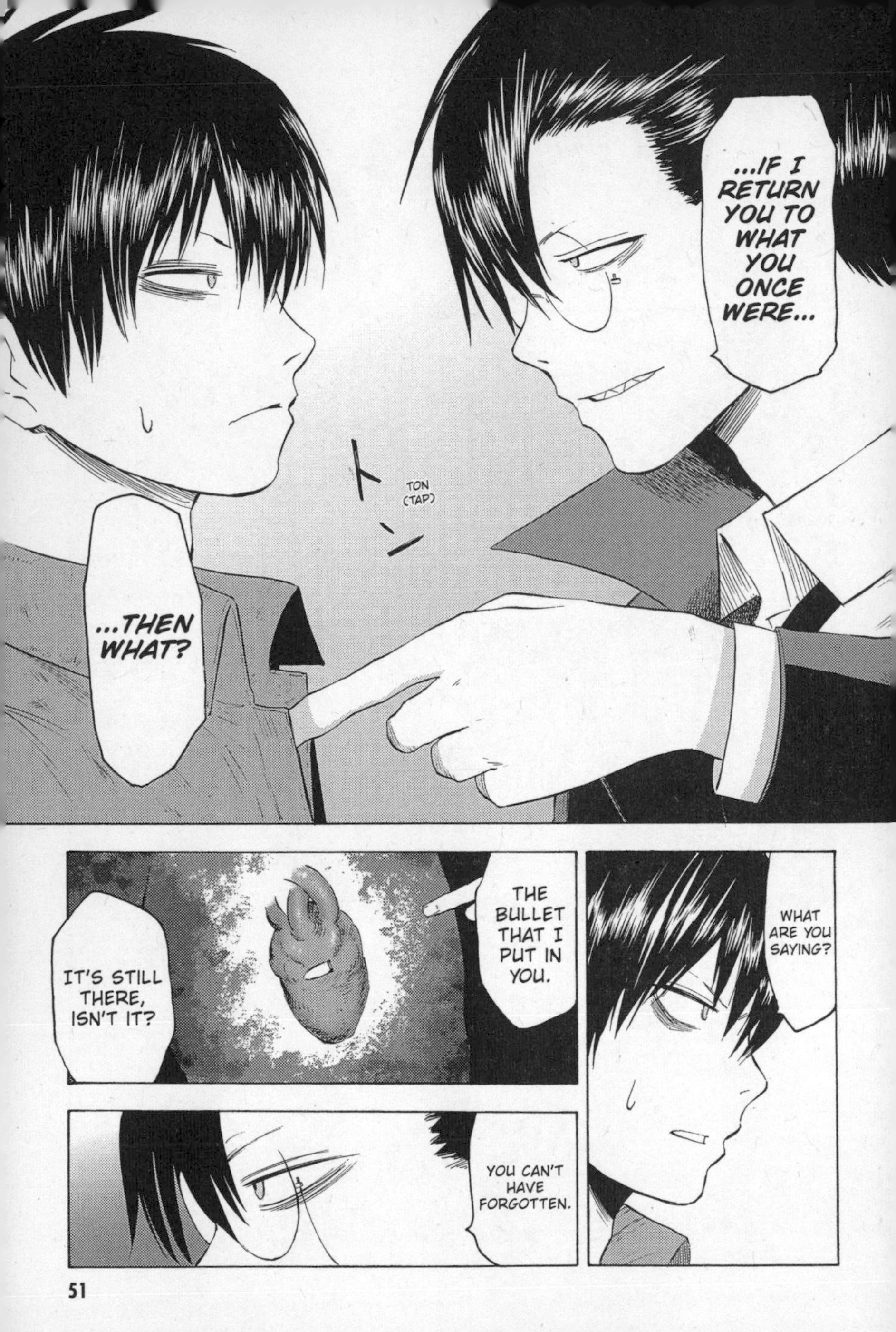

...IF I RETURN YOU TO WHAT YOU ONCE WERE...
TON (TAP)
...THEN WHAT?
WHAT ARE YOU SAYING?
THE BULLET THAT I PUT IN YOU.
IT'S STILL THERE, ISN'T IT?
YOU CAN'T HAVE FORGOTTEN.

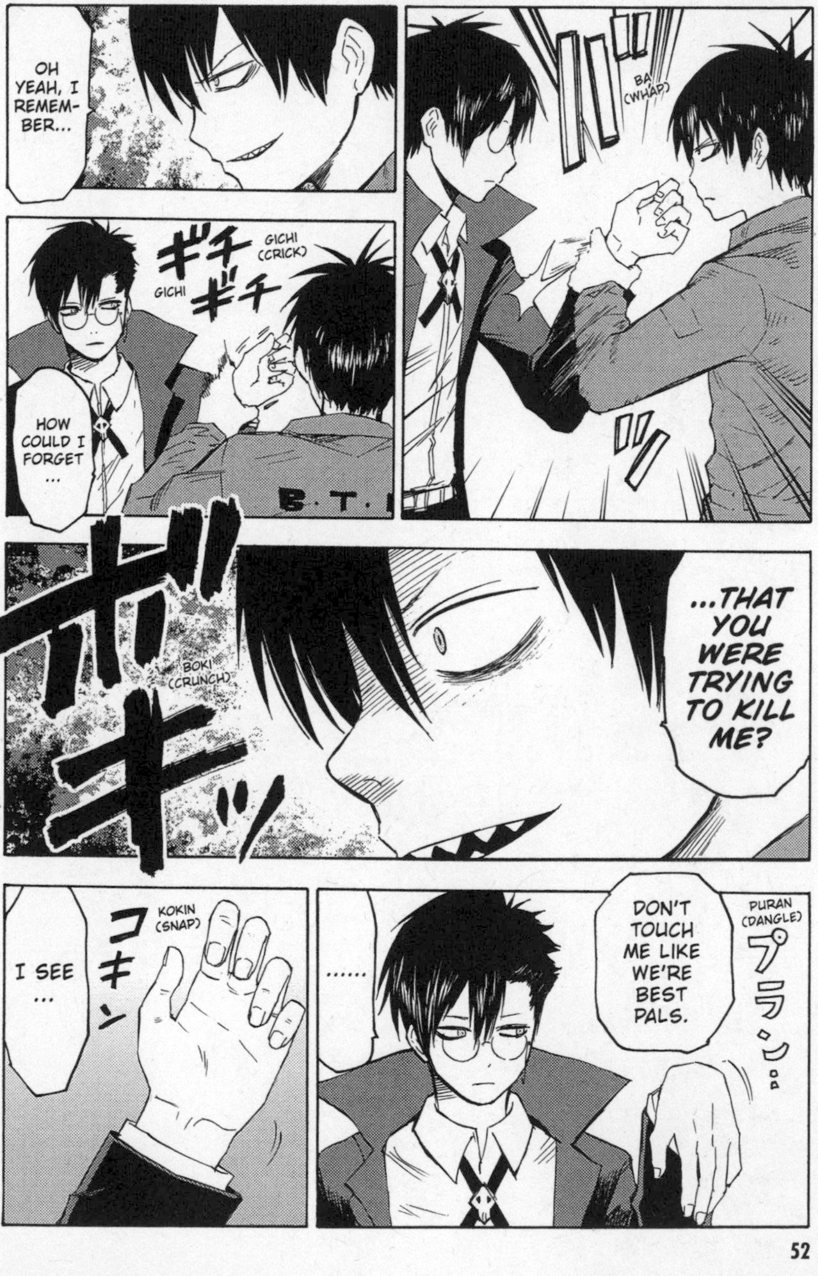
BA (WHAP)
OH YEAH, I REMEMBER...
GICHI (CRICK)
GICHI
HOW COULD I FORGET...
B.T.I
...THAT YOU WERE TRYING TO KILL ME?
BOKI (CRUNCH)
PURAN (DANGLE)
DON'T TOUCH ME LIKE WE'RE BEST PALS.
......
KOKIN (SNAP)
I SEE...

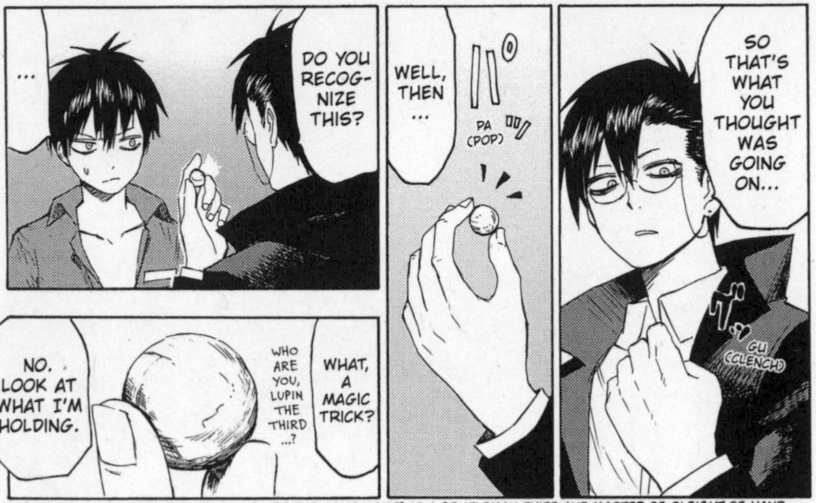
SO THAT'S WHAT YOU THOUGHT WAS GOING ON...
GU (CLENCH)
WELL, THEN...
PA (POP)
DO YOU RECOG-NIZE THIS?
...
WHAT, A MAGIC TRICK?
WHO ARE YOU, LUPIN THE THIRD...?
NO. LOOK AT WHAT I'M HOLDING.

NOTE: LUPIN THE THIRD (OF THE MANGA BY THE SAME NAME) IS A GENTLEMAN THIEF AND MASTER OF SLEIGHT OF HAND.

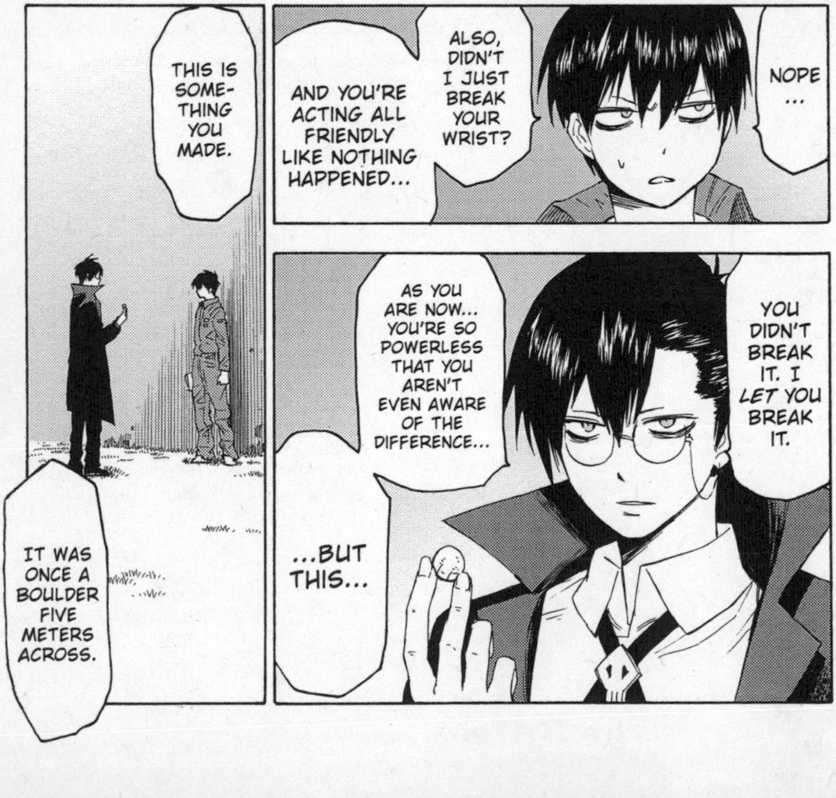
NOPE...
ALSO, DIDN'T I JUST BREAK YOUR WRIST?
AND YOU'RE ACTING ALL FRIENDLY LIKE NOTHING HAPPENED...
YOU DIDN'T BREAK IT. I *LET* YOU BREAK IT.
AS YOU ARE NOW... YOU'RE SO POWERLESS THAT YOU AREN'T EVEN AWARE OF THE DIFFERENCE...
...BUT THIS...
THIS IS SOME-THING YOU MADE.
IT WAS ONCE A BOULDER FIVE METERS ACROSS.

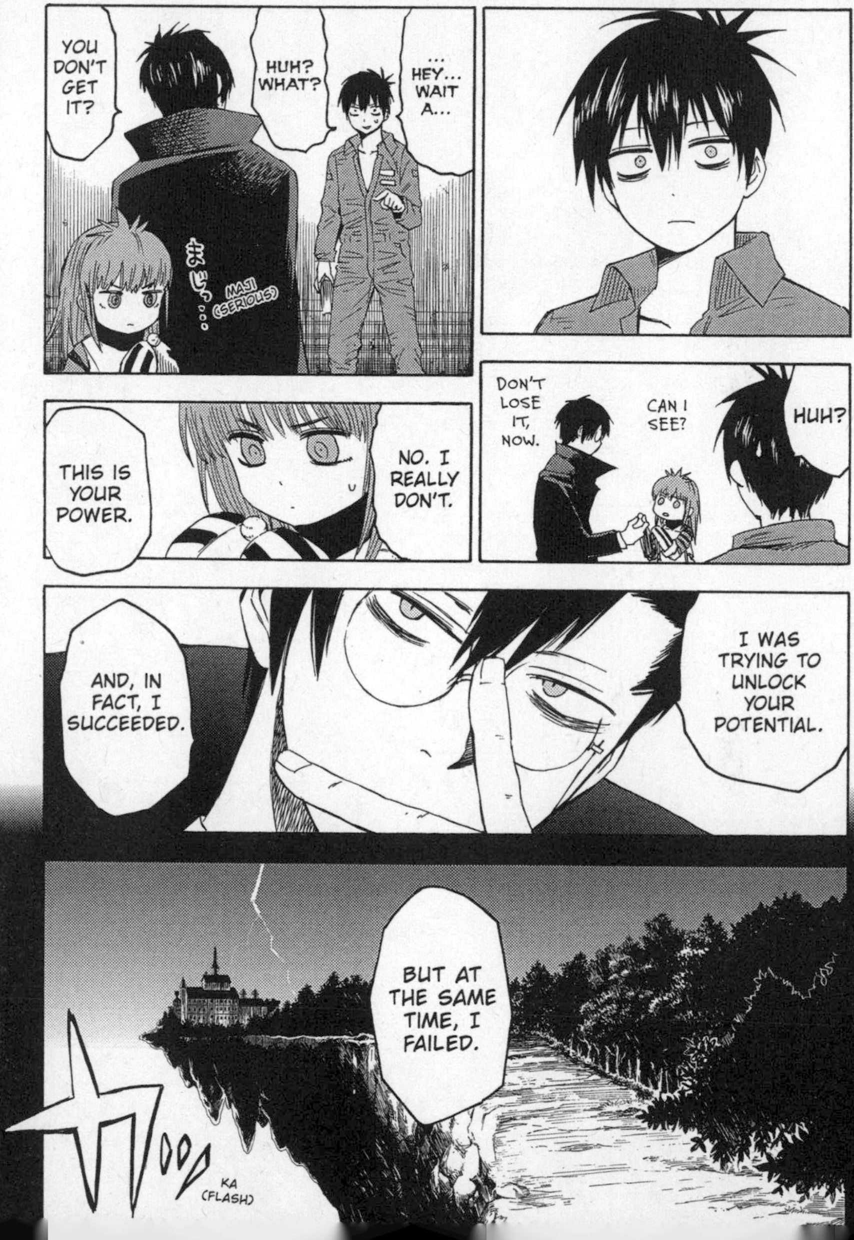
... HEY... WAIT A...
HUH? WHAT?
YOU DON'T GET IT?
まじ...
MAJI (SERIOUS)
HUH?
CAN I SEE?
DON'T LOSE IT, NOW.
NO. I REALLY DON'T.
THIS IS YOUR POWER.
I WAS TRYING TO UNLOCK YOUR POTENTIAL.
AND, IN FACT, I SUCCEEDED.
BUT AT THE SAME TIME, I FAILED.
KA (FLASH)

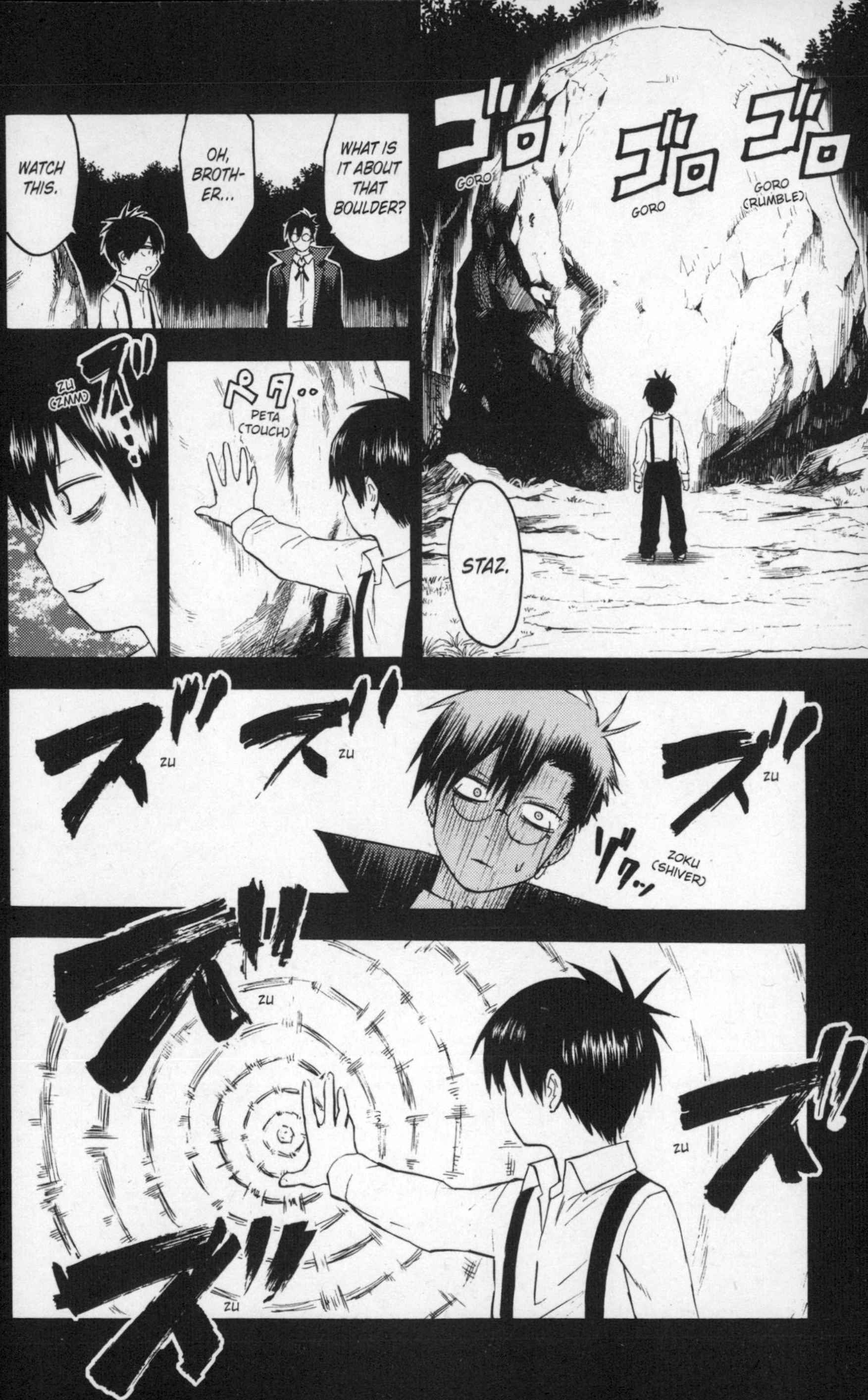

ゴロ
GORO (RUMBLE)
ゴロ
GORO
ゴロ
GORO
STAZ.
WHAT IS IT ABOUT THAT BOULDER?
OH, BROTHER...
WATCH THIS.
ペタ..
PETA (TOUCH)
ズ
ZU (ZMM)
ズ
ZU
ズ
ZU
ズ
ZU
ゾクッ
ZOKU (SHIVER)
ズ
ZU
ズ
ZU
ズ
ZU

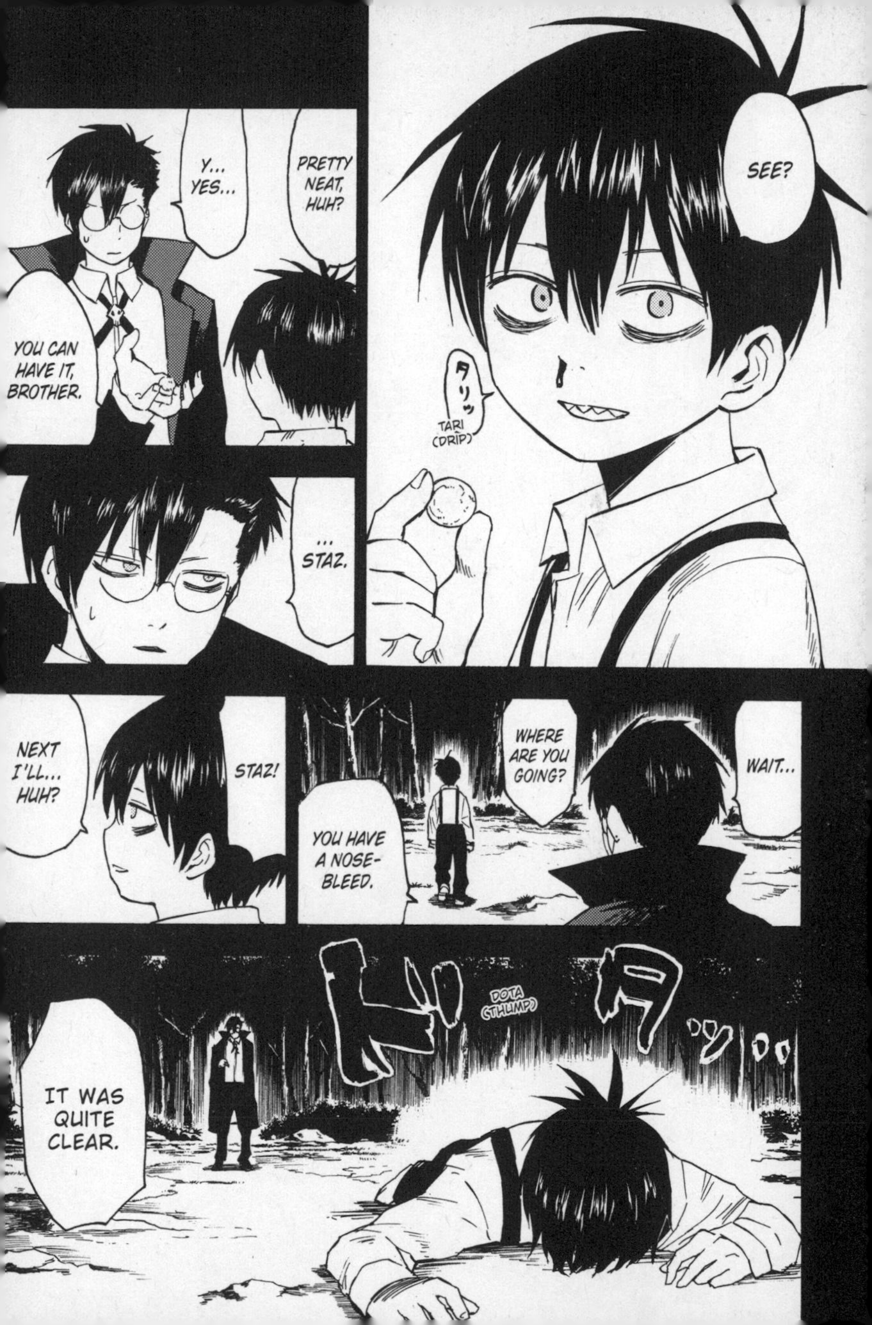
SEE?
タリッ
TARI (DRIP)
PRETTY NEAT, HUH?
Y... YES...
YOU CAN HAVE IT, BROTHER.
... STAZ.
WAIT...
WHERE ARE YOU GOING?
YOU HAVE A NOSE-BLEED.
STAZ!
NEXT I'LL... HUH?
ドタッ
DOTA (THUMP)
IT WAS QUITE CLEAR.

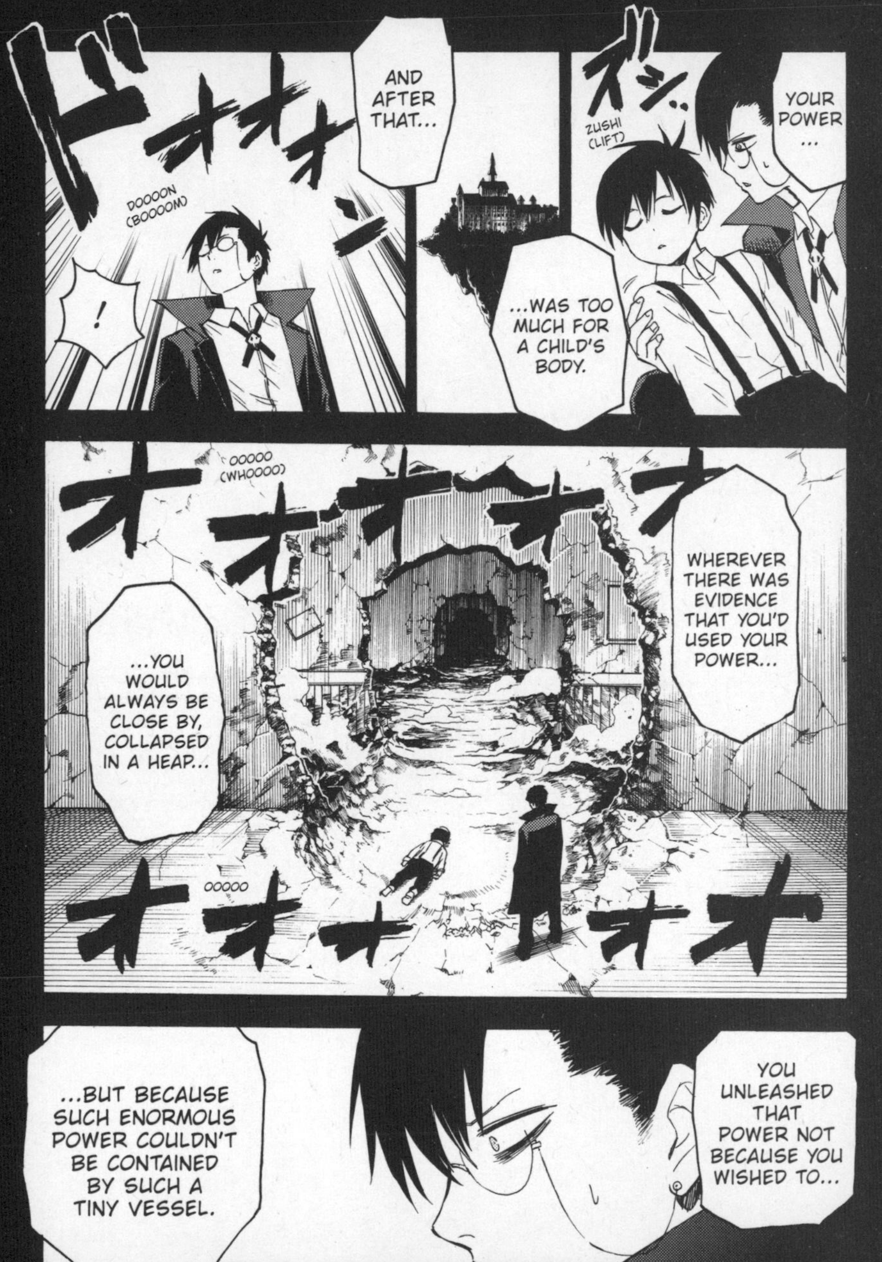
ZUSHI (LIFT)
YOUR POWER ...
...WAS TOO MUCH FOR A CHILD'S BODY.
AND AFTER THAT...
DOOOON (BOOOOM)
!
OOOOO (WHOOOO)
WHEREVER THERE WAS EVIDENCE THAT YOU'D USED YOUR POWER...
...YOU WOULD ALWAYS BE CLOSE BY, COLLAPSED IN A HEAP...
OOOOO
YOU UNLEASHED THAT POWER NOT BECAUSE YOU WISHED TO...
...BUT BECAUSE SUCH ENORMOUS POWER COULDN'T BE CONTAINED BY SUCH A TINY VESSEL.

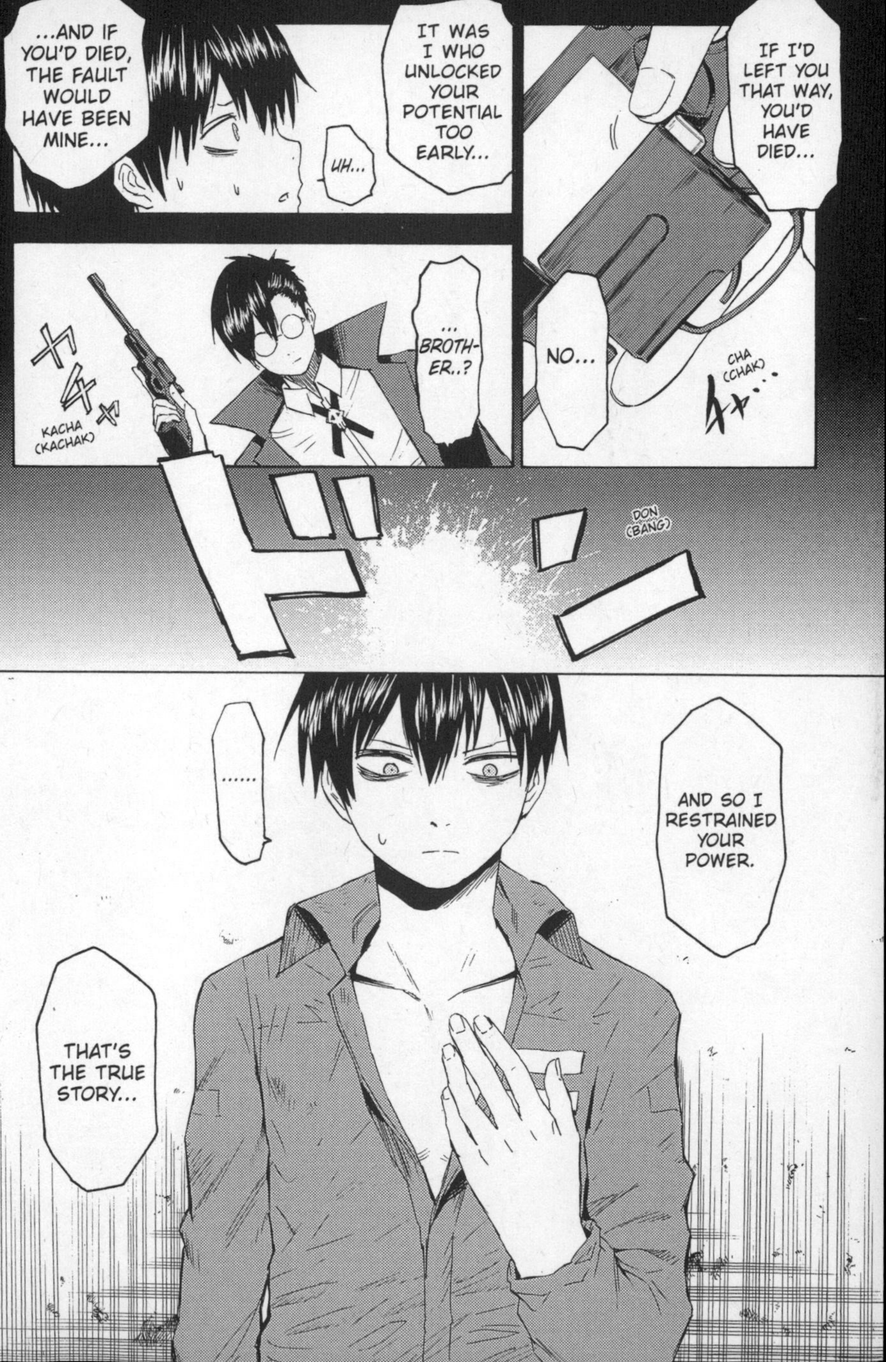
IF I'D LEFT YOU THAT WAY, YOU'D HAVE DIED...
NO...
CHA (CHAK)
IT WAS I WHO UNLOCKED YOUR POTENTIAL TOO EARLY...
UH...
...AND IF YOU'D DIED, THE FAULT WOULD HAVE BEEN MINE...
... BROTHER-ER..?
KACHA (KACHAK)
DON (BANG)
AND SO I RESTRAINED YOUR POWER.
......
THAT'S THE TRUE STORY...

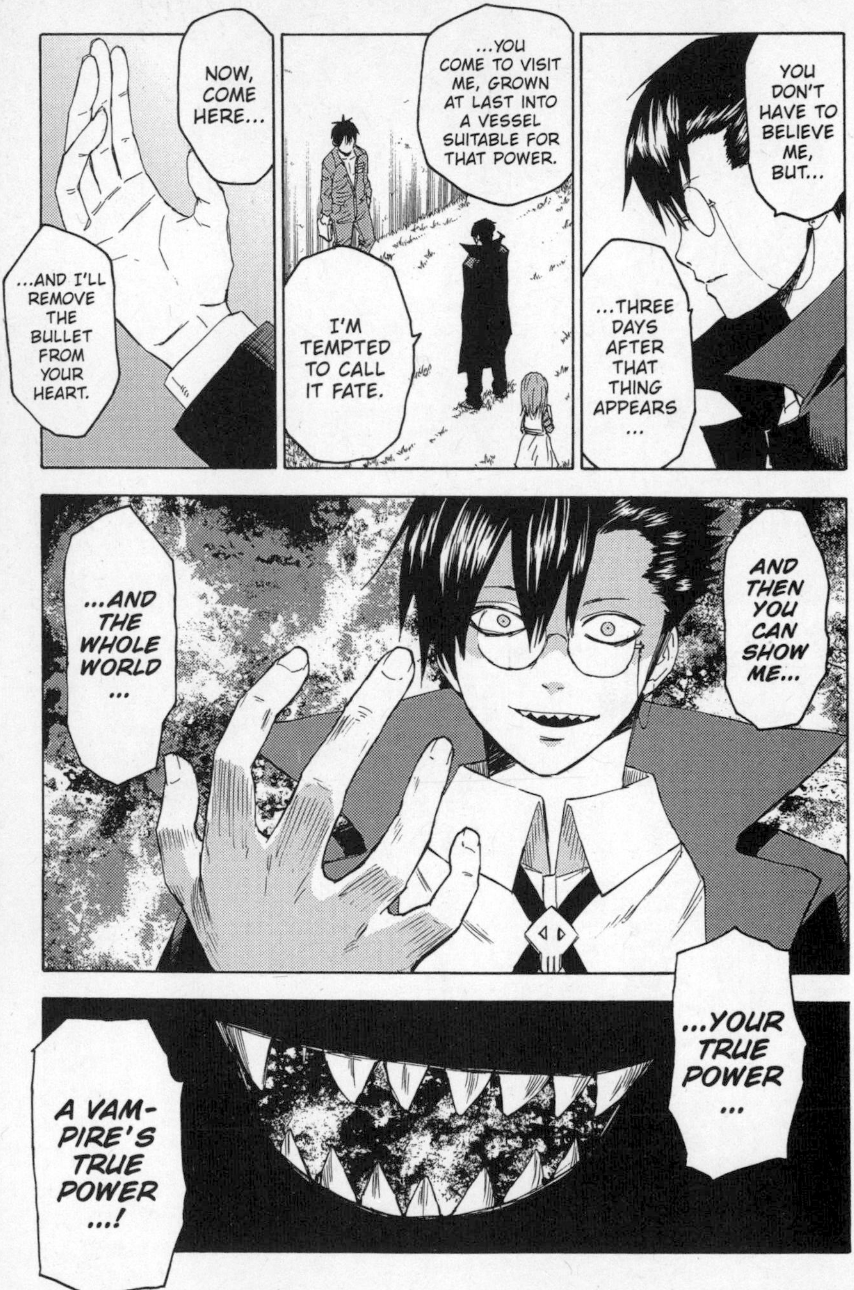
YOU DON'T HAVE TO BELIEVE ME, BUT...
...THREE DAYS AFTER THAT THING APPEARS ...
...YOU COME TO VISIT ME, GROWN AT LAST INTO A VESSEL SUITABLE FOR THAT POWER.
I'M TEMPTED TO CALL IT FATE.
NOW, COME HERE...
...AND I'LL REMOVE THE BULLET FROM YOUR HEART.
AND THEN YOU CAN SHOW ME...
...AND THE WHOLE WORLD ...
...YOUR TRUE POWER ...
A VAMPIRE'S TRUE POWER ...!

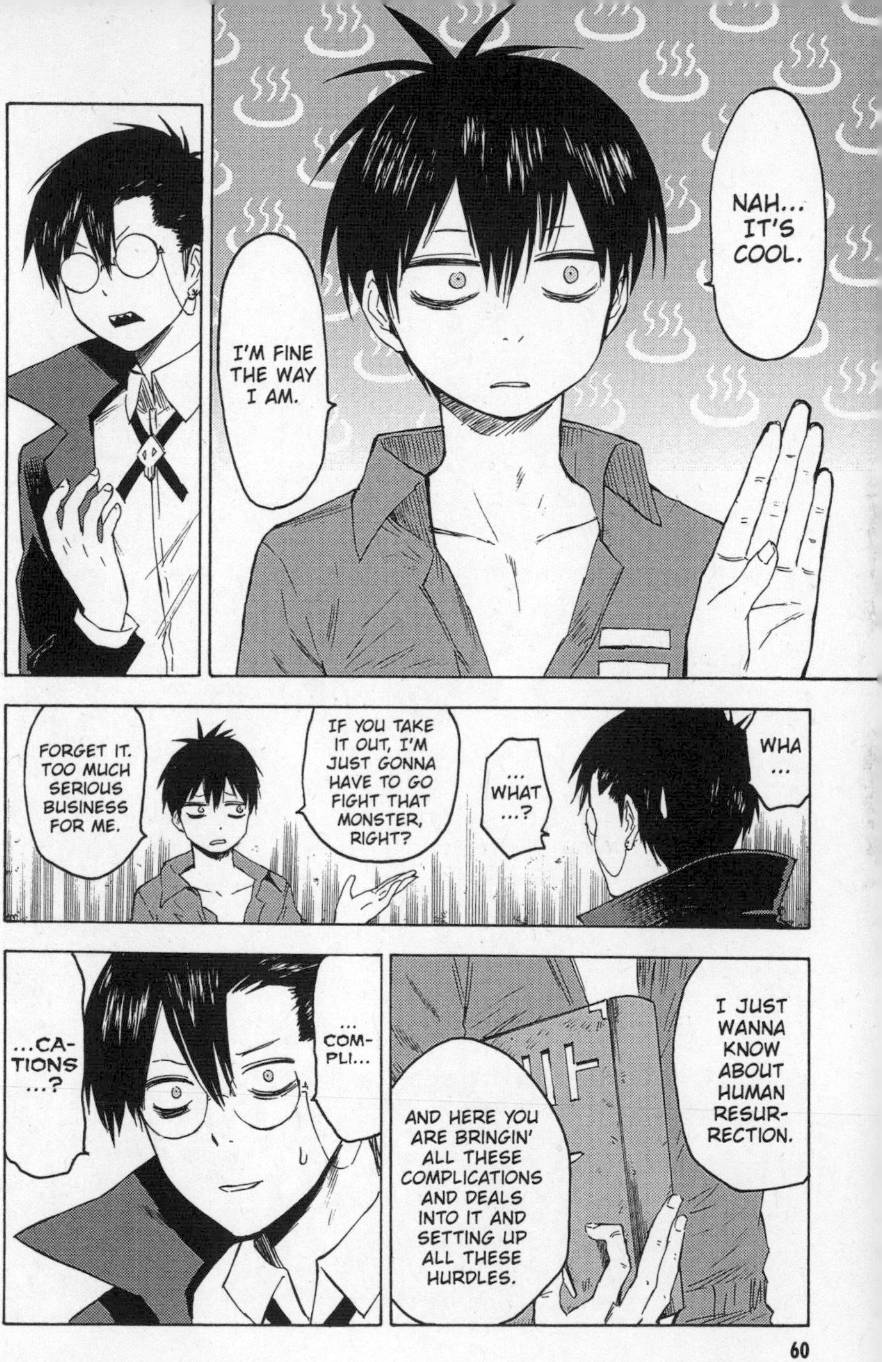
NAH... IT'S COOL.
I'M FINE THE WAY I AM.
WHA ...
... WHAT ...?
IF YOU TAKE IT OUT, I'M JUST GONNA HAVE TO GO FIGHT THAT MONSTER, RIGHT?
FORGET IT. TOO MUCH SERIOUS BUSINESS FOR ME.
I JUST WANNA KNOW ABOUT HUMAN RESUR-RECTION.
AND HERE YOU ARE BRINGIN' ALL THESE COMPLICATIONS AND DEALS INTO IT AND SETTING UP ALL THESE HURDLES.
... COMPLI...
...CA-TIONS ...?

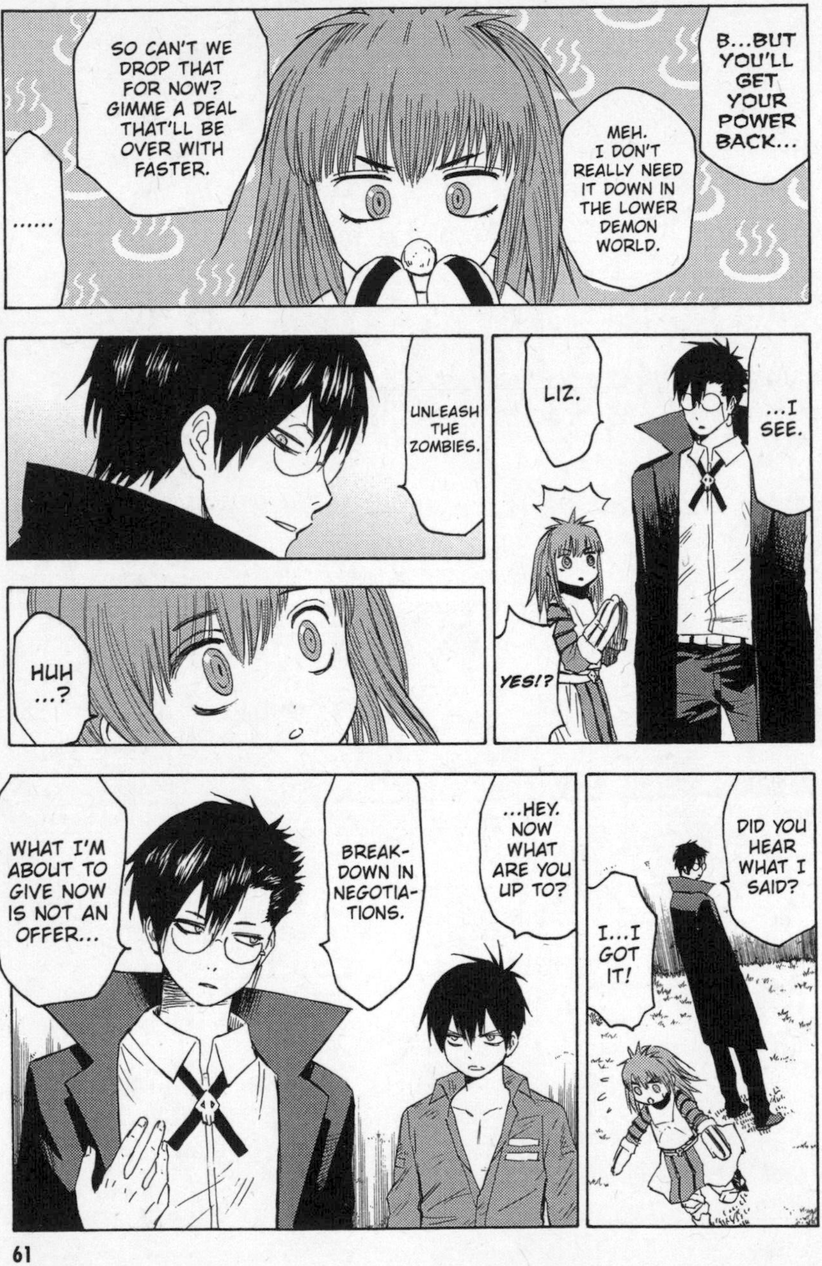
B...BUT YOU'LL GET YOUR POWER BACK...
MEH. I DON'T REALLY NEED IT DOWN IN THE LOWER DEMON WORLD.
SO CAN'T WE DROP THAT FOR NOW? GIMME A DEAL THAT'LL BE OVER WITH FASTER.
......
...I SEE.
LIZ.
YES!?
UNLEASH THE ZOMBIES.
HUH ...?
DID YOU HEAR WHAT I SAID?
I...I GOT IT!
...HEY. NOW WHAT ARE YOU UP TO?
BREAK-DOWN IN NEGOTIA-TIONS.
WHAT I'M ABOUT TO GIVE NOW IS NOT AN OFFER...

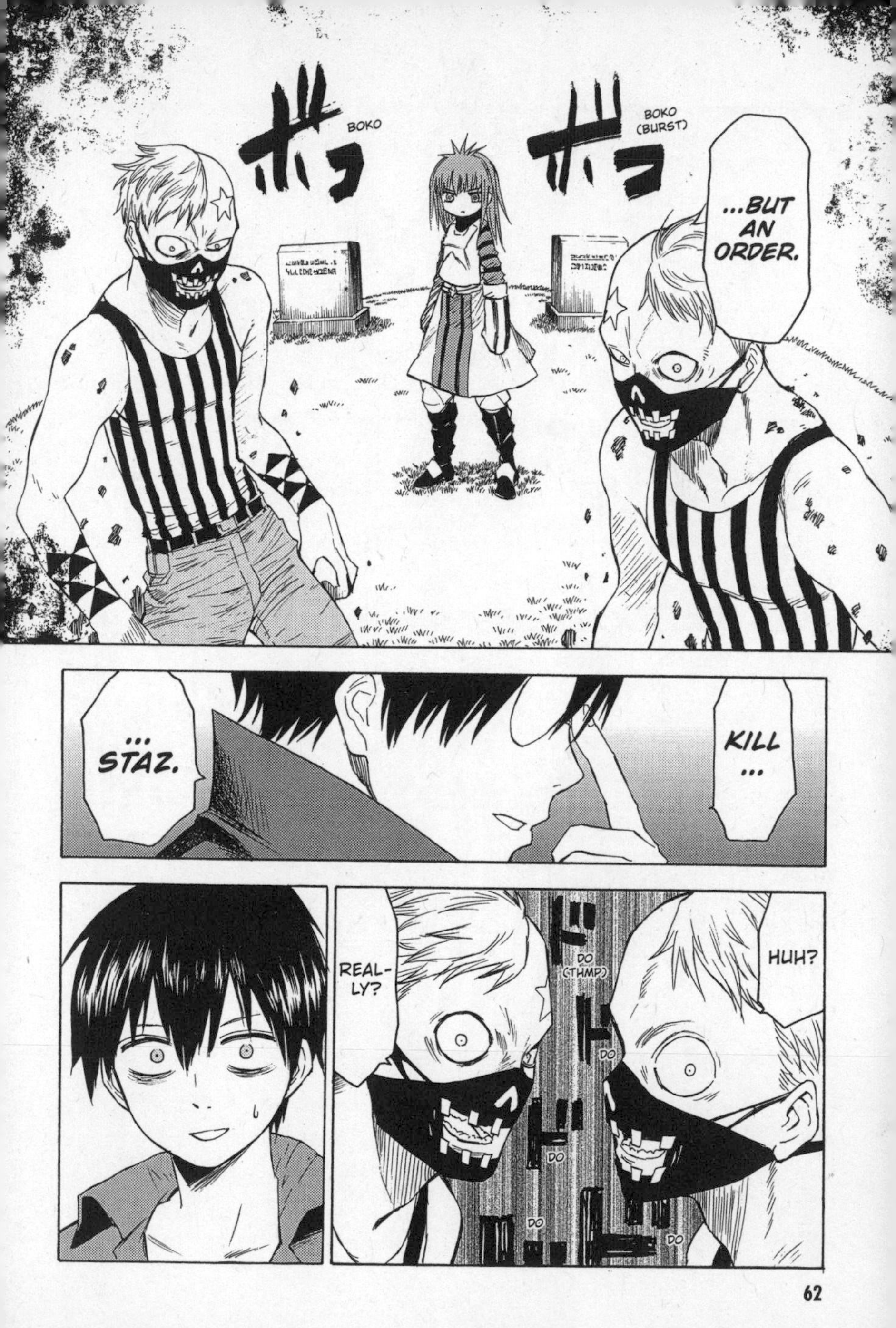
...BUT AN ORDER.
BOKO (BURST)
BOKO
KILL...
...STAZ.
HUH?
DO (THMP)
REAL-LY?
DO
DO
DO
DO

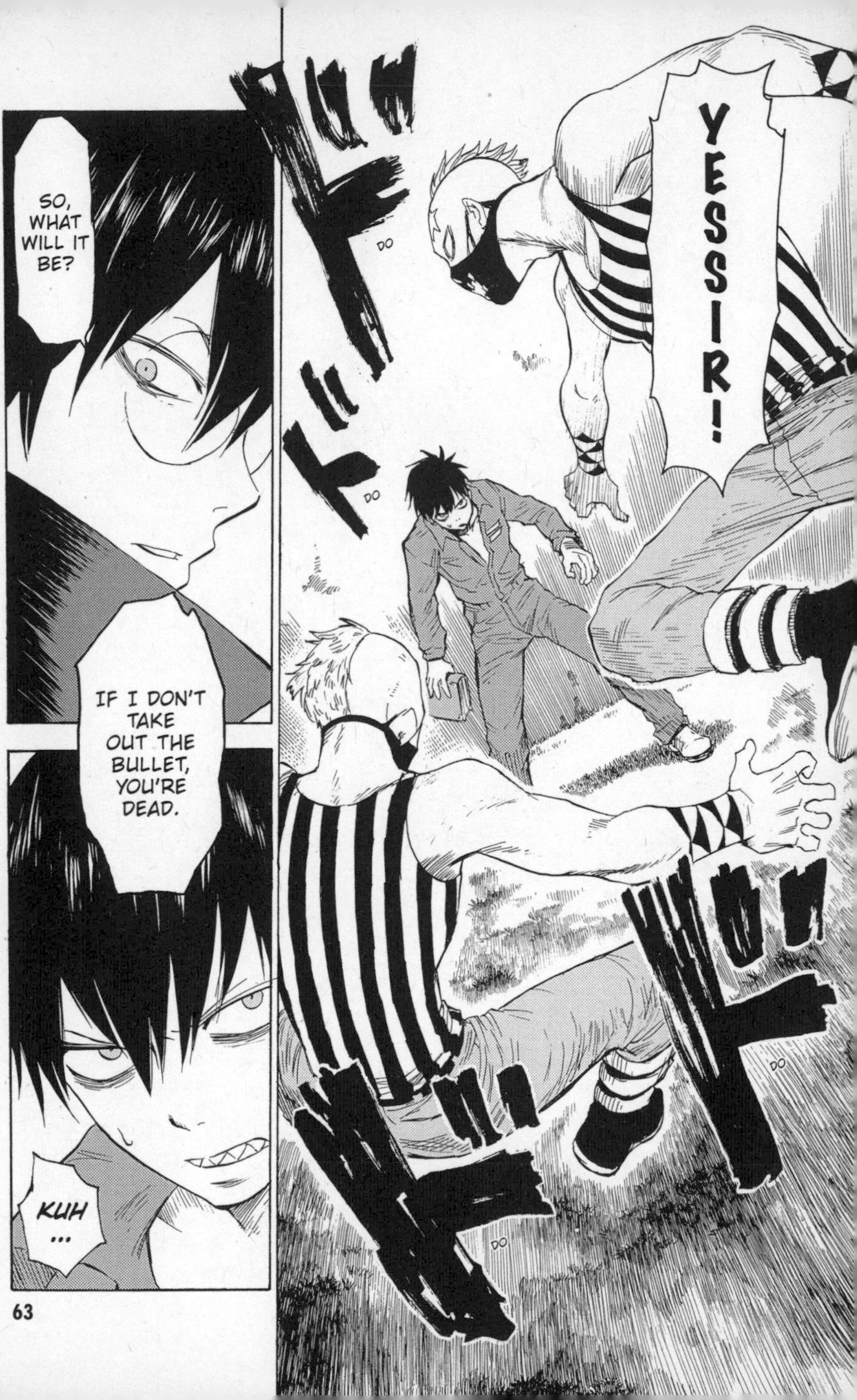
YESSIR!
DO
DO
DO
DO
SO, WHAT WILL IT BE?
IF I DON'T TAKE OUT THE BULLET, YOU'RE DEAD.
KUH ...

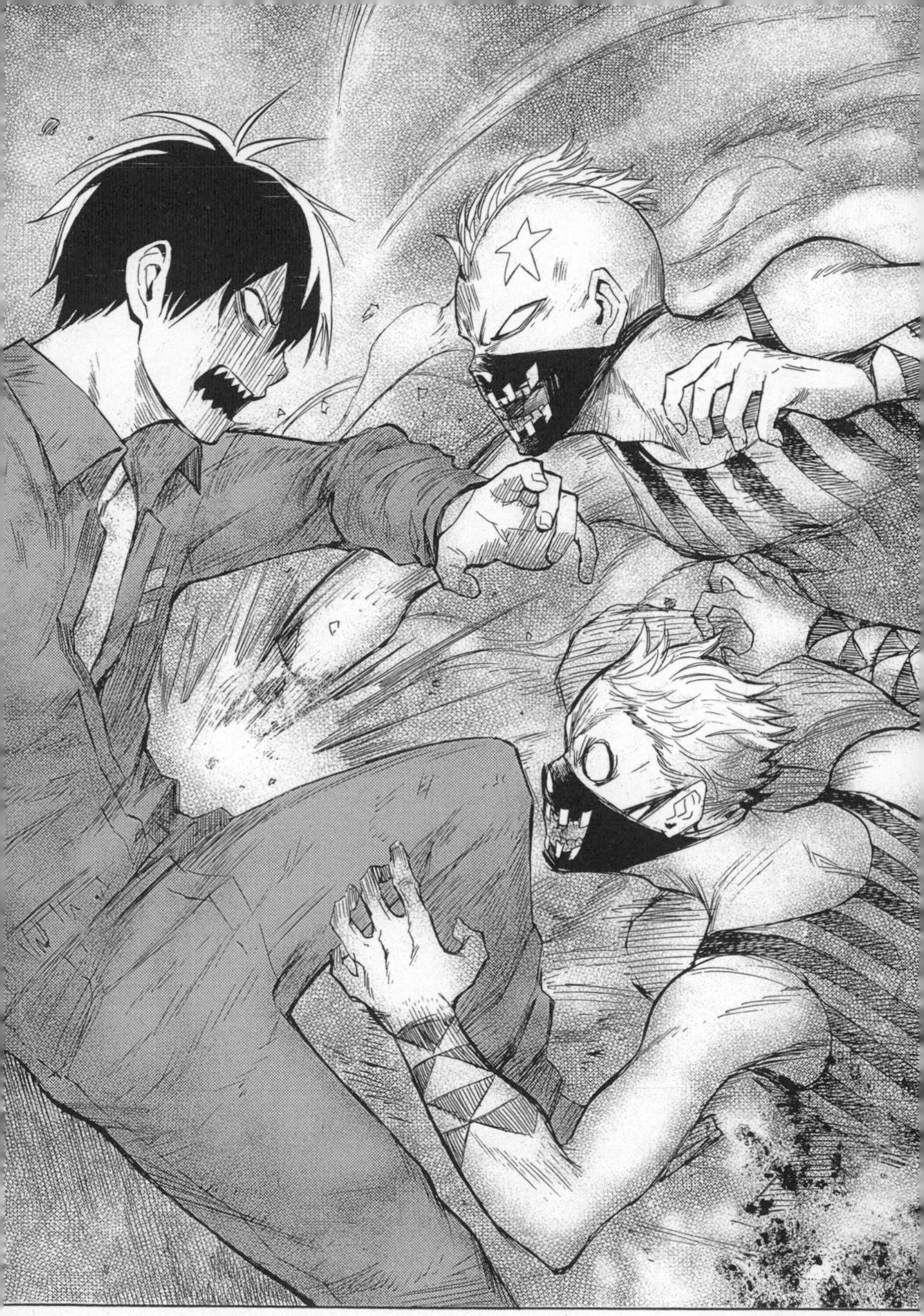

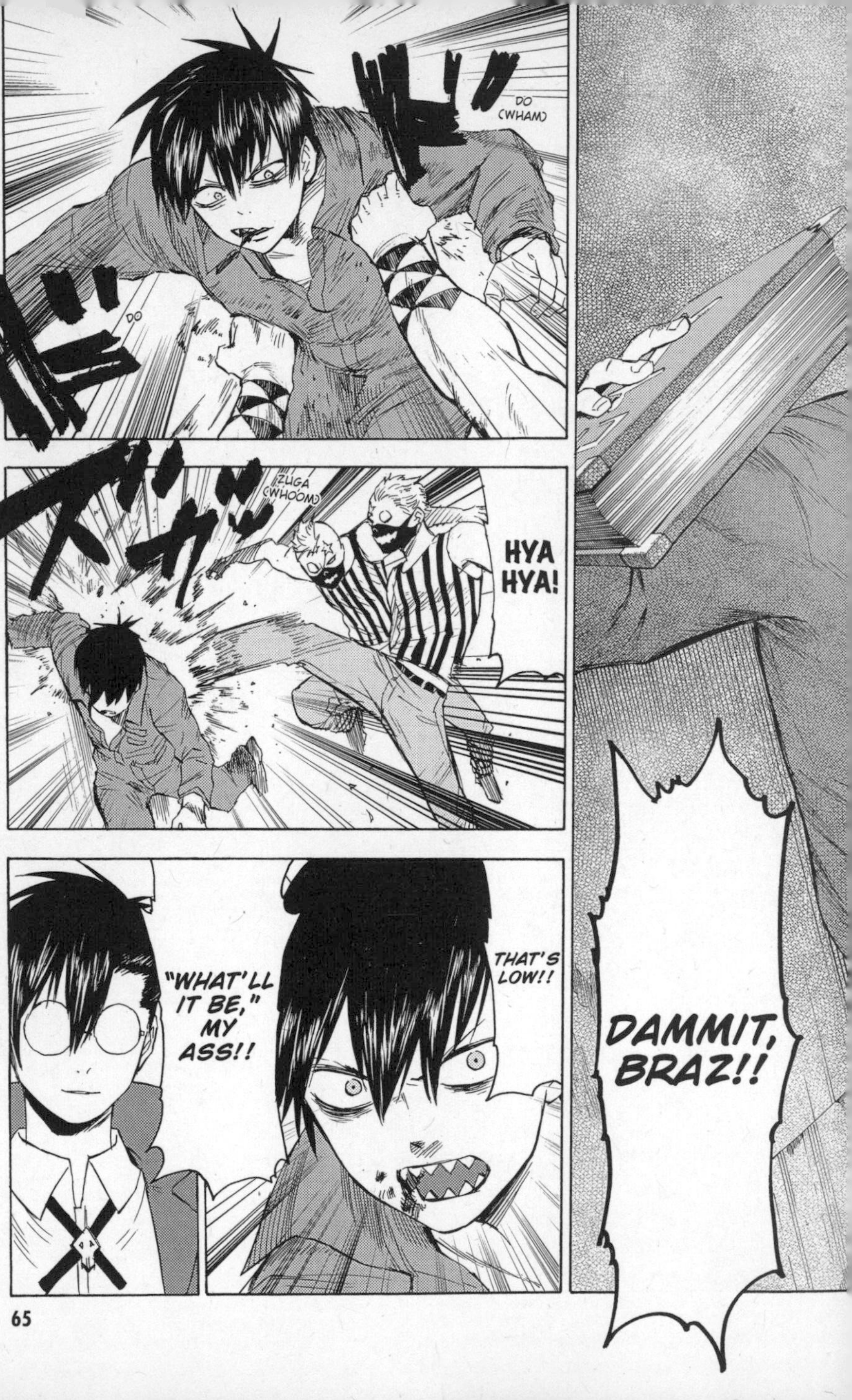
DAMMIT, BRAZ!!
DO (WHAM)
DO
ZUGA (WHOOM)
HYA HYA!
THAT'S LOW!!
"WHAT'LL IT BE," MY ASS!!

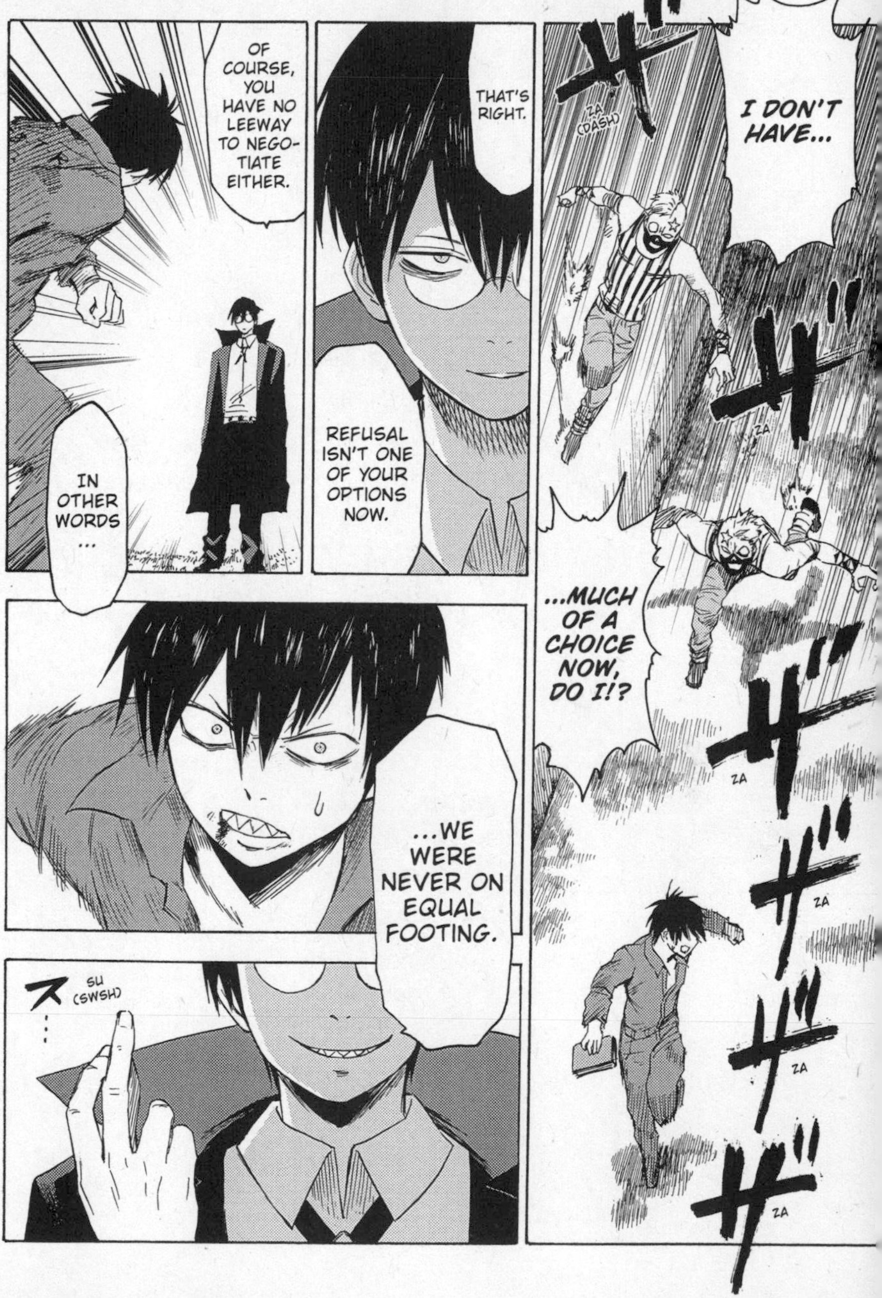
ザ
ZA (DASH)
I DON'T HAVE...
ザ
ZA
...MUCH OF A CHOICE NOW, DO I!?
ザ
ZA
ザ
ZA
ザ
ZA
ザ
ZA
THAT'S RIGHT.
REFUSAL ISN'T ONE OF YOUR OPTIONS NOW.
OF COURSE, YOU HAVE NO LEEWAY TO NEGO-TIATE EITHER.
IN OTHER WORDS...
...WE WERE NEVER ON EQUAL FOOTING.
ス
SU (SWSH)
...

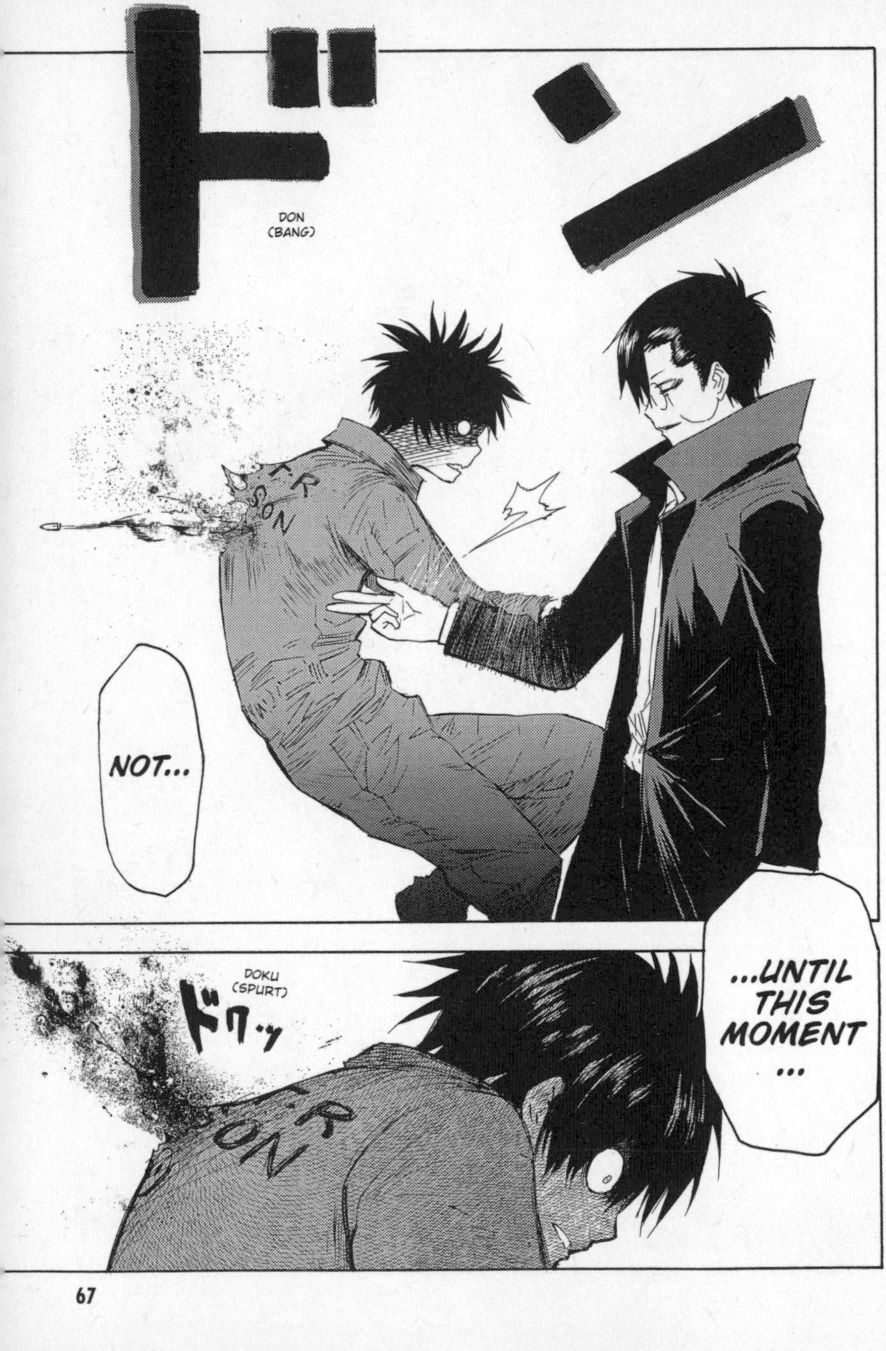
ドン
DON
(BANG)
NOT...
...UNTIL THIS MOMENT ...
DOKU
(SPURT)
ドクッ

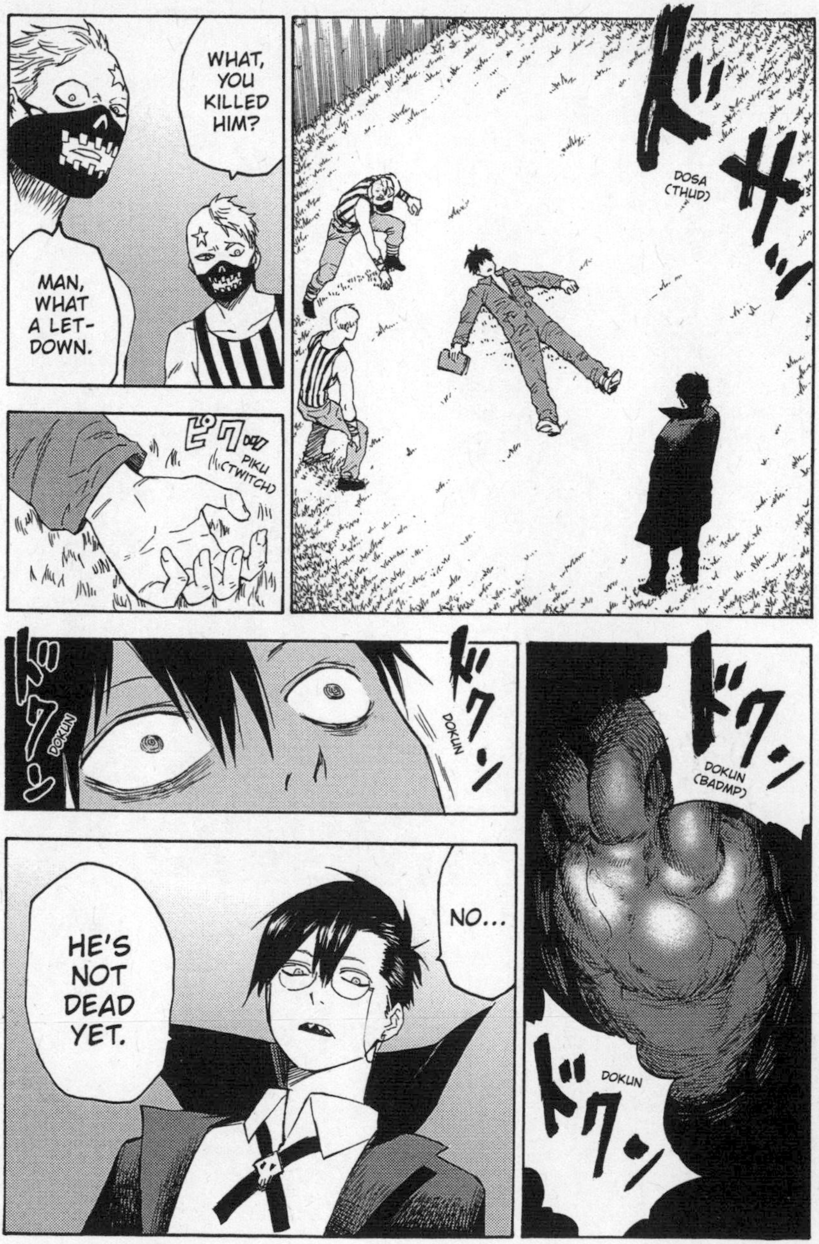
DOSA (THUD)
WHAT, YOU KILLED HIM?
MAN, WHAT A LET-DOWN.
PIKU (TWITCH)
DOKUN (BADMP)
DOKUN
DOKUN
DOKUN
NO...
HE'S NOT DEAD YET.

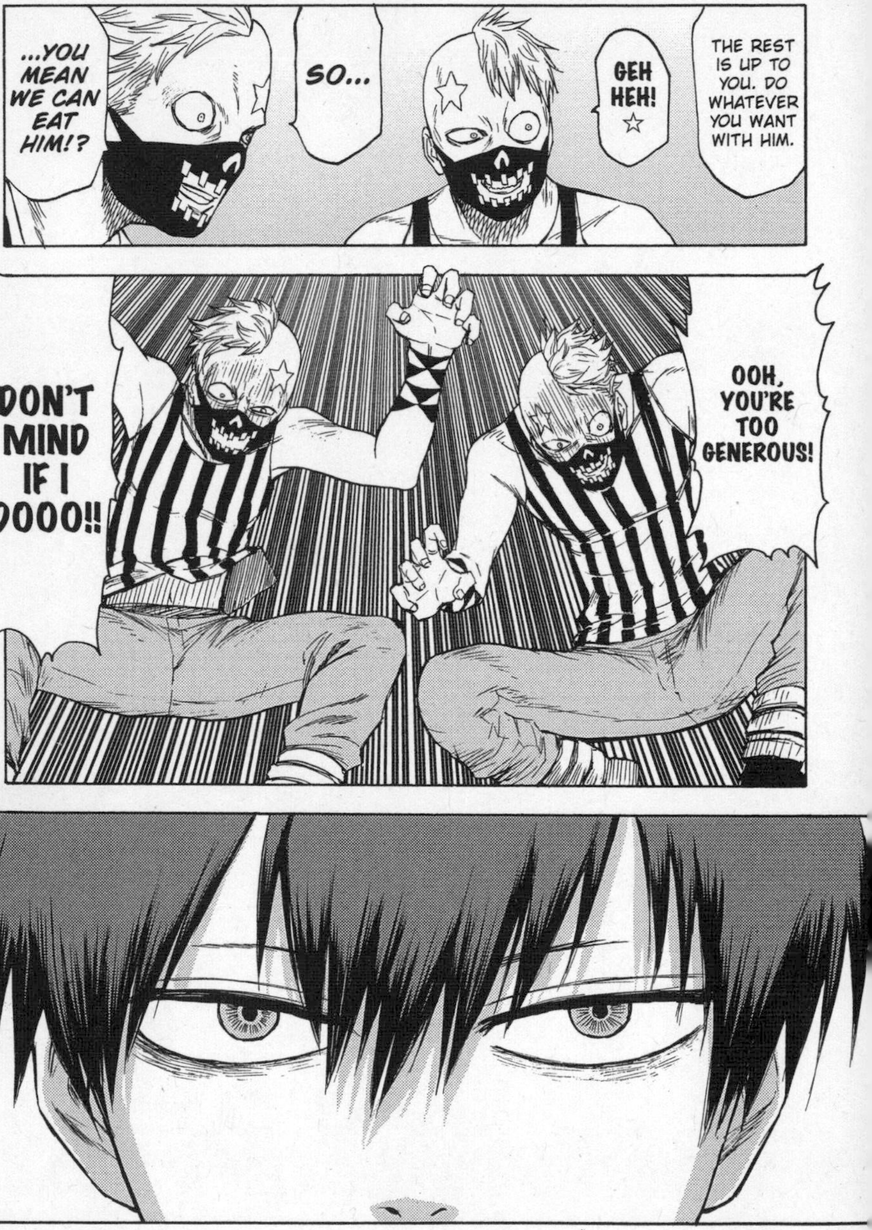
THE REST IS UP TO YOU. DO WHATEVER YOU WANT WITH HIM.
GEH HEH! ☆
SO...
...YOU MEAN WE CAN EAT HIM!?
OOH, YOU'RE TOO GENEROUS!
DON'T MIND IF I DOOO!!

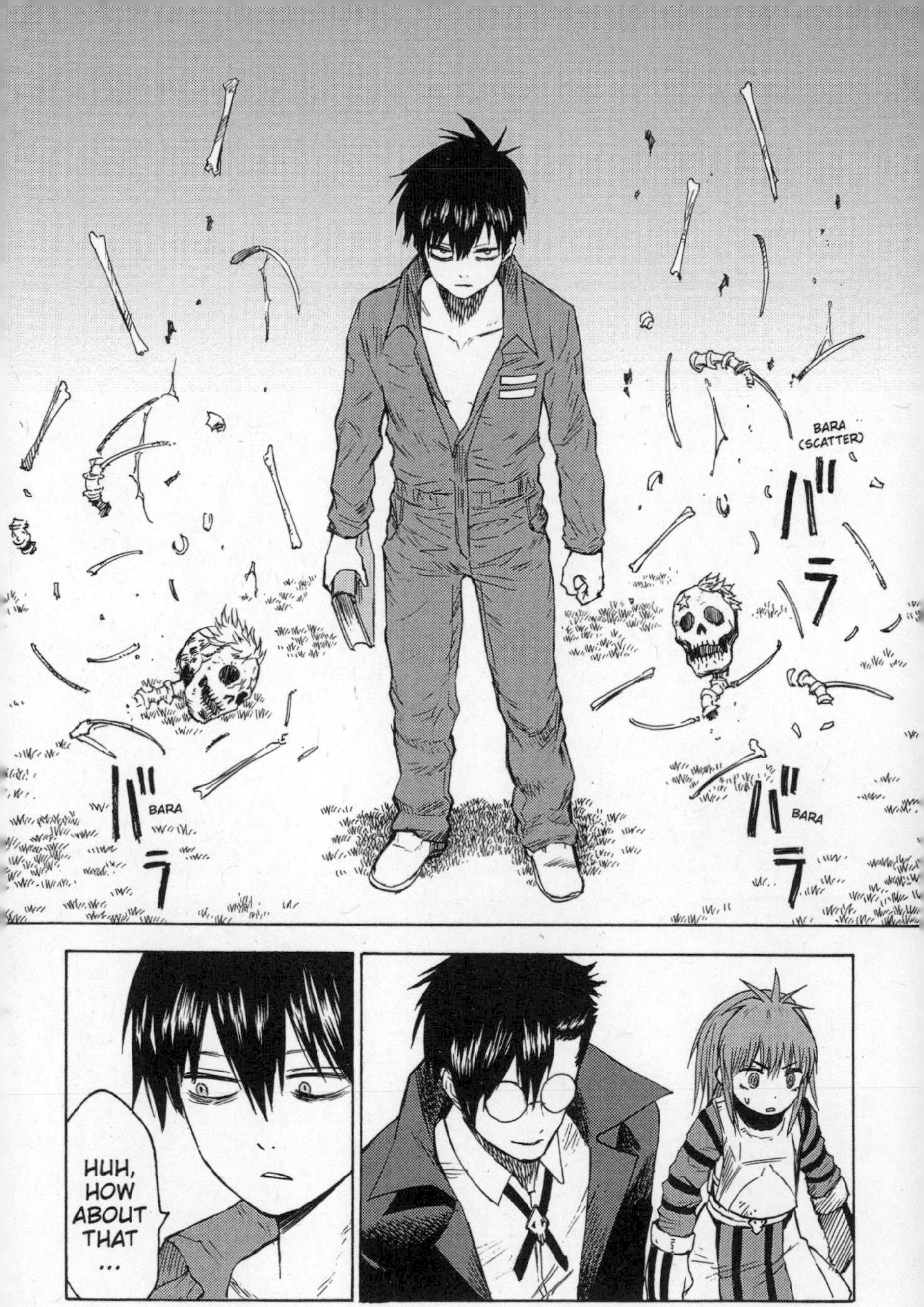
BARA (SCATTER)
バラ
BARA
バラ
BARA
バラ
HUH, HOW ABOUT THAT ...

♠ To Be Continued ♠

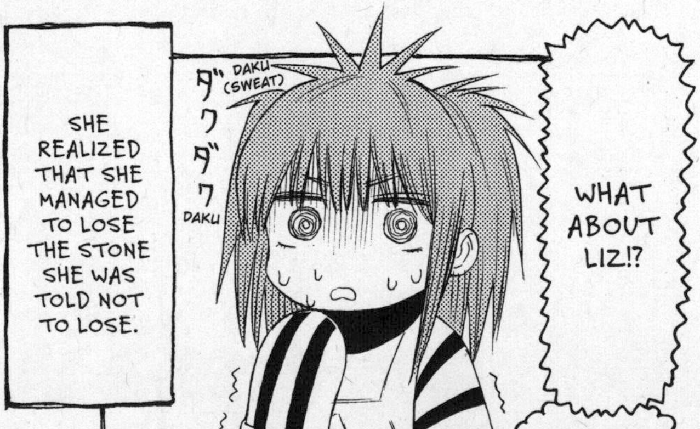
WHAT ABOUT LIZ!?
PART 2
ダクダク
DAKU (SWEAT) DAKU
SHE REALIZED THAT SHE MANAGED TO LOSE THE STONE SHE WAS TOLD NOT TO LOSE.

BLOOD LAD

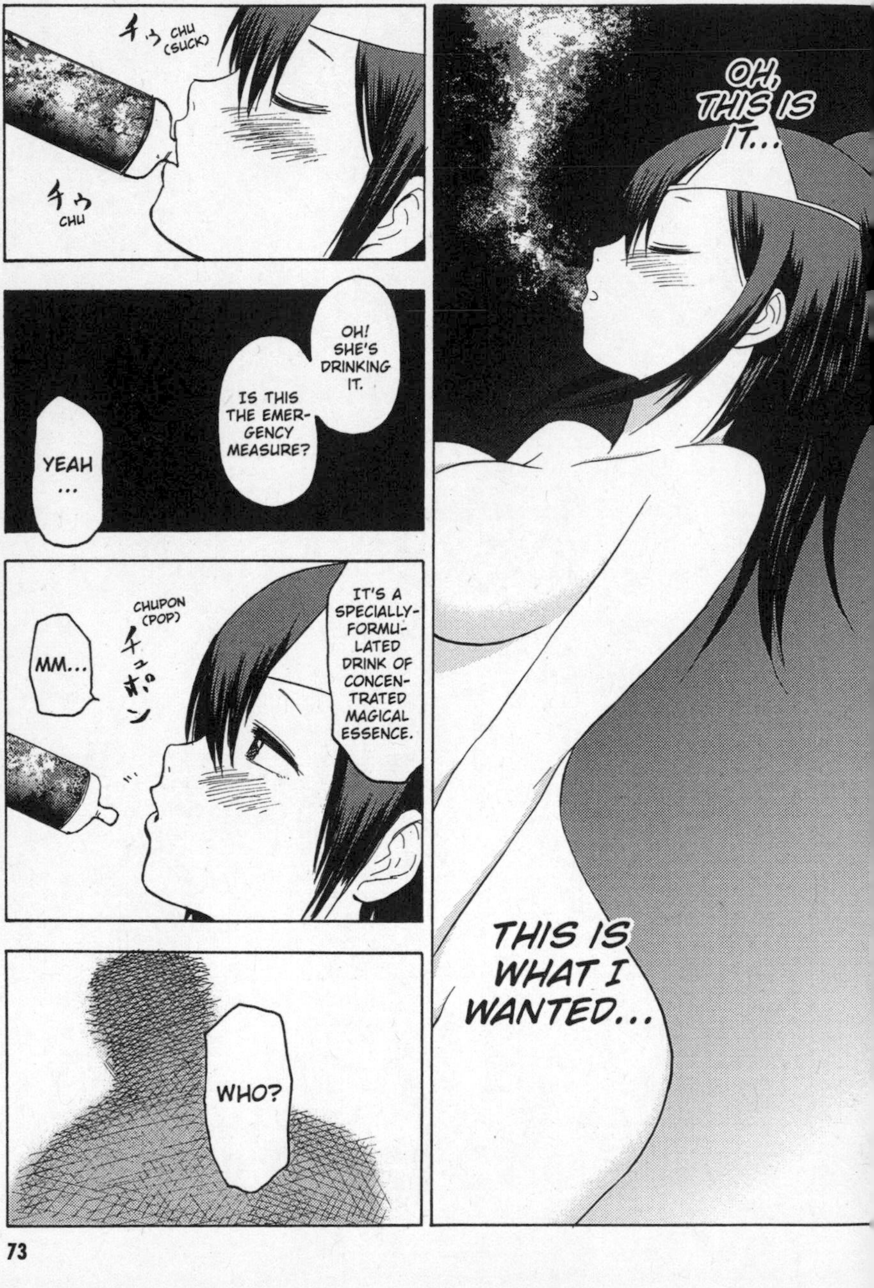
OH, THIS IS IT...
THIS IS WHAT I WANTED...
チゥ CHU (SUCK)
チゥ CHU
OH! SHE'S DRINKING IT.
IS THIS THE EMERGENCY MEASURE?
YEAH...
IT'S A SPECIALLY-FORMULATED DRINK OF CONCENTRATED MAGICAL ESSENCE.
チュポン CHUPON (POP)
MM...
WHO?

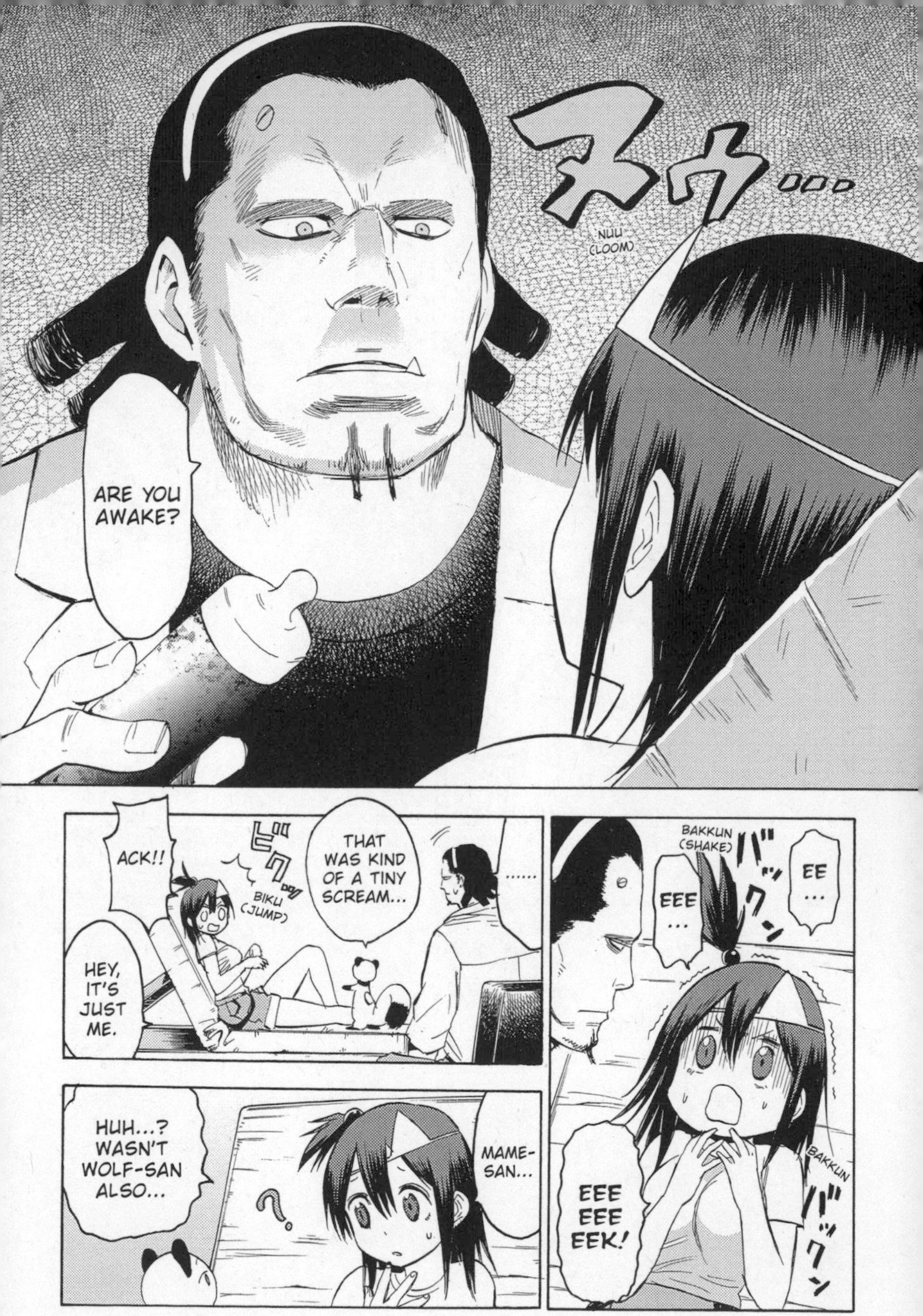

ヌウ
NUU (LOOM)
ARE YOU AWAKE?
BAKKUN (SHAKE)
バックン
EE...
EEE...
EEE EEE EEK!
BAKKUN
バックン
......
THAT WAS KIND OF A TINY SCREAM...
ビク
BIKU (JUMP)
ACK!!
HEY, IT'S JUST ME.
MAME-SAN...
HUH...? WASN'T WOLF-SAN ALSO...

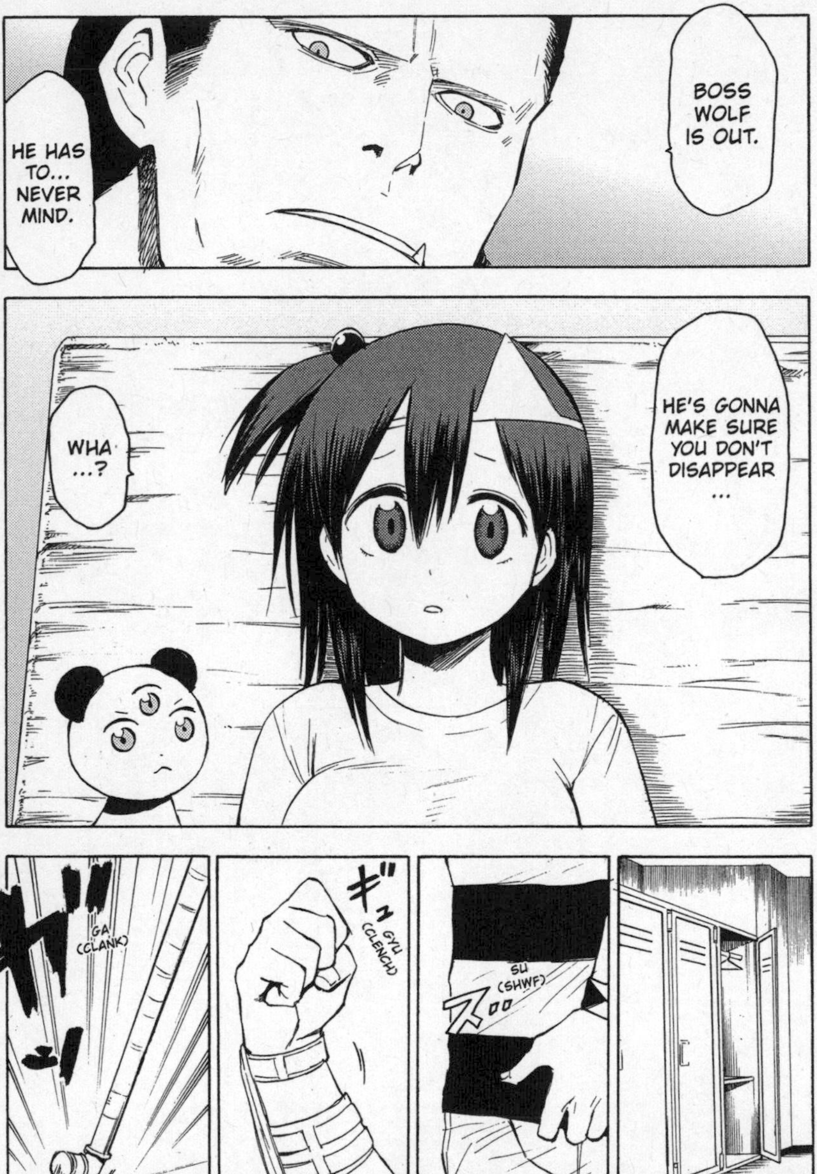

BOSS WOLF IS OUT.
HE HAS TO... NEVER MIND.
HE'S GONNA MAKE SURE YOU DON'T DISAPPEAR ...
WHA ...?
SU (SHWF)
GYU (CLENCH)
GA (CLANK)

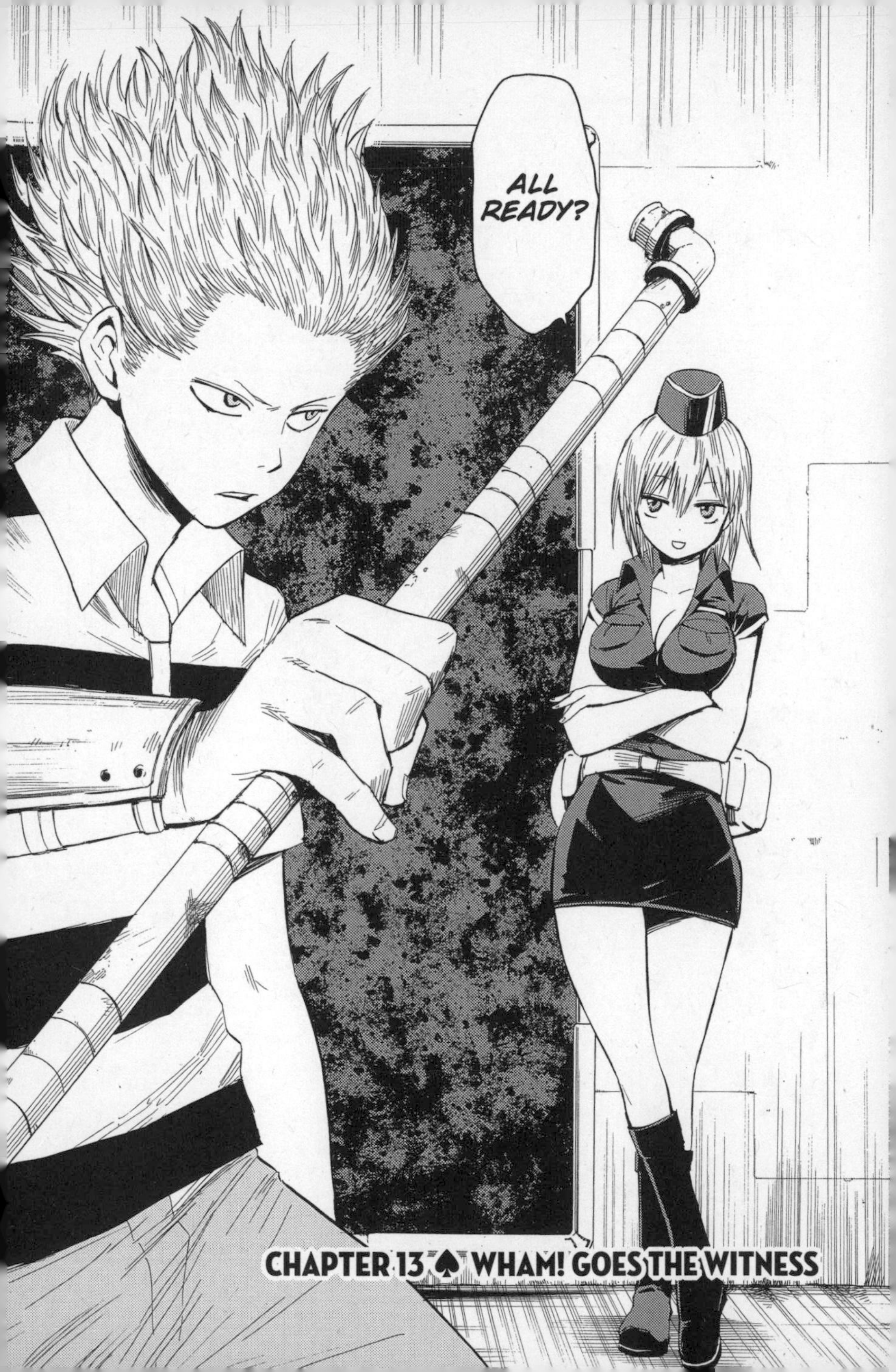
ALL READY?
CHAPTER 13 ♠ WHAM! GOES THE WITNESS

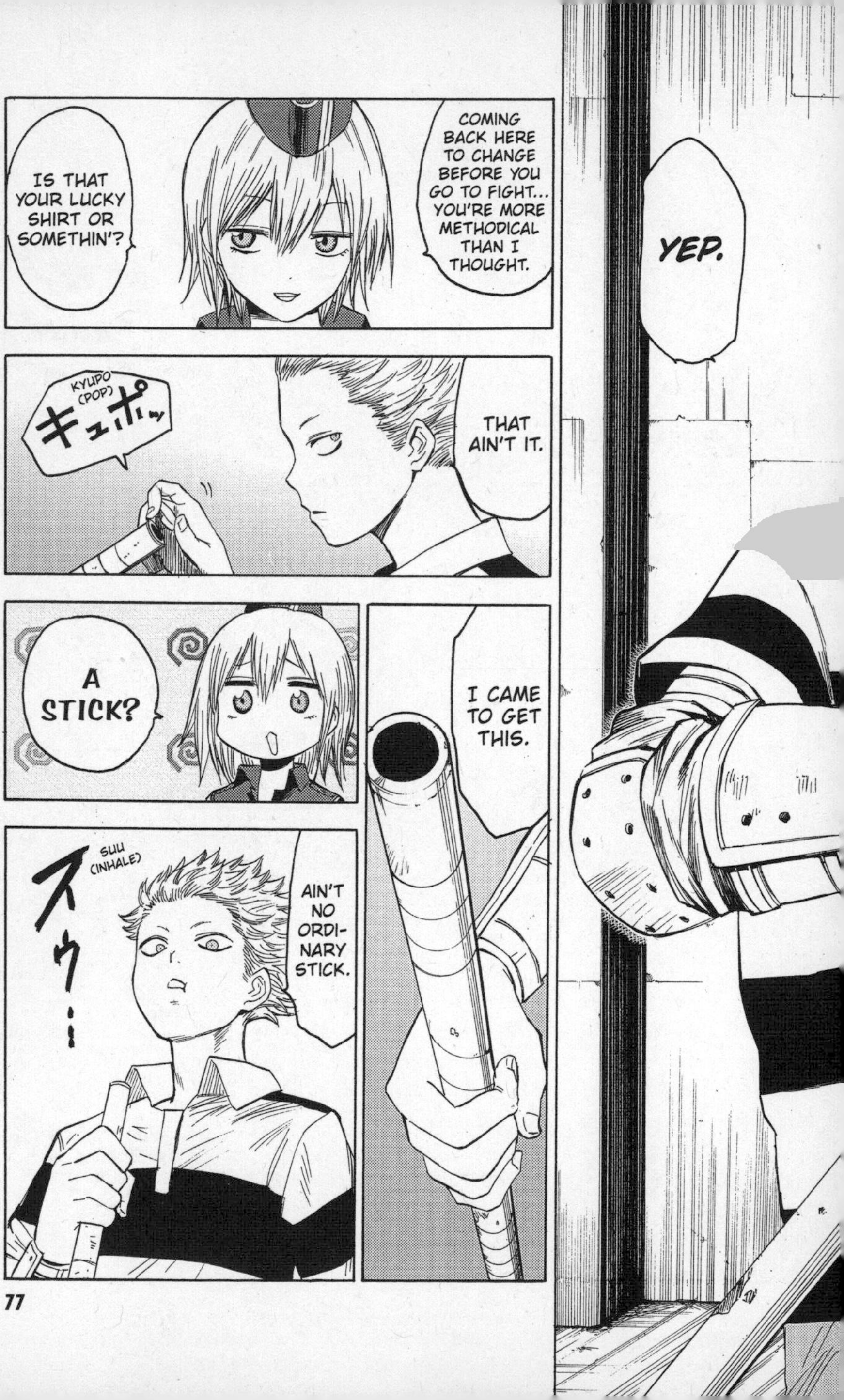
YEP.
COMING BACK HERE TO CHANGE BEFORE YOU GO TO FIGHT... YOU'RE MORE METHODICAL THAN I THOUGHT.
IS THAT YOUR LUCKY SHIRT OR SOMETHIN'?
KYUPO (POP)
キュポ
THAT AIN'T IT.
I CAME TO GET THIS.
A STICK?
SUU (INHALE)
スゥ…
AIN'T NO ORDINARY STICK.

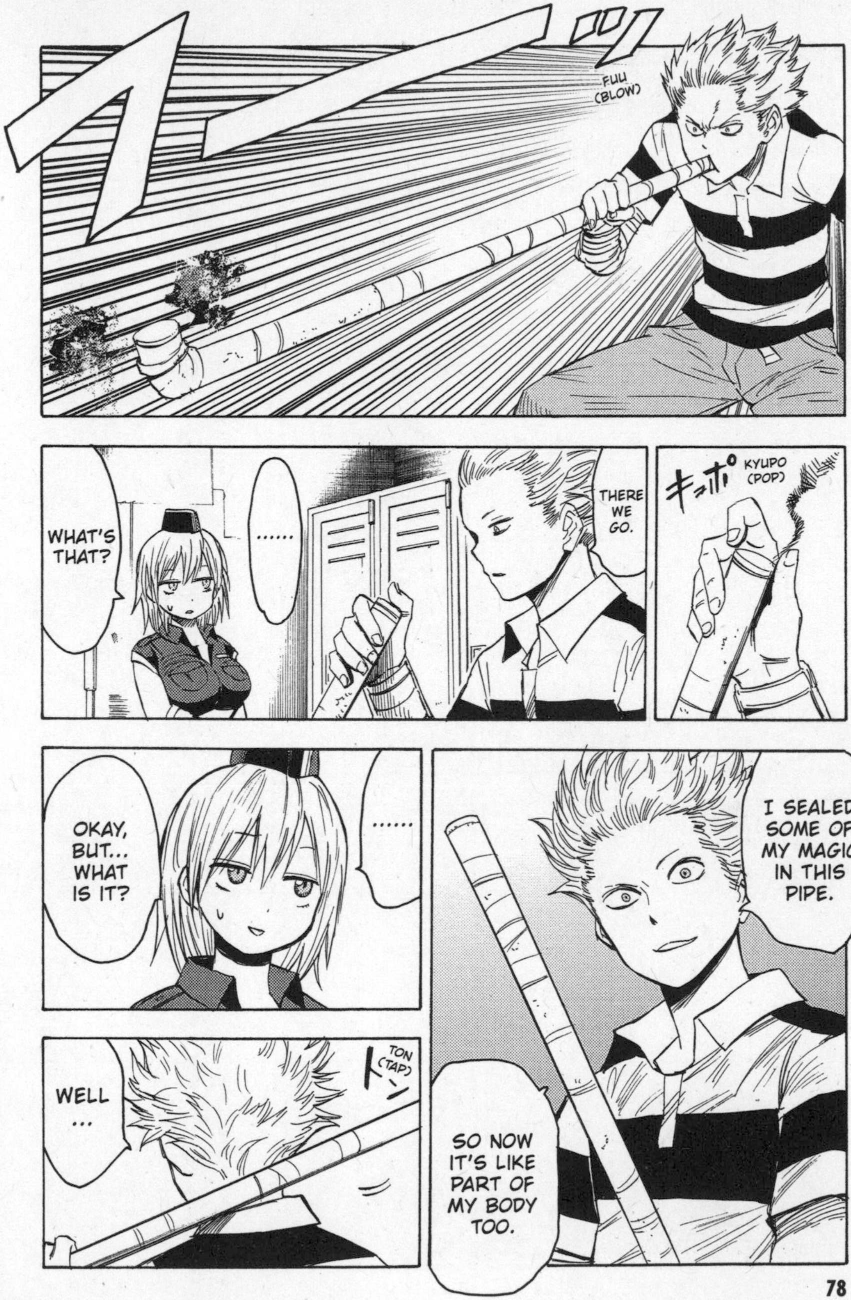
FUU (BLOW)
KYUPO (POP)
キュポ
THERE WE GO.
......
WHAT'S THAT?
I SEALED SOME OF MY MAGIC IN THIS PIPE.
SO NOW IT'S LIKE PART OF MY BODY TOO.
......
OKAY, BUT... WHAT IS IT?
TON (TAP)
WELL ...

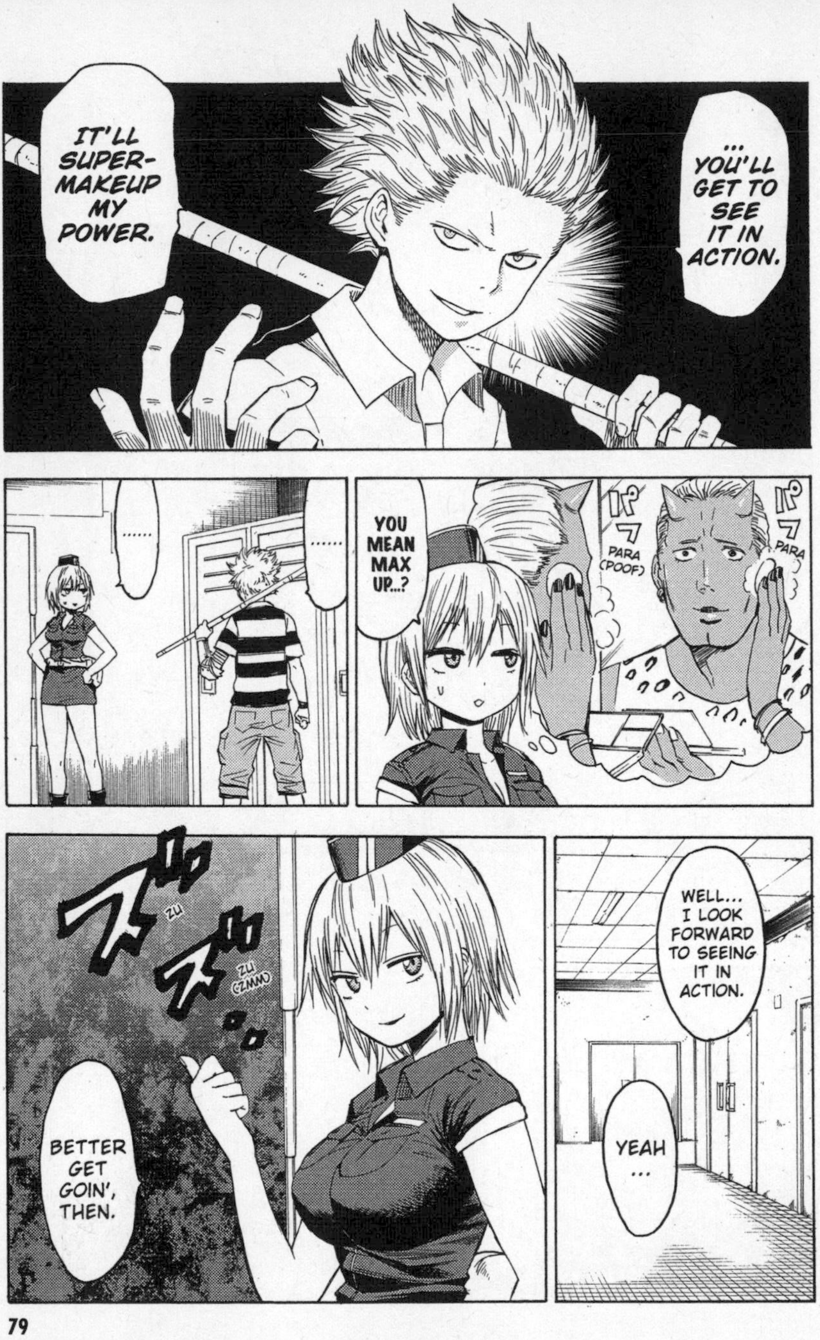
... YOU'LL GET TO SEE IT IN ACTION.
IT'LL SUPER-MAKEUP MY POWER.
PARA (POOF)
PARA
YOU MEAN MAX UP...?
......
......
WELL... I LOOK FORWARD TO SEEING IT IN ACTION.
YEAH ...
ZU
ZU (ZMM)
BETTER GET GOIN', THEN.

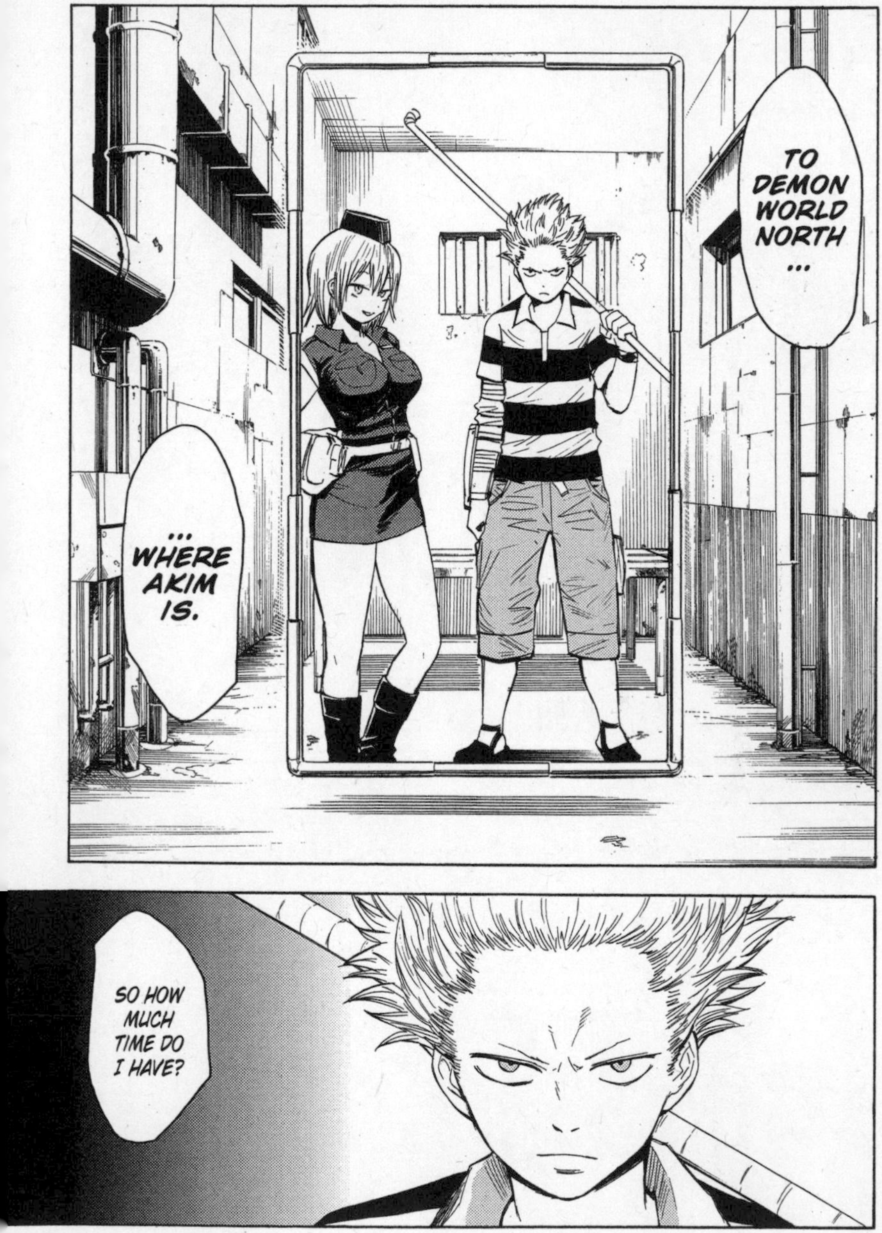
TO DEMON WORLD NORTH ...
... WHERE AKIM IS.
SO HOW MUCH TIME DO I HAVE?

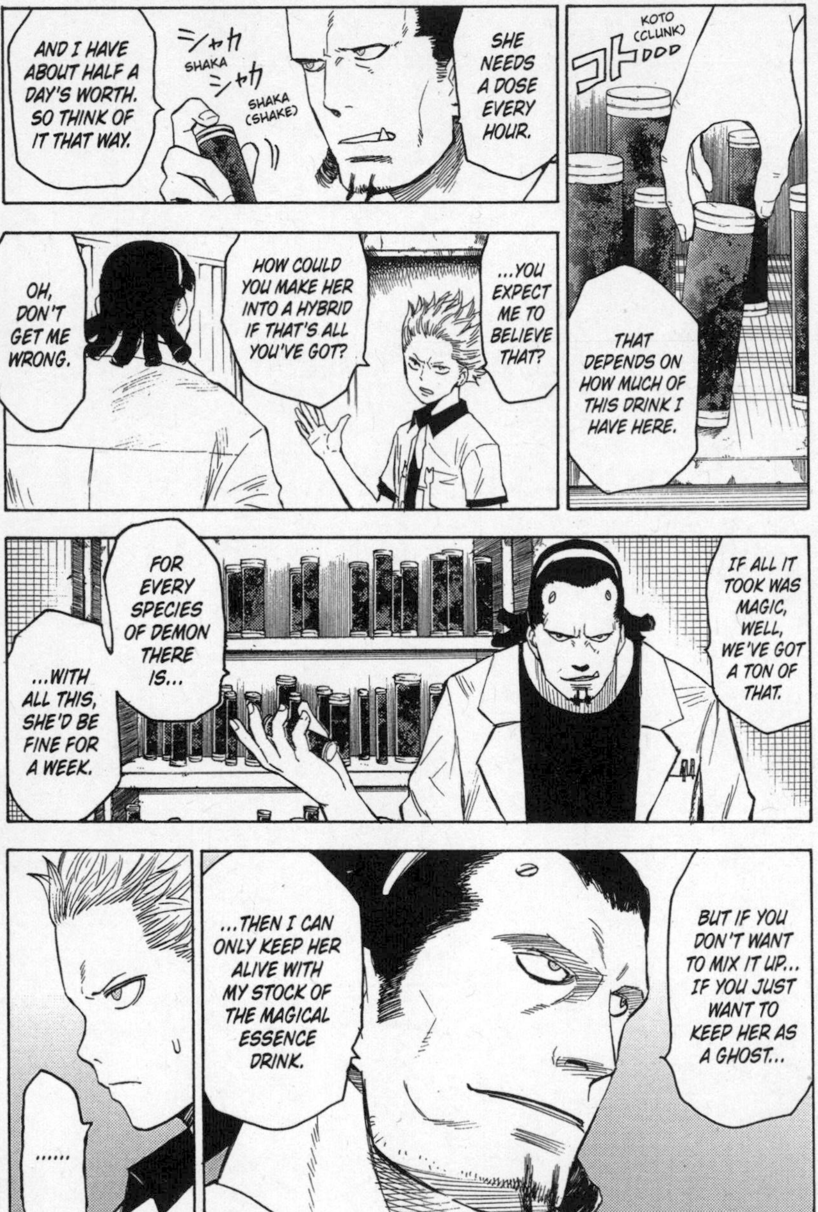

コト KOTO (CLUNK)
THAT DEPENDS ON HOW MUCH OF THIS DRINK I HAVE HERE.
SHE NEEDS A DOSE EVERY HOUR.
シャカ SHAKA シャカ SHAKA (SHAKE)
AND I HAVE ABOUT HALF A DAY'S WORTH. SO THINK OF IT THAT WAY.
...YOU EXPECT ME TO BELIEVE THAT?
HOW COULD YOU MAKE HER INTO A HYBRID IF THAT'S ALL YOU'VE GOT?
OH, DON'T GET ME WRONG.
IF ALL IT TOOK WAS MAGIC, WELL, WE'VE GOT A TON OF THAT.
FOR EVERY SPECIES OF DEMON THERE IS...
...WITH ALL THIS, SHE'D BE FINE FOR A WEEK.
BUT IF YOU DON'T WANT TO MIX IT UP... IF YOU JUST WANT TO KEEP HER AS A GHOST...
...THEN I CAN ONLY KEEP HER ALIVE WITH MY STOCK OF THE MAGICAL ESSENCE DRINK.
......

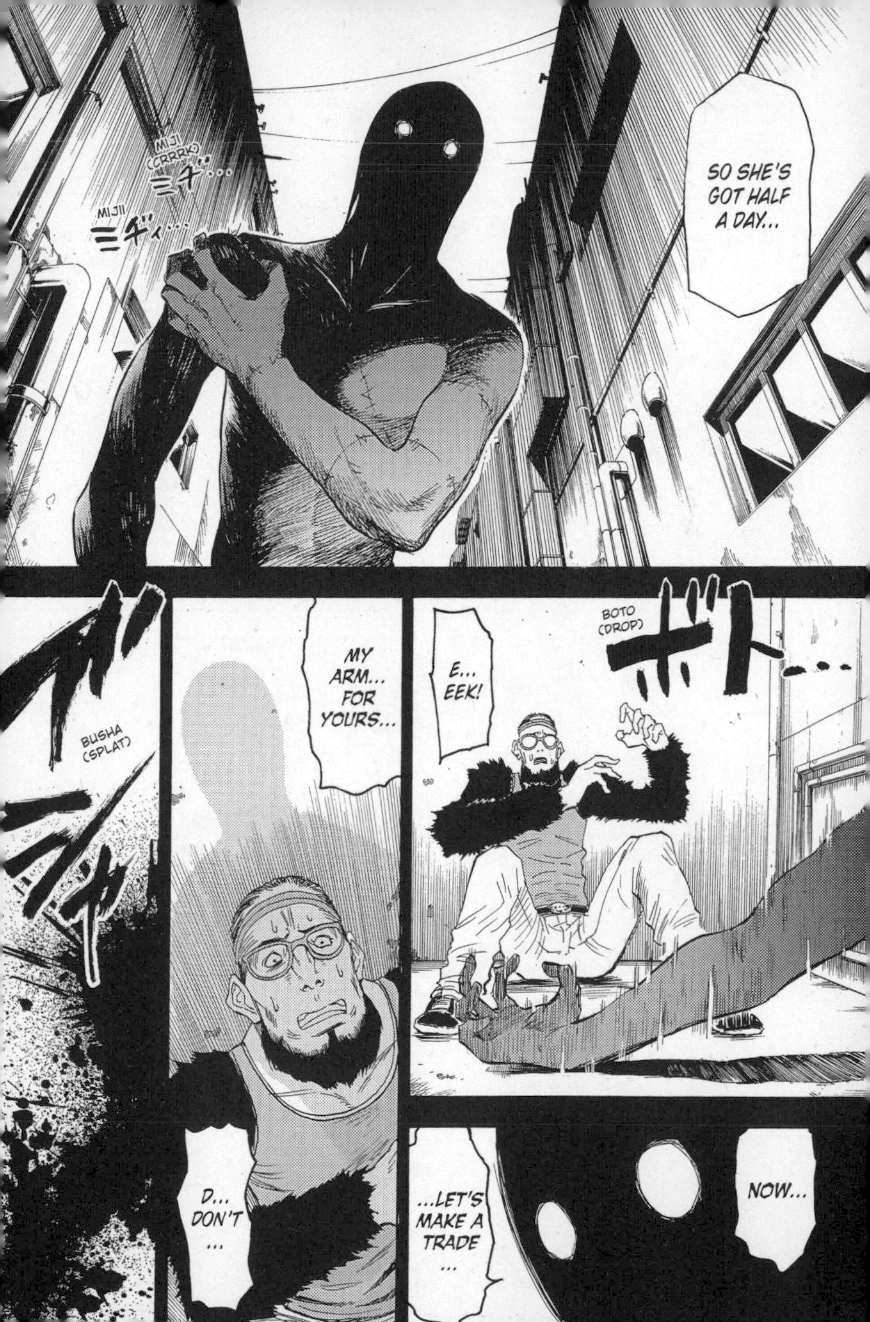
SO SHE'S GOT HALF A DAY...
MIJI (CRRRK)
ミヂ...
MIJI
ミヂィ...
BOTO (DROP)
ボト...
E... EEK!
NOW...
...LET'S MAKE A TRADE ...
MY ARM... FOR YOURS...
D... DON'T ...
BUSHA (SPLAT)
ブシャ

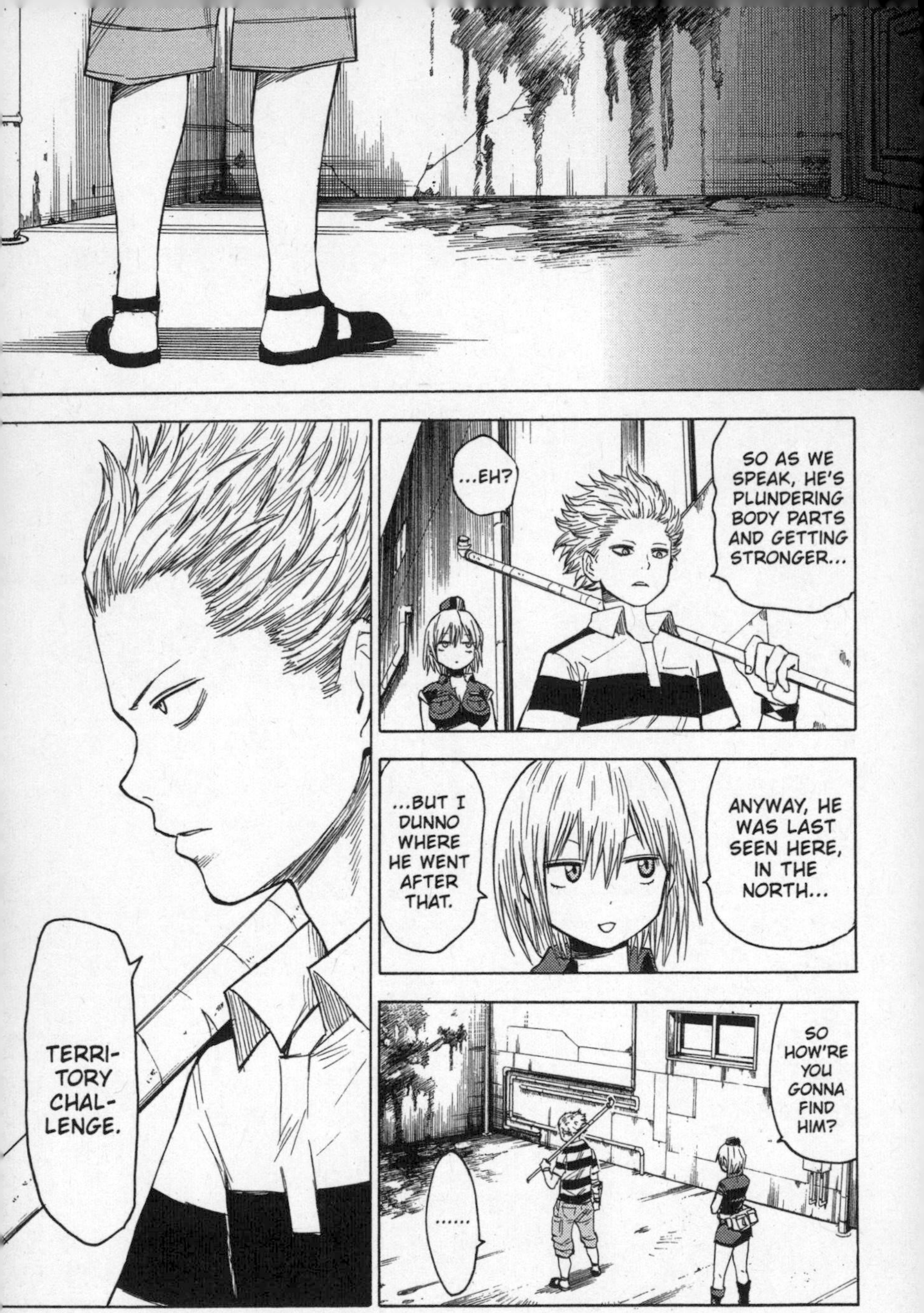
SO AS WE SPEAK, HE'S PLUNDERING BODY PARTS AND GETTING STRONGER...
...EH?
ANYWAY, HE WAS LAST SEEN HERE, IN THE NORTH...
...BUT I DUNNO WHERE HE WENT AFTER THAT.
SO HOW'RE YOU GONNA FIND HIM?
......
TERRI-TORY CHAL-LENGE.

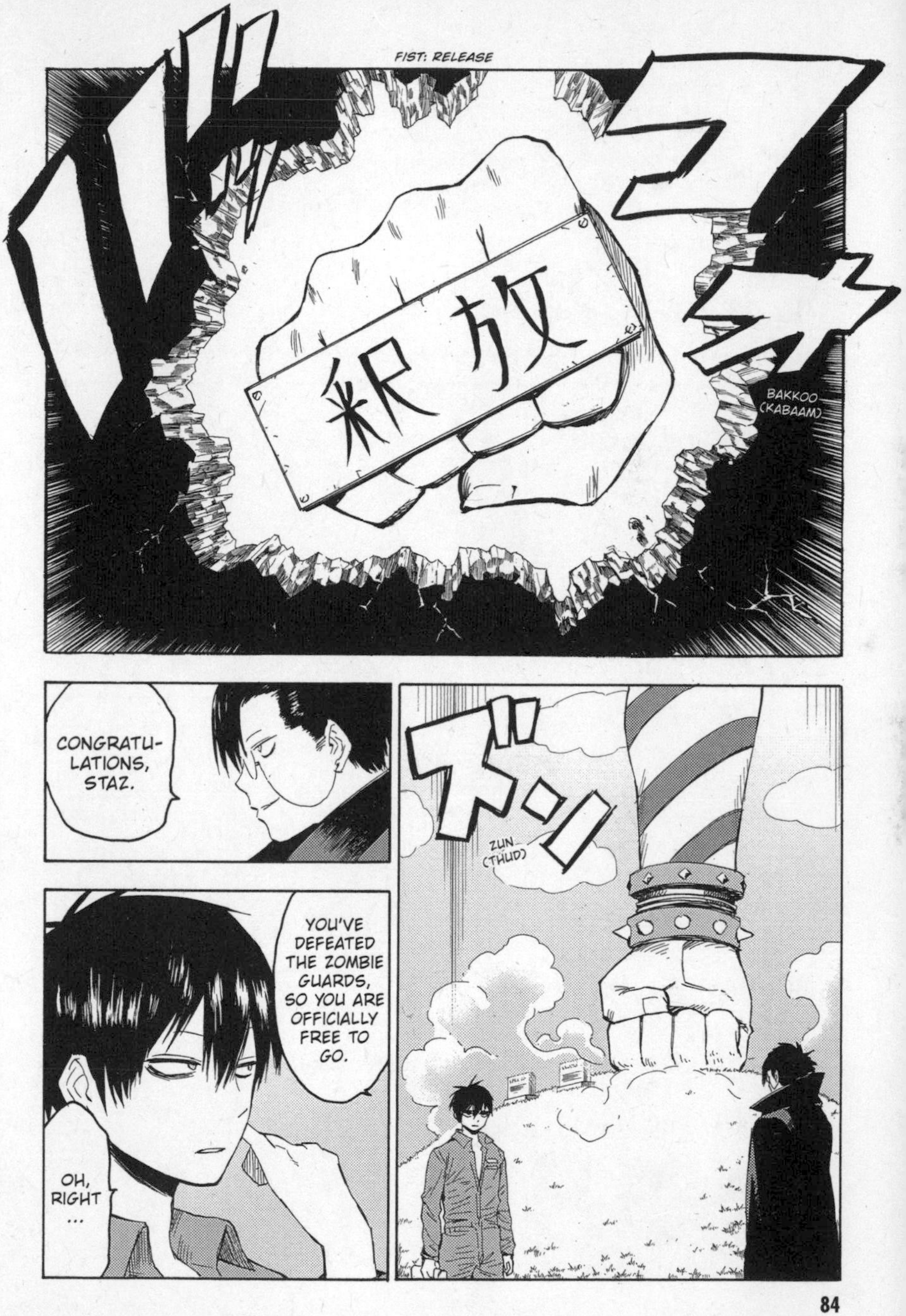
FIST: RELEASE
釈放
BAKKOO (KABAAM)
ZUN (THUD)
CONGRATULATIONS, STAZ.
YOU'VE DEFEATED THE ZOMBIE GUARDS, SO YOU ARE OFFICIALLY FREE TO GO.
OH, RIGHT ...

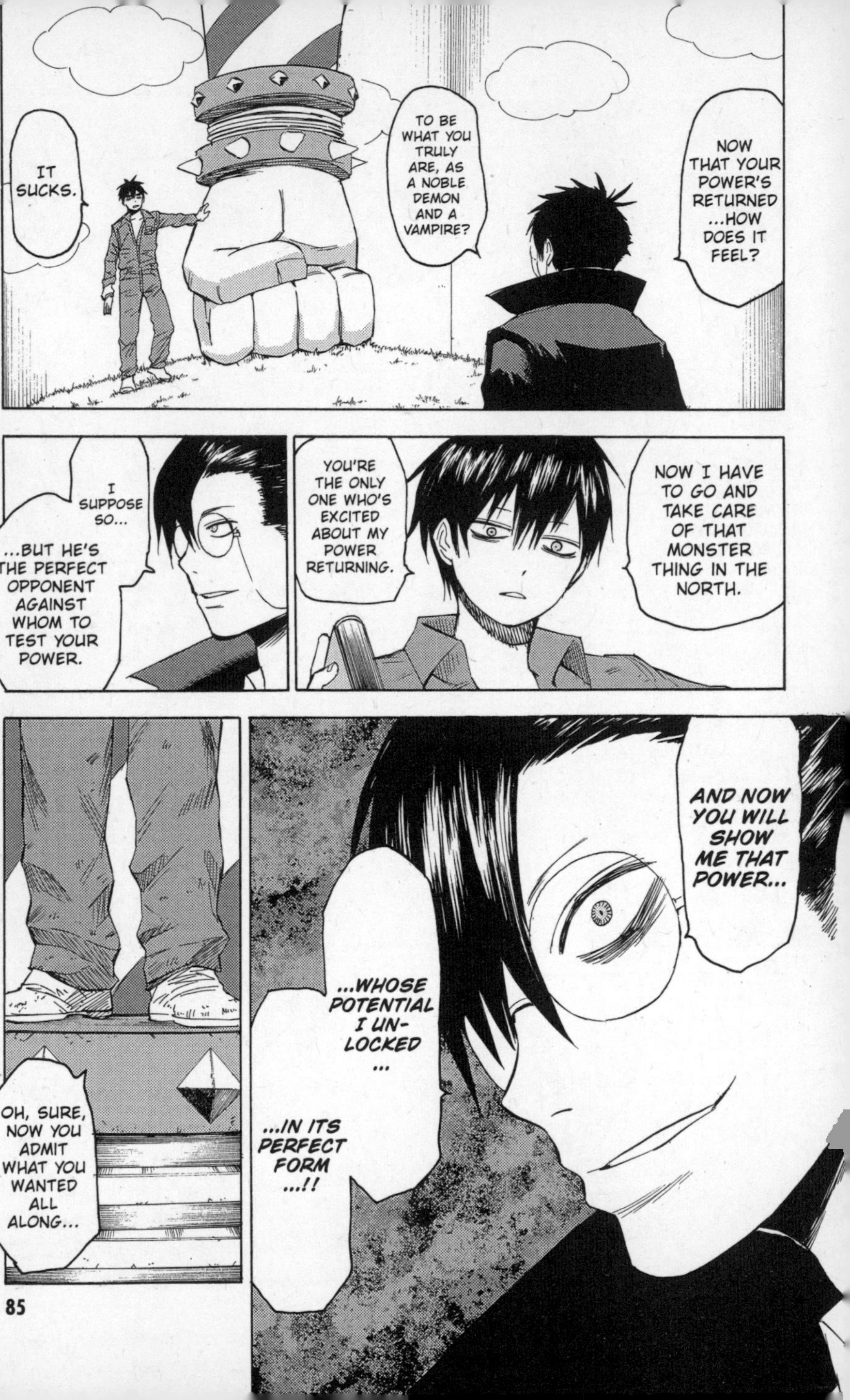
NOW THAT YOUR POWER'S RETURNED ...HOW DOES IT FEEL?
TO BE WHAT YOU TRULY ARE, AS A NOBLE DEMON AND A VAMPIRE?
IT SUCKS.
NOW I HAVE TO GO AND TAKE CARE OF THAT MONSTER THING IN THE NORTH.
YOU'RE THE ONLY ONE WHO'S EXCITED ABOUT MY POWER RETURNING.
I SUPPOSE SO...
...BUT HE'S THE PERFECT OPPONENT AGAINST WHOM TO TEST YOUR POWER.
AND NOW YOU WILL SHOW ME THAT POWER...
...WHOSE POTENTIAL I UN-LOCKED ...
...IN ITS PERFECT FORM ...!!
OH, SURE, NOW YOU ADMIT WHAT YOU WANTED ALL ALONG...

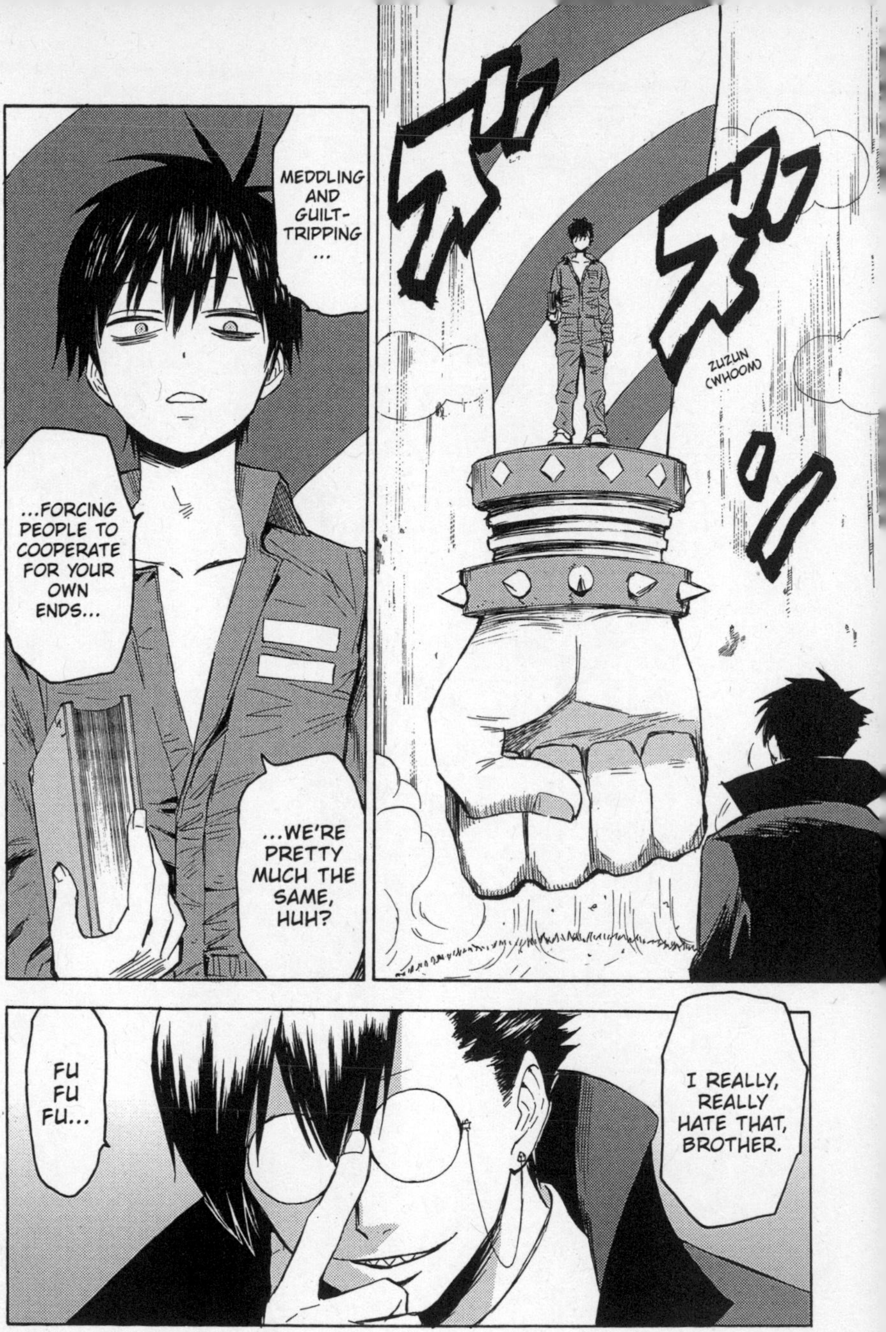
ZUZUN (WHOOM)
MEDDLING AND GUILT-TRIPPING ...
...FORCING PEOPLE TO COOPERATE FOR YOUR OWN ENDS...
...WE'RE PRETTY MUCH THE SAME, HUH?
I REALLY, REALLY HATE THAT, BROTHER.
FU FU FU...

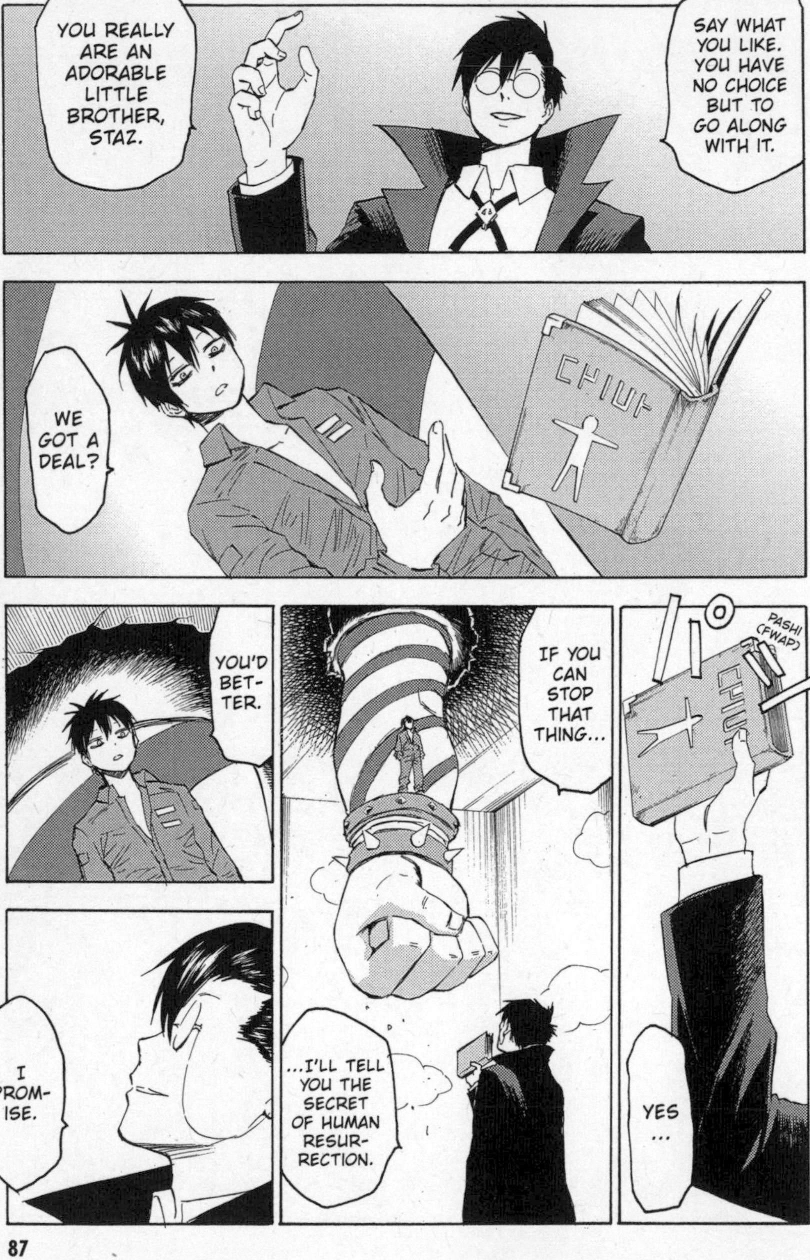
SAY WHAT YOU LIKE. YOU HAVE NO CHOICE BUT TO GO ALONG WITH IT.
YOU REALLY ARE AN ADORABLE LITTLE BROTHER, STAZ.
WE GOT A DEAL?
PASHI (FWAP)
YES...
IF YOU CAN STOP THAT THING...
...I'LL TELL YOU THE SECRET OF HUMAN RESURRECTION.
YOU'D BET-TER.
I PROM-ISE.

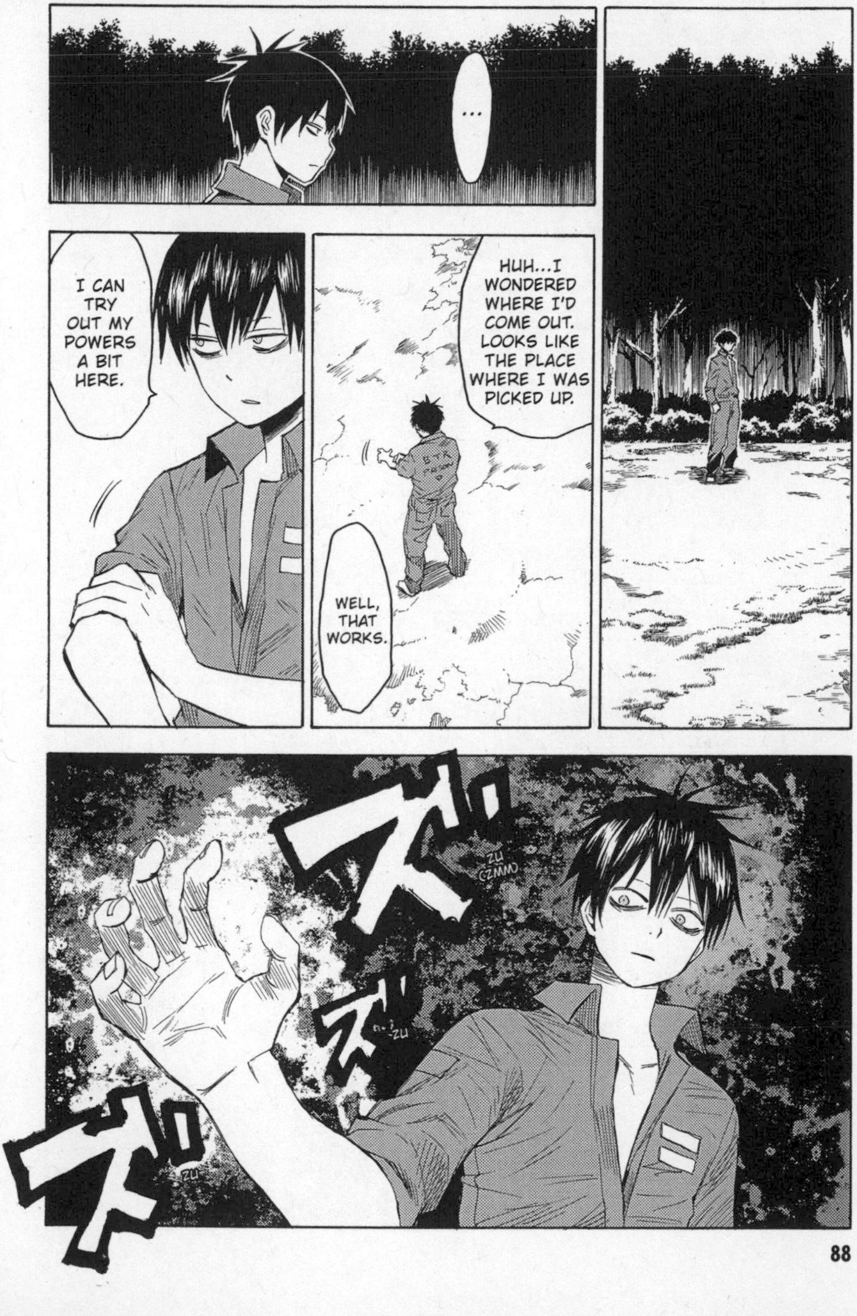
...
HUH...I WONDERED WHERE I'D COME OUT. LOOKS LIKE THE PLACE WHERE I WAS PICKED UP.
WELL, THAT WORKS.
I CAN TRY OUT MY POWERS A BIT HERE.
ZU (ZMM)
ZU
ZU

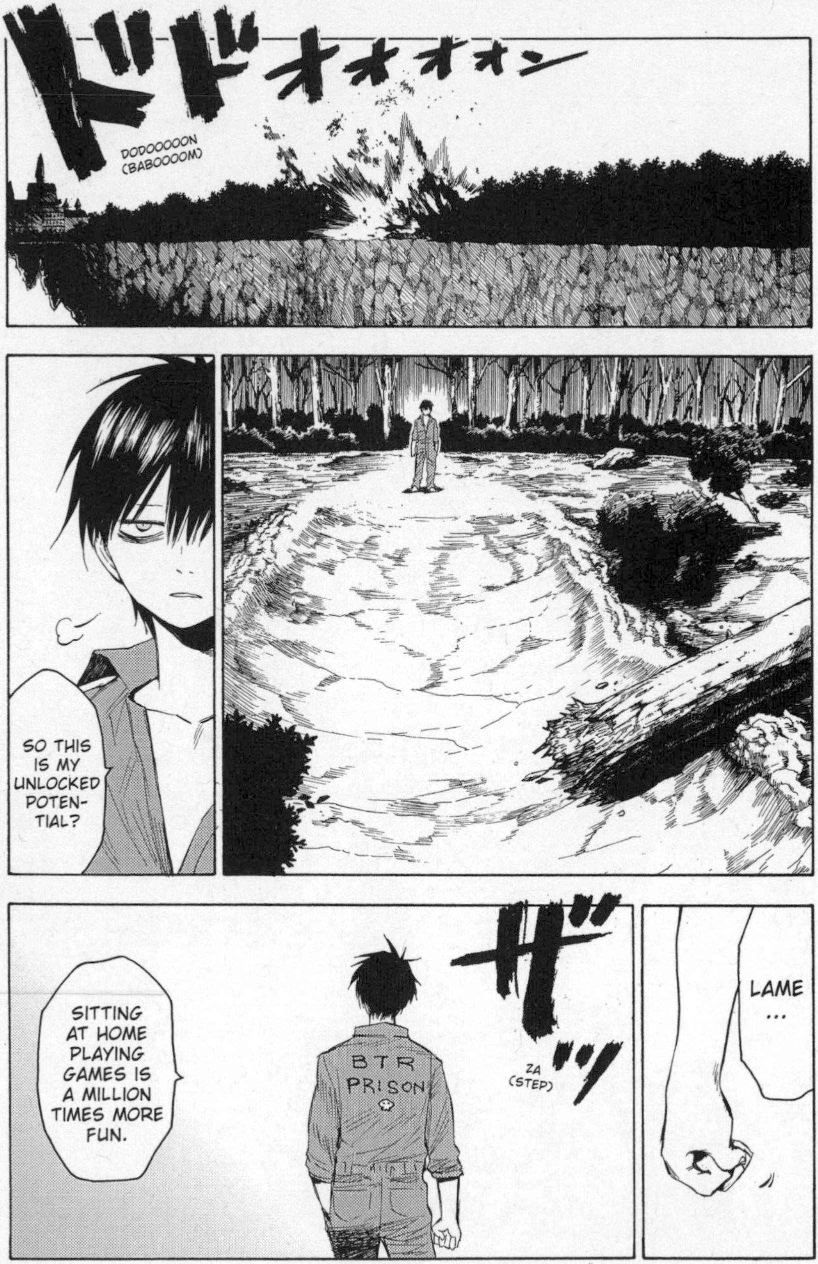
ドドオオオオン
DODOOOOON (BABOOOOM)
SO THIS IS MY UNLOCKED POTEN-TIAL?
LAME ...
ザッ
ZA (STEP)
BTR PRISON
SITTING AT HOME PLAYING GAMES IS A MILLION TIMES MORE FUN.

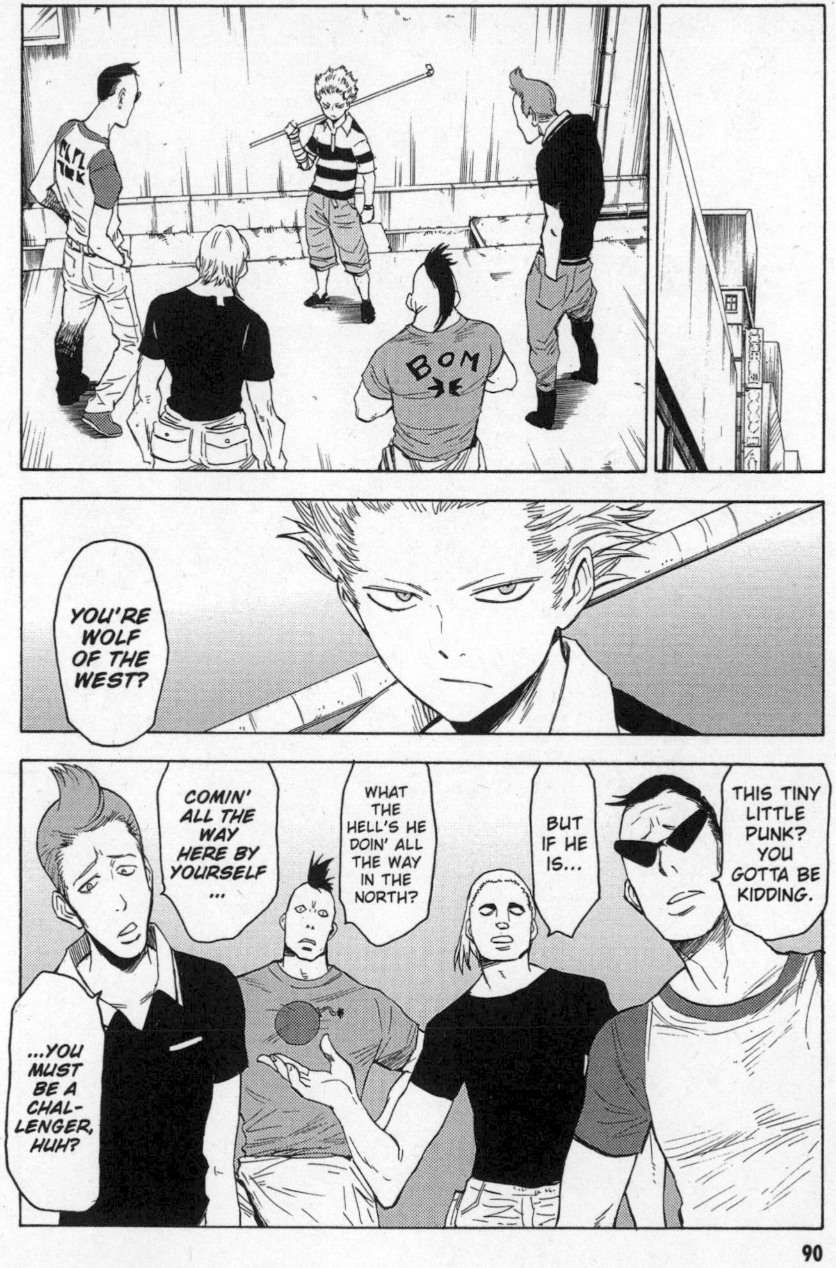
BOM
YOU'RE WOLF OF THE WEST?
THIS TINY LITTLE PUNK? YOU GOTTA BE KIDDING.
BUT IF HE IS...
WHAT THE HELL'S HE DOIN' ALL THE WAY IN THE NORTH?
COMIN' ALL THE WAY HERE BY YOURSELF...
...YOU MUST BE A CHALLENGER, HUH?

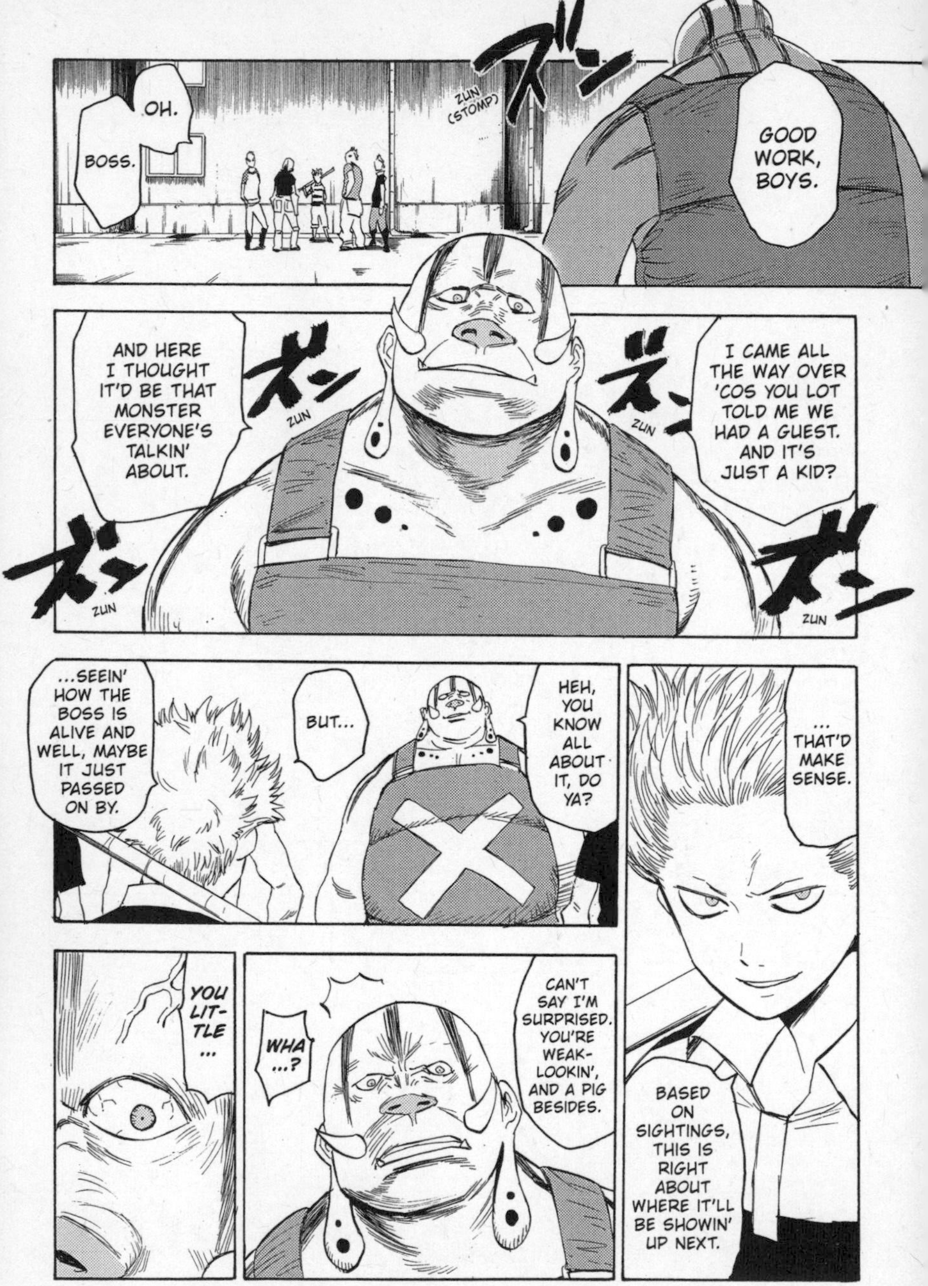
GOOD WORK, BOYS.
ZUN (STOMP)
OH.
BOSS.
I CAME ALL THE WAY OVER 'COS YOU LOT TOLD ME WE HAD A GUEST. AND IT'S JUST A KID?
ZUN
ZUN
AND HERE I THOUGHT IT'D BE THAT MONSTER EVERYONE'S TALKIN' ABOUT.
ZUN
ZUN
...THAT'D MAKE SENSE.
BASED ON SIGHTINGS, THIS IS RIGHT ABOUT WHERE IT'LL BE SHOWIN' UP NEXT.
HEH, YOU KNOW ALL ABOUT IT, DO YA?
BUT...
...SEEIN' HOW THE BOSS IS ALIVE AND WELL, MAYBE IT JUST PASSED ON BY.
CAN'T SAY I'M SURPRISED. YOU'RE WEAK-LOOKIN', AND A PIG BESIDES.
WHA ...?
YOU LIT-TLE ...

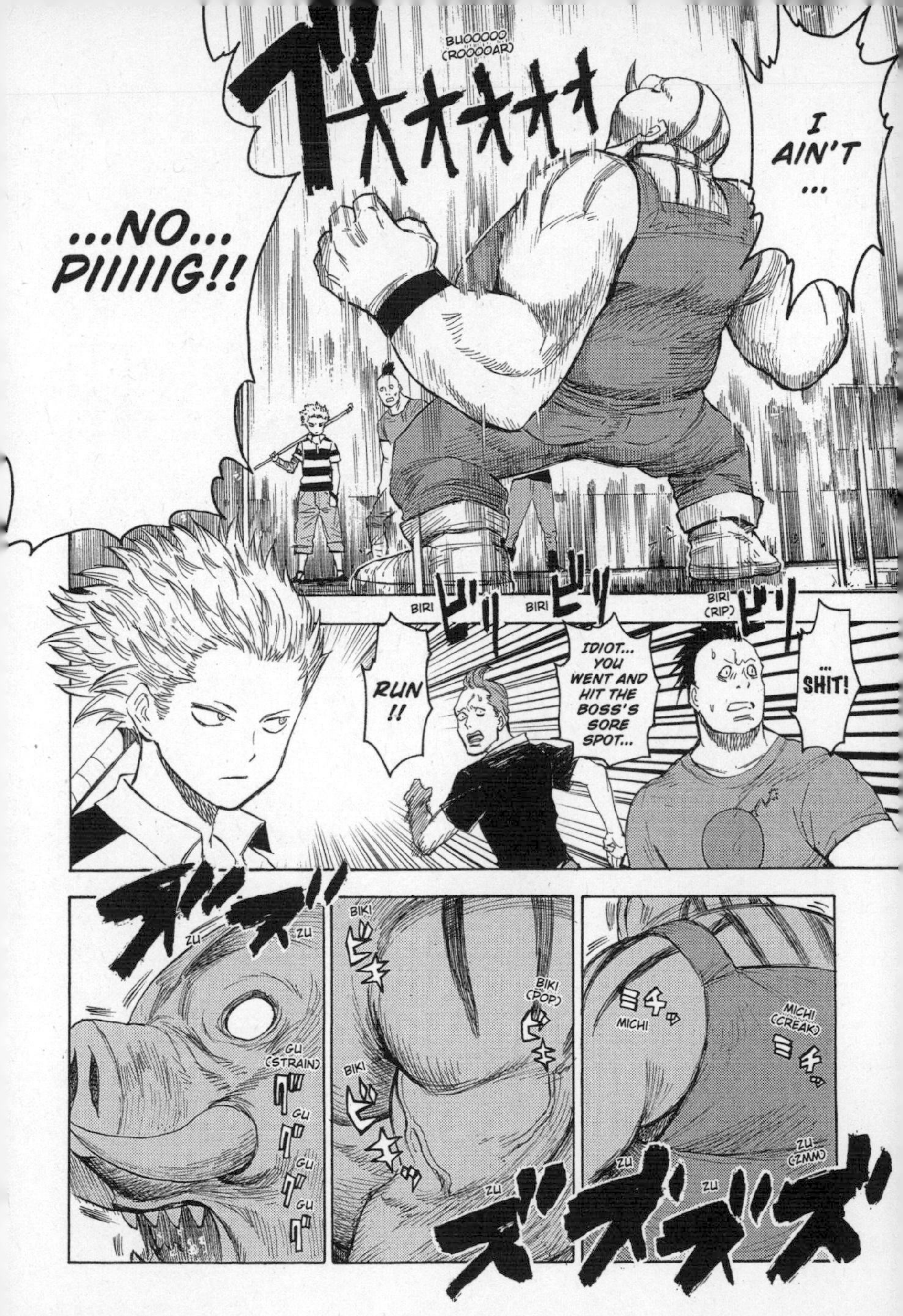
BUOOOOO (ROOOOAR)
I AIN'T ...
...NO... PIIIIG!!
BIRI (RIP)
... SHIT!
IDIOT... YOU WENT AND HIT THE BOSS'S SORE SPOT...
BIRI
RUN !!
BIRI
MICHI (CREAK)
MICHI
ZU (ZMM)
ZU
ZU
BIKI
BIKI (POP)
BIKI
ZU
ZU
GU (STRAIN)
GU
GU
GU

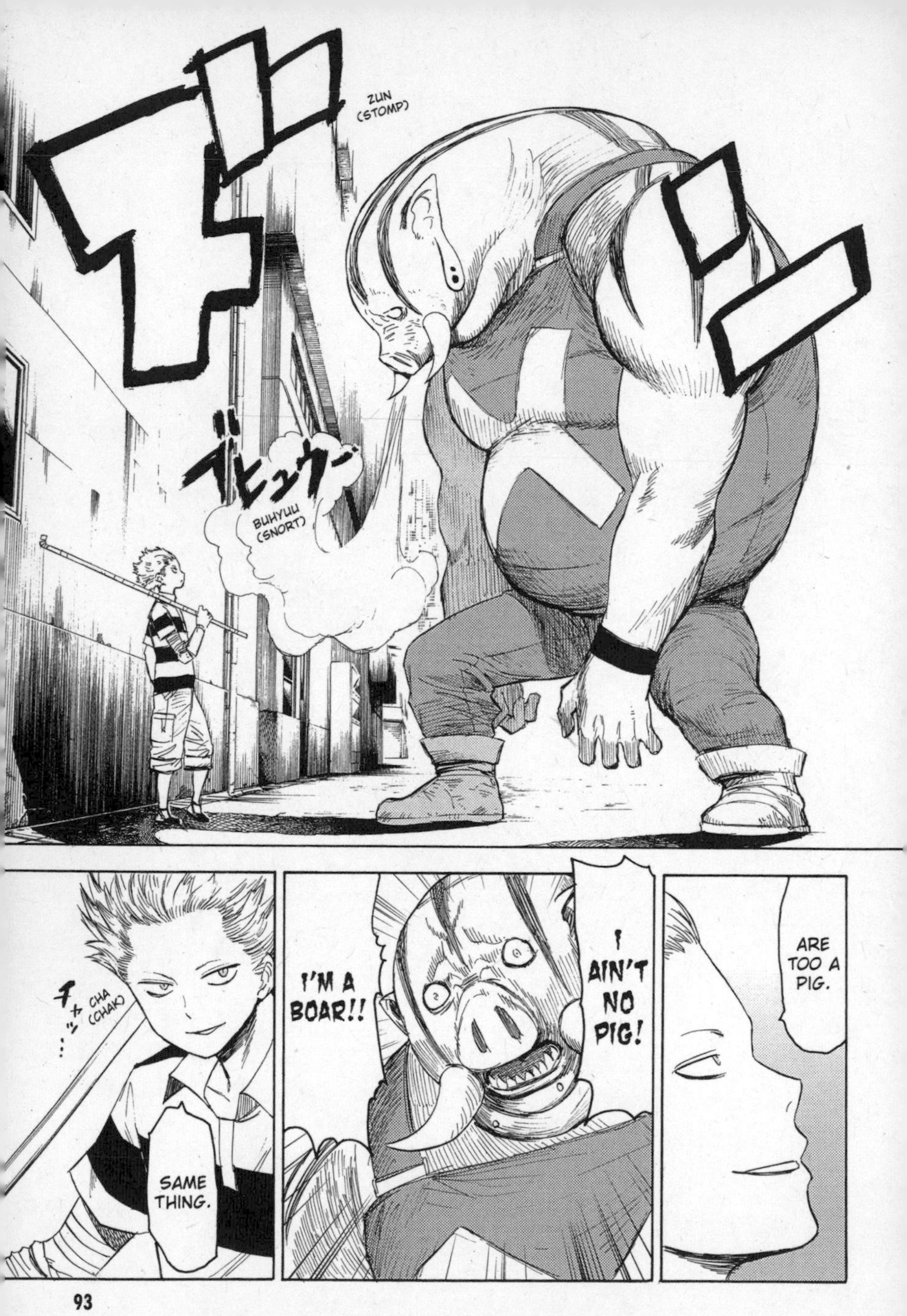
ZUN
(STOMP)
BUHYUU
(SNORT)
ARE TOO A PIG.
I AIN'T NO PIG!
I'M A BOAR!!
CHA
(CHAK)
SAME THING.

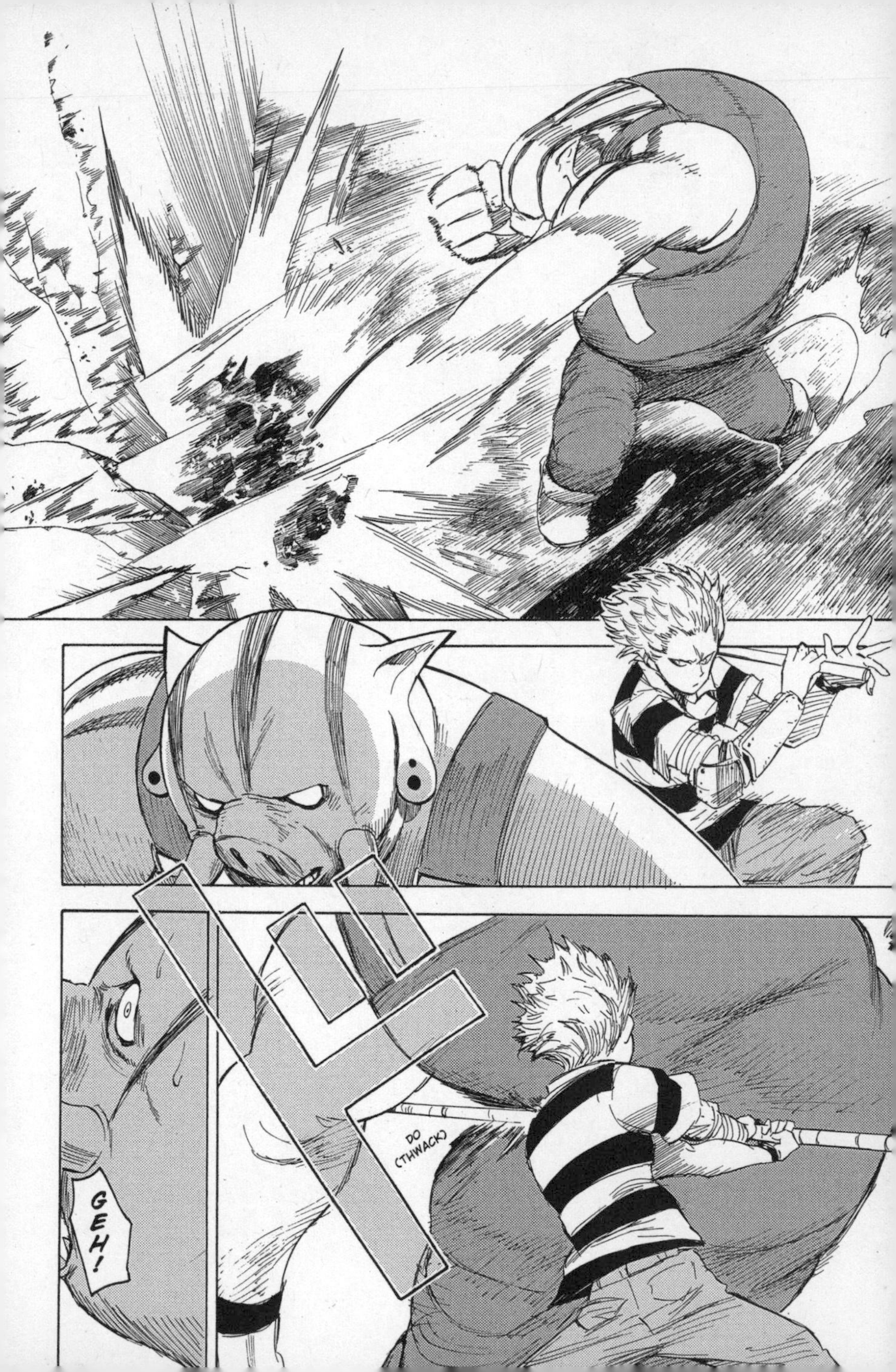
DO (THWACK)
GEH!

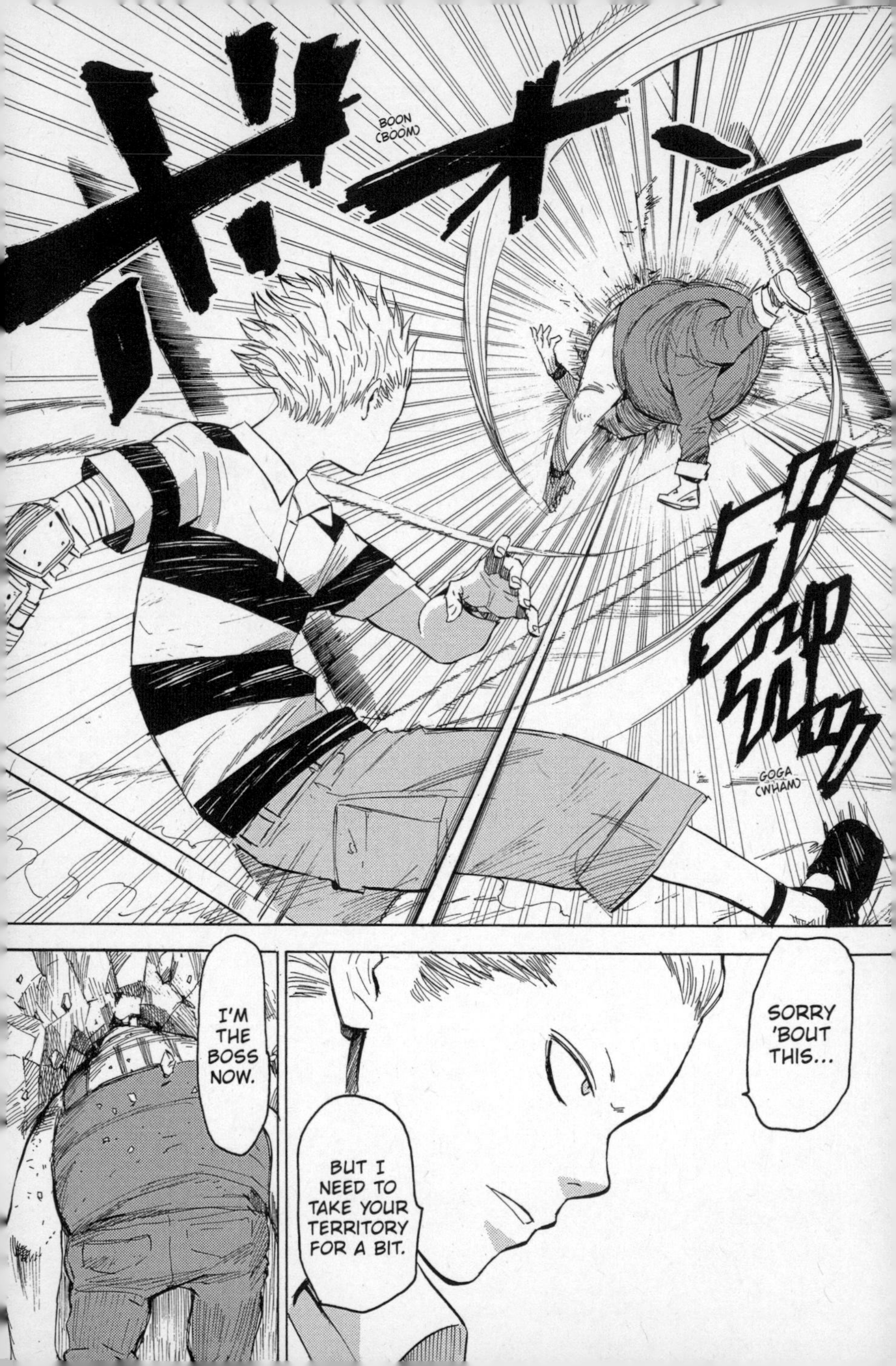
BOON (BOOM)
GOGA (WHAM)
SORRY 'BOUT THIS...
BUT I NEED TO TAKE YOUR TERRITORY FOR A BIT.
I'M THE BOSS NOW.

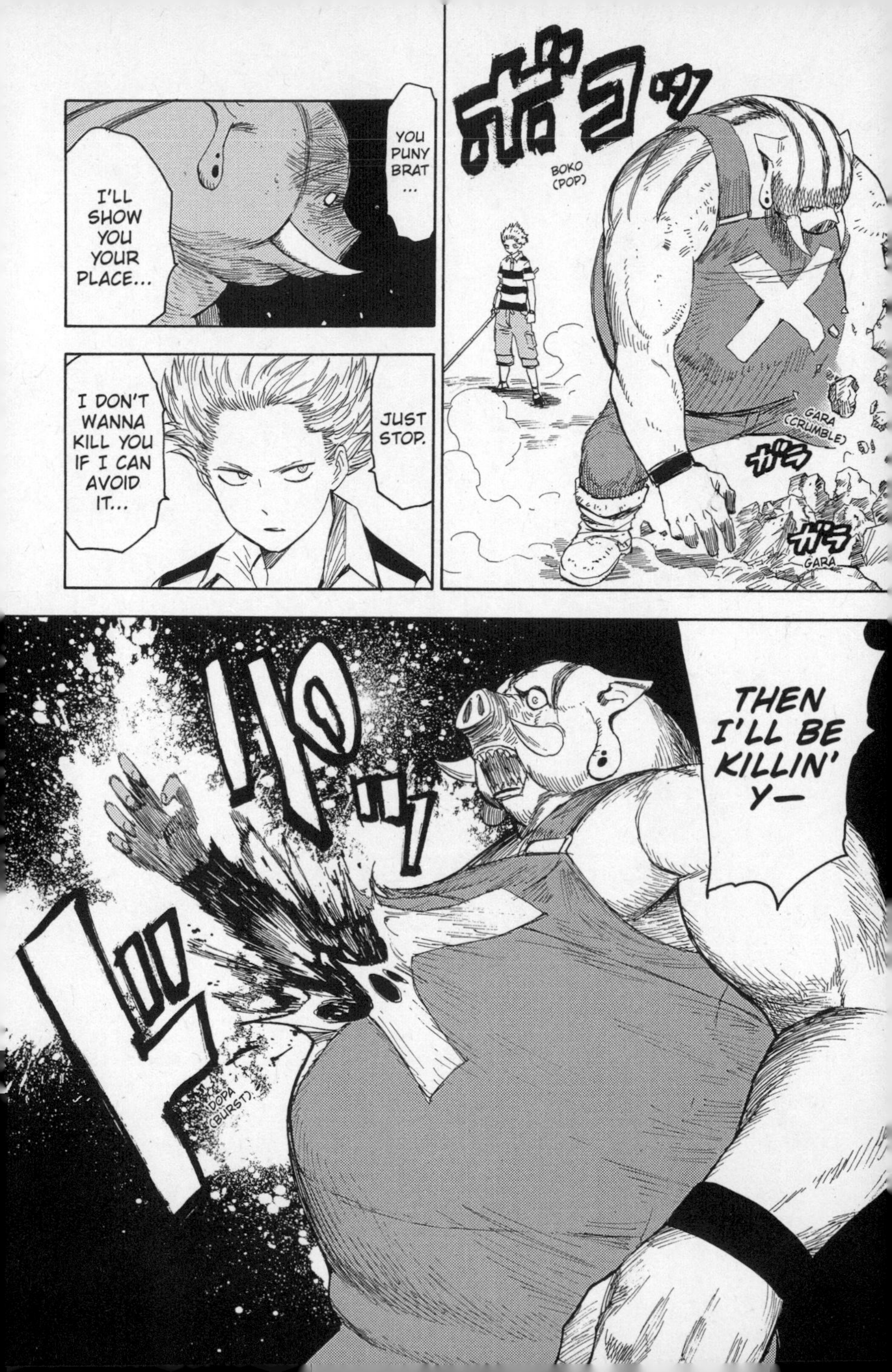

BOKO (POP)
GARA (CRUMBLE)
GARA
YOU PUNY BRAT ...
I'LL SHOW YOU YOUR PLACE...
JUST STOP.
I DON'T WANNA KILL YOU IF I CAN AVOID IT...
THEN I'LL BE KILLIN' Y—
DOPA (BURST)

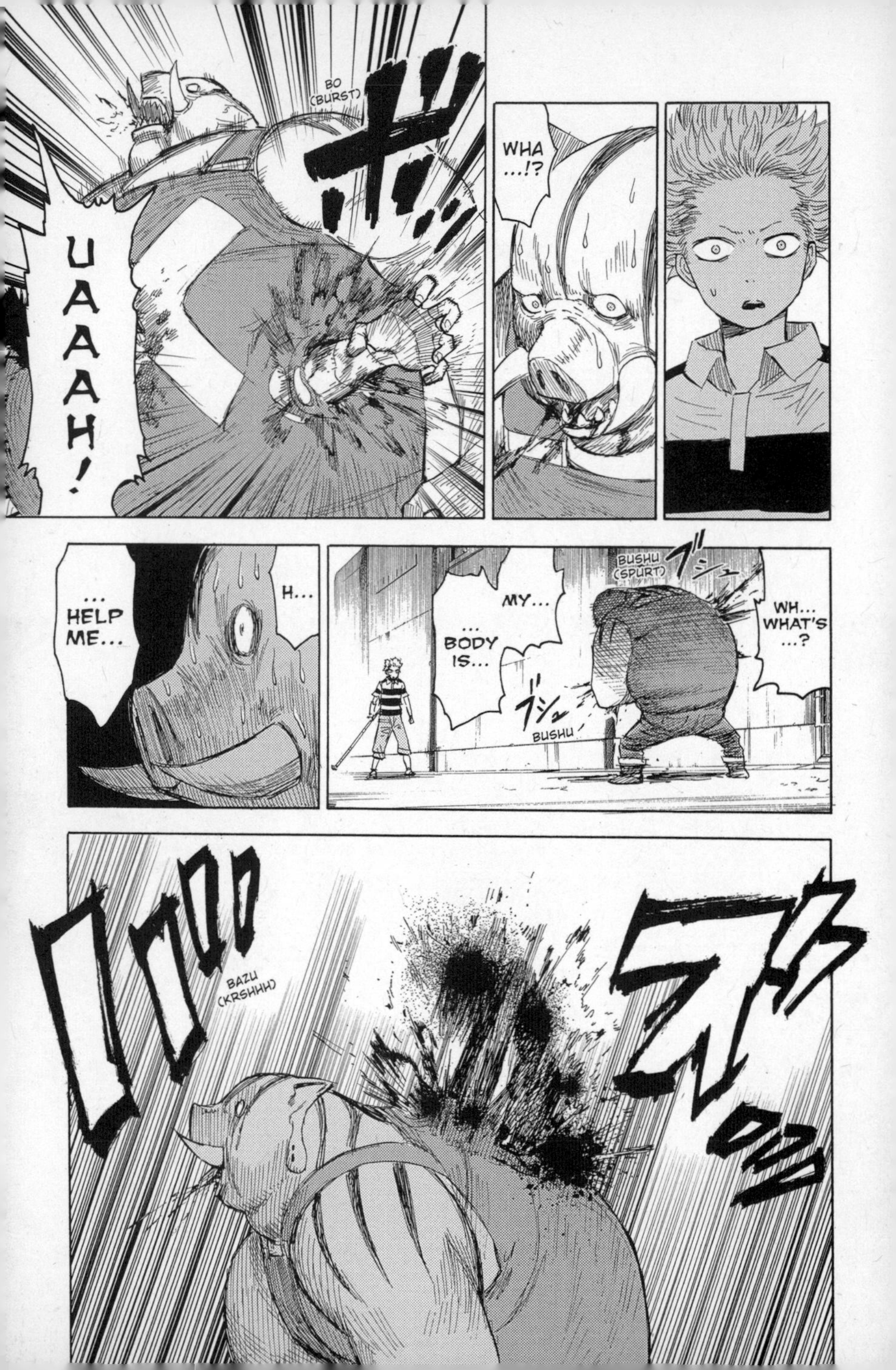
WHA ...!?
BO (BURST)
UAAAAH!
BUSHU (SPURT)
WH... WHAT'S ...?
MY...
... BODY IS...
BUSHU
H...
... HELP ME...
BAZU (KRSHHH)

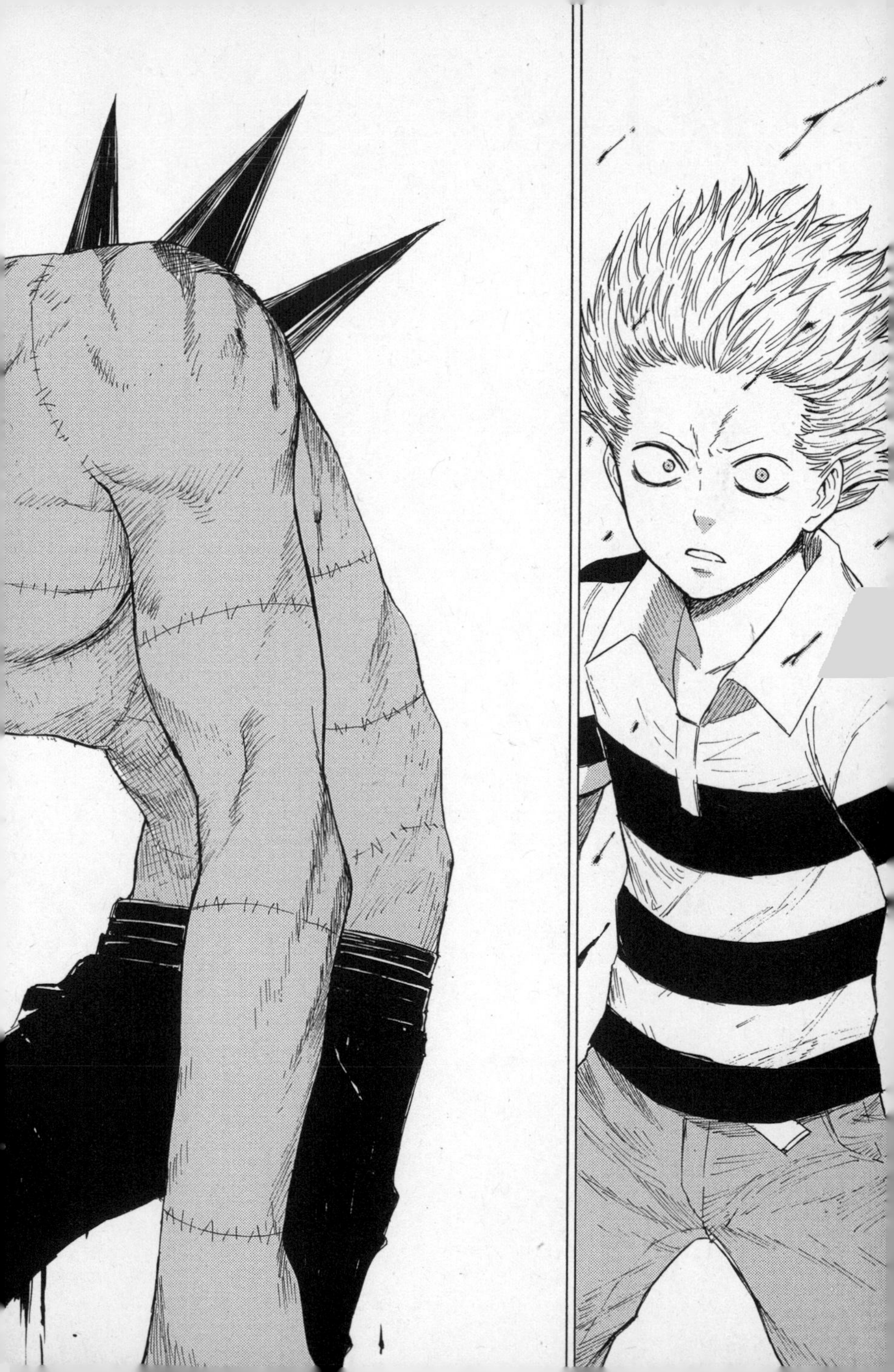

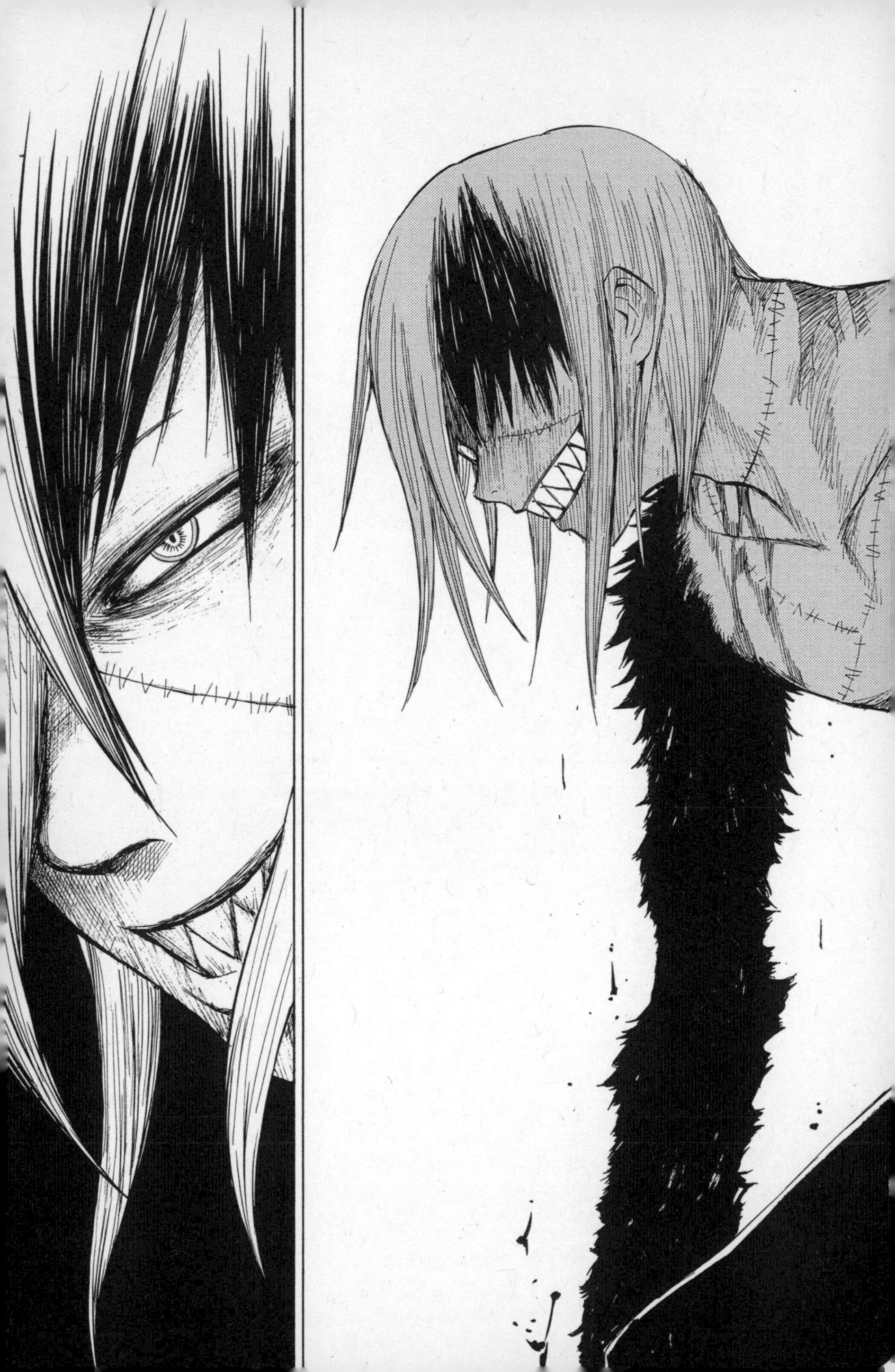

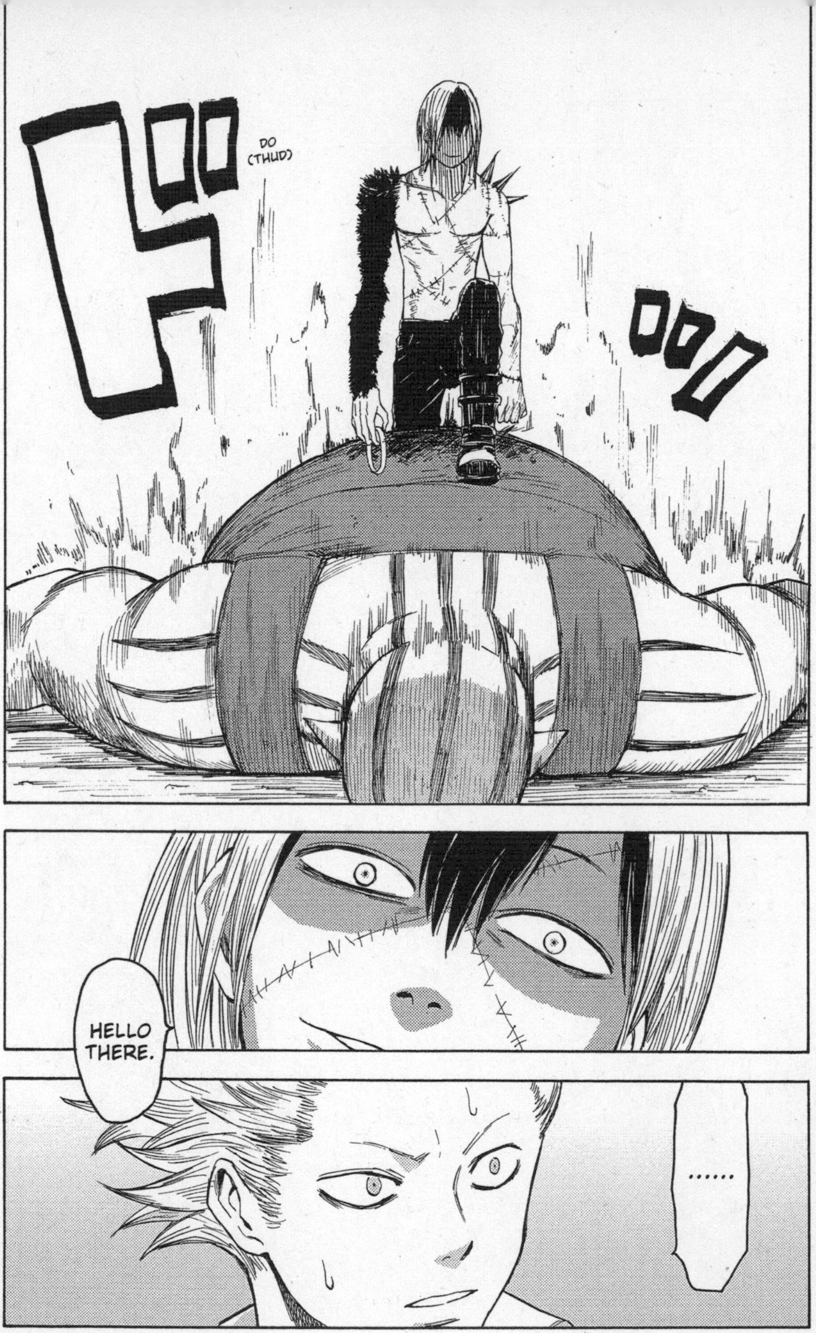

DO
(THUD)
HELLO THERE.
......

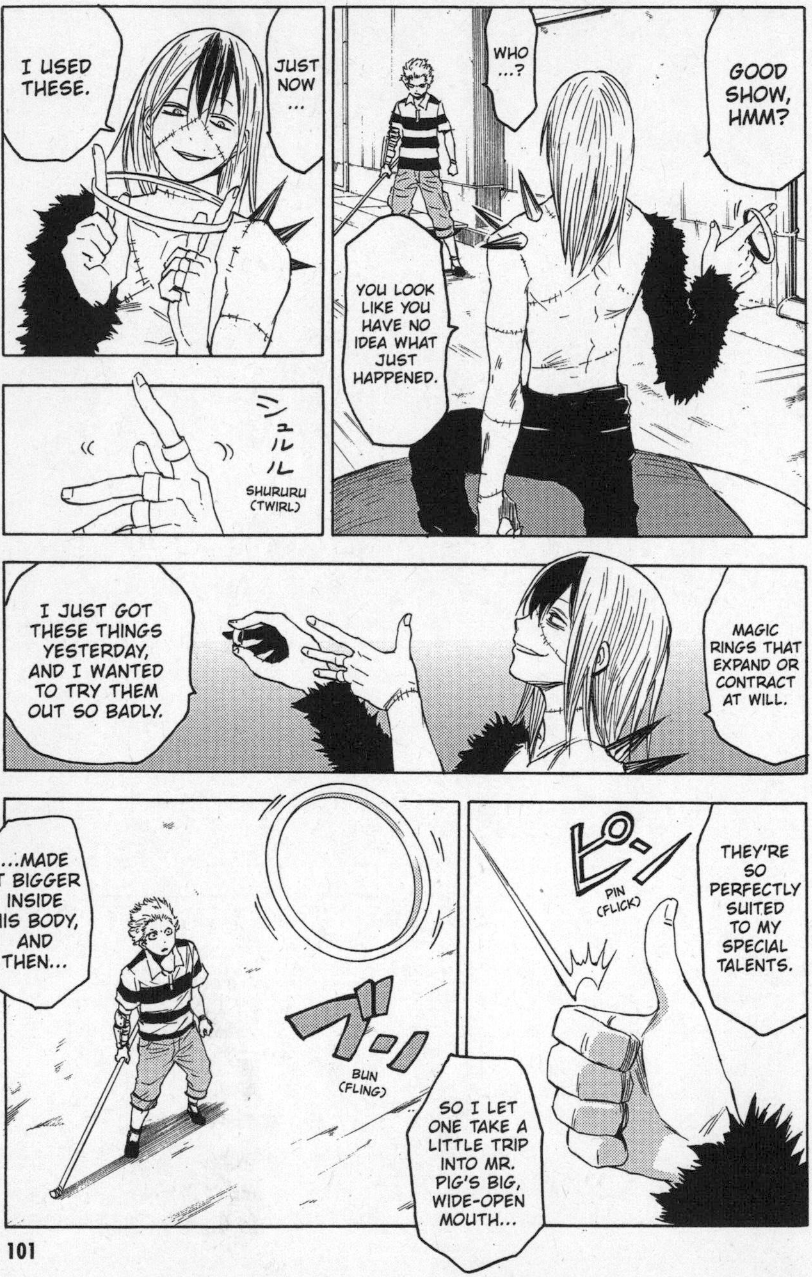
GOOD SHOW, HMM?
WHO ...?
YOU LOOK LIKE YOU HAVE NO IDEA WHAT JUST HAPPENED.
JUST NOW ...
I USED THESE.
シュルル
SHURURU (TWIRL)
MAGIC RINGS THAT EXPAND OR CONTRACT AT WILL.
I JUST GOT THESE THINGS YESTERDAY, AND I WANTED TO TRY THEM OUT SO BADLY.
THEY'RE SO PERFECTLY SUITED TO MY SPECIAL TALENTS.
PIN (FLICK)
SO I LET ONE TAKE A LITTLE TRIP INTO MR. PIG'S BIG, WIDE-OPEN MOUTH...
BUN (FLING)
...MADE IT BIGGER INSIDE HIS BODY, AND THEN...

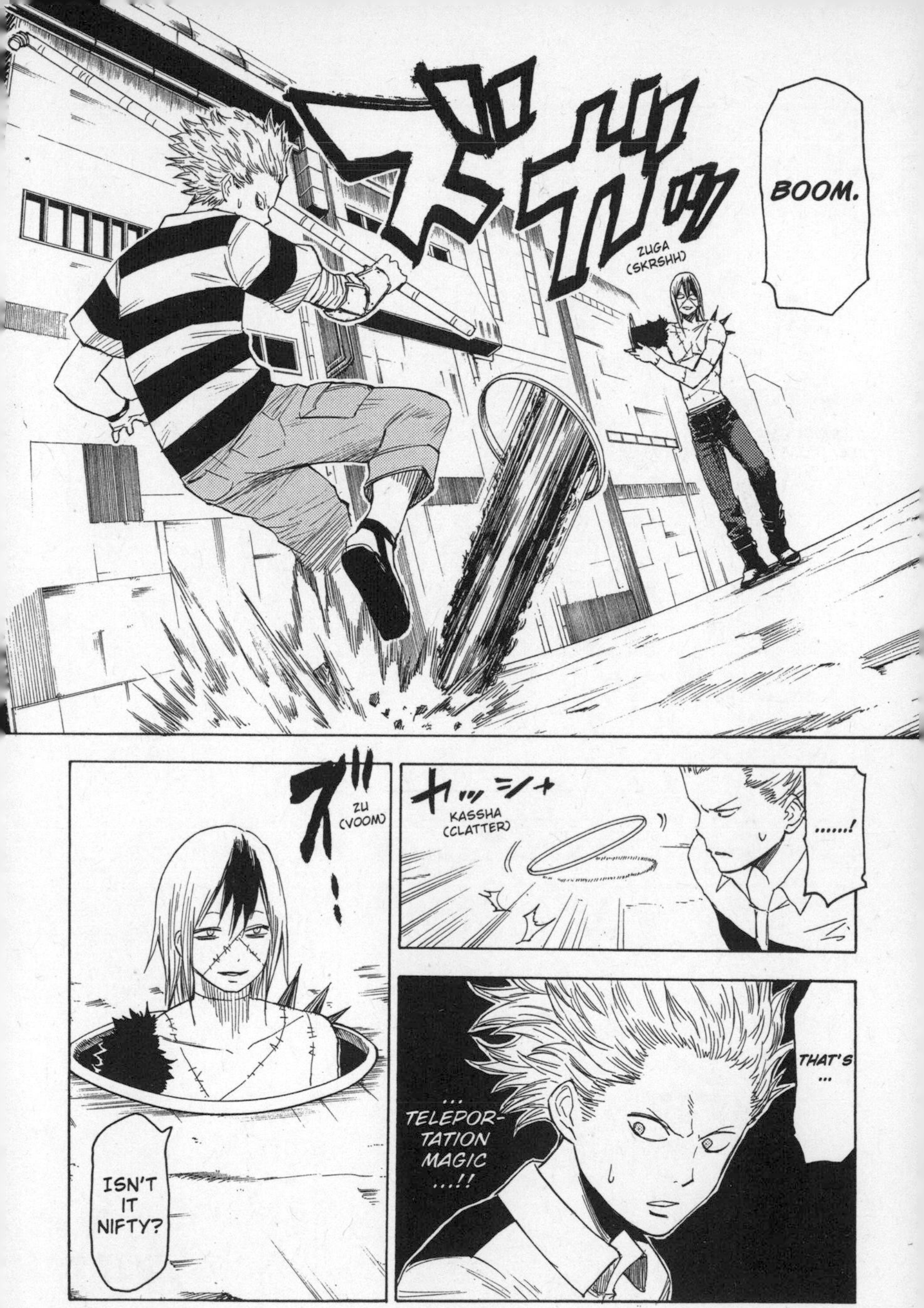
BOOM.
ZUGA (SKRSHH)
......!
KASSHA (CLATTER)
THAT'S ...
... TELEPORTATION MAGIC ...!!
ZU (VOOM)
ISN'T IT NIFTY?

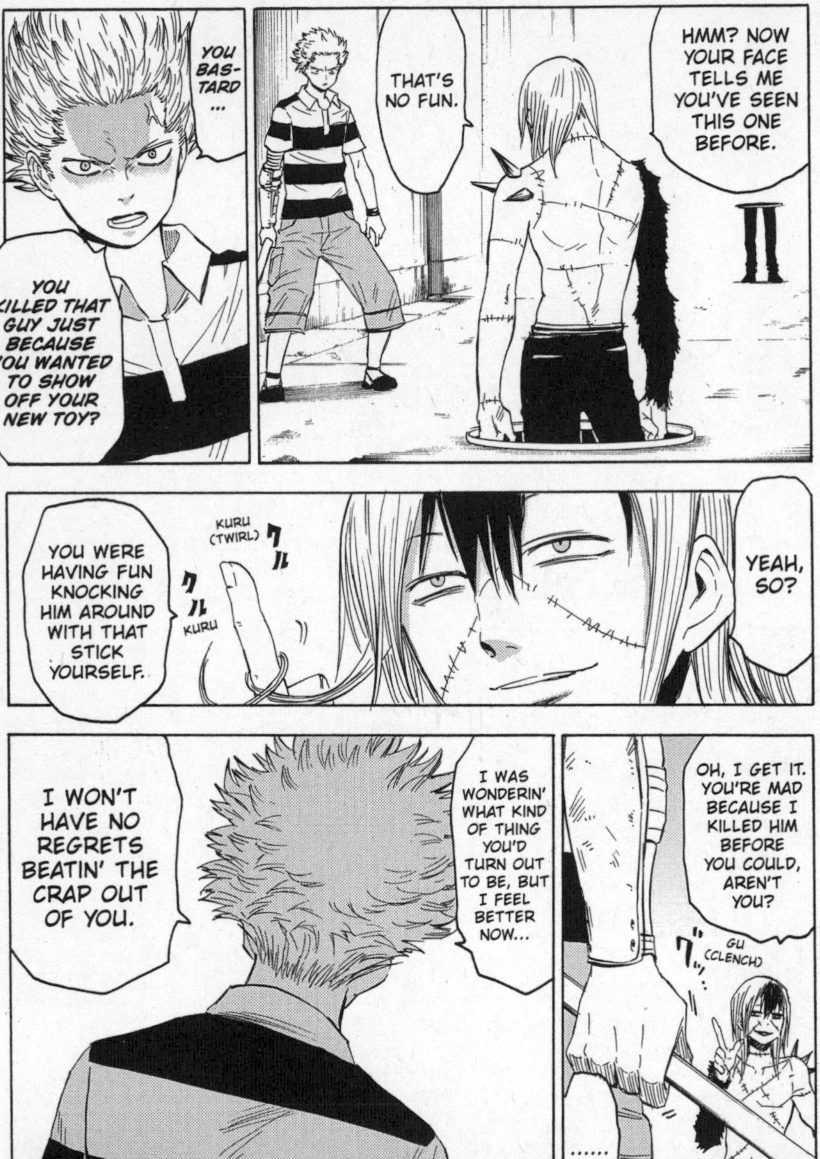
HMM? NOW YOUR FACE TELLS ME YOU'VE SEEN THIS ONE BEFORE.
THAT'S NO FUN.
YOU BASTARD...
YOU KILLED THAT GUY JUST BECAUSE YOU WANTED TO SHOW OFF YOUR NEW TOY?
YEAH, SO?
KURU (TWIRL) クル
クル KURU
YOU WERE HAVING FUN KNOCKING HIM AROUND WITH THAT STICK YOURSELF.
OH, I GET IT. YOU'RE MAD BECAUSE I KILLED HIM BEFORE YOU COULD, AREN'T YOU?
GU (CLENCH)
......
I WAS WONDERIN' WHAT KIND OF THING YOU'D TURN OUT TO BE, BUT I FEEL BETTER NOW...
I WON'T HAVE NO REGRETS BEATIN' THE CRAP OUT OF YOU.

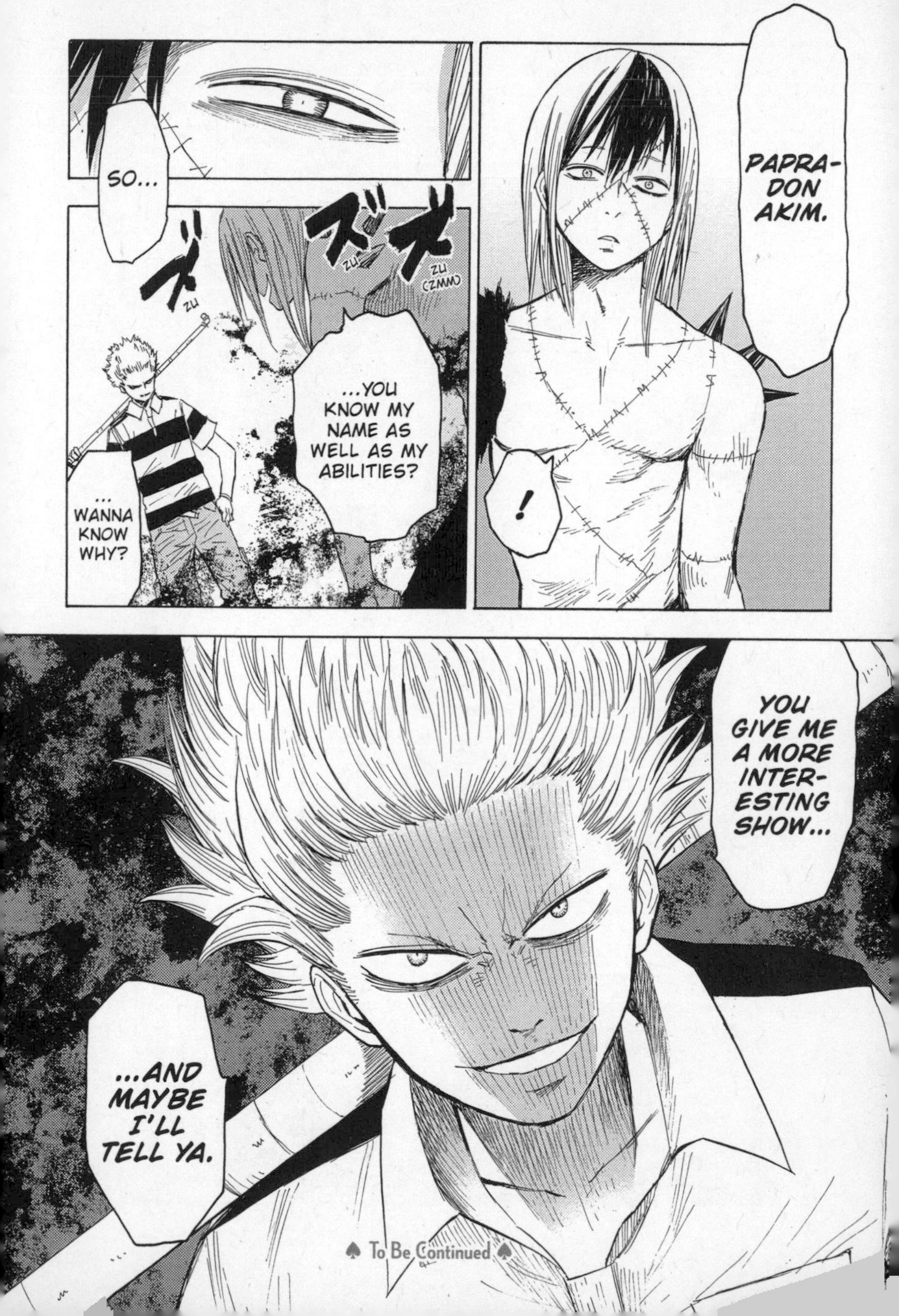
PAPRA-DON AKIM.
!
SO...
ズ ZU (ZMM)
ズ ZU
ズ ZU
...YOU KNOW MY NAME AS WELL AS MY ABILITIES?
...WANNA KNOW WHY?
YOU GIVE ME A MORE INTER-ESTING SHOW...
...AND MAYBE I'LL TELL YA.
To Be Continued

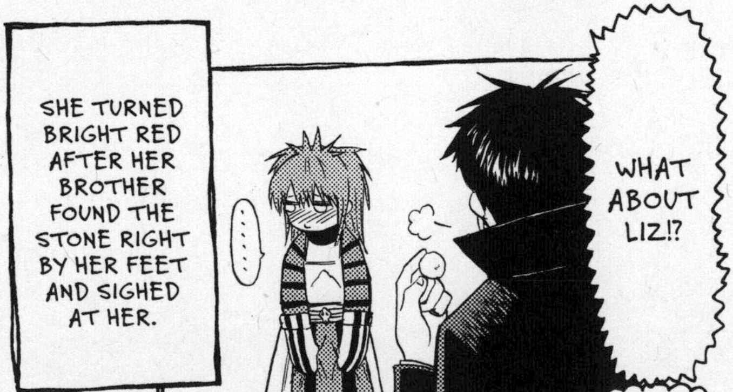
WHAT ABOUT LIZ!?
PART 3
......
SHE TURNED BRIGHT RED AFTER HER BROTHER FOUND THE STONE RIGHT BY HER FEET AND SIGHED AT HER.

BLOOD LAD

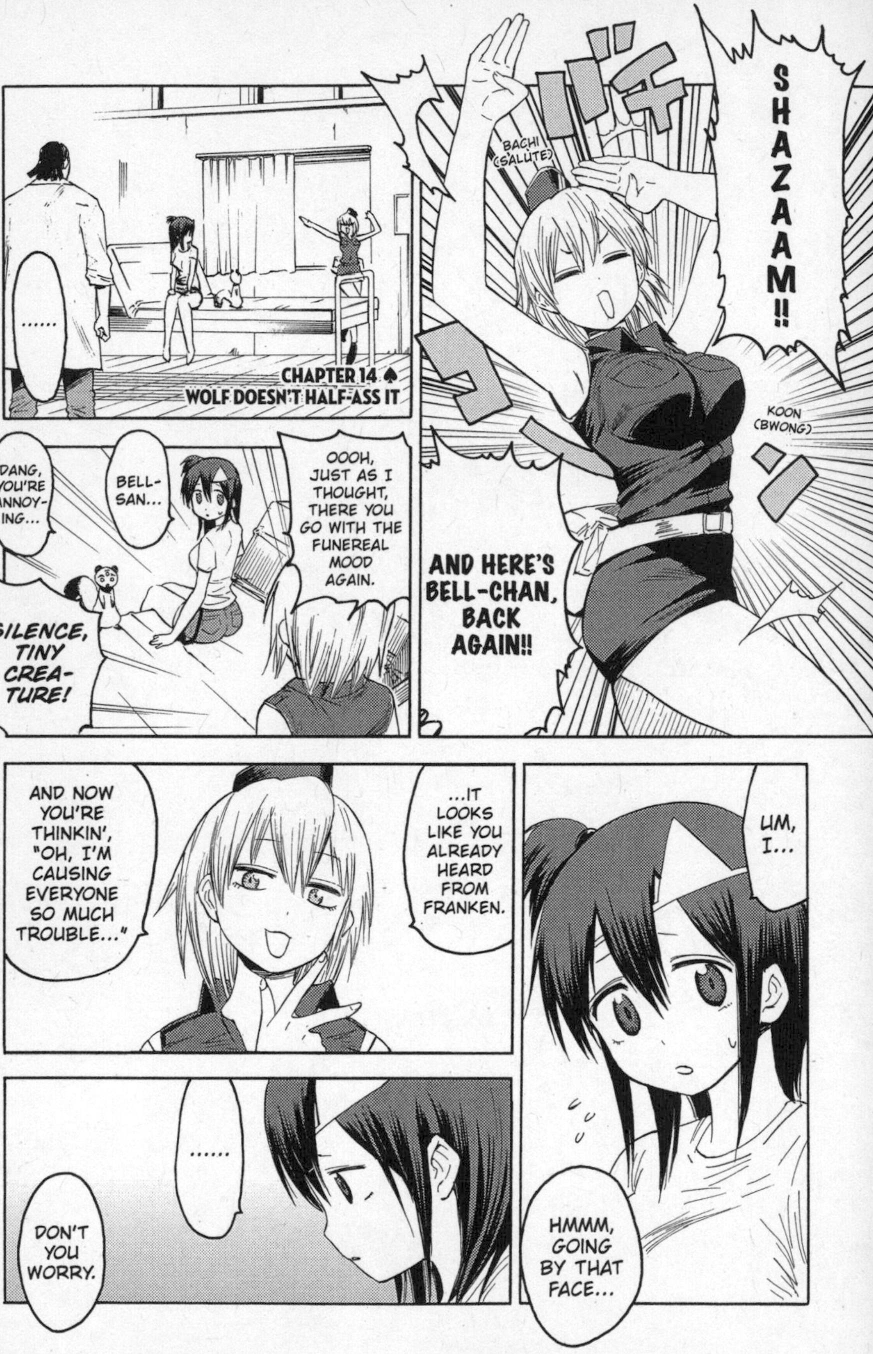

SHAZAAM!!
バチ
BACHI (SALUTE)
KOON (BWONG)
AND HERE'S BELL-CHAN, BACK AGAIN!!
......
CHAPTER 14 ♠
WOLF DOESN'T HALF-ASS IT
OOOH, JUST AS I THOUGHT, THERE YOU GO WITH THE FUNEREAL MOOD AGAIN.
BELL-SAN...
DANG, YOU'RE ANNOY-ING...
SILENCE, TINY CREA-TURE!
UM, I...
HMMM, GOING BY THAT FACE...
...IT LOOKS LIKE YOU ALREADY HEARD FROM FRANKEN.
AND NOW YOU'RE THINKIN', "OH, I'M CAUSING EVERYONE SO MUCH TROUBLE..."
......
DON'T YOU WORRY.

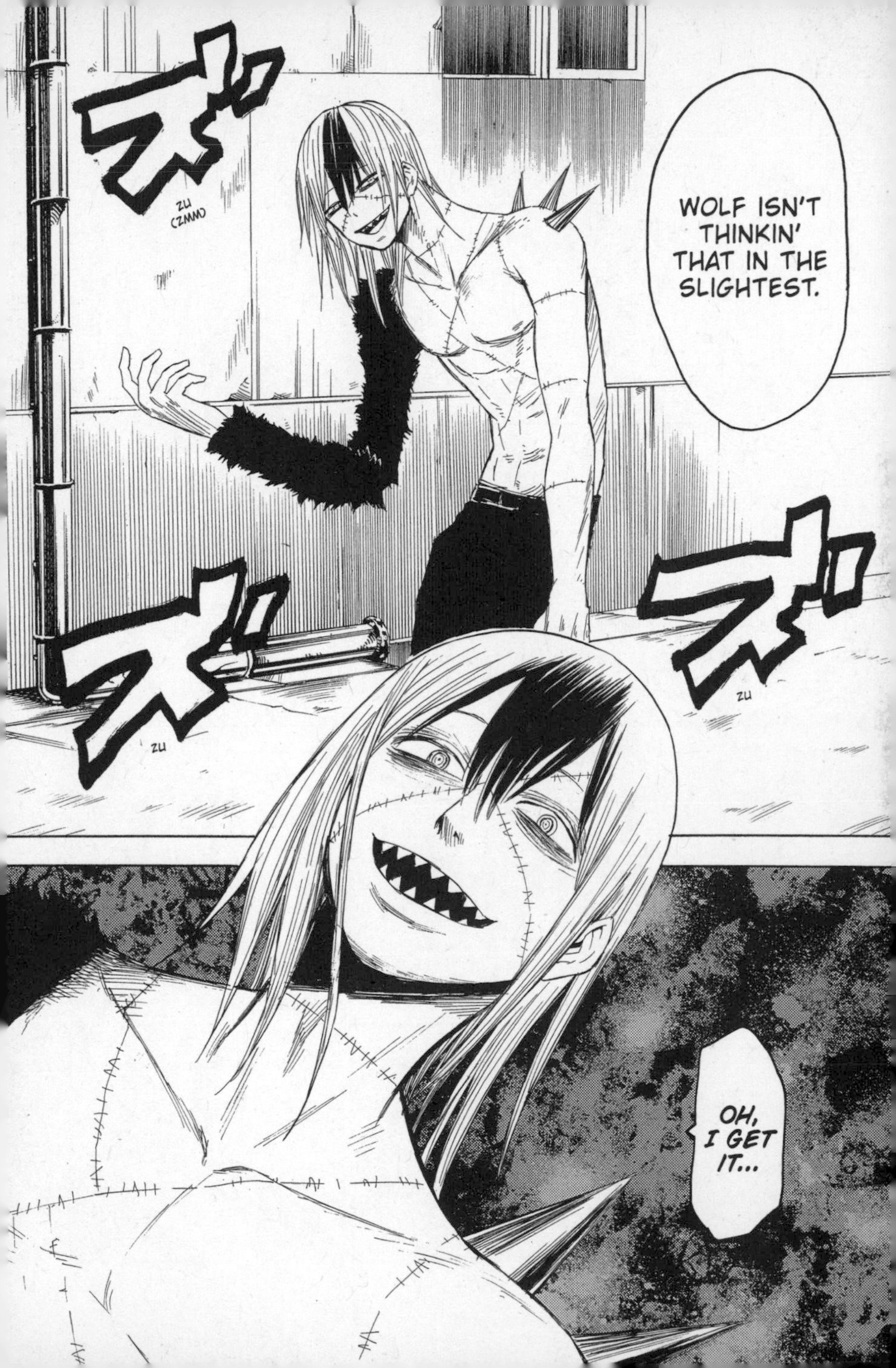
WOLF ISN'T THINKIN' THAT IN THE SLIGHTEST.
ZU (ZMM)
ZU
ZU
OH, I GET IT...

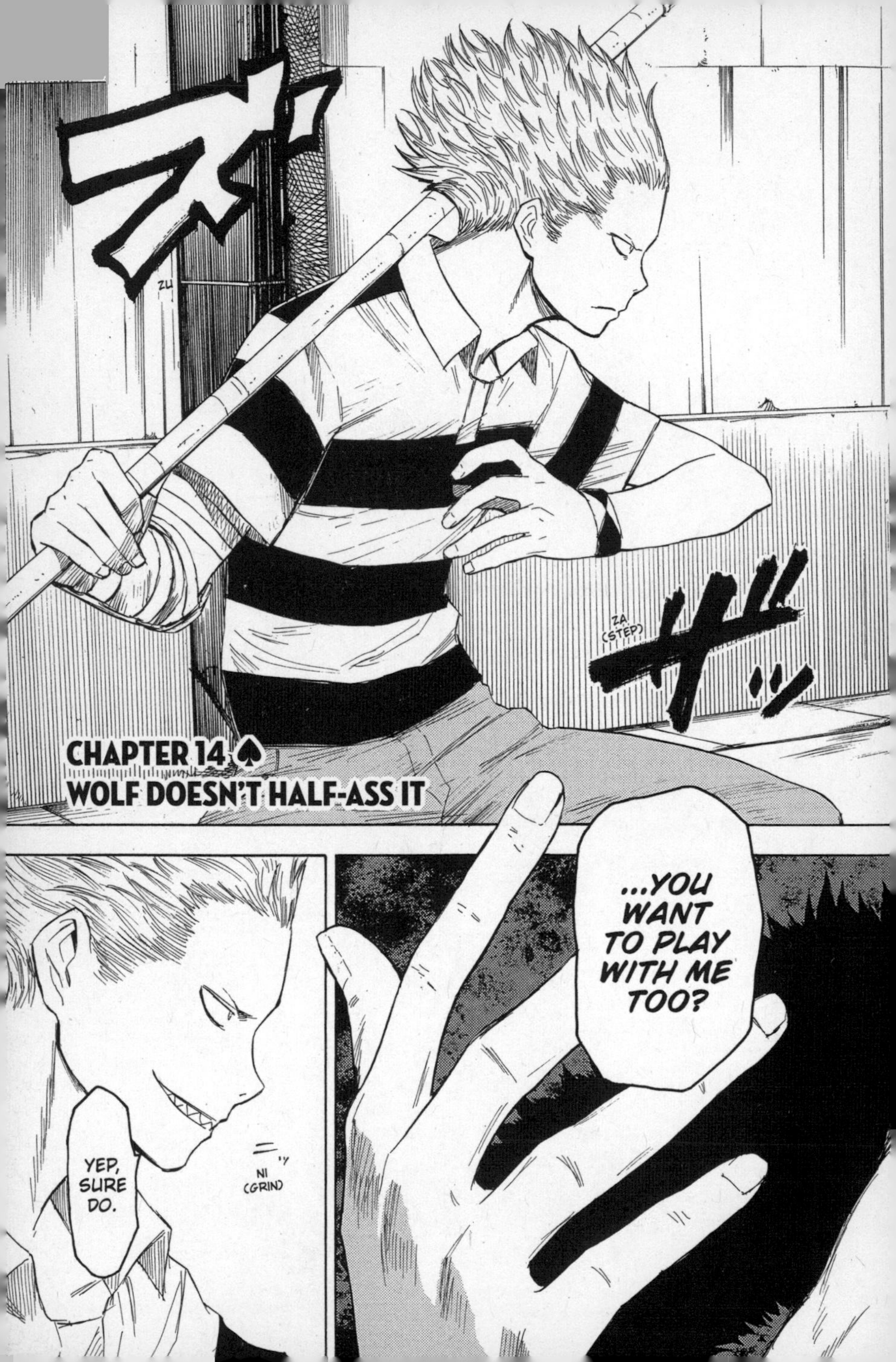
ZU
ZA (STEP)
CHAPTER 14
WOLF DOESN'T HALF-ASS IT
...YOU WANT TO PLAY WITH ME TOO?
NI (GRIN)
YEP, SURE DO.

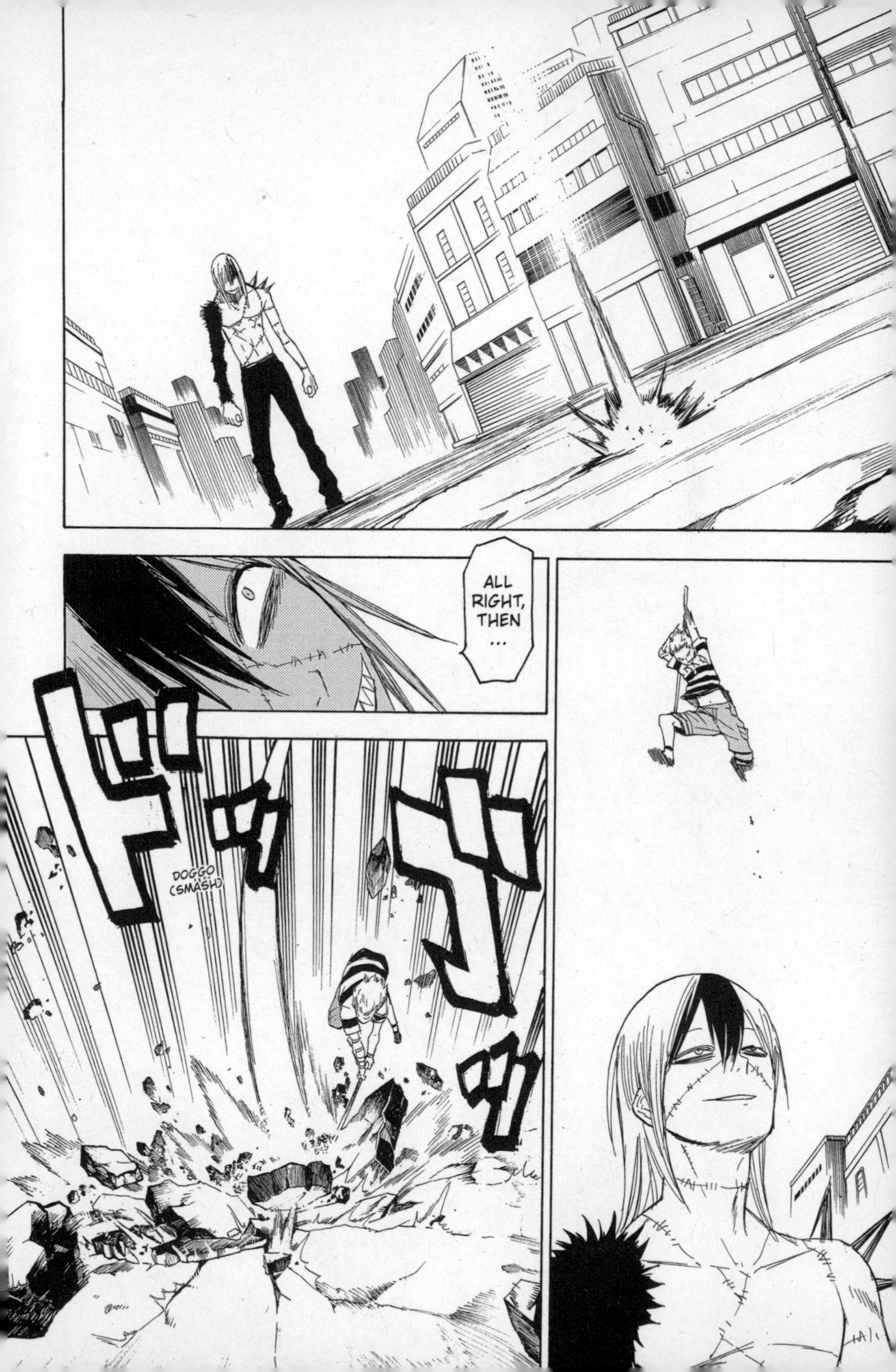
ALL RIGHT, THEN ...
DOGGO (SMASH)

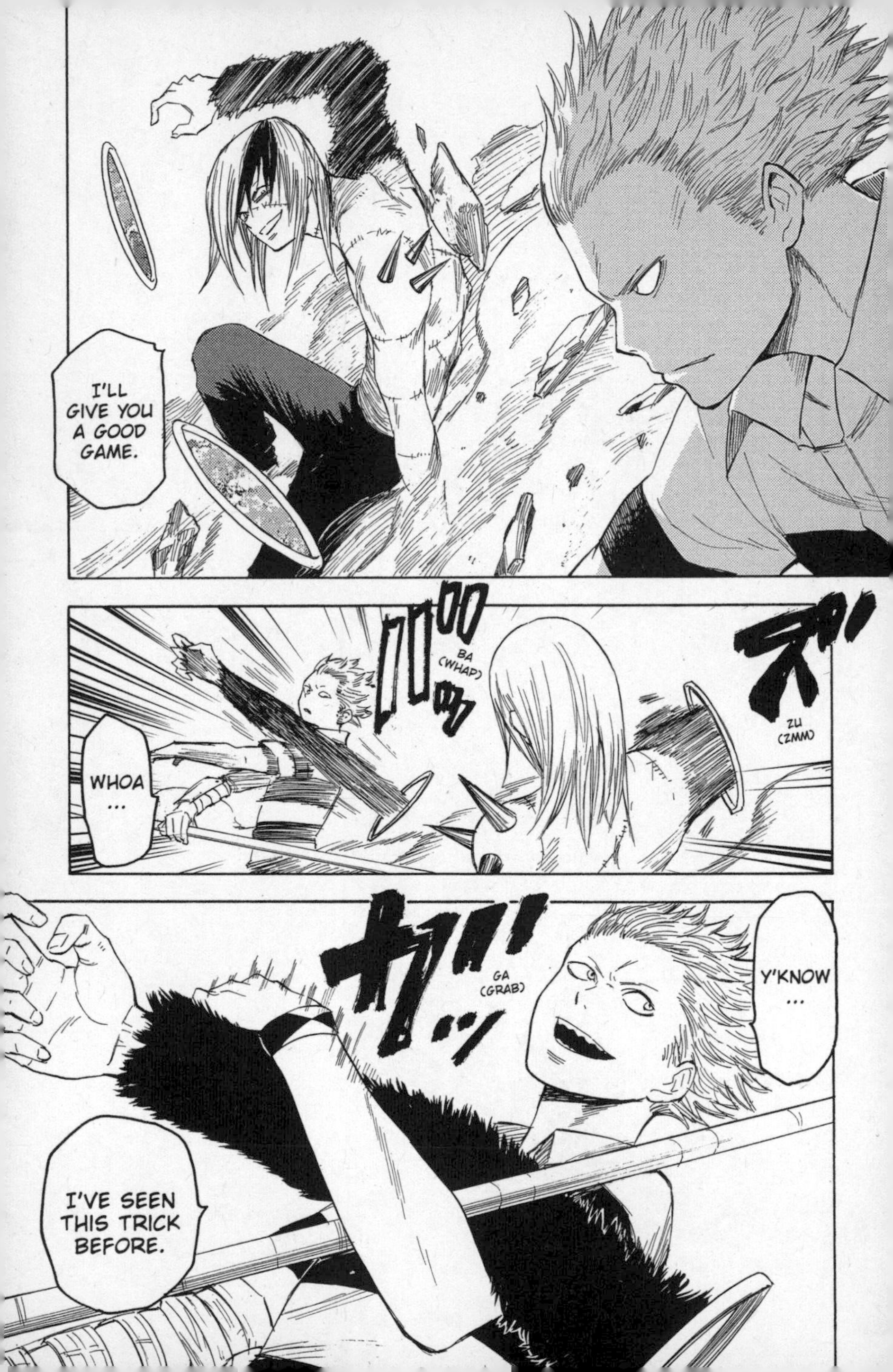
I'LL GIVE YOU A GOOD GAME.
ZU (ZMM)
BA (WHAP)
WHOA ...
Y'KNOW ...
GA (GRAB)
I'VE SEEN THIS TRICK BEFORE.

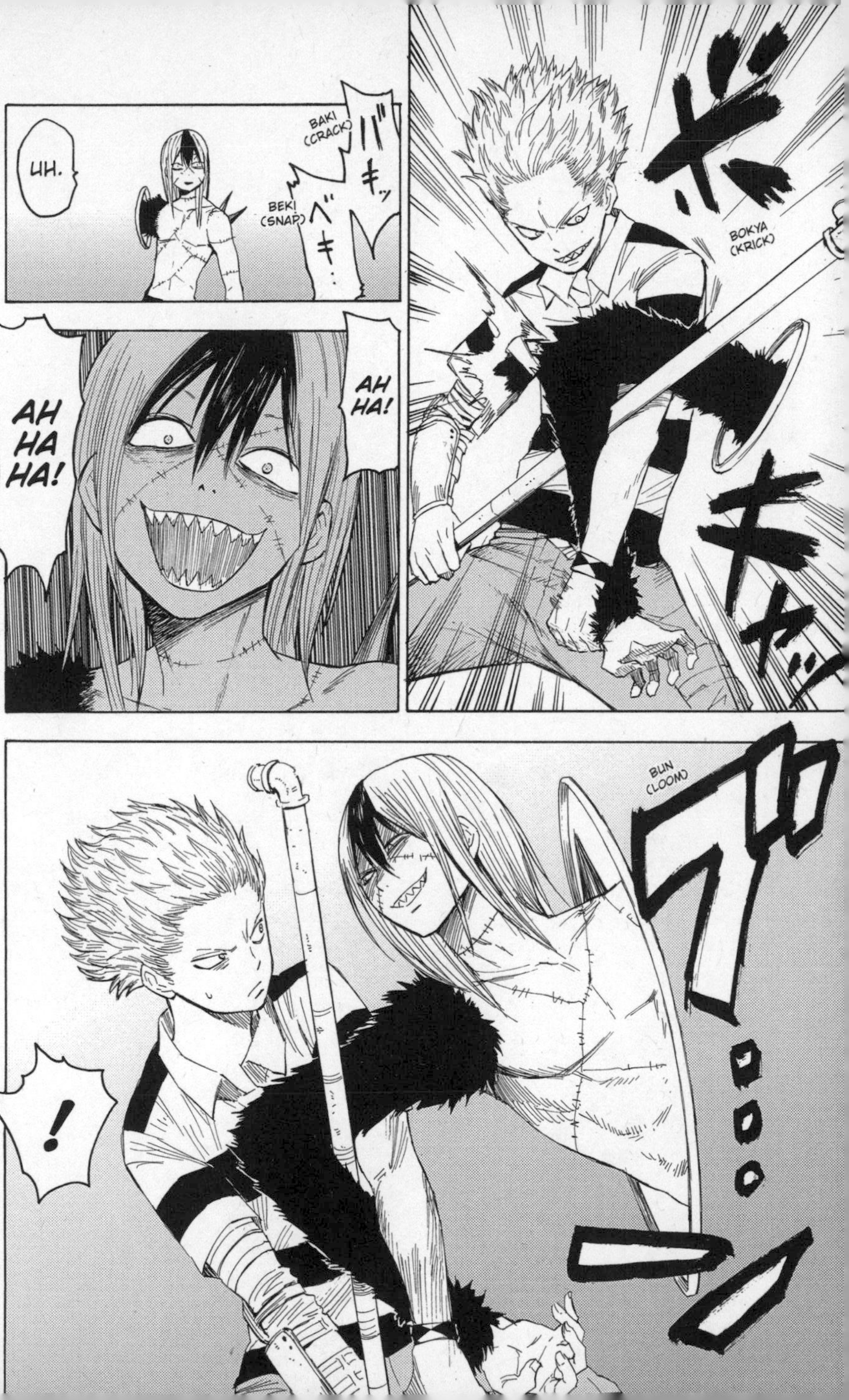
ボキャッ
BOKYA (KRICK)
バキッ
BAKI (CRACK)
ベキ…
BEKI (SNAP)
UH.
AH HA!
AH HA HA HA!
BUN (LOOM)
!

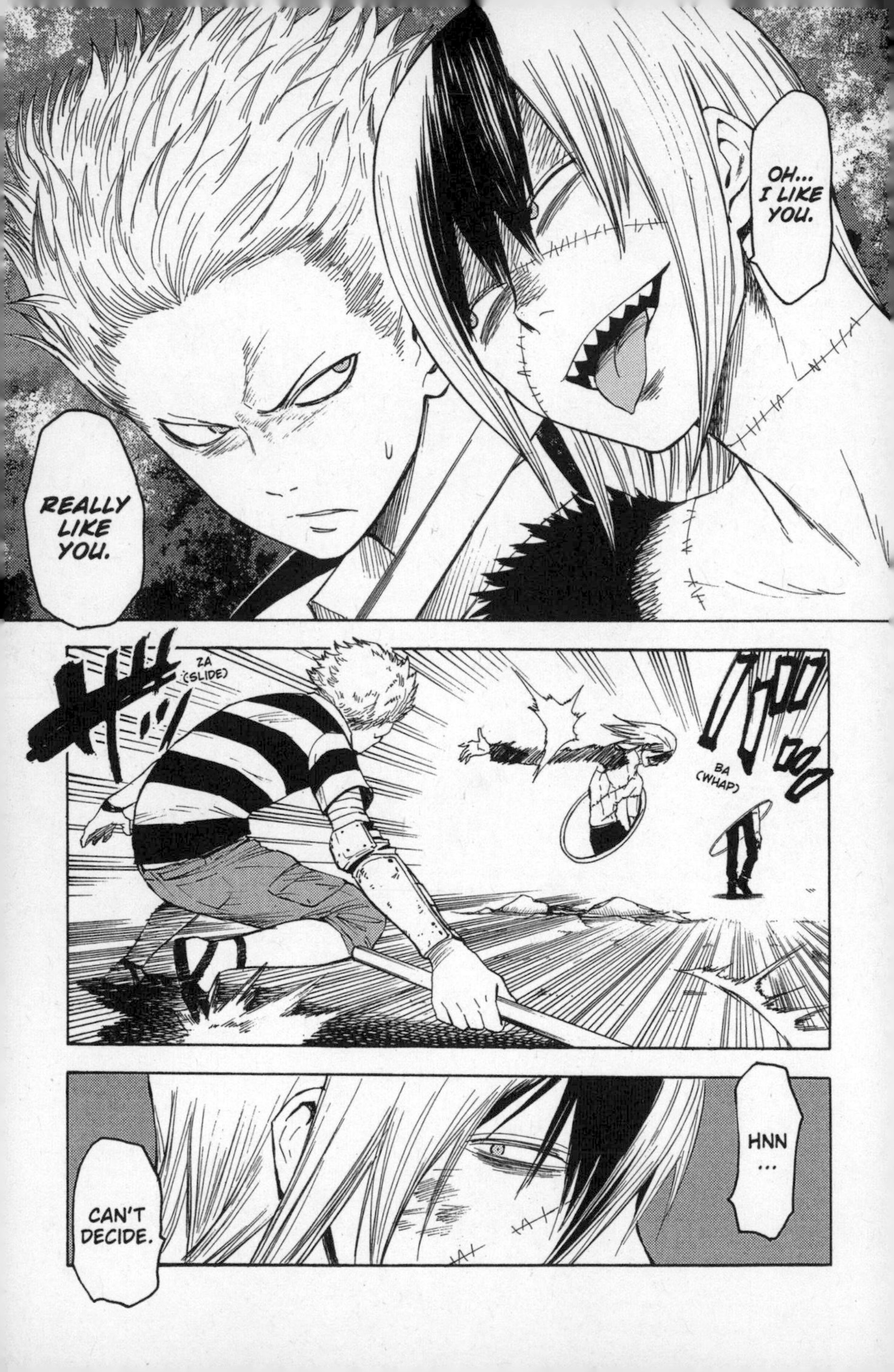
OH... I LIKE YOU.
REALLY LIKE YOU.
BA (WHAP)
ZA (SLIDE)
HNN ...
CAN'T DECIDE.

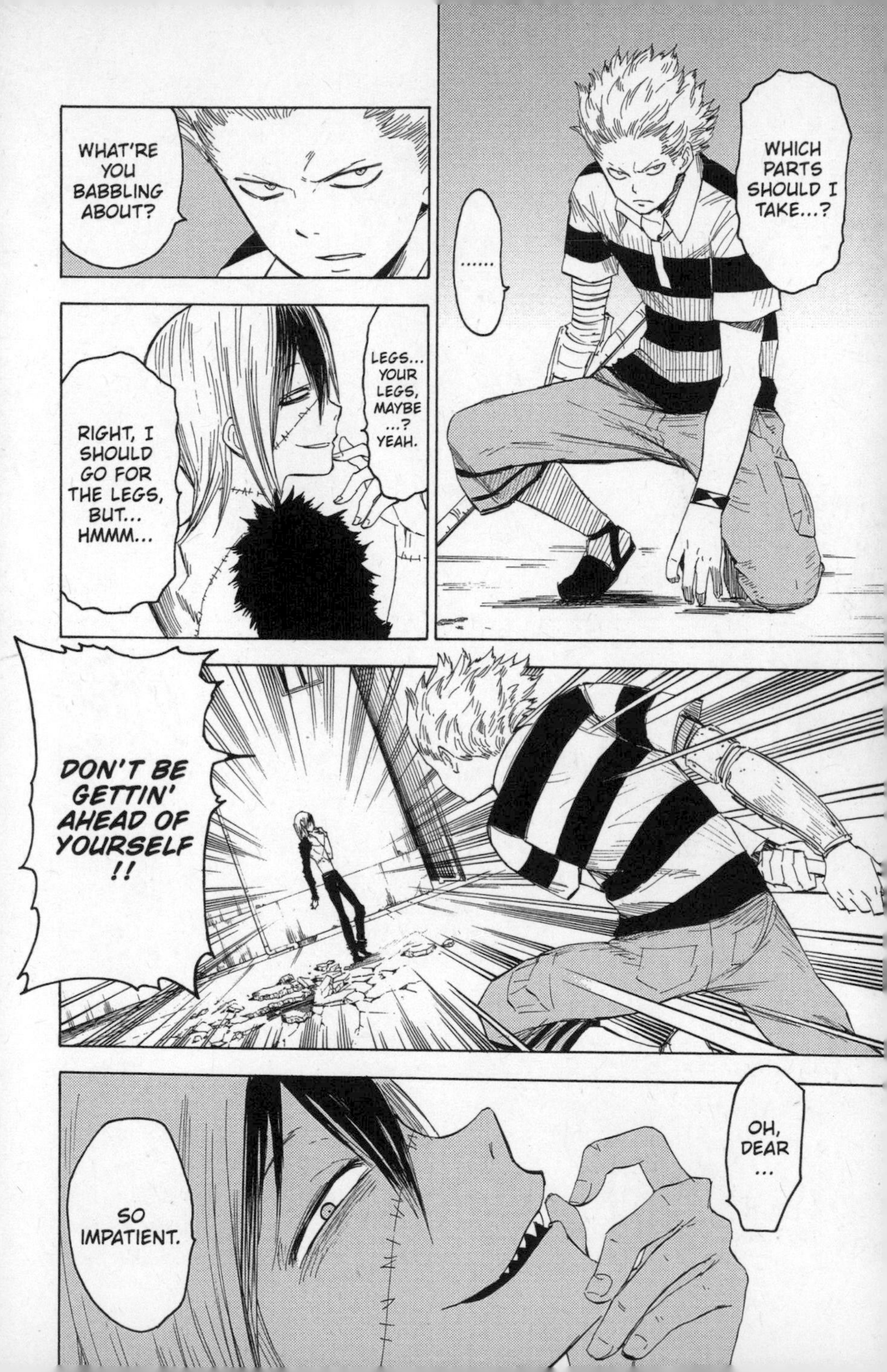
WHICH PARTS SHOULD I TAKE...?
......
WHAT'RE YOU BABBLING ABOUT?
LEGS... YOUR LEGS, MAYBE ...? YEAH.
RIGHT, I SHOULD GO FOR THE LEGS, BUT... HMMM...
DON'T BE GETTIN' AHEAD OF YOURSELF!!
OH, DEAR ...
SO IMPATIENT.

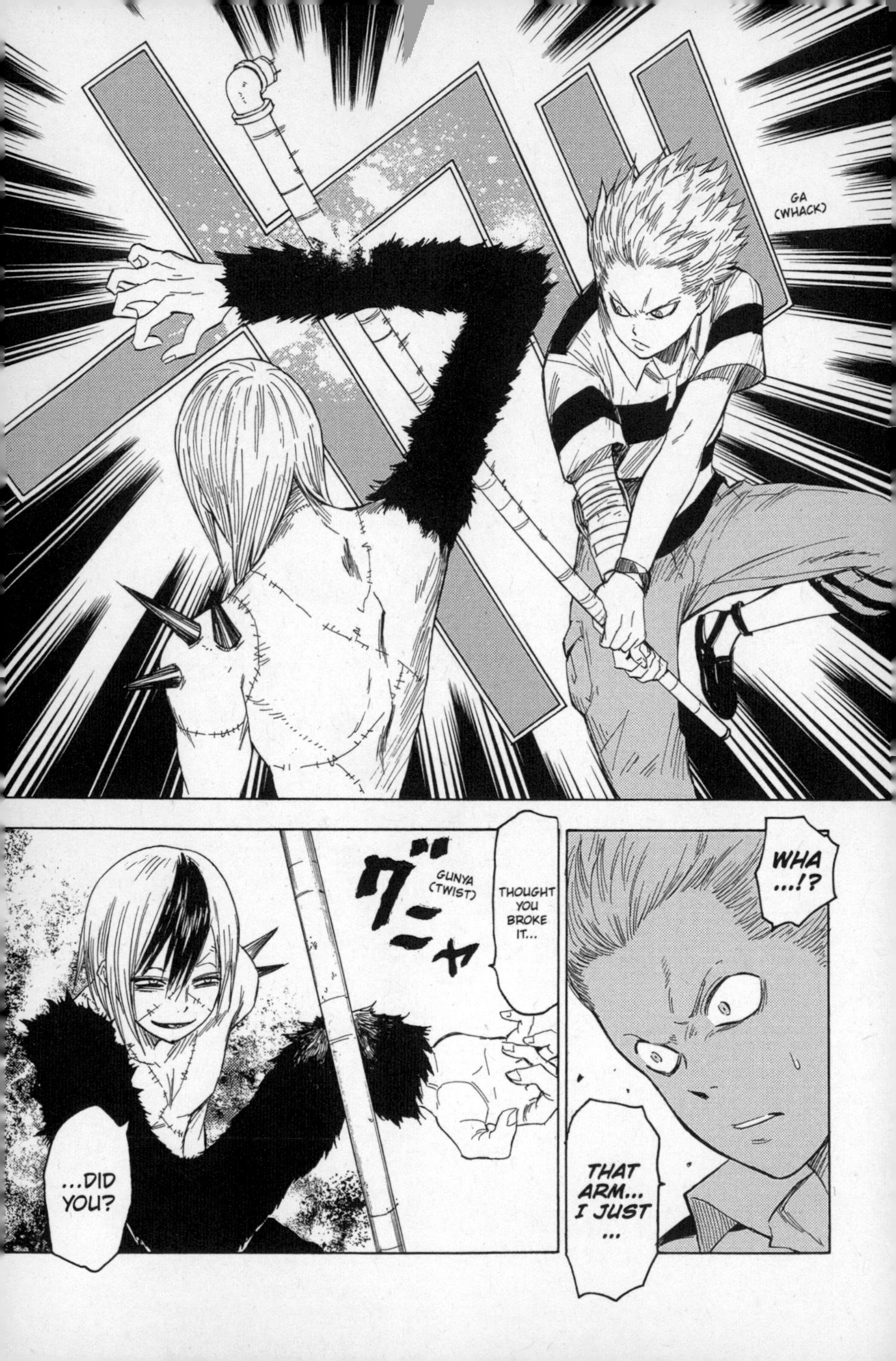
GA (WHACK)
WHA ...!?
THAT ARM... I JUST ...
THOUGHT YOU BROKE IT...
グニャ
GUNYA (TWIST)
...DID YOU?

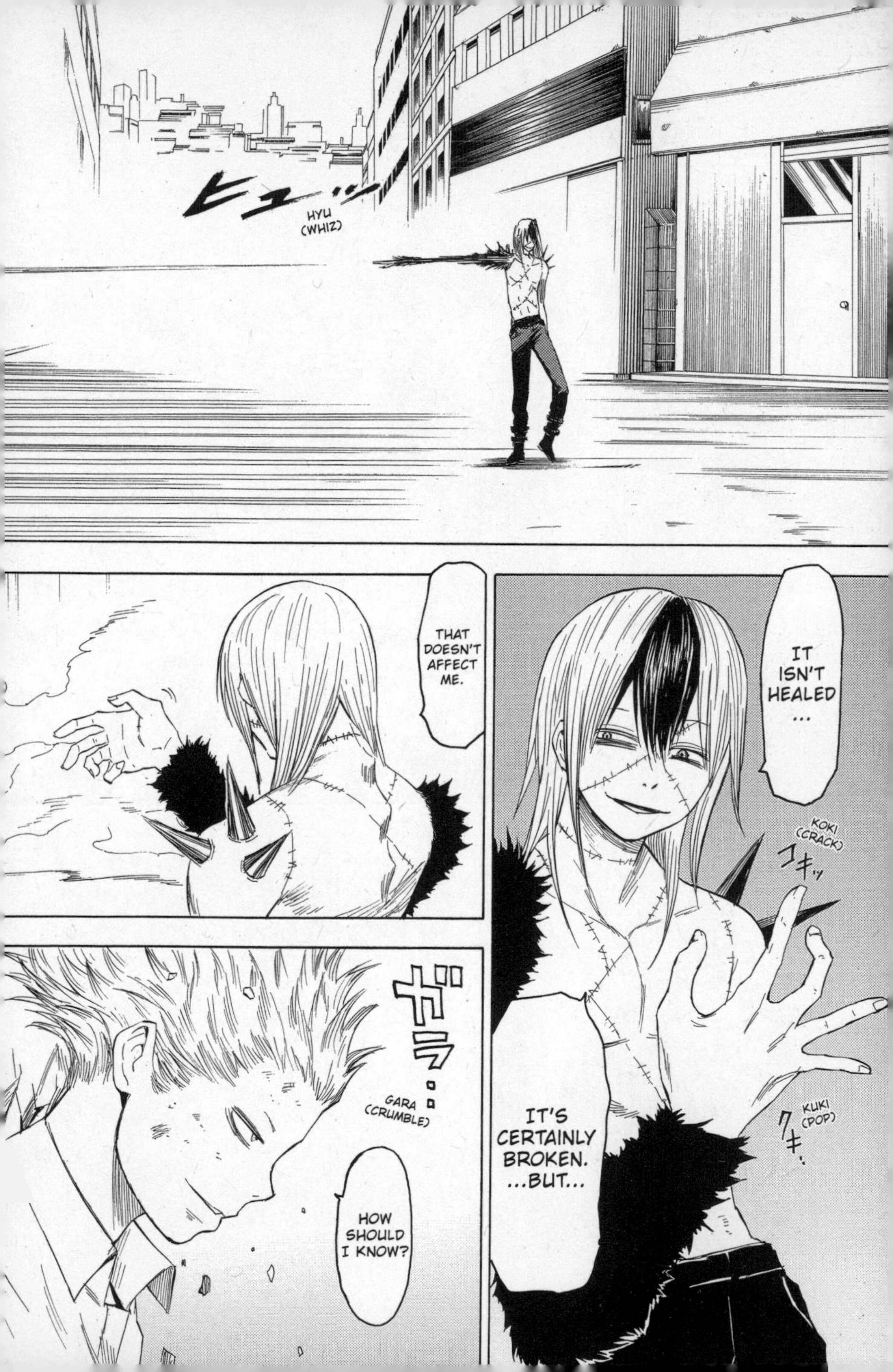

ヒュッ
HYU (WHIZ)
IT ISN'T HEALED ...
コキッ
KOKI (CRACK)
IT'S CERTAINLY BROKEN. ...BUT...
クキ
KUKI (POP)
THAT DOESN'T AFFECT ME.
ガラ
GARA (CRUMBLE)
HOW SHOULD I KNOW?

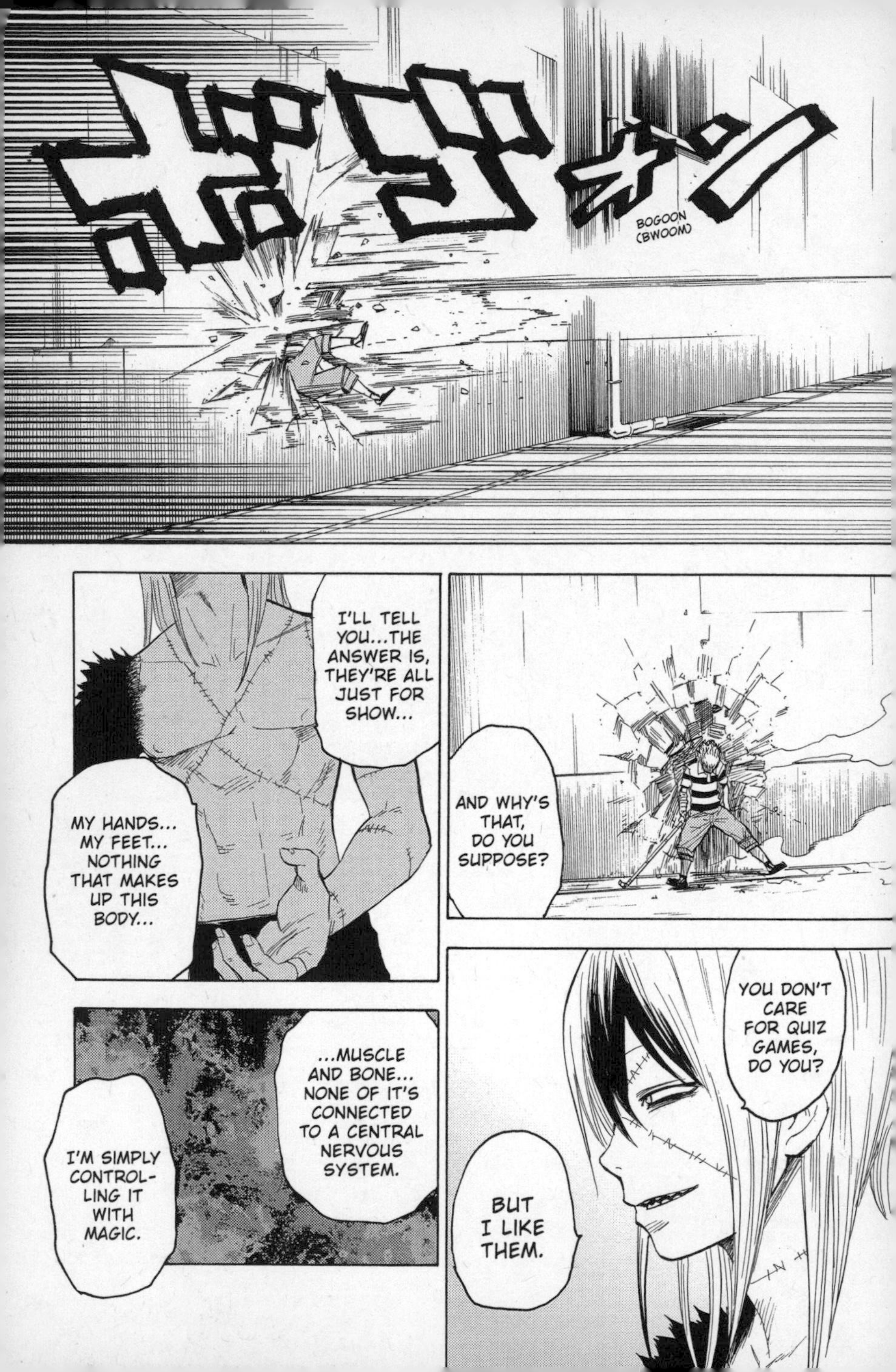
BOGOON
(BWOOM)
AND WHY'S THAT, DO YOU SUPPOSE?
YOU DON'T CARE FOR QUIZ GAMES, DO YOU?
BUT I LIKE THEM.
I'LL TELL YOU...THE ANSWER IS, THEY'RE ALL JUST FOR SHOW...
MY HANDS... MY FEET... NOTHING THAT MAKES UP THIS BODY...
...MUSCLE AND BONE... NONE OF IT'S CONNECTED TO A CENTRAL NERVOUS SYSTEM.
I'M SIMPLY CONTROL-LING IT WITH MAGIC.

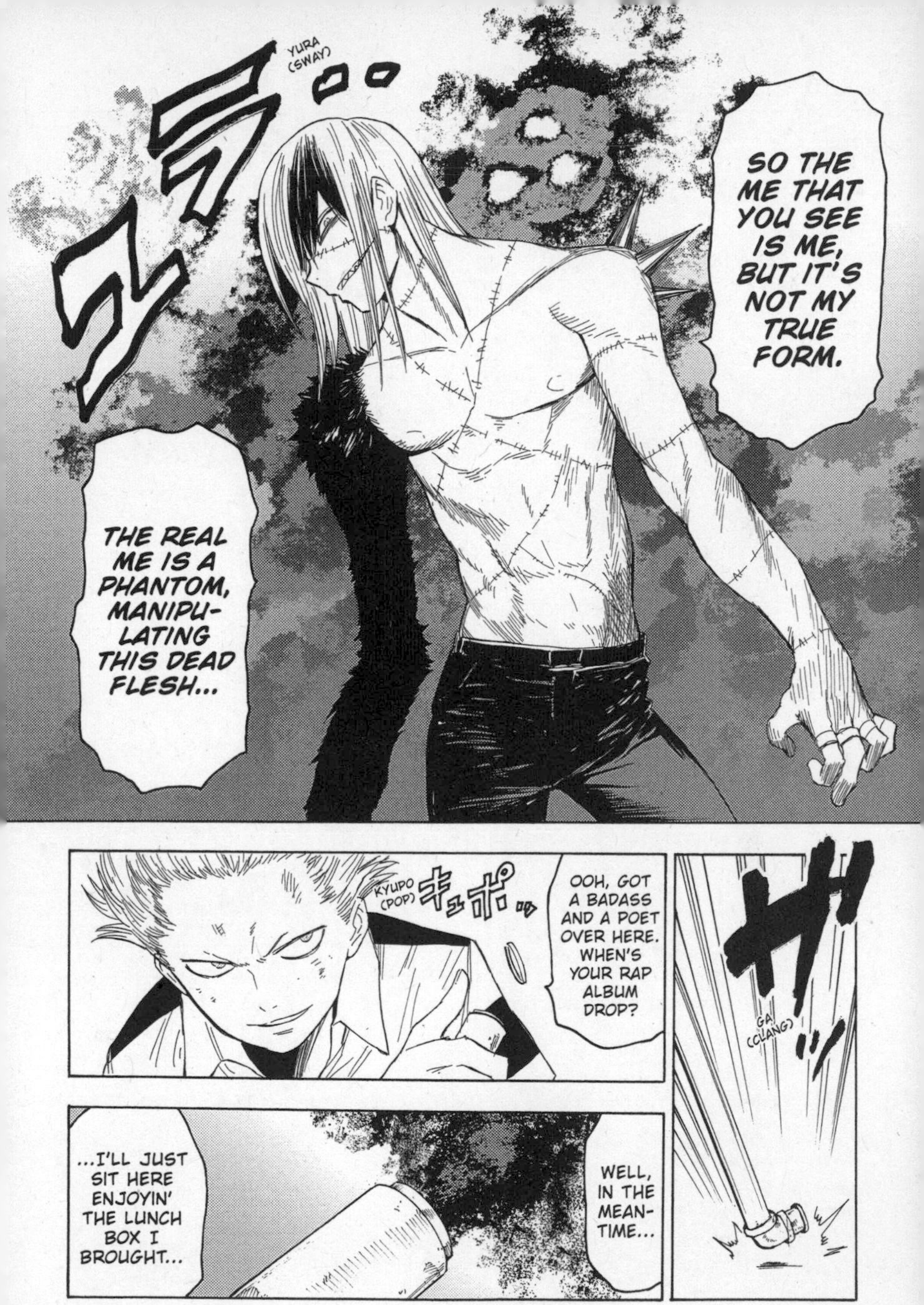
YURA (SWAY)
SO THE ME THAT YOU SEE IS ME, BUT IT'S NOT MY TRUE FORM.
THE REAL ME IS A PHANTOM, MANIPU-LATING THIS DEAD FLESH...
GA (CLANG)
KYUPO (POP)
OOH, GOT A BADASS AND A POET OVER HERE. WHEN'S YOUR RAP ALBUM DROP?
WELL, IN THE MEAN-TIME...
...I'LL JUST SIT HERE ENJOYIN' THE LUNCH BOX I BROUGHT...

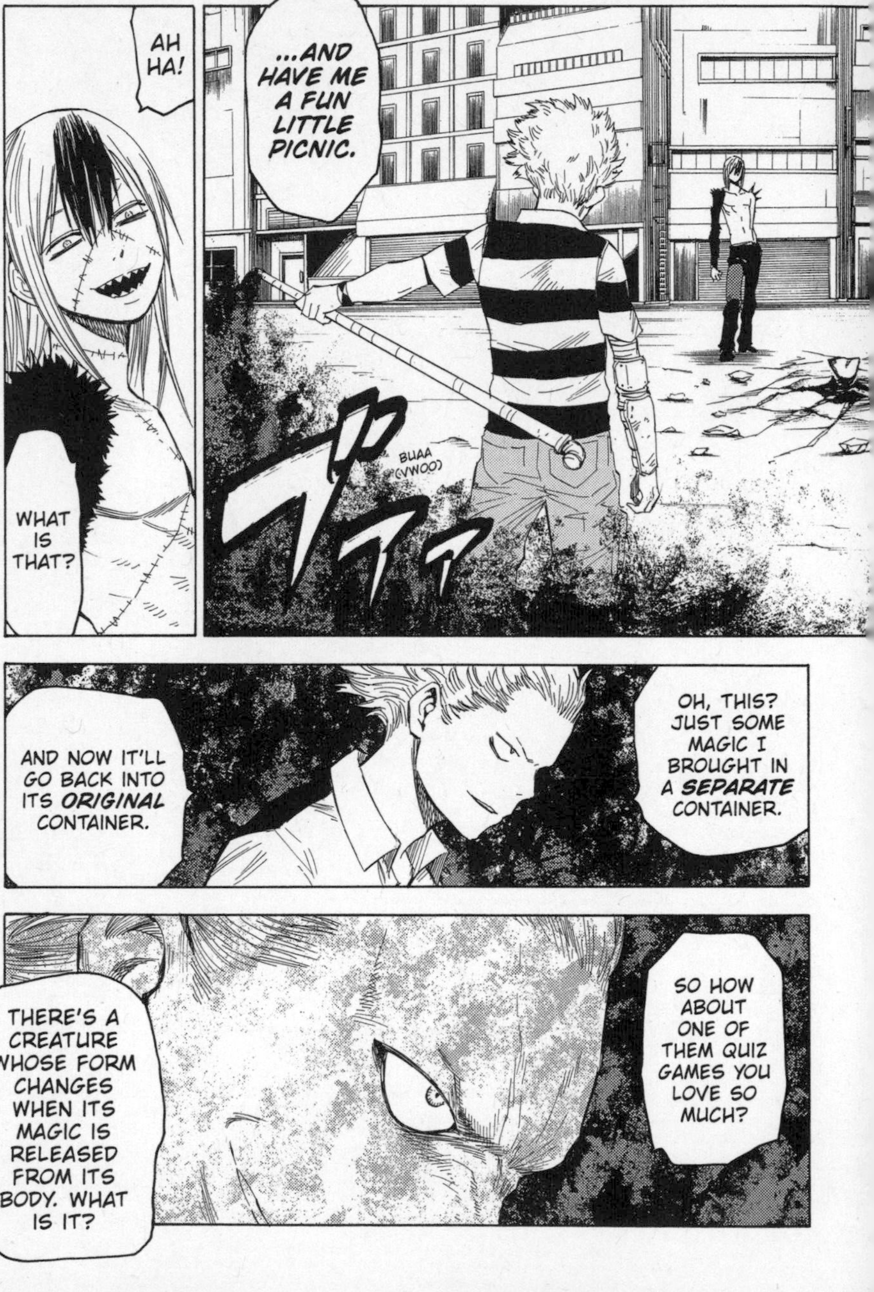
...AND HAVE ME A FUN LITTLE PICNIC.
BUAA (VWOO)
AH HA!
WHAT IS THAT?
OH, THIS? JUST SOME MAGIC I BROUGHT IN A *SEPARATE* CONTAINER.
AND NOW IT'LL GO BACK INTO ITS *ORIGINAL* CONTAINER.
SO HOW ABOUT ONE OF THEM QUIZ GAMES YOU LOVE SO MUCH?
THERE'S A CREATURE WHOSE FORM CHANGES WHEN ITS MAGIC IS RELEASED FROM ITS BODY. WHAT IS IT?

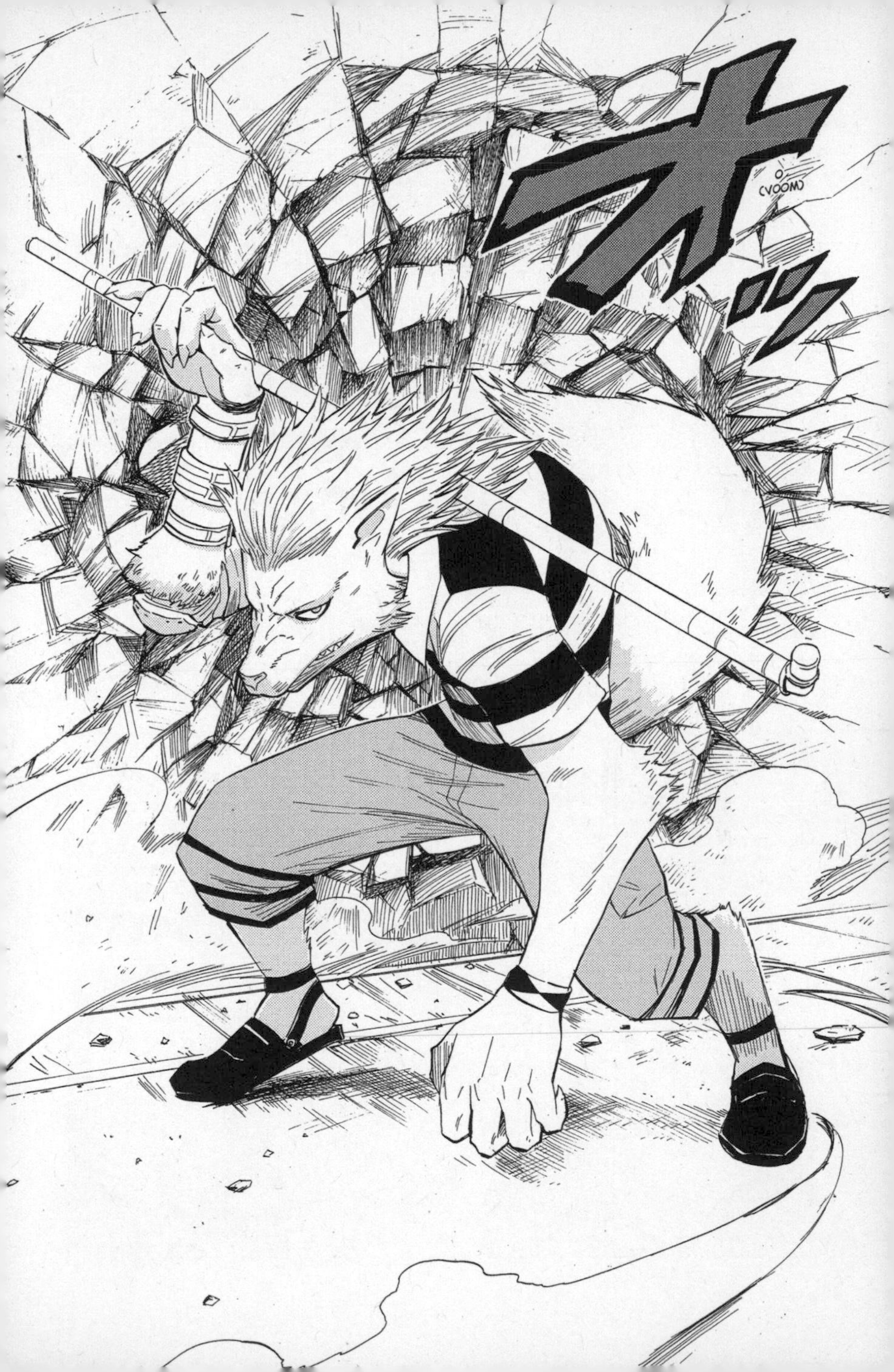

ォ゛ッ
O
(VOOM)

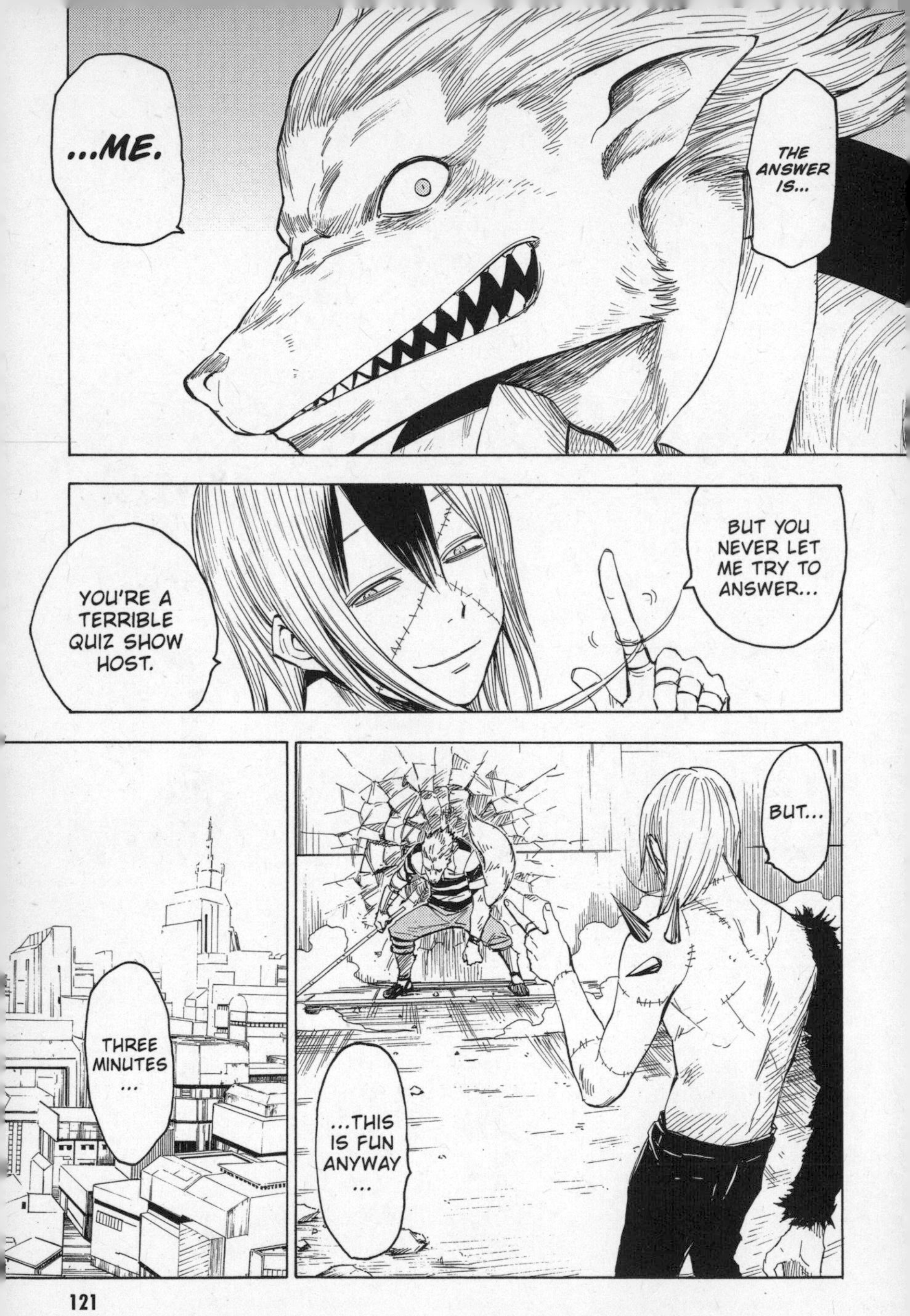
THE ANSWER IS...
...ME.
BUT YOU NEVER LET ME TRY TO ANSWER...
YOU'RE A TERRIBLE QUIZ SHOW HOST.
BUT...
...THIS IS FUN ANYWAY...
THREE MINUTES...

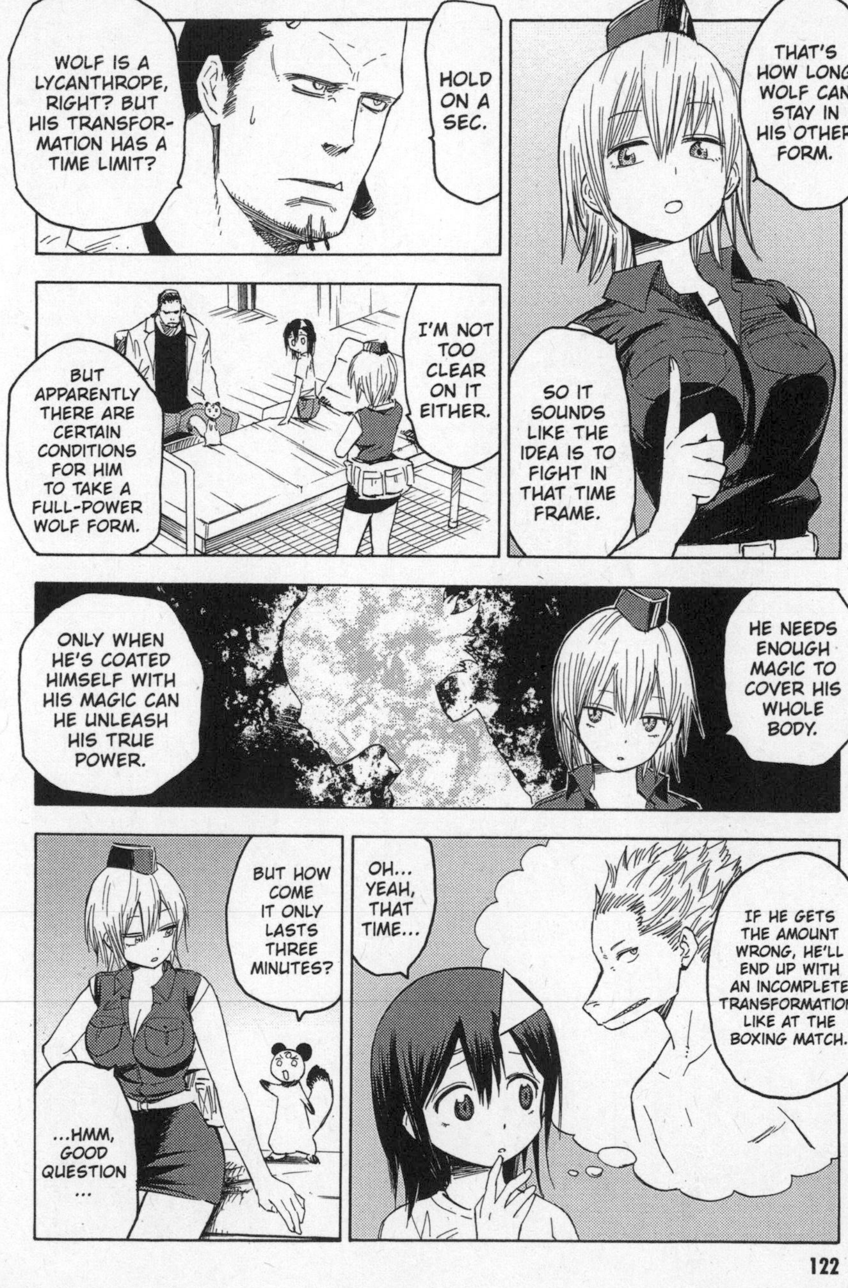
THAT'S HOW LONG WOLF CAN STAY IN HIS OTHER FORM.
SO IT SOUNDS LIKE THE IDEA IS TO FIGHT IN THAT TIME FRAME.
HOLD ON A SEC.
WOLF IS A LYCANTHROPE, RIGHT? BUT HIS TRANSFORMATION HAS A TIME LIMIT?
I'M NOT TOO CLEAR ON IT EITHER.
BUT APPARENTLY THERE ARE CERTAIN CONDITIONS FOR HIM TO TAKE A FULL-POWER WOLF FORM.
HE NEEDS ENOUGH MAGIC TO COVER HIS WHOLE BODY.
ONLY WHEN HE'S COATED HIMSELF WITH HIS MAGIC CAN HE UNLEASH HIS TRUE POWER.
IF HE GETS THE AMOUNT WRONG, HE'LL END UP WITH AN INCOMPLETE TRANSFORMATION, LIKE AT THE BOXING MATCH.
OH... YEAH, THAT TIME...
BUT HOW COME IT ONLY LASTS THREE MINUTES?
...HMM, GOOD QUESTION...

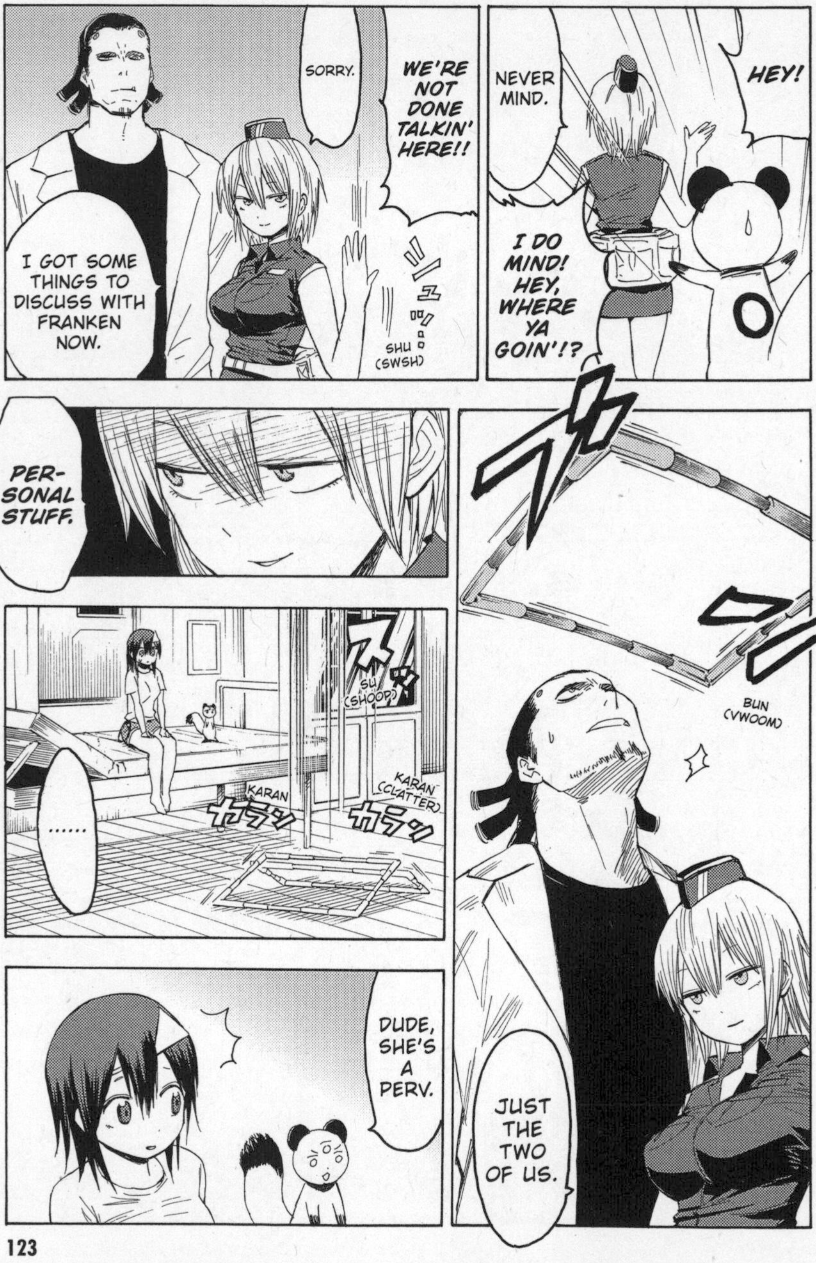
HEY!
NEVER MIND.
I DO MIND! HEY, WHERE YA GOIN'!?
WE'RE NOT DONE TALKIN' HERE!!
SORRY.
I GOT SOME THINGS TO DISCUSS WITH FRANKEN NOW.
SHU (SWSH)
BUN (VWOOM)
JUST THE TWO OF US.
PER-SONAL STUFF.
SU (SHOOP)
KARAN (CLATTER)
KARAN
......
DUDE, SHE'S A PERV.

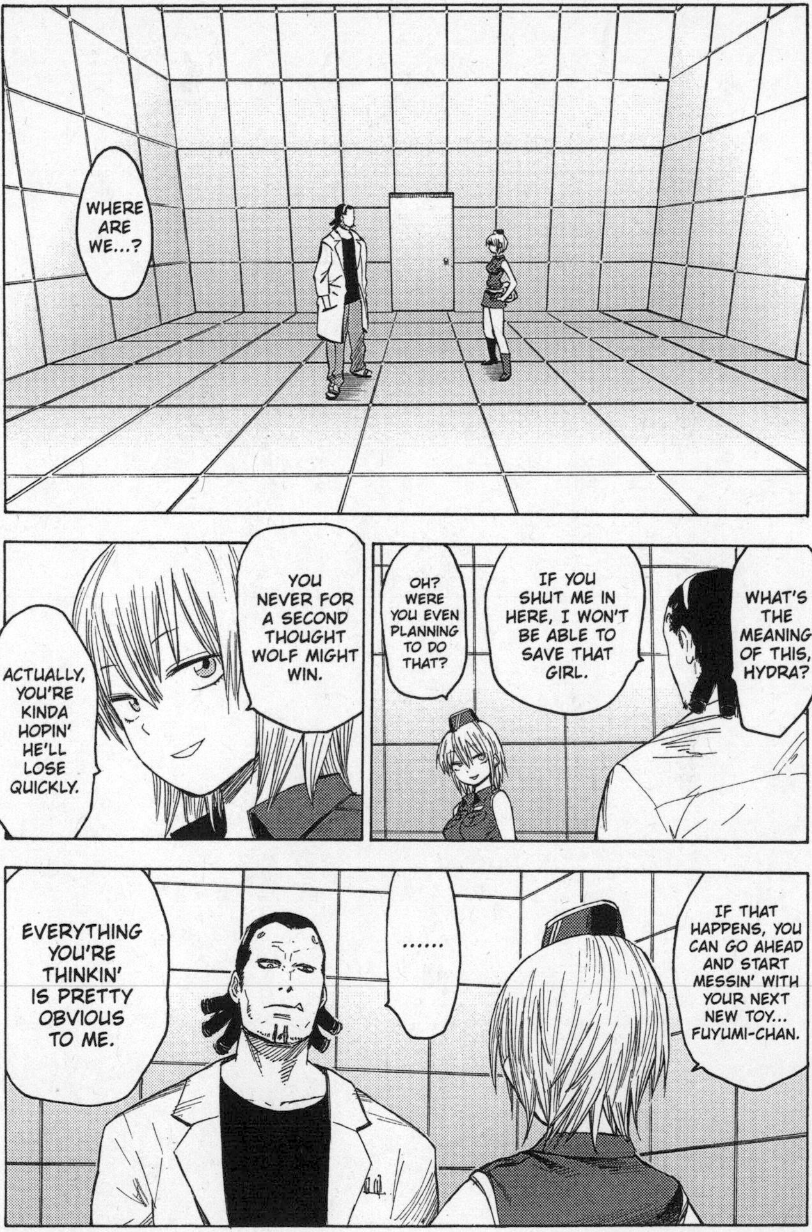
WHERE ARE WE...?
WHAT'S THE MEANING OF THIS, HYDRA?
IF YOU SHUT ME IN HERE, I WON'T BE ABLE TO SAVE THAT GIRL.
OH? WERE YOU EVEN PLANNING TO DO THAT?
YOU NEVER FOR A SECOND THOUGHT WOLF MIGHT WIN.
ACTUALLY, YOU'RE KINDA HOPIN' HE'LL LOSE QUICKLY.
IF THAT HAPPENS, YOU CAN GO AHEAD AND START MESSIN' WITH YOUR NEXT NEW TOY... FUYUMI-CHAN.
......
EVERYTHING YOU'RE THINKIN' IS PRETTY OBVIOUS TO ME.

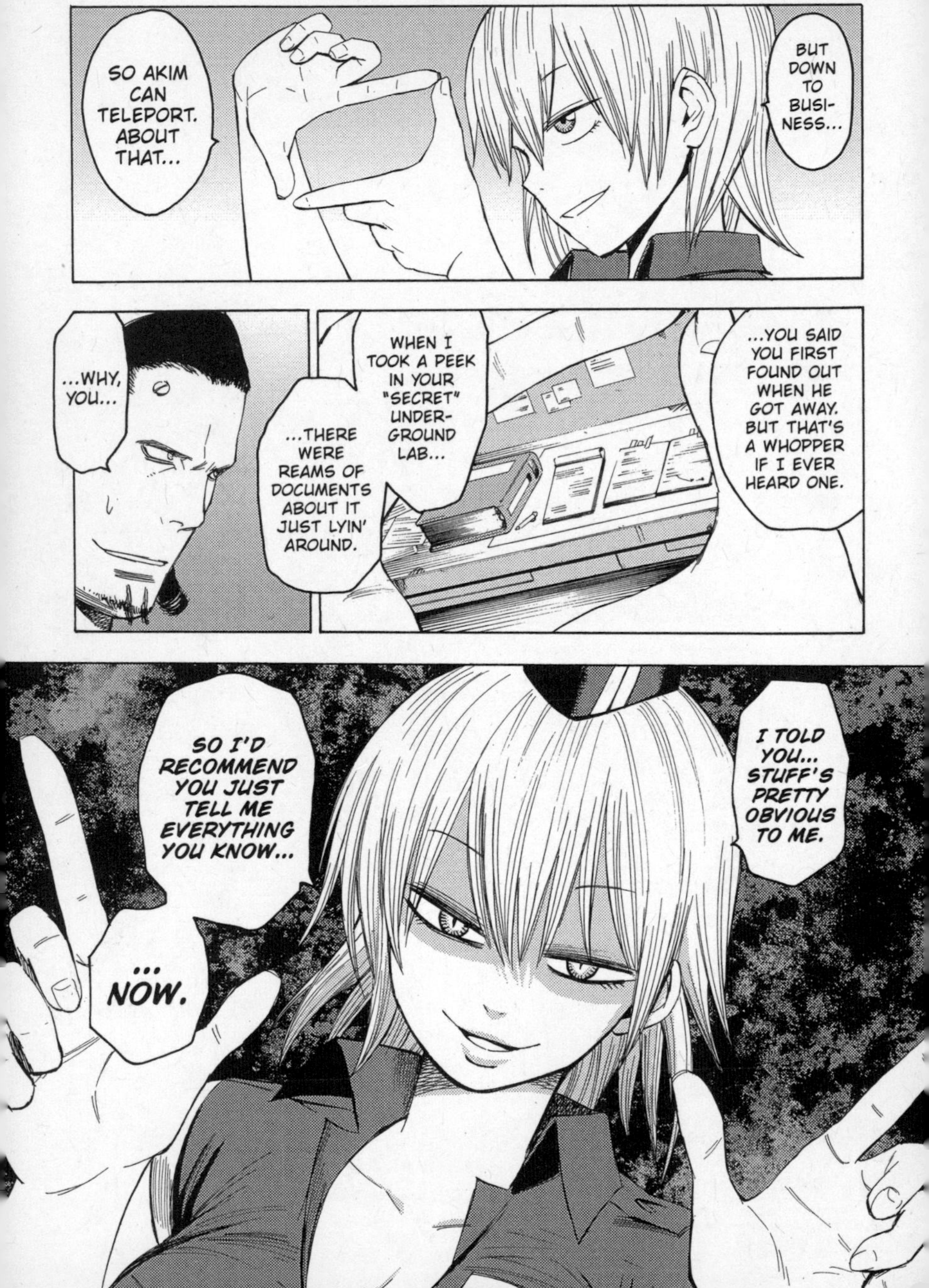
BUT DOWN TO BUSI-NESS...
SO AKIM CAN TELEPORT. ABOUT THAT...
...YOU SAID YOU FIRST FOUND OUT WHEN HE GOT AWAY. BUT THAT'S A WHOPPER IF I EVER HEARD ONE.
WHEN I TOOK A PEEK IN YOUR "SECRET" UNDER-GROUND LAB...
...THERE WERE REAMS OF DOCUMENTS ABOUT IT JUST LYIN' AROUND.
...WHY, YOU...
I TOLD YOU... STUFF'S PRETTY OBVIOUS TO ME.
SO I'D RECOMMEND YOU JUST TELL ME EVERYTHING YOU KNOW...
... NOW.

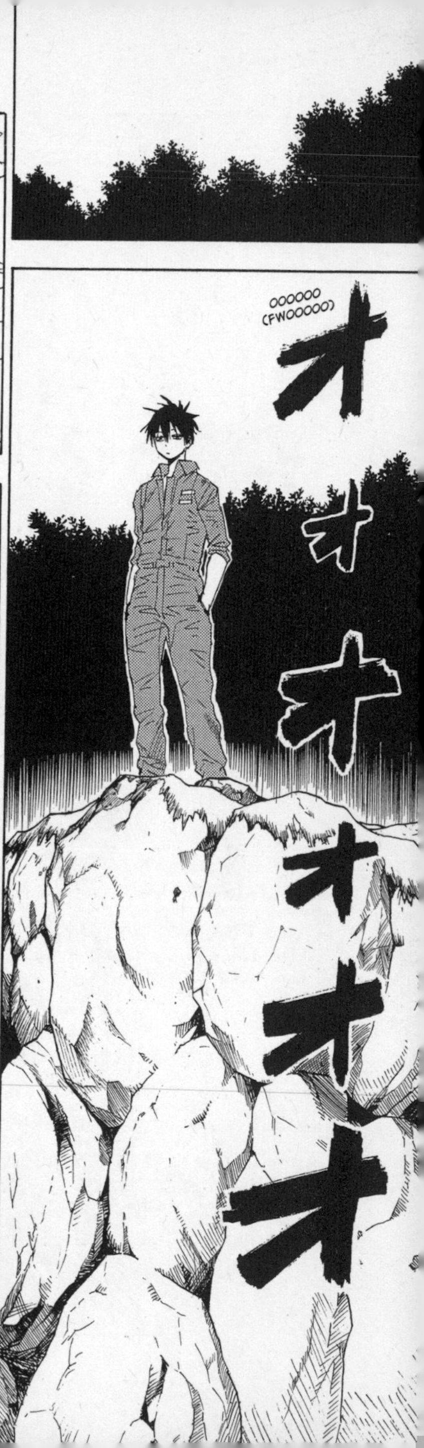
オオオオオオ
OOOOOO
(FWOOOOO)

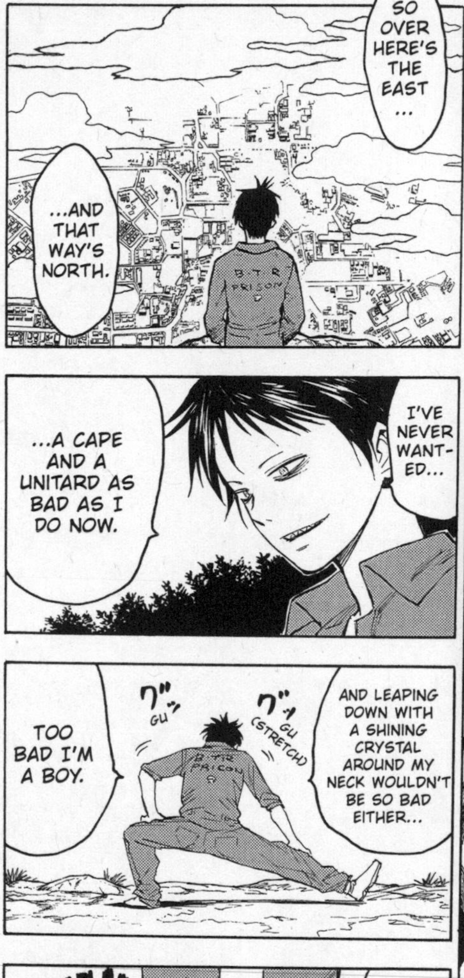
SO OVER HERE'S THE EAST ...
...AND THAT WAY'S NORTH.
B.T.R PRISON
I'VE NEVER WANTED...
...A CAPE AND A UNITARD AS BAD AS I DO NOW.
AND LEAPING DOWN WITH A SHINING CRYSTAL AROUND MY NECK WOULDN'T BE SO BAD EITHER...
グッ
GU (STRETCH)
グッ
GU
TOO BAD I'M A BOY.
SO I'LL HAVE TO FLY DOWN BRAVELY ...
ザッ
ZA (CRUNCH)
...WITH ATOMIC POWER!

NOTE: THE "SHINING CRYSTAL" IS A REFERENCE TO PRINCESS SHEETA'S PROTECTIVE CRYSTAL AMULET IN THE STUDIO GHIBLI FILM *LAPUTA: CASTLE IN THE SKY*. OPPOSITE, STAZ IS SINGING THE ORIGINAL THEME SONG TO THE CLASSIC *ASTRO BOY*.

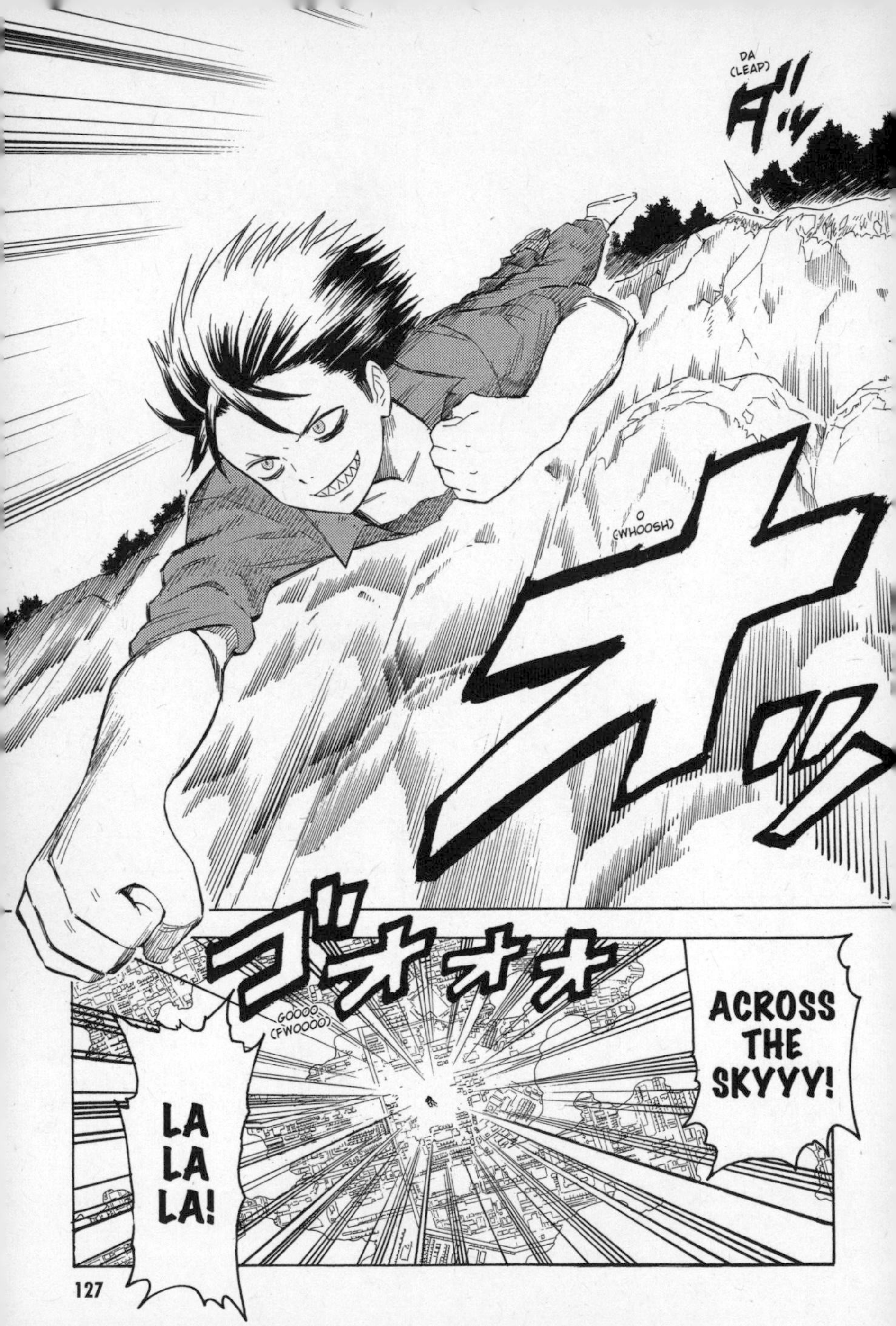
DA (LEAP)
O (WHOOSH)
GOOOO (FWOOOO)
ACROSS THE SKYYY!
LA LA LA!

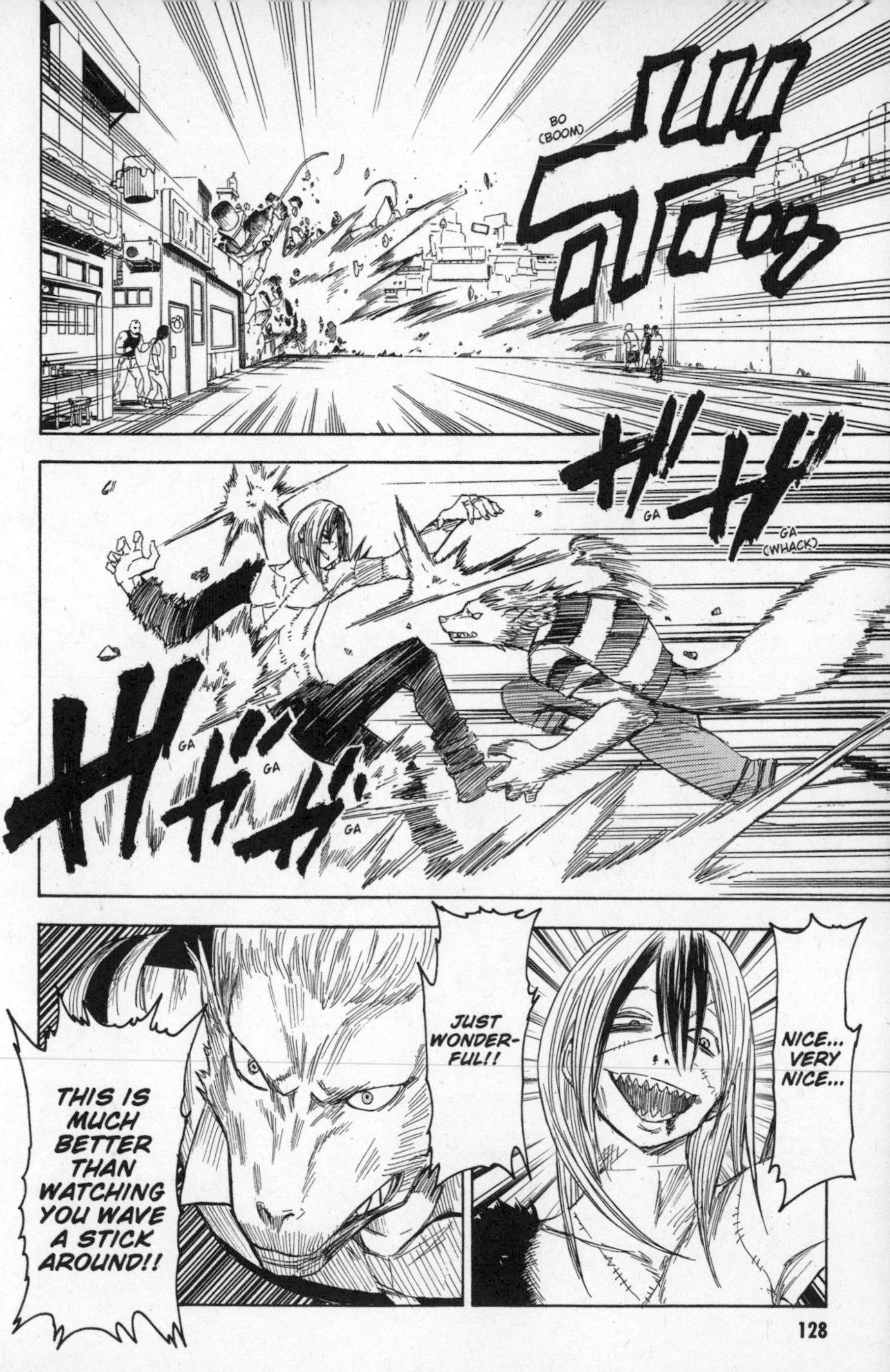
BO (BOOM)
GA
GA (WHACK)
GA
GA
GA
NICE... VERY NICE...
JUST WONDERFUL!!
THIS IS MUCH BETTER THAN WATCHING YOU WAVE A STICK AROUND!!

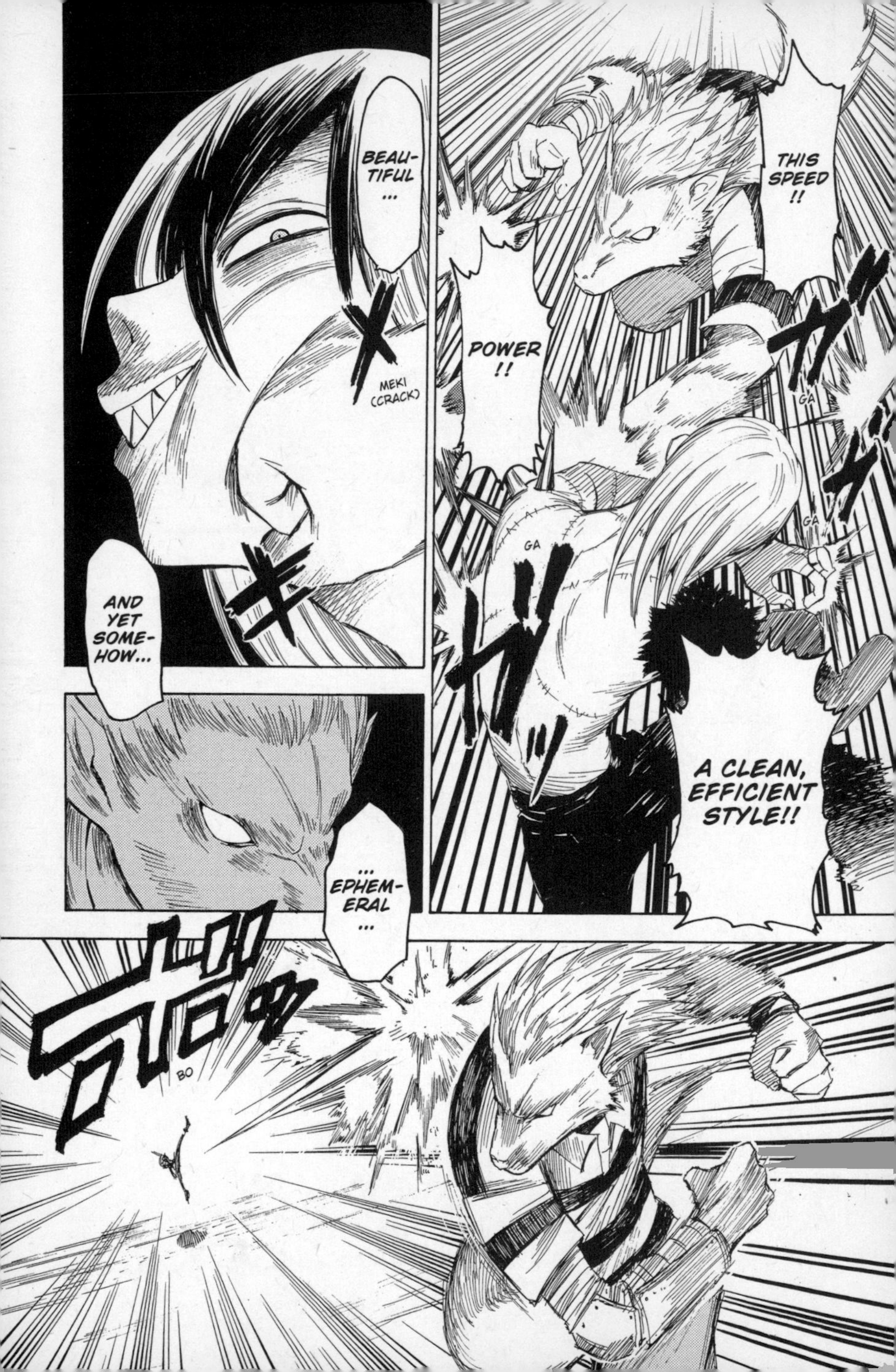

THIS SPEED !!
GA
GA
POWER !!
GA
A CLEAN, EFFICIENT STYLE!!
BEAUTIFUL ...
MEKI (CRACK)
AND YET SOMEHOW...
... EPHEMERAL ...
BO

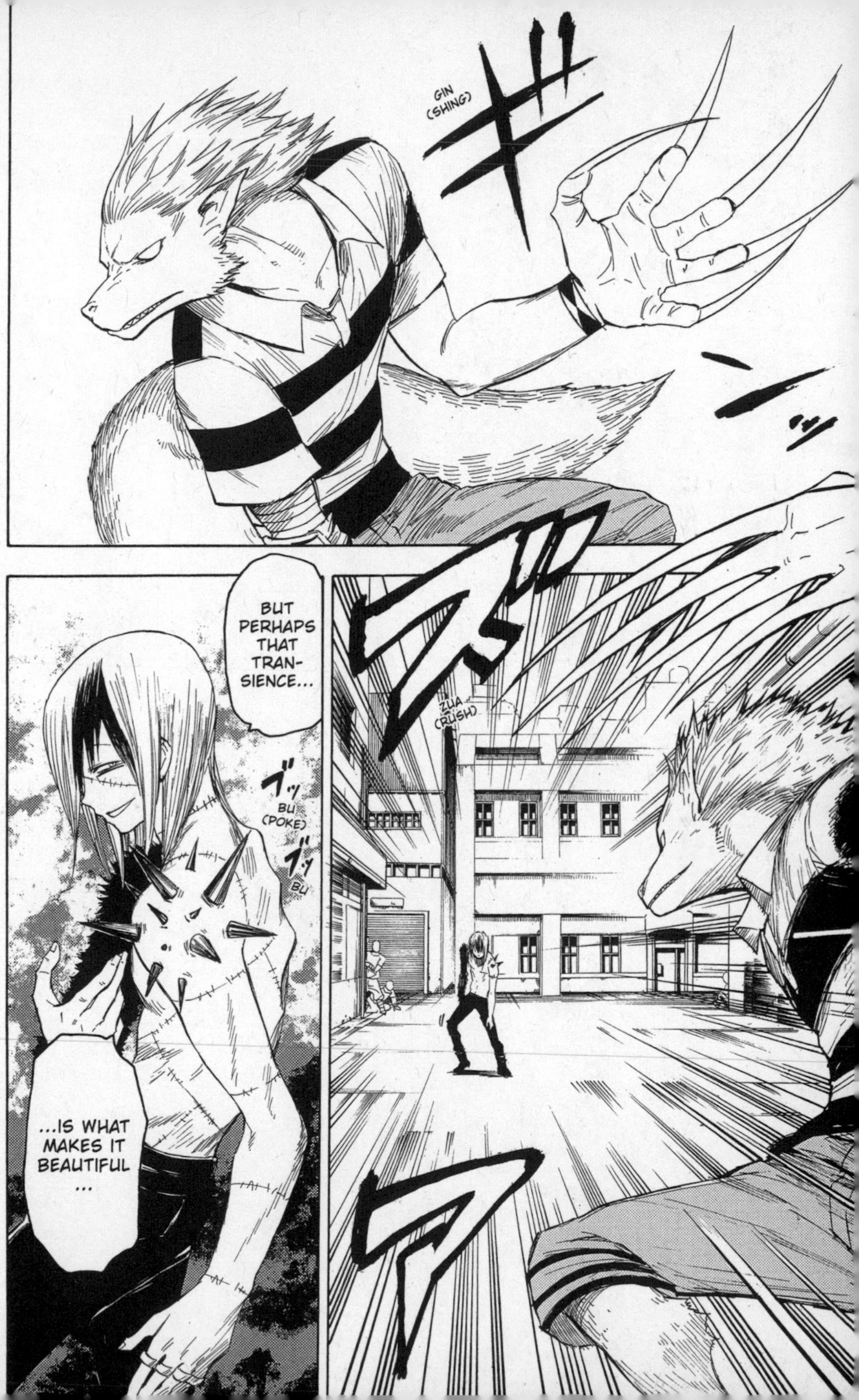
GIN (SHING)
ZUA (RUSH)
BUT PERHAPS THAT TRANSIENCE...
BU (POKE)
BU
...IS WHAT MAKES IT BEAUTIFUL...

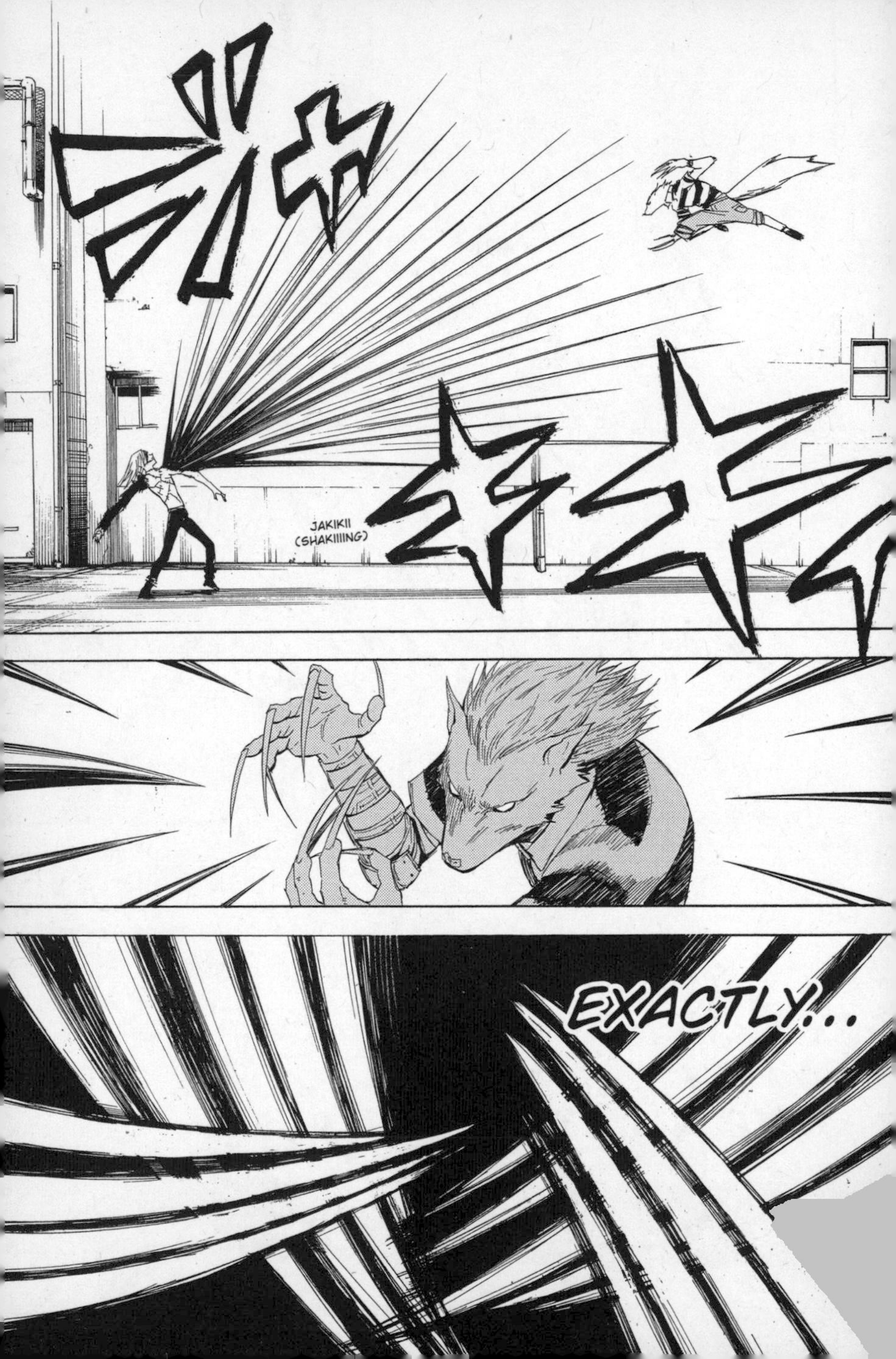
JAKIKII
(SHAKIIIING)
EXACTLY...

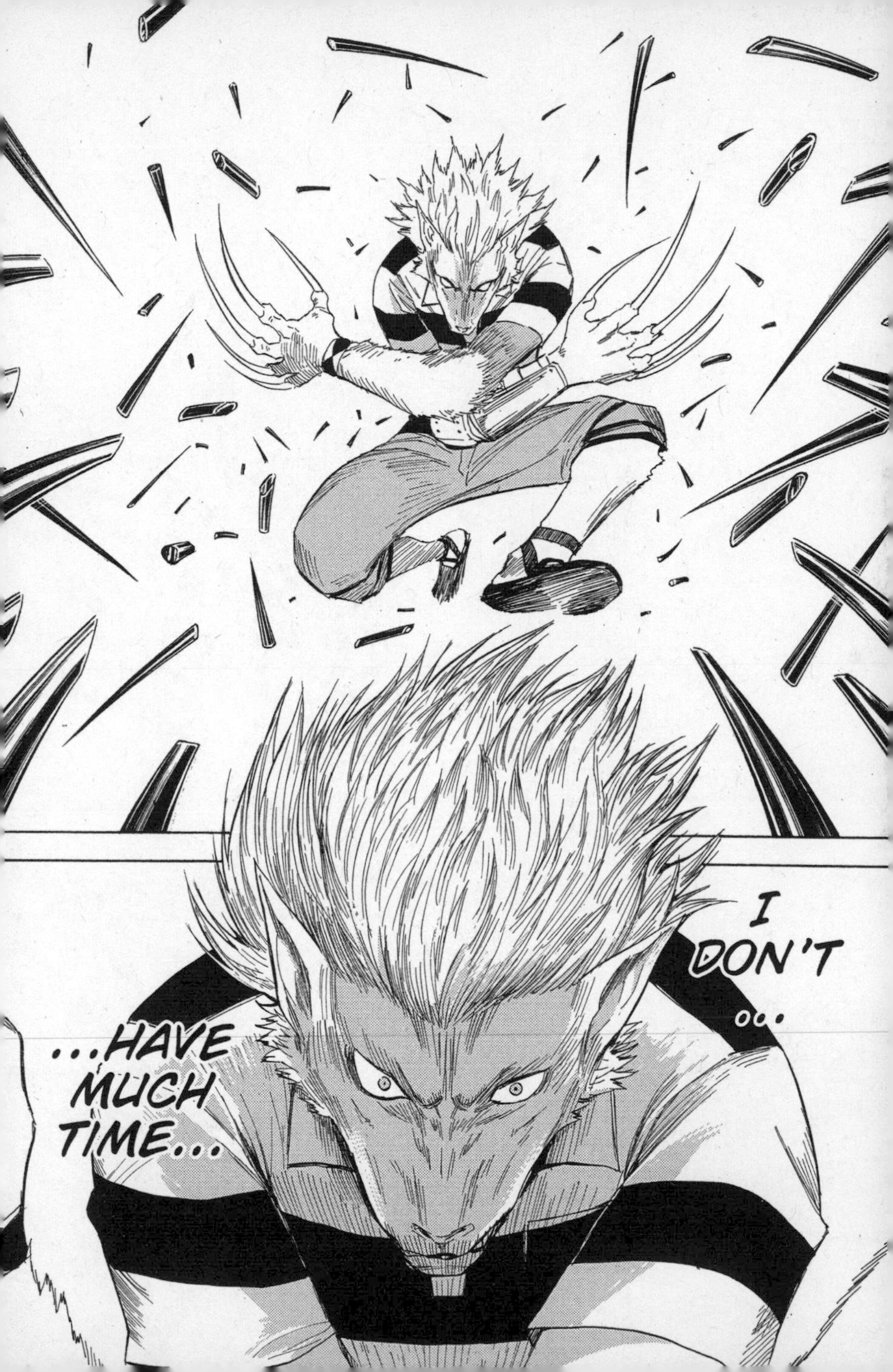
I DON'T ...
...HAVE MUCH TIME...

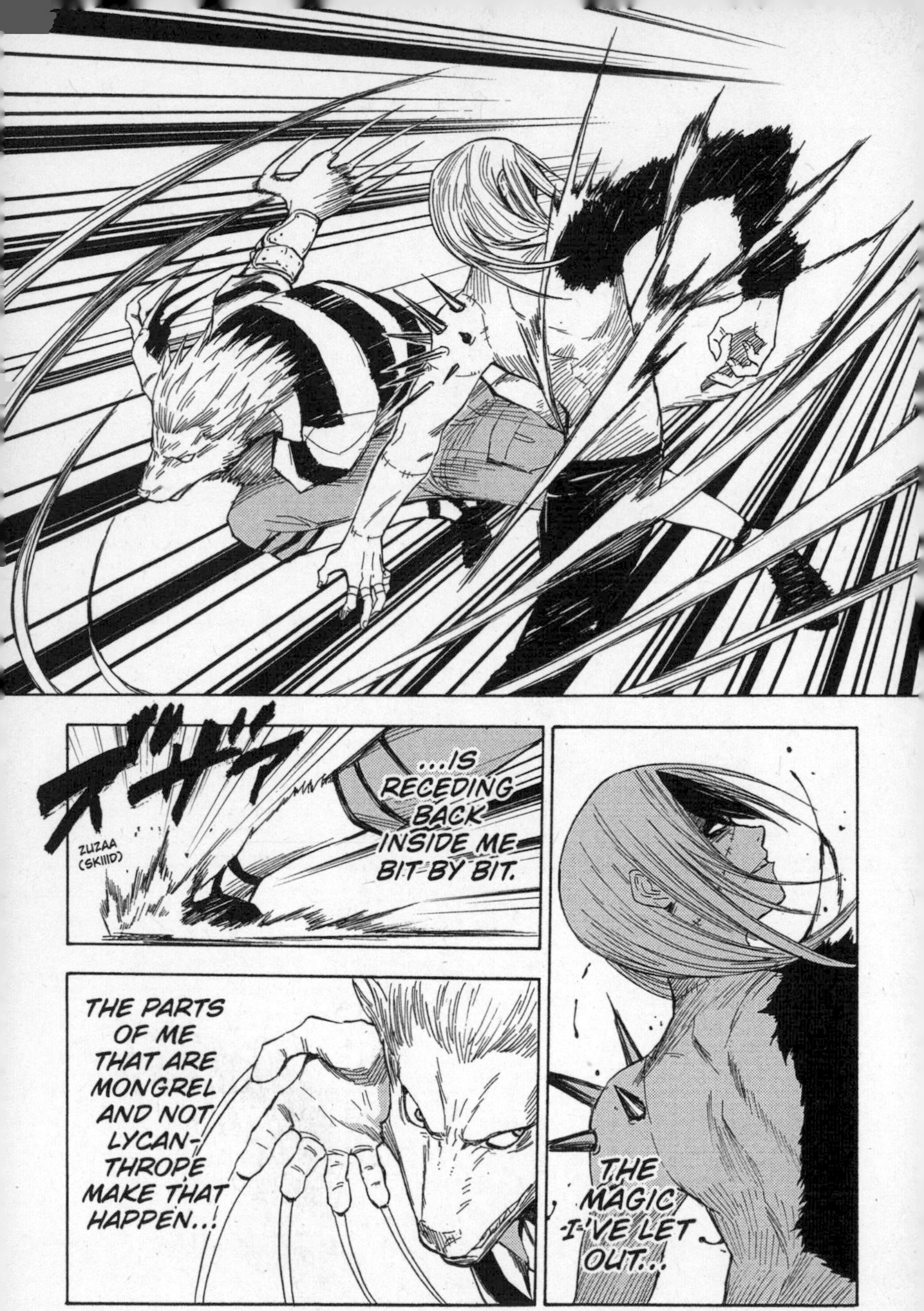
THE MAGIC I'VE LET OUT...
...IS RECEDING BACK INSIDE ME BIT BY BIT.
ZUZAA (SKIIID)
THE PARTS OF ME THAT ARE MONGREL AND NOT LYCAN-THROPE MAKE THAT HAPPEN...

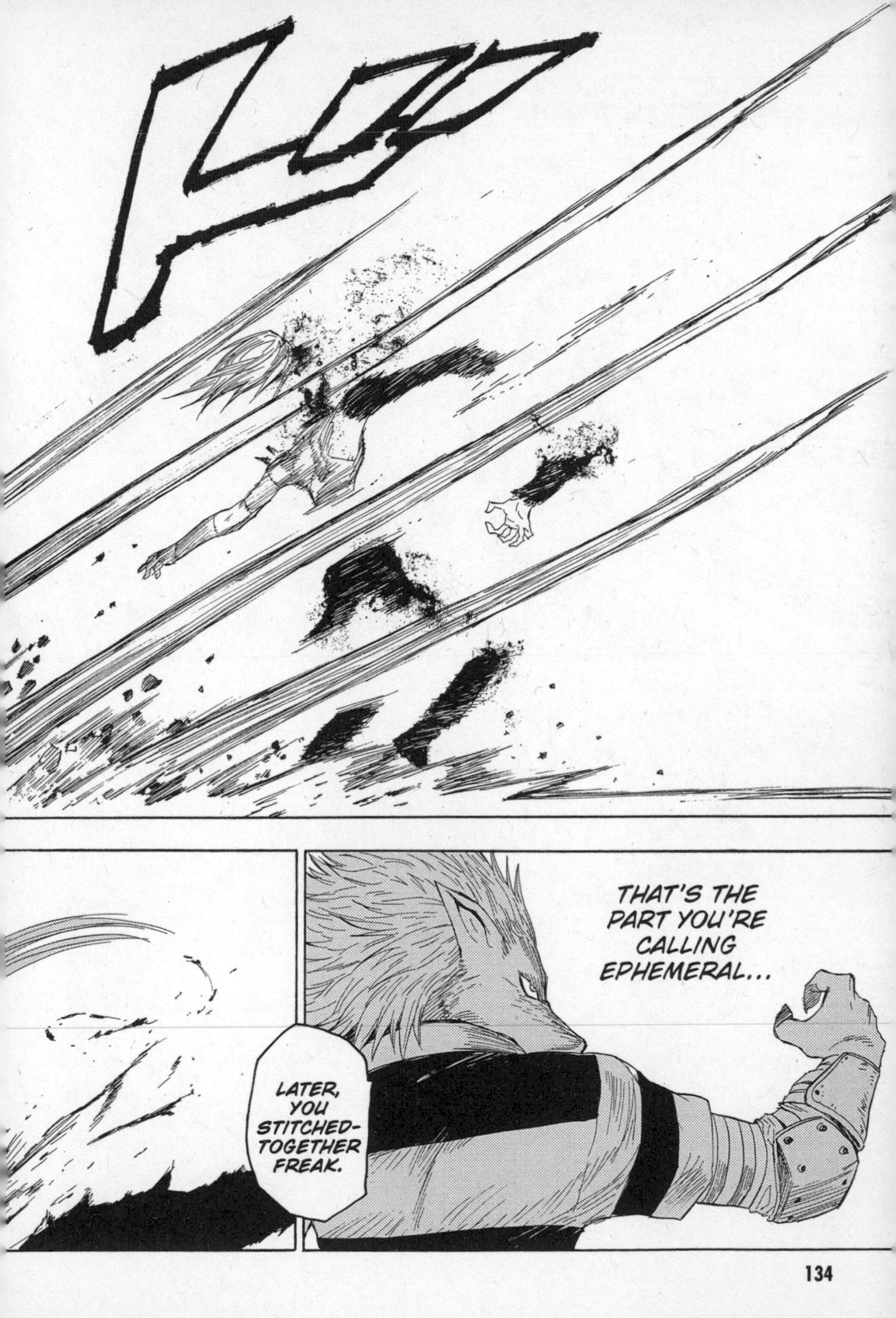
THAT'S THE PART YOU'RE CALLING EPHEMERAL...
LATER, YOU STITCHED-TOGETHER FREAK.

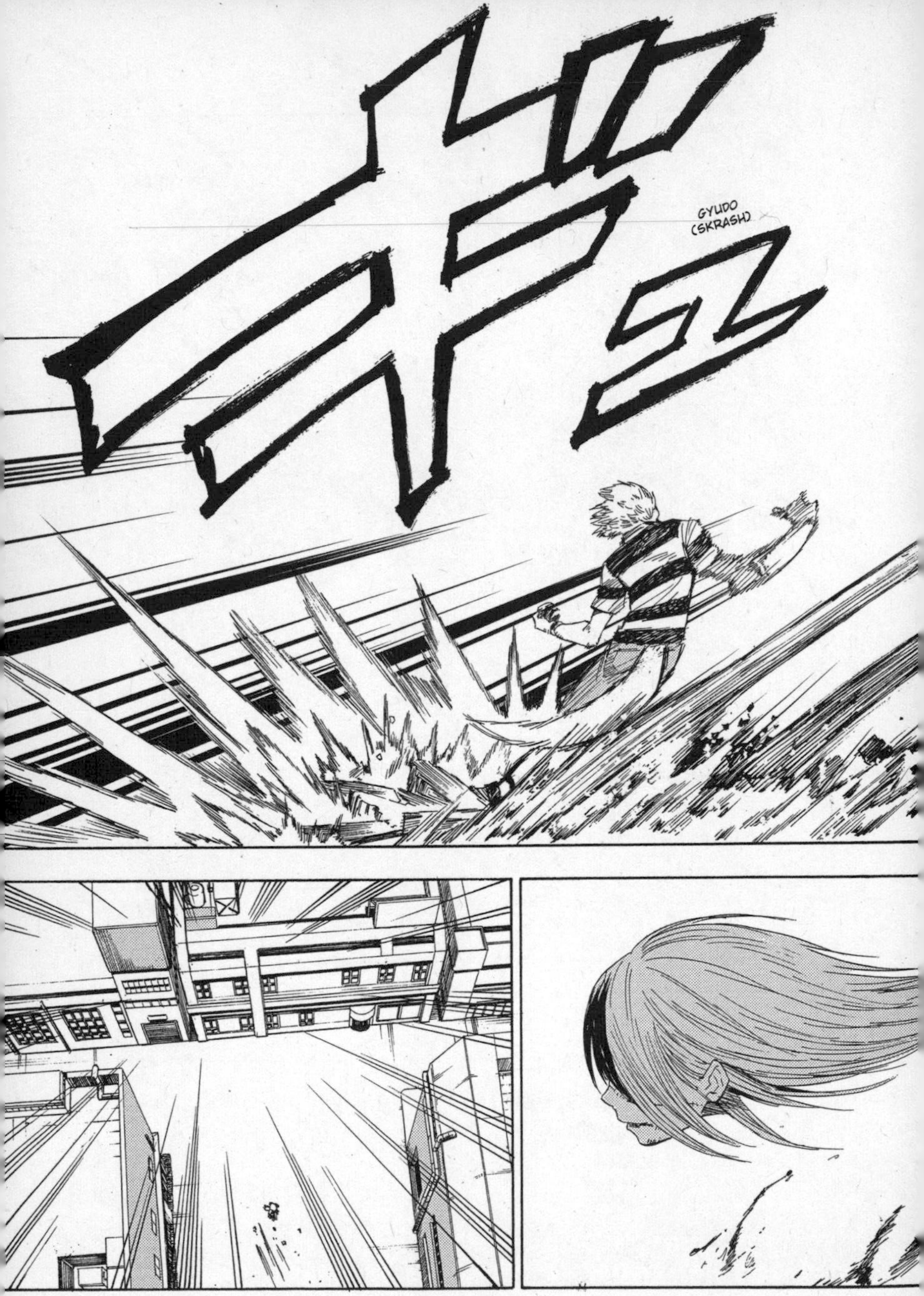
GYUDO
(SKRASH)

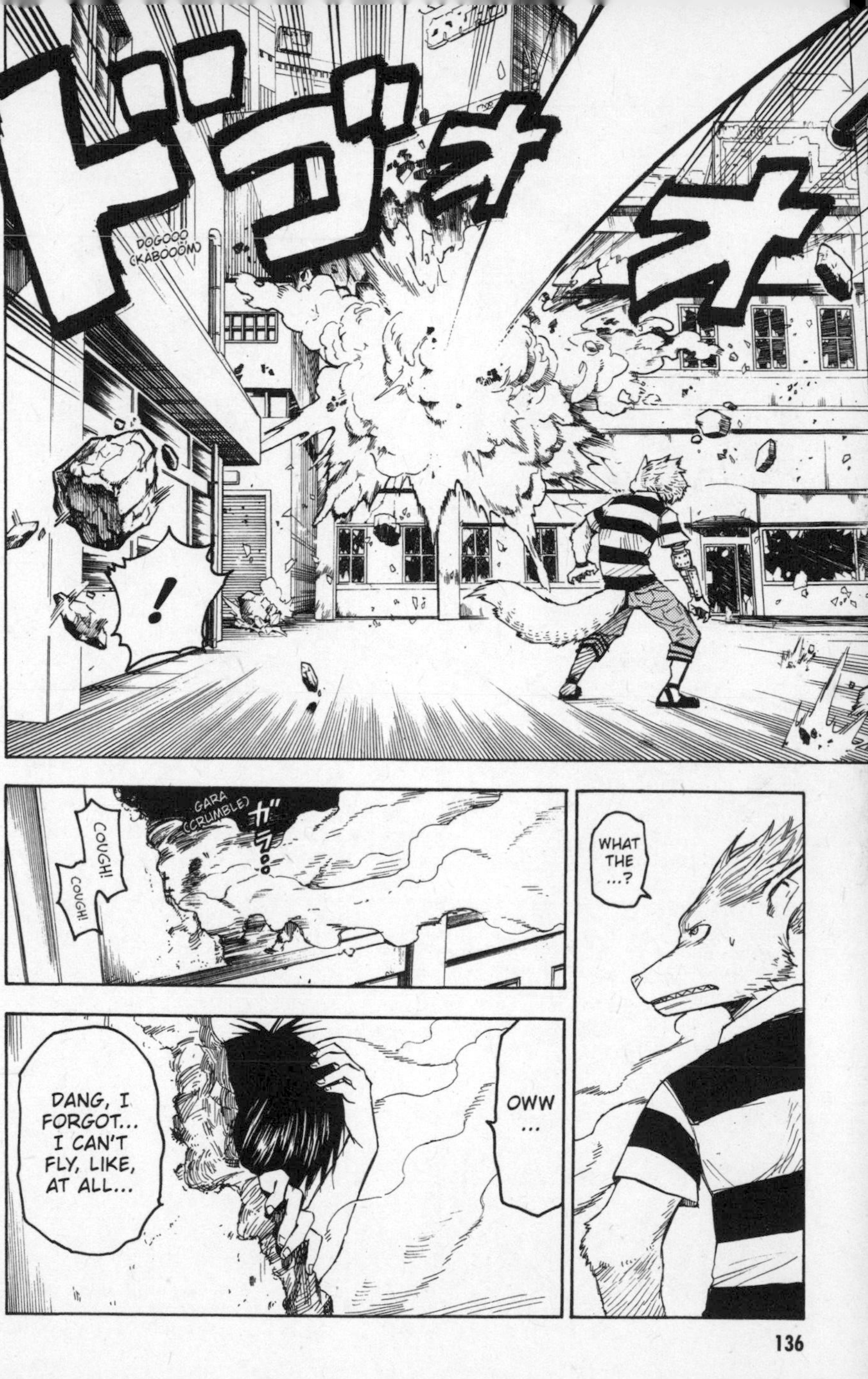
DOGOOO (KABOOOM)
!
WHAT THE ...?
GARA (CRUMBLE)
COUGH! COUGH!
OWW ...
DANG, I FORGOT... I CAN'T FLY, LIKE, AT ALL...

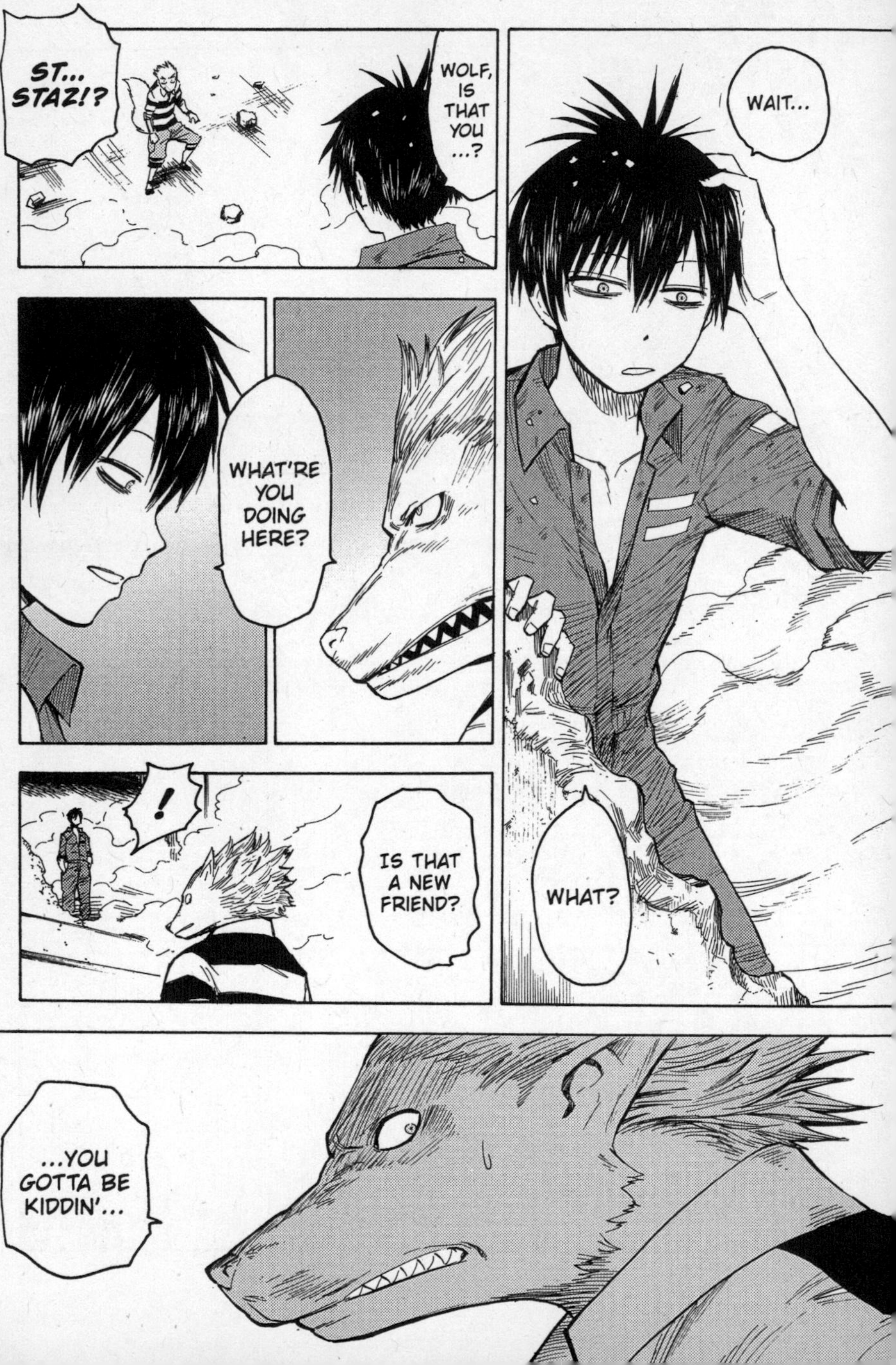
WAIT...
WHAT?
WOLF, IS THAT YOU ...?
ST... STAZ!?
WHAT'RE YOU DOING HERE?
IS THAT A NEW FRIEND?
!
...YOU GOTTA BE KIDDIN'...

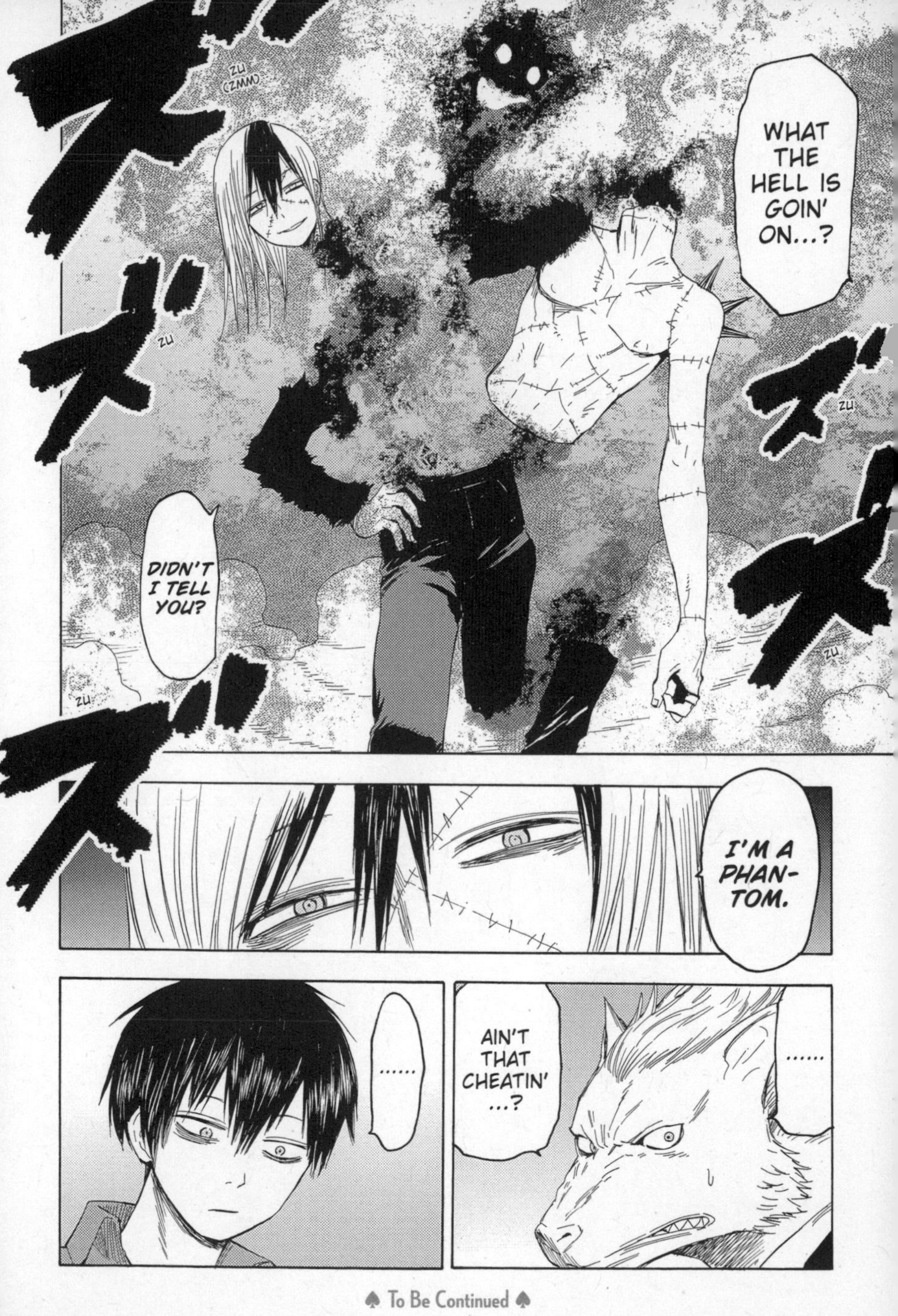
WHAT THE HELL IS GOIN' ON...?
ZU (ZMM)
ZU
ZU
DIDN'T I TELL YOU?
ZU
ZU
I'M A PHANTOM.
......
AIN'T THAT CHEATIN' ...?
......

♠ To Be Continued ♠

WHAT ABOUT LIZ!?
PART 4
GAPO (POP)
SHE WAS THINKING ABOUT HOW GREAT MASKS ARE, SINCE THEY HIDE HER EXPRESSION.

BLOOD LAD

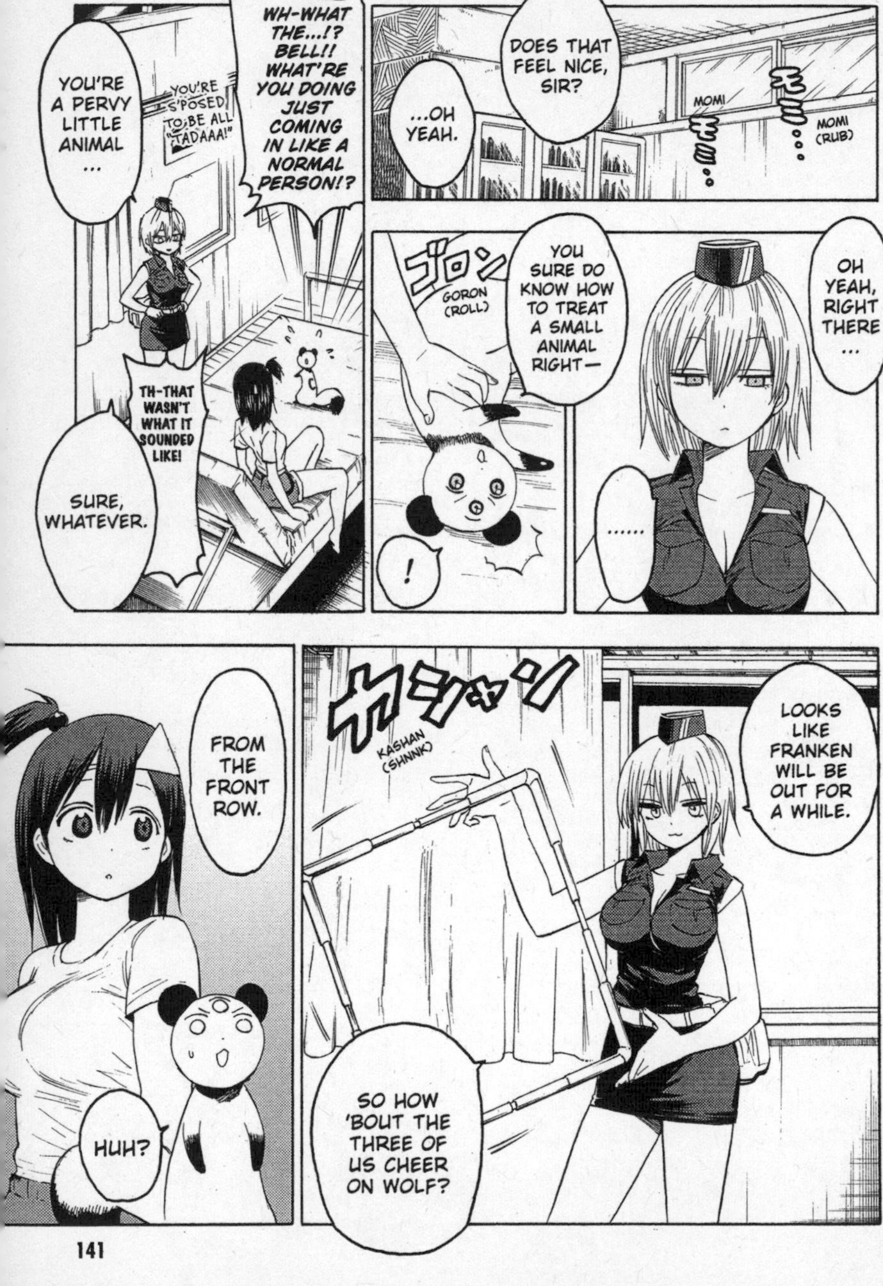
モミ…
MOMI (RUB)
モミ…
MOMI
DOES THAT FEEL NICE, SIR?
...OH YEAH.
OH YEAH, RIGHT THERE...
......
ゴロン
GORON (ROLL)
YOU SURE DO KNOW HOW TO TREAT A SMALL ANIMAL RIGHT—
!
WH-WHAT THE...!? BELL!! WHAT'RE YOU DOING JUST COMING IN LIKE A NORMAL PERSON!?
YOU'RE A PERVY LITTLE ANIMAL...
YOU'RE S'POSED TO BE ALL "TADAAA!"
TH-THAT WASN'T WHAT IT SOUNDED LIKE!
SURE, WHATEVER.
LOOKS LIKE FRANKEN WILL BE OUT FOR A WHILE.
カシャン
KASHAN (SHNNK)
SO HOW 'BOUT THE THREE OF US CHEER ON WOLF?
FROM THE FRONT ROW.
HUH?

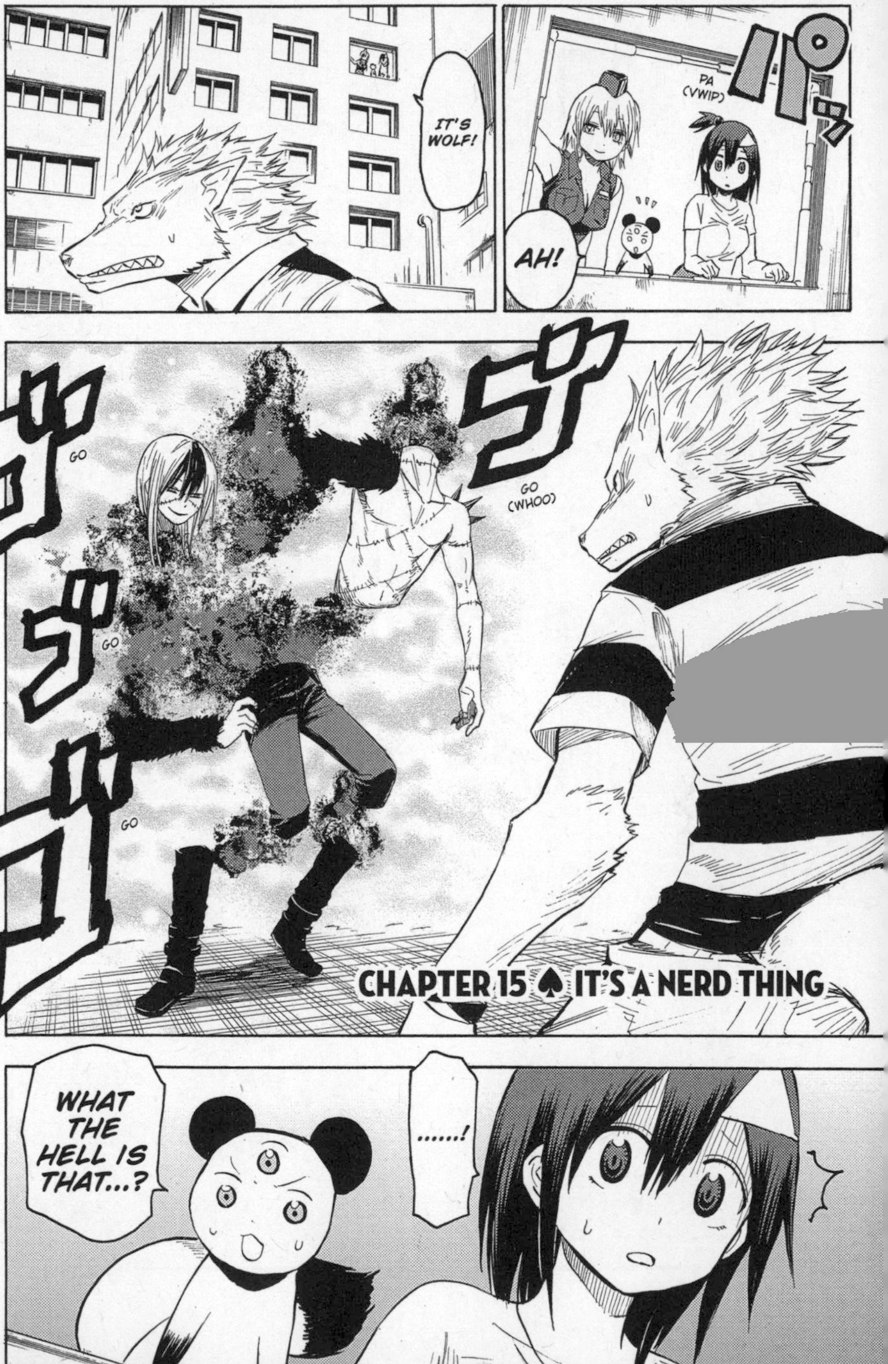
PA (VWIP)
AH!
IT'S WOLF!
GO (WHOO)
GO
GO
GO
CHAPTER 15 ♠ IT'S A NERD THING
......!
WHAT THE HELL IS THAT...?

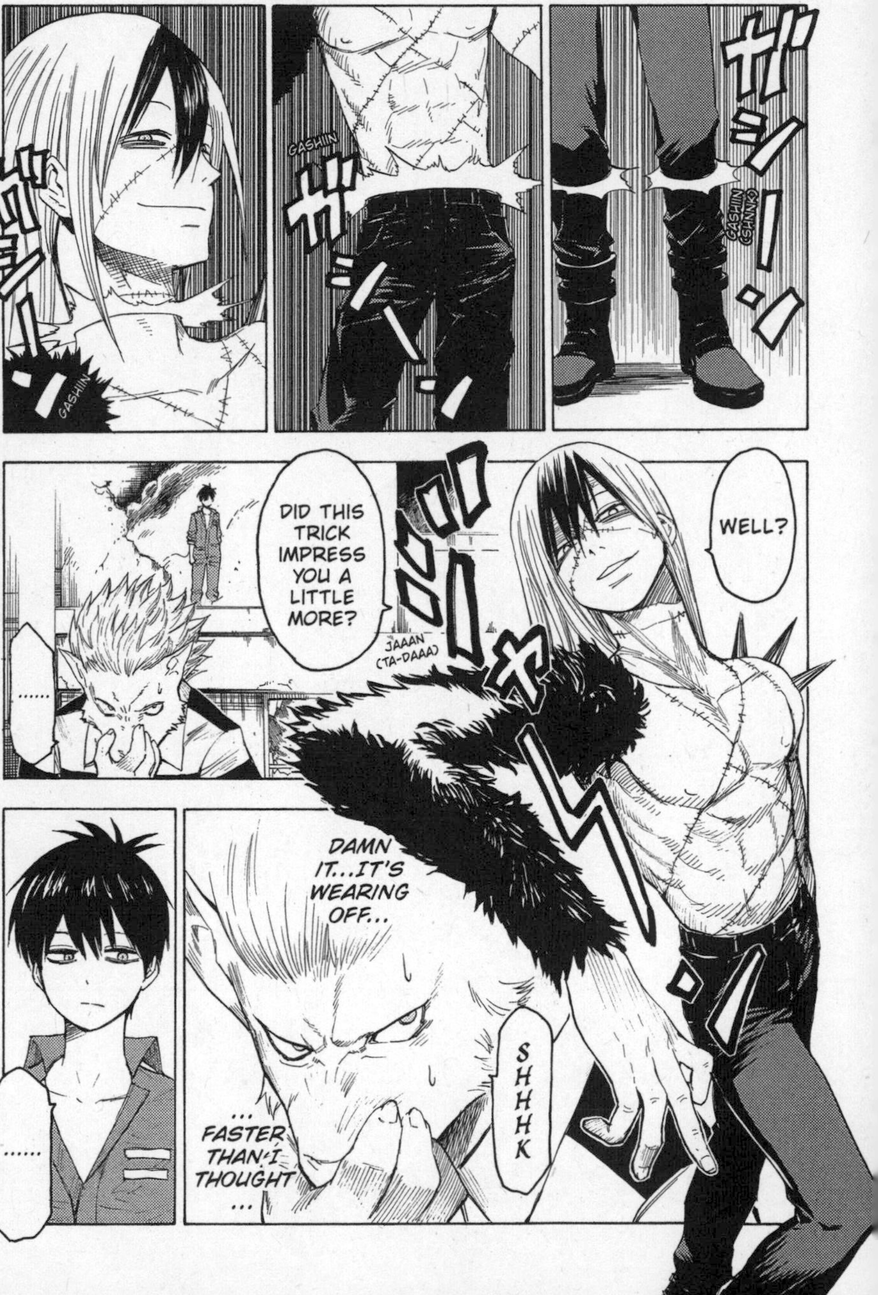
GASHIIN (SHNK)
GASHIIN
GASHIIN
WELL?
JAAAN (TA-DAAA)
DID THIS TRICK IMPRESS YOU A LITTLE MORE?
......
DAMN IT...IT'S WEARING OFF...
SHHHK
...FASTER THAN I THOUGHT...
......

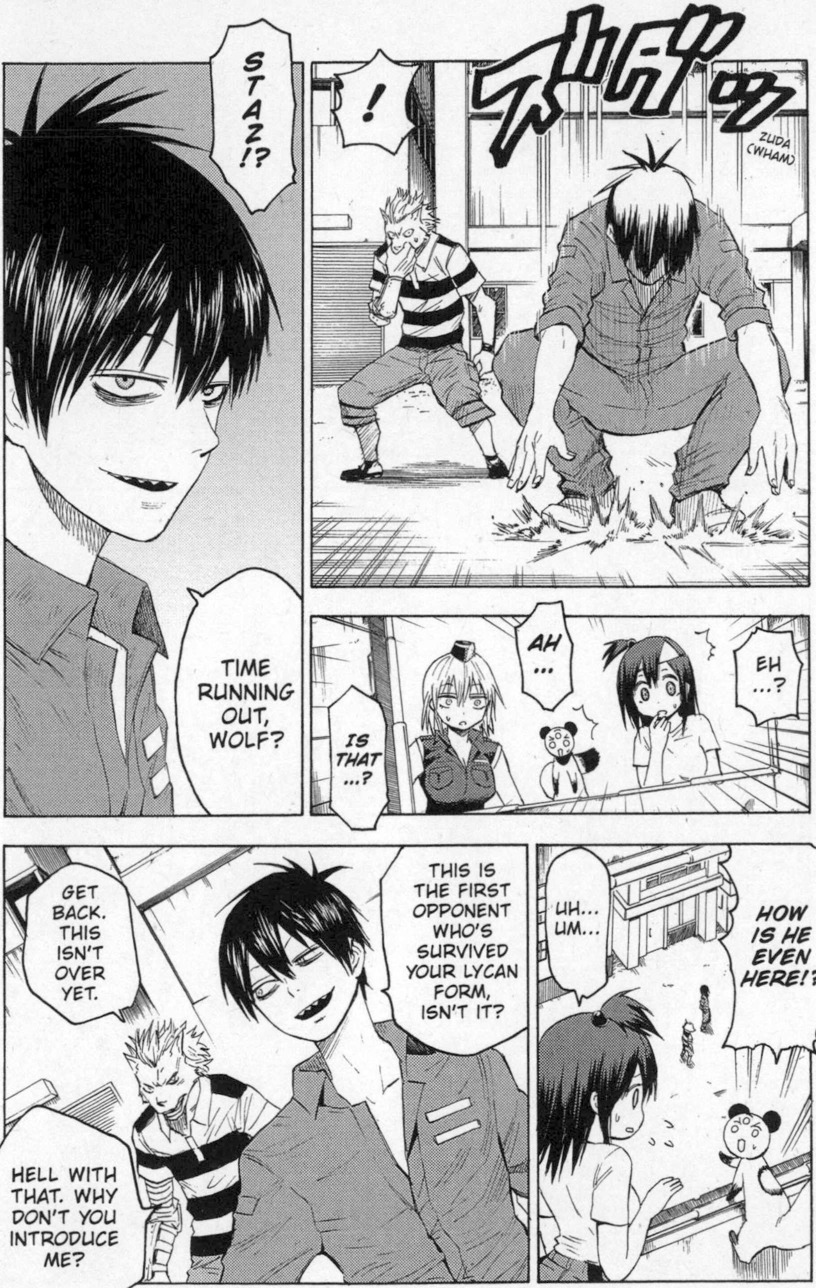
ZUDA (WHAM)
!
EH ...?
AH ...
IS THAT ...?
STAZ!?
TIME RUNNING OUT, WOLF?
HOW IS HE EVEN HERE!?
UH... UM...
THIS IS THE FIRST OPPONENT WHO'S SURVIVED YOUR LYCAN FORM, ISN'T IT?
GET BACK. THIS ISN'T OVER YET.
HELL WITH THAT. WHY DON'T YOU INTRODUCE ME?

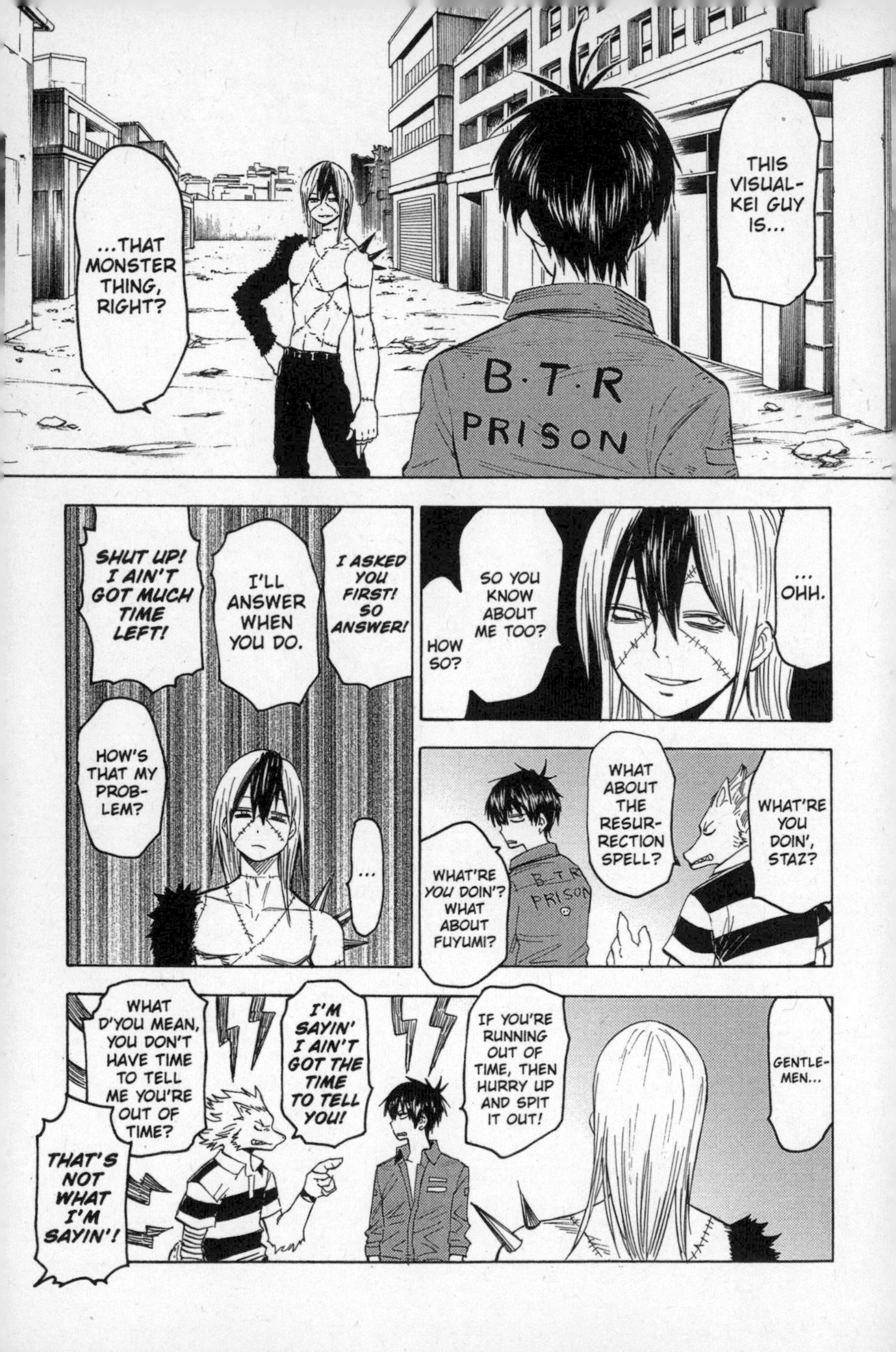
THIS VISUAL-KEI GUY IS...
B·T·R PRISON
...THAT MONSTER THING, RIGHT?
...OHH.
SO YOU KNOW ABOUT ME TOO?
HOW SO?
WHAT'RE YOU DOIN', STAZ?
WHAT ABOUT THE RESURRECTION SPELL?
WHAT'RE *YOU* DOIN'? WHAT ABOUT FUYUMI?
I ASKED YOU FIRST! SO ANSWER!
I'LL ANSWER WHEN YOU DO.
SHUT UP! I AIN'T GOT MUCH TIME LEFT!
...
HOW'S THAT MY PROBLEM?
GENTLEMEN...
IF YOU'RE RUNNING OUT OF TIME, THEN HURRY UP AND SPIT IT OUT!
I'M SAYIN' I AIN'T GOT THE TIME TO TELL YOU!
WHAT D'YOU MEAN, YOU DON'T HAVE TIME TO TELL ME YOU'RE OUT OF TIME?
THAT'S NOT WHAT I'M SAYIN'!

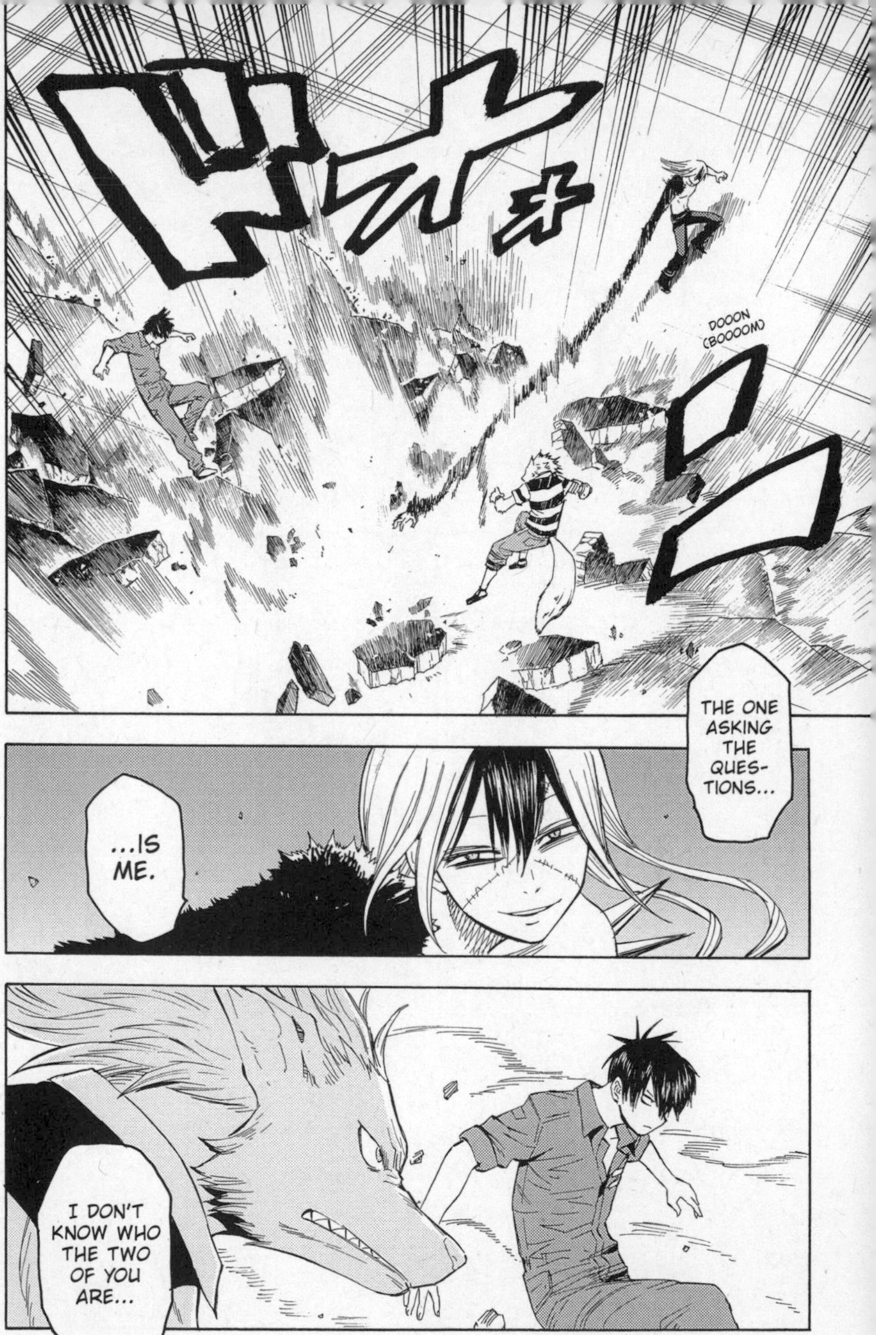
DOOON (BOOOOM)
THE ONE ASKING THE QUES- TIONS...
...IS ME.
I DON'T KNOW WHO THE TWO OF YOU ARE...

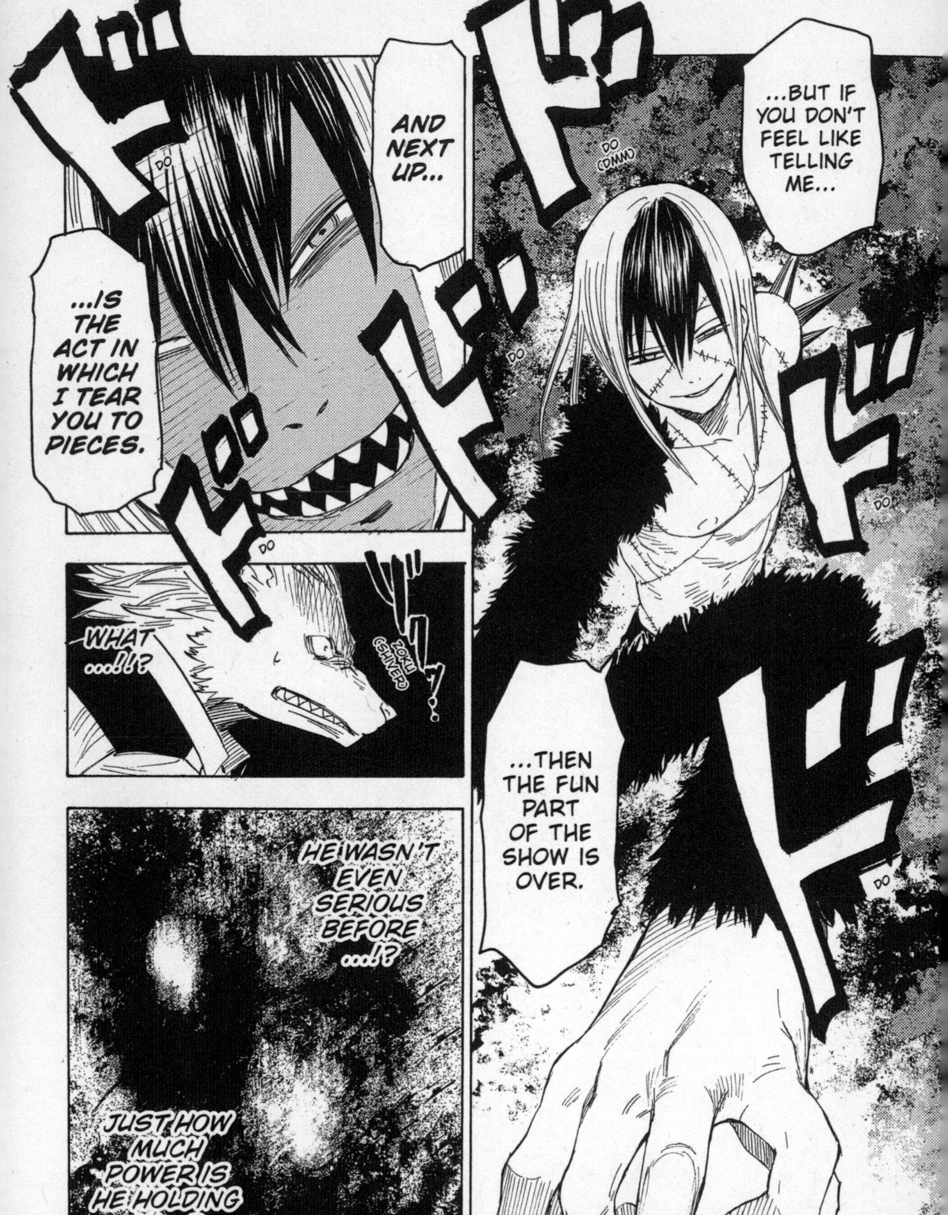
...BUT IF YOU DON'T FEEL LIKE TELLING ME...
DO (DMM)
DO
DO
...THEN THE FUN PART OF THE SHOW IS OVER.
DO
AND NEXT UP...
...IS THE ACT IN WHICH I TEAR YOU TO PIECES.
DO
DO
ZOKU (SHIVER)
WHAT ...!!?
HE WASN'T EVEN SERIOUS BEFORE ...!?
JUST HOW MUCH POWER IS HE HOLDING IN...?

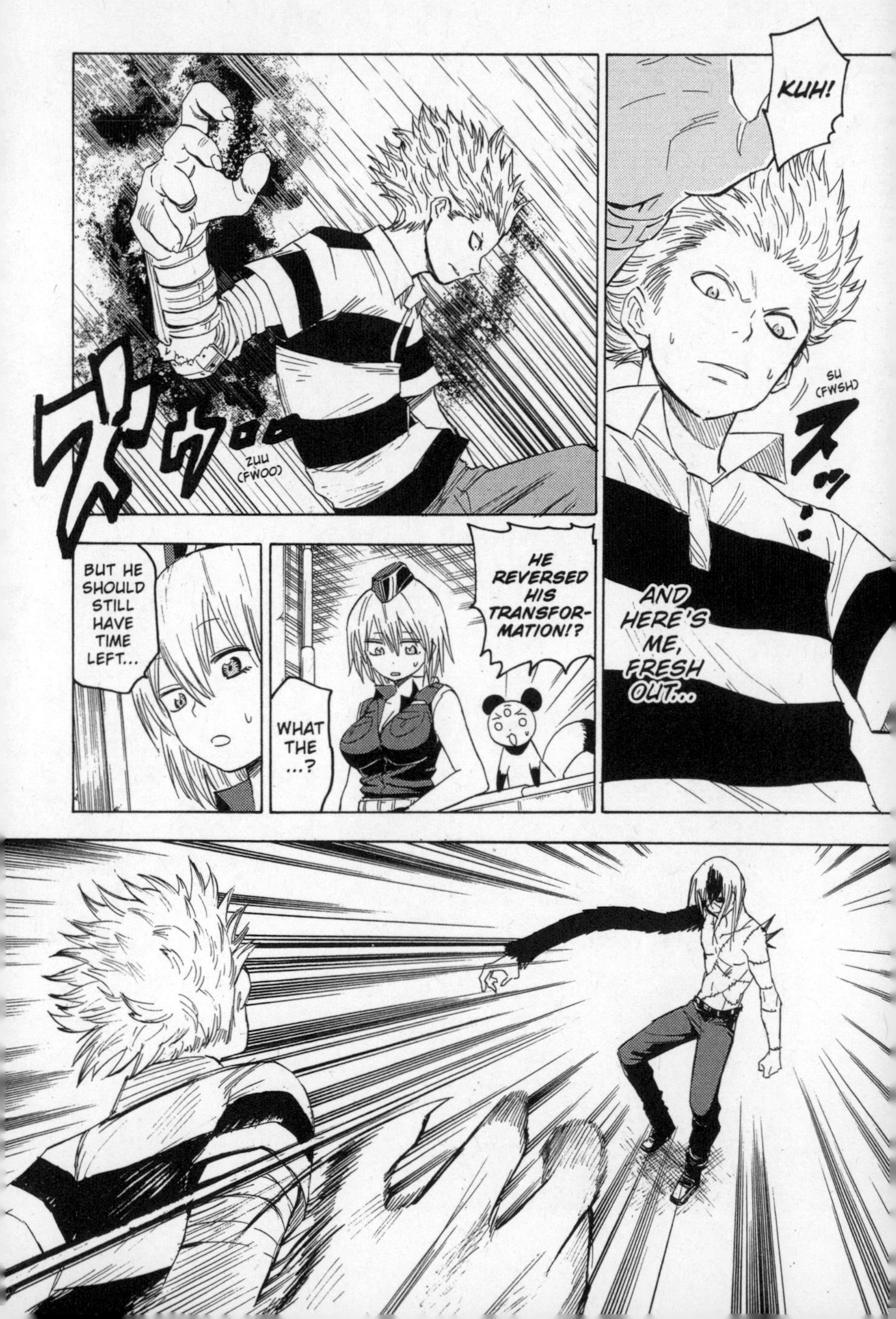
KUH!
SU (FWSH)
AND HERE'S ME, FRESH OUT...
ZUU (FWOO)
HE REVERSED HIS TRANSFOR-MATION!?
WHAT THE ...?
BUT HE SHOULD STILL HAVE TIME LEFT...

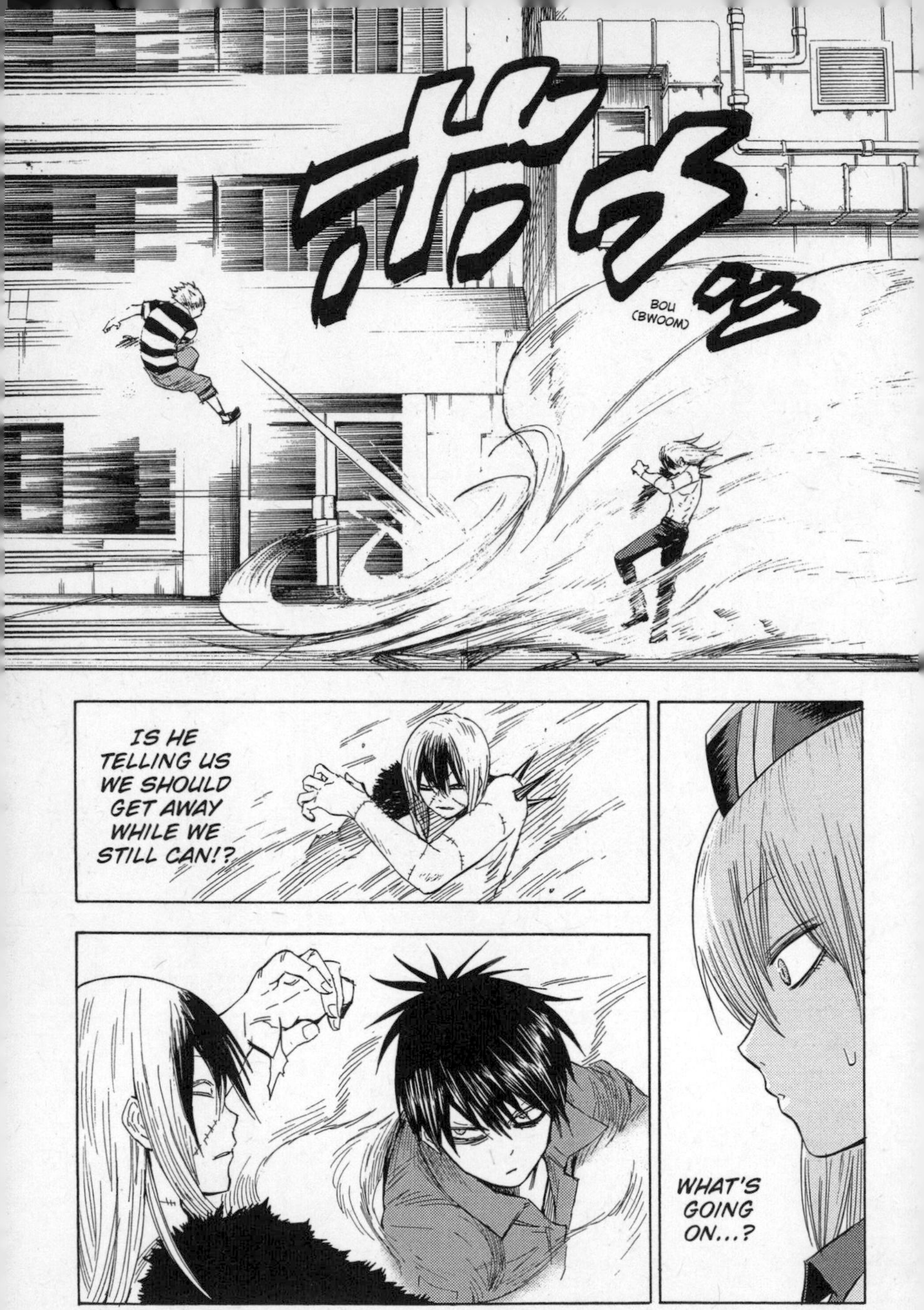
BOU
(BWOOM)
WHAT'S GOING ON...?
IS HE TELLING US WE SHOULD GET AWAY WHILE WE STILL CAN!?

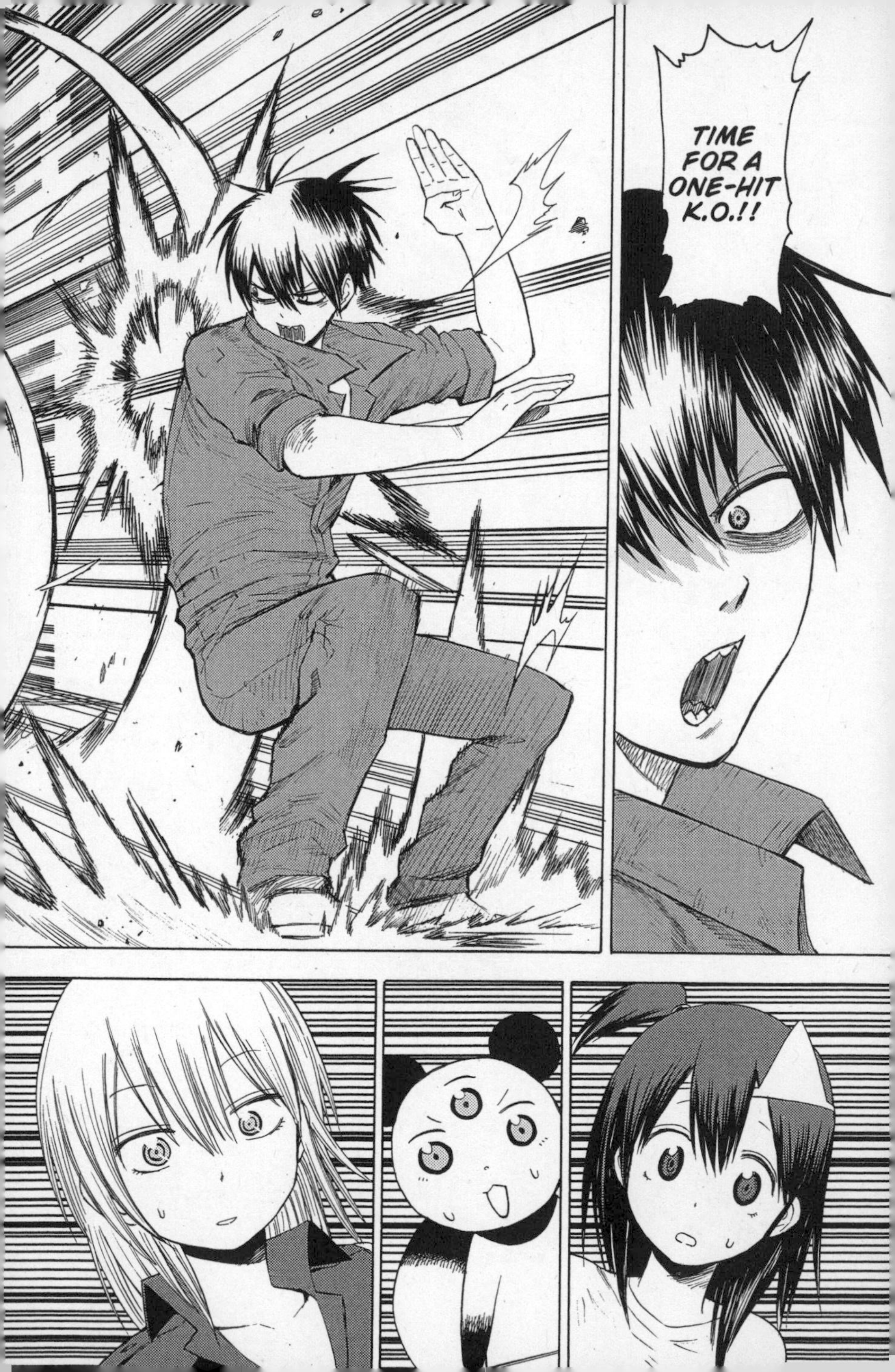
TIME FOR A ONE-HIT K.O.!!

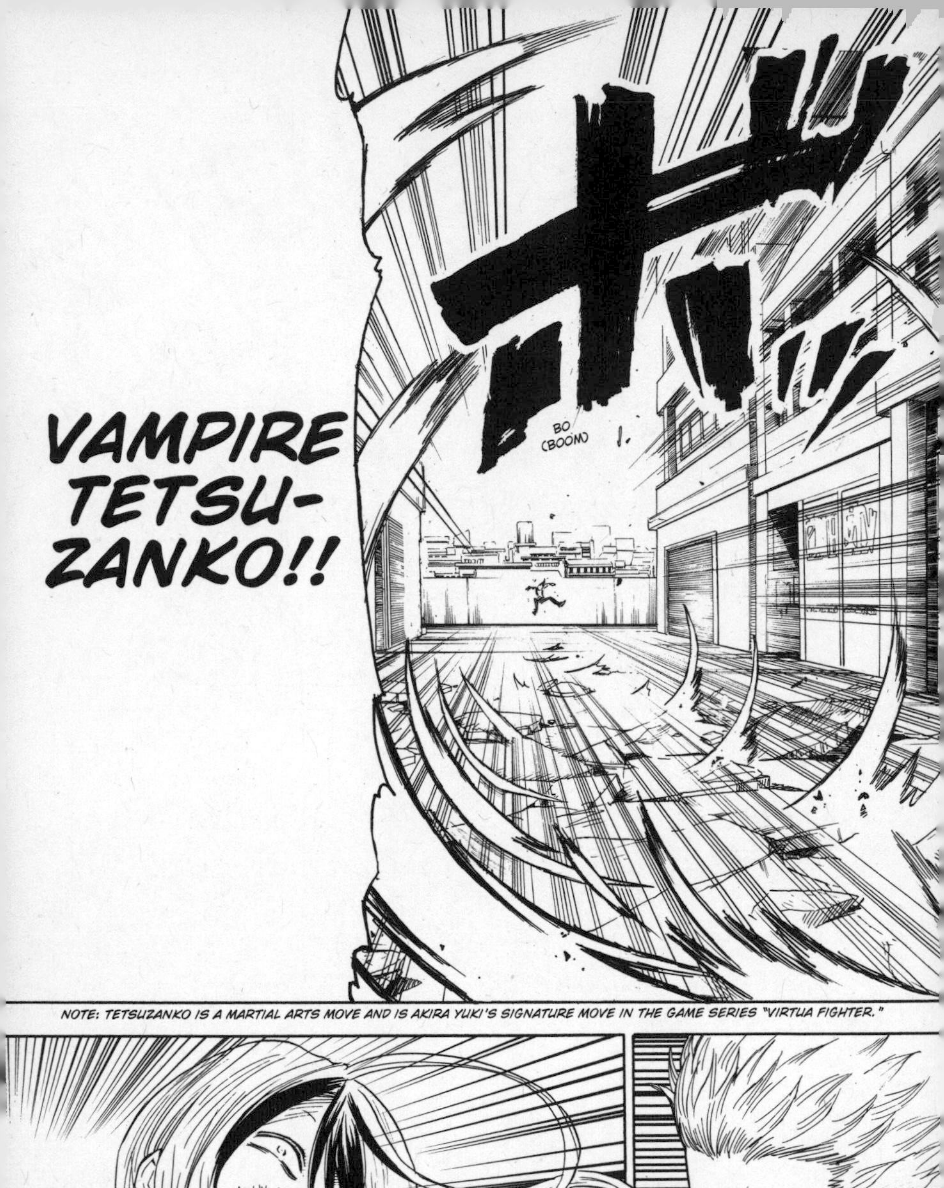
BO
(BOOM)
VAMPIRE TETSU-ZANKO!!

NOTE: TETSUZANKO IS A MARTIAL ARTS MOVE AND IS AKIRA YUKI'S SIGNATURE MOVE IN THE GAME SERIES "VIRTUA FIGHTER."

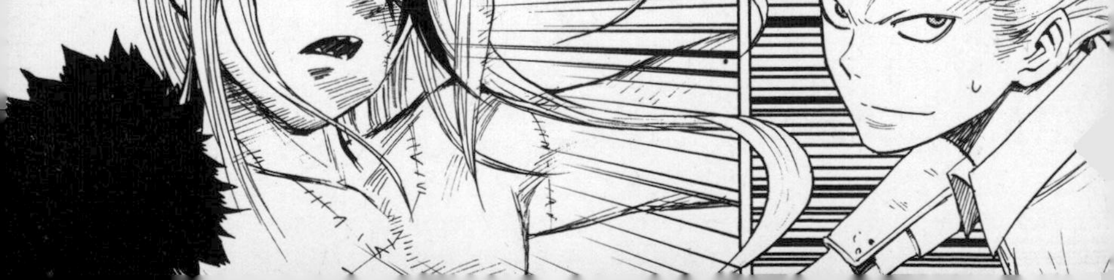

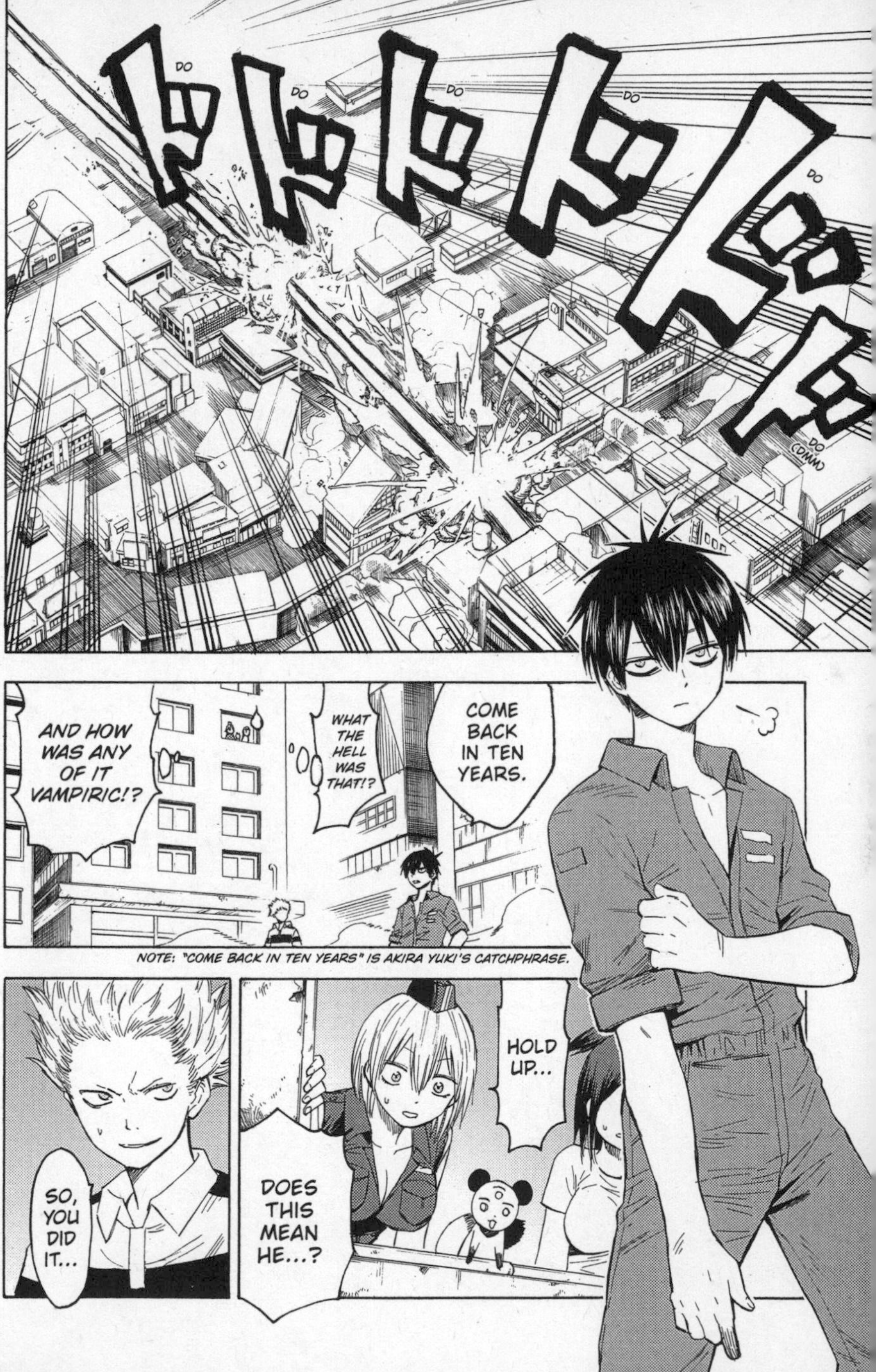
DO
DO
DO
DO
DO
DO
(DMM)
COME BACK IN TEN YEARS.
WHAT THE HELL WAS THAT!?
AND HOW WAS ANY OF IT VAMPIRIC!?
HOLD UP...
DOES THIS MEAN HE...?
SO, YOU DID IT...
NOTE: "COME BACK IN TEN YEARS" IS AKIRA YUKI'S CATCHPHRASE.

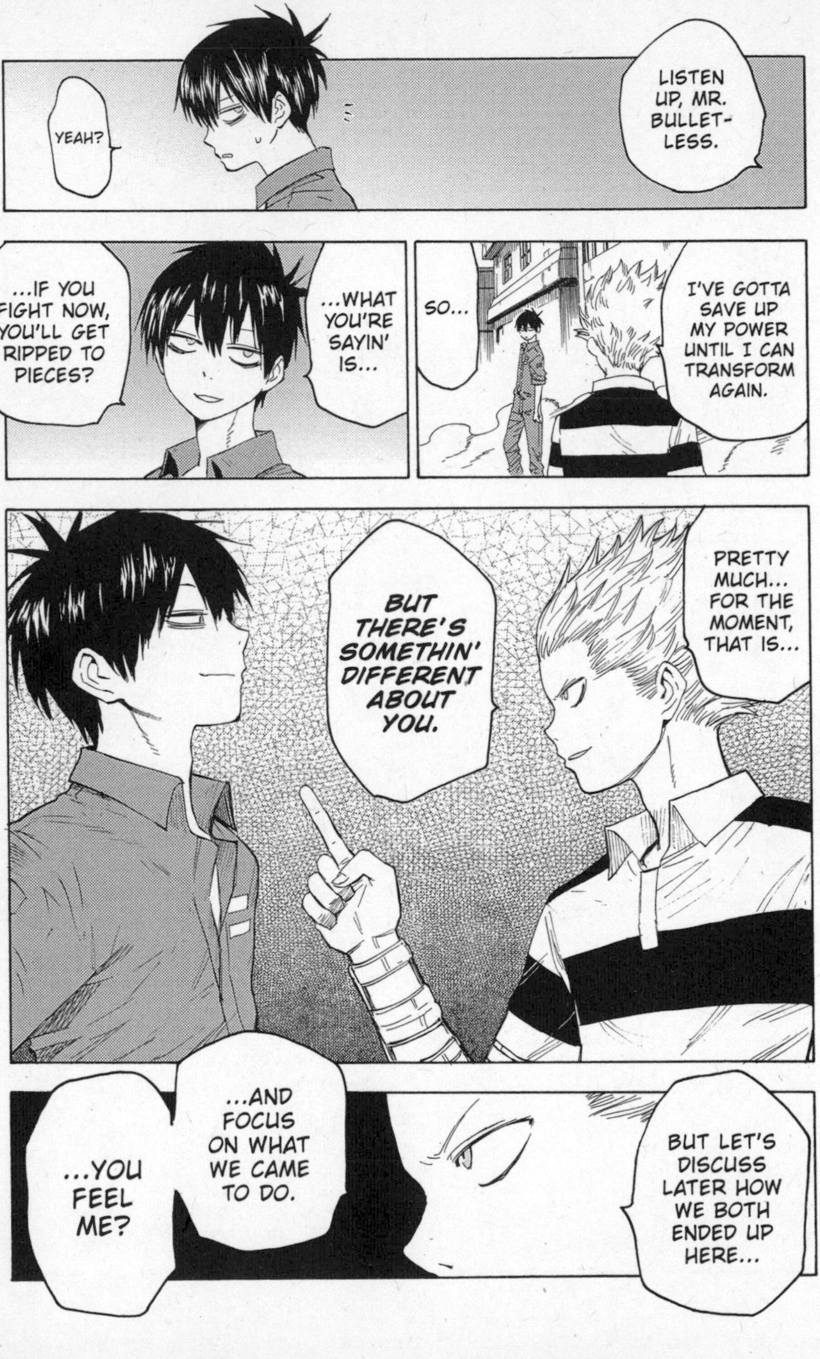
LISTEN UP, MR. BULLET-LESS.
YEAH?
I'VE GOTTA SAVE UP MY POWER UNTIL I CAN TRANSFORM AGAIN.
SO...
...WHAT YOU'RE SAYIN' IS...
...IF YOU FIGHT NOW, YOU'LL GET RIPPED TO PIECES?
PRETTY MUCH... FOR THE MOMENT, THAT IS...
BUT THERE'S SOMETHIN' DIFFERENT ABOUT YOU.
BUT LET'S DISCUSS LATER HOW WE BOTH ENDED UP HERE...
...AND FOCUS ON WHAT WE CAME TO DO.
...YOU FEEL ME?

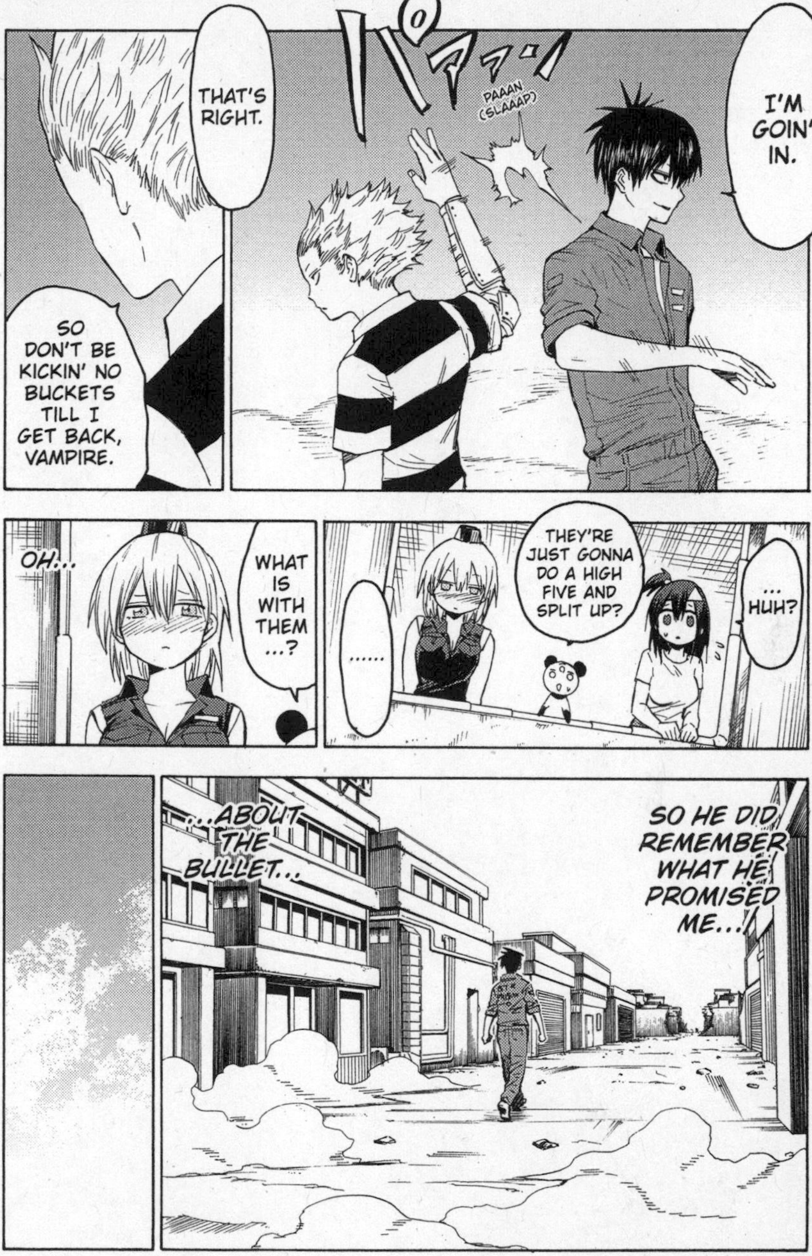
I'M GOIN' IN.
パァァーン
PAAAN (SLAAAP)
THAT'S RIGHT.
SO DON'T BE KICKIN' NO BUCKETS TILL I GET BACK, VAMPIRE.
... HUH?
THEY'RE JUST GONNA DO A HIGH FIVE AND SPLIT UP?
......
WHAT IS WITH THEM ...?
OH...
SO HE DID REMEMBER WHAT HE PROMISED ME...!
...ABOUT THE BULLET...

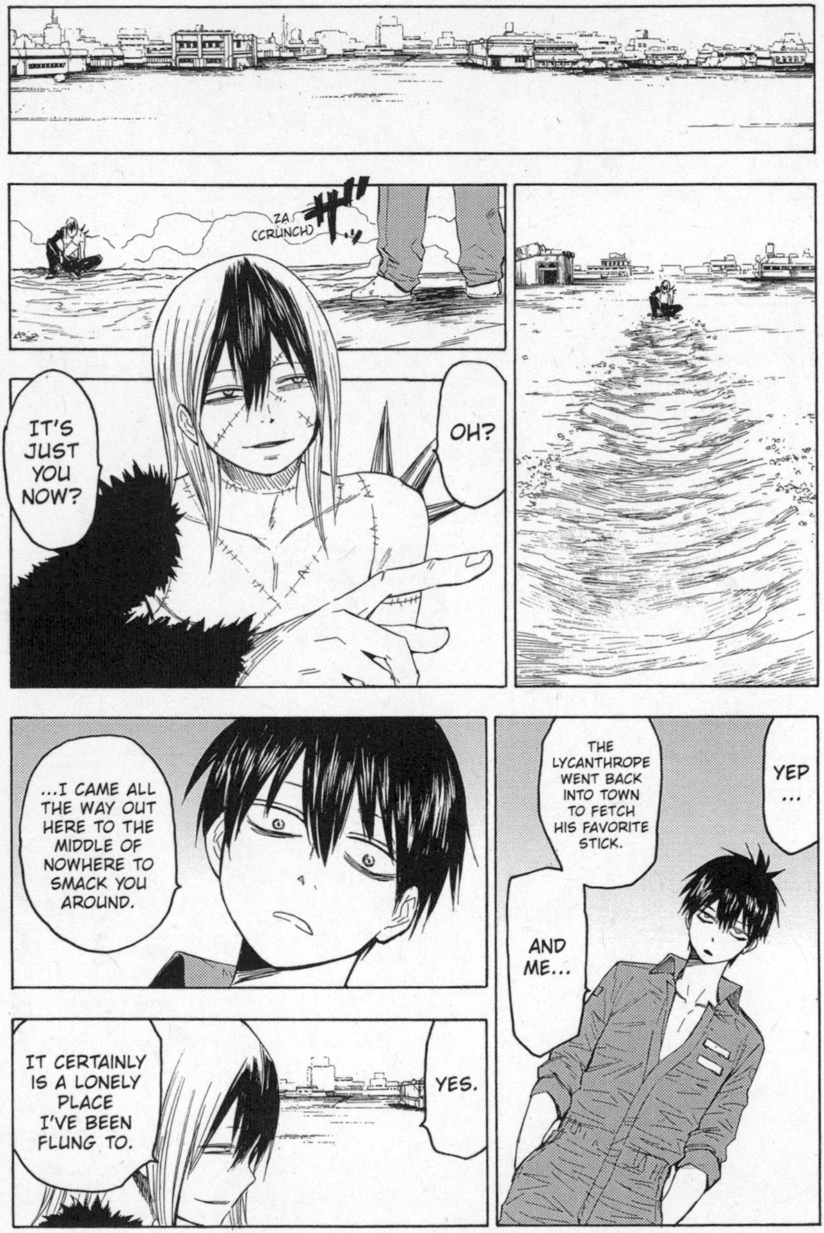
ZA (CRUNCH)
OH?
IT'S JUST YOU NOW?
YEP ...
THE LYCANTHROPE WENT BACK INTO TOWN TO FETCH HIS FAVORITE STICK.
AND ME...
...I CAME ALL THE WAY OUT HERE TO THE MIDDLE OF NOWHERE TO SMACK YOU AROUND.
YES.
IT CERTAINLY IS A LONELY PLACE I'VE BEEN FLUNG TO.

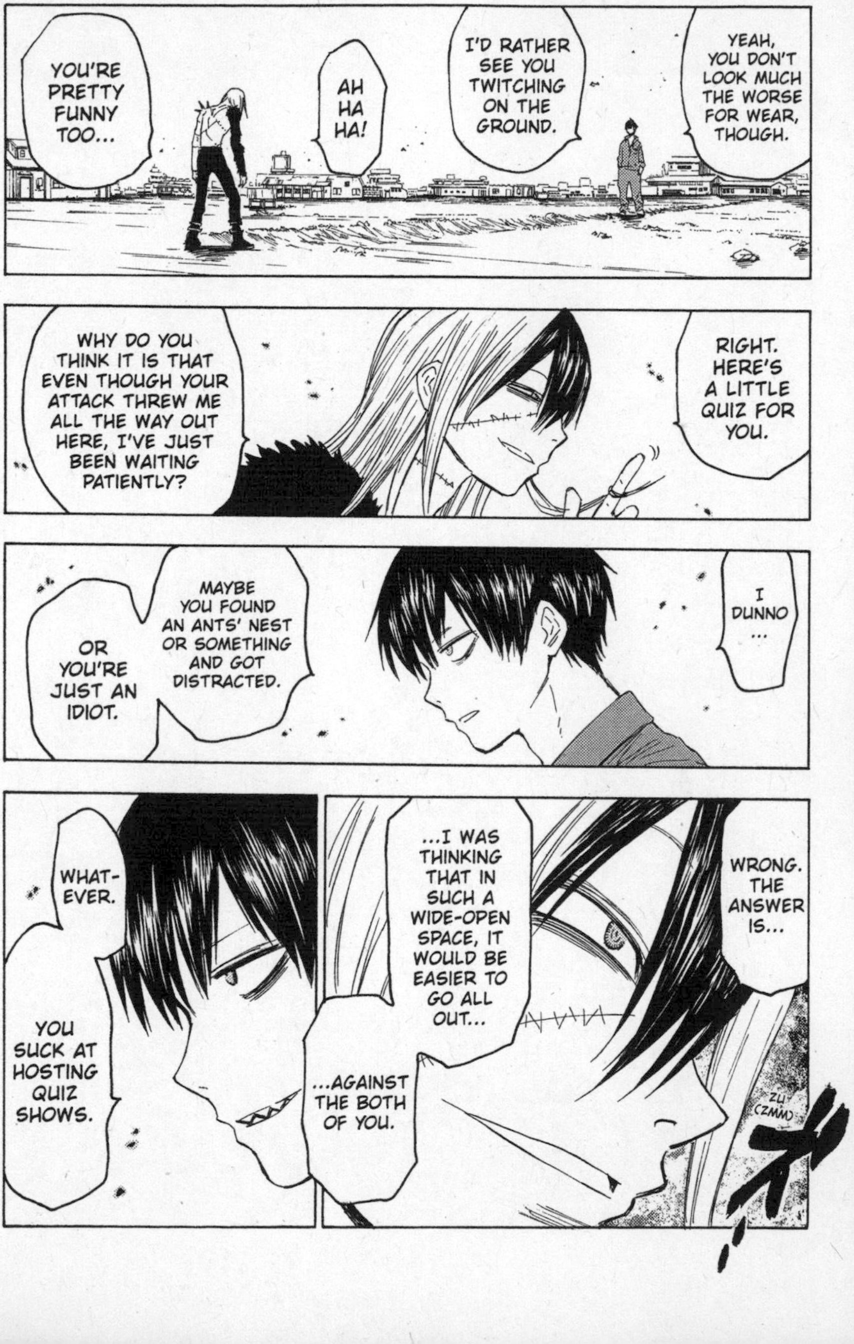
YEAH, YOU DON'T LOOK MUCH THE WORSE FOR WEAR, THOUGH.
I'D RATHER SEE YOU TWITCHING ON THE GROUND.
AH HA HA!
YOU'RE PRETTY FUNNY TOO...
RIGHT. HERE'S A LITTLE QUIZ FOR YOU.
WHY DO YOU THINK IT IS THAT EVEN THOUGH YOUR ATTACK THREW ME ALL THE WAY OUT HERE, I'VE JUST BEEN WAITING PATIENTLY?
I DUNNO ...
MAYBE YOU FOUND AN ANTS' NEST OR SOMETHING AND GOT DISTRACTED.
OR YOU'RE JUST AN IDIOT.
WRONG. THE ANSWER IS...
...I WAS THINKING THAT IN SUCH A WIDE-OPEN SPACE, IT WOULD BE EASIER TO GO ALL OUT...
...AGAINST THE BOTH OF YOU.
ZU (ZMM)
WHAT-EVER.
YOU SUCK AT HOSTING QUIZ SHOWS.

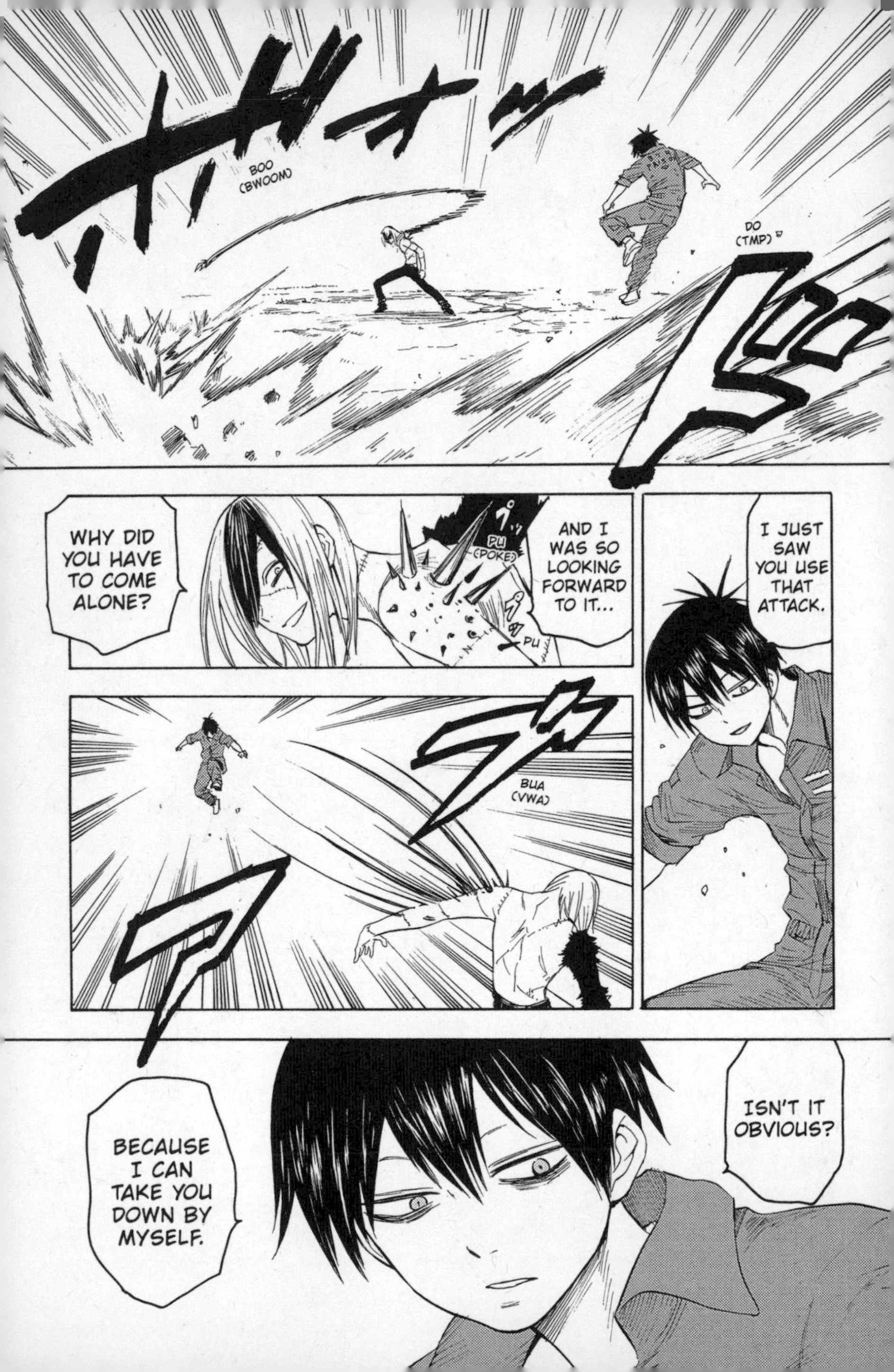
BOO (BWOOM)
DO (TMP)
I JUST SAW YOU USE THAT ATTACK.
PU (POKE)
AND I WAS SO LOOKING FORWARD TO IT...
PU
WHY DID YOU HAVE TO COME ALONE?
BUA (VWA)
ISN'T IT OBVIOUS?
BECAUSE I CAN TAKE YOU DOWN BY MYSELF.

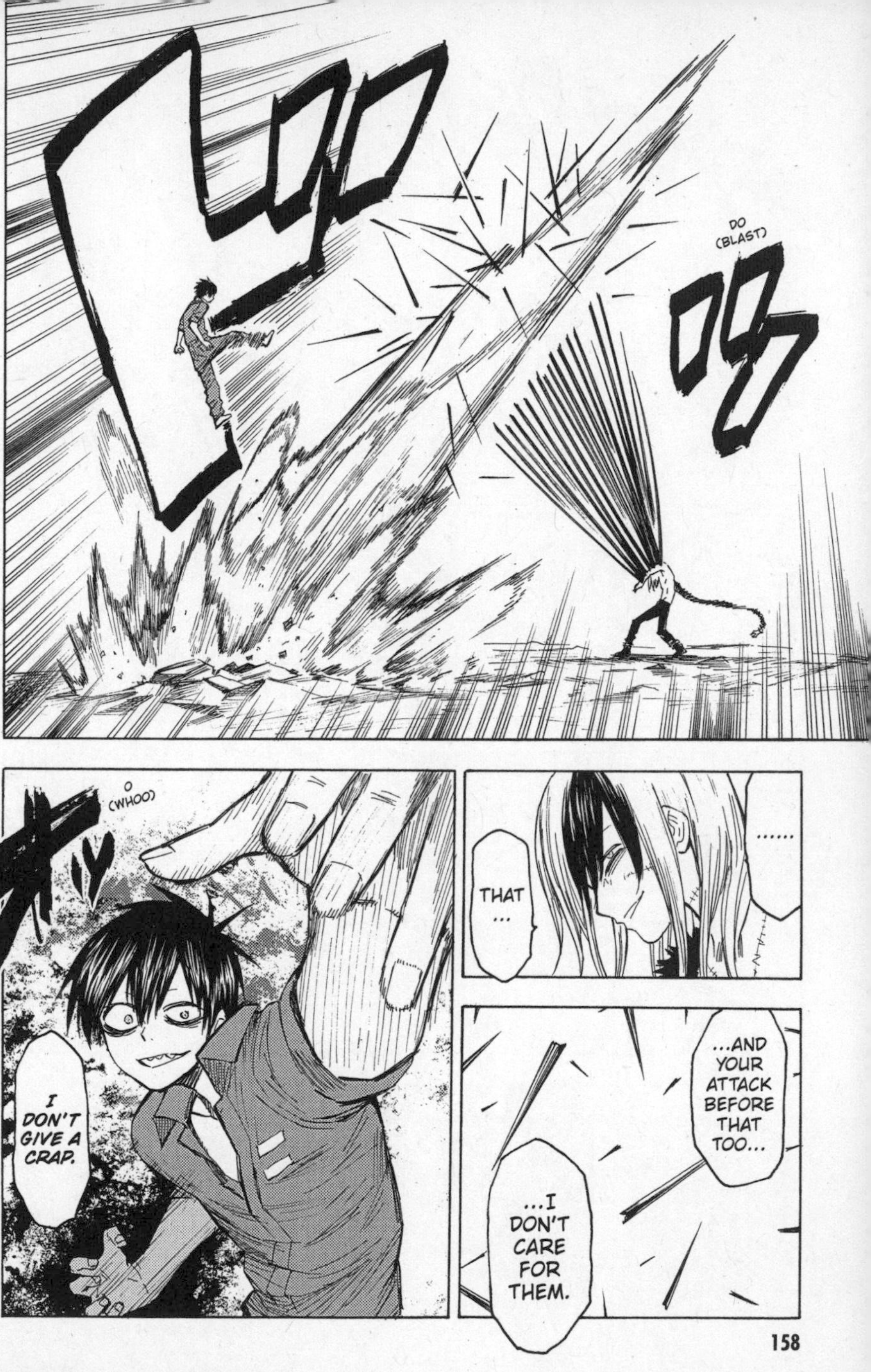
DO
(BLAST)
......
THAT ...
...AND YOUR ATTACK BEFORE THAT TOO...
...I DON'T CARE FOR THEM.
O
(WHOO)
I DON'T GIVE A CRAP.

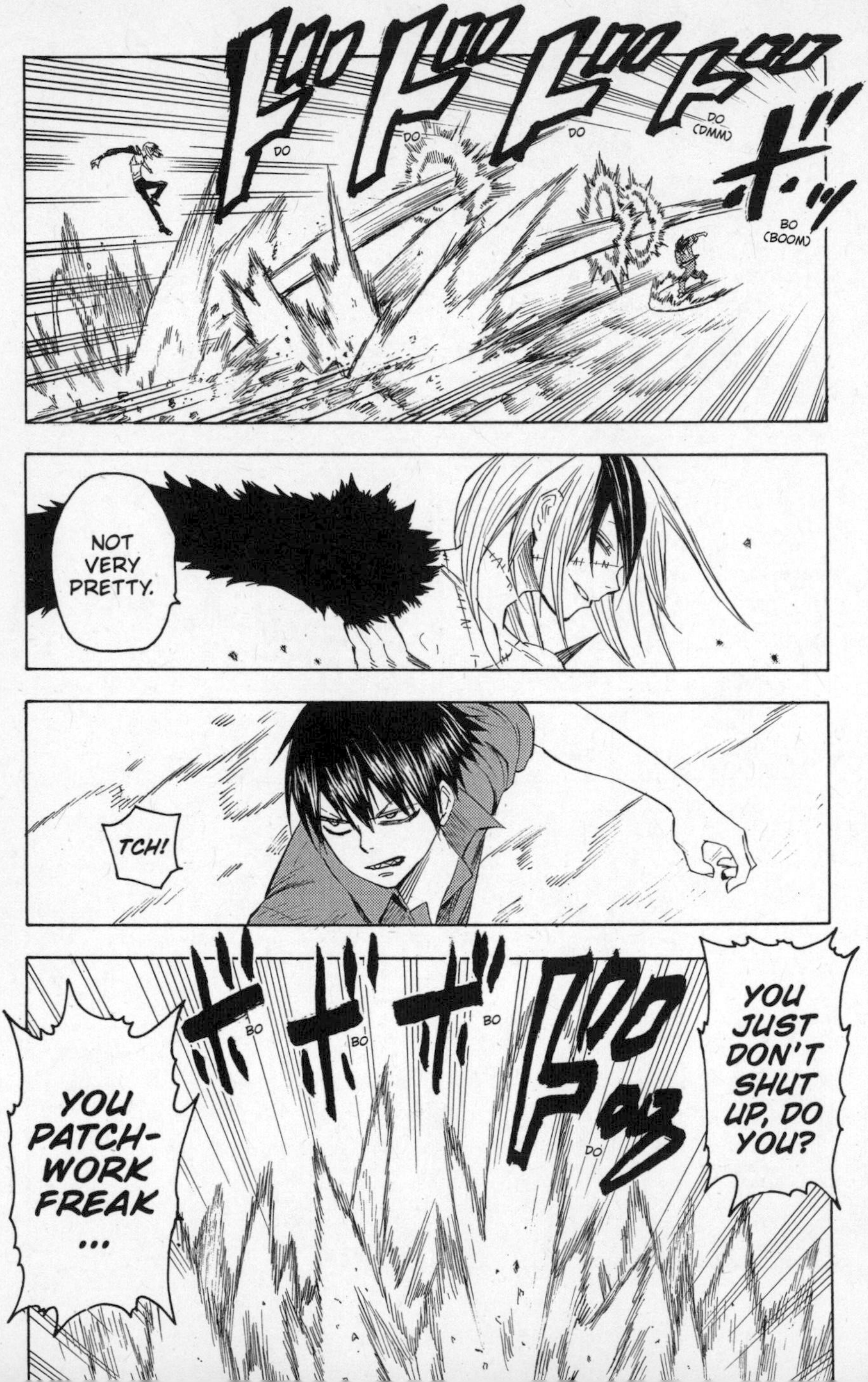
DO (DMM)
DO
DO
DO
BO (BOOM)
NOT VERY PRETTY.
TCH!
YOU JUST DON'T SHUT UP, DO YOU?
DO
BO
BO
BO
YOU PATCH-WORK FREAK ...

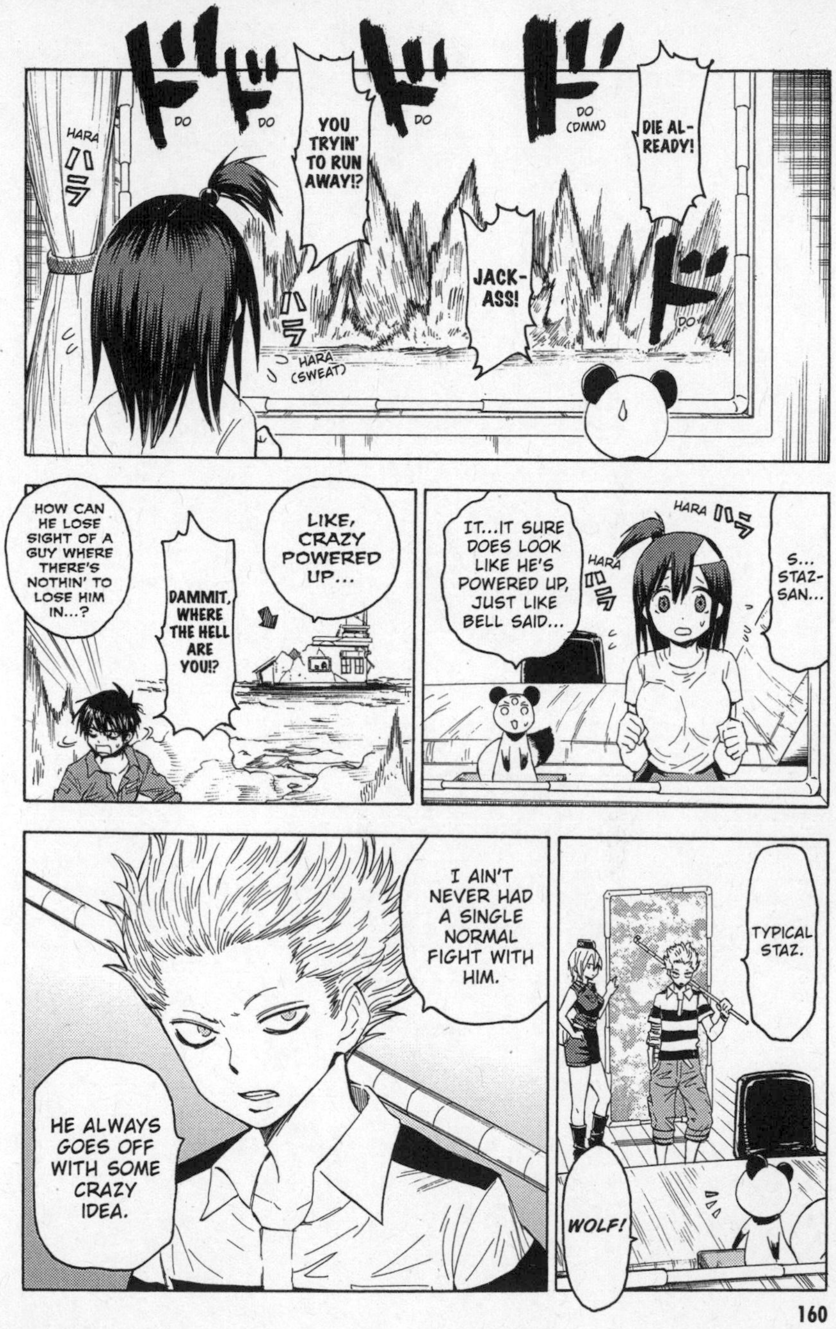
DIE AL-
READY!
DO
(DMM)
DO
YOU
TRYIN'
TO RUN
AWAY!?
DO
DO
DO
HARA
JACK-
ASS!
HARA
(SWEAT)
S...
STAZ-
SAN...
HARA
HARA
IT...IT SURE
DOES LOOK
LIKE HE'S
POWERED UP,
JUST LIKE
BELL SAID...
LIKE,
CRAZY
POWERED
UP...
DAMMIT,
WHERE
THE HELL
ARE
YOU!?
HOW CAN
HE LOSE
SIGHT OF A
GUY WHERE
THERE'S
NOTHIN' TO
LOSE HIM
IN...?
TYPICAL
STAZ.
WOLF!
I AIN'T
NEVER HAD
A SINGLE
NORMAL
FIGHT WITH
HIM.
HE ALWAYS
GOES OFF
WITH SOME
CRAZY
IDEA.

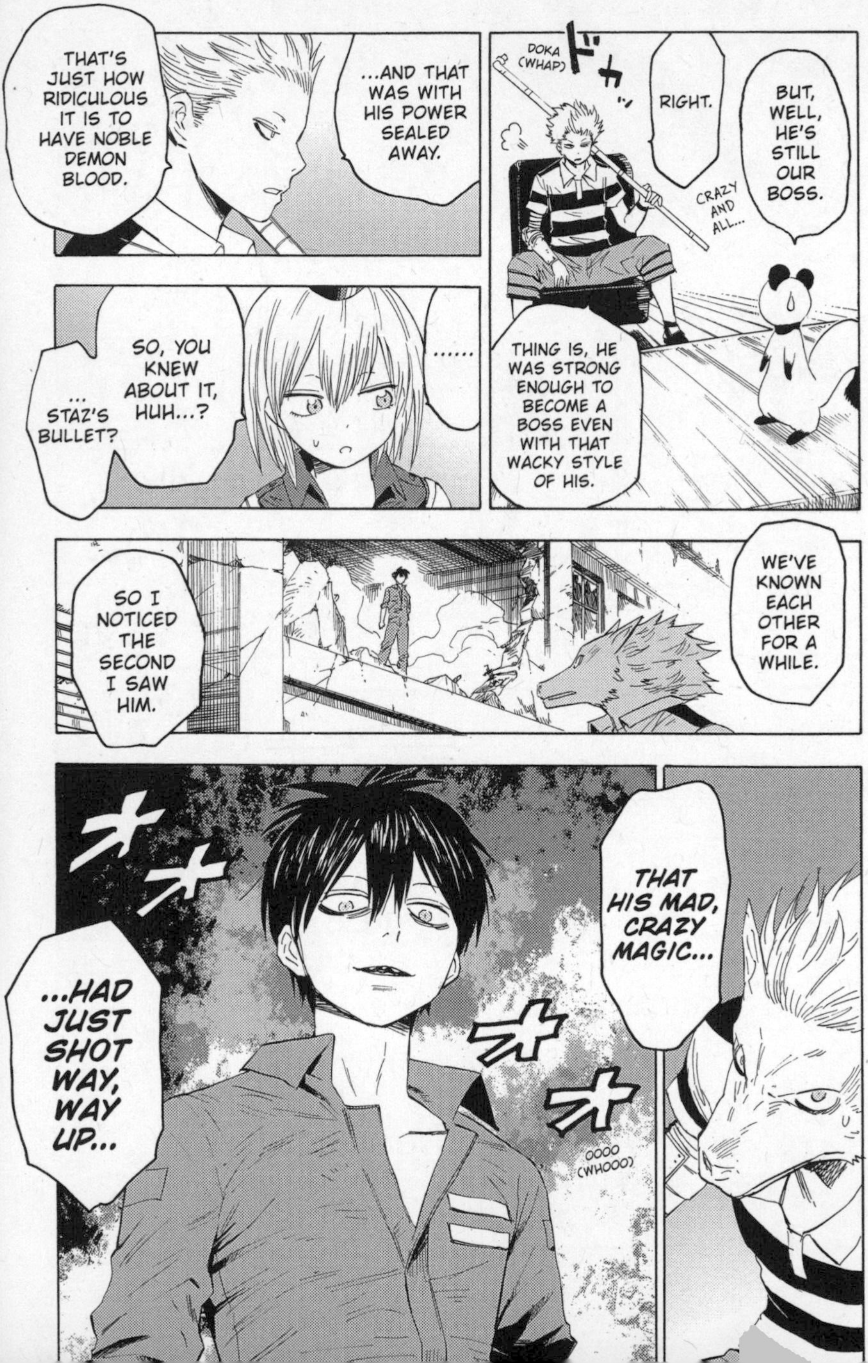
BUT, WELL, HE'S STILL OUR BOSS.
RIGHT.
DOKA (WHAP)
CRAZY AND ALL...
THING IS, HE WAS STRONG ENOUGH TO BECOME A BOSS EVEN WITH THAT WACKY STYLE OF HIS.
THAT'S JUST HOW RIDICULOUS IT IS TO HAVE NOBLE DEMON BLOOD.
...AND THAT WAS WITH HIS POWER SEALED AWAY.
......
SO, YOU KNEW ABOUT IT, HUH...?
... STAZ'S BULLET?
WE'VE KNOWN EACH OTHER FOR A WHILE.
SO I NOTICED THE SECOND I SAW HIM.
THAT HIS MAD, CRAZY MAGIC...
OOOO (WHOOO)
...HAD JUST SHOT WAY, WAY UP...

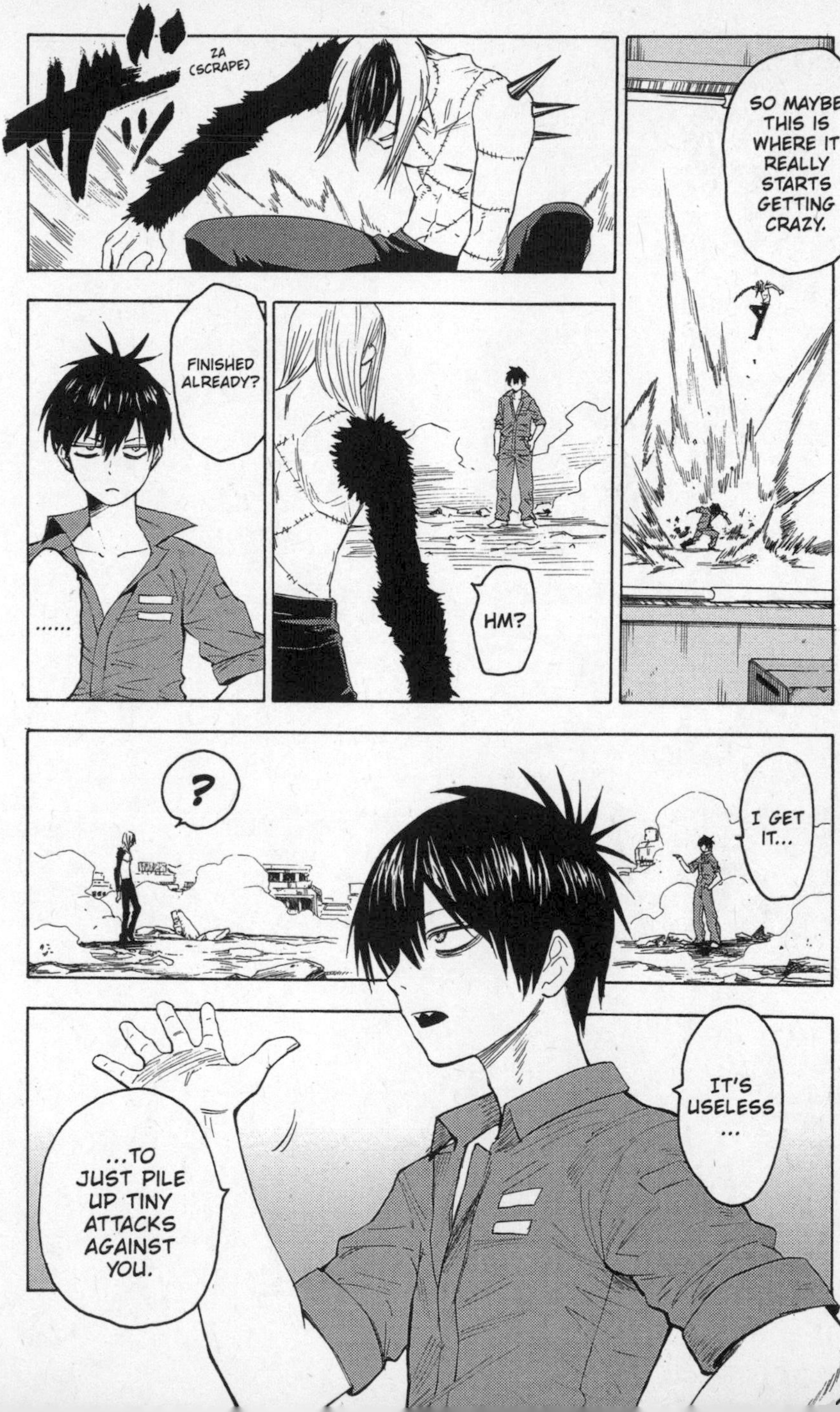
SO MAYBE THIS IS WHERE IT REALLY STARTS GETTING CRAZY.
ZA (SCRAPE)
HM?
FINISHED ALREADY?
......
I GET IT...
?
IT'S USELESS...
...TO JUST PILE UP TINY ATTACKS AGAINST YOU.

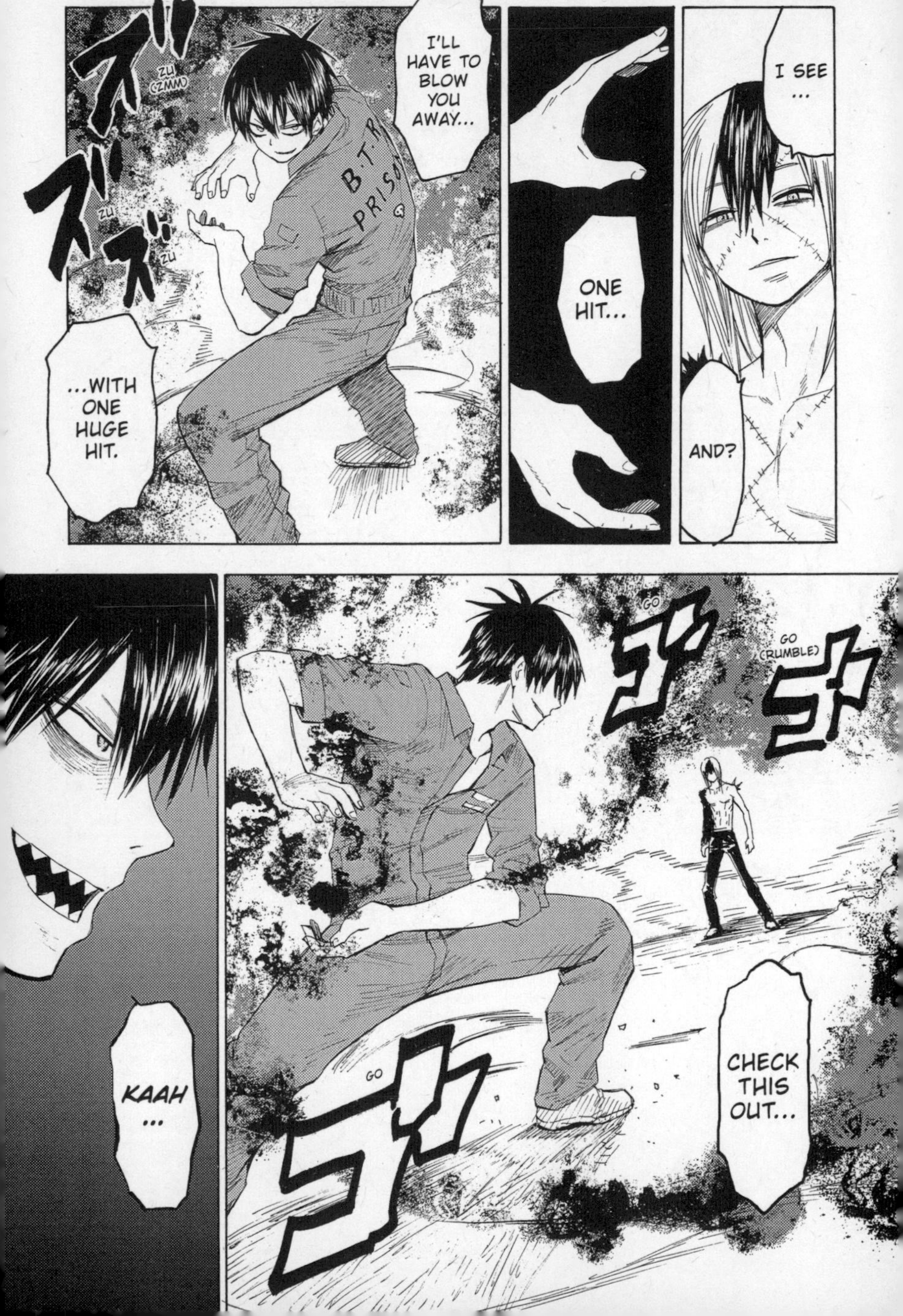
I SEE ...
AND?
ONE HIT...
I'LL HAVE TO BLOW YOU AWAY...
ZU (ZMM)
ZU
ZU
...WITH ONE HUGE HIT.
GO
GO (RUMBLE)
CHECK THIS OUT...
GO
KAAH ...

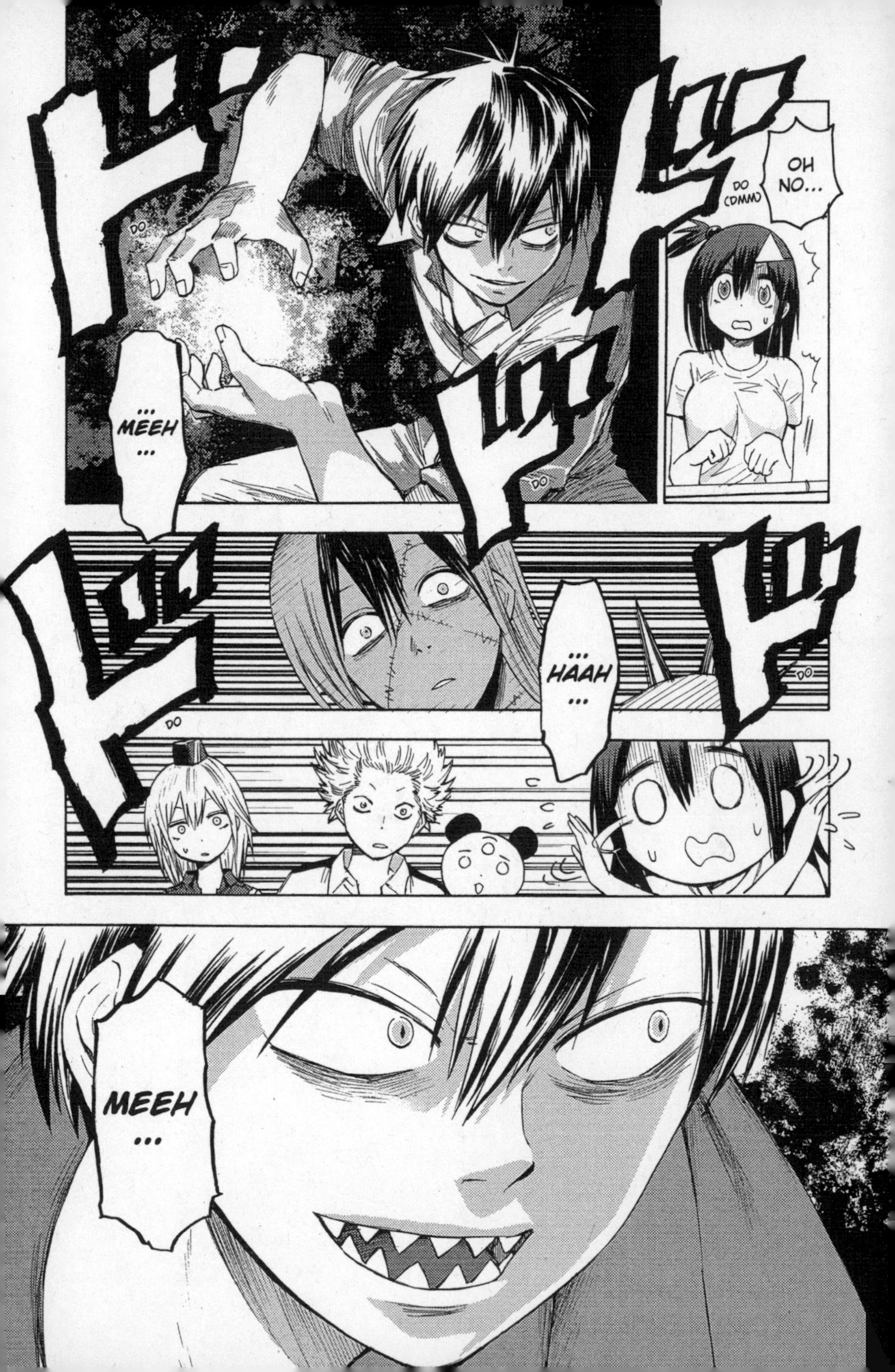
OH NO...
DO (DMM)
DO
... MEEH ...
DO
... HÄÄH ...
DO
DO
MEEH ...

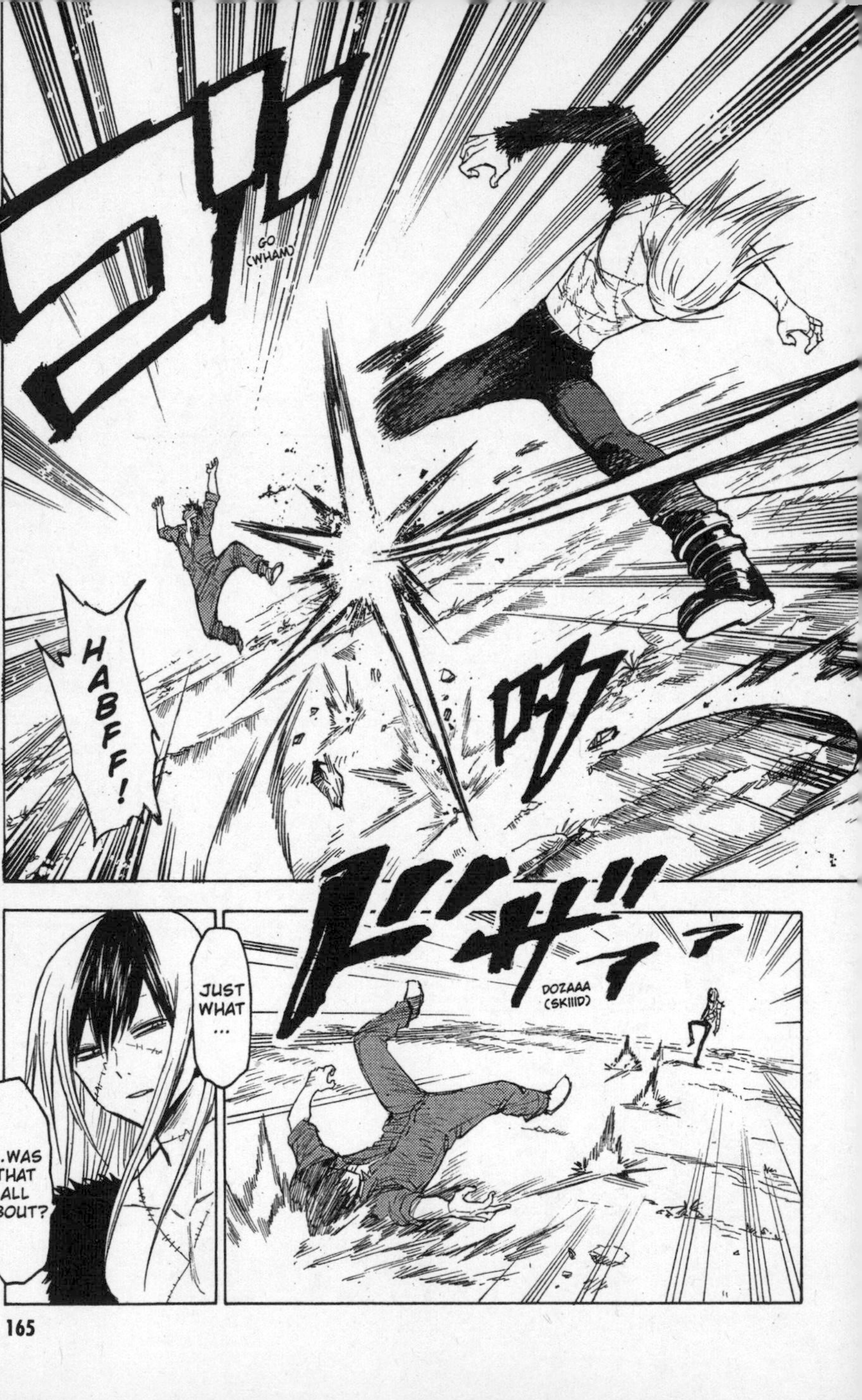
GO
(WHAM)
HABFFF!
DOZAAA
(SKIIID)
JUST WHAT...
...WAS THAT ALL ABOUT?

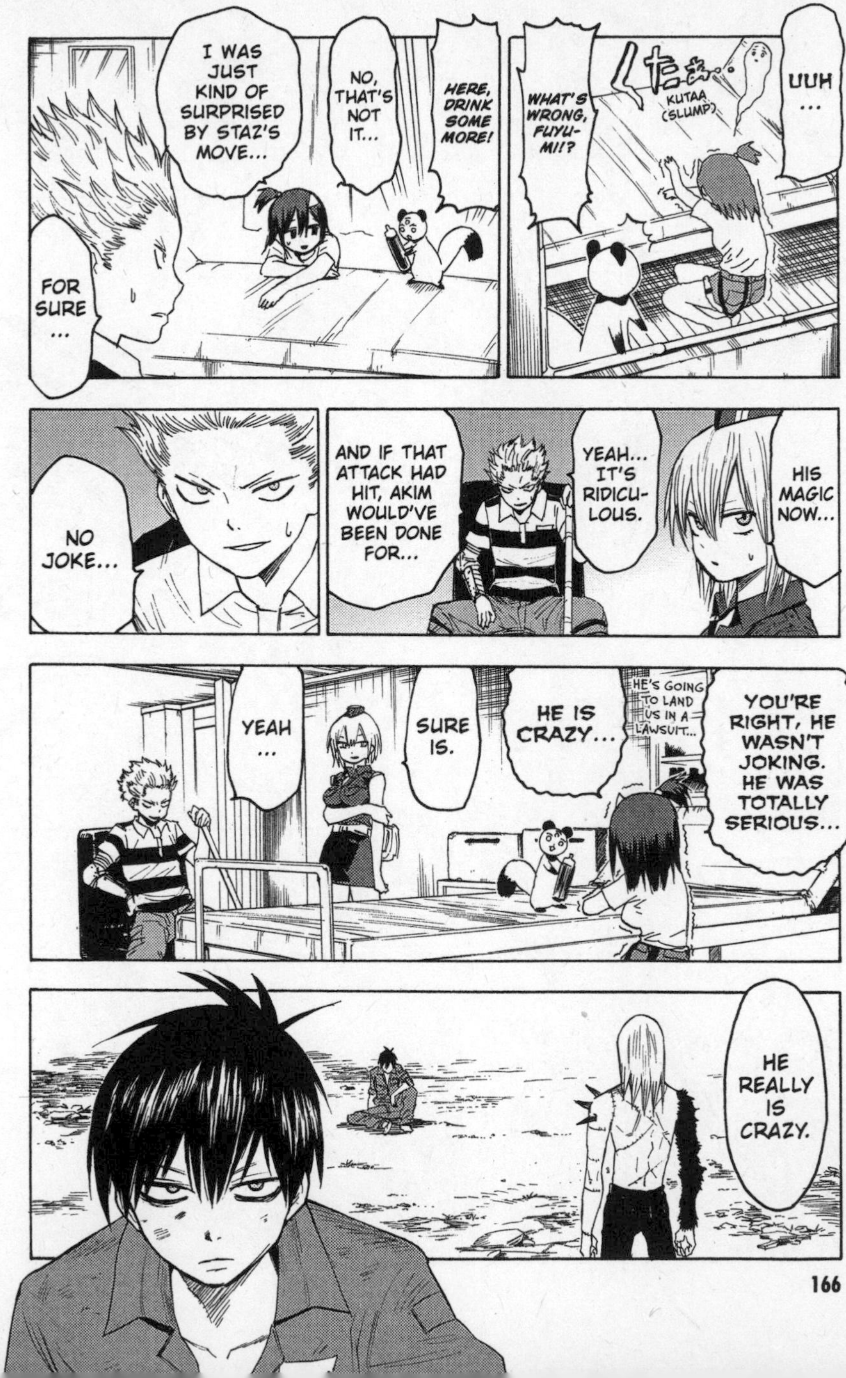
UUH ...
WHAT'S WRONG, FUYUMI!?
KUTAA (SLUMP)
HERE, DRINK SOME MORE!
NO, THAT'S NOT IT...
I WAS JUST KIND OF SURPRISED BY STAZ'S MOVE...
FOR SURE ...
HIS MAGIC NOW...
YEAH... IT'S RIDICULOUS.
AND IF THAT ATTACK HAD HIT, AKIM WOULD'VE BEEN DONE FOR...
NO JOKE...
YOU'RE RIGHT, HE WASN'T JOKING. HE WAS TOTALLY SERIOUS...
HE'S GOING TO LAND US IN A LAWSUIT...
HE IS CRAZY...
SURE IS.
YEAH ...
HE REALLY IS CRAZY.

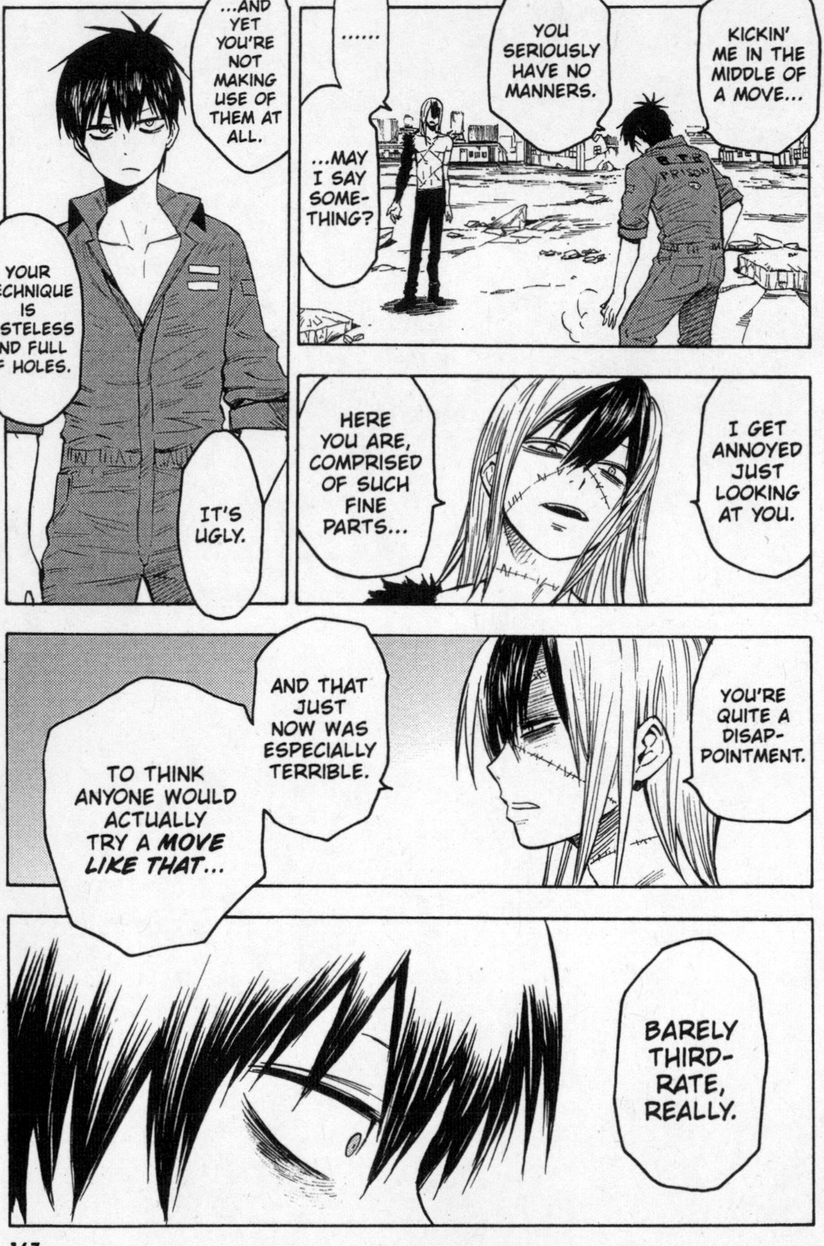
KICKIN' ME IN THE MIDDLE OF A MOVE...
YOU SERIOUSLY HAVE NO MANNERS.
......
...MAY I SAY SOMETHING?
I GET ANNOYED JUST LOOKING AT YOU.
HERE YOU ARE, COMPRISED OF SUCH FINE PARTS...
...AND YET YOU'RE NOT MAKING USE OF THEM AT ALL.
YOUR TECHNIQUE IS TASTELESS AND FULL OF HOLES.
IT'S UGLY.
YOU'RE QUITE A DISAPPOINTMENT.
AND THAT JUST NOW WAS ESPECIALLY TERRIBLE.
TO THINK ANYONE WOULD ACTUALLY TRY A *MOVE LIKE THAT*...
BARELY THIRD-RATE, REALLY.

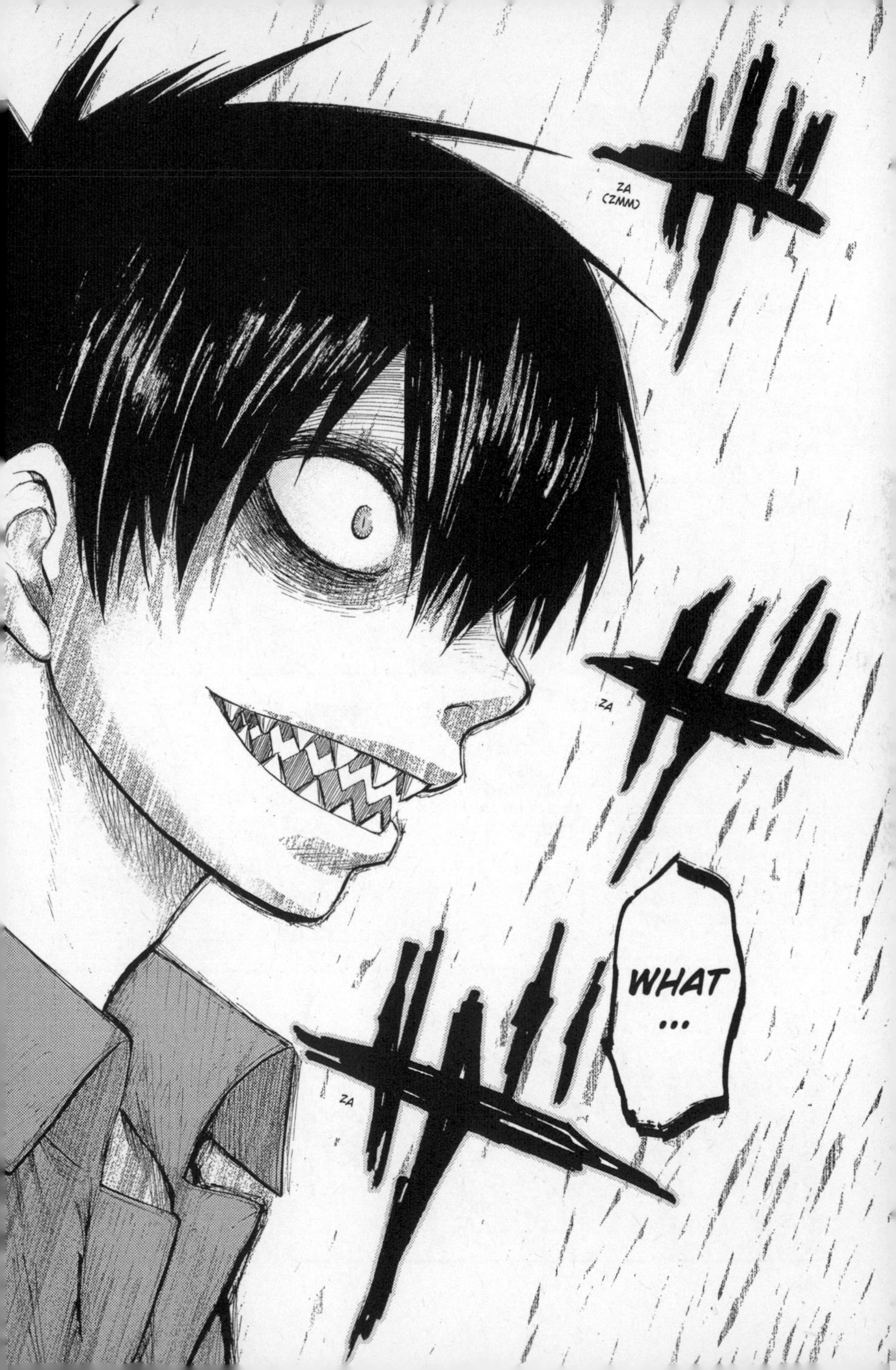

ZA (ZMM)
ZA
WHAT ...
ZA

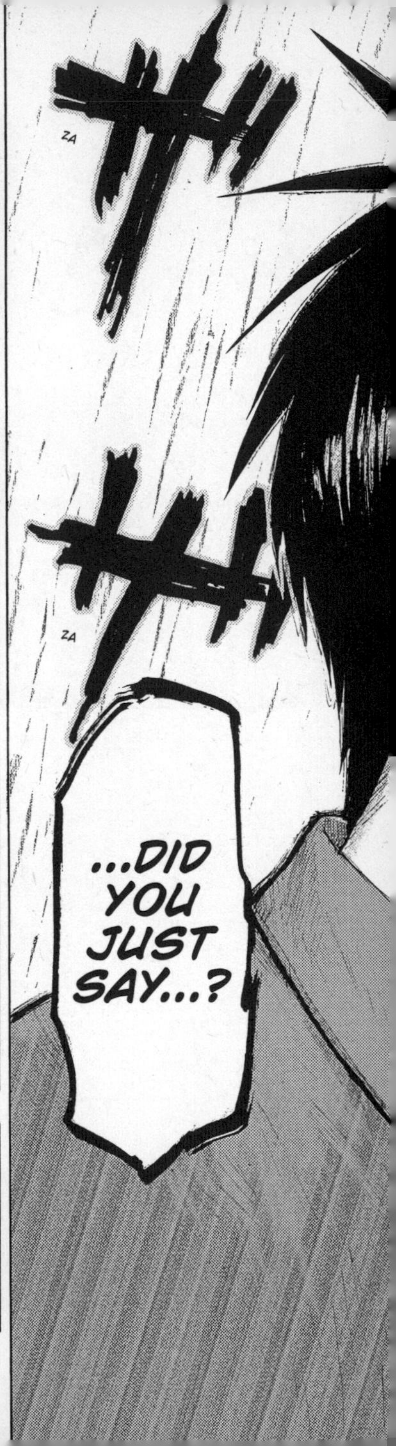
ZA
ZA
...DID YOU JUST SAY...?

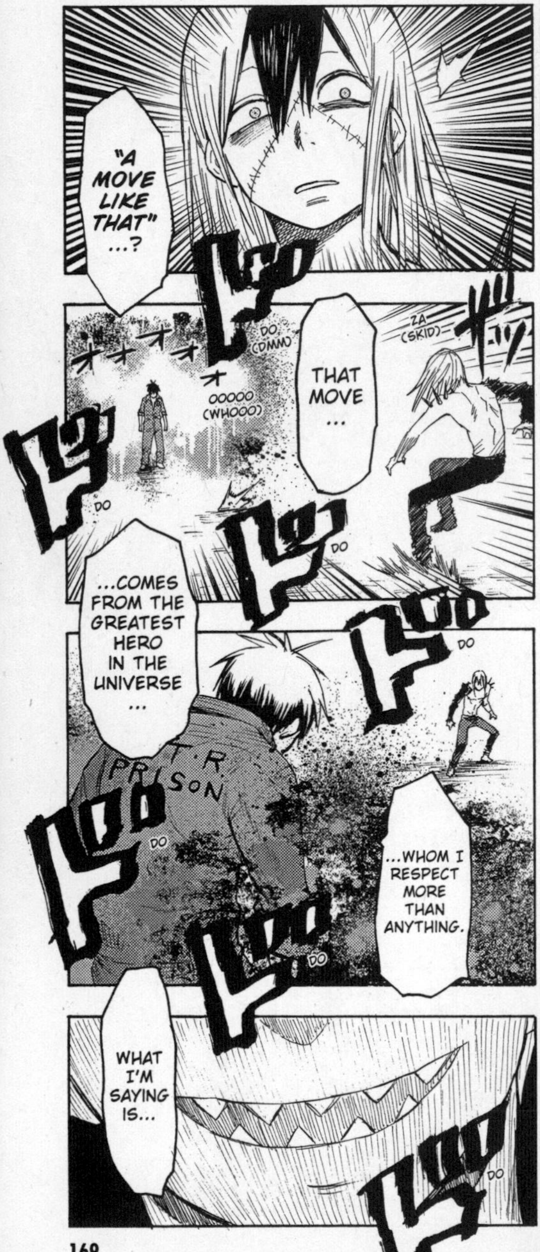
"A MOVE LIKE THAT" ...?
DO (DMM)
ZA (SKID)
THAT MOVE ...
OOOOO (WHOOO)
DO
DO
DO
...COMES FROM THE GREATEST HERO IN THE UNIVERSE ...
PRISON
...WHOM I RESPECT MORE THAN ANYTHING.
DO
DO
WHAT I'M SAYING IS...
DO

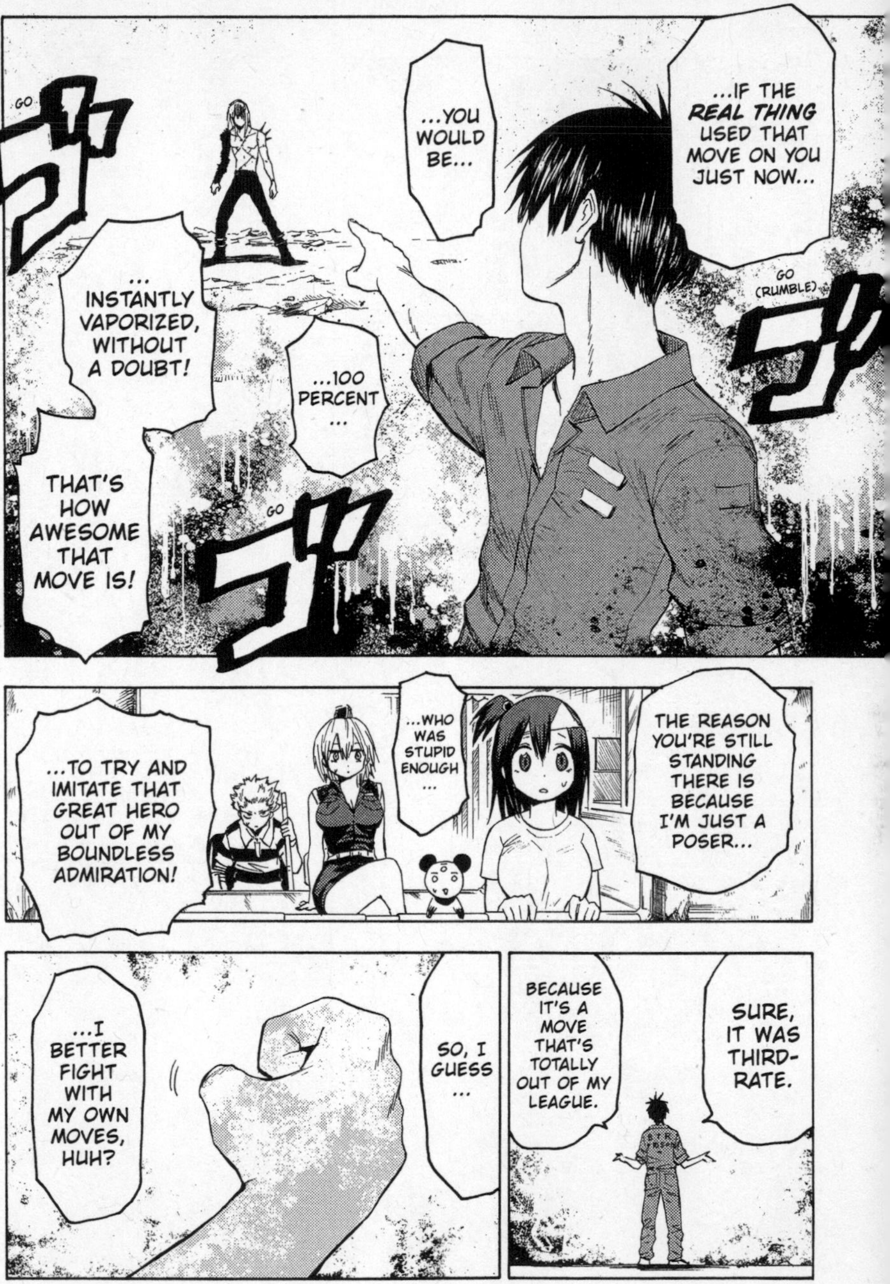
...IF THE *REAL THING* USED THAT MOVE ON YOU JUST NOW...
GO (RUMBLE)
...YOU WOULD BE...
GO
...100 PERCENT...
...INSTANTLY VAPORIZED, WITHOUT A DOUBT!
GO
THAT'S HOW AWESOME THAT MOVE IS!
THE REASON YOU'RE STILL STANDING THERE IS BECAUSE I'M JUST A POSER...
...WHO WAS STUPID ENOUGH...
...TO TRY AND IMITATE THAT GREAT HERO OUT OF MY BOUNDLESS ADMIRATION!
SURE, IT WAS THIRD-RATE.
BECAUSE IT'S A MOVE THAT'S TOTALLY OUT OF MY LEAGUE.
SO, I GUESS...
...I BETTER FIGHT WITH MY OWN MOVES, HUH?

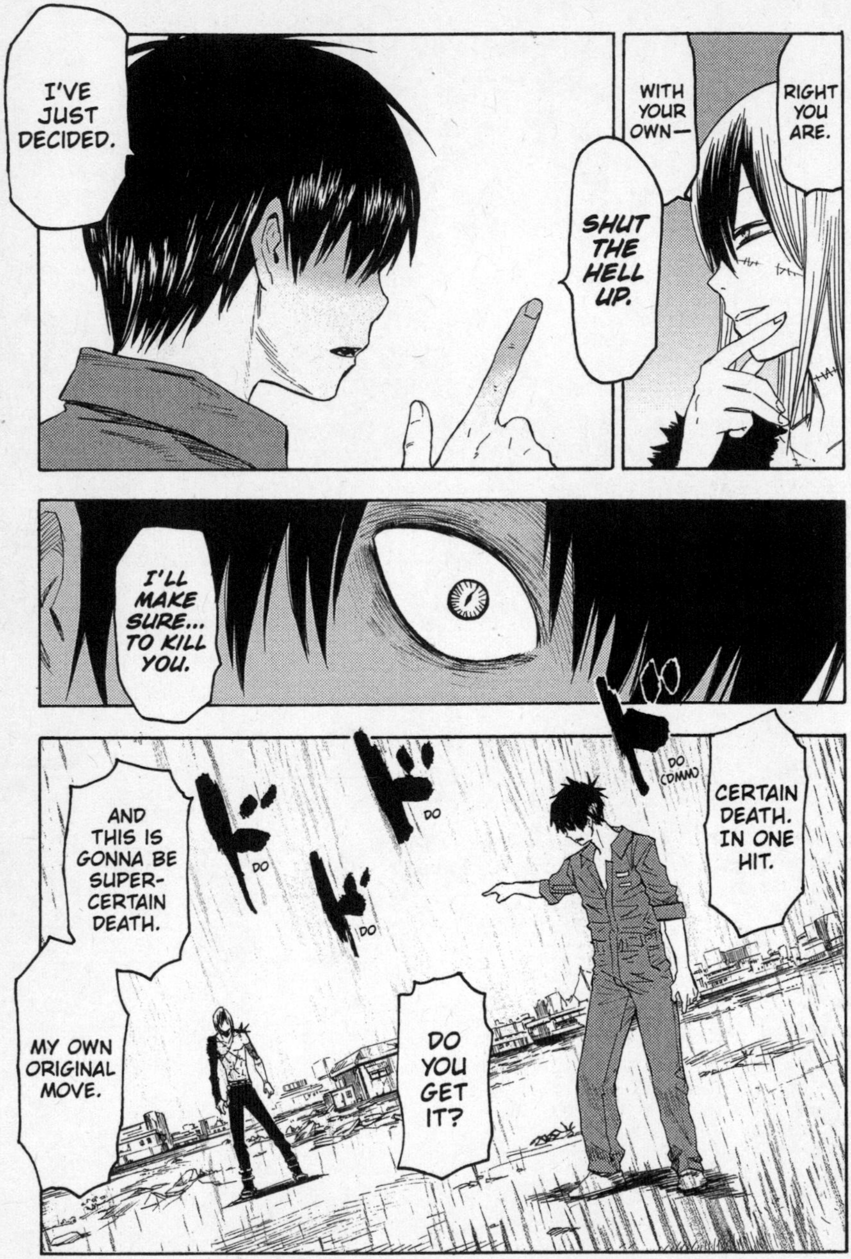
RIGHT YOU ARE.
WITH YOUR OWN—
SHUT THE HELL UP.
I'VE JUST DECIDED.
I'LL MAKE SURE... TO KILL YOU.
DO (DMM)
CERTAIN DEATH. IN ONE HIT.
DO
DO
DO
AND THIS IS GONNA BE SUPER-CERTAIN DEATH.
DO YOU GET IT?
MY OWN ORIGINAL MOVE.

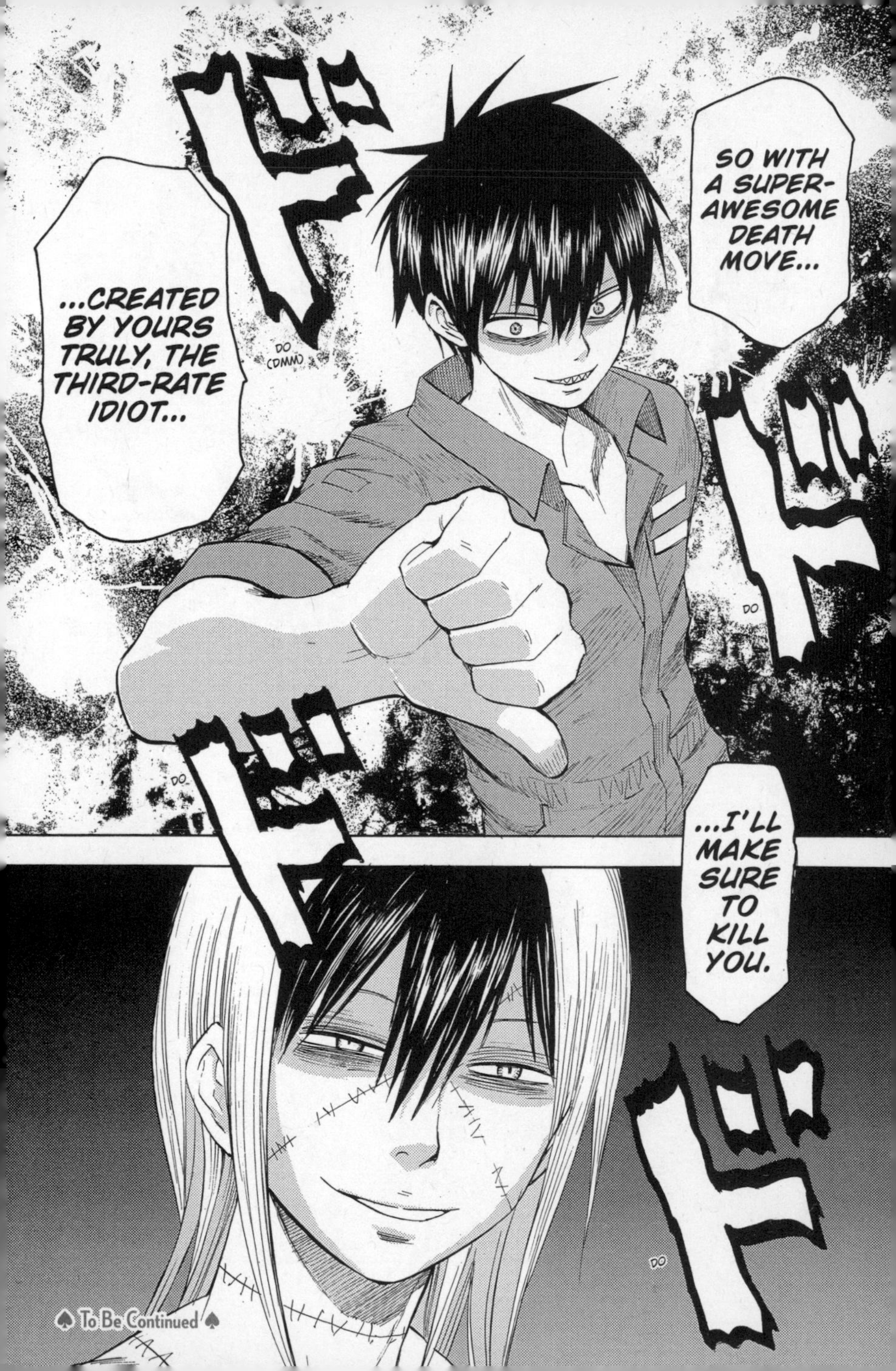
SO WITH A SUPER-AWESOME DEATH MOVE...
...CREATED BY YOURS TRULY, THE THIRD-RATE IDIOT...
DO
DO (DMM)
DO
...I'LL MAKE SURE TO KILL YOU.
DO
To Be Continued

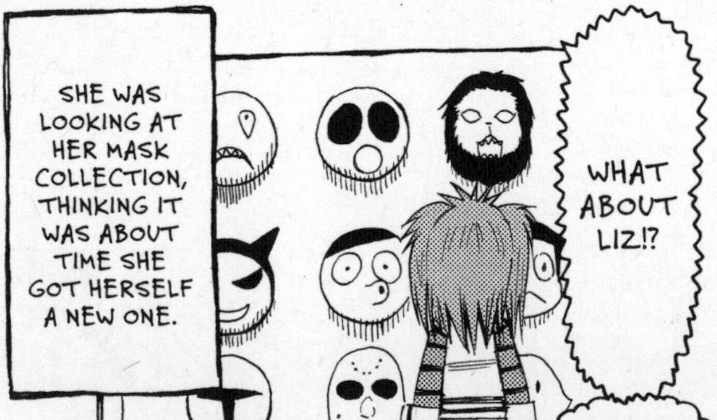
WHAT ABOUT LIZ!?
PART 5
SHE WAS LOOKING AT HER MASK COLLECTION, THINKING IT WAS ABOUT TIME SHE GOT HERSELF A NEW ONE.

BLOOD LAD

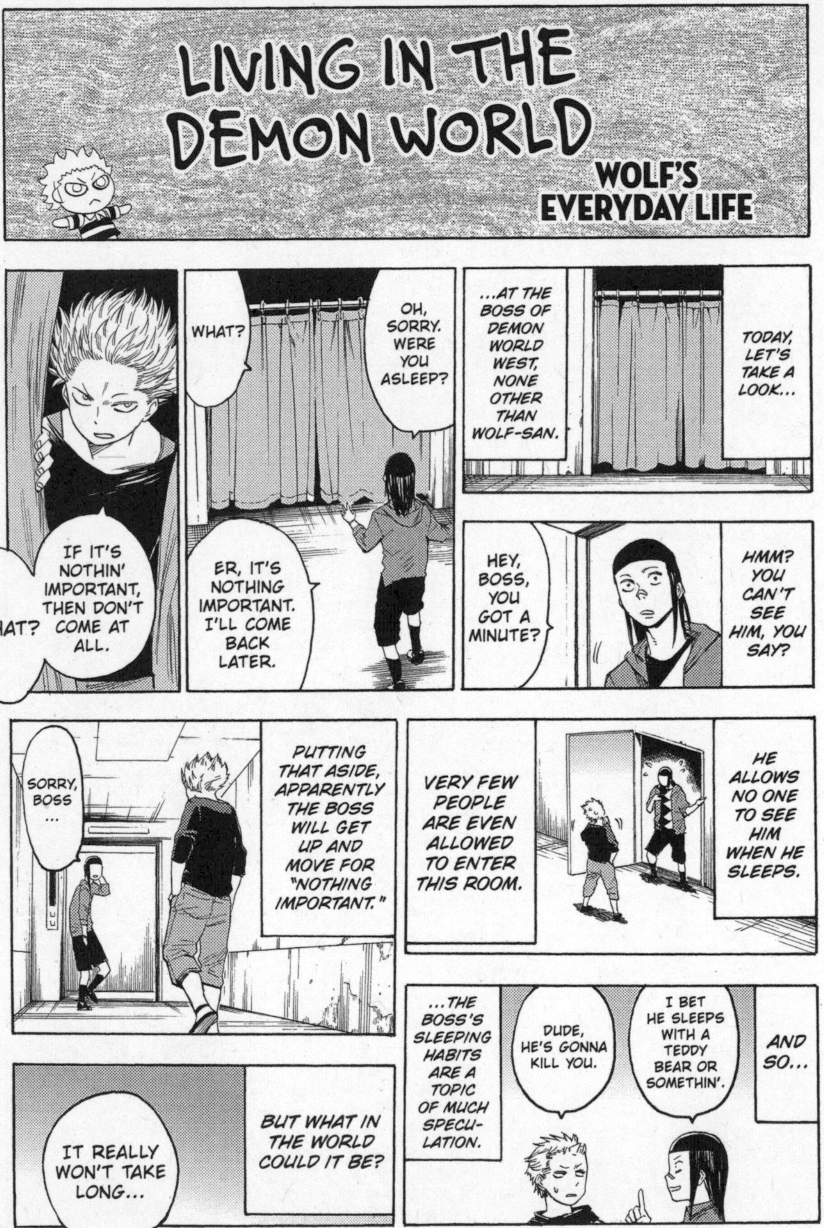
LIVING IN THE DEMON WORLD
WOLF'S EVERYDAY LIFE
TODAY, LET'S TAKE A LOOK...
...AT THE BOSS OF DEMON WORLD WEST, NONE OTHER THAN WOLF-SAN.
HMM? YOU CAN'T SEE HIM, YOU SAY?
HEY, BOSS, YOU GOT A MINUTE?
OH, SORRY. WERE YOU ASLEEP?
WHAT?
ER, IT'S NOTHING IMPORTANT. I'LL COME BACK LATER.
IF IT'S NOTHIN' IMPORTANT, THEN DON'T COME AT ALL.
WHAT?
HE ALLOWS NO ONE TO SEE HIM WHEN HE SLEEPS.
VERY FEW PEOPLE ARE EVEN ALLOWED TO ENTER THIS ROOM.
PUTTING THAT ASIDE, APPARENTLY THE BOSS WILL GET UP AND MOVE FOR "NOTHING IMPORTANT."
SORRY, BOSS ...
AND SO...
I BET HE SLEEPS WITH A TEDDY BEAR OR SOMETHIN'.
DUDE, HE'S GONNA KILL YOU.
...THE BOSS'S SLEEPING HABITS ARE A TOPIC OF MUCH SPECULATION.
BUT WHAT IN THE WORLD COULD IT BE?
IT REALLY WON'T TAKE LONG...

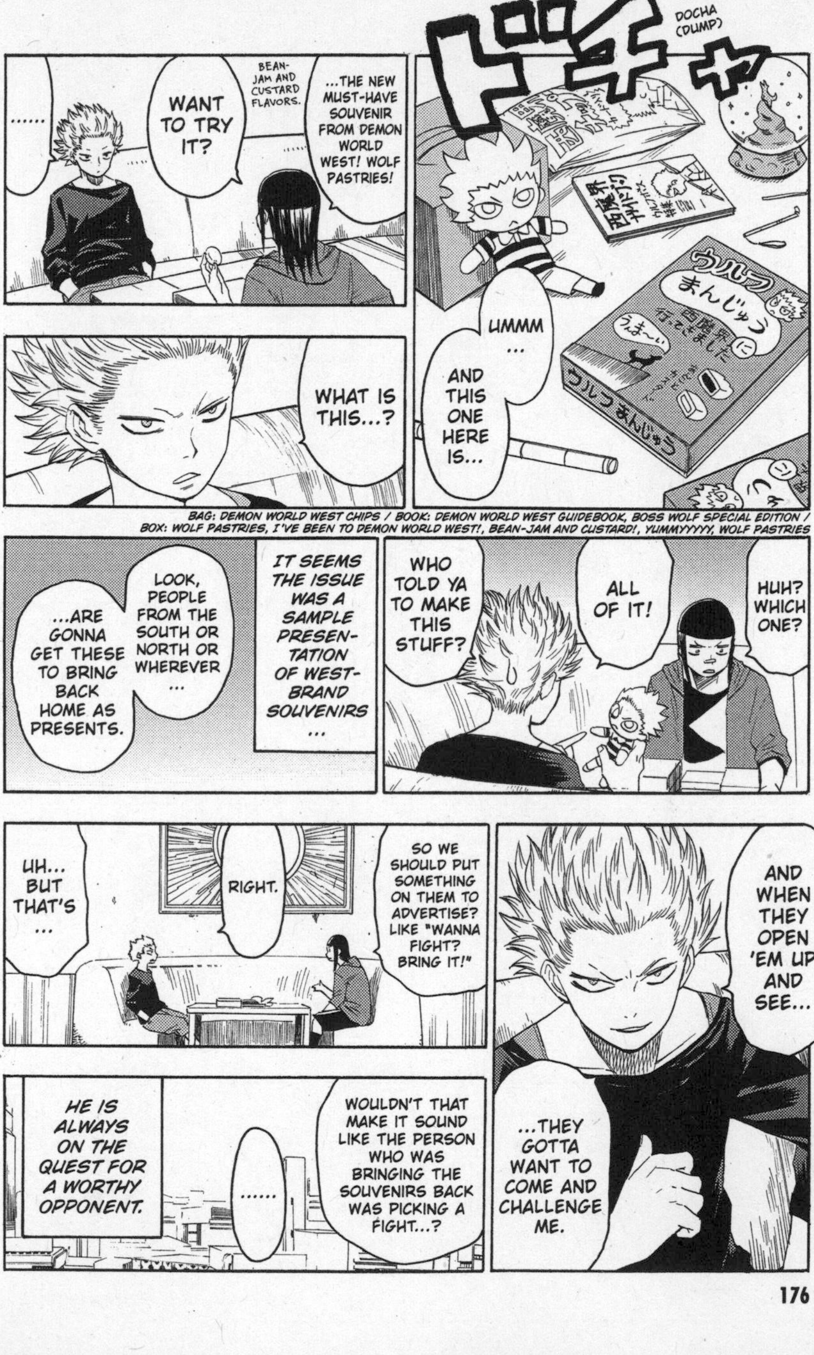
DOCHA (DUMP)
UMMM...
AND THIS ONE HERE IS...
...THE NEW MUST-HAVE SOUVENIR FROM DEMON WORLD WEST! WOLF PASTRIES!
BEAN-JAM AND CUSTARD FLAVORS.
WANT TO TRY IT?
......
WHAT IS THIS...?
BAG: DEMON WORLD WEST CHIPS / BOOK: DEMON WORLD WEST GUIDEBOOK, BOSS WOLF SPECIAL EDITION / BOX: WOLF PASTRIES, I'VE BEEN TO DEMON WORLD WEST!, BEAN-JAM AND CUSTARD!, YUMMYYYYY, WOLF PASTRIES
HUH? WHICH ONE?
ALL OF IT!
WHO TOLD YA TO MAKE THIS STUFF?
IT SEEMS THE ISSUE WAS A SAMPLE PRESEN-TATION OF WEST-BRAND SOUVENIRS...
LOOK, PEOPLE FROM THE SOUTH OR NORTH OR WHEREVER...
...ARE GONNA GET THESE TO BRING BACK HOME AS PRESENTS.
AND WHEN THEY OPEN 'EM UP AND SEE...
...THEY GOTTA WANT TO COME AND CHALLENGE ME.
SO WE SHOULD PUT SOMETHING ON THEM TO ADVERTISE? LIKE "WANNA FIGHT? BRING IT!"
RIGHT.
UH... BUT THAT'S...
WOULDN'T THAT MAKE IT SOUND LIKE THE PERSON WHO WAS BRINGING THE SOUVENIRS BACK WAS PICKING A FIGHT...?
......
HE IS ALWAYS ON THE QUEST FOR A WORTHY OPPONENT.

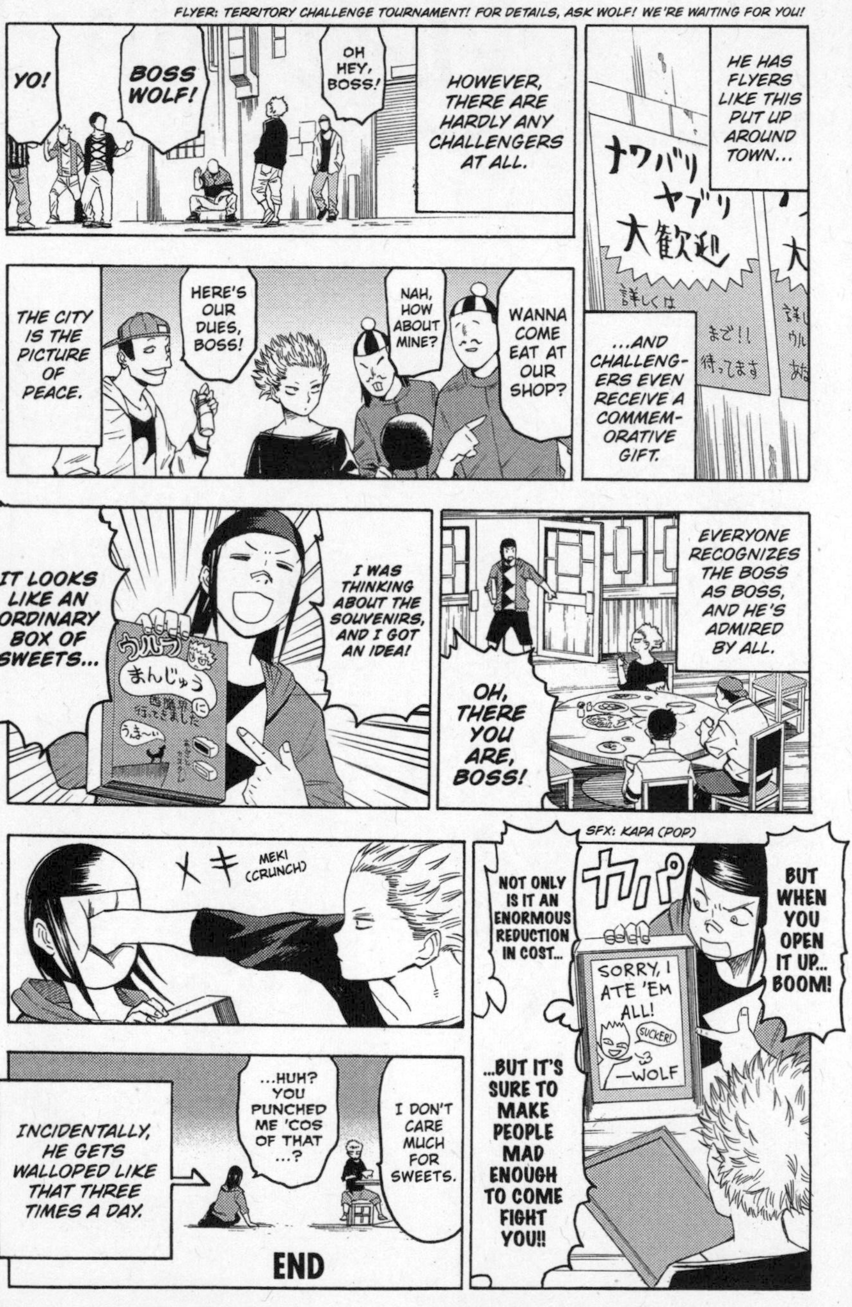
FLYER: TERRITORY CHALLENGE TOURNAMENT! FOR DETAILS, ASK WOLF! WE'RE WAITING FOR YOU!
HE HAS FLYERS LIKE THIS PUT UP AROUND TOWN...
ナワバリ ヤブリ 大歓迎
詳しくは
まで!! 待ってます
...AND CHALLENGERS EVEN RECEIVE A COMMEMORATIVE GIFT.
HOWEVER, THERE ARE HARDLY ANY CHALLENGERS AT ALL.
OH HEY, BOSS!
BOSS WOLF!
YO!
WANNA COME EAT AT OUR SHOP?
NAH, HOW ABOUT MINE?
HERE'S OUR DUES, BOSS!
THE CITY IS THE PICTURE OF PEACE.
EVERYONE RECOGNIZES THE BOSS AS BOSS, AND HE'S ADMIRED BY ALL.
OH, THERE YOU ARE, BOSS!
I WAS THINKING ABOUT THE SOUVENIRS, AND I GOT AN IDEA!
IT LOOKS LIKE AN ORDINARY BOX OF SWEETS...
ウルフ
まんじゅう
SFX: KAPA (POP)
BUT WHEN YOU OPEN IT UP... BOOM!
SORRY, I ATE 'EM ALL!
SUCKER!
—WOLF
NOT ONLY IS IT AN ENORMOUS REDUCTION IN COST...
...BUT IT'S SURE TO MAKE PEOPLE MAD ENOUGH TO COME FIGHT YOU!!
MEKI (CRUNCH)
I DON'T CARE MUCH FOR SWEETS.
...HUH? YOU PUNCHED ME 'COS OF THAT ...?
INCIDENTALLY, HE GETS WALLOPED LIKE THAT THREE TIMES A DAY.
END

BLOOD LAD 1

These images appeared under the jackets of the original editions of *Blood Lad*!

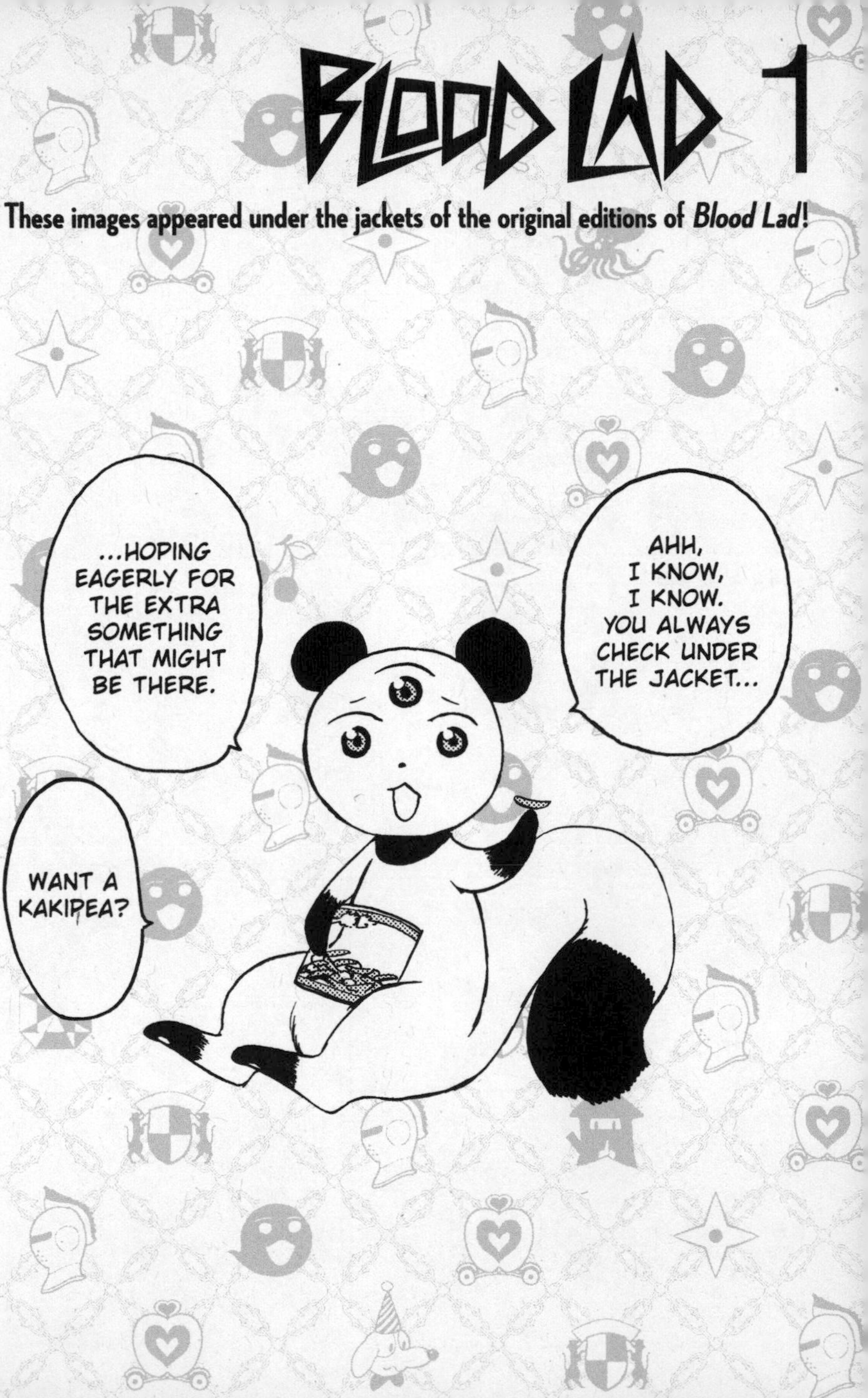
AHH, I KNOW, I KNOW. YOU ALWAYS CHECK UNDER THE JACKET...
...HOPING EAGERLY FOR THE EXTRA SOMETHING THAT MIGHT BE THERE.
WANT A KAKIPEA?

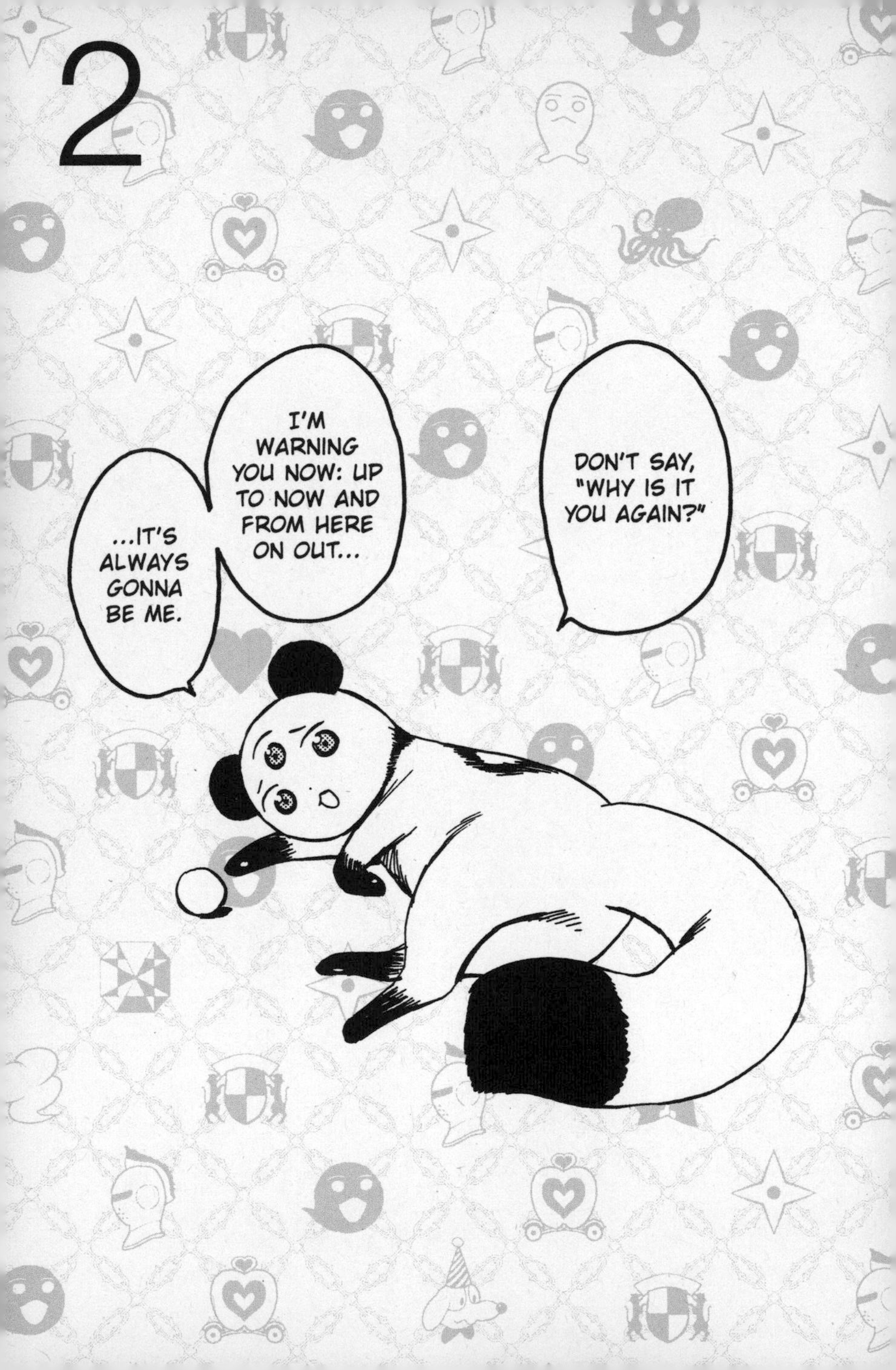
2
DON'T SAY, "WHY IS IT YOU AGAIN?"
I'M WARNING YOU NOW: UP TO NOW AND FROM HERE ON OUT...
...IT'S ALWAYS GONNA BE ME.

BLOOD LAD

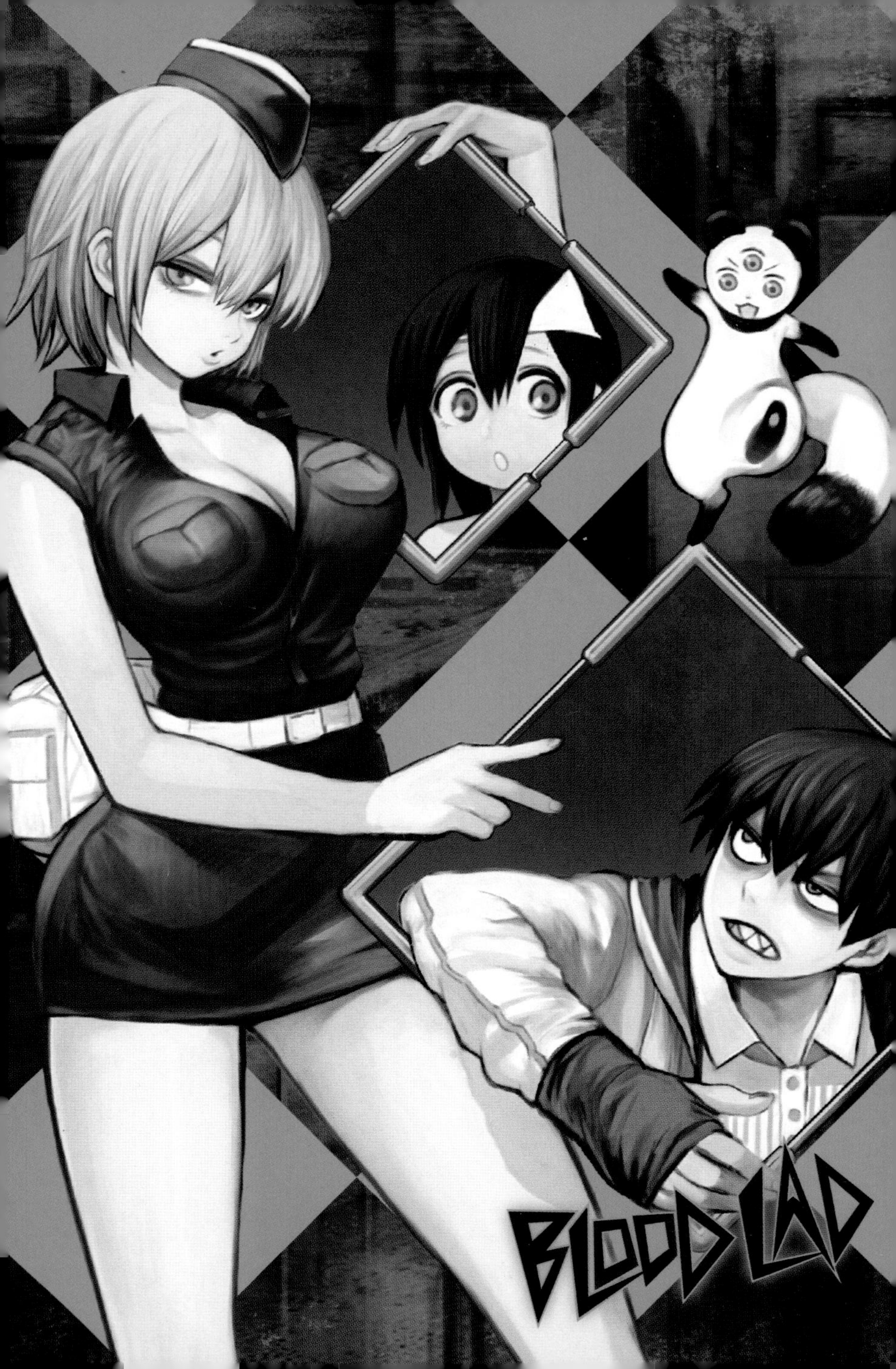
BLOOD LAD

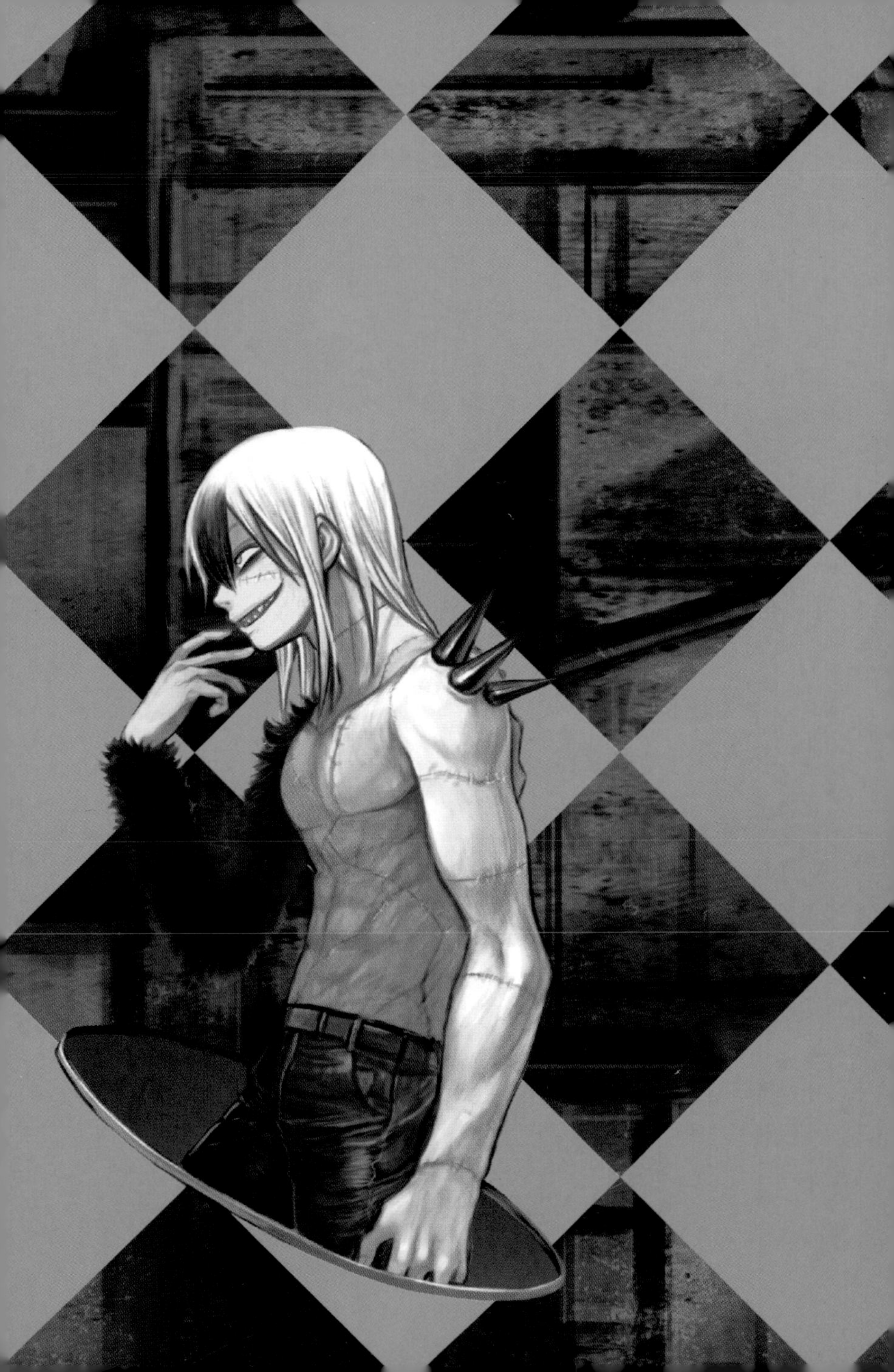

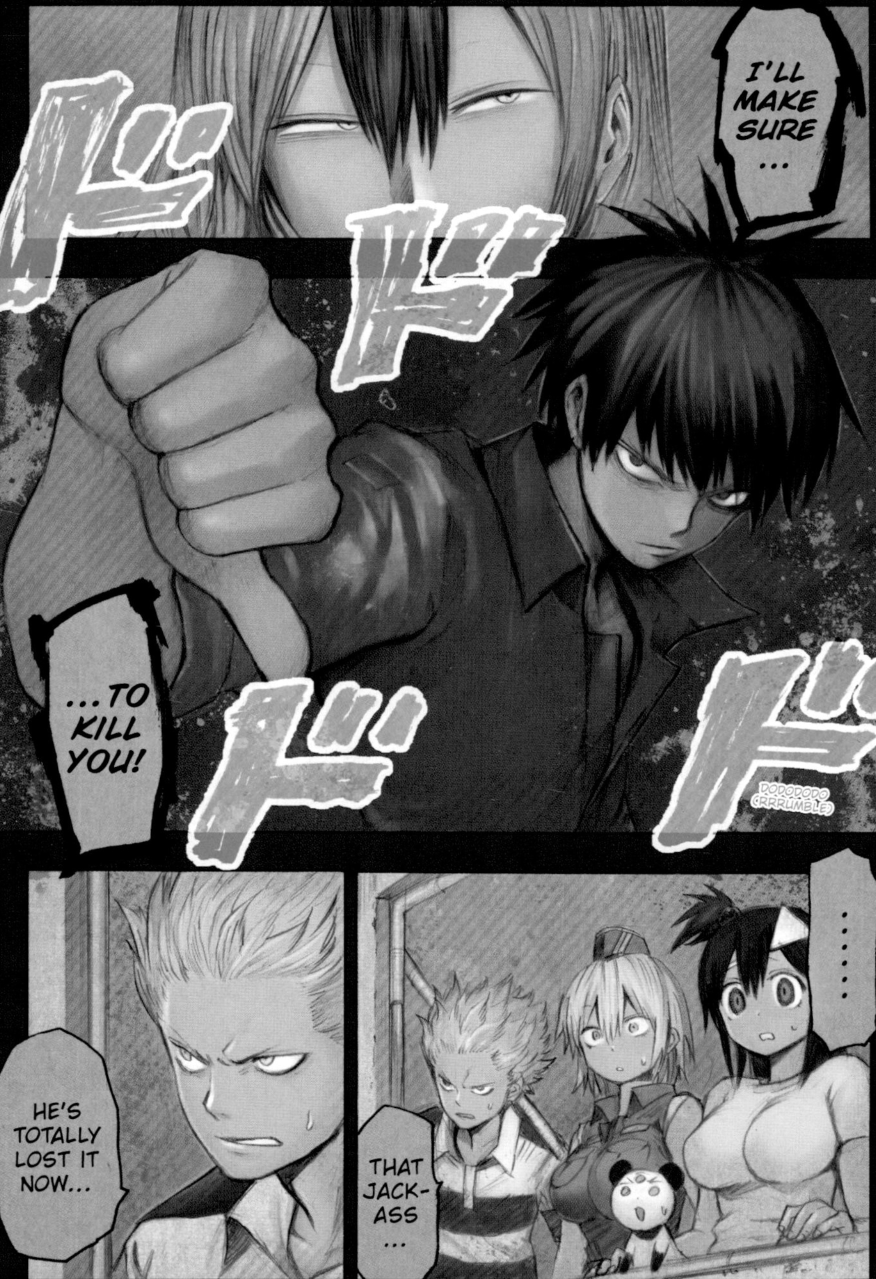
I'LL MAKE SURE...
...TO KILL YOU!
DODODODO (RRRUMBLE)
......
THAT JACK-ASS...
HE'S TOTALLY LOST IT NOW...

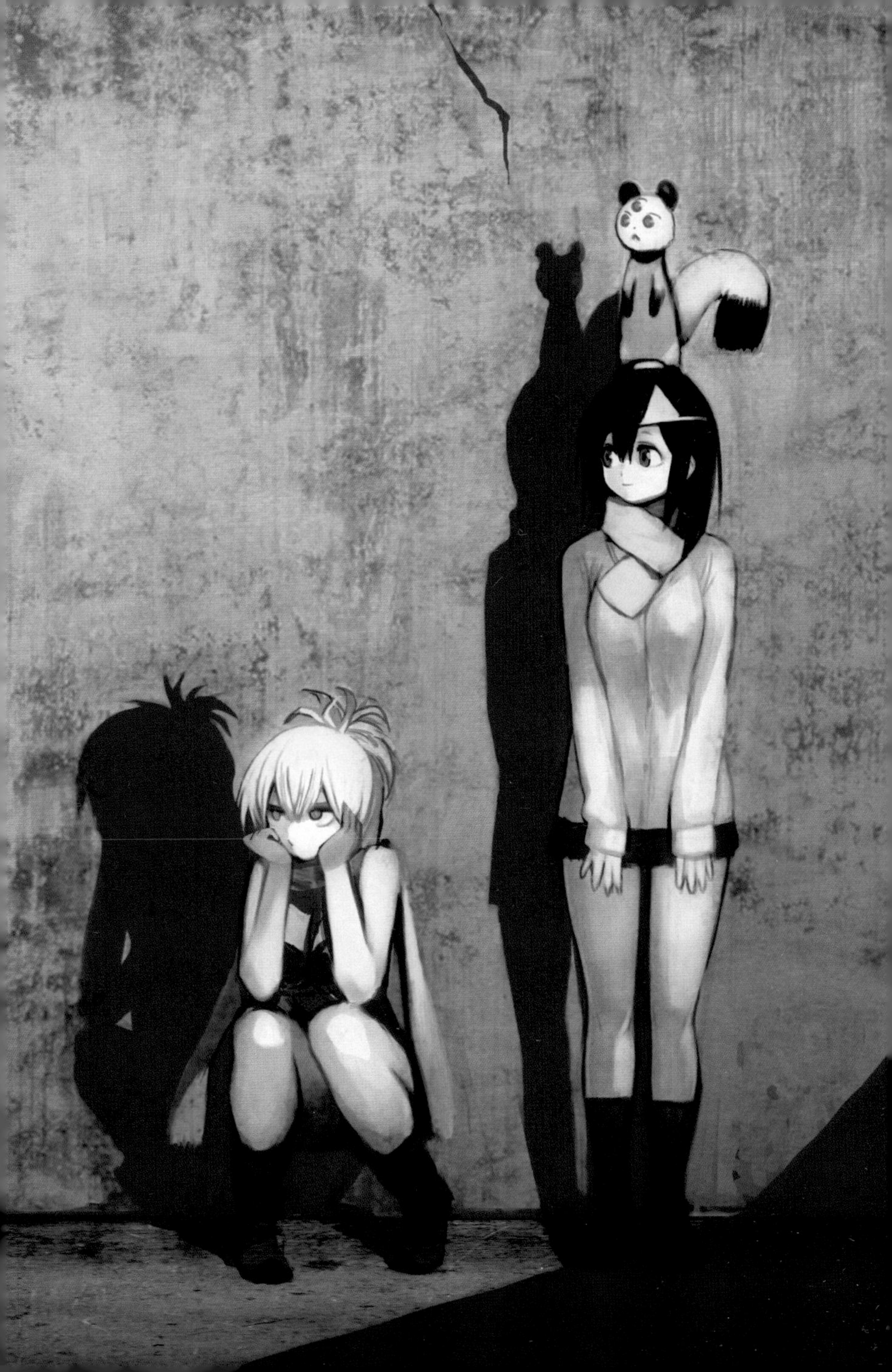

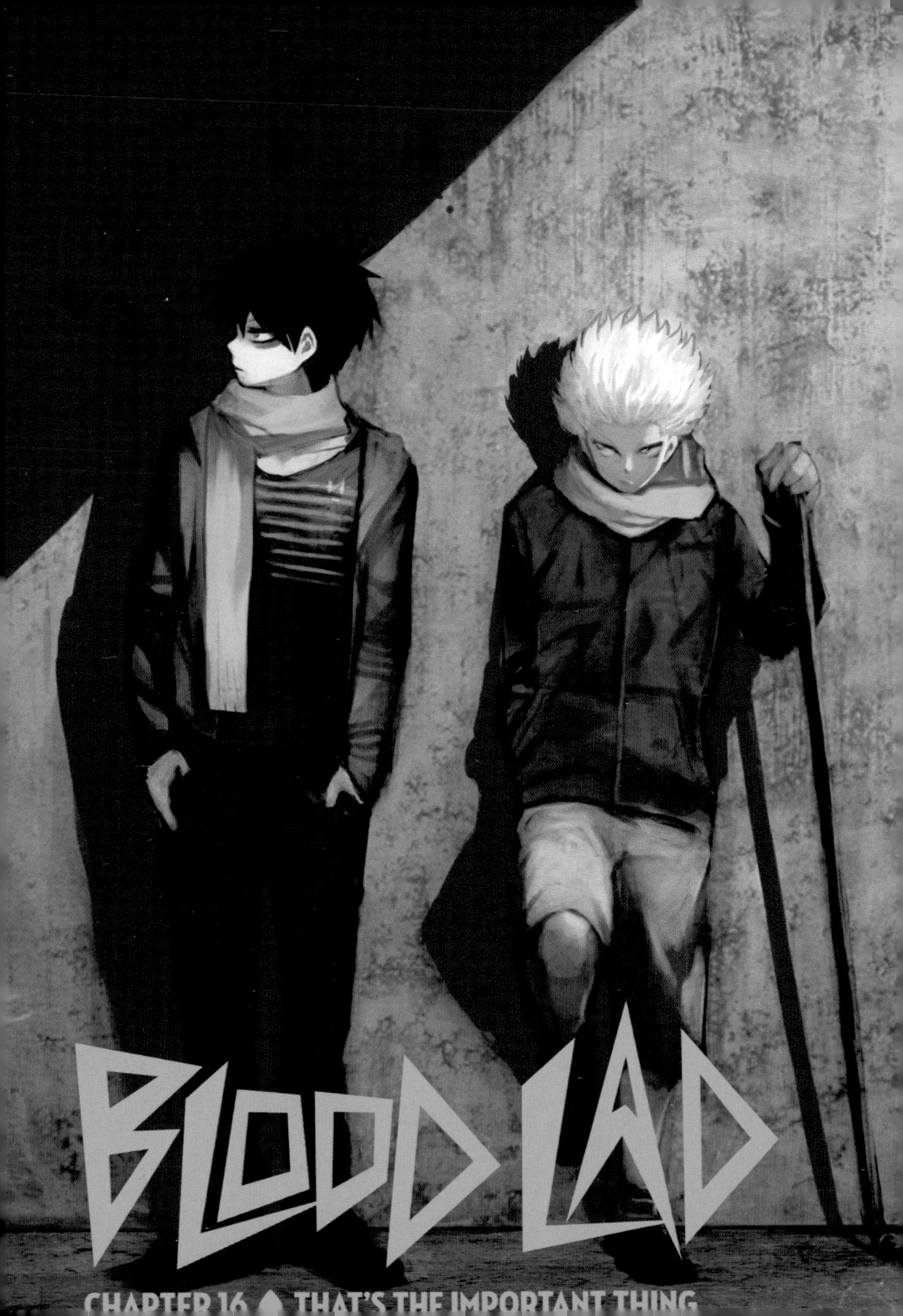
BLOOD LAD
CHAPTER 16 ♠ THAT'S THE IMPORTANT THING

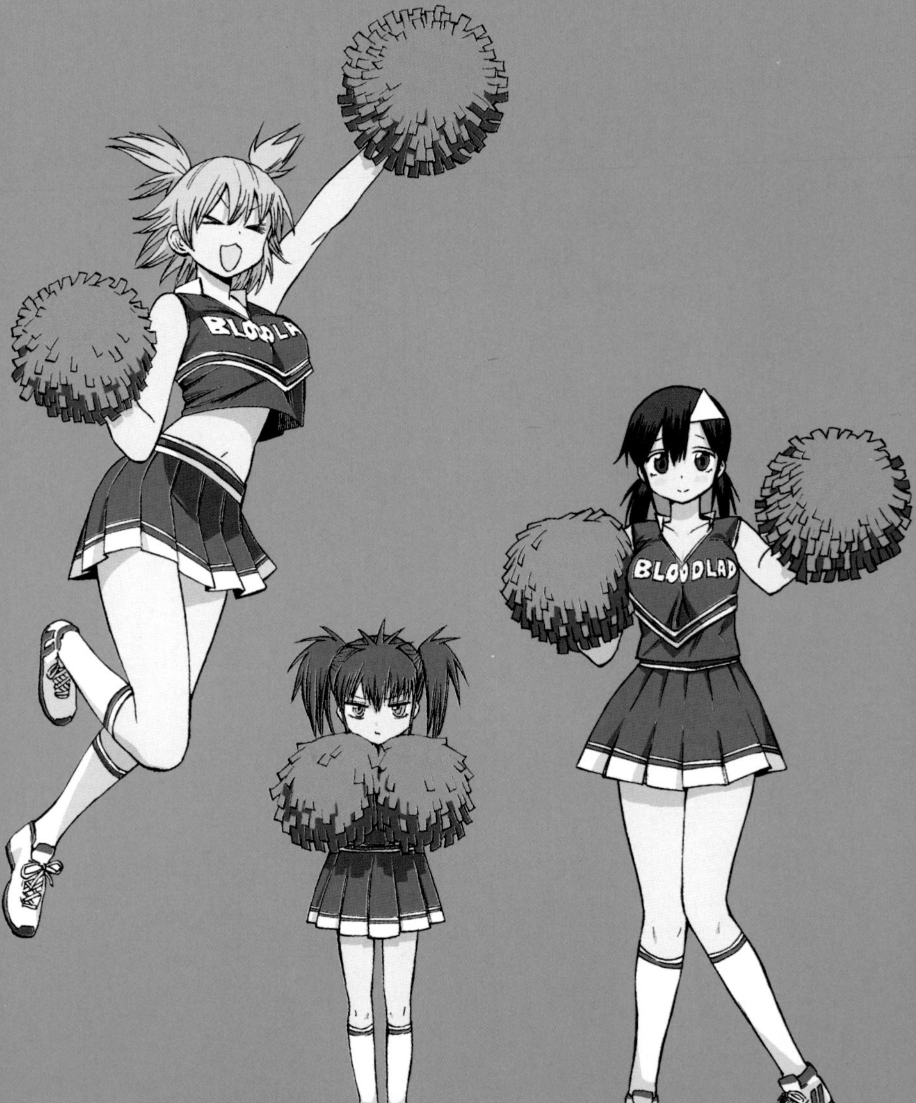
BLOODLAD
BLOODLA

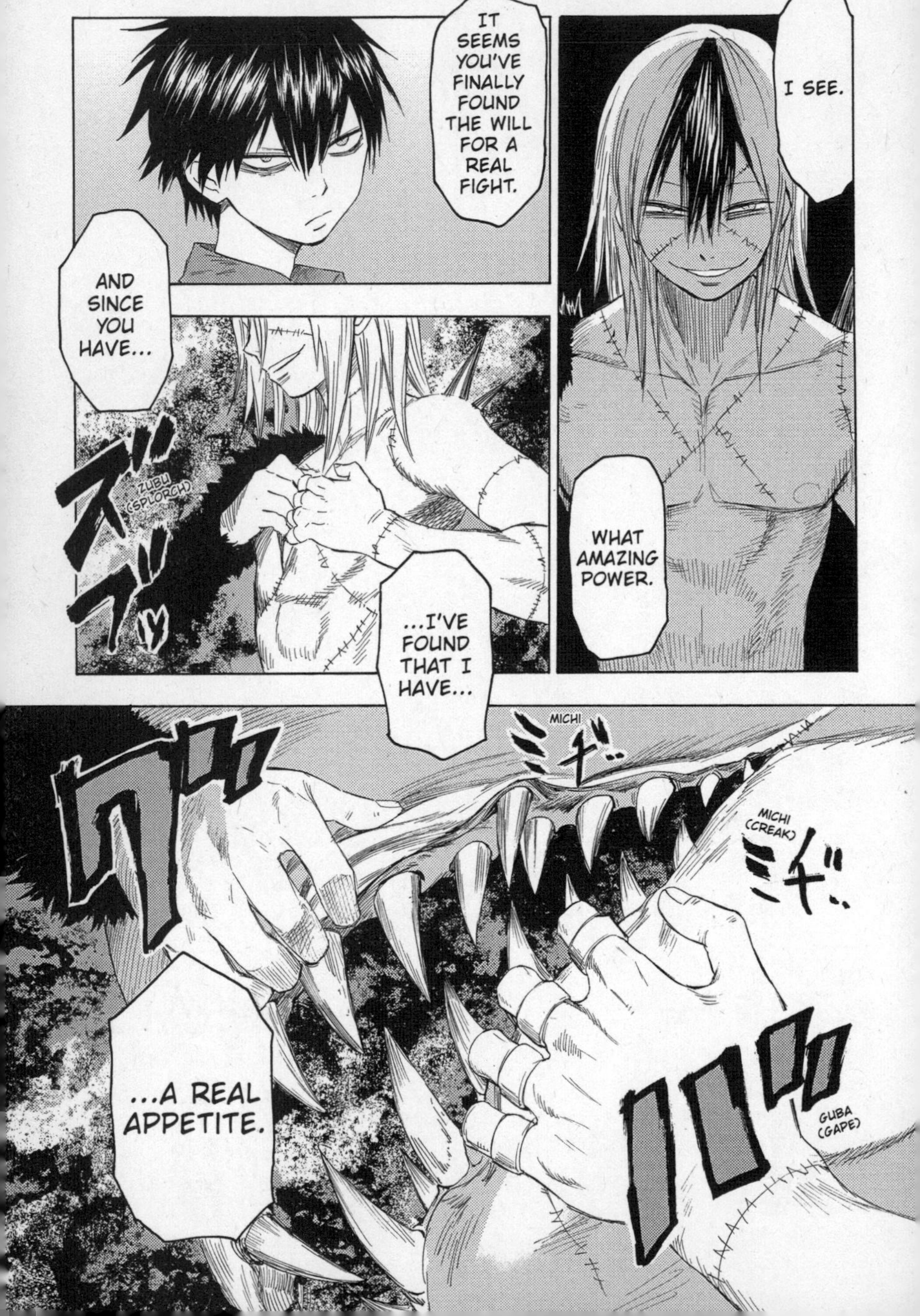
I SEE.
WHAT AMAZING POWER.
IT SEEMS YOU'VE FINALLY FOUND THE WILL FOR A REAL FIGHT.
AND SINCE YOU HAVE...
ZUBU (SPLORCH)
...I'VE FOUND THAT I HAVE...
MICHI
MICHI (CREAK)
GUBA (GAPE)
...A REAL APPETITE.

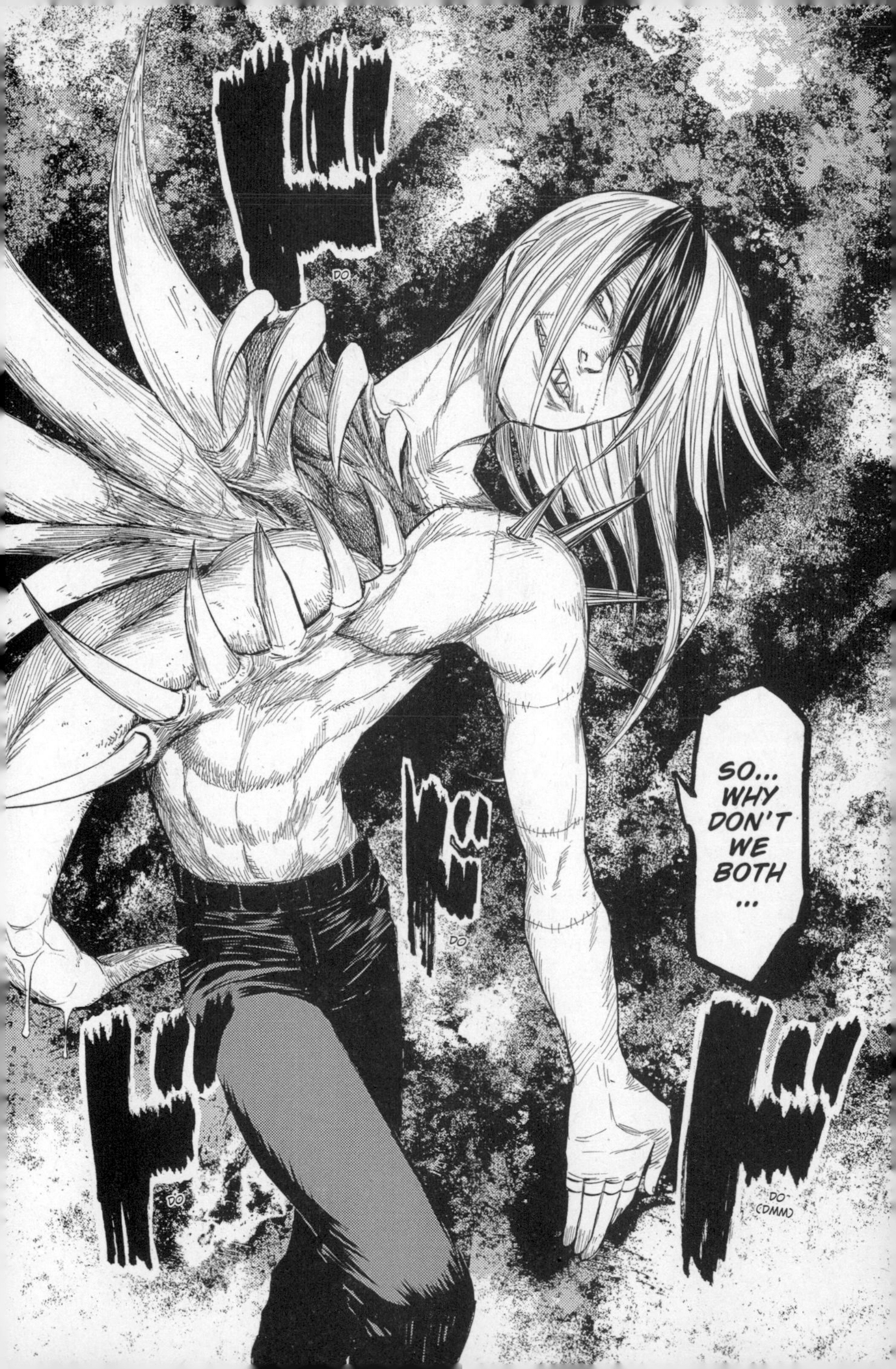
DO
SO... WHY DON'T WE BOTH ...
DO
DO (DMM)
DO

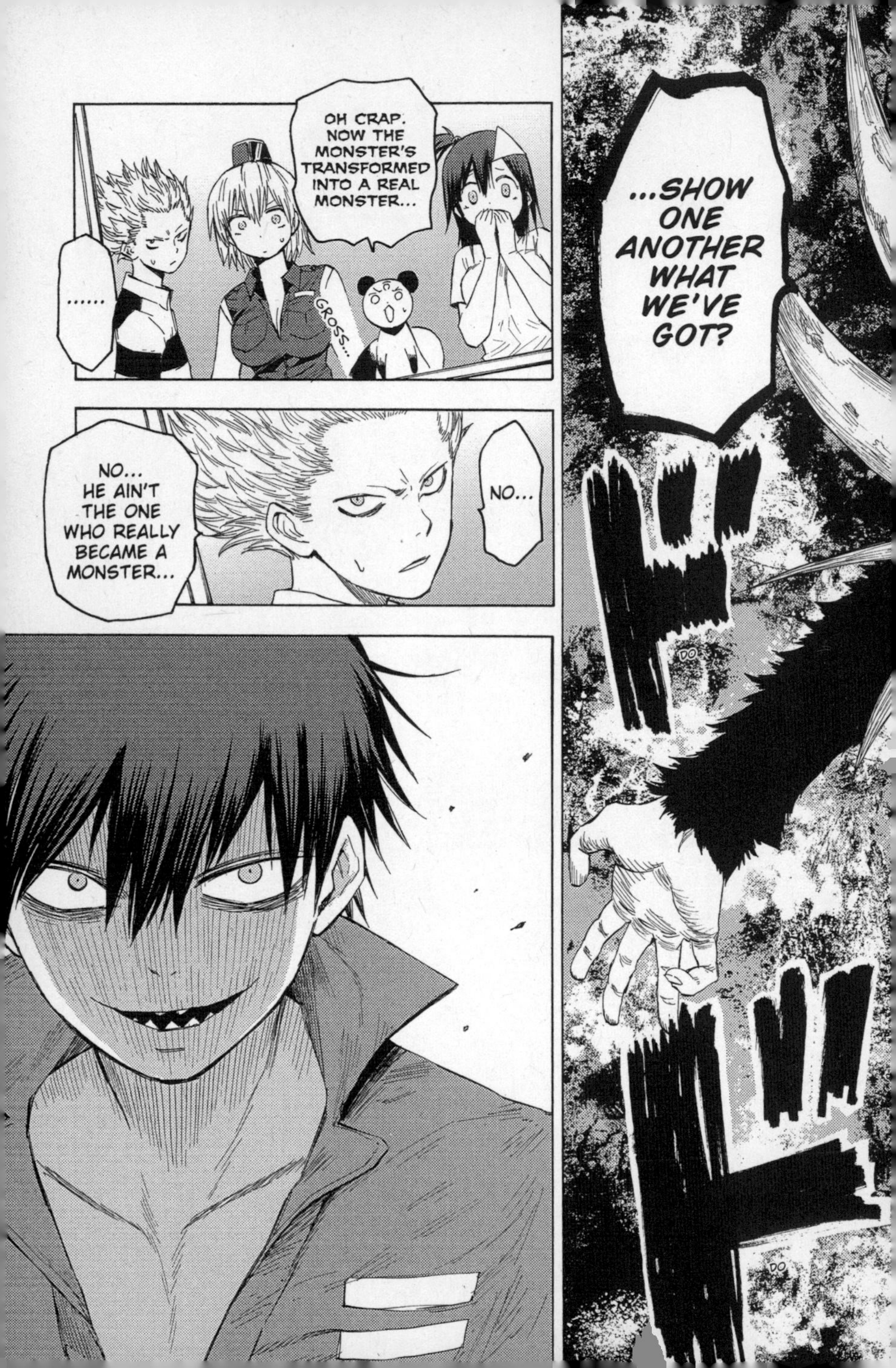
...SHOW ONE ANOTHER WHAT WE'VE GOT?
DO
DO
OH CRAP. NOW THE MONSTER'S TRANSFORMED INTO A REAL MONSTER...
GROSS...
......
NO...
NO... HE AIN'T THE ONE WHO REALLY BECAME A MONSTER...

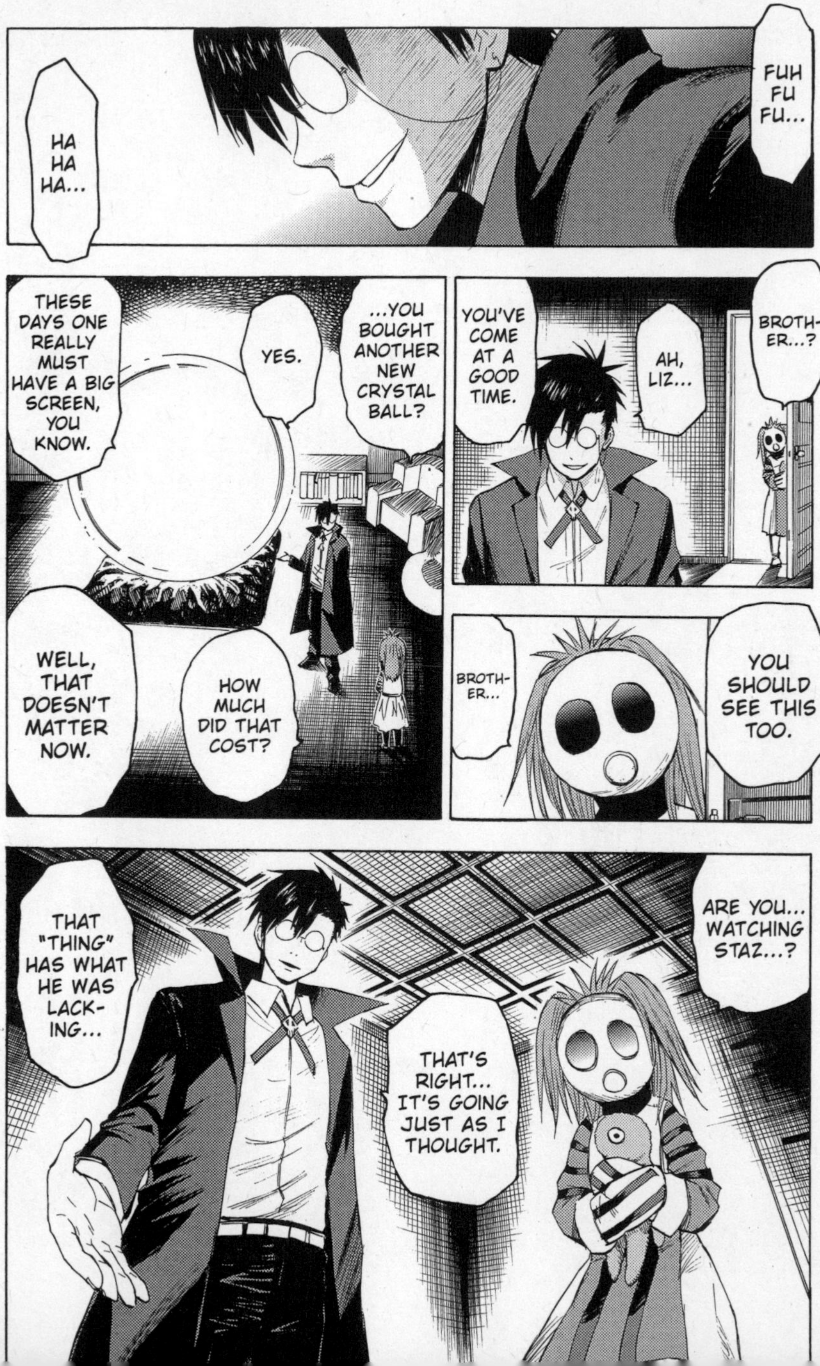
FUH FU FU...
HA HA HA...
BROTHER...?
AH, LIZ...
YOU'VE COME AT A GOOD TIME.
YOU SHOULD SEE THIS TOO.
BROTHER...
...YOU BOUGHT ANOTHER NEW CRYSTAL BALL?
YES.
THESE DAYS ONE REALLY MUST HAVE A BIG SCREEN, YOU KNOW.
HOW MUCH DID THAT COST?
WELL, THAT DOESN'T MATTER NOW.
ARE YOU... WATCHING STAZ...?
THAT'S RIGHT... IT'S GOING JUST AS I THOUGHT.
THAT "THING" HAS WHAT HE WAS LACKING...

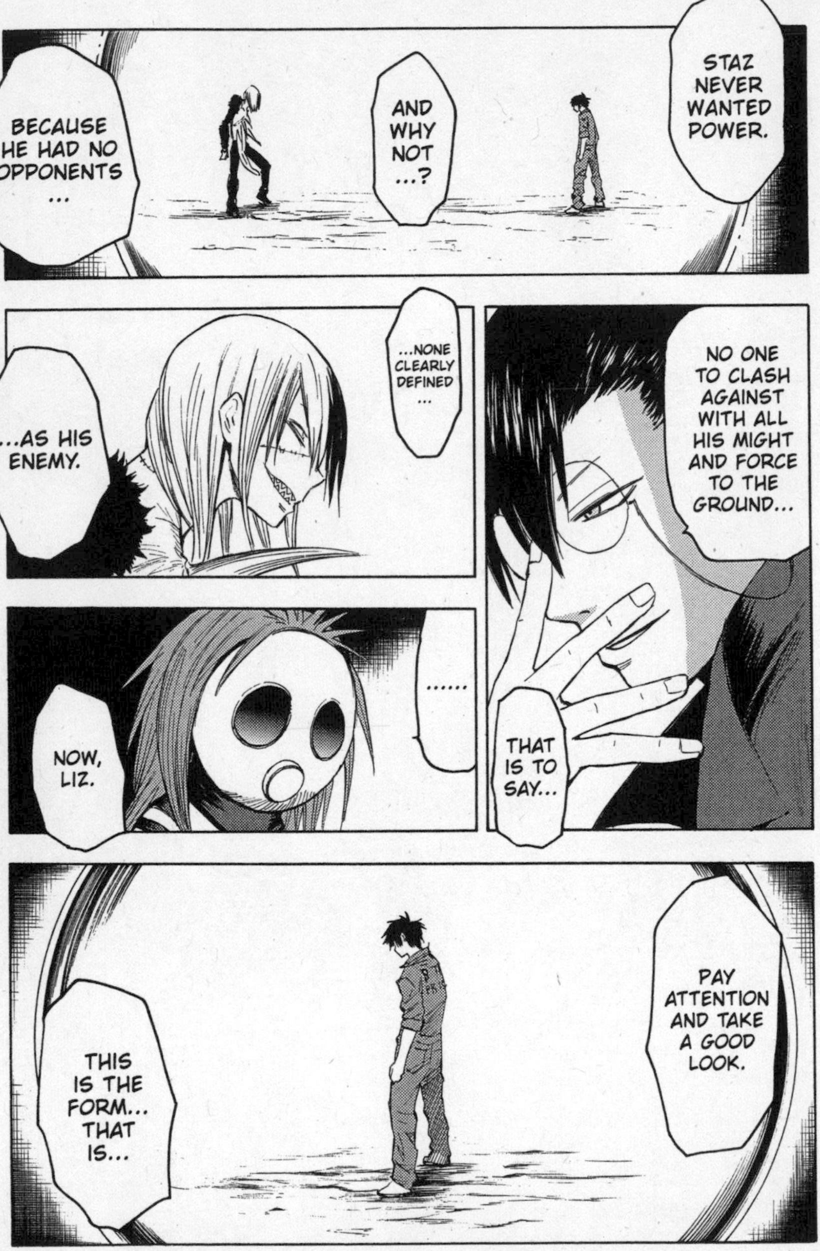
STAZ NEVER WANTED POWER.
AND WHY NOT...?
BECAUSE HE HAD NO OPPONENTS...
NO ONE TO CLASH AGAINST WITH ALL HIS MIGHT AND FORCE TO THE GROUND...
THAT IS TO SAY...
...NONE CLEARLY DEFINED...
...AS HIS ENEMY.
......
NOW, LIZ.
PAY ATTENTION AND TAKE A GOOD LOOK.
THIS IS THE FORM... THAT IS...

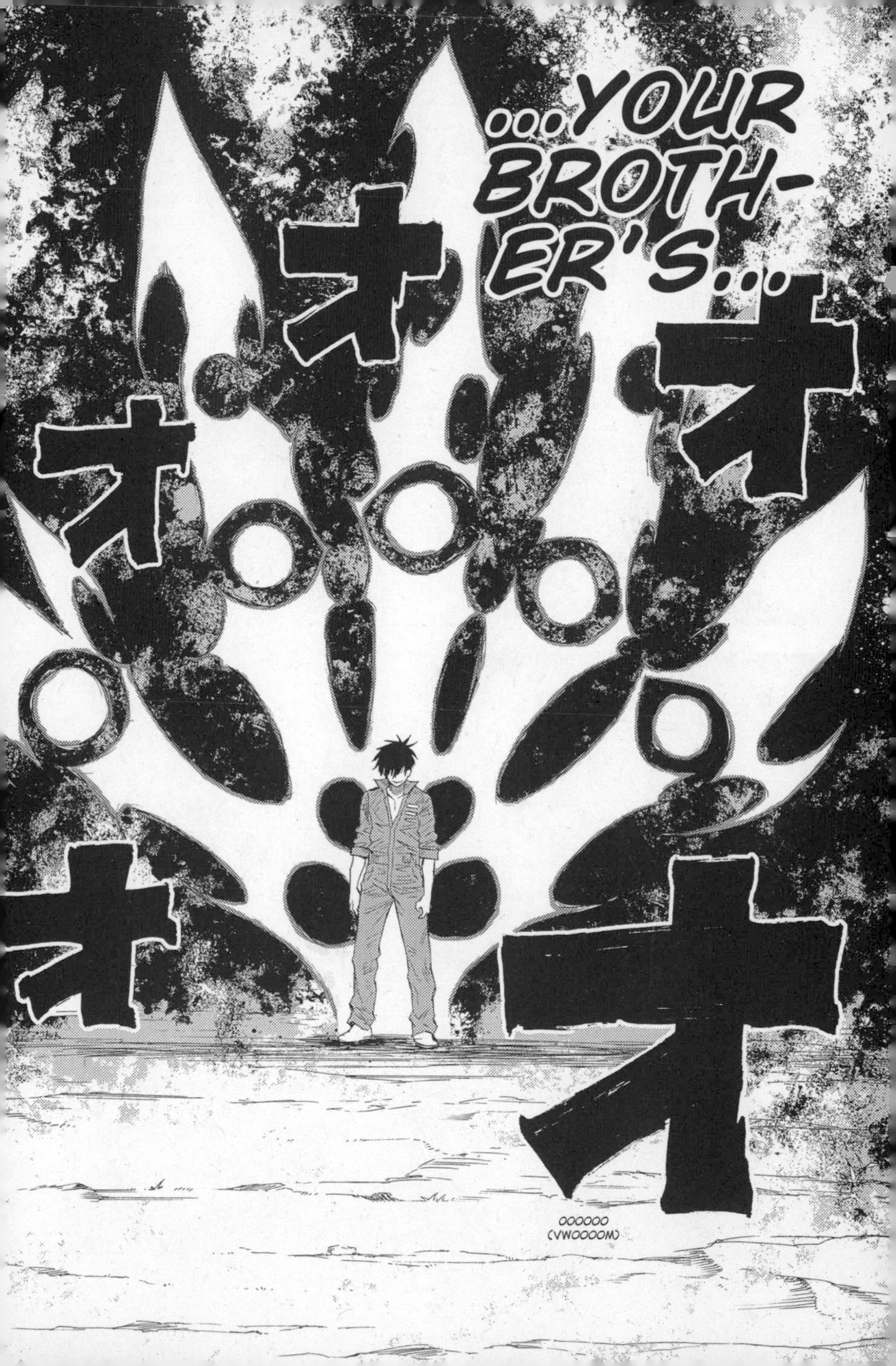
...YOUR BROTHER'S...
オオオオオオ
OOOOOO (VWOOOOM)

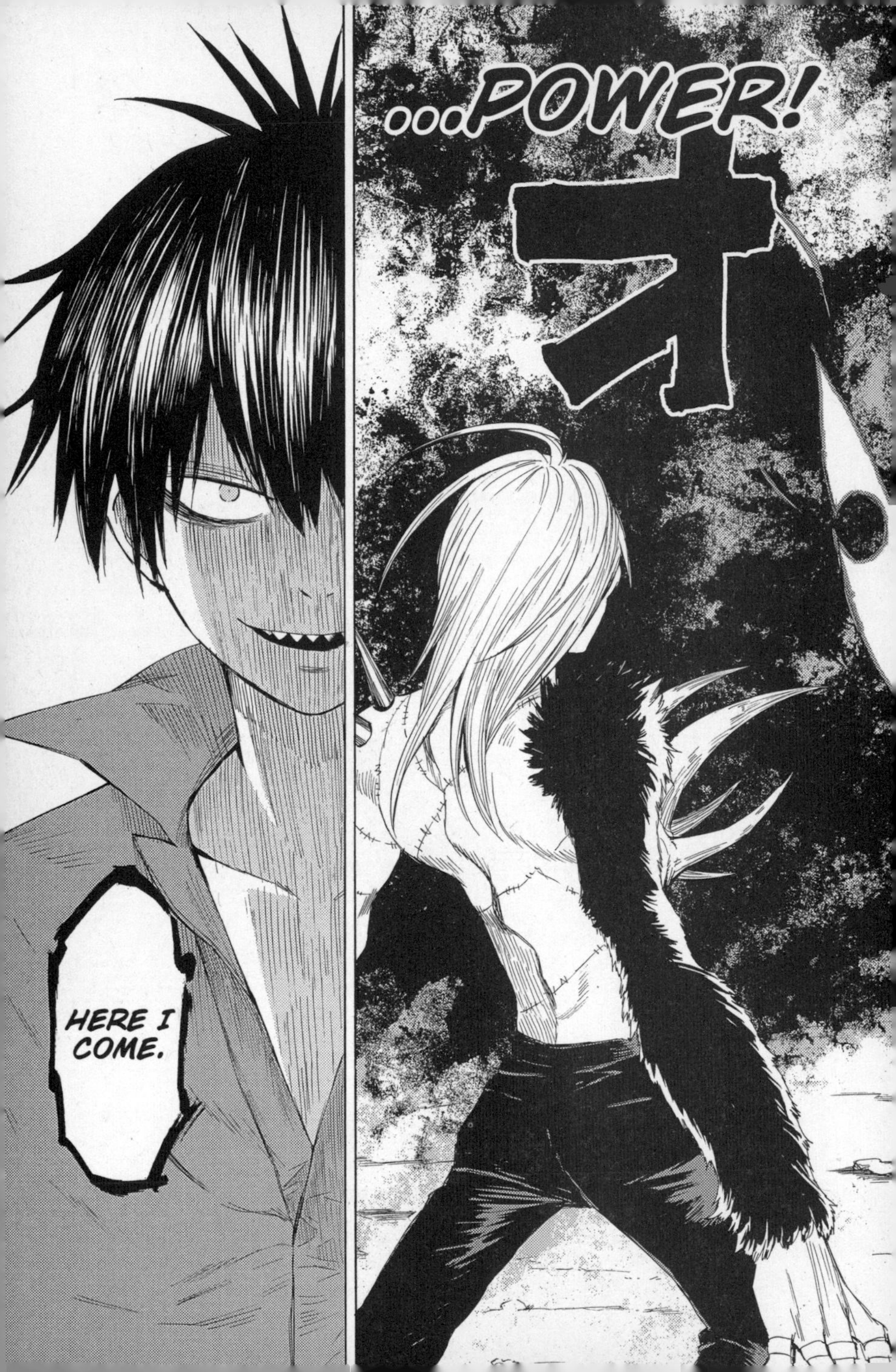
...POWER!
オ
HERE I COME.

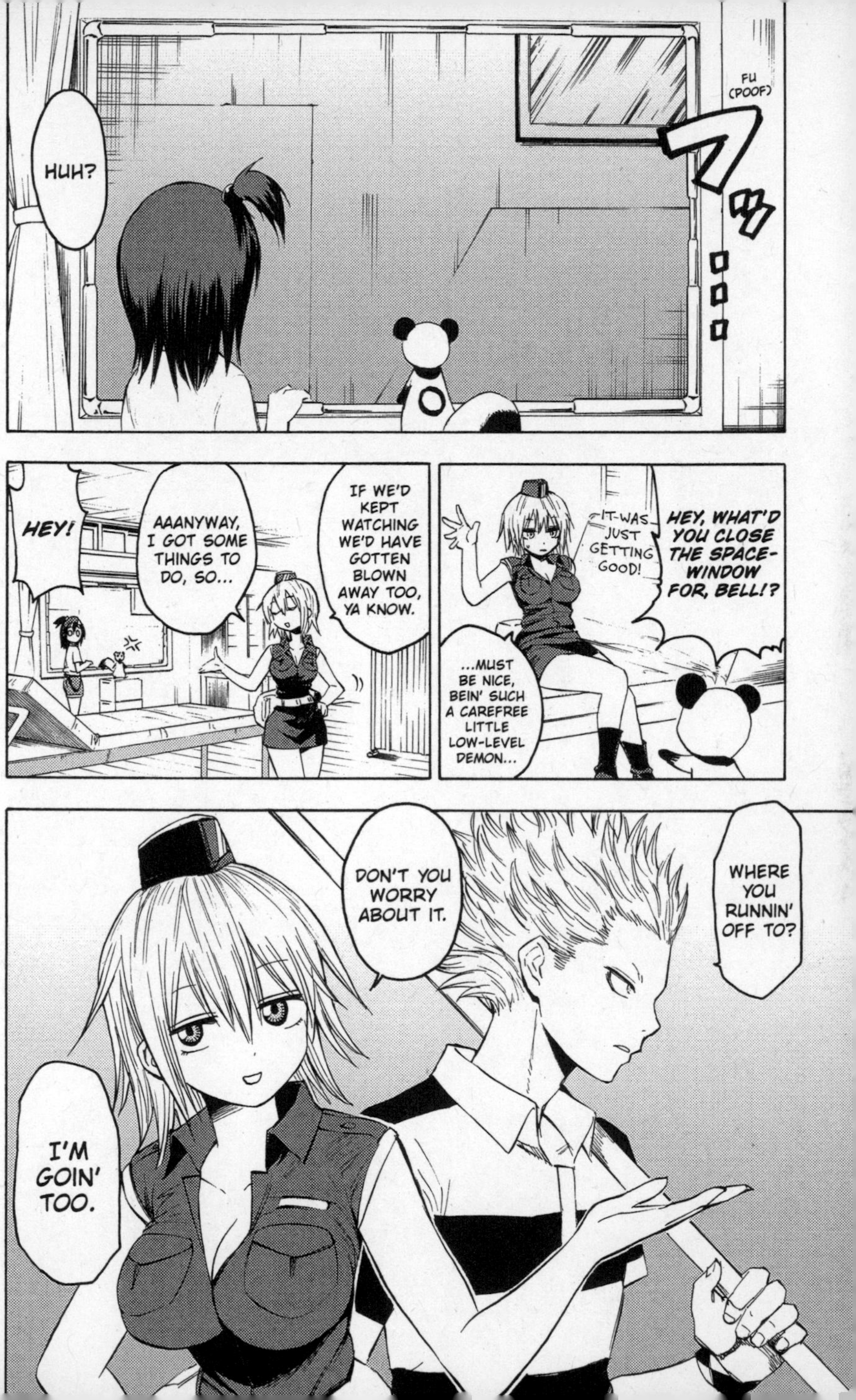
FU (POOF)
HUH?
HEY, WHAT'D YOU CLOSE THE SPACE-WINDOW FOR, BELL!?
IT WAS JUST GETTING GOOD!
...MUST BE NICE, BEIN' SUCH A CAREFREE LITTLE LOW-LEVEL DEMON...
IF WE'D KEPT WATCHING WE'D HAVE GOTTEN BLOWN AWAY TOO, YA KNOW.
AAANYWAY, I GOT SOME THINGS TO DO, SO...
HEY!
WHERE YOU RUNNIN' OFF TO?
DON'T YOU WORRY ABOUT IT.
I'M GOIN' TOO.

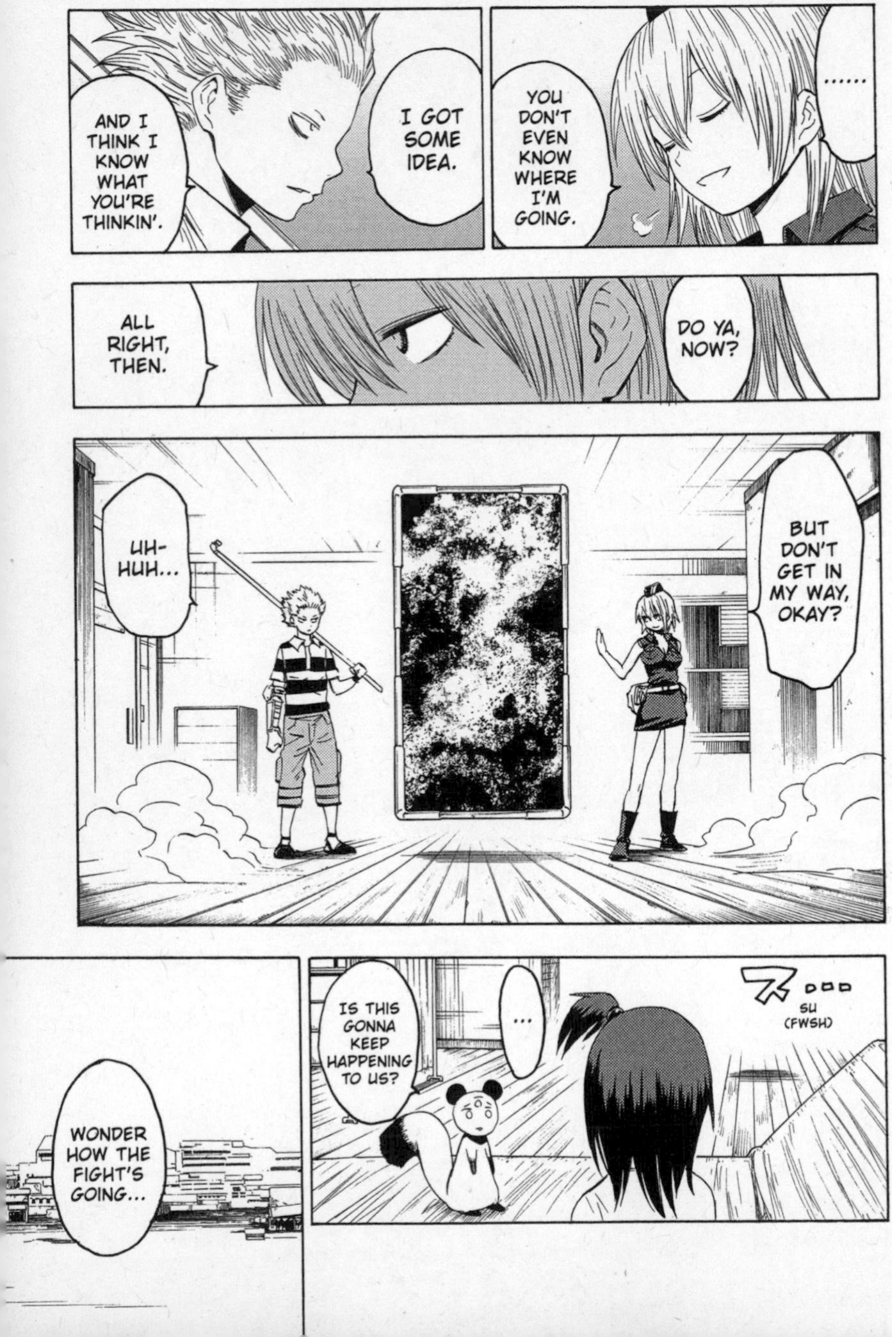
......
YOU DON'T EVEN KNOW WHERE I'M GOING.
I GOT SOME IDEA.
AND I THINK I KNOW WHAT YOU'RE THINKIN'.
DO YA, NOW?
ALL RIGHT, THEN.
BUT DON'T GET IN MY WAY, OKAY?
UH-HUH...
SU (FWSH)
...
IS THIS GONNA KEEP HAPPENING TO US?
WONDER HOW THE FIGHT'S GOING...

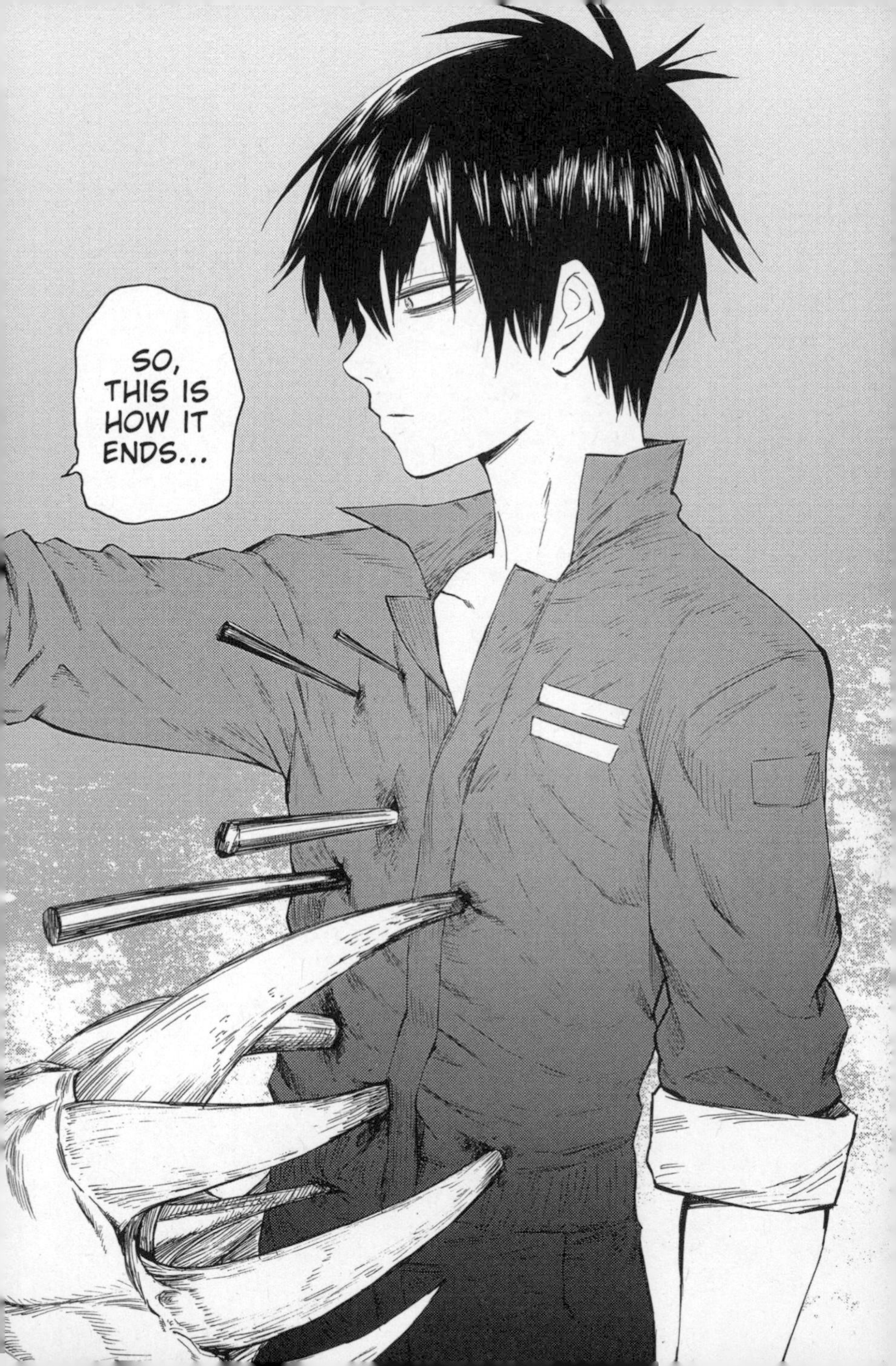
SO, THIS IS HOW IT ENDS...

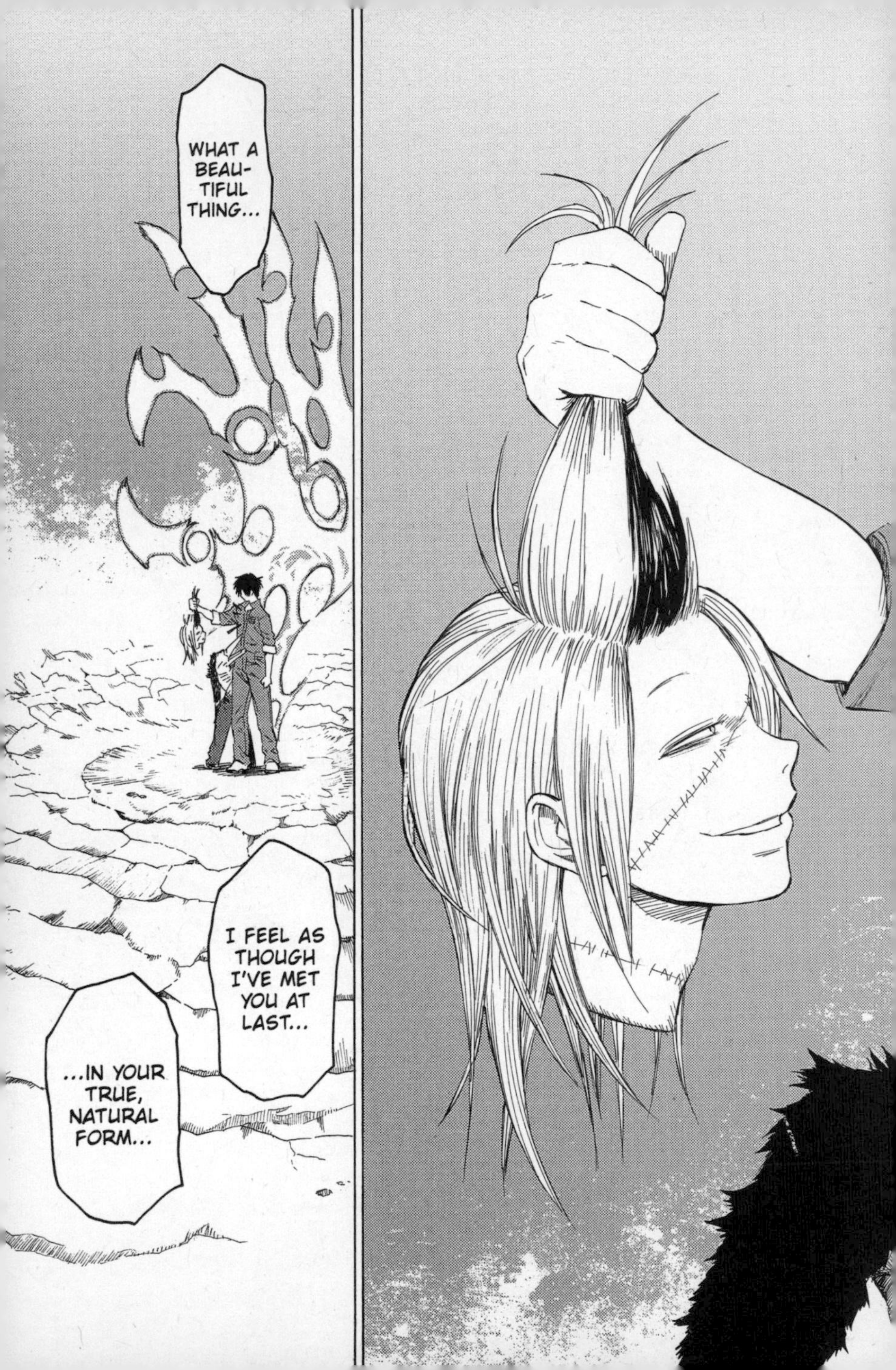
WHAT A BEAU-TIFUL THING...
I FEEL AS THOUGH I'VE MET YOU AT LAST...
...IN YOUR TRUE, NATURAL FORM...

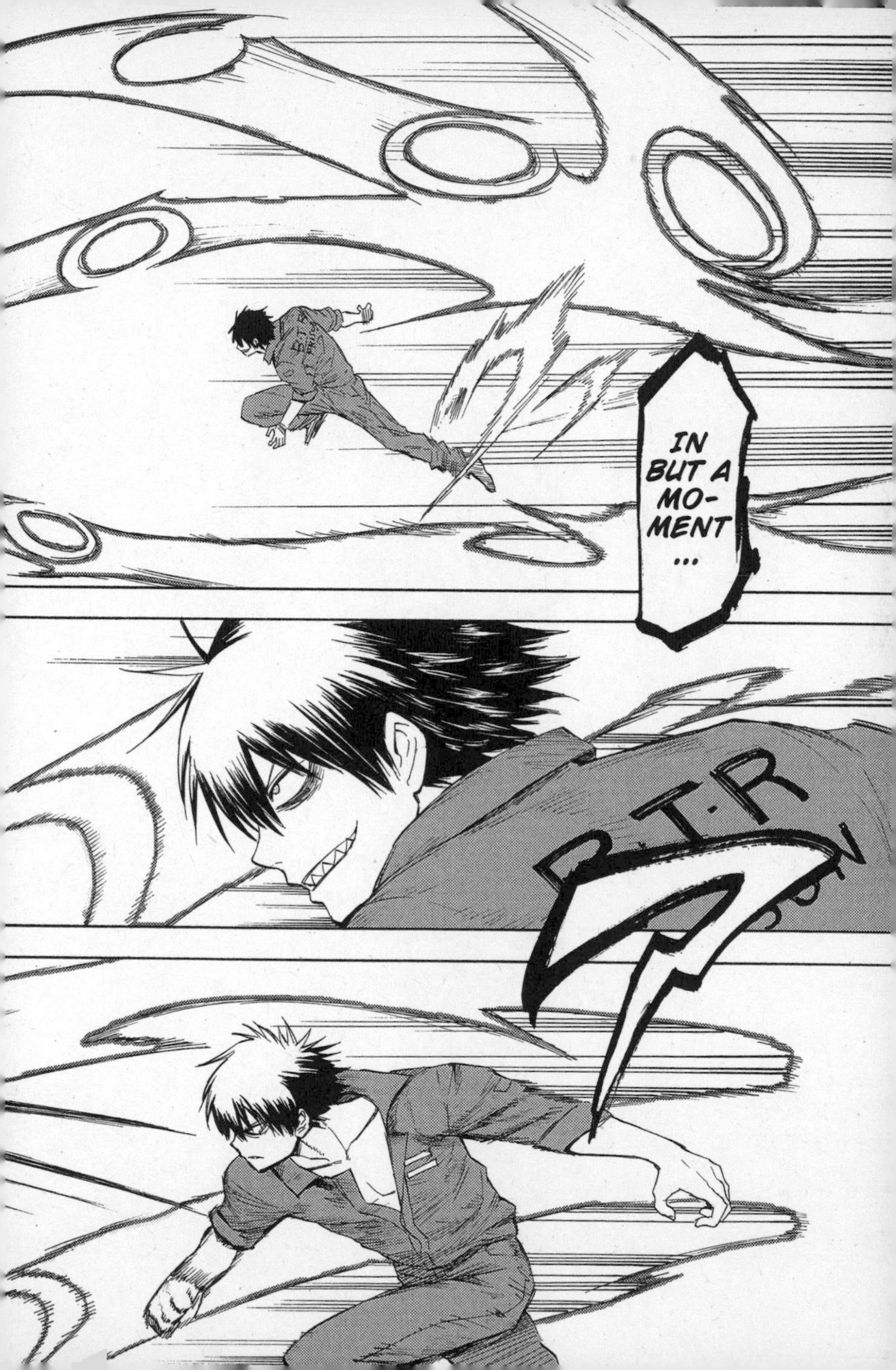
IN BUT A MO-MENT ...

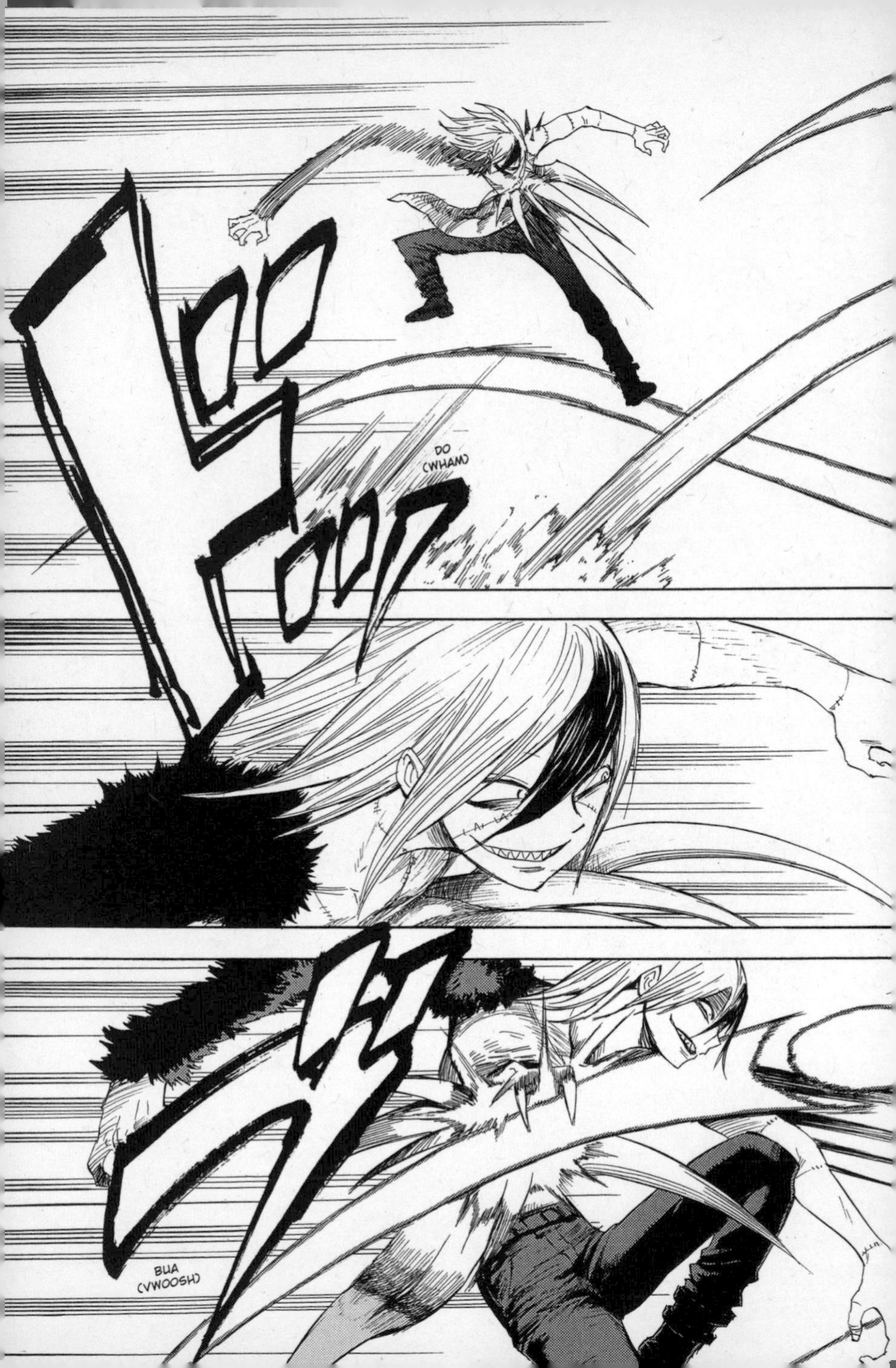
DO
(WHAM)
BUA
(VWOOSH)

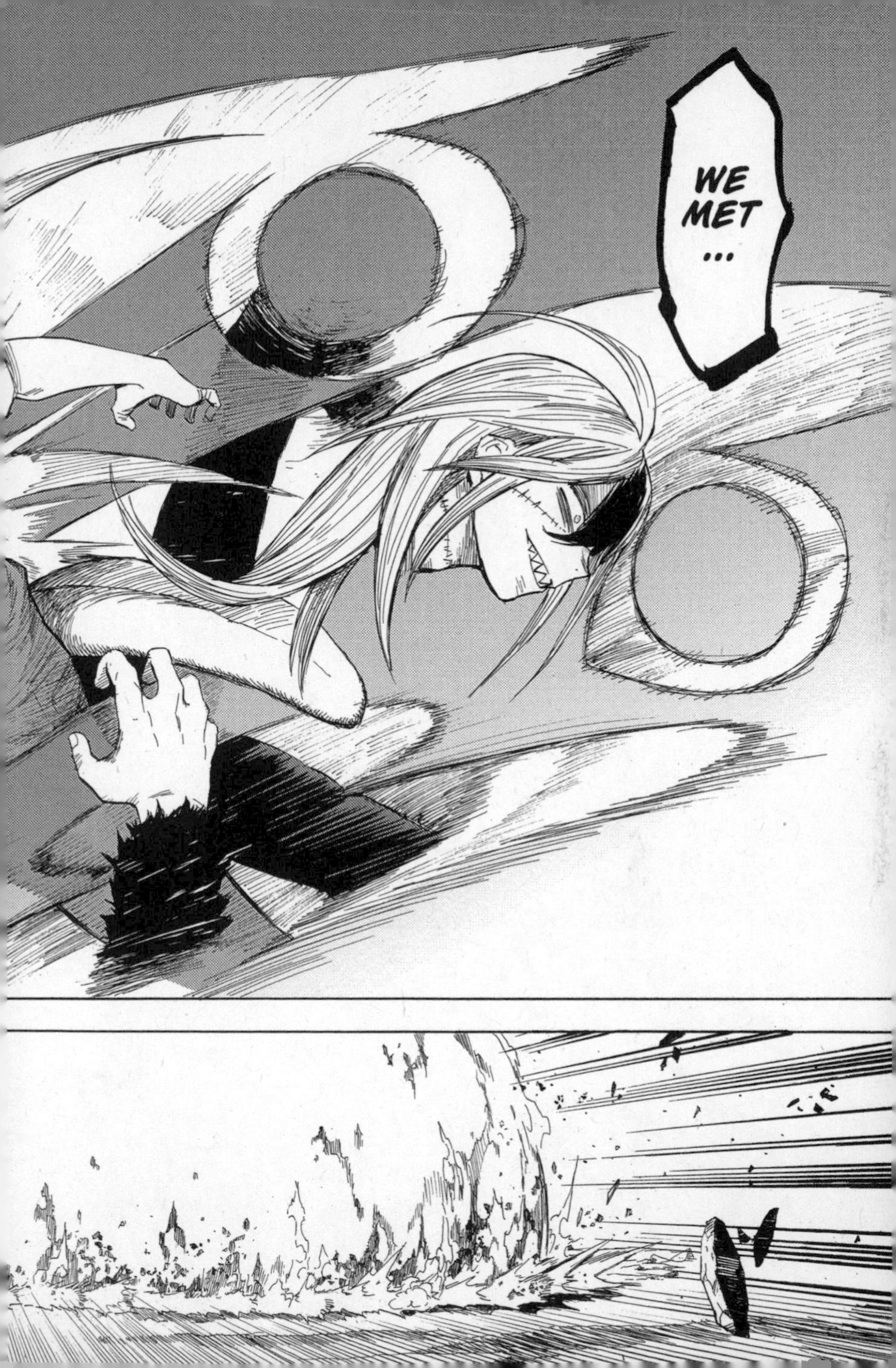
WE MET ...

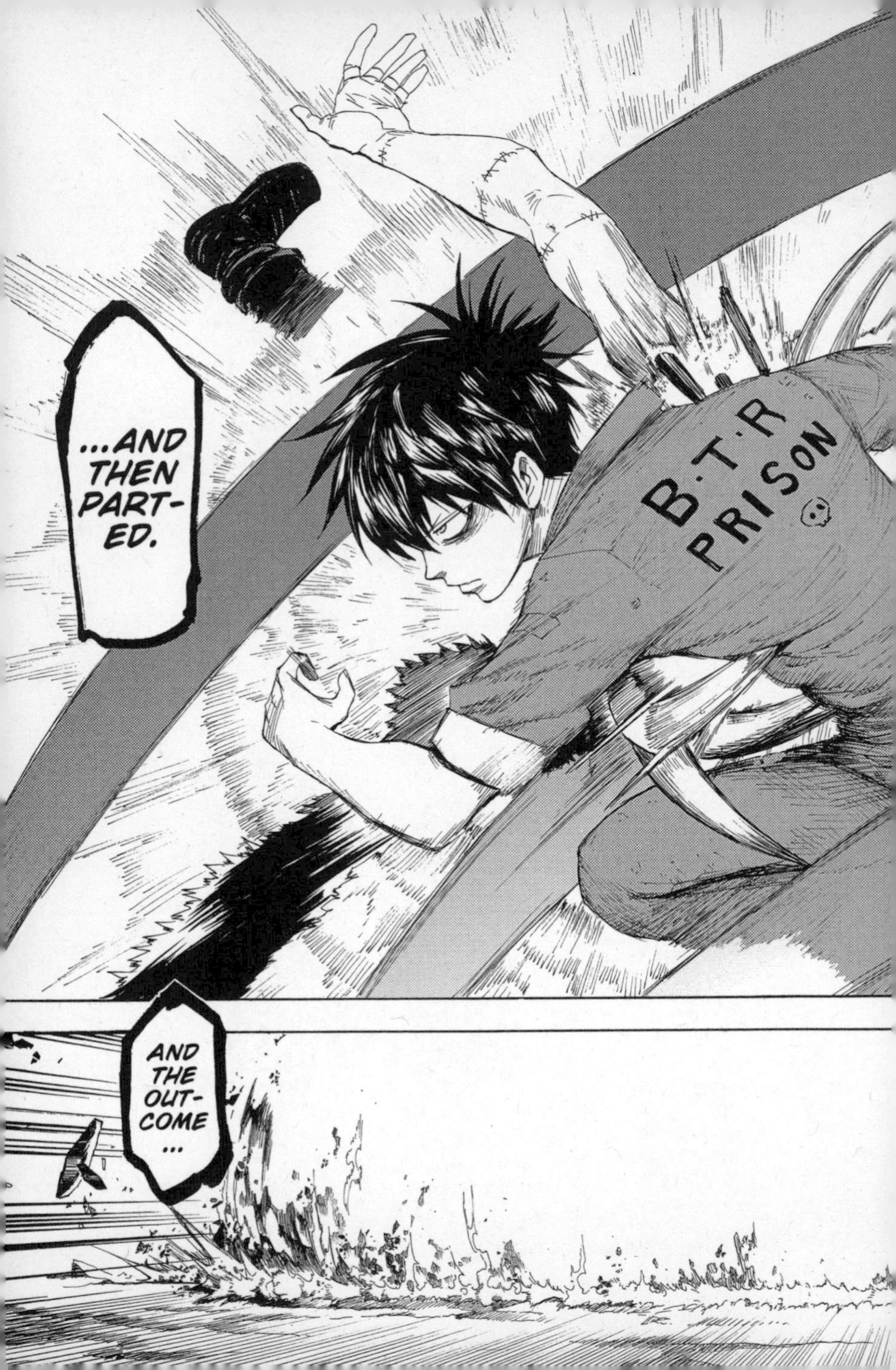
...AND THEN PART-ED.
B.T.R PRISON
AND THE OUT-COME ...

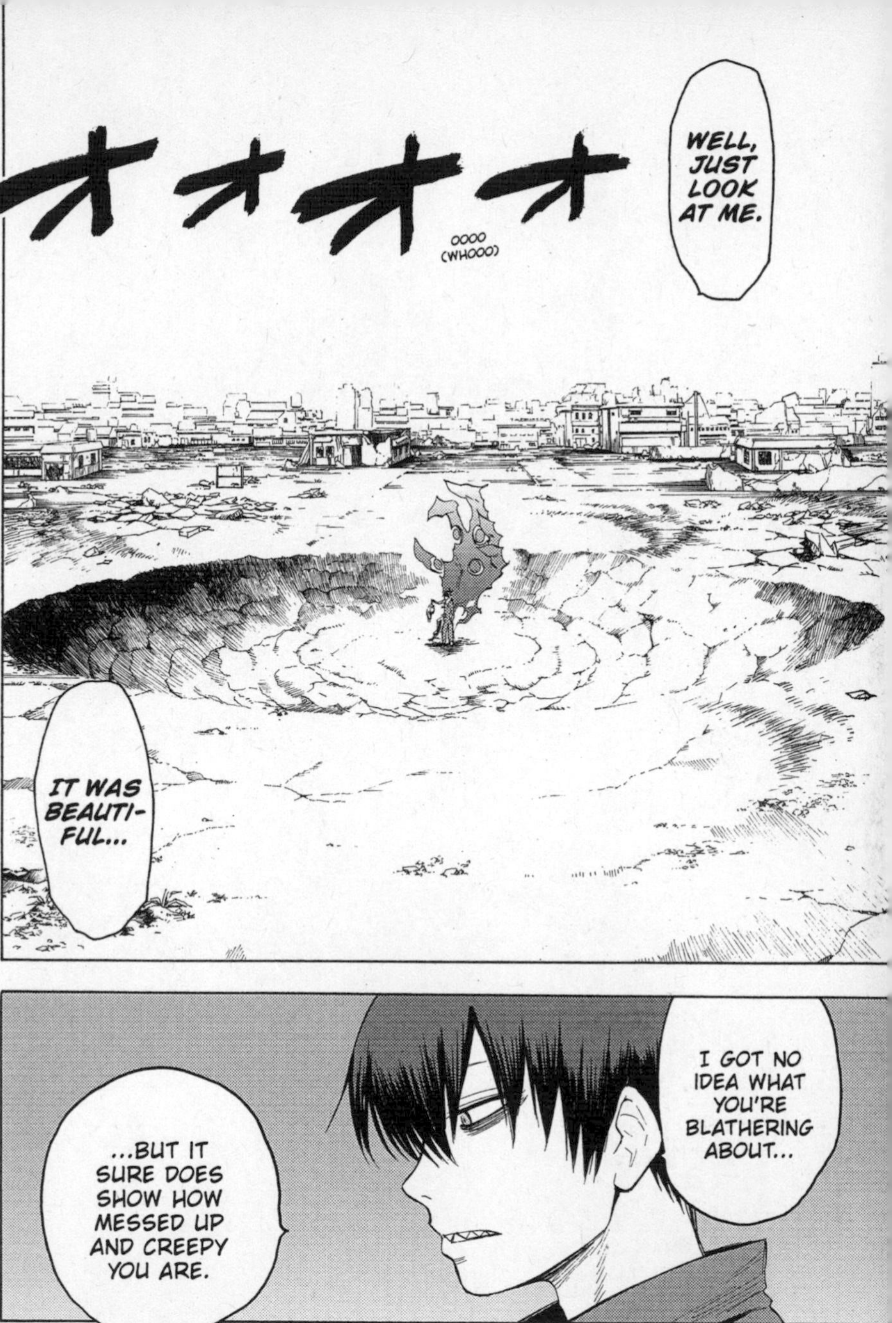
WELL, JUST LOOK AT ME.
オオオオ
OOOO (WHOOO)
IT WAS BEAUTI-FUL...
I GOT NO IDEA WHAT YOU'RE BLATHERING ABOUT...
...BUT IT SURE DOES SHOW HOW MESSED UP AND CREEPY YOU ARE.

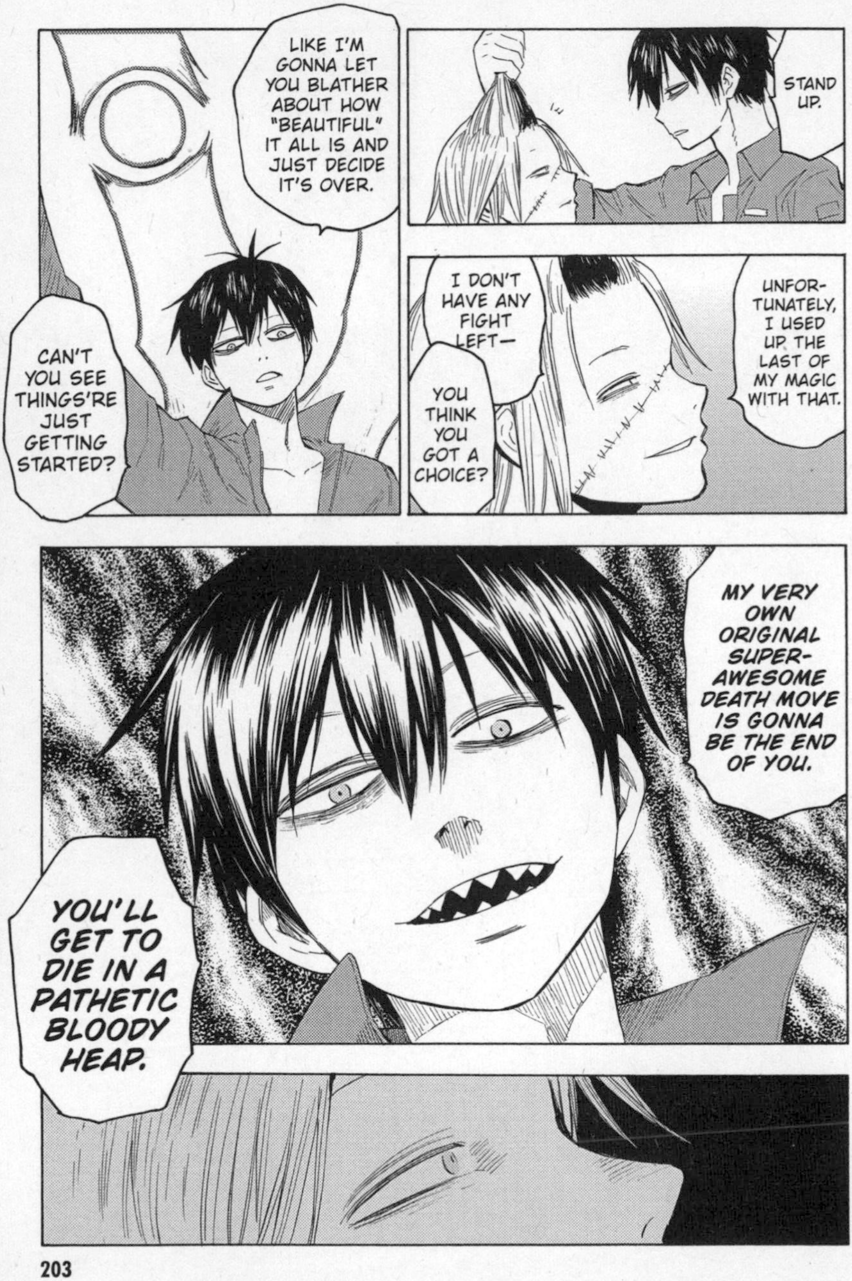
STAND UP.
UNFORTUNATELY, I USED UP THE LAST OF MY MAGIC WITH THAT.
I DON'T HAVE ANY FIGHT LEFT—
YOU THINK YOU GOT A CHOICE?
LIKE I'M GONNA LET YOU BLATHER ABOUT HOW "BEAUTIFUL" IT ALL IS AND JUST DECIDE IT'S OVER.
CAN'T YOU SEE THINGS'RE JUST GETTING STARTED?
MY VERY OWN ORIGINAL SUPER-AWESOME DEATH MOVE IS GONNA BE THE END OF YOU.
YOU'LL GET TO DIE IN A PATHETIC BLOODY HEAP.

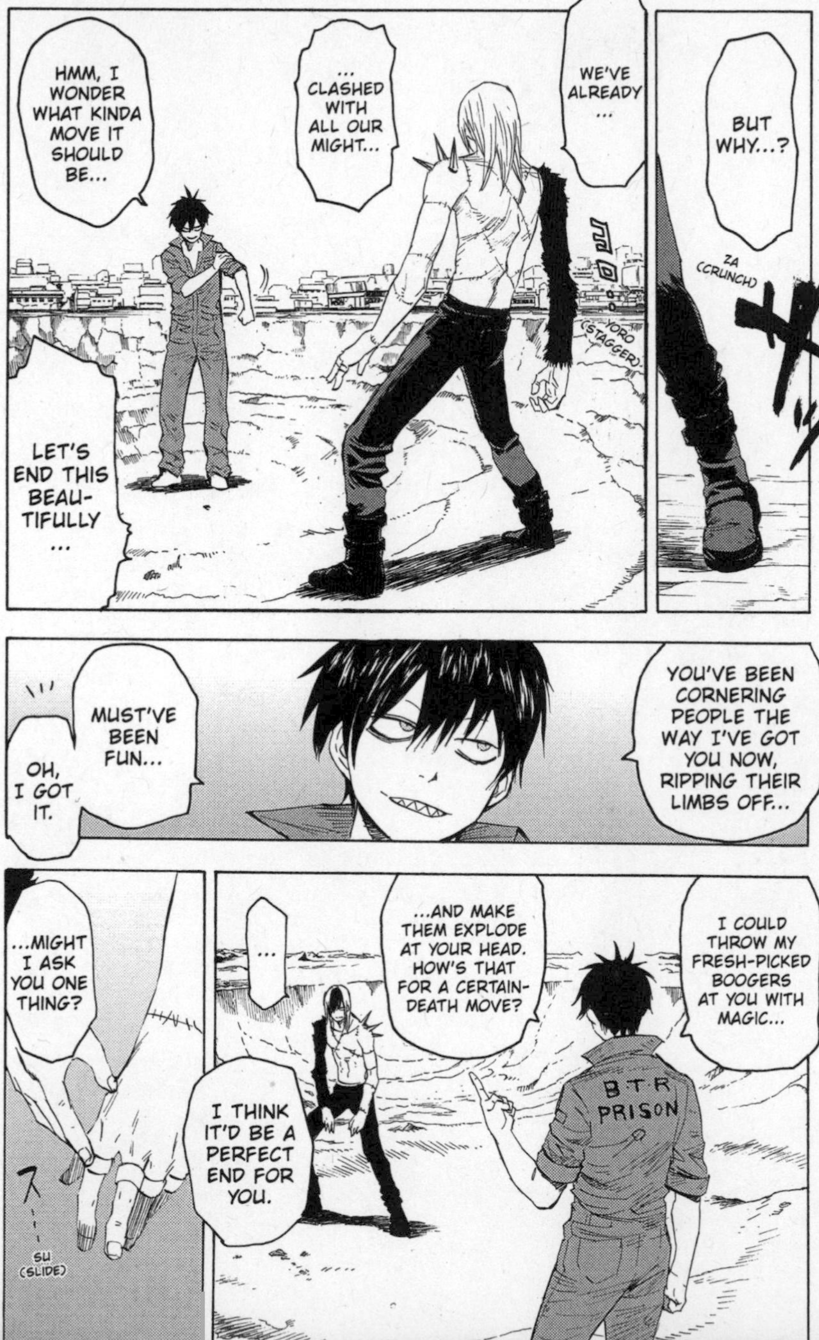
BUT WHY...?
ZA (CRUNCH)
WE'VE ALREADY ...
... CLASHED WITH ALL OUR MIGHT...
YORO (STAGGER)
HMM, I WONDER WHAT KINDA MOVE IT SHOULD BE...
LET'S END THIS BEAU-TIFULLY ...
YOU'VE BEEN CORNERING PEOPLE THE WAY I'VE GOT YOU NOW, RIPPING THEIR LIMBS OFF...
MUST'VE BEEN FUN...
OH, I GOT IT.
I COULD THROW MY FRESH-PICKED BOOGERS AT YOU WITH MAGIC...
...AND MAKE THEM EXPLODE AT YOUR HEAD. HOW'S THAT FOR A CERTAIN-DEATH MOVE?
B·T·R PRISON
...
I THINK IT'D BE A PERFECT END FOR YOU.
...MIGHT I ASK YOU ONE THING?
SU (SLIDE)

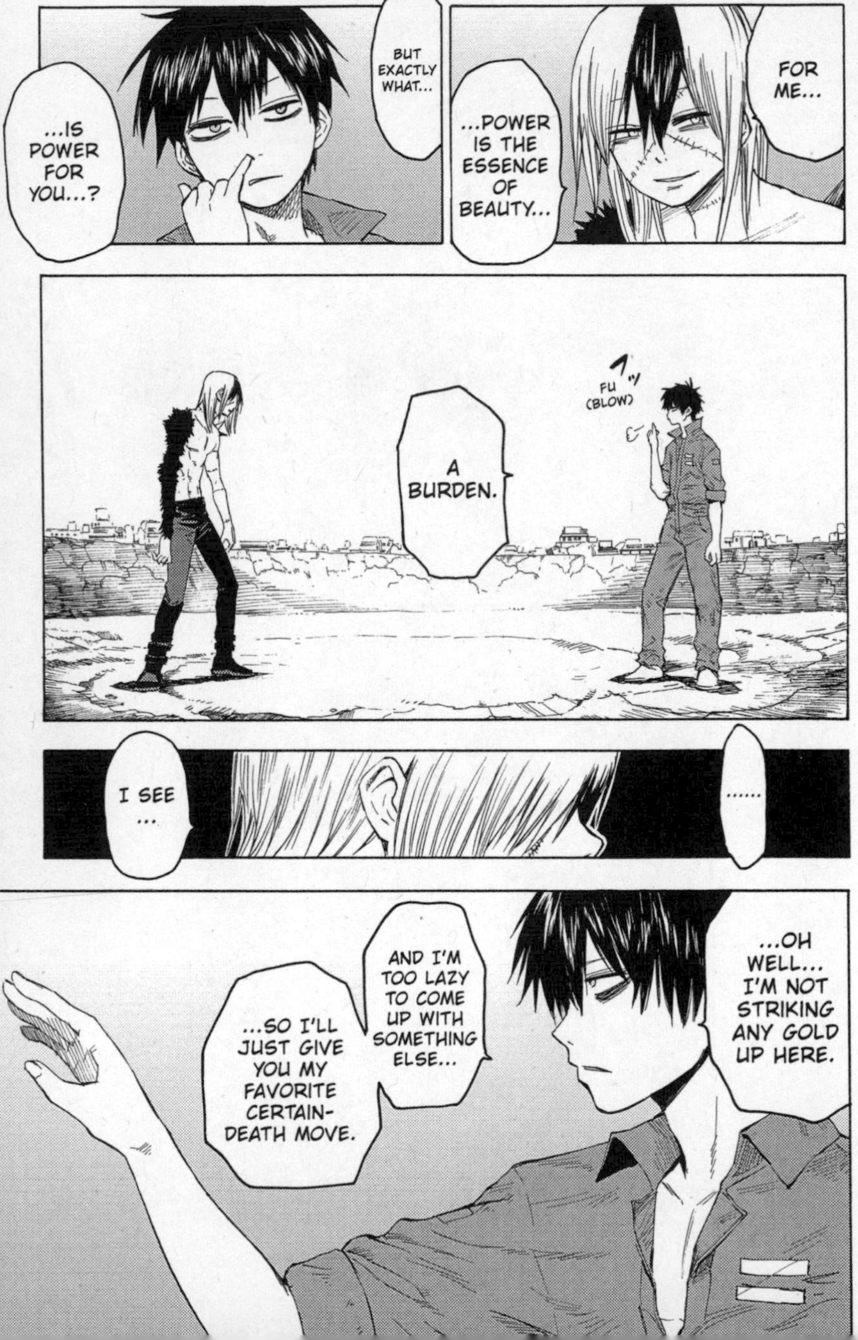
FOR ME...
...POWER IS THE ESSENCE OF BEAUTY...
BUT EXACTLY WHAT...
...IS POWER FOR YOU...?
フッ
FU (BLOW)
A BURDEN.
......
I SEE ...
...OH WELL... I'M NOT STRIKING ANY GOLD UP HERE.
AND I'M TOO LAZY TO COME UP WITH SOMETHING ELSE...
...SO I'LL JUST GIVE YOU MY FAVORITE CERTAIN-DEATH MOVE.

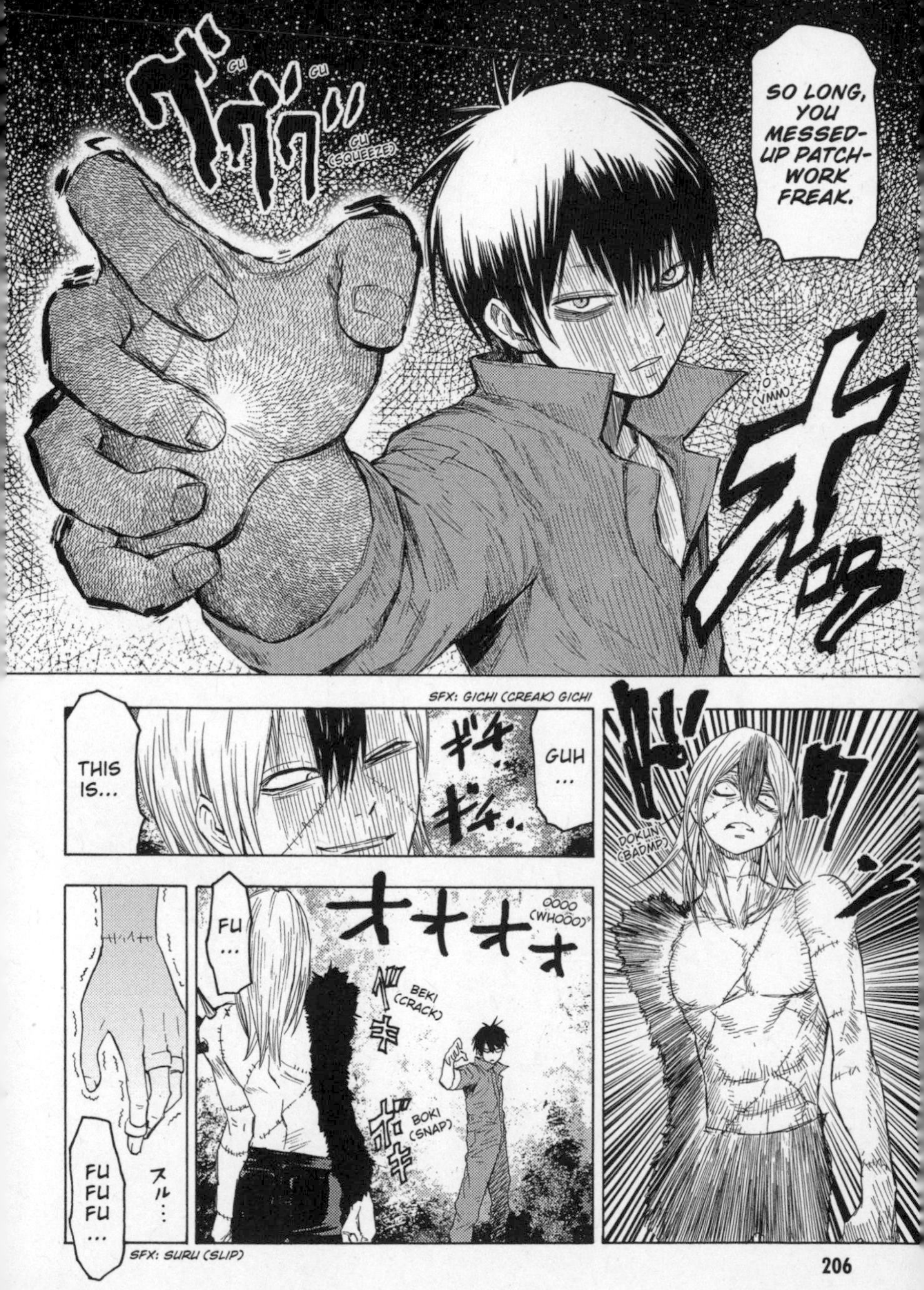
SO LONG, YOU MESSED-UP PATCH-WORK FREAK.
O (VMM)
GU GU GU (SQUEEZE)
DOKUN (BADMP)
GUH ...
SFX: GICHI (CREAK) GICHI
THIS IS...
OOOO (WHOOO)
BEKI (CRACK)
BOKI (SNAP)
FU ...
スル…
FU FU FU ...
SFX: SURU (SLIP)

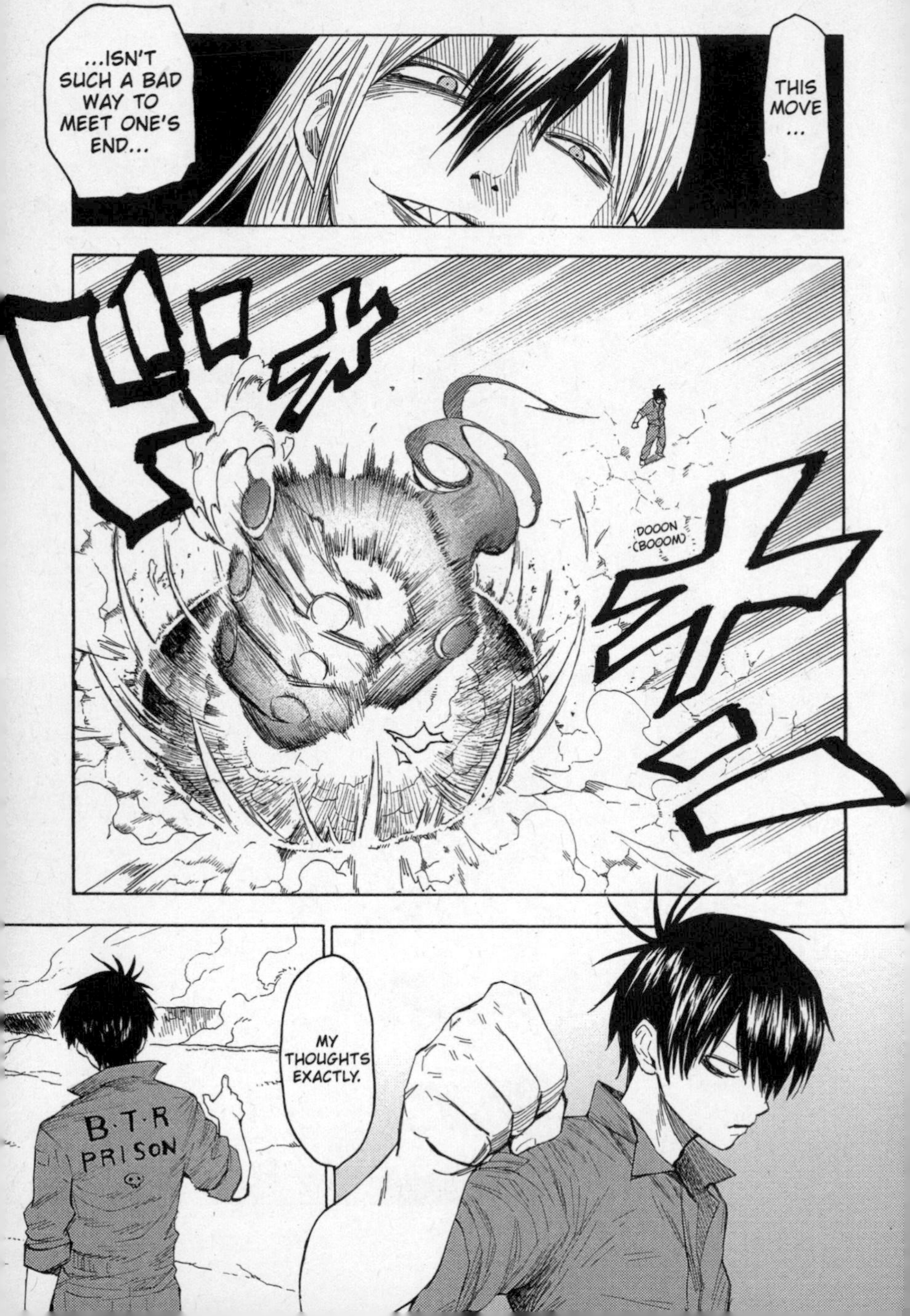
THIS MOVE ...
...ISN'T SUCH A BAD WAY TO MEET ONE'S END...
DOOON (BOOOM)
MY THOUGHTS EXACTLY.

オオオオオオオ
OOOOOOO
(WHOOOOOOO)
HEY.

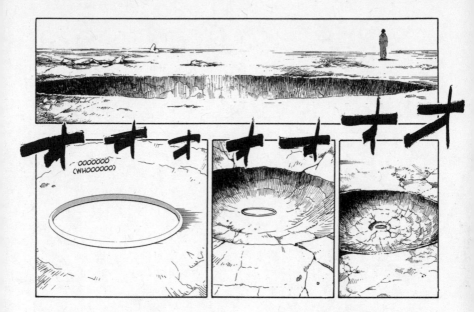

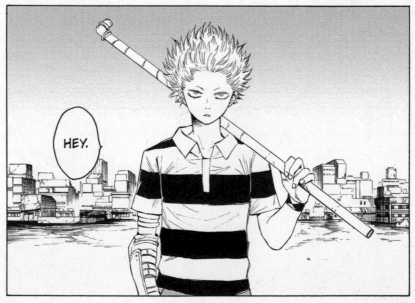

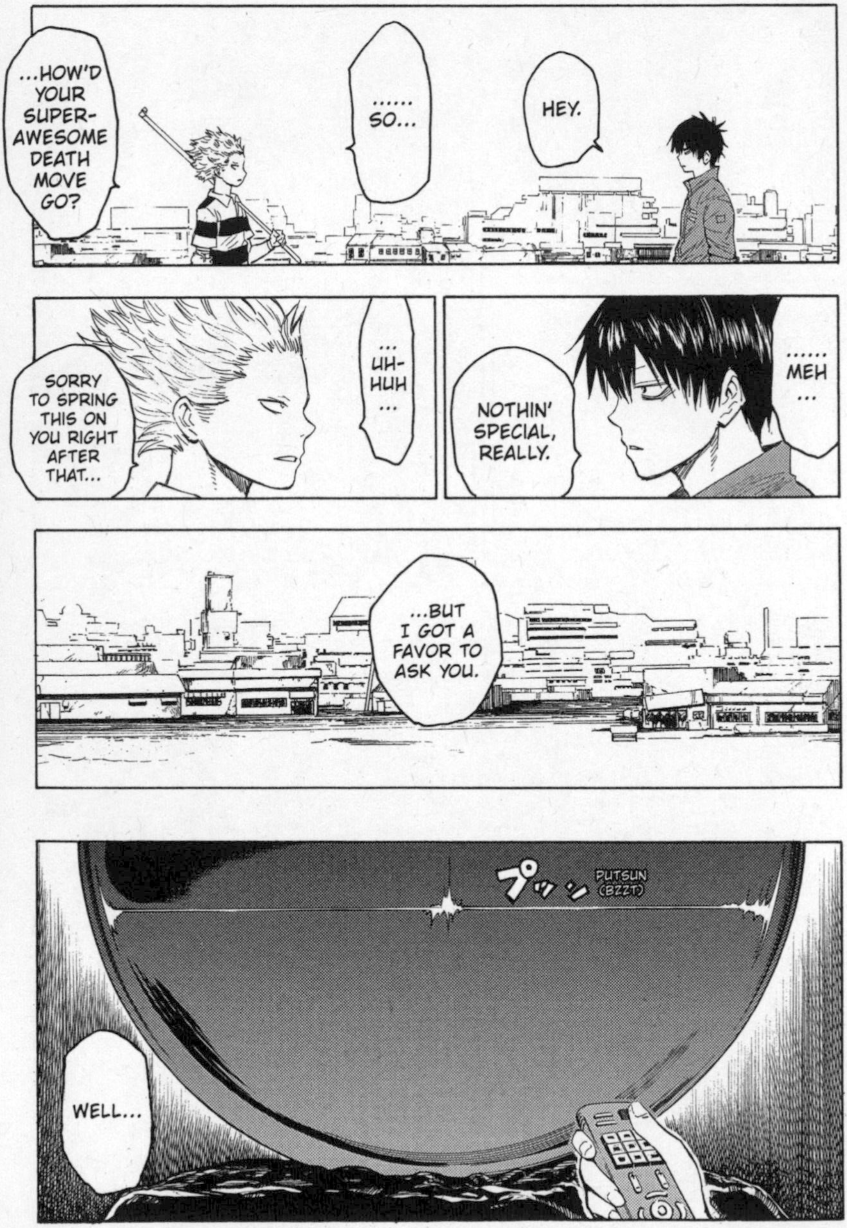
HEY.
...... SO...
...HOW'D YOUR SUPER-AWESOME DEATH MOVE GO?
...... MEH ...
NOTHIN' SPECIAL, REALLY.
... UH-HUH ...
SORRY TO SPRING THIS ON YOU RIGHT AFTER THAT...
...BUT I GOT A FAVOR TO ASK YOU.
プッン
PUTSUN (BZZT)
WELL...

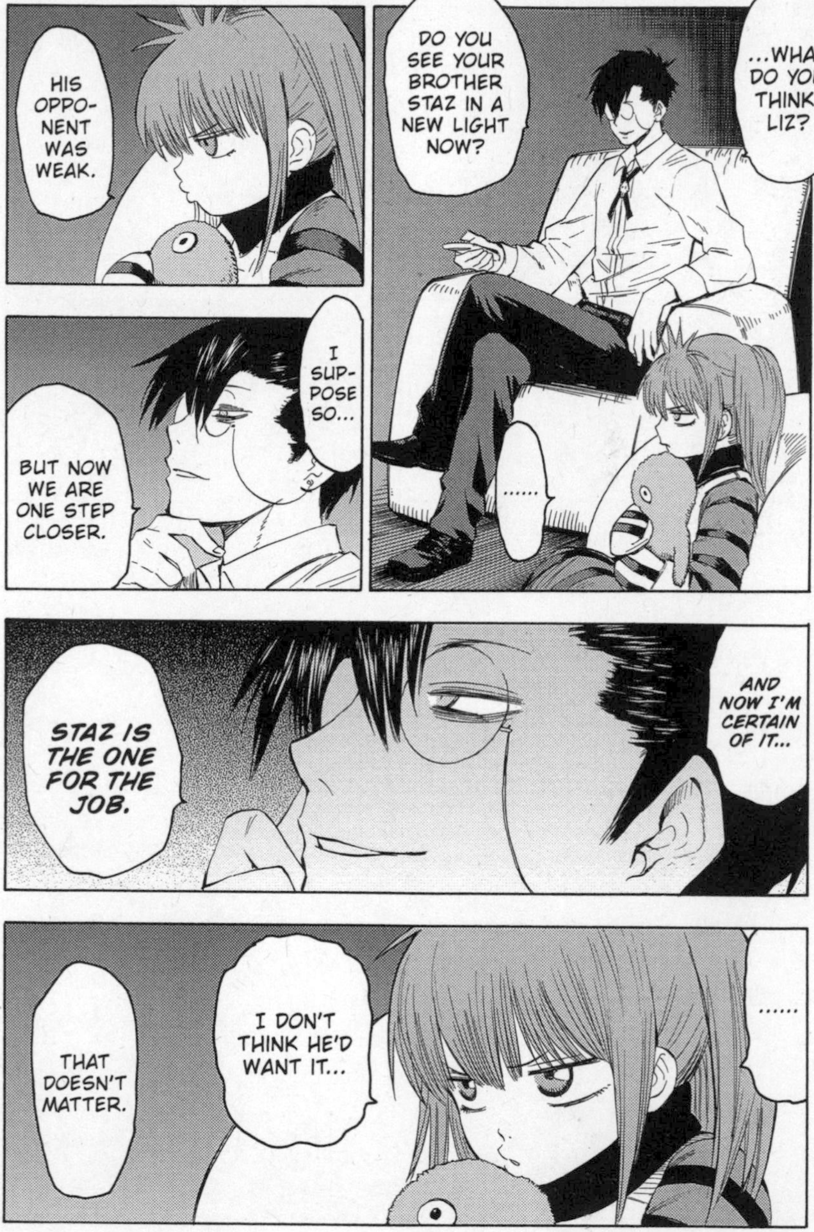
...WHAT DO YOU THINK, LIZ?
DO YOU SEE YOUR BROTHER STAZ IN A NEW LIGHT NOW?
......
HIS OPPONENT WAS WEAK.
I SUPPOSE SO...
BUT NOW WE ARE ONE STEP CLOSER.
AND NOW I'M CERTAIN OF IT...
STAZ IS THE ONE FOR THE JOB.
......
I DON'T THINK HE'D WANT IT...
THAT DOESN'T MATTER.

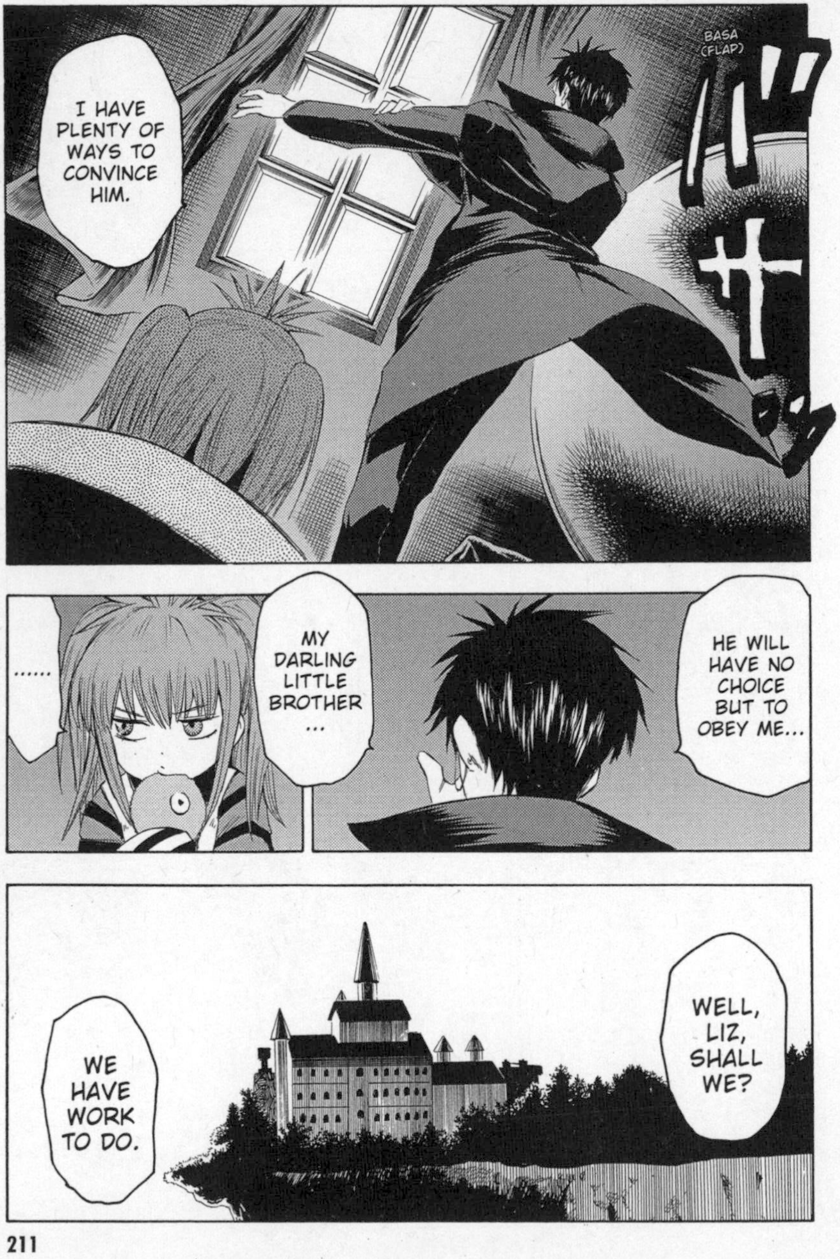
BASA (FLAP)
I HAVE PLENTY OF WAYS TO CONVINCE HIM.
HE WILL HAVE NO CHOICE BUT TO OBEY ME...
MY DARLING LITTLE BROTHER ...
......
WELL, LIZ, SHALL WE?
WE HAVE WORK TO DO.

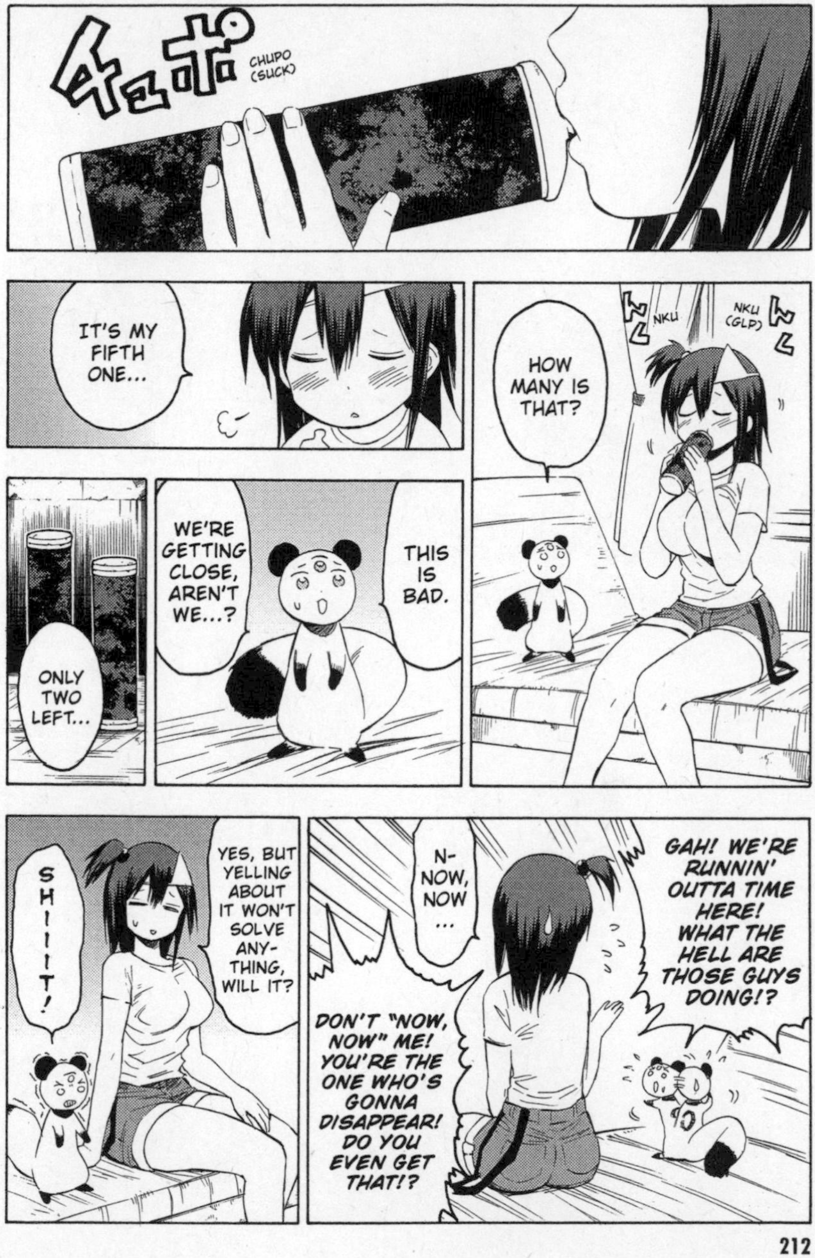
チュポ
CHUPO (SUCK)
NKU (GLP)
NKU
HOW MANY IS THAT?
IT'S MY FIFTH ONE...
THIS IS BAD.
WE'RE GETTING CLOSE, AREN'T WE...?
ONLY TWO LEFT...
GAH! WE'RE RUNNIN' OUTTA TIME HERE! WHAT THE HELL ARE THOSE GUYS DOING!?
N-NOW, NOW...
DON'T "NOW, NOW" ME! YOU'RE THE ONE WHO'S GONNA DISAPPEAR! DO YOU EVEN GET THAT!?
YES, BUT YELLING ABOUT IT WON'T SOLVE ANY-THING, WILL IT?
SH!!!T!

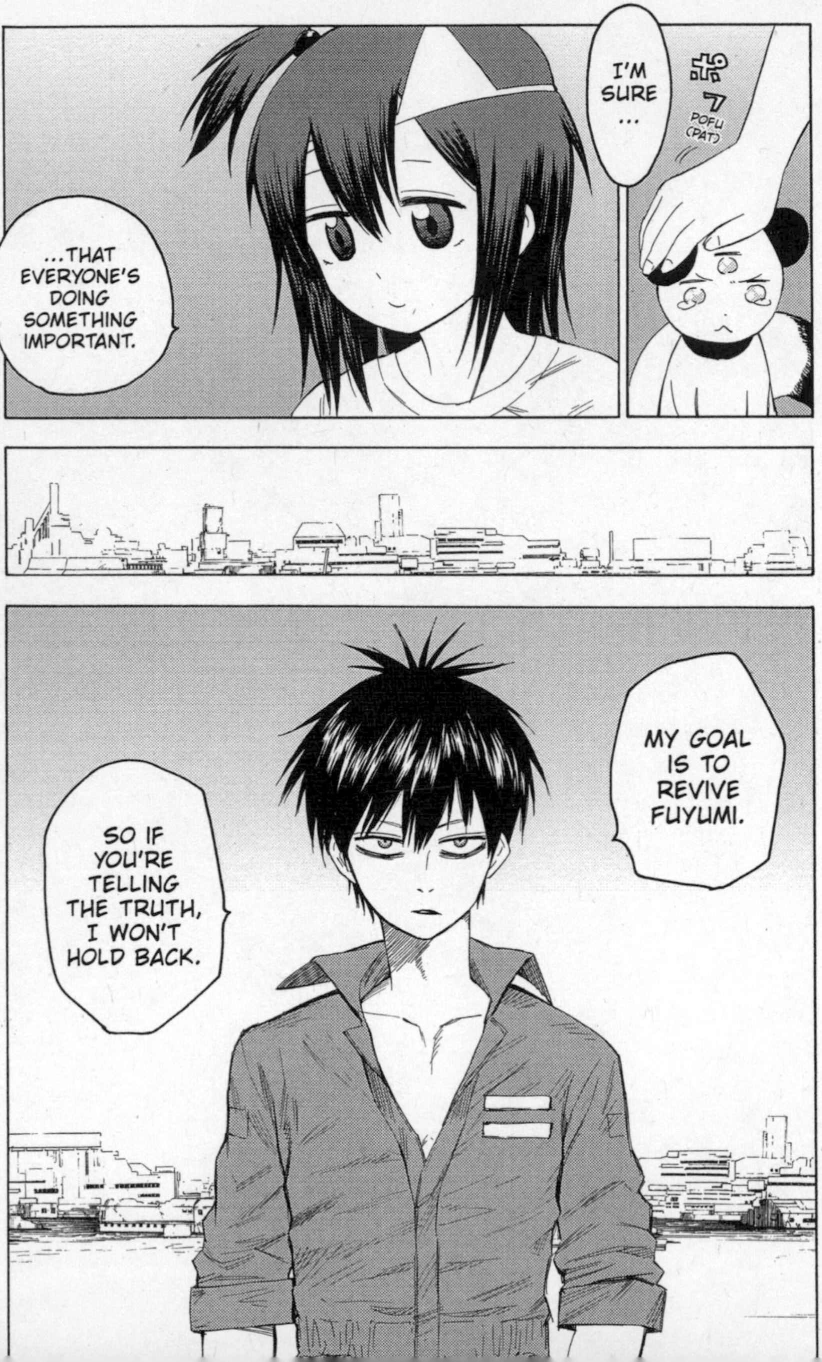
ポフ
POFU (PAT)
I'M SURE...
...THAT EVERYONE'S DOING SOMETHING IMPORTANT.
MY GOAL IS TO REVIVE FUYUMI.
SO IF YOU'RE TELLING THE TRUTH, I WON'T HOLD BACK.

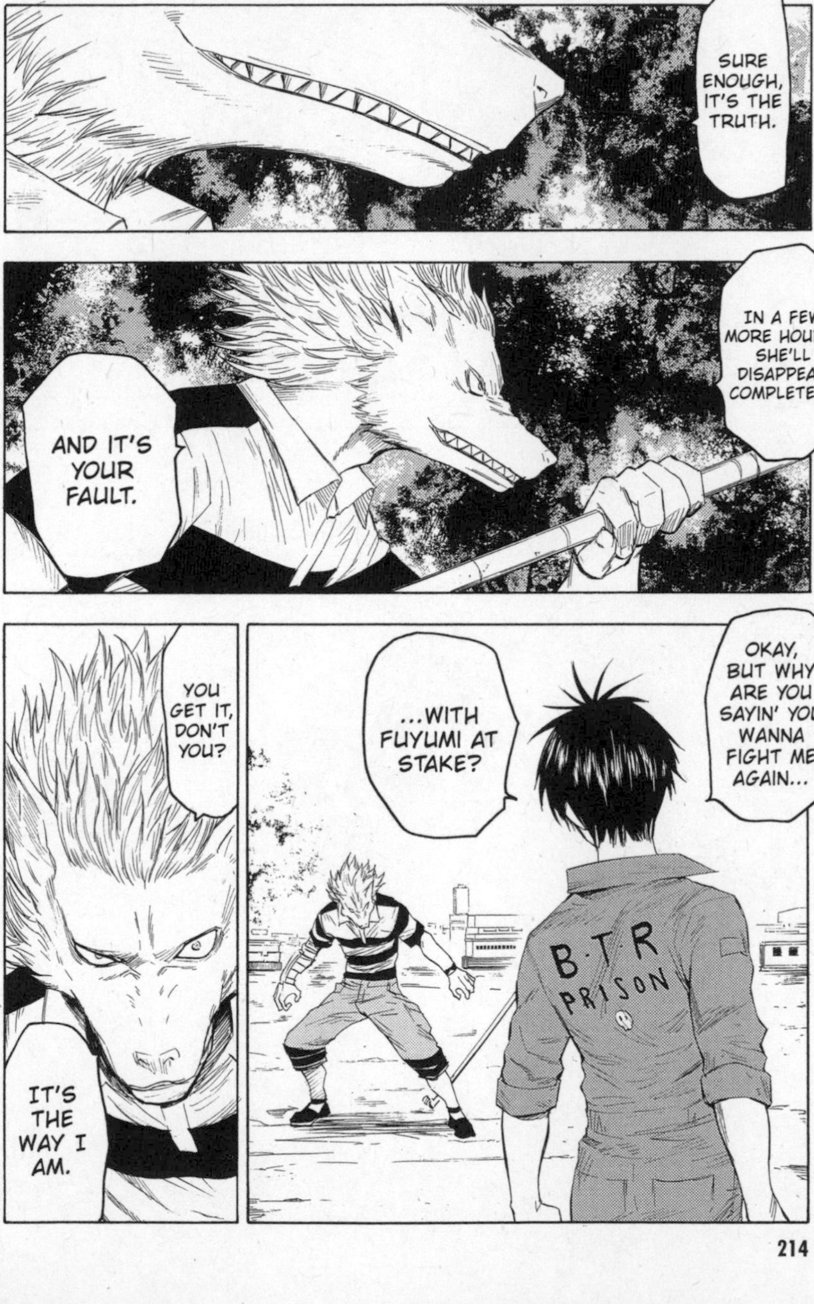
SURE ENOUGH, IT'S THE TRUTH.
IN A FEW MORE HOURS, SHE'LL DISAPPEAR COMPLETELY.
AND IT'S YOUR FAULT.
OKAY, BUT WHY ARE YOU SAYIN' YOU WANNA FIGHT ME AGAIN...
...WITH FUYUMI AT STAKE?
B.T.R PRISON
YOU GET IT, DON'T YOU?
IT'S THE WAY I AM.

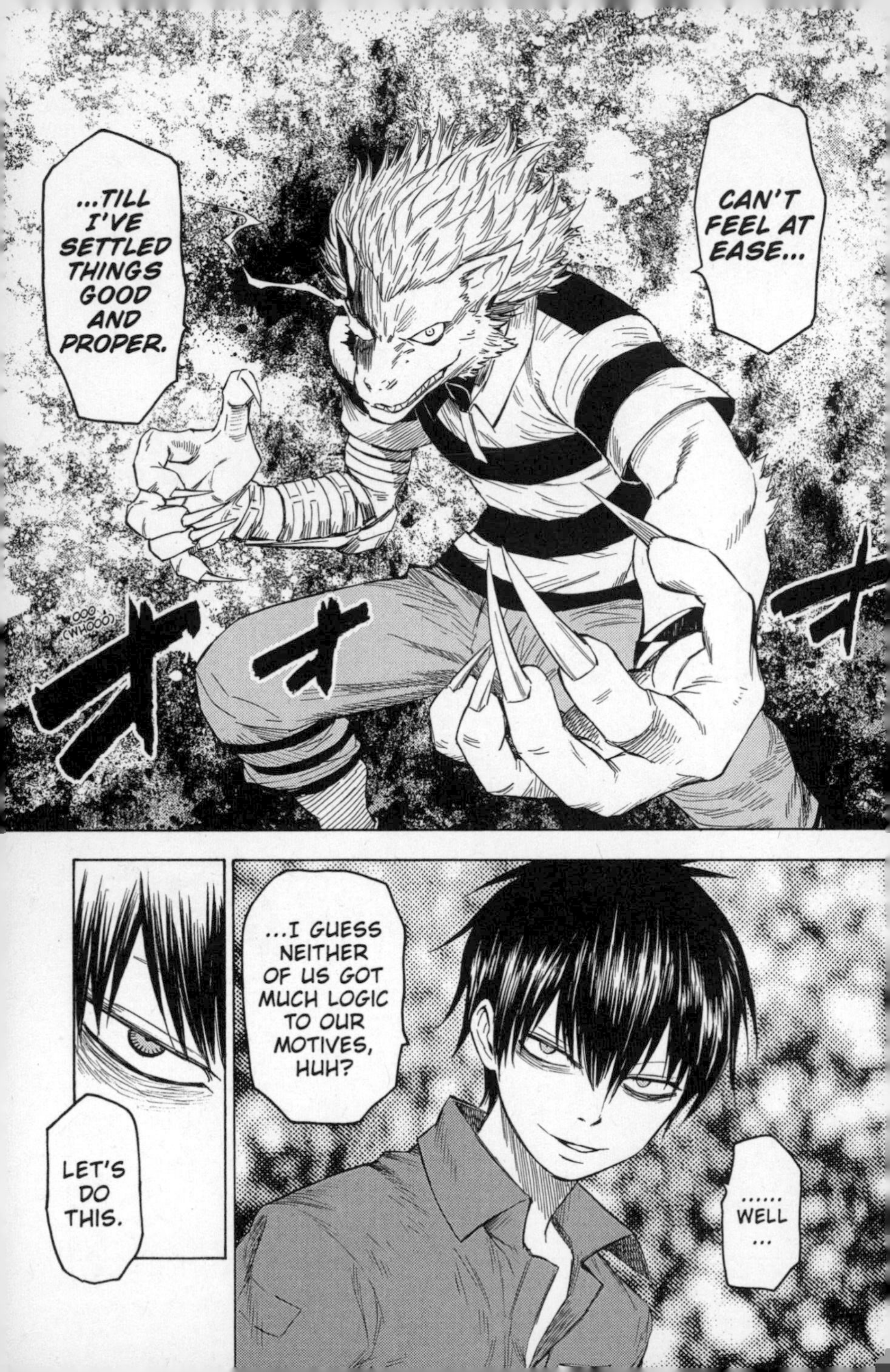CAN'T FEEL AT EASE...
...TILL I'VE SETTLED THINGS GOOD AND PROPER.
OOO (WHOOO)
......WELL...
...I GUESS NEITHER OF US GOT MUCH LOGIC TO OUR MOTIVES, HUH?
LET'S DO THIS.

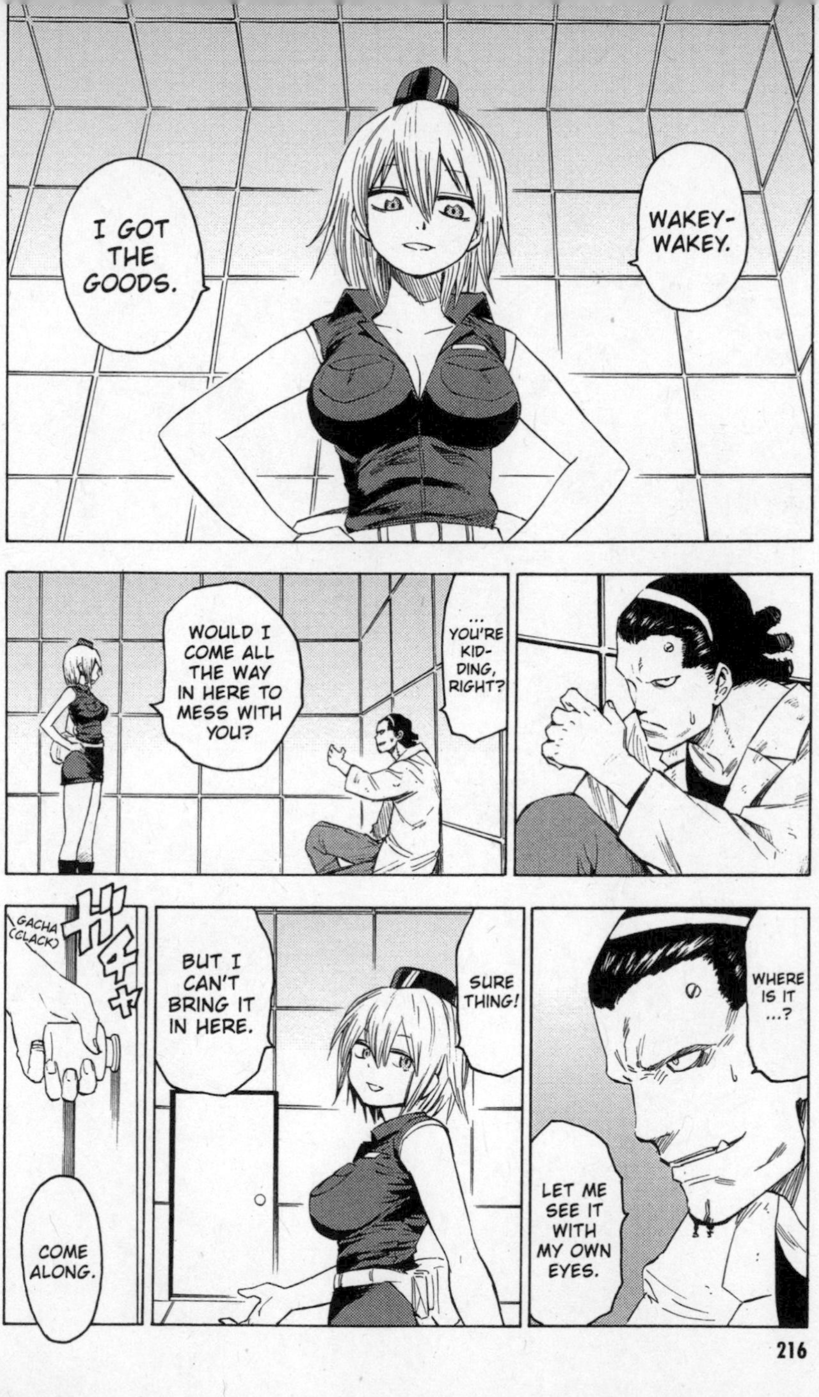
WAKEY-WAKEY.
I GOT THE GOODS.
... YOU'RE KID-DING, RIGHT?
WOULD I COME ALL THE WAY IN HERE TO MESS WITH YOU?
WHERE IS IT ...?
LET ME SEE IT WITH MY OWN EYES.
SURE THING!
BUT I CAN'T BRING IT IN HERE.
GACHA (CLACK)
COME ALONG.

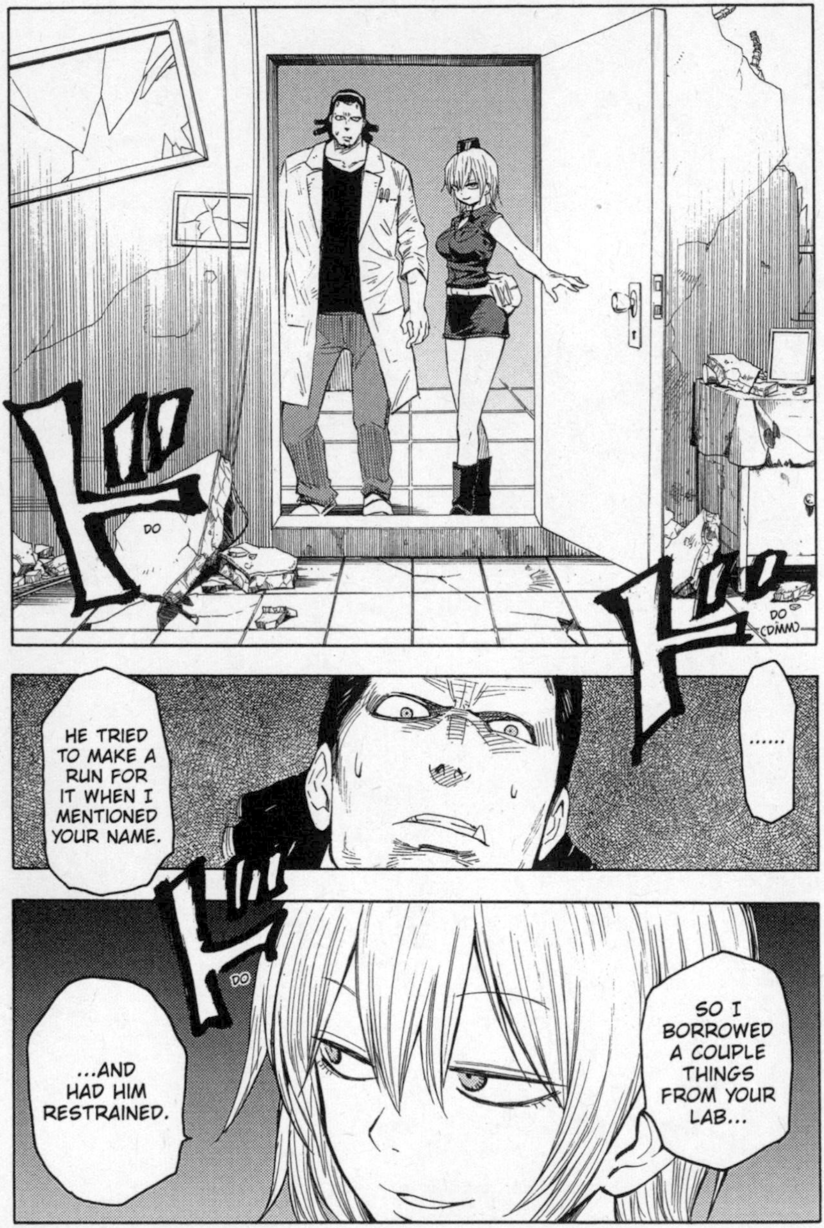
DO (DMM)
DO
......
HE TRIED TO MAKE A RUN FOR IT WHEN I MENTIONED YOUR NAME.
DO
SO I BORROWED A COUPLE THINGS FROM YOUR LAB...
...AND HAD HIM RESTRAINED.

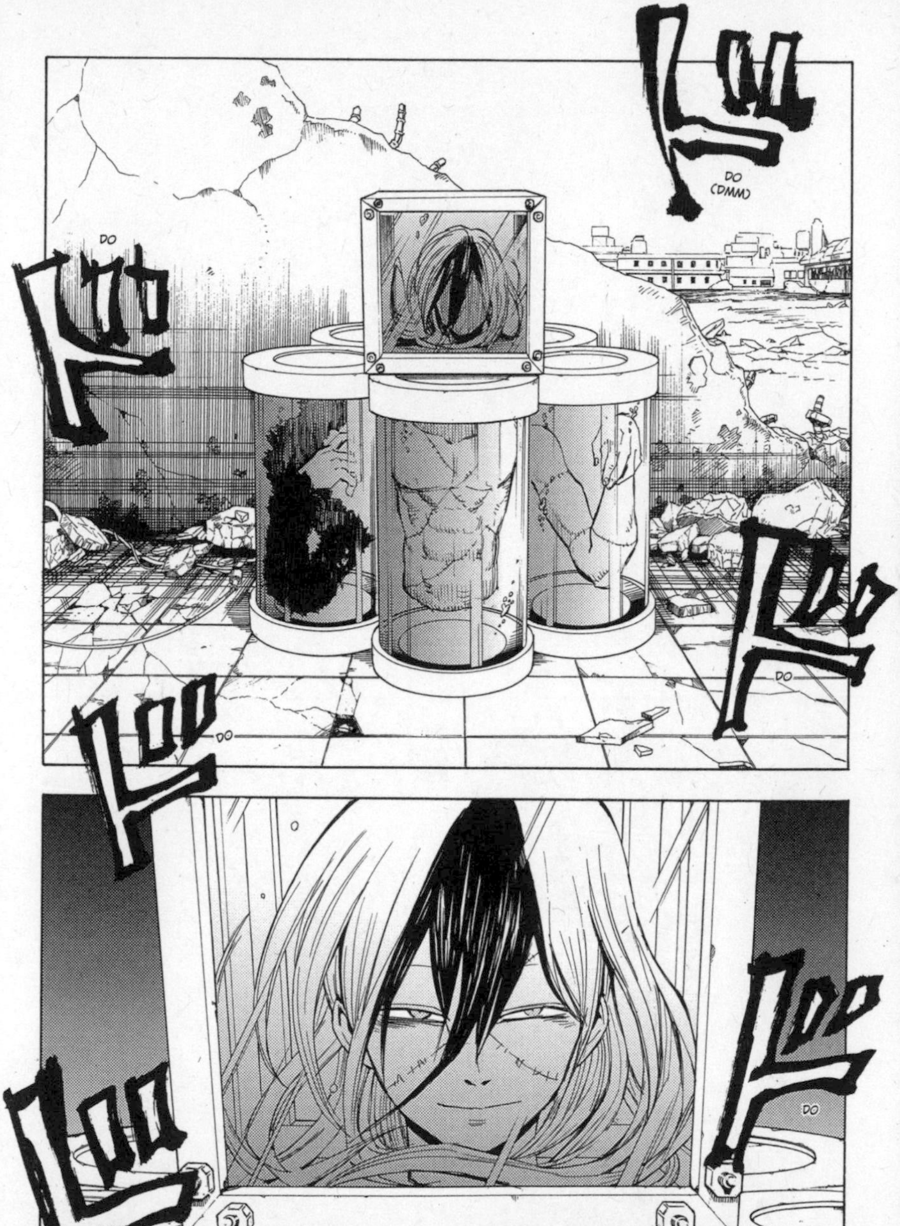
DO
(DMM)
DO
DO
DO
DO
DO

♠ To Be Continued ♠

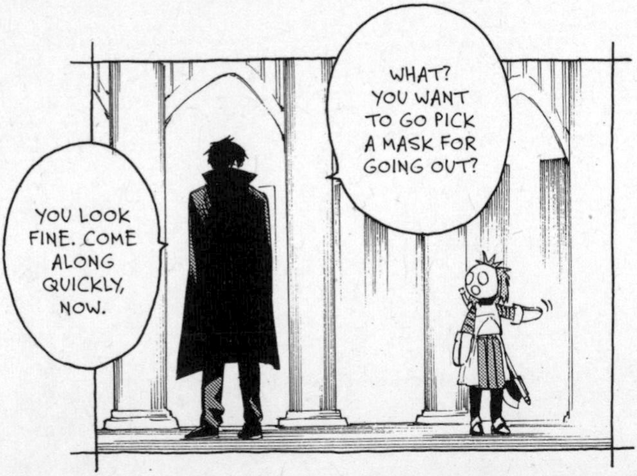
WHAT? YOU WANT TO GO PICK A MASK FOR GOING OUT?
YOU LOOK FINE. COME ALONG QUICKLY, NOW.

BLOOD LAD

CHAPTER 17 ♠ THAT'S FRIENDSHIP

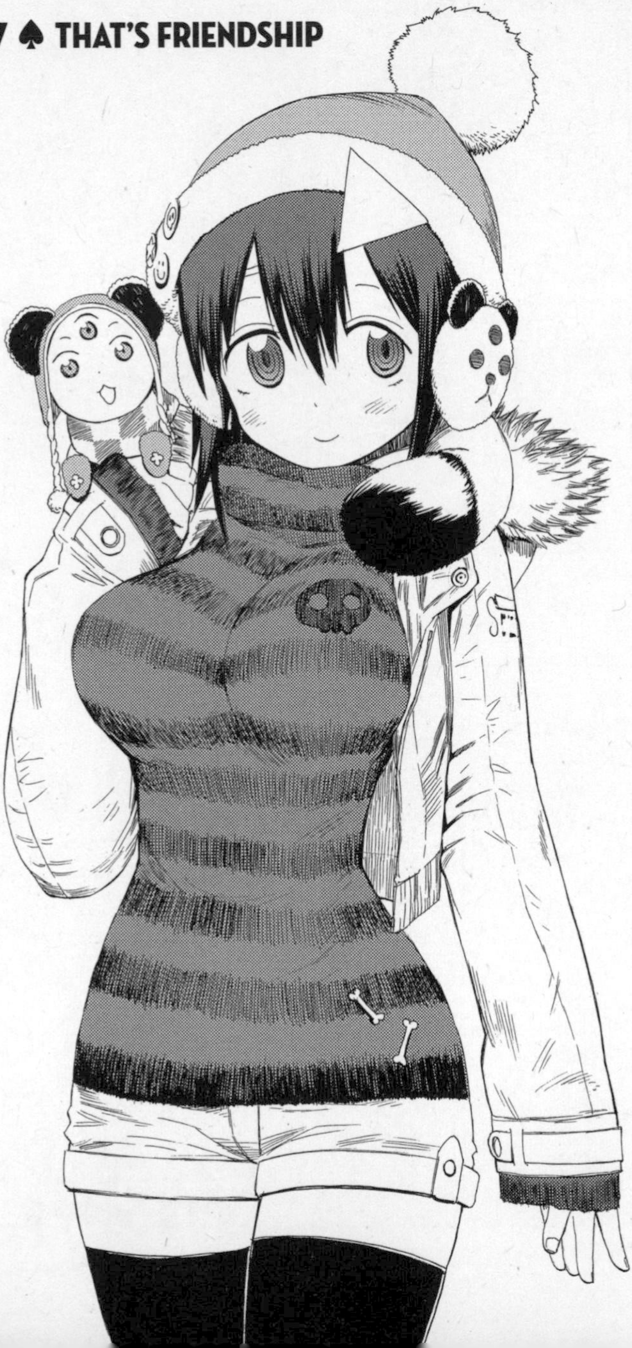

... THAT'S ...
...HIS FORM IS DIFFERENT FROM WHEN I LAST SAW HIM, BUT...
...IT'S DEFINITELY AKIM...
...HOW IN THE WORLD DID YOU...?
WELL, I AM A PRO-FESSIONAL TELEPORTER, Y'KNOW!
NOW, A PRO...
...WOULD NEVER FIGHT IN A BIG, WIDE-OPEN, EMPTY SPOT LIKE THAT.
IT LIMITS ONE'S MEANS OF MOVING ABOUT, YOU SEE.
BUN (SWING)
AND JUST AS I THOUGHT, AKIM HAD NO CHOICE BUT TO USE THIS LITTLE TOY.
SO I WENT OUT THERE TO CATCH HIM.

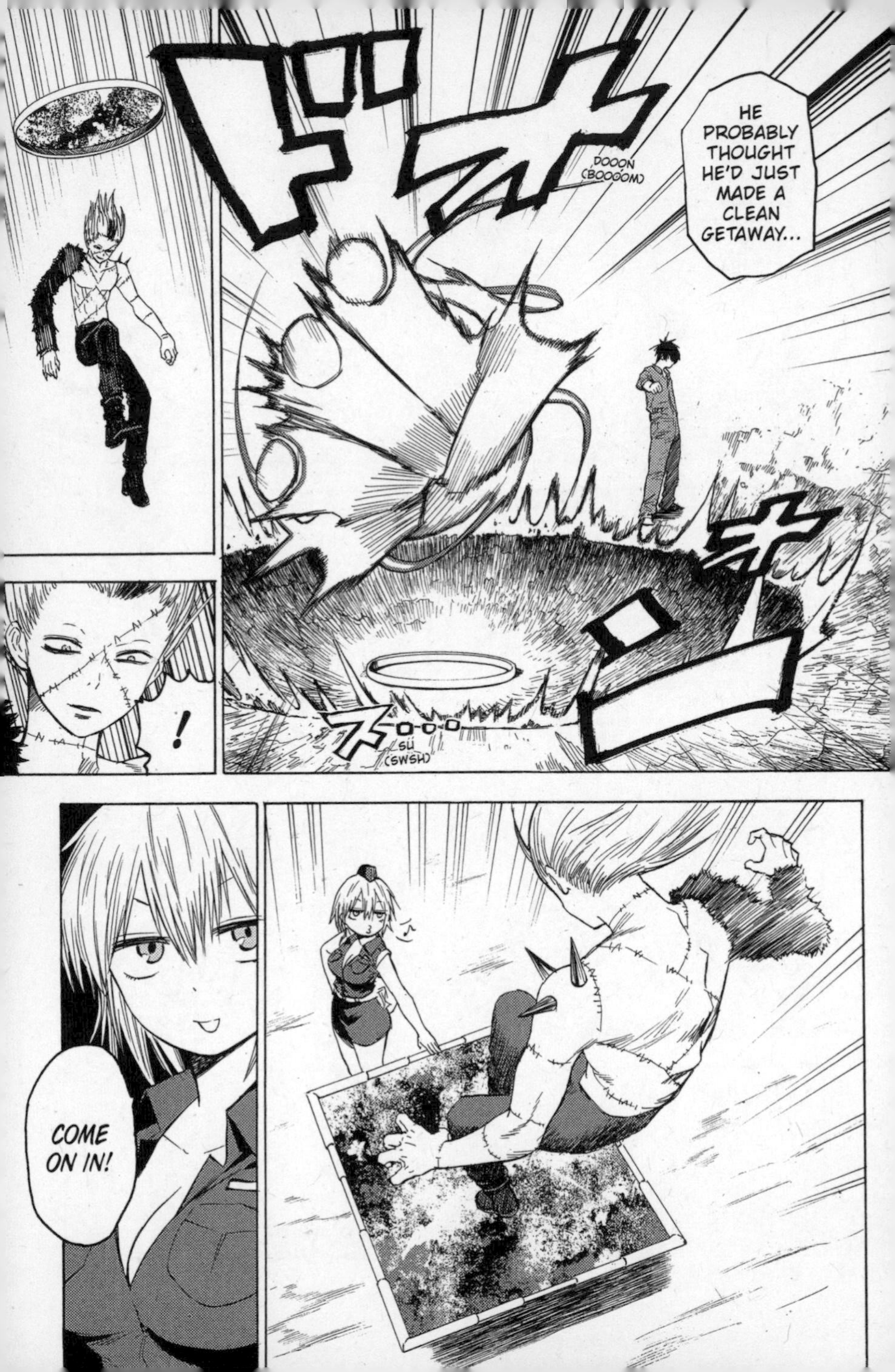
HE PROBABLY THOUGHT HE'D JUST MADE A CLEAN GETAWAY...
DOOON (BOOOOM)
SU (SWSH)
!
COME ON IN!

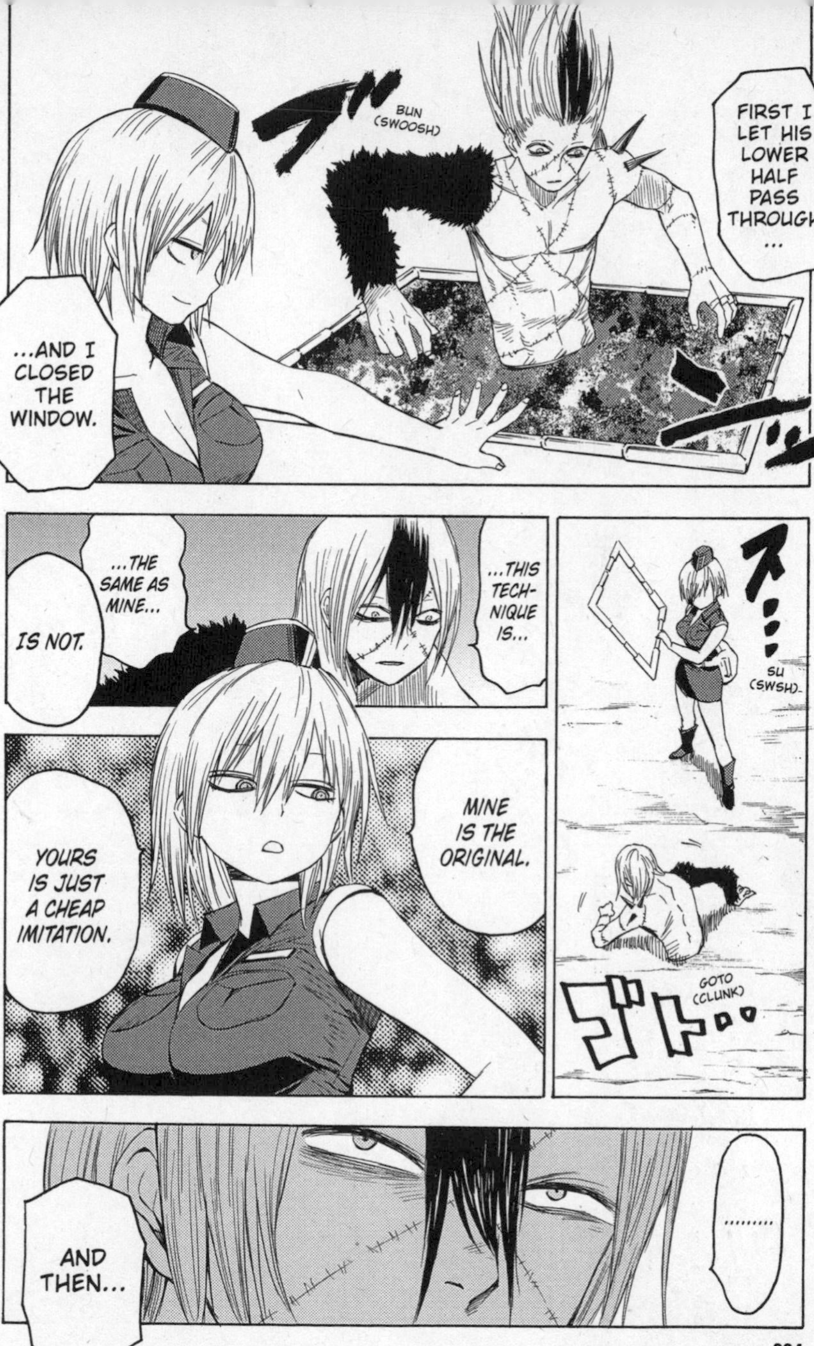
FIRST I LET HIS LOWER HALF PASS THROUGH...
BUN (SWOOSH)
...AND I CLOSED THE WINDOW.
SU (SWSH)
GOTO (CLUNK)
...THIS TECHNIQUE IS...
...THE SAME AS MINE...
IS NOT.
MINE IS THE ORIGINAL.
YOURS IS JUST A CHEAP IMITATION.
....
AND THEN...

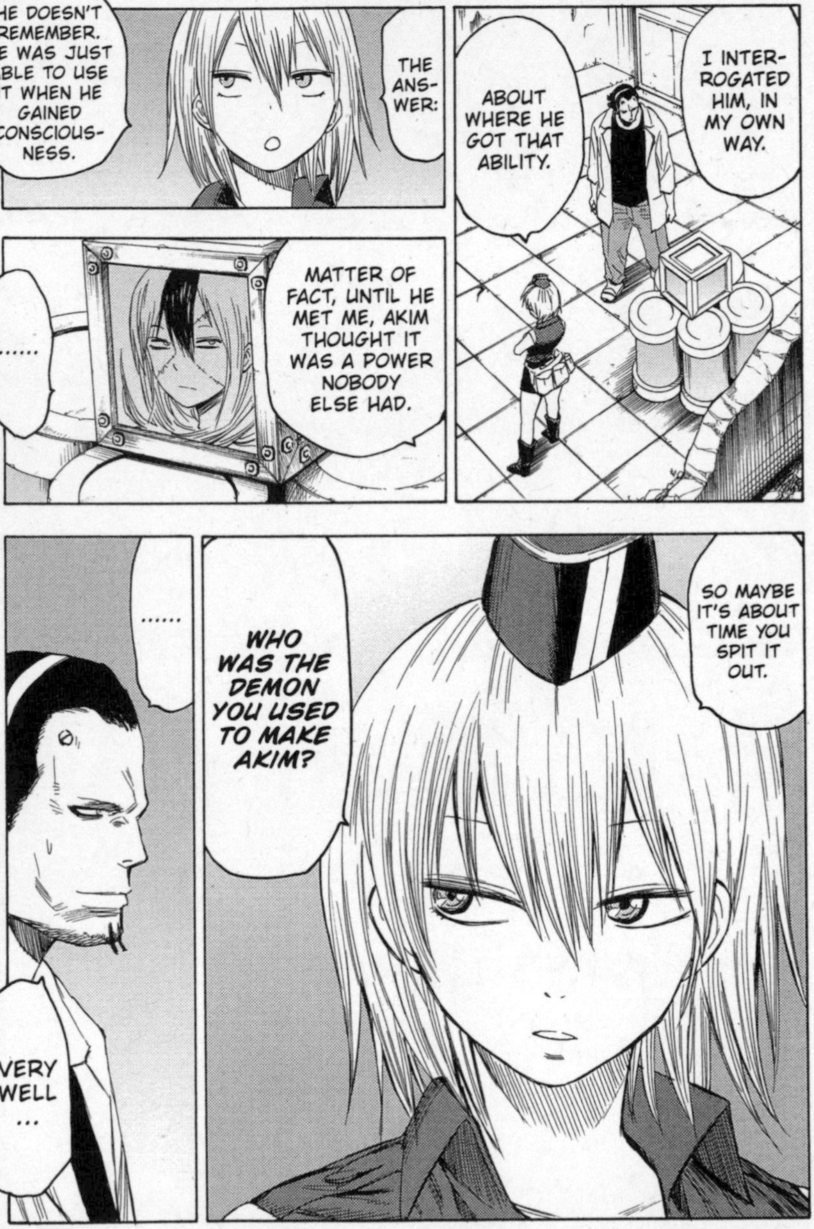
I INTER-ROGATED HIM, IN MY OWN WAY.
ABOUT WHERE HE GOT THAT ABILITY.
THE ANS-WER:
HE DOESN'T REMEMBER. HE WAS JUST ABLE TO USE IT WHEN HE GAINED CONSCIOUS-NESS.
MATTER OF FACT, UNTIL HE MET ME, AKIM THOUGHT IT WAS A POWER NOBODY ELSE HAD.
......
SO MAYBE IT'S ABOUT TIME YOU SPIT IT OUT.
WHO WAS THE DEMON YOU USED TO MAKE AKIM?
......
VERY WELL ...

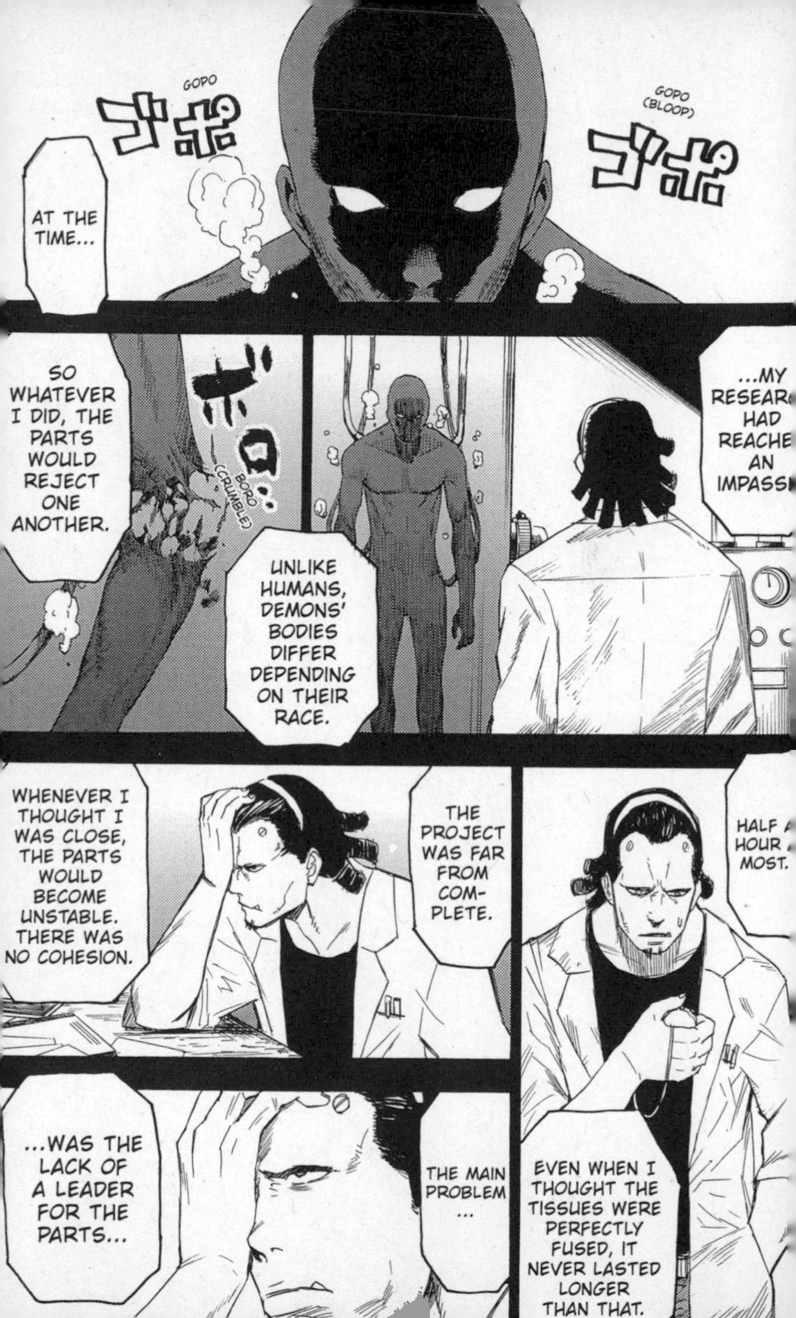

GOPO (BLOOP)
GOPO
AT THE TIME...
...MY RESEAR HAD REACHE AN IMPASS
UNLIKE HUMANS, DEMONS' BODIES DIFFER DEPENDING ON THEIR RACE.
BORO (CRUMBLE)
SO WHATEVER I DID, THE PARTS WOULD REJECT ONE ANOTHER.
HALF A HOUR A MOST.
EVEN WHEN I THOUGHT THE TISSUES WERE PERFECTLY FUSED, IT NEVER LASTED LONGER THAN THAT.
THE PROJECT WAS FAR FROM COM-PLETE.
WHENEVER I THOUGHT I WAS CLOSE, THE PARTS WOULD BECOME UNSTABLE. THERE WAS NO COHESION.
THE MAIN PROBLEM ...
...WAS THE LACK OF A LEADER FOR THE PARTS...

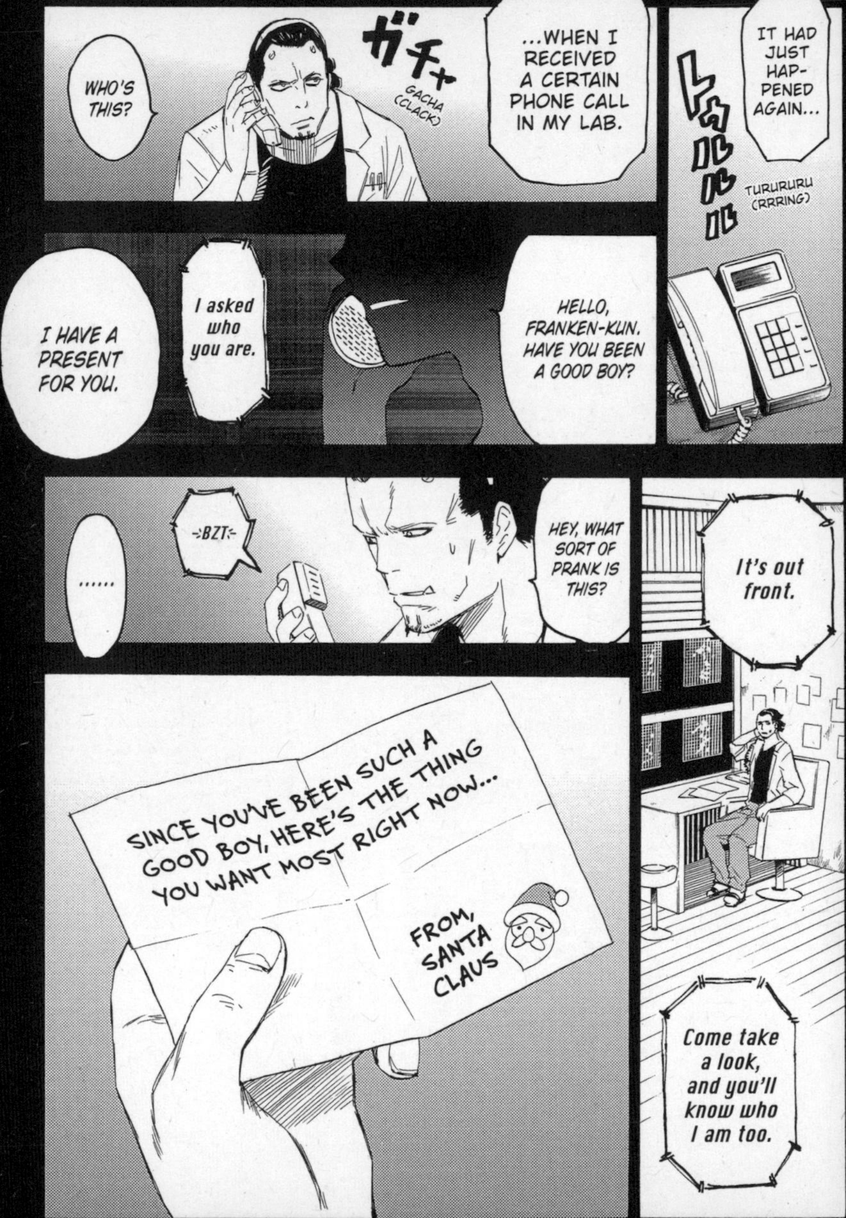
IT HAD JUST HAP-PENED AGAIN...
トゥルルル
TURURURU (RRRING)
...WHEN I RECEIVED A CERTAIN PHONE CALL IN MY LAB.
ガチャ
GACHA (CLACK)
WHO'S THIS?
HELLO, FRANKEN-KUN. HAVE YOU BEEN A GOOD BOY?
I asked who you are.
I HAVE A PRESENT FOR YOU.
It's out front.
Come take a look, and you'll know who I am too.
HEY, WHAT SORT OF PRANK IS THIS?
-BZT-
......
SINCE YOU'VE BEEN SUCH A GOOD BOY, HERE'S THE THING YOU WANT MOST RIGHT NOW...
FROM, SANTA CLAUS

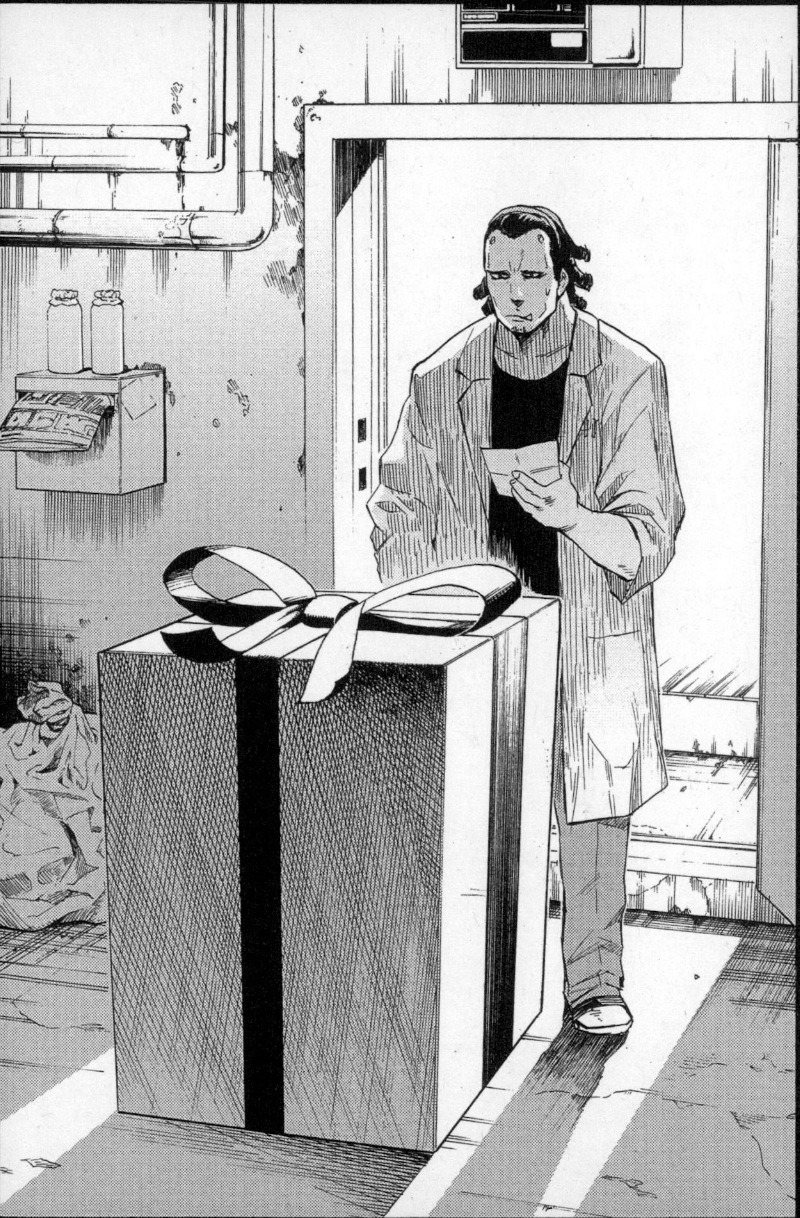

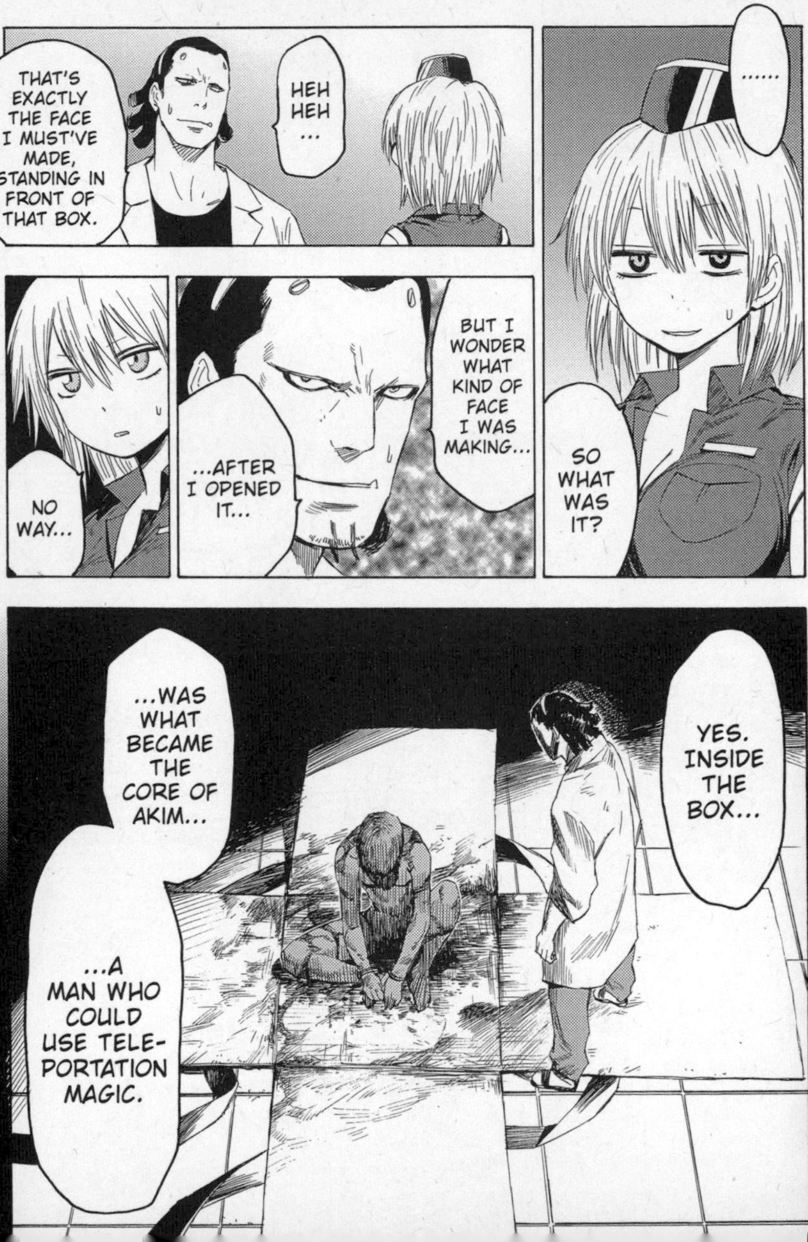
......
SO WHAT WAS IT?
HEH HEH ...
THAT'S EXACTLY THE FACE I MUST'VE MADE, STANDING IN FRONT OF THAT BOX.
BUT I WONDER WHAT KIND OF FACE I WAS MAKING...
...AFTER I OPENED IT...
NO WAY...
YES. INSIDE THE BOX...
...WAS WHAT BECAME THE CORE OF AKIM...
...A MAN WHO COULD USE TELE-PORTATION MAGIC.

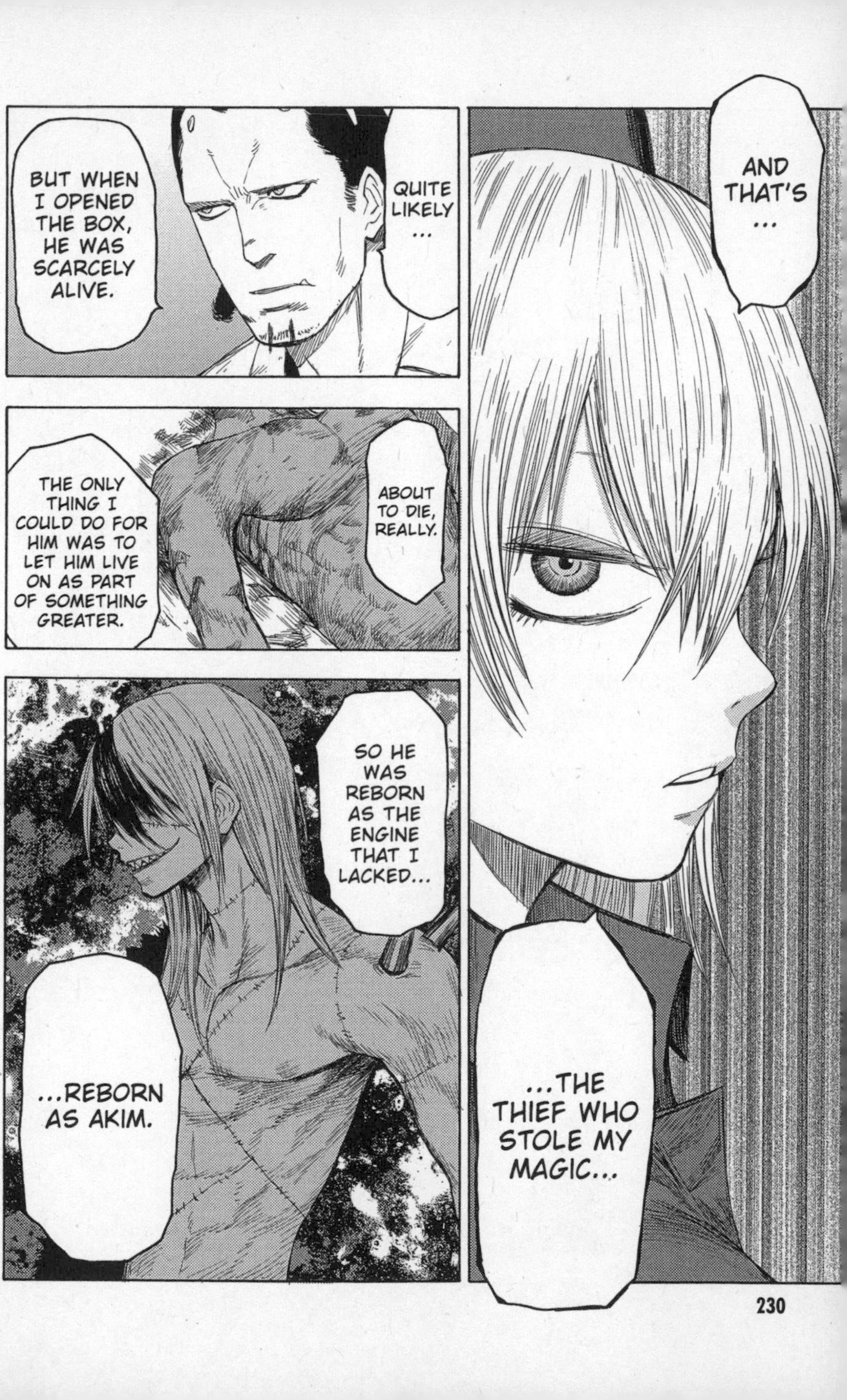
AND THAT'S ...
...THE THIEF WHO STOLE MY MAGIC...
QUITE LIKELY ...
BUT WHEN I OPENED THE BOX, HE WAS SCARCELY ALIVE.
ABOUT TO DIE, REALLY.
THE ONLY THING I COULD DO FOR HIM WAS TO LET HIM LIVE ON AS PART OF SOMETHING GREATER.
SO HE WAS REBORN AS THE ENGINE THAT I LACKED...
...REBORN AS AKIM.

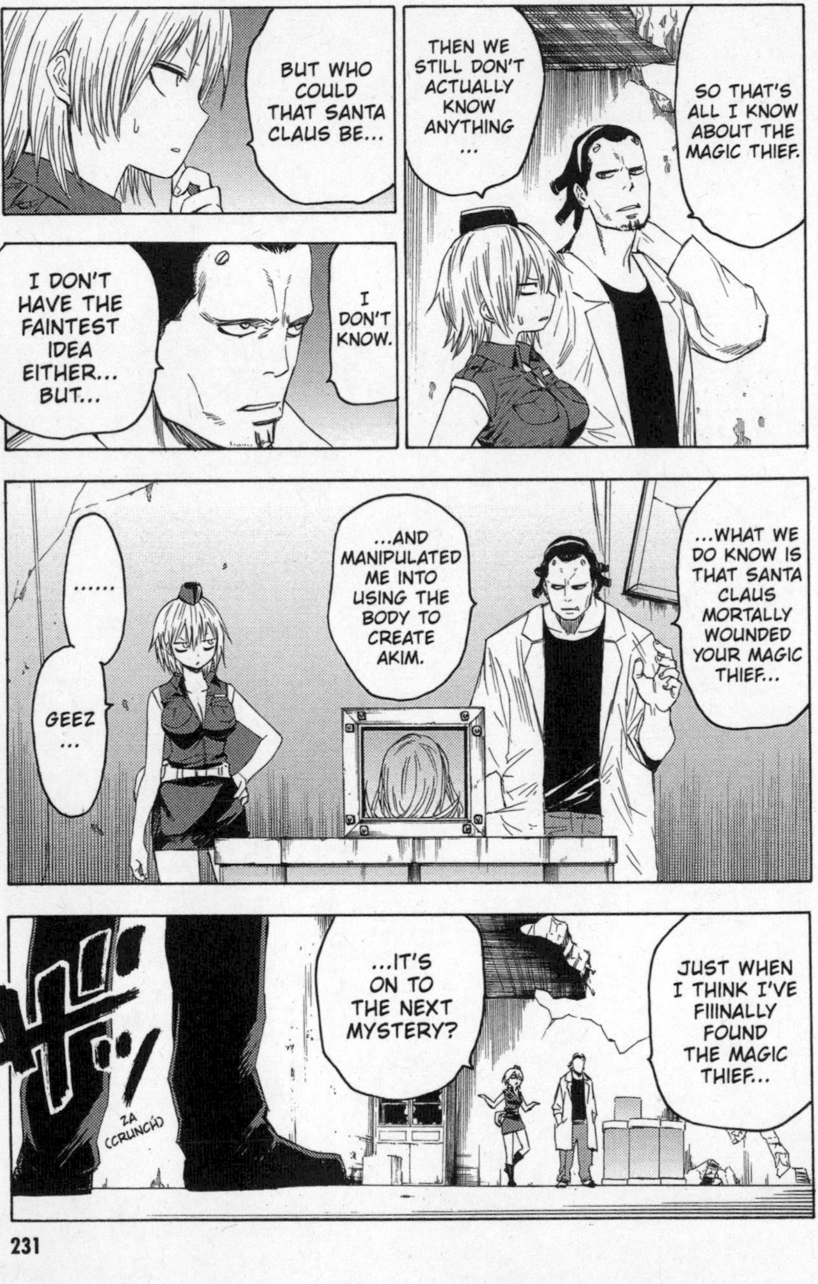
SO THAT'S ALL I KNOW ABOUT THE MAGIC THIEF.
THEN WE STILL DON'T ACTUALLY KNOW ANYTHING ...
BUT WHO COULD THAT SANTA CLAUS BE...
I DON'T KNOW.
I DON'T HAVE THE FAINTEST IDEA EITHER... BUT...
...WHAT WE DO KNOW IS THAT SANTA CLAUS MORTALLY WOUNDED YOUR MAGIC THIEF...
...AND MANIPULATED ME INTO USING THE BODY TO CREATE AKIM.
......
GEEZ ...
JUST WHEN I THINK I'VE FIIINALLY FOUND THE MAGIC THIEF...
...IT'S ON TO THE NEXT MYSTERY?
ZA (CRUNCH)

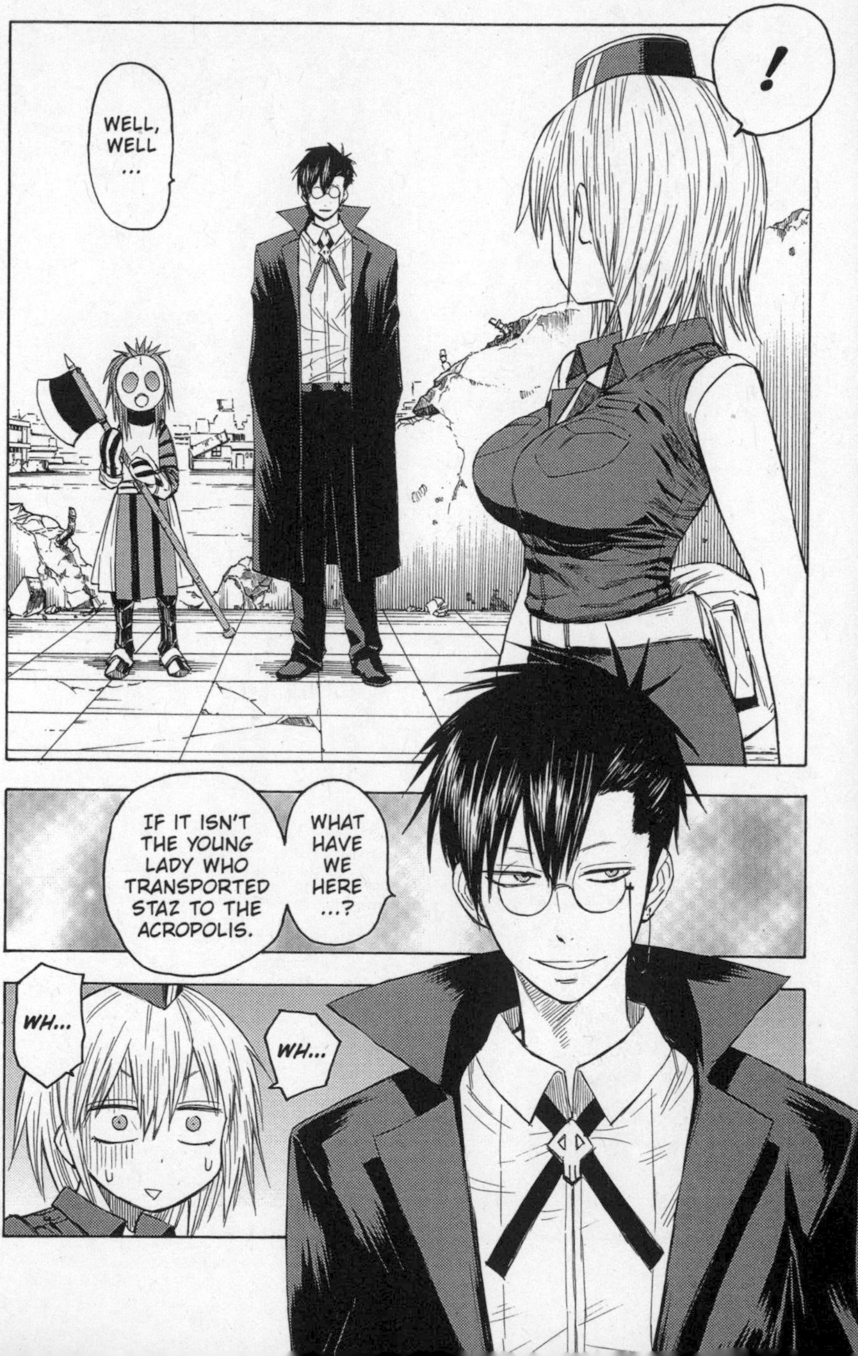
!
WELL, WELL ...
WHAT HAVE WE HERE ...?
IF IT ISN'T THE YOUNG LADY WHO TRANSPORTED STAZ TO THE ACROPOLIS.
WH...
WH...

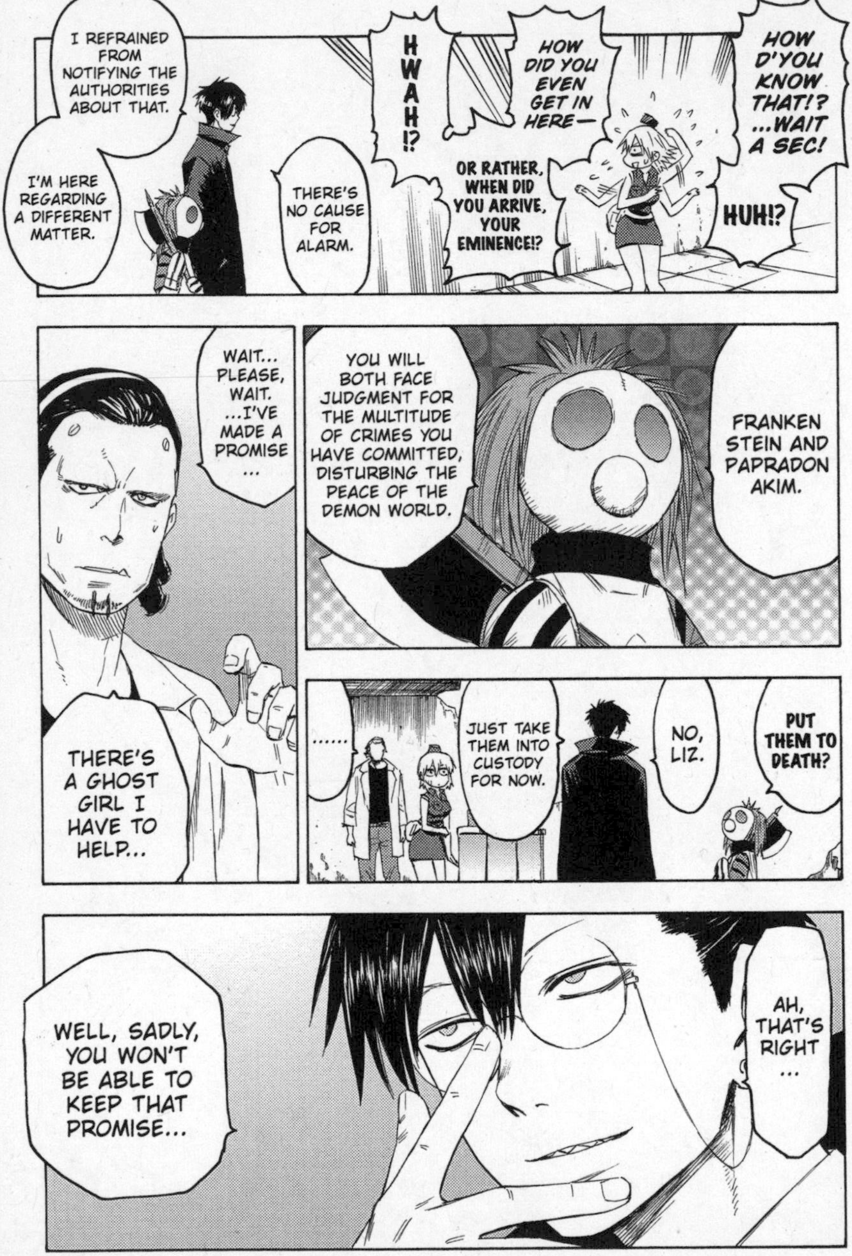
HOW D'YOU KNOW THAT!? ...WAIT A SEC!
HUH!?
HOW DID YOU EVEN GET IN HERE—
OR RATHER, WHEN DID YOU ARRIVE, YOUR EMINENCE!?
HWAH!?
THERE'S NO CAUSE FOR ALARM.
I REFRAINED FROM NOTIFYING THE AUTHORITIES ABOUT THAT.
I'M HERE REGARDING A DIFFERENT MATTER.
FRANKEN STEIN AND PAPRADON AKIM.
YOU WILL BOTH FACE JUDGMENT FOR THE MULTITUDE OF CRIMES YOU HAVE COMMITTED, DISTURBING THE PEACE OF THE DEMON WORLD.
PUT THEM TO DEATH?
NO, LIZ.
JUST TAKE THEM INTO CUSTODY FOR NOW.
......
WAIT... PLEASE, WAIT. ...I'VE MADE A PROMISE ...
THERE'S A GHOST GIRL I HAVE TO HELP...
AH, THAT'S RIGHT ...
WELL, SADLY, YOU WON'T BE ABLE TO KEEP THAT PROMISE...

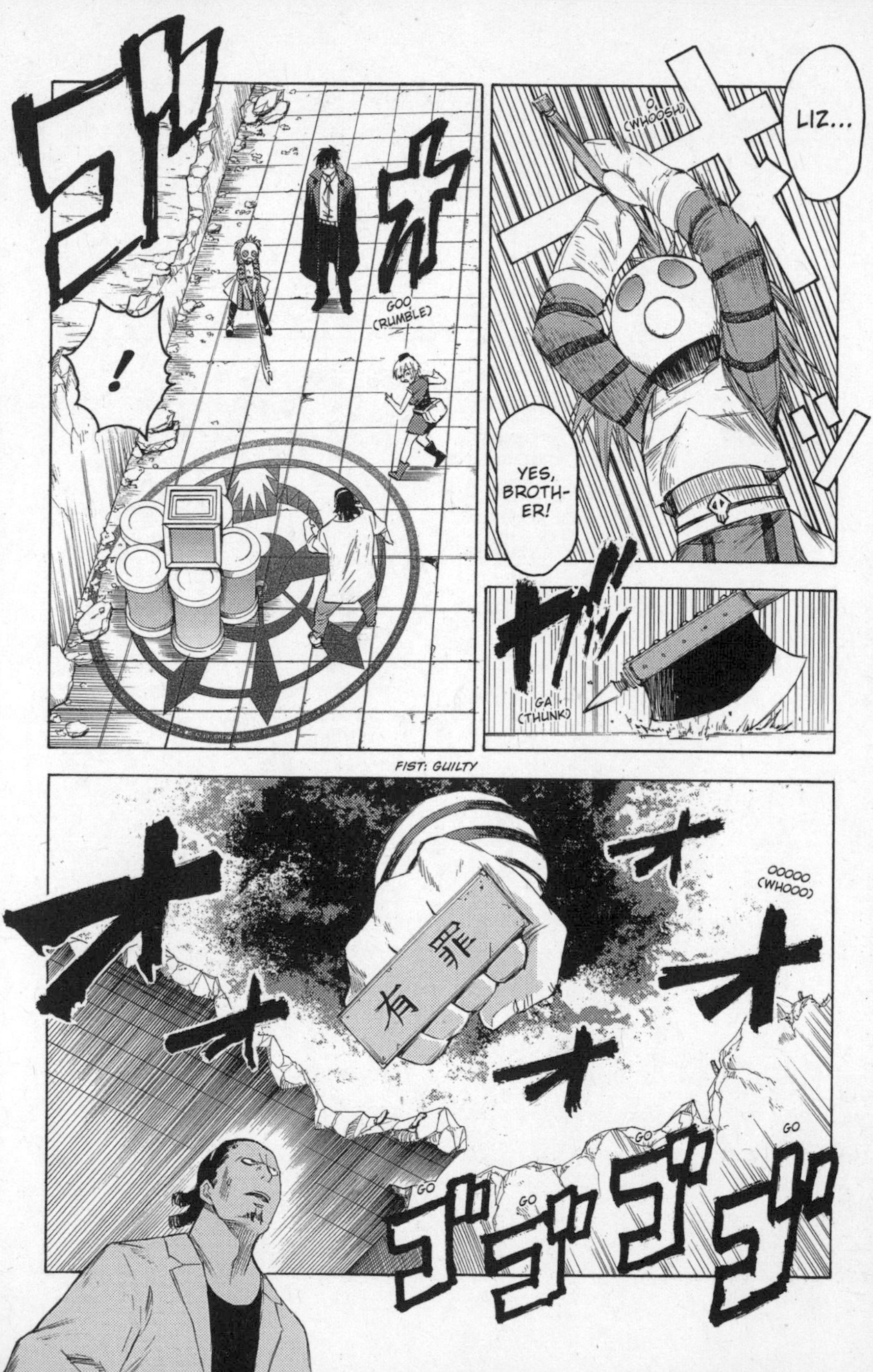
LIZ...
O (WHOOSH)
YES, BROTHER!
GA (THUNK)
GOO (RUMBLE)
!
FIST: GUILTY
OOOOO (WHOOO)
有罪
GO
GO
GO
GO

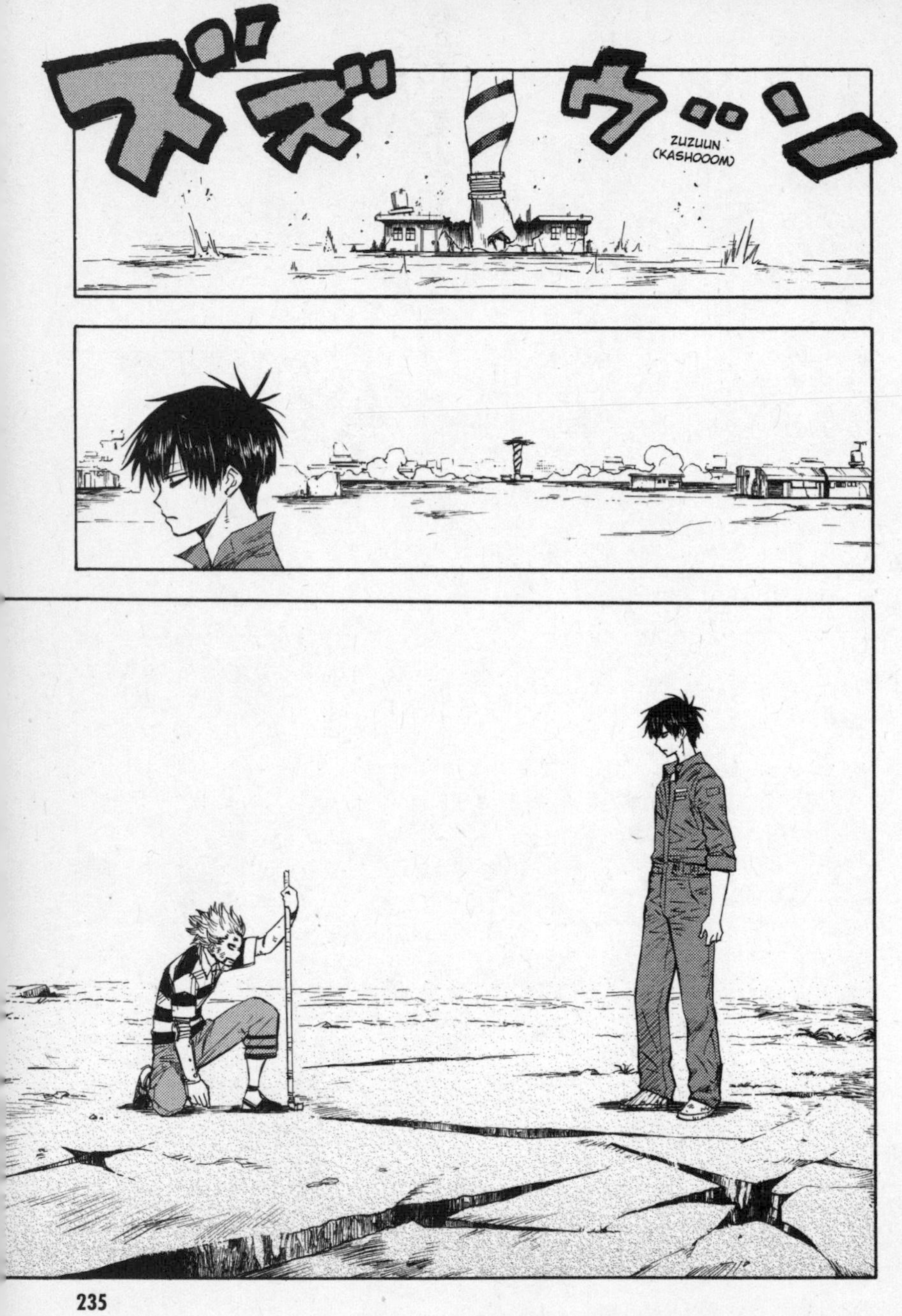
ZUZUUN
(KASHOOOM)

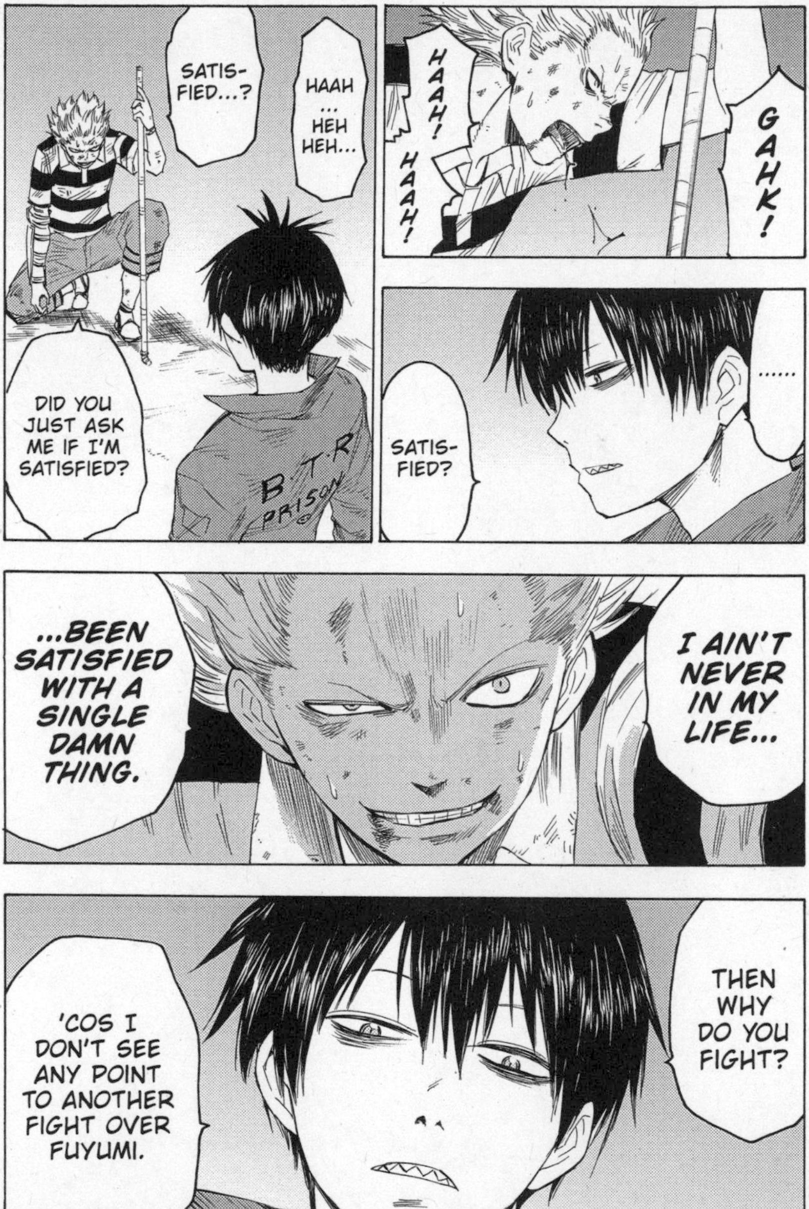
GAHK!
HAAH! HAAH!
......
SATIS-FIED?
HAAH ... HEH HEH...
SATIS-FIED...?
DID YOU JUST ASK ME IF I'M SATISFIED?
B.T.R PRISON
I AIN'T NEVER IN MY LIFE...
...BEEN SATISFIED WITH A SINGLE DAMN THING.
THEN WHY DO YOU FIGHT?
'COS I DON'T SEE ANY POINT TO ANOTHER FIGHT OVER FUYUMI.

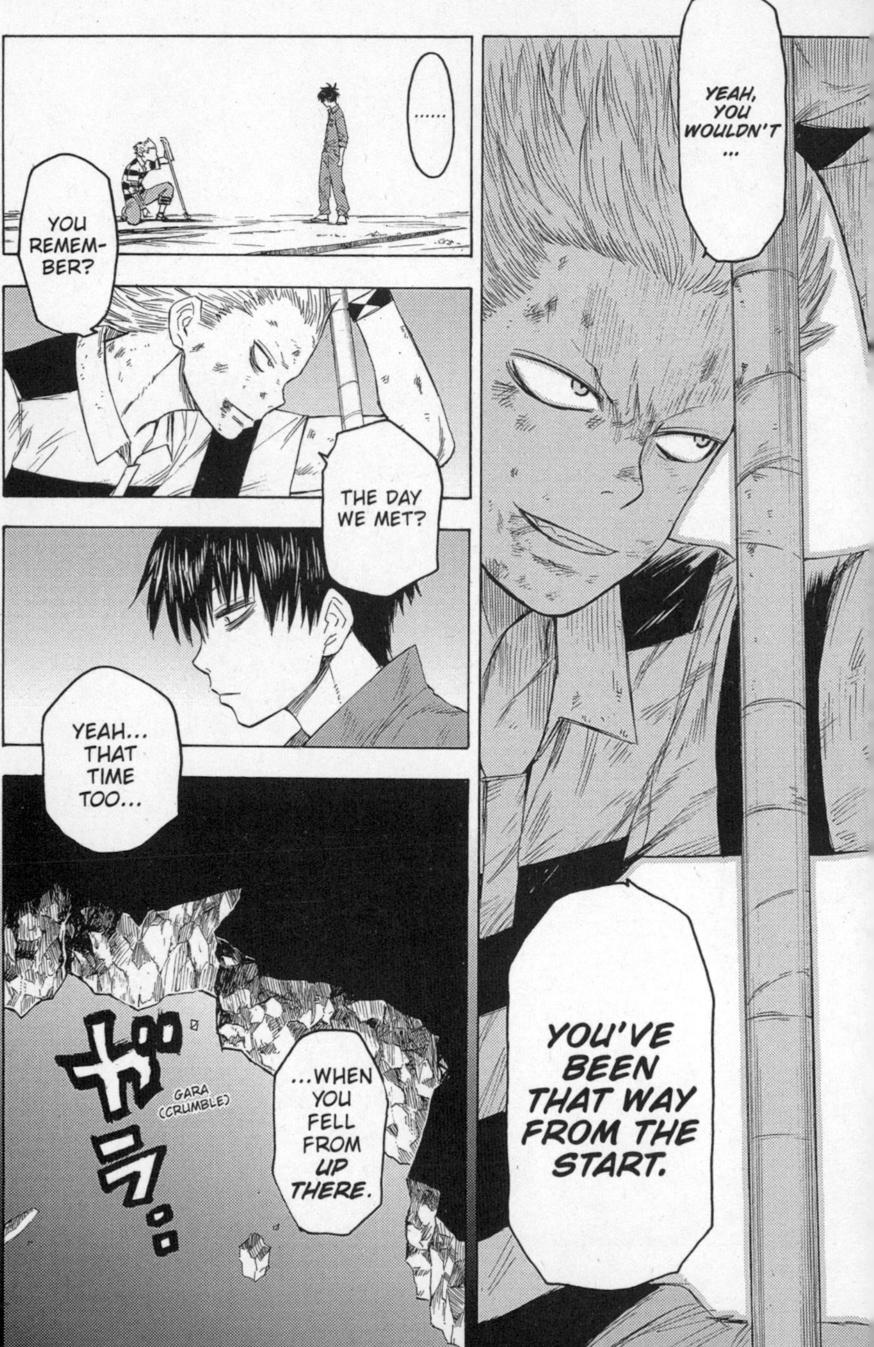
YEAH, YOU WOULDN'T ...
YOU'VE BEEN THAT WAY FROM THE START.
......
YOU REMEMBER?
THE DAY WE MET?
YEAH... THAT TIME TOO...
GARA (CRUMBLE)
...WHEN YOU FELL FROM UP THERE.

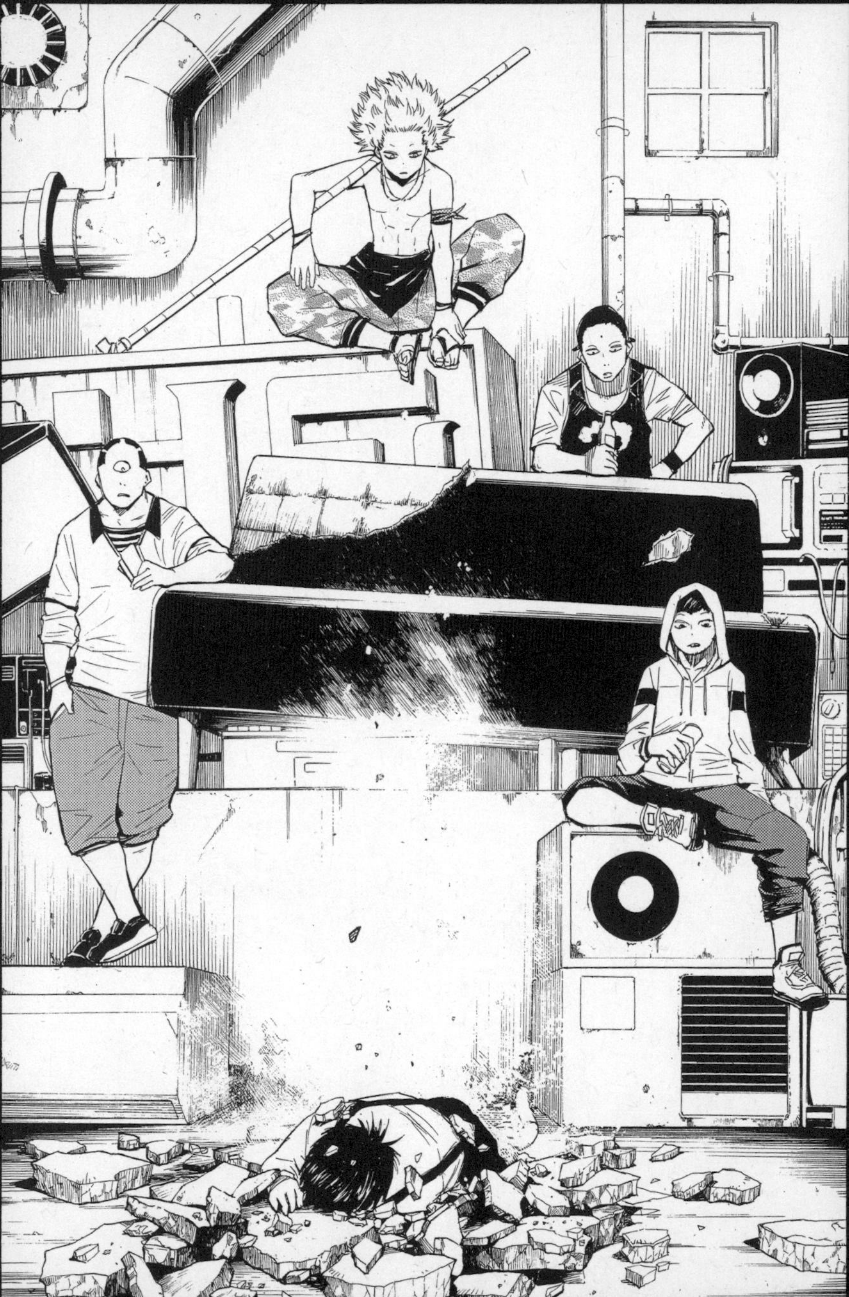

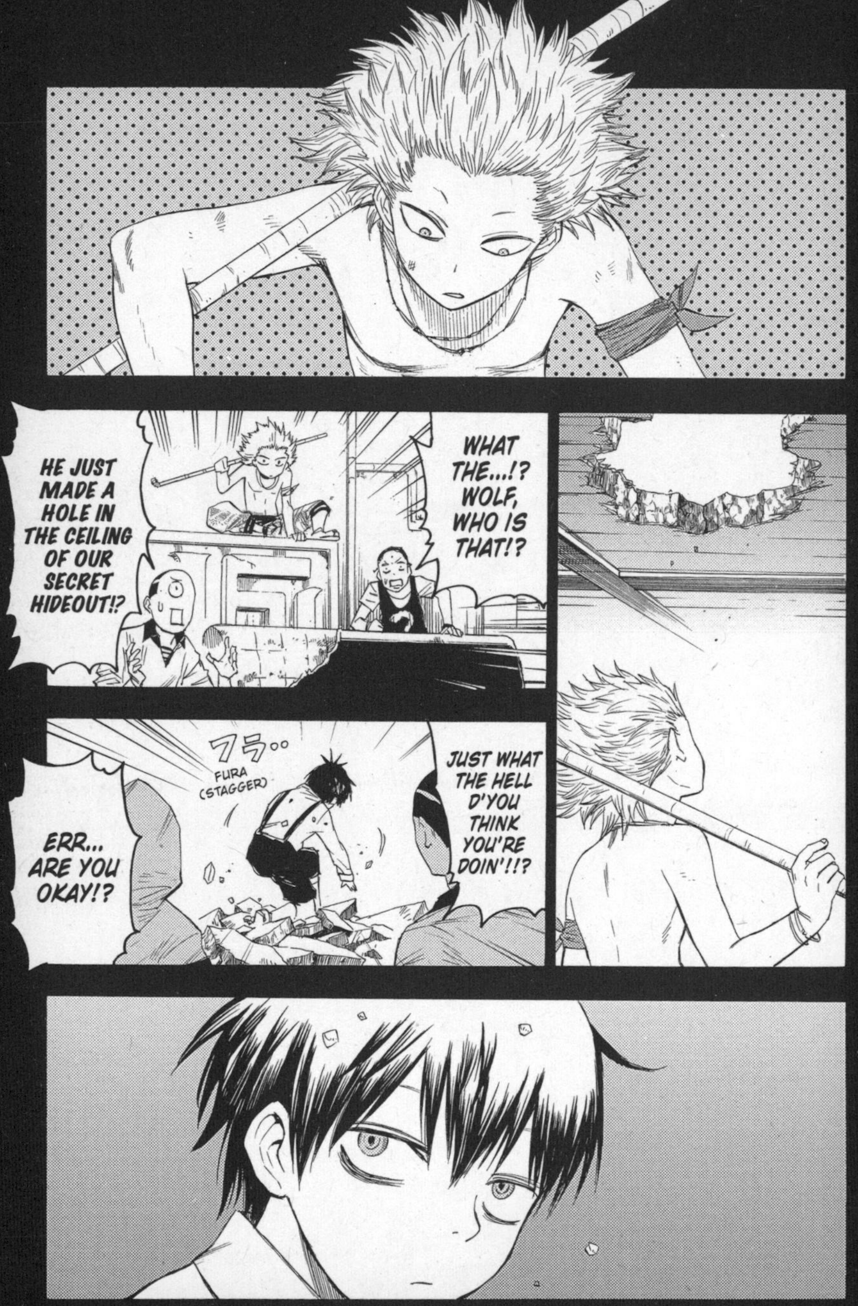
WHAT THE...!? WOLF, WHO IS THAT!?
HE JUST MADE A HOLE IN THE CEILING OF OUR SECRET HIDEOUT!?
JUST WHAT THE HELL D'YOU THINK YOU'RE DOIN'!!?
フラ
FURA (STAGGER)
ERR... ARE YOU OKAY!?

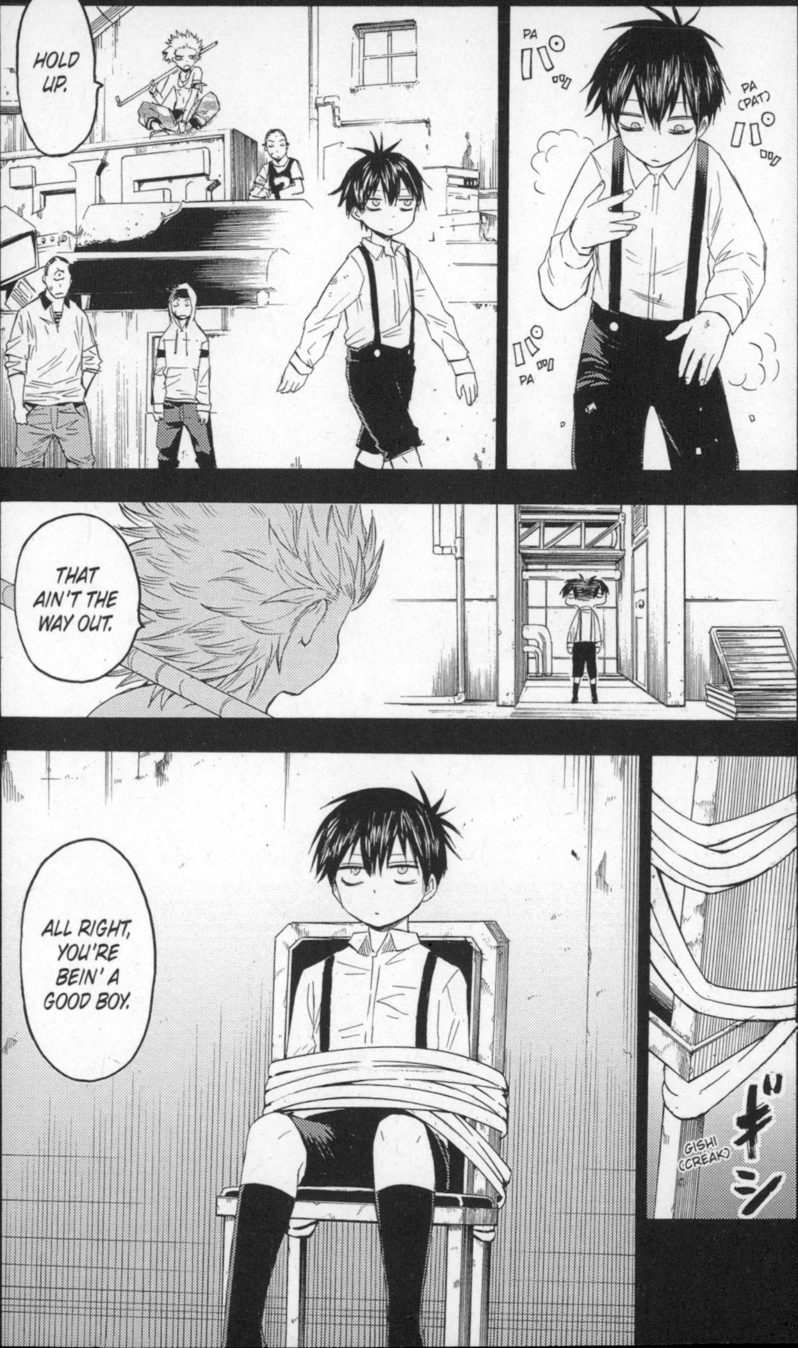
PA (PAT)
PA
PA
HOLD UP.
THAT AIN'T THE WAY OUT.
GISHI (CREAK)
ALL RIGHT, YOU'RE BEIN' A GOOD BOY.

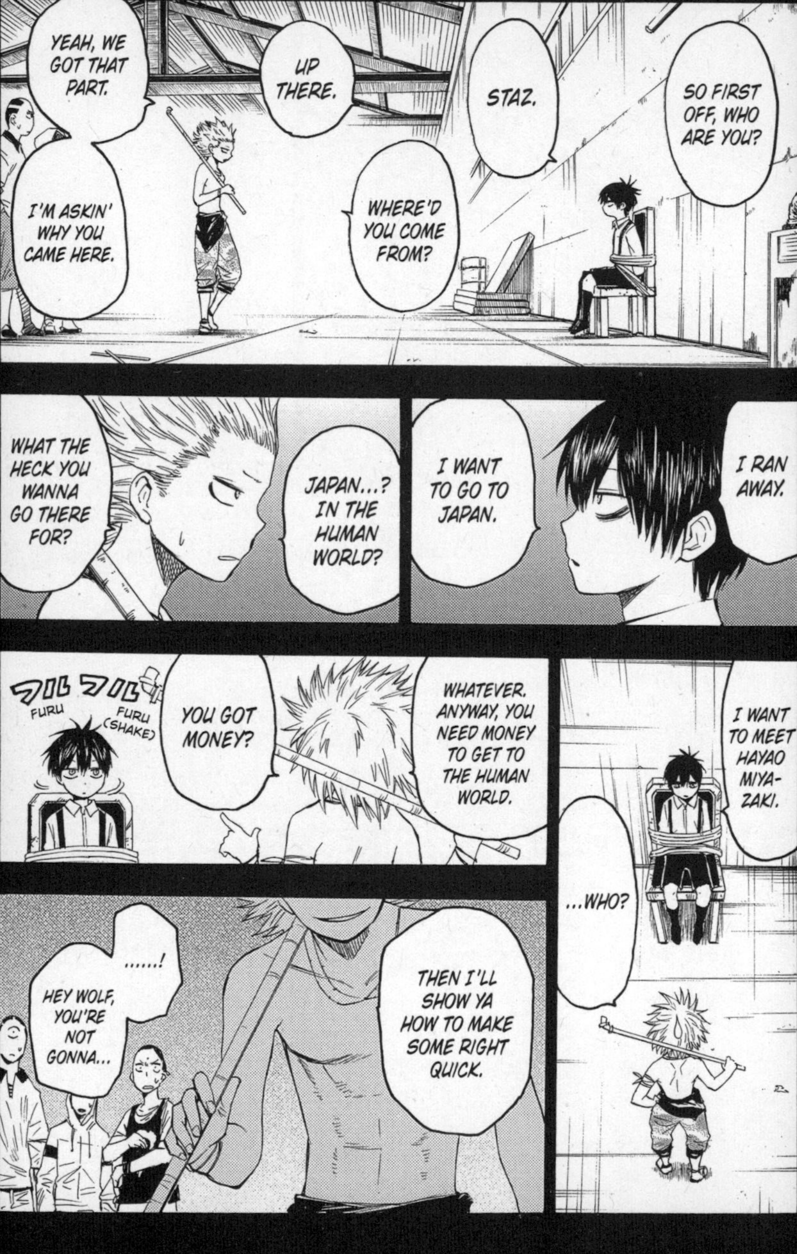
SO FIRST OFF, WHO ARE YOU?
STAZ.
WHERE'D YOU COME FROM?
UP THERE.
YEAH, WE GOT THAT PART.
I'M ASKIN' WHY YOU CAME HERE.
I RAN AWAY.
I WANT TO GO TO JAPAN.
JAPAN...? IN THE HUMAN WORLD?
WHAT THE HECK YOU WANNA GO THERE FOR?
I WANT TO MEET HAYAO MIYA-ZAKI.
...WHO?
WHATEVER. ANYWAY, YOU NEED MONEY TO GET TO THE HUMAN WORLD.
YOU GOT MONEY?
FURU FURU (SHAKE)
THEN I'LL SHOW YA HOW TO MAKE SOME RIGHT QUICK.
......!
HEY WOLF, YOU'RE NOT GONNA...

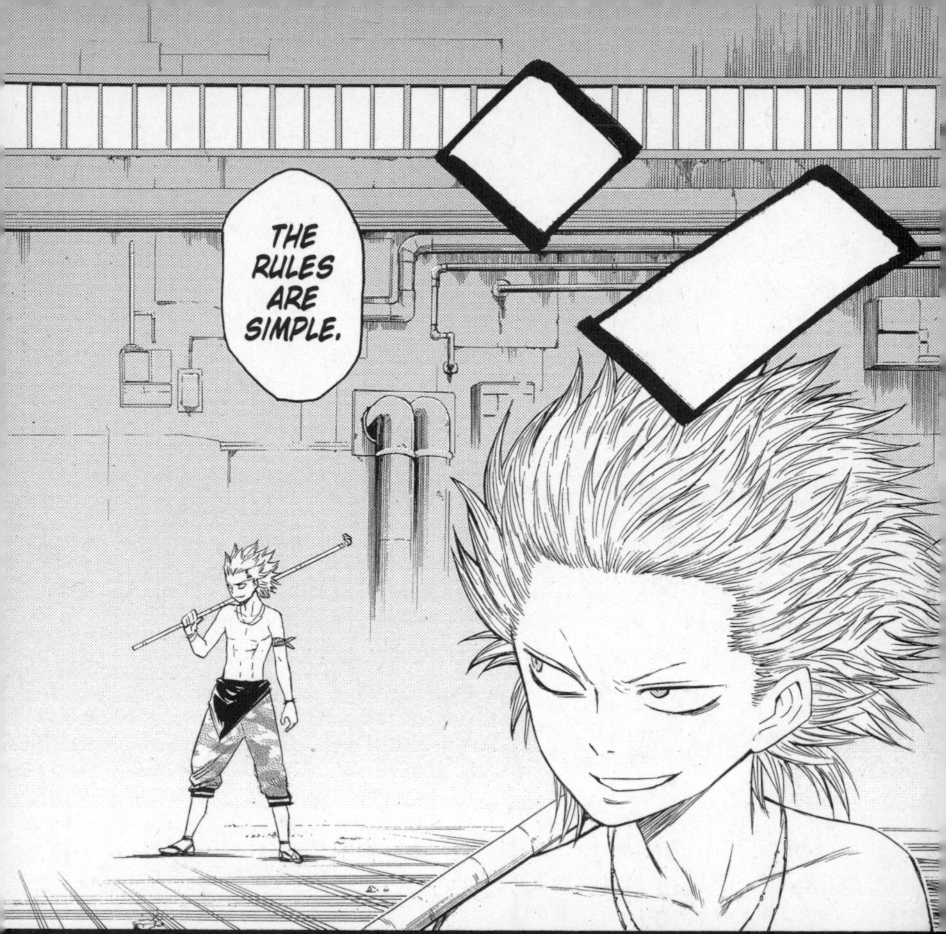
THE RULES ARE SIMPLE.
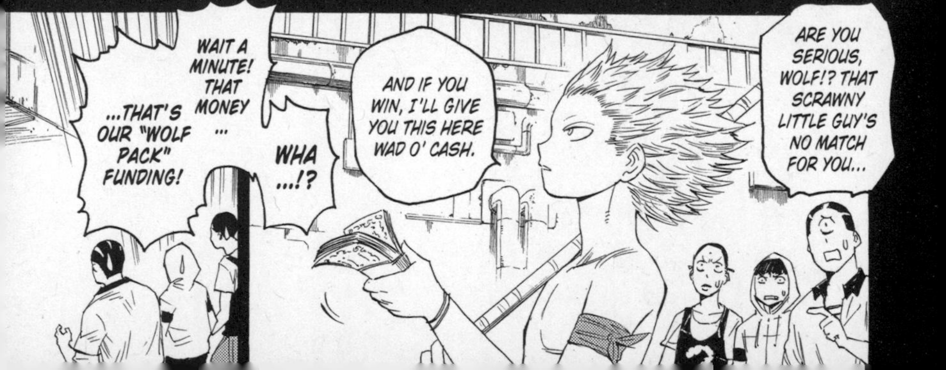
ARE YOU SERIOUS, WOLF!? THAT SCRAWNY LITTLE GUY'S NO MATCH FOR YOU...
AND IF YOU WIN, I'LL GIVE YOU THIS HERE WAD O' CASH.
WHA ...!?
WAIT A MINUTE! THAT MONEY ...
...THAT'S OUR "WOLF PACK" FUNDING!

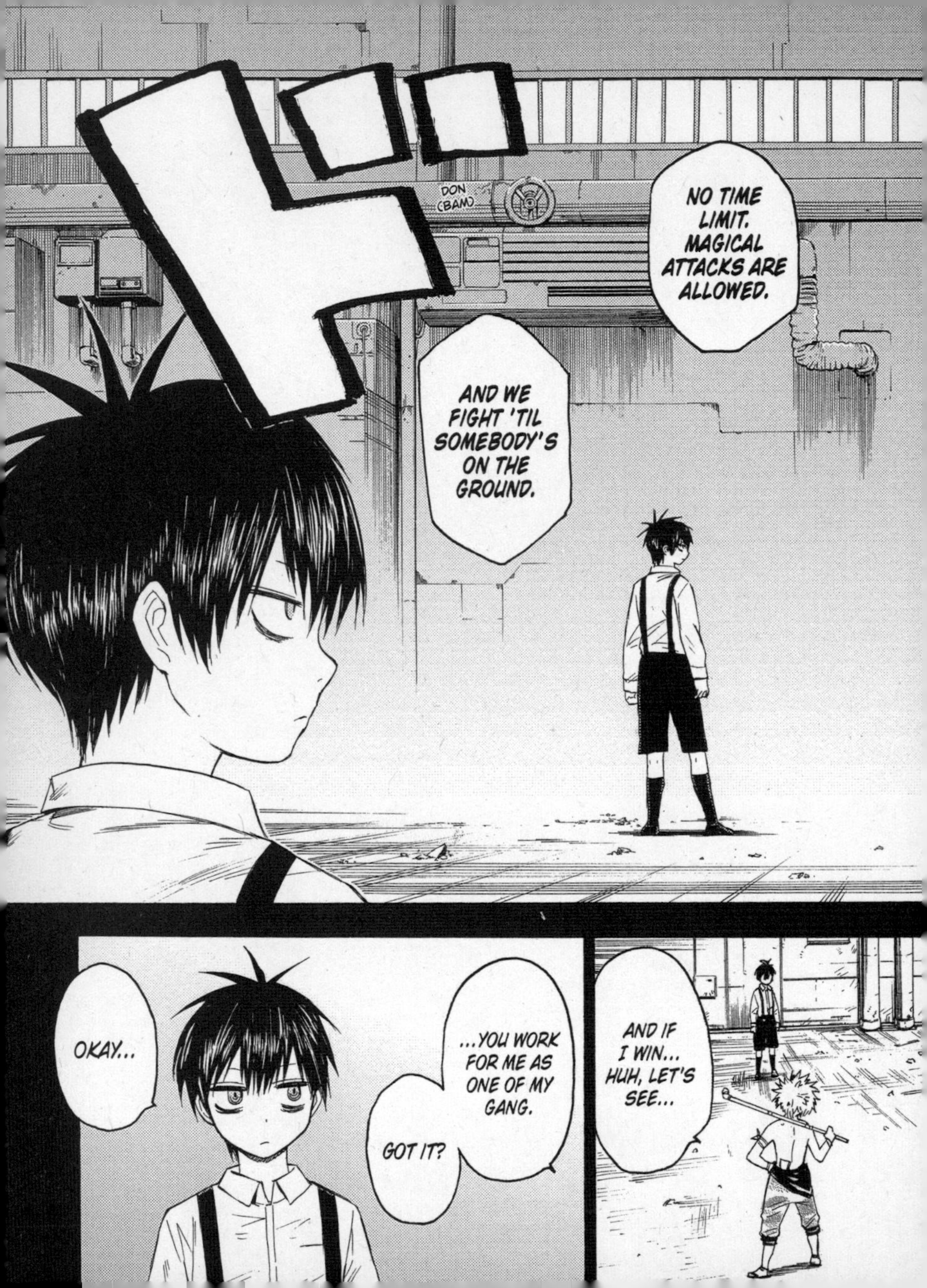
DON
(BAM)
NO TIME LIMIT. MAGICAL ATTACKS ARE ALLOWED.
AND WE FIGHT 'TIL SOMEBODY'S ON THE GROUND.
AND IF I WIN... HUH, LET'S SEE...
...YOU WORK FOR ME AS ONE OF MY GANG.
GOT IT?
OKAY...

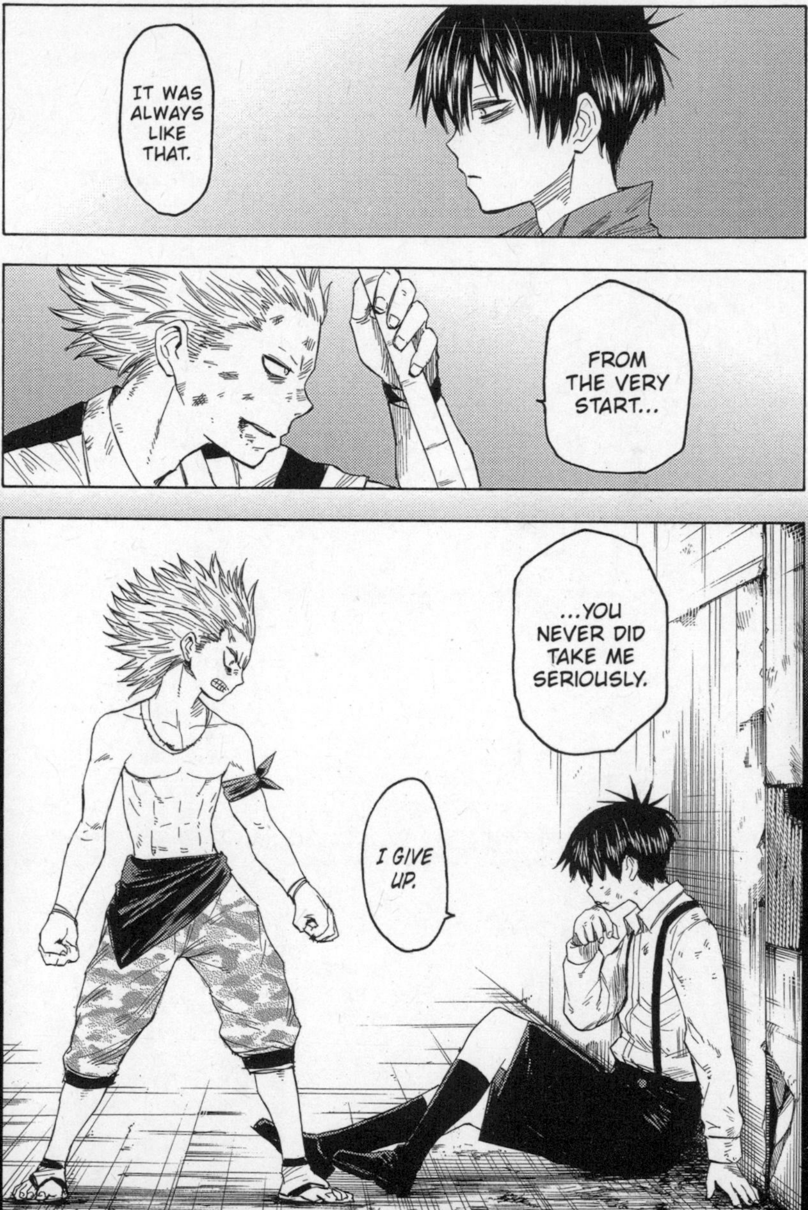
IT WAS ALWAYS LIKE THAT.
FROM THE VERY START...
...YOU NEVER DID TAKE ME SERIOUSLY.
I GIVE UP.

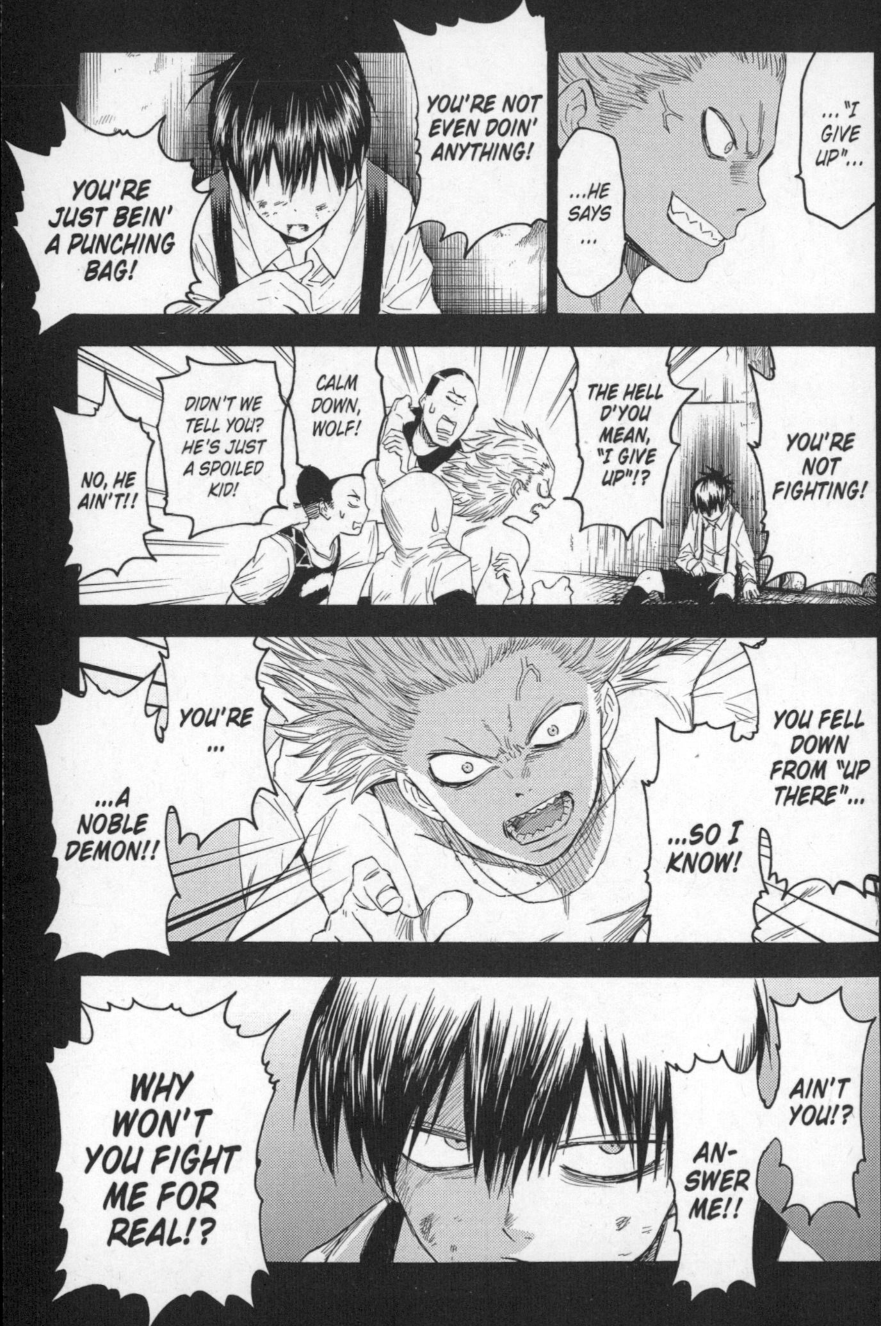
..."I GIVE UP"...
...HE SAYS ...
YOU'RE NOT EVEN DOIN' ANYTHING!
YOU'RE JUST BEIN' A PUNCHING BAG!
YOU'RE NOT FIGHTING!
THE HELL D'YOU MEAN, "I GIVE UP"!?
CALM DOWN, WOLF!
DIDN'T WE TELL YOU? HE'S JUST A SPOILED KID!
NO, HE AIN'T!!
YOU FELL DOWN FROM "UP THERE"...
...SO I KNOW!
YOU'RE ...
...A NOBLE DEMON!!
AIN'T YOU!?
AN-SWER ME!!
WHY WON'T YOU FIGHT ME FOR REAL!?

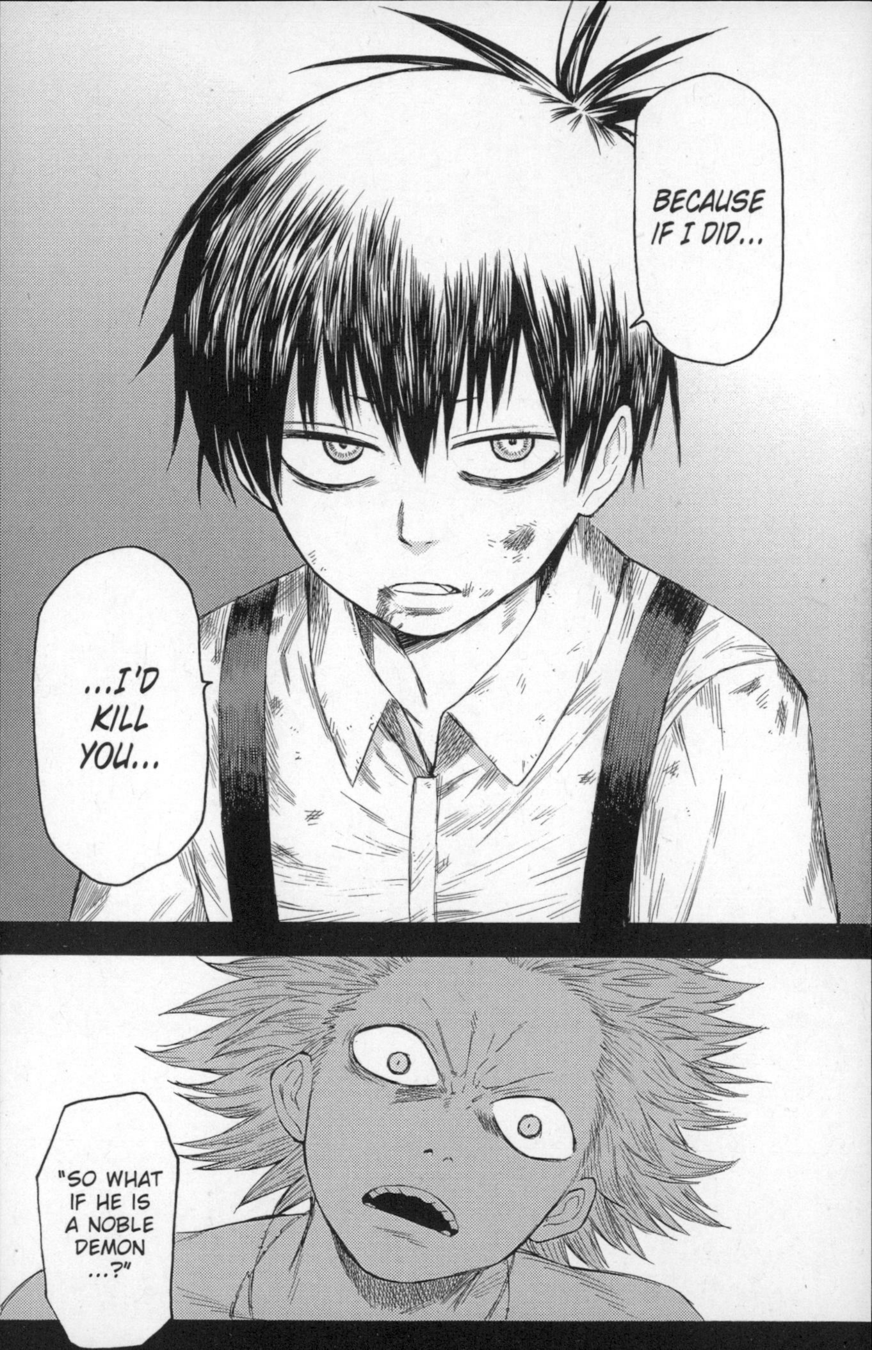
BECAUSE IF I DID...
...I'D KILL YOU...
"SO WHAT IF HE IS A NOBLE DEMON ...?"

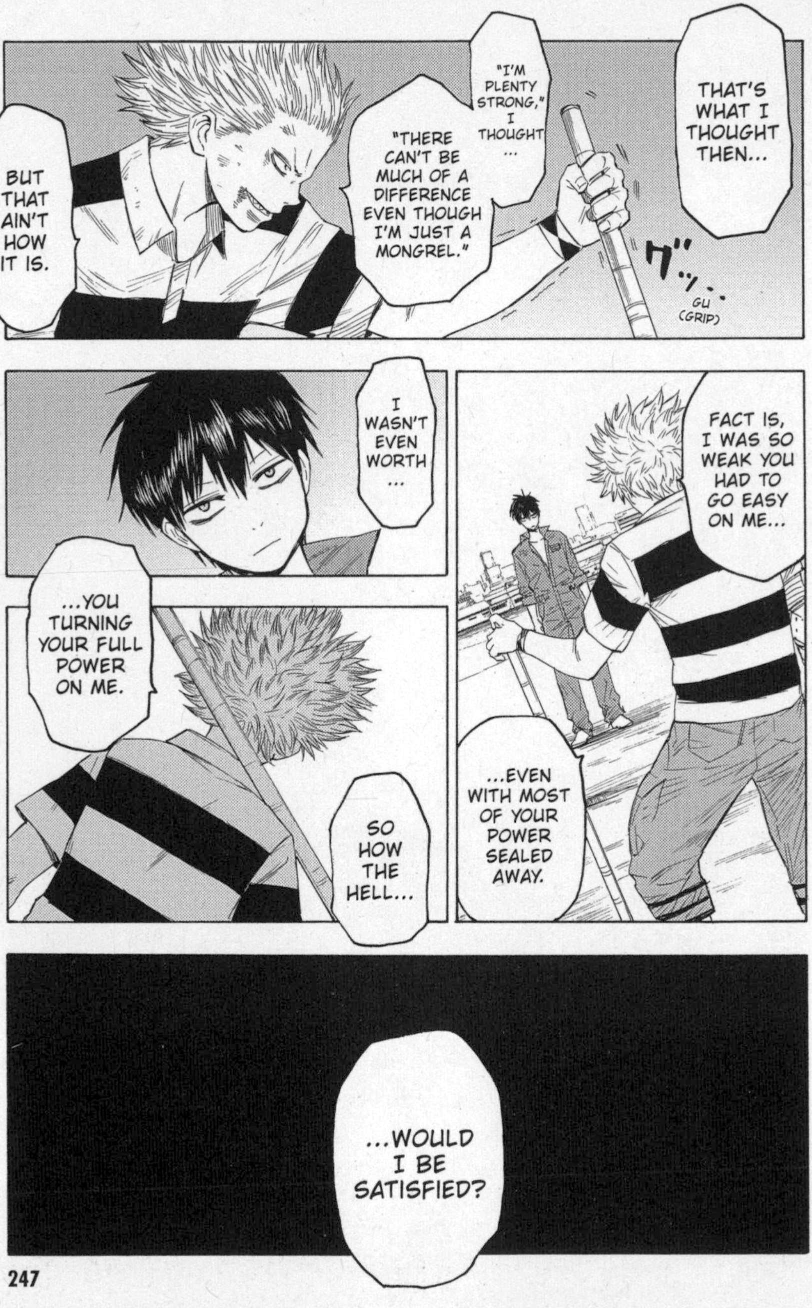
THAT'S WHAT I THOUGHT THEN...
"I'M PLENTY STRONG," I THOUGHT...
"THERE CAN'T BE MUCH OF A DIFFERENCE EVEN THOUGH I'M JUST A MONGREL."
グッ‥
GU (GRIP)
BUT THAT AIN'T HOW IT IS.
FACT IS, I WAS SO WEAK YOU HAD TO GO EASY ON ME...
...EVEN WITH MOST OF YOUR POWER SEALED AWAY.
I WASN'T EVEN WORTH...
...YOU TURNING YOUR FULL POWER ON ME.
SO HOW THE HELL...
...WOULD I BE SATISFIED?

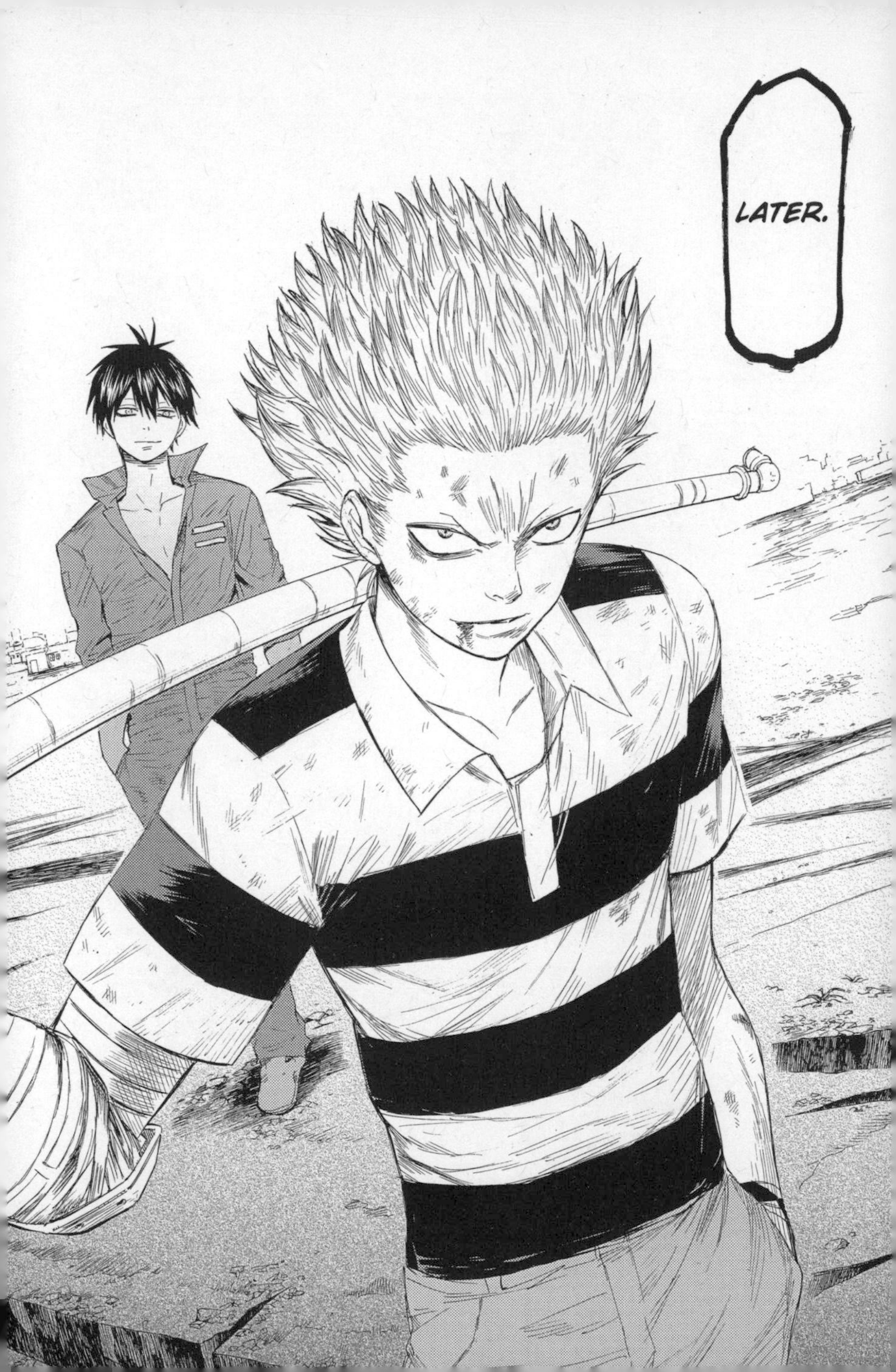
LATER.

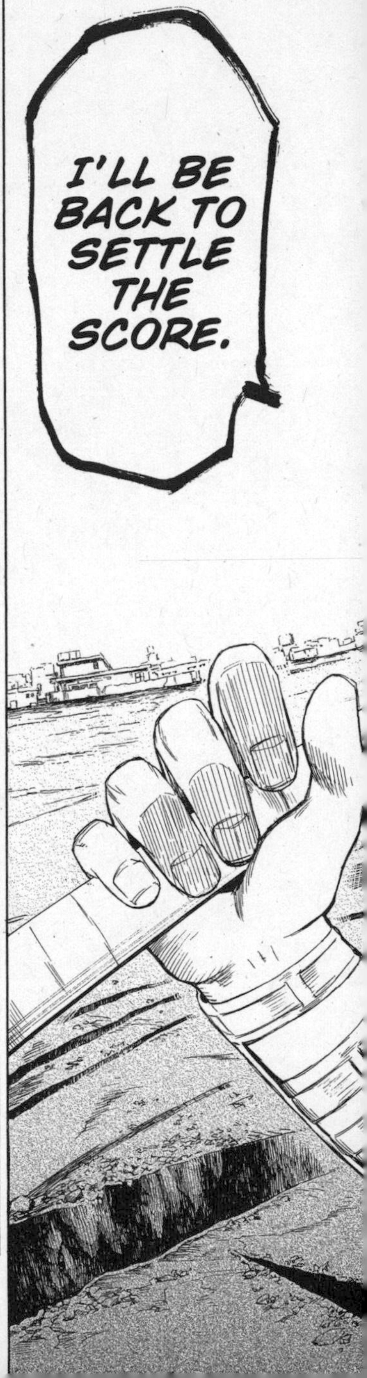
I'LL BE BACK TO SETTLE THE SCORE.

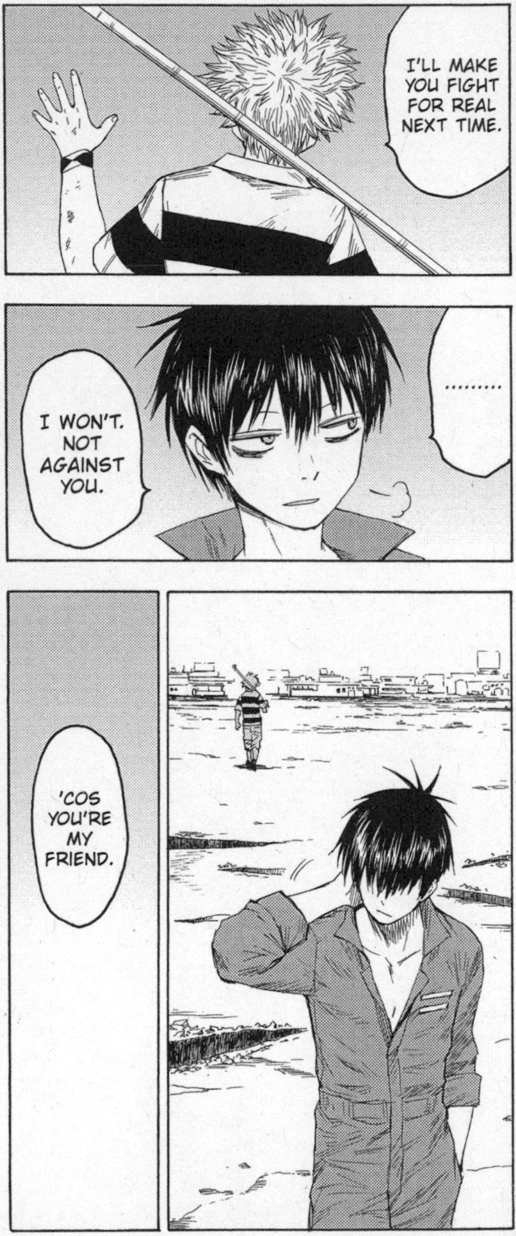
I'LL MAKE YOU FIGHT FOR REAL NEXT TIME.
....
I WON'T. NOT AGAINST YOU.
'COS YOU'RE MY FRIEND.

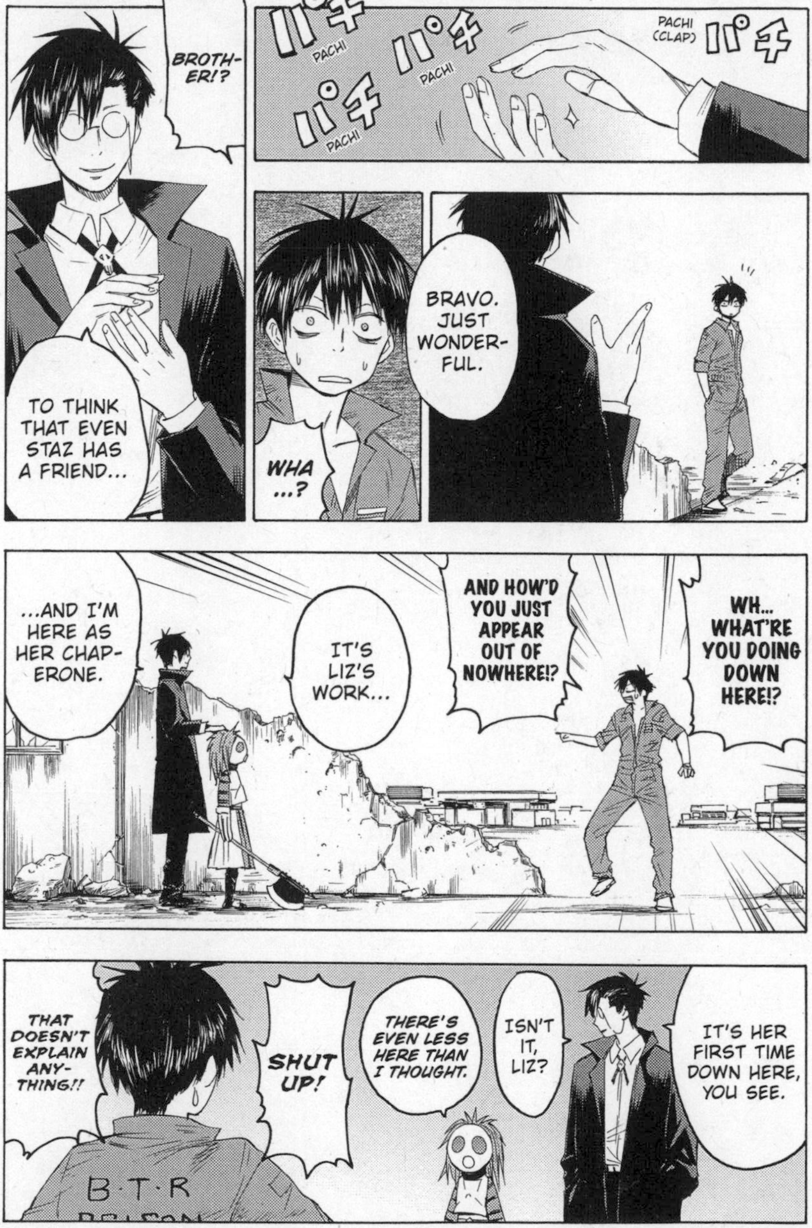
PACHI (CLAP)
パチ
パチ
PACHI
パチ
PACHI
パチ
PACHI
BRAVO. JUST WONDERFUL.
WHA ...?
BROTHER!?
TO THINK THAT EVEN STAZ HAS A FRIEND...
WH... WHAT'RE YOU DOING DOWN HERE!?
AND HOW'D YOU JUST APPEAR OUT OF NOWHERE!?
IT'S LIZ'S WORK...
...AND I'M HERE AS HER CHAPERONE.
IT'S HER FIRST TIME DOWN HERE, YOU SEE.
ISN'T IT, LIZ?
THERE'S EVEN LESS HERE THAN I THOUGHT.
SHUT UP!
THAT DOESN'T EXPLAIN ANYTHING!!
B·T·R

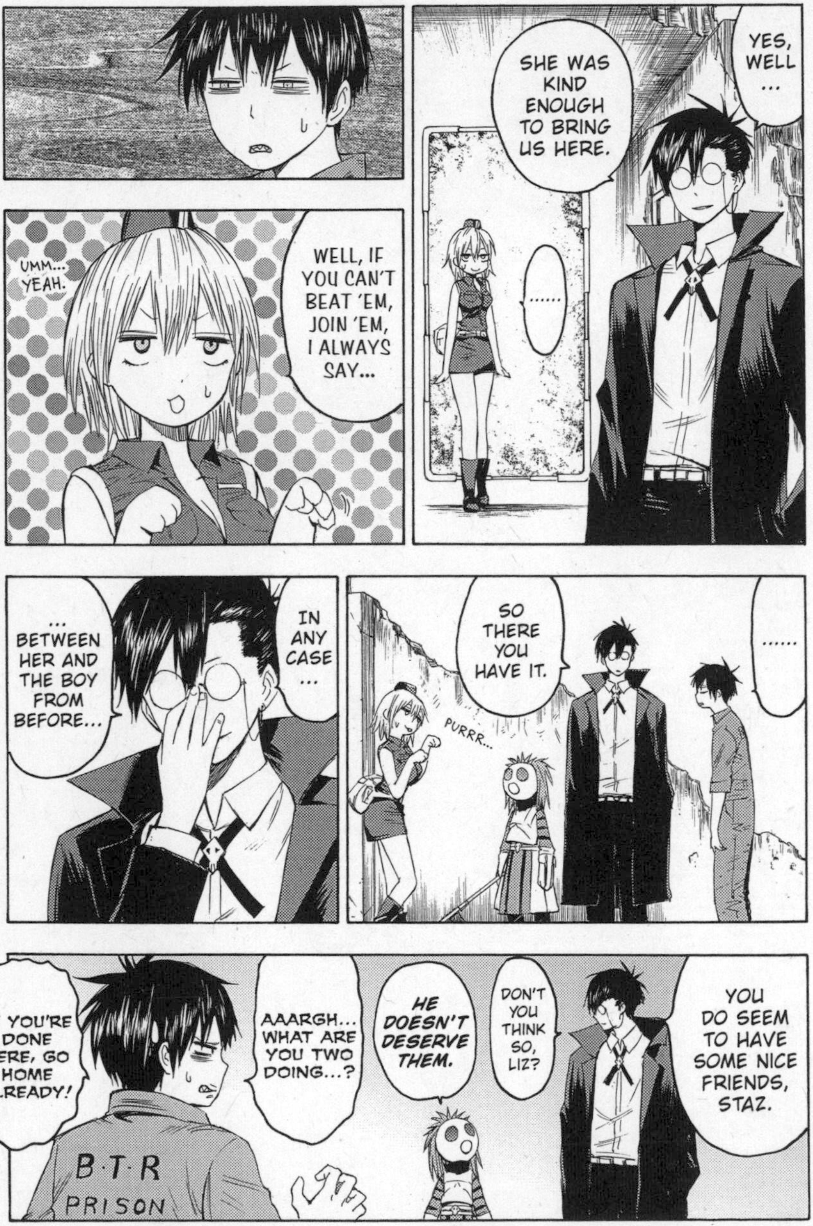
YES, WELL ...
SHE WAS KIND ENOUGH TO BRING US HERE.
......
WELL, IF YOU CAN'T BEAT 'EM, JOIN 'EM, I ALWAYS SAY...
UMM... YEAH.
......
SO THERE YOU HAVE IT.
PURRR...
IN ANY CASE ...
... BETWEEN HER AND THE BOY FROM BEFORE...
YOU DO SEEM TO HAVE SOME NICE FRIENDS, STAZ.
DON'T YOU THINK SO, LIZ?
HE DOESN'T DESERVE THEM.
AAARGH... WHAT ARE YOU TWO DOING...?
IF YOU'RE DONE HERE, GO HOME ALREADY!
B·T·R
PRISON

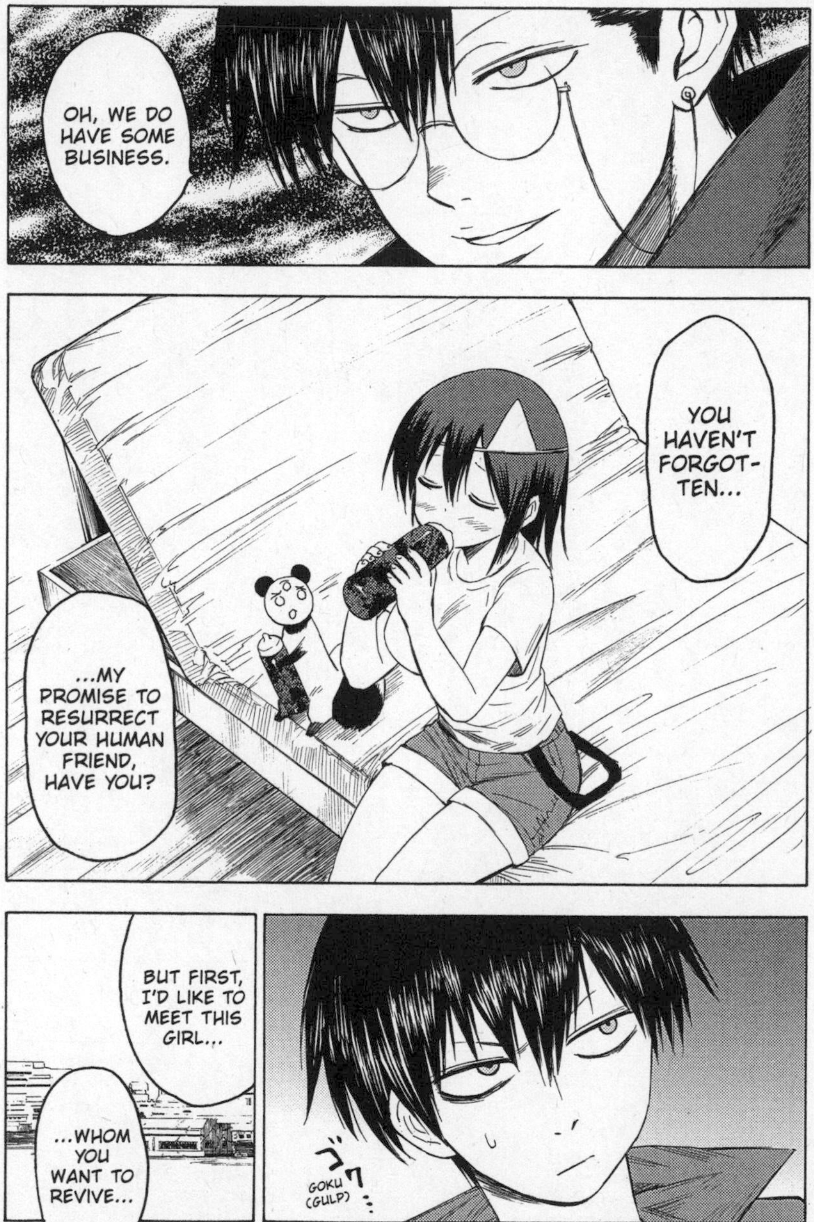
OH, WE DO HAVE SOME BUSINESS.
YOU HAVEN'T FORGOT-TEN...
...MY PROMISE TO RESURRECT YOUR HUMAN FRIEND, HAVE YOU?
ゴク
GOKU (GULP)
BUT FIRST, I'D LIKE TO MEET THIS GIRL...
...WHOM YOU WANT TO REVIVE...

♠ To Be Continued ♠

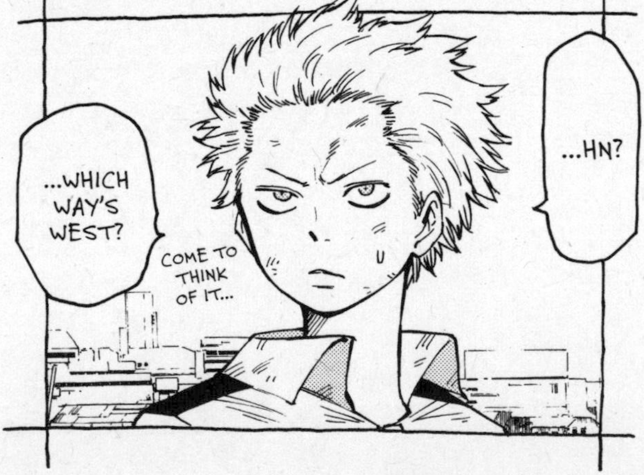
...HN?
COME TO THINK OF IT...
...WHICH WAY'S WEST?

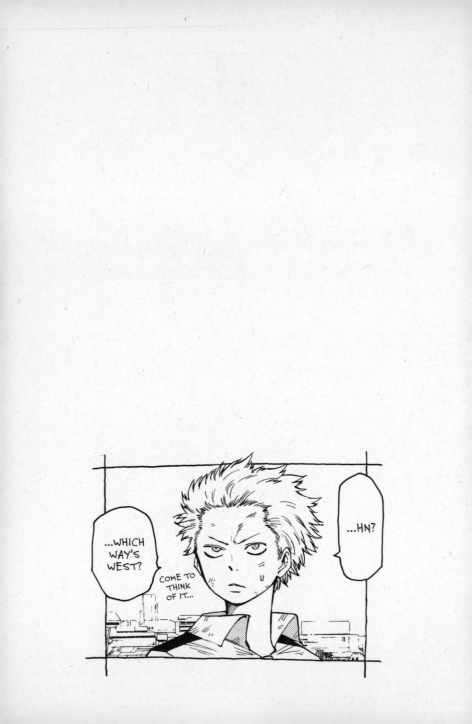

BLOOD LAD

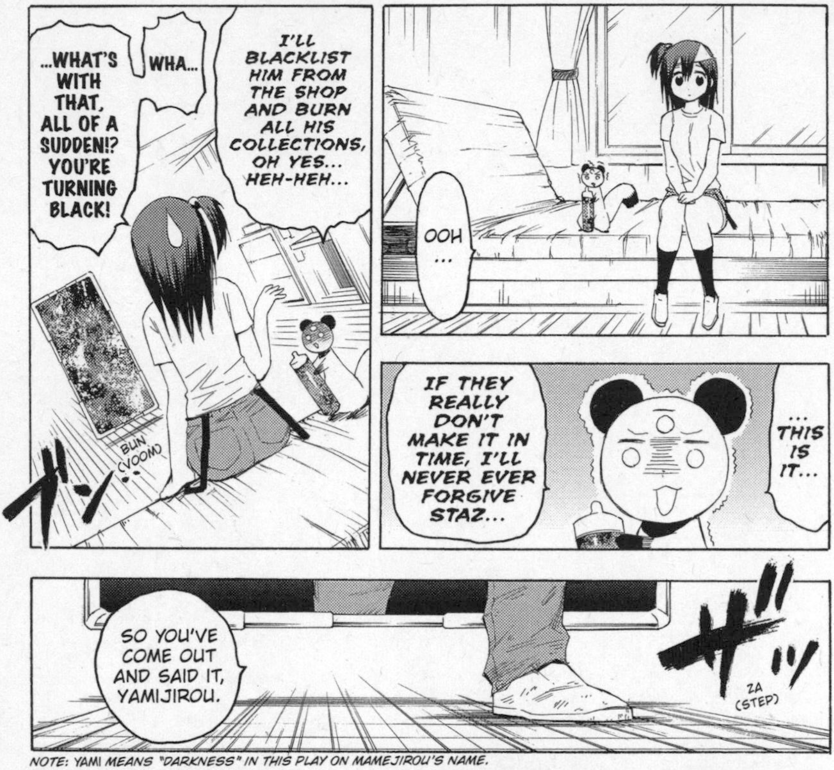
OOH ...
... THIS IS IT...
IF THEY REALLY DON'T MAKE IT IN TIME, I'LL NEVER EVER FORGIVE STAZ...
I'LL BLACKLIST HIM FROM THE SHOP AND BURN ALL HIS COLLECTIONS, OH YES... HEH-HEH...
WHA...
...WHAT'S WITH THAT, ALL OF A SUDDEN!? YOU'RE TURNING BLACK!
BUN (VOOM)
ZA (STEP)
SO YOU'VE COME OUT AND SAID IT, YAMIJIROU.

NOTE: YAMI MEANS "DARKNESS" IN THIS PLAY ON MAMEJIROU'S NAME.

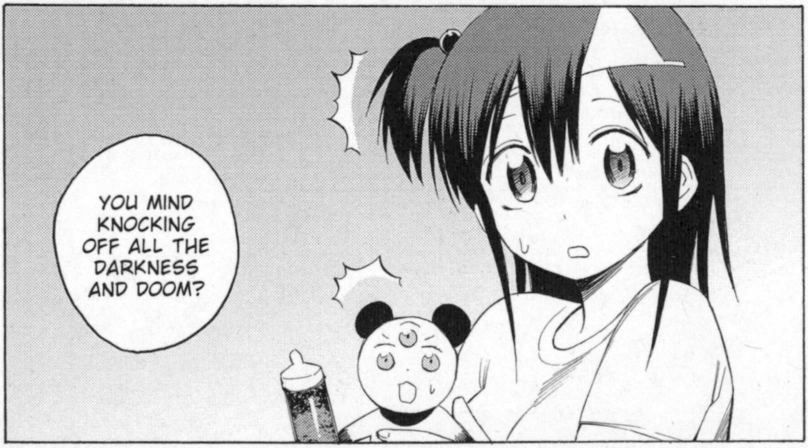
YOU MIND KNOCKING OFF ALL THE DARKNESS AND DOOM?

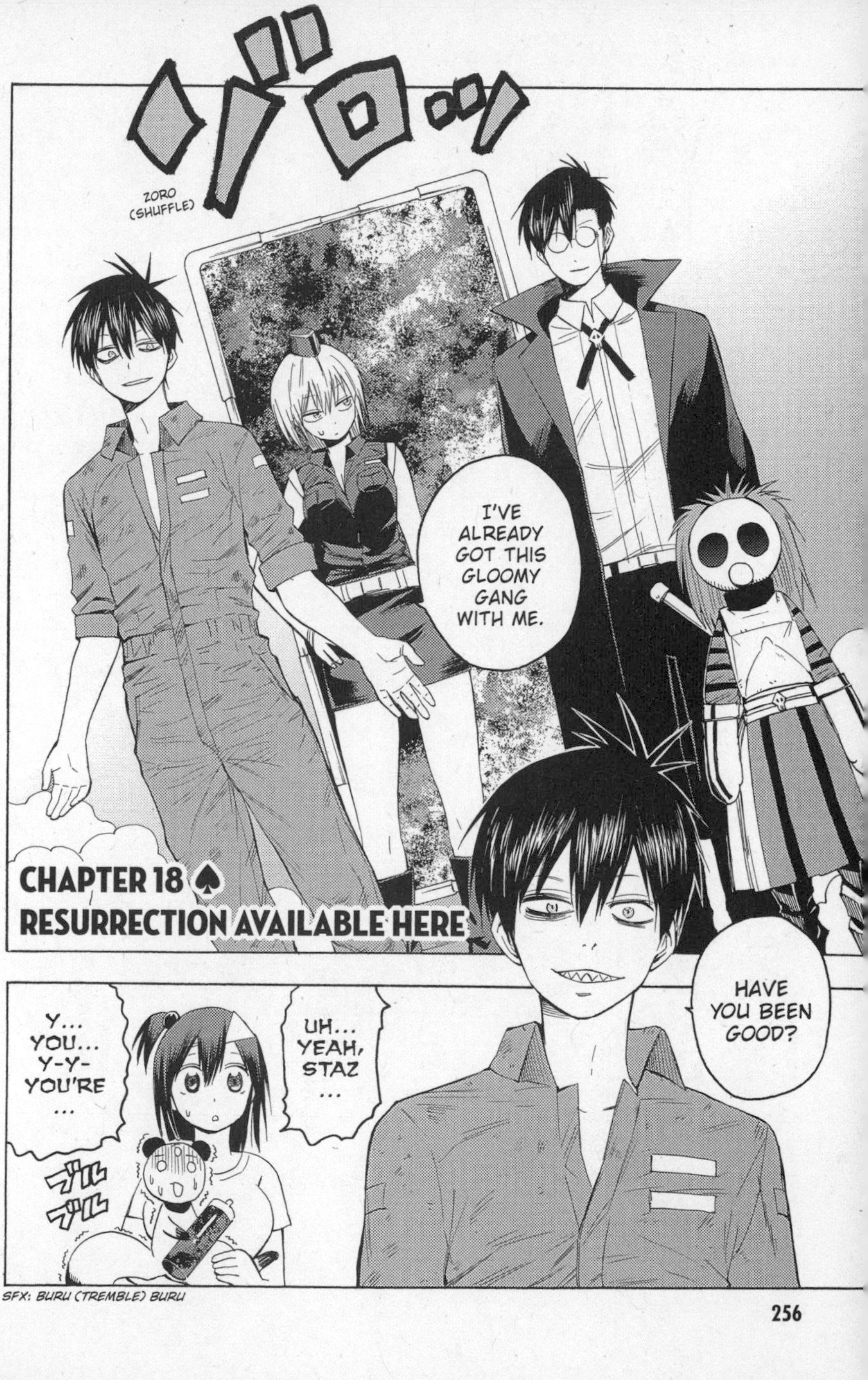
ZORO (SHUFFLE)
I'VE ALREADY GOT THIS GLOOMY GANG WITH ME.
CHAPTER 18 ♠ RESURRECTION AVAILABLE HERE
HAVE YOU BEEN GOOD?
UH... YEAH, STAZ...
Y... YOU... Y-Y-YOU'RE...

SFX: BURU (TREMBLE) BURU

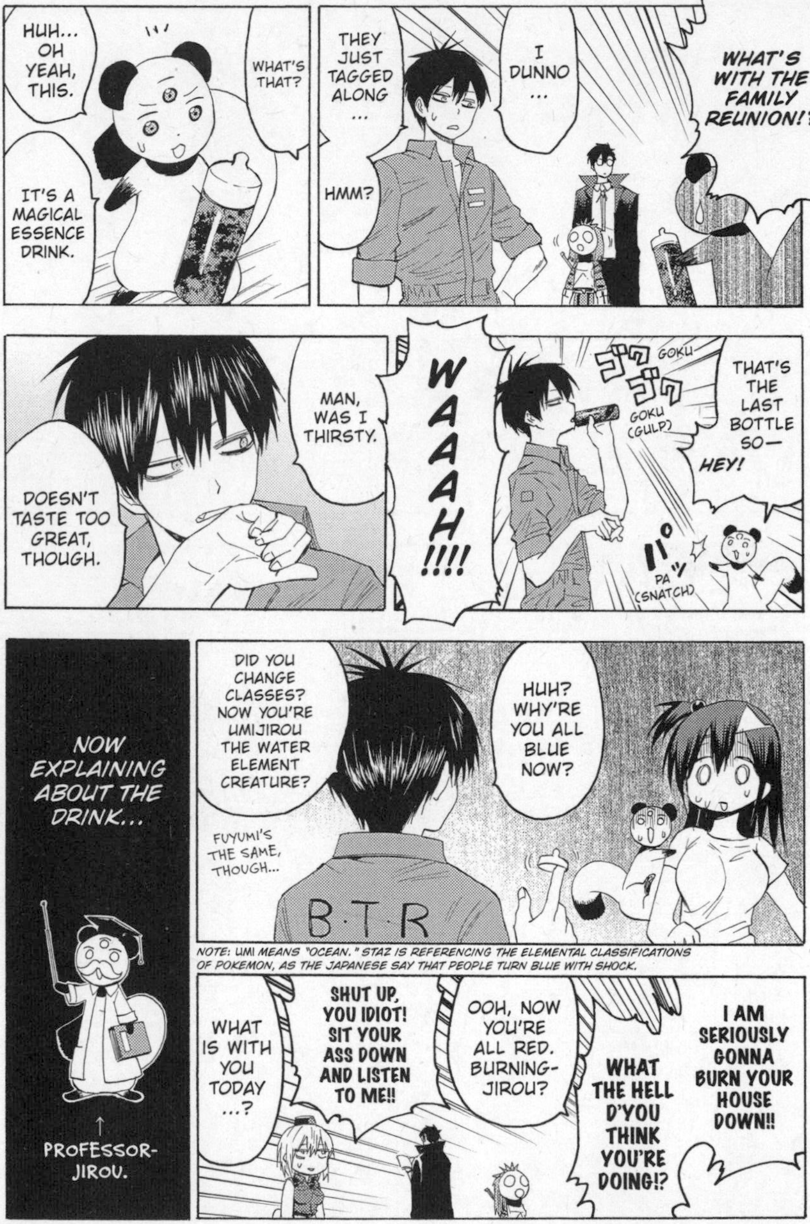
WHAT'S WITH THE FAMILY REUNION!?
I DUNNO...
THEY JUST TAGGED ALONG...
HMM?
WHAT'S THAT?
HUH... OH YEAH, THIS.
IT'S A MAGICAL ESSENCE DRINK.
THAT'S THE LAST BOTTLE SO—
HEY!
ゴクゴク GOKU GOKU (GULP)
パッ PA (SNATCH)
WAAAAH!!!!
MAN, WAS I THIRSTY.
DOESN'T TASTE TOO GREAT, THOUGH.
HUH? WHY'RE YOU ALL BLUE NOW?
DID YOU CHANGE CLASSES? NOW YOU'RE UMIJIROU THE WATER ELEMENT CREATURE?
FUYUMI'S THE SAME, THOUGH...
B·T·R
I AM SERIOUSLY GONNA BURN YOUR HOUSE DOWN!!
WHAT THE HELL D'YOU THINK YOU'RE DOING!?
OOH, NOW YOU'RE ALL RED. BURNING-JIROU?
SHUT UP, YOU IDIOT! SIT YOUR ASS DOWN AND LISTEN TO ME!!
WHAT IS WITH YOU TODAY...?
NOW EXPLAINING ABOUT THE DRINK...
↑ PROFESSOR-JIROU.
NOTE: UMI MEANS "OCEAN." STAZ IS REFERENCING THE ELEMENTAL CLASSIFICATIONS OF POKEMON, AS THE JAPANESE SAY THAT PEOPLE TURN BLUE WITH SHOCK.

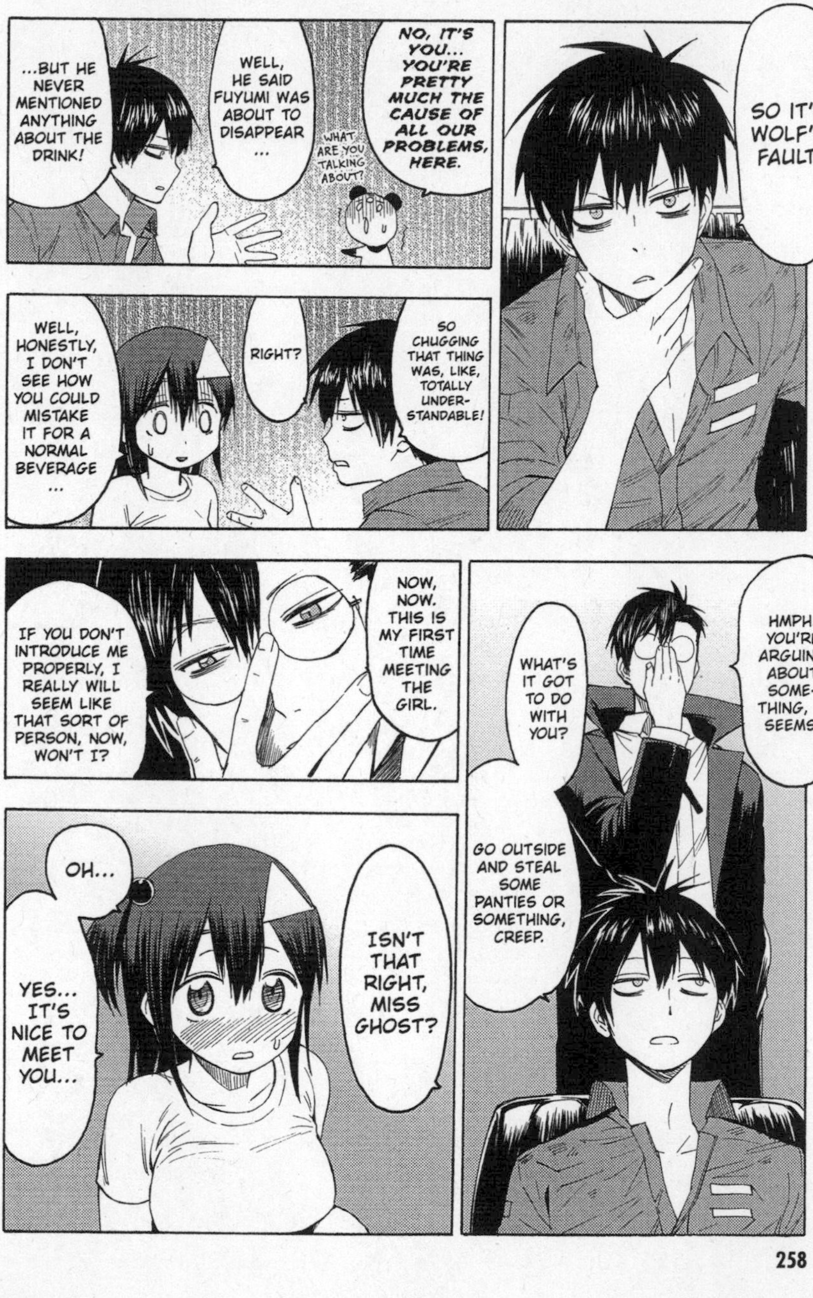
SO IT'S WOLF'S FAULT.
NO, IT'S YOU... YOU'RE PRETTY MUCH THE CAUSE OF ALL OUR PROBLEMS, HERE.
WHAT ARE YOU TALKING ABOUT?
WELL, HE SAID FUYUMI WAS ABOUT TO DISAPPEAR...
...BUT HE NEVER MENTIONED ANYTHING ABOUT THE DRINK!
SO CHUGGING THAT THING WAS, LIKE, TOTALLY UNDER-STANDABLE!
RIGHT?
WELL, HONESTLY, I DON'T SEE HOW YOU COULD MISTAKE IT FOR A NORMAL BEVERAGE...
HMPH. YOU'RE ARGUING ABOUT SOME-THING, IT SEEMS.
WHAT'S IT GOT TO DO WITH YOU?
GO OUTSIDE AND STEAL SOME PANTIES OR SOMETHING, CREEP.
NOW, NOW. THIS IS MY FIRST TIME MEETING THE GIRL.
IF YOU DON'T INTRODUCE ME PROPERLY, I REALLY WILL SEEM LIKE THAT SORT OF PERSON, NOW, WON'T I?
ISN'T THAT RIGHT, MISS GHOST?
OH...
YES... IT'S NICE TO MEET YOU...

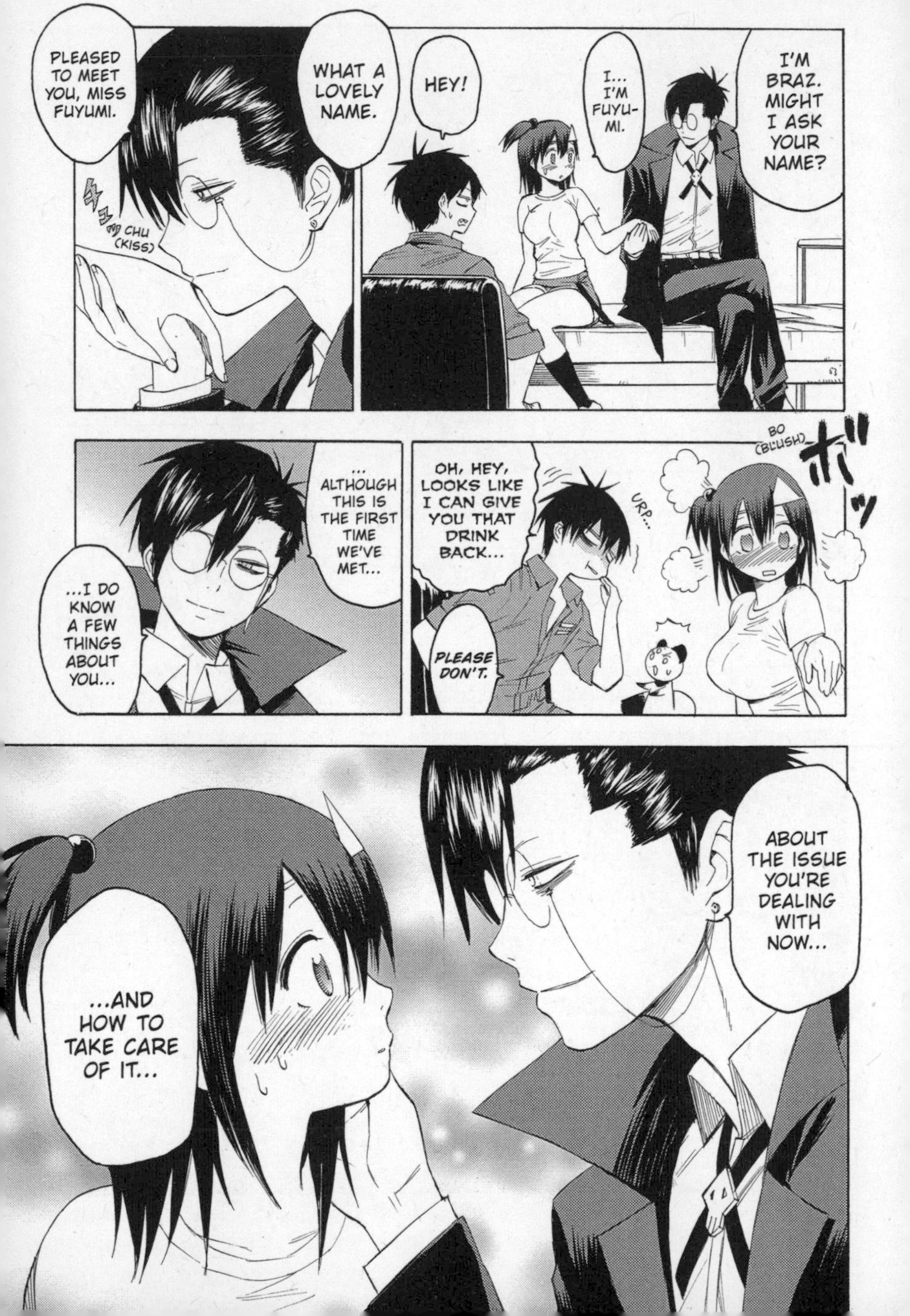
I'M BRAZ. MIGHT I ASK YOUR NAME?
I... I'M FUYU-MI.
HEY!
WHAT A LOVELY NAME.
PLEASED TO MEET YOU, MISS FUYUMI.
CHU (KISS)
ボッ
BO (BLUSH)
OH, HEY, LOOKS LIKE I CAN GIVE YOU THAT DRINK BACK...
URP...
PLEASE DON'T.
... ALTHOUGH THIS IS THE FIRST TIME WE'VE MET...
...I DO KNOW A FEW THINGS ABOUT YOU...
ABOUT THE ISSUE YOU'RE DEALING WITH NOW...
...AND HOW TO TAKE CARE OF IT...

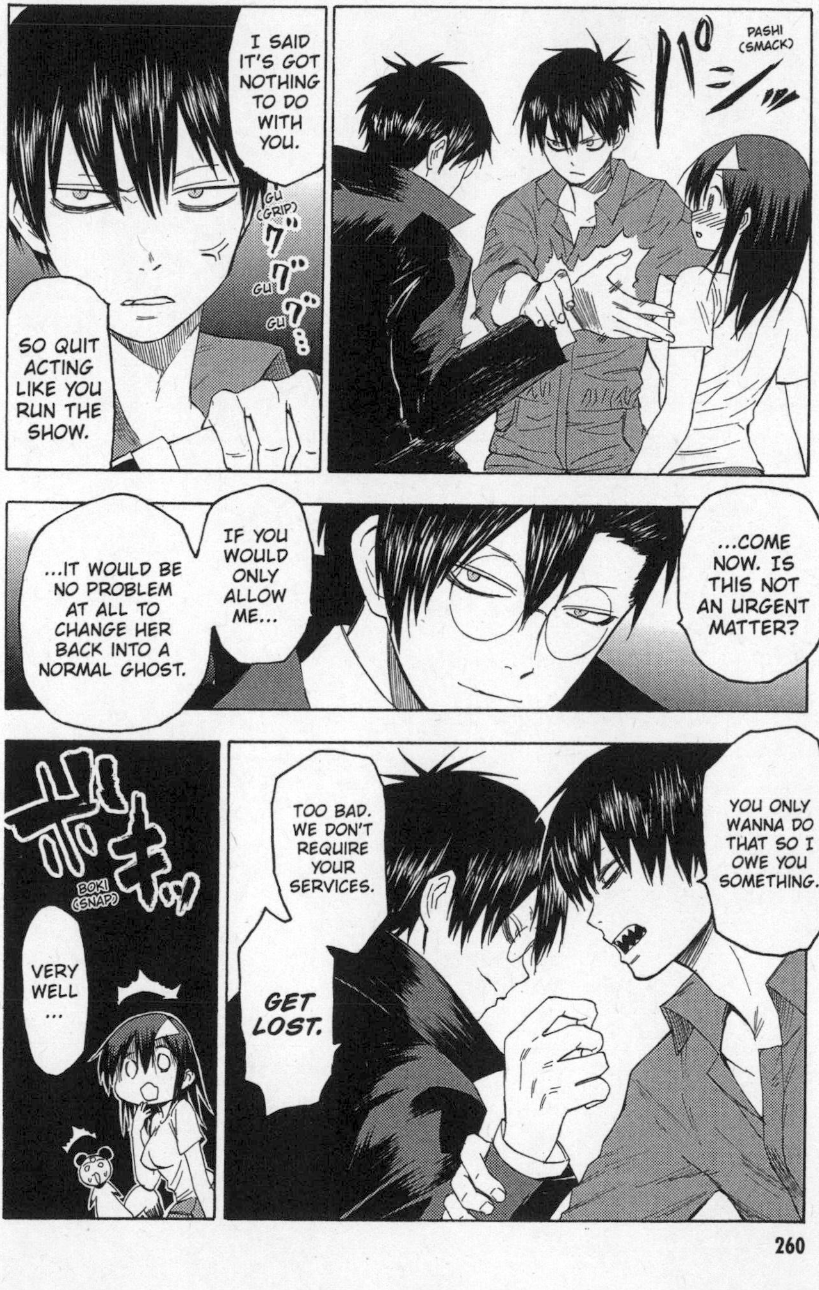
PASHI (SMACK)
I SAID IT'S GOT NOTHING TO DO WITH YOU.
GU (GRIP) GU GU
SO QUIT ACTING LIKE YOU RUN THE SHOW.
...COME NOW. IS THIS NOT AN URGENT MATTER?
IF YOU WOULD ONLY ALLOW ME...
...IT WOULD BE NO PROBLEM AT ALL TO CHANGE HER BACK INTO A NORMAL GHOST.
YOU ONLY WANNA DO THAT SO I OWE YOU SOMETHING.
TOO BAD. WE DON'T REQUIRE YOUR SERVICES.
GET LOST.
BOKI (SNAP)
VERY WELL ...

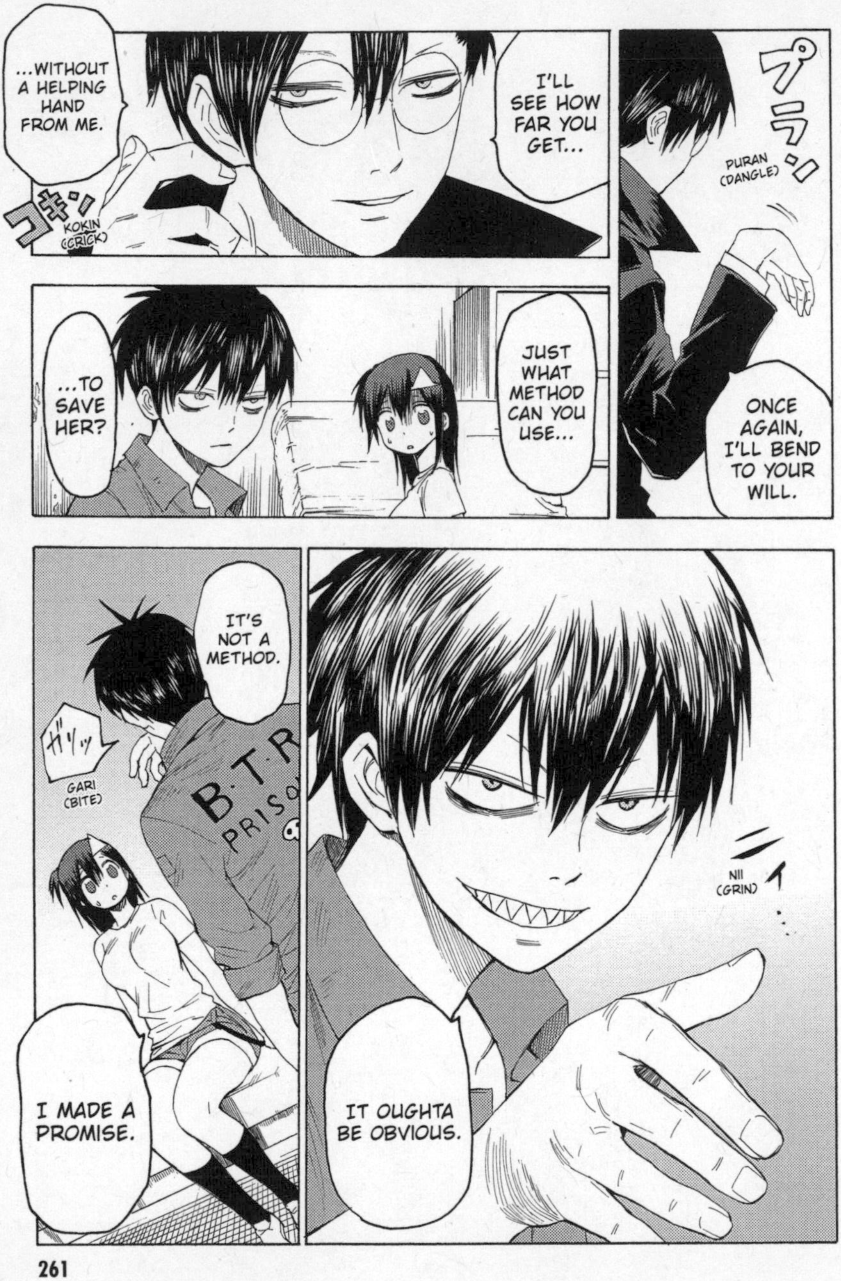

プラン
PURAN (DANGLE)
ONCE AGAIN, I'LL BEND TO YOUR WILL.
I'LL SEE HOW FAR YOU GET...
...WITHOUT A HELPING HAND FROM ME.
コキン
KOKIN (CRICK)
JUST WHAT METHOD CAN YOU USE...
...TO SAVE HER?
NII (GRIN)
IT OUGHTA BE OBVIOUS.
IT'S NOT A METHOD.
ガリッ
GARI (BITE)
I MADE A PROMISE.

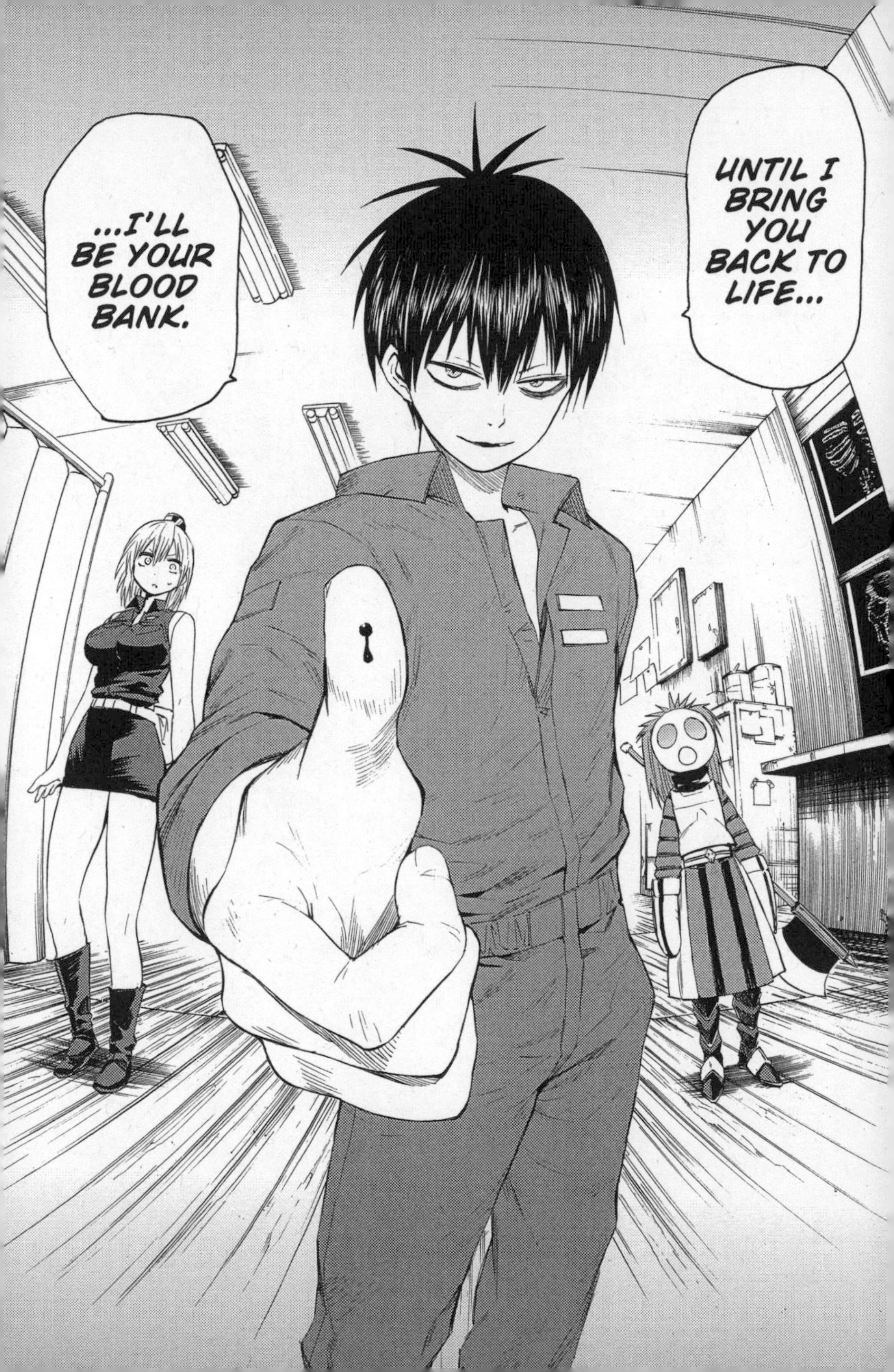
UNTIL I BRING YOU BACK TO LIFE...
...I'LL BE YOUR BLOOD BANK.

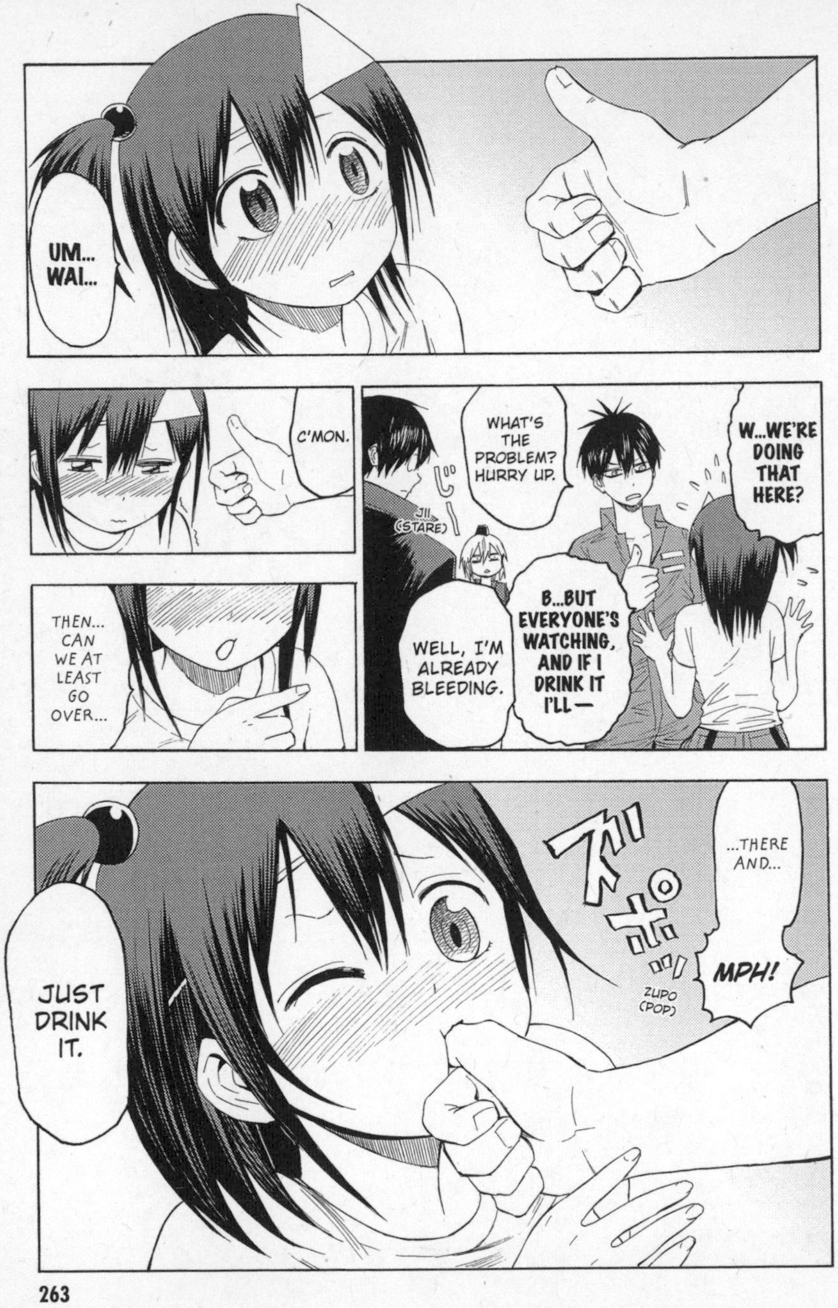
UM... WAI...
W...WE'RE DOING THAT HERE?
WHAT'S THE PROBLEM? HURRY UP.
JII (STARE)
B...BUT EVERYONE'S WATCHING, AND IF I DRINK IT I'LL—
WELL, I'M ALREADY BLEEDING.
C'MON.
THEN... CAN WE AT LEAST GO OVER...
...THERE AND...
MPH!
ZUPO (POP)
JUST DRINK IT.

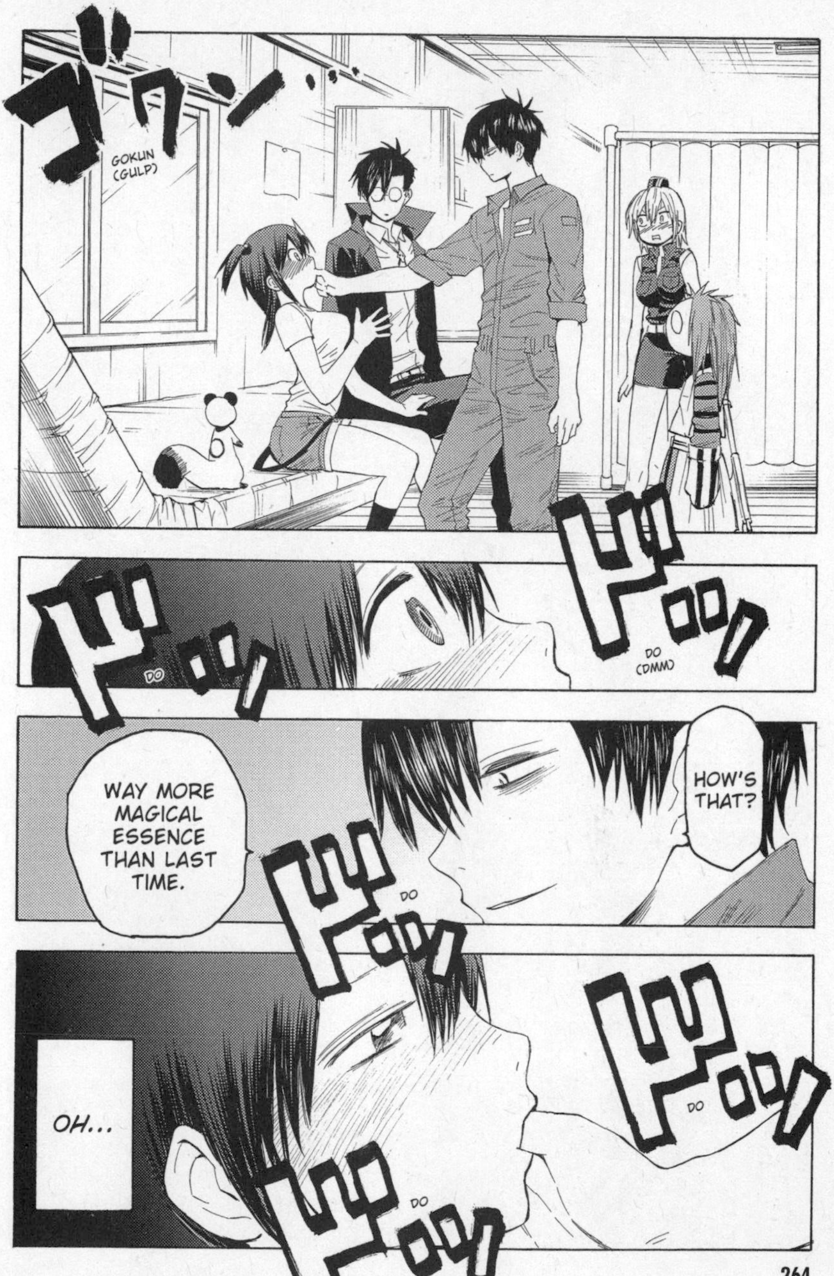
GOKUN (GULP)
DO (DMM)
DO
HOW'S THAT?
WAY MORE MAGICAL ESSENCE THAN LAST TIME.
DO
DO
OH...
DO

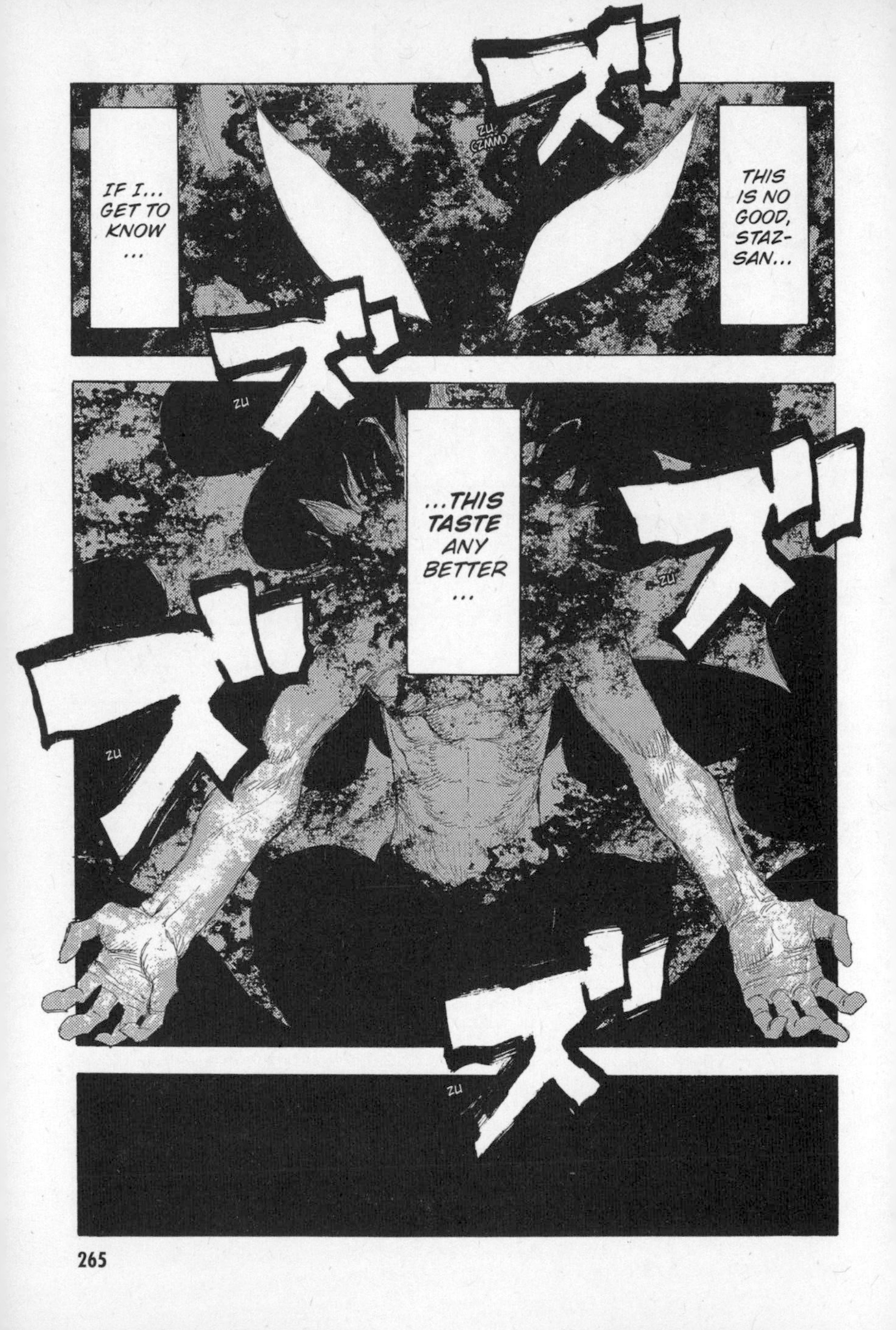
THIS IS NO GOOD, STAZ-SAN...
ZU (ZMM)
IF I... GET TO KNOW ...
ZU
...THIS TASTE ANY BETTER ...
ZU
ZU
ZU

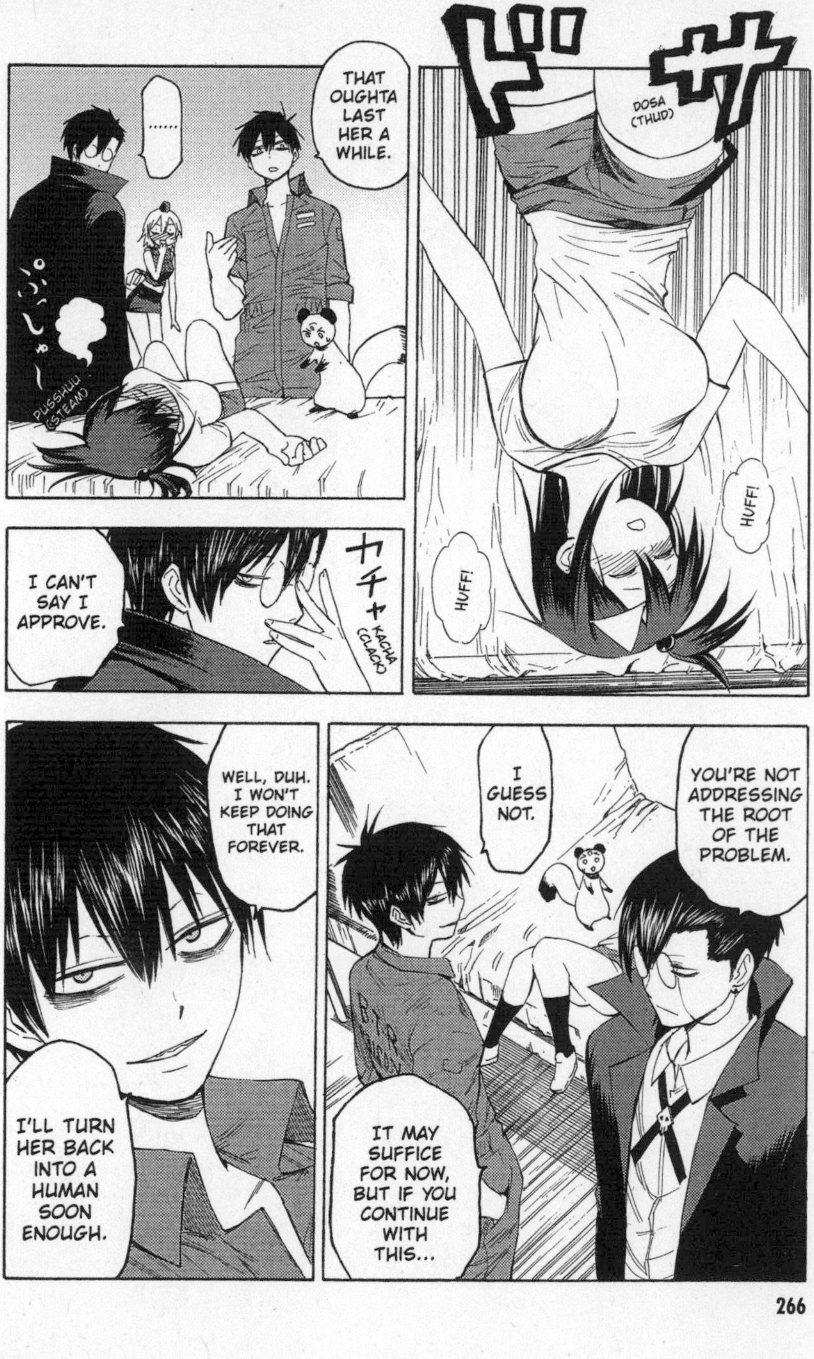
ドサ
DOSA (THUD)
HUFF!
HUFF!
THAT OUGHTA LAST HER A WHILE.
......
PUSSHUU (STEAM)
カチャ
KACHA (CLACK)
I CAN'T SAY I APPROVE.
YOU'RE NOT ADDRESSING THE ROOT OF THE PROBLEM.
I GUESS NOT.
IT MAY SUFFICE FOR NOW, BUT IF YOU CONTINUE WITH THIS...
WELL, DUH. I WON'T KEEP DOING THAT FOREVER.
I'LL TURN HER BACK INTO A HUMAN SOON ENOUGH.

THAT WAS OUR DEAL.
RIGHT, BROTHER?
......
I SUPPOSE SO...
IN DEMON WORLD EAST...
...WHERE YOU MET THE HUMAN FUYUMI...
...AND THEN LOST HER.
WELL THEN, IT'S TIME TO GO AND MEET THE *ORIGINAL* GIRL.
IN THE TERRITORY OF BOSS STAZ.

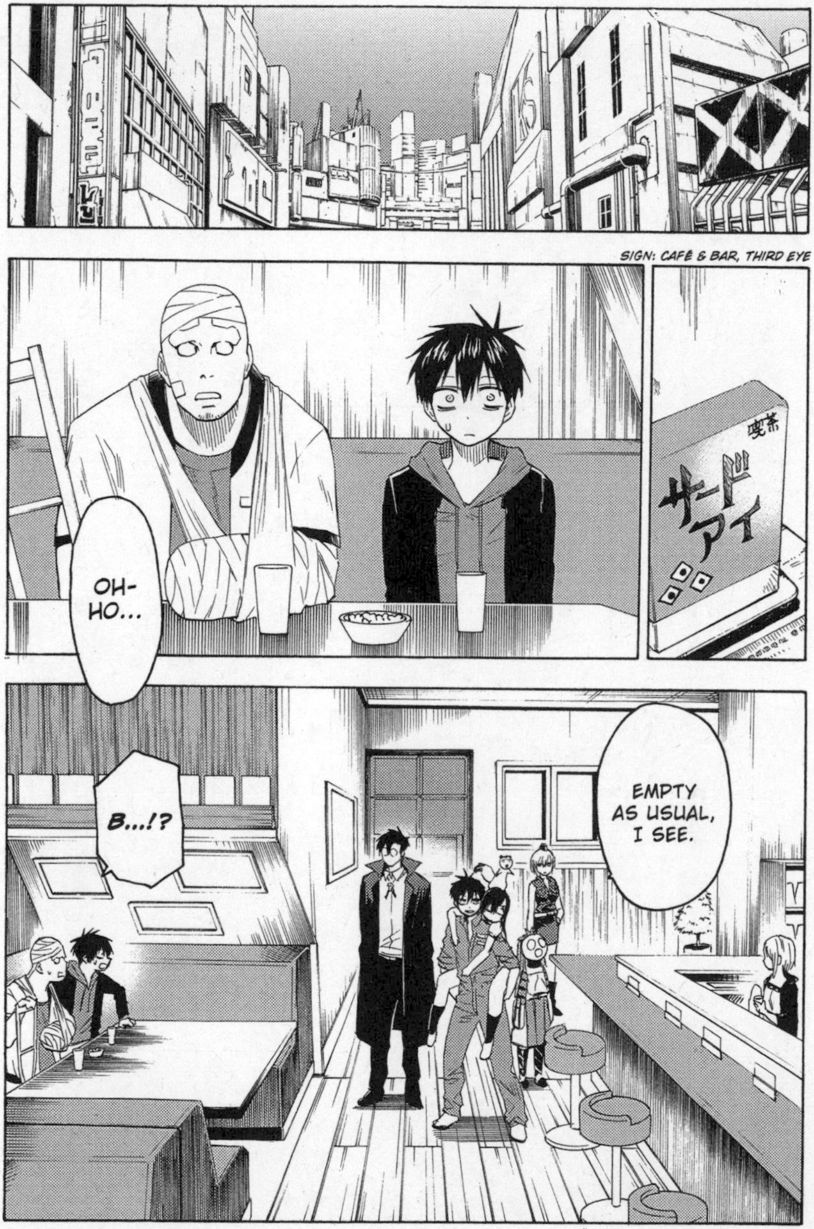
SIGN: CAFÉ & BAR, THIRD EYE
喫茶
サードアイ
OH-HO...
EMPTY AS USUAL, I SEE.
B...!?

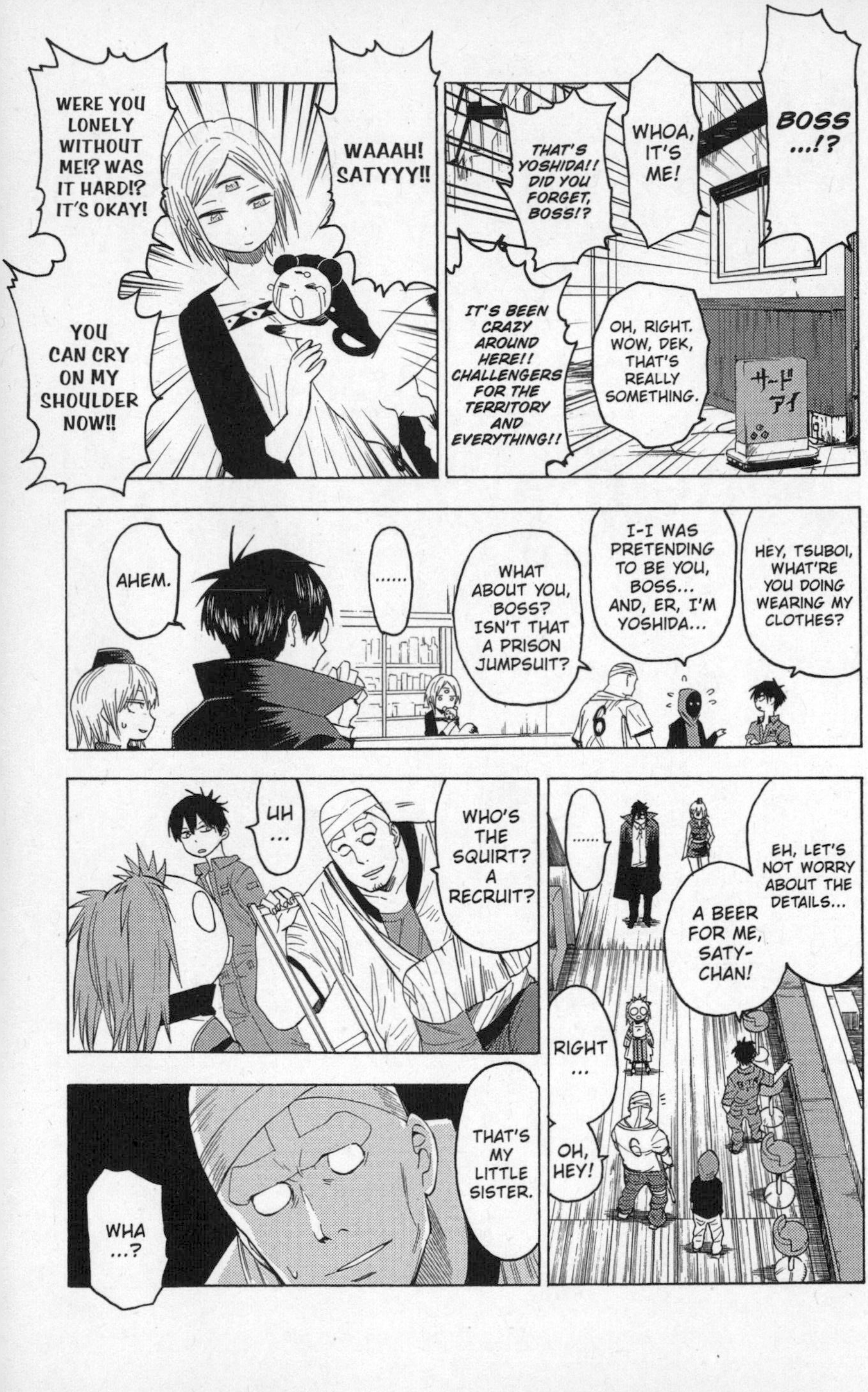
BOSS ...!?
WHOA, IT'S ME!
THAT'S YOSHIDA!! DID YOU FORGET, BOSS!?
OH, RIGHT. WOW, DEK, THAT'S REALLY SOMETHING.
IT'S BEEN CRAZY AROUND HERE!! CHALLENGERS FOR THE TERRITORY AND EVERYTHING!!
サード アイ
WAAAH! SATYYY!!
WERE YOU LONELY WITHOUT ME!? WAS IT HARD!? IT'S OKAY!
YOU CAN CRY ON MY SHOULDER NOW!!
HEY, TSUBOI, WHAT'RE YOU DOING WEARING MY CLOTHES?
I-I WAS PRETENDING TO BE YOU, BOSS... AND, ER, I'M YOSHIDA...
WHAT ABOUT YOU, BOSS? ISN'T THAT A PRISON JUMPSUIT?
......
AHEM.
EH, LET'S NOT WORRY ABOUT THE DETAILS...
A BEER FOR ME, SATY-CHAN!
......
RIGHT ...
OH, HEY!
WHO'S THE SQUIRT? A RECRUIT?
UH ...
THAT'S MY LITTLE SISTER.
WHA ...?

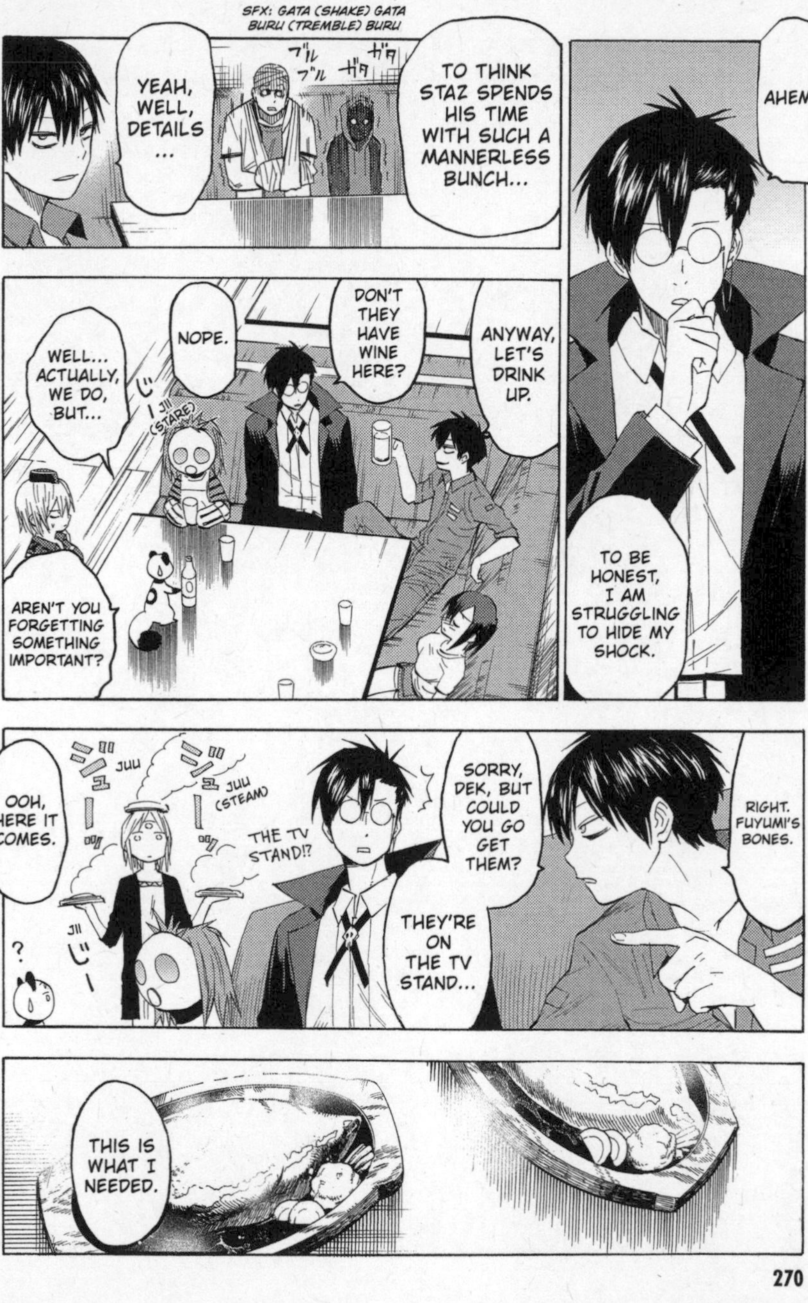
AHEM.
TO BE HONEST, I AM STRUGGLING TO HIDE MY SHOCK.
SFX: GATA (SHAKE) GATA BURU (TREMBLE) BURU
TO THINK STAZ SPENDS HIS TIME WITH SUCH A MANNERLESS BUNCH...
YEAH, WELL, DETAILS...
ANYWAY, LET'S DRINK UP.
DON'T THEY HAVE WINE HERE?
NOPE.
JII (STARE)
WELL... ACTUALLY, WE DO, BUT...
AREN'T YOU FORGETTING SOMETHING IMPORTANT?
RIGHT. FUYUMI'S BONES.
SORRY, DEK, BUT COULD YOU GO GET THEM?
THEY'RE ON THE TV STAND...
THE TV STAND!?
JUU (STEAM)
JUU
JII
OOH, HERE IT COMES.
?
THIS IS WHAT I NEEDED.

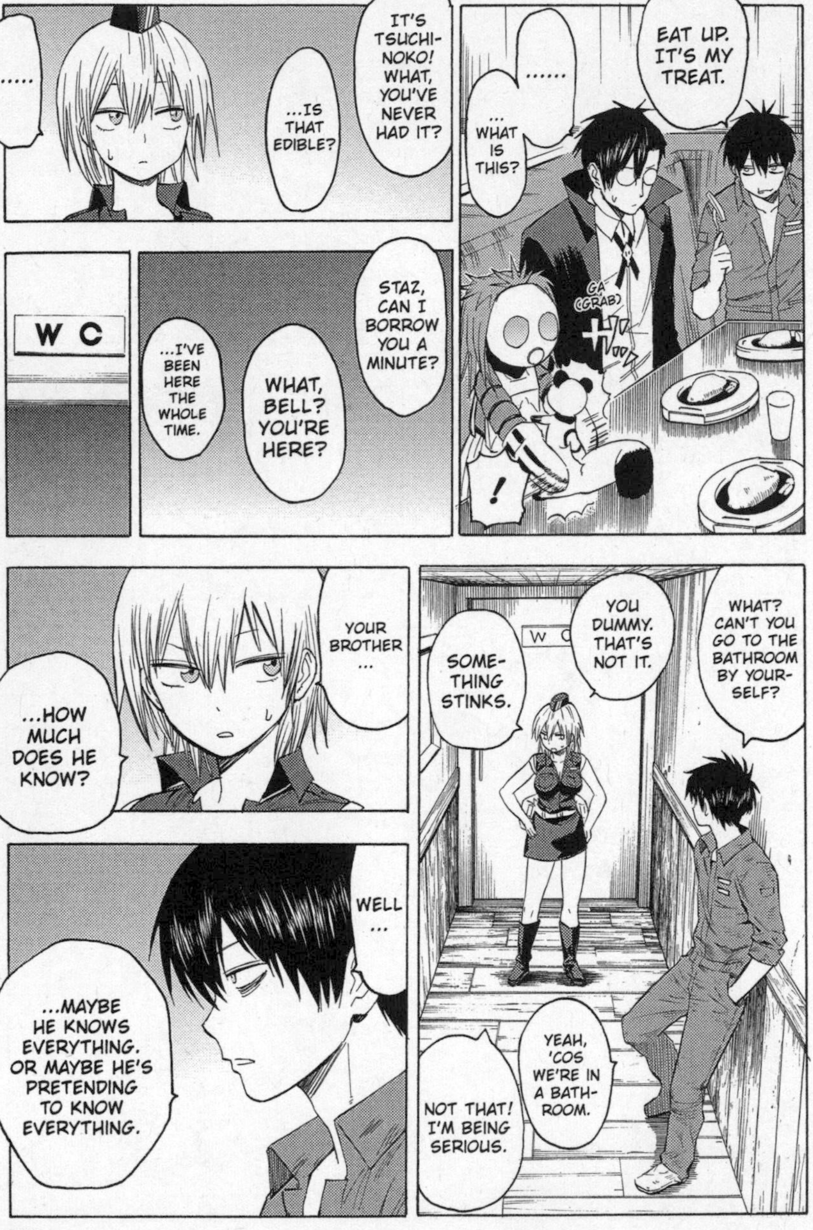
EAT UP. IT'S MY TREAT.
......
...WHAT IS THIS?
GA (GRAB)
!
IT'S TSUCHINOKO! WHAT, YOU'VE NEVER HAD IT?
...IS THAT EDIBLE?
......
STAZ, CAN I BORROW YOU A MINUTE?
WHAT, BELL? YOU'RE HERE?
...I'VE BEEN HERE THE WHOLE TIME.
W C
WHAT? CAN'T YOU GO TO THE BATHROOM BY YOURSELF?
YOU DUMMY. THAT'S NOT IT.
SOMETHING STINKS.
W C
YEAH, 'COS WE'RE IN A BATHROOM.
NOT THAT! I'M BEING SERIOUS.
YOUR BROTHER...
...HOW MUCH DOES HE KNOW?
WELL...
...MAYBE HE KNOWS EVERYTHING. OR MAYBE HE'S PRETENDING TO KNOW EVERYTHING.

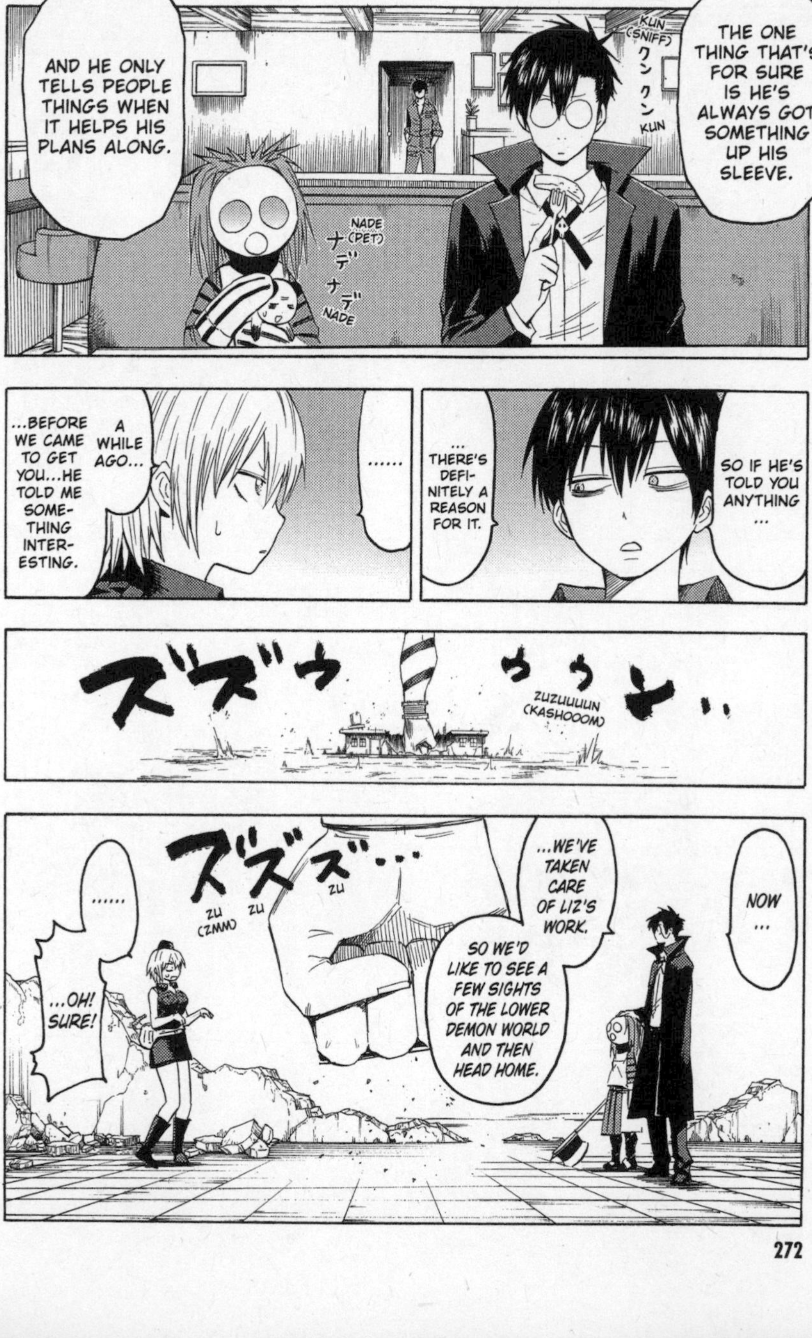
THE ONE THING THAT'S FOR SURE IS HE'S ALWAYS GOT SOMETHING UP HIS SLEEVE.
KUN (SNIFF) クン クン KUN
NADE (PET) ナデ ナデ NADE
AND HE ONLY TELLS PEOPLE THINGS WHEN IT HELPS HIS PLANS ALONG.
SO IF HE'S TOLD YOU ANYTHING ...
... THERE'S DEFINITELY A REASON FOR IT.
......
A WHILE AGO...
...BEFORE WE CAME TO GET YOU...HE TOLD ME SOMETHING INTERESTING.
ズズゥ ゥゥン、、
ZUZUUUUN (KASHOOOM)
NOW ...
...WE'VE TAKEN CARE OF LIZ'S WORK.
SO WE'D LIKE TO SEE A FEW SIGHTS OF THE LOWER DEMON WORLD AND THEN HEAD HOME.
ズズズ...
ZU ZU ZU (ZMM)
......
...OH! SURE!

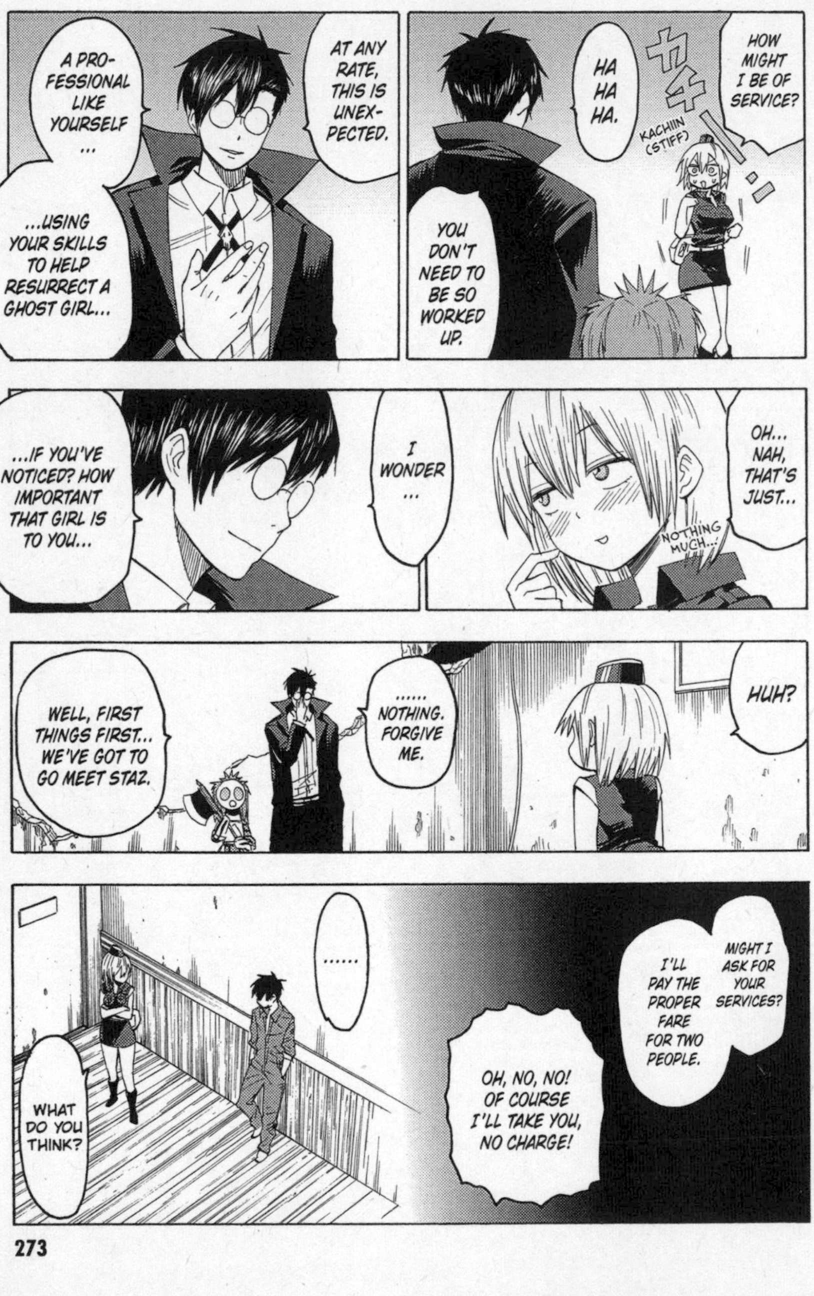
HOW MIGHT I BE OF SERVICE?
KACHIIN (STIFF)
HA HA HA.
YOU DON'T NEED TO BE SO WORKED UP.
AT ANY RATE, THIS IS UNEXPECTED.
A PRO-FESSIONAL LIKE YOURSELF ...
...USING YOUR SKILLS TO HELP RESURRECT A GHOST GIRL...
OH... NAH, THAT'S JUST...
NOTHING MUCH...!
I WONDER ...
...IF YOU'VE NOTICED? HOW IMPORTANT THAT GIRL IS TO YOU...
HUH?
...... NOTHING. FORGIVE ME.
WELL, FIRST THINGS FIRST... WE'VE GOT TO GO MEET STAZ.
MIGHT I ASK FOR YOUR SERVICES?
I'LL PAY THE PROPER FARE FOR TWO PEOPLE.
OH, NO, NO! OF COURSE I'LL TAKE YOU, NO CHARGE!
......
WHAT DO YOU THINK?

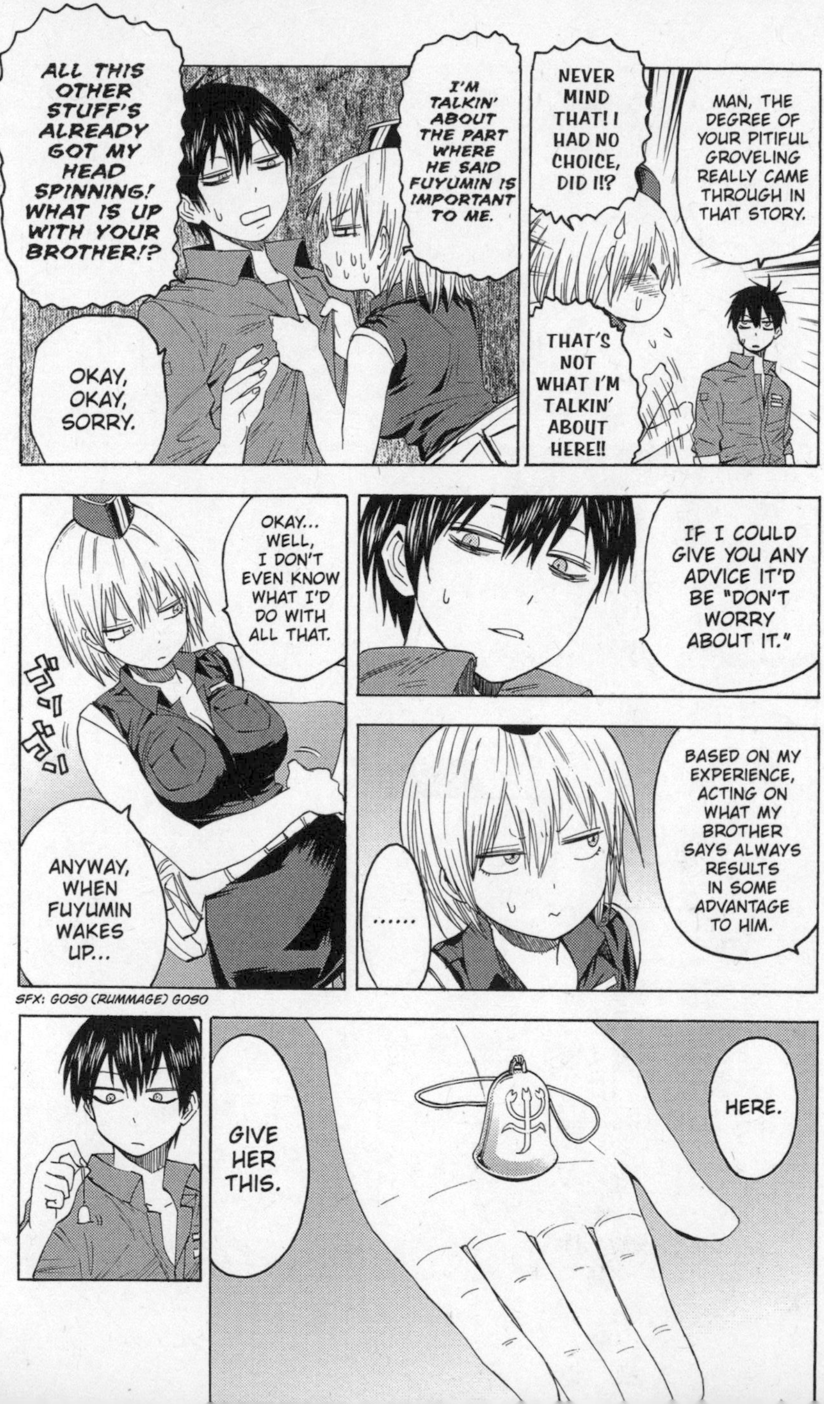
MAN, THE DEGREE OF YOUR PITIFUL GROVELING REALLY CAME THROUGH IN THAT STORY.
NEVER MIND THAT!! I HAD NO CHOICE, DID I!?
THAT'S NOT WHAT I'M TALKIN' ABOUT HERE!!
I'M TALKIN' ABOUT THE PART WHERE HE SAID FUYUMIN IS IMPORTANT TO ME.
ALL THIS OTHER STUFF'S ALREADY GOT MY HEAD SPINNING! WHAT IS UP WITH YOUR BROTHER!?
OKAY, OKAY, SORRY.
IF I COULD GIVE YOU ANY ADVICE IT'D BE "DON'T WORRY ABOUT IT."
BASED ON MY EXPERIENCE, ACTING ON WHAT MY BROTHER SAYS ALWAYS RESULTS IN SOME ADVANTAGE TO HIM.
......
OKAY... WELL, I DON'T EVEN KNOW WHAT I'D DO WITH ALL THAT.
ANYWAY, WHEN FUYUMIN WAKES UP...
SFX: GOSO (RUMMAGE) GOSO
HERE.
GIVE HER THIS.

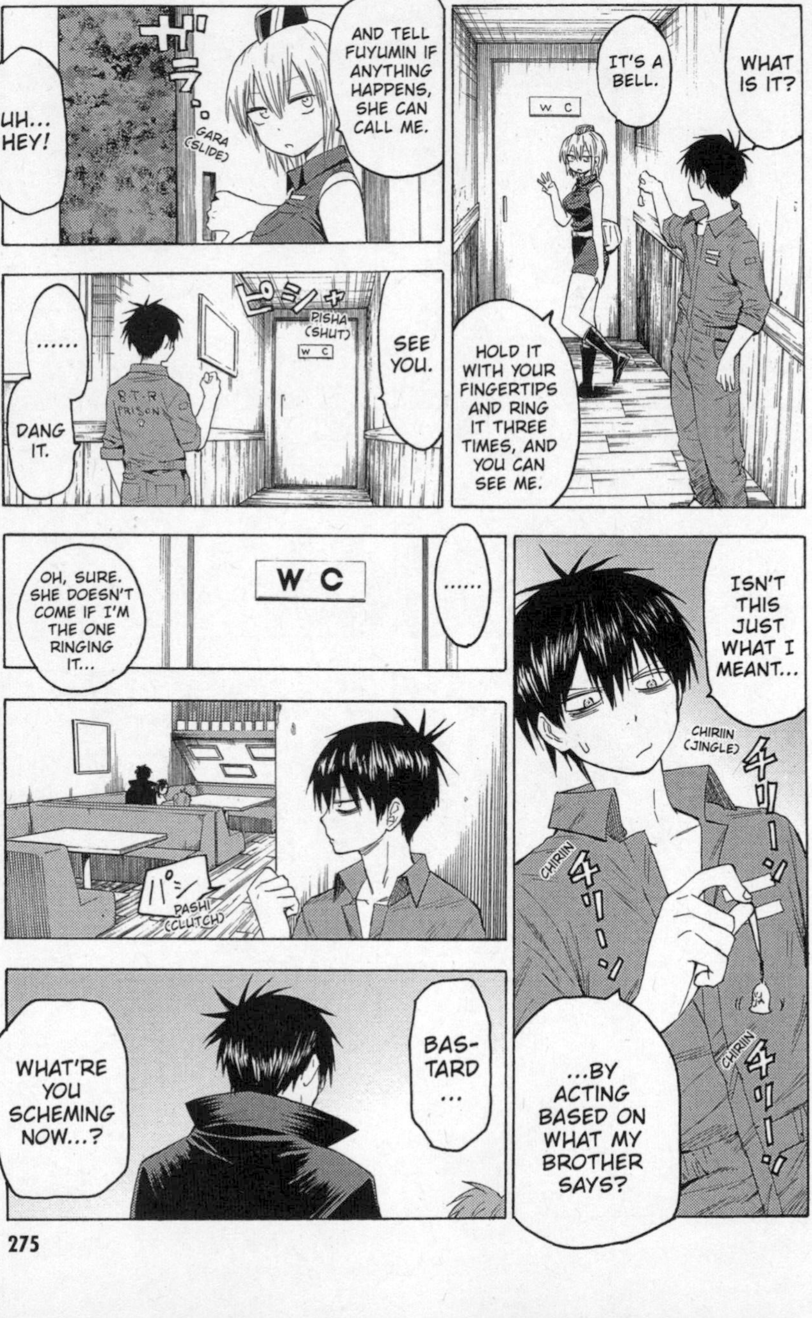
WHAT IS IT?
IT'S A BELL.
W C
HOLD IT WITH YOUR FINGERTIPS AND RING IT THREE TIMES, AND YOU CAN SEE ME.
AND TELL FUYUMIN IF ANYTHING HAPPENS, SHE CAN CALL ME.
GARA (SLIDE)
UH... HEY!
SEE YOU.
PISHA (SHUT)
W C
......
DANG IT.
ISN'T THIS JUST WHAT I MEANT...
CHIRIIN (JINGLE)
CHIRIIN
CHIRIIN
...BY ACTING BASED ON WHAT MY BROTHER SAYS?
......
W C
OH, SURE. SHE DOESN'T COME IF I'M THE ONE RINGING IT...
PASHI (CLUTCH)
BAS-TARD...
WHAT'RE YOU SCHEMING NOW...?

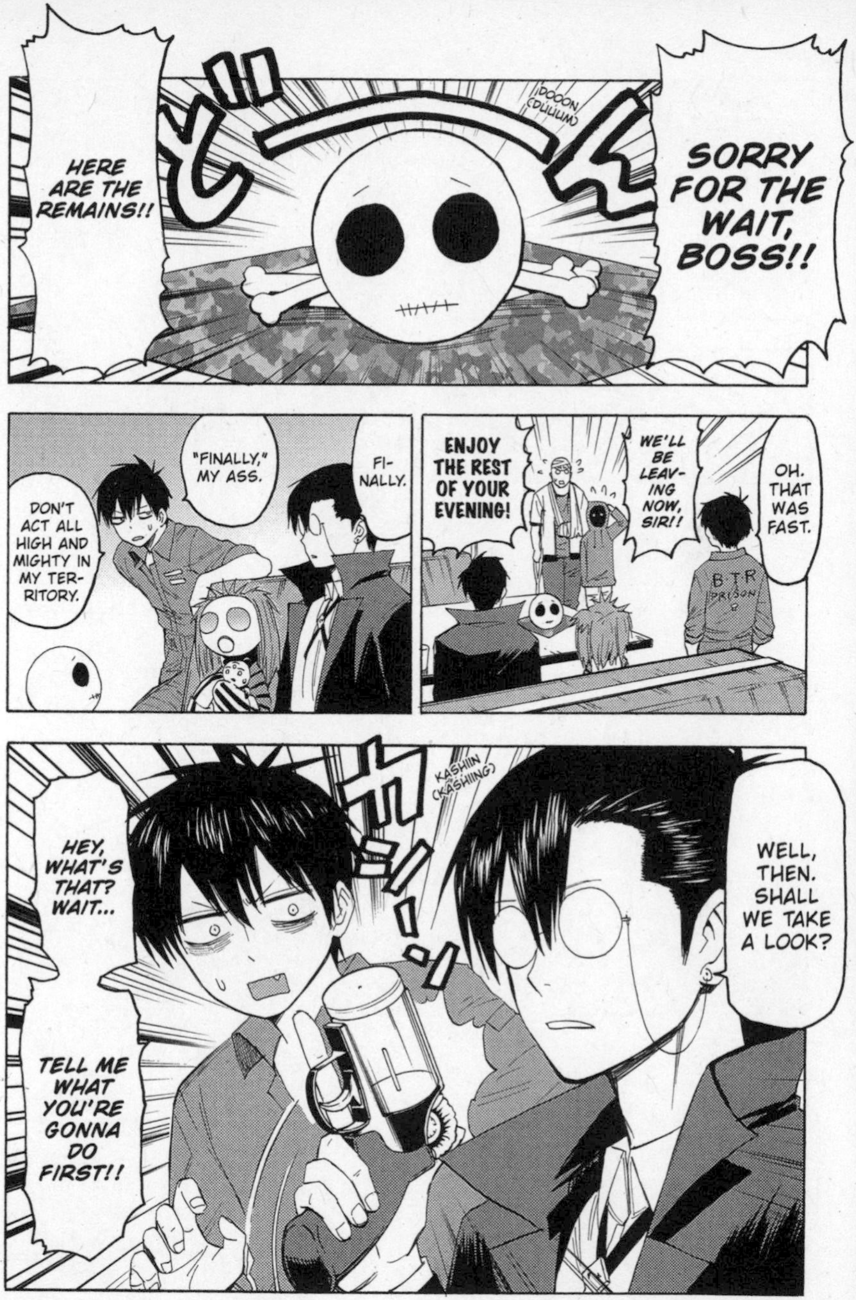
SORRY FOR THE WAIT, BOSS!!
DOOOON (DUUUN)
HERE ARE THE REMAINS!!
OH. THAT WAS FAST.
WE'LL BE LEAVING NOW, SIR!!
ENJOY THE REST OF YOUR EVENING!
FI-NALLY.
"FINALLY," MY ASS.
DON'T ACT ALL HIGH AND MIGHTY IN MY TERRITORY.
BTR PRISON
WELL, THEN. SHALL WE TAKE A LOOK?
KASHIIN (KASHIING)
HEY, WHAT'S THAT? WAIT...
TELL ME WHAT YOU'RE GONNA DO FIRST!!

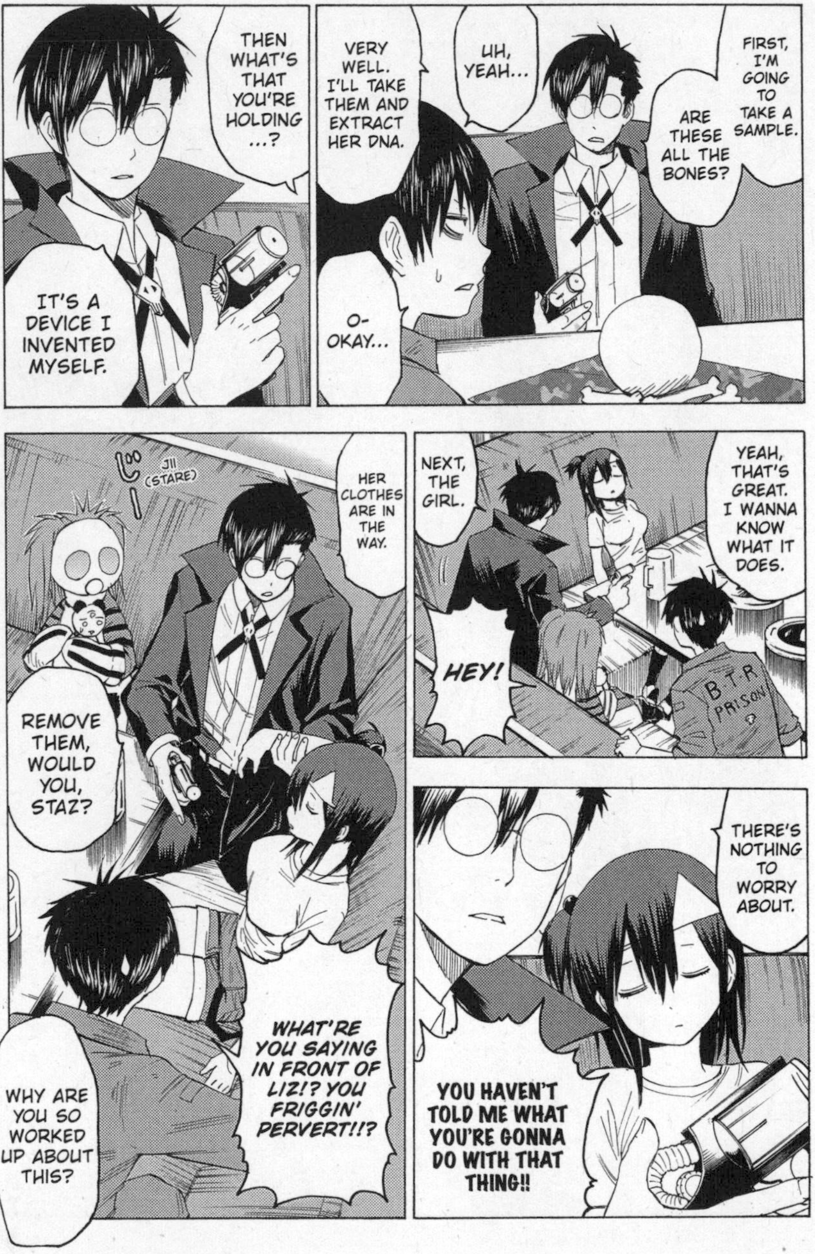
FIRST, I'M GOING TO TAKE A SAMPLE.
ARE THESE ALL THE BONES?
UH, YEAH...
VERY WELL. I'LL TAKE THEM AND EXTRACT HER DNA.
O-OKAY...
THEN WHAT'S THAT YOU'RE HOLDING ...?
IT'S A DEVICE I INVENTED MYSELF.
YEAH, THAT'S GREAT. I WANNA KNOW WHAT IT DOES.
NEXT, THE GIRL.
HEY!
THERE'S NOTHING TO WORRY ABOUT.
YOU HAVEN'T TOLD ME WHAT YOU'RE GONNA DO WITH THAT THING!!
HER CLOTHES ARE IN THE WAY.
じー
JII (STARE)
REMOVE THEM, WOULD YOU, STAZ?
WHAT'RE YOU SAYING IN FRONT OF LIZ!? YOU FRIGGIN' PERVERT!!?
WHY ARE YOU SO WORKED UP ABOUT THIS?
B.T.R PRISON

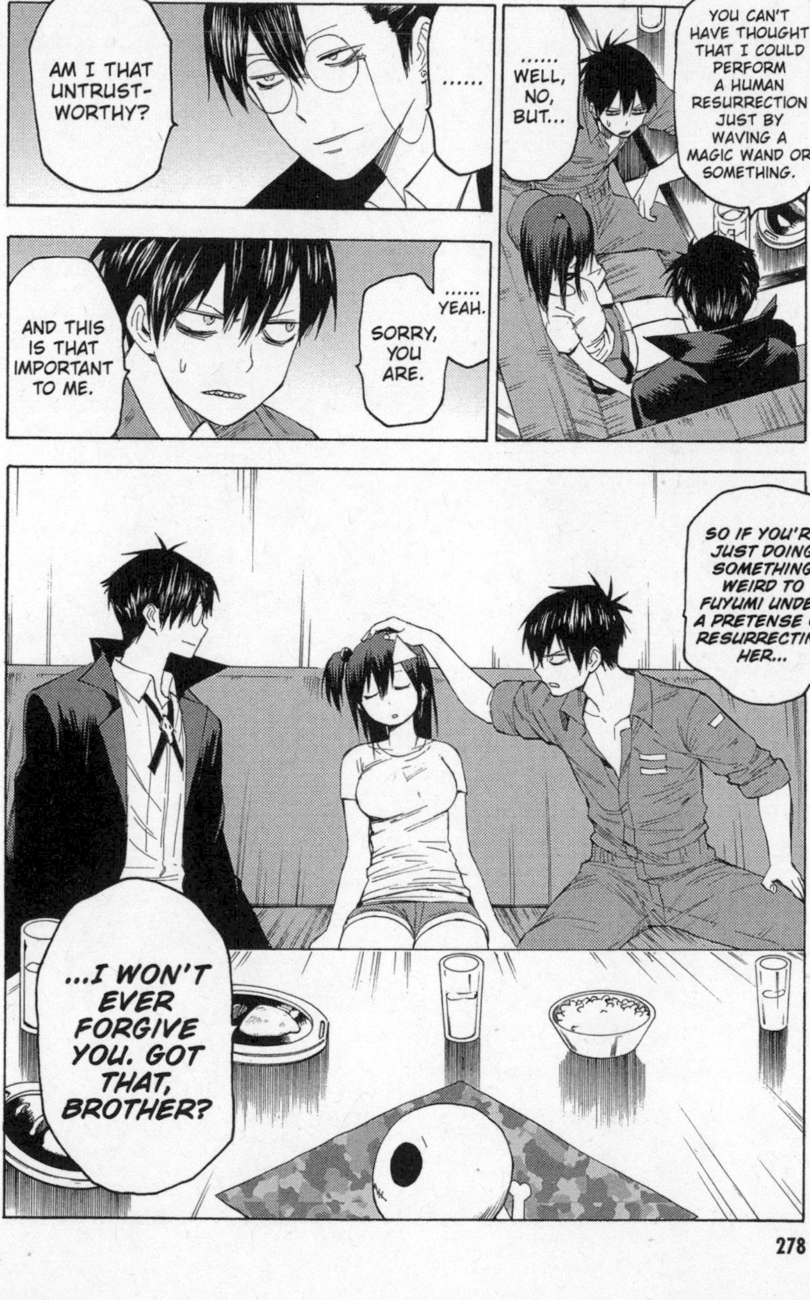
YOU CAN'T HAVE THOUGHT THAT I COULD PERFORM A HUMAN RESURRECTION JUST BY WAVING A MAGIC WAND OR SOMETHING.
......WELL, NO, BUT...
......
AM I THAT UNTRUST-WORTHY?
......YEAH.
SORRY, YOU ARE.
AND THIS IS THAT IMPORTANT TO ME.
SO IF YOU'RE JUST DOING SOMETHING WEIRD TO FUYUMI UNDER A PRETENSE OF RESURRECTING HER...
...I WON'T EVER FORGIVE YOU. GOT THAT, BROTHER?

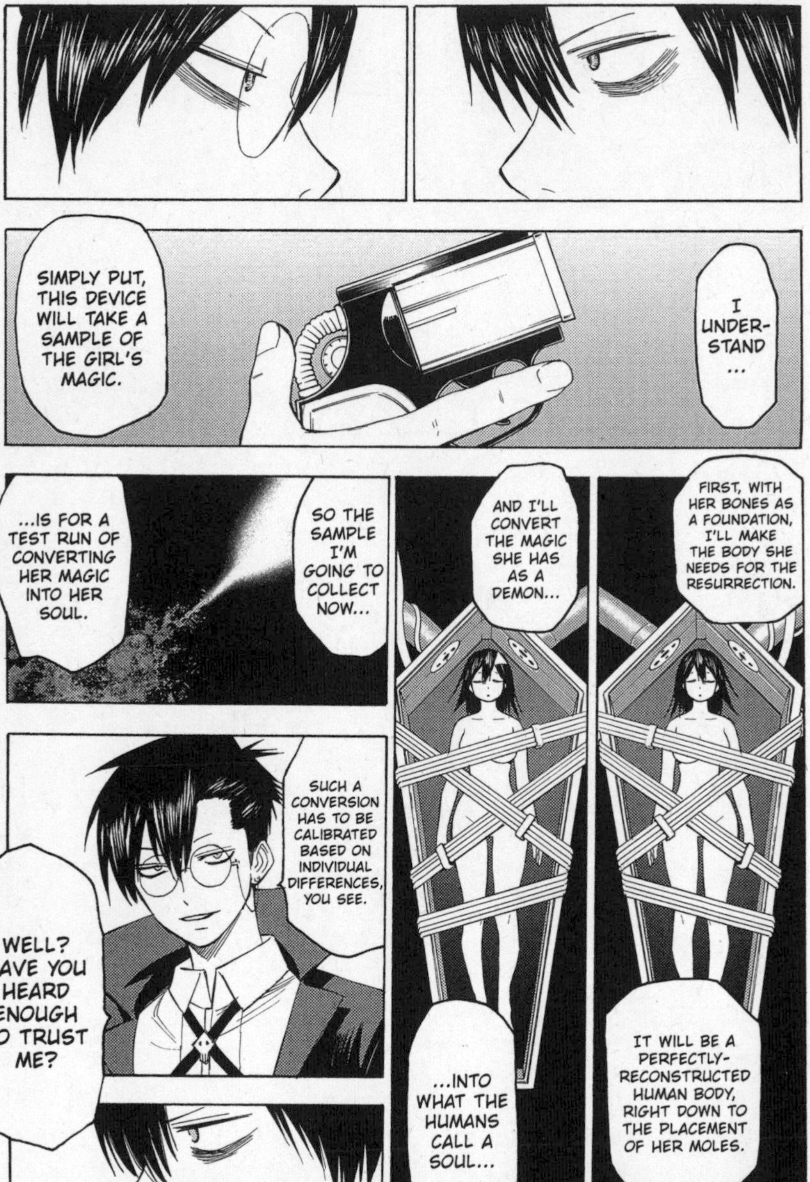
I UNDER-STAND...
SIMPLY PUT, THIS DEVICE WILL TAKE A SAMPLE OF THE GIRL'S MAGIC.
FIRST, WITH HER BONES AS A FOUNDATION, I'LL MAKE THE BODY SHE NEEDS FOR THE RESURRECTION.
IT WILL BE A PERFECTLY-RECONSTRUCTED HUMAN BODY, RIGHT DOWN TO THE PLACEMENT OF HER MOLES.
AND I'LL CONVERT THE MAGIC SHE HAS AS A DEMON...
...INTO WHAT THE HUMANS CALL A SOUL...
SO THE SAMPLE I'M GOING TO COLLECT NOW...
...IS FOR A TEST RUN OF CONVERTING HER MAGIC INTO HER SOUL.
SUCH A CONVERSION HAS TO BE CALIBRATED BASED ON INDIVIDUAL DIFFERENCES, YOU SEE.
WELL? HAVE YOU HEARD ENOUGH TO TRUST ME?

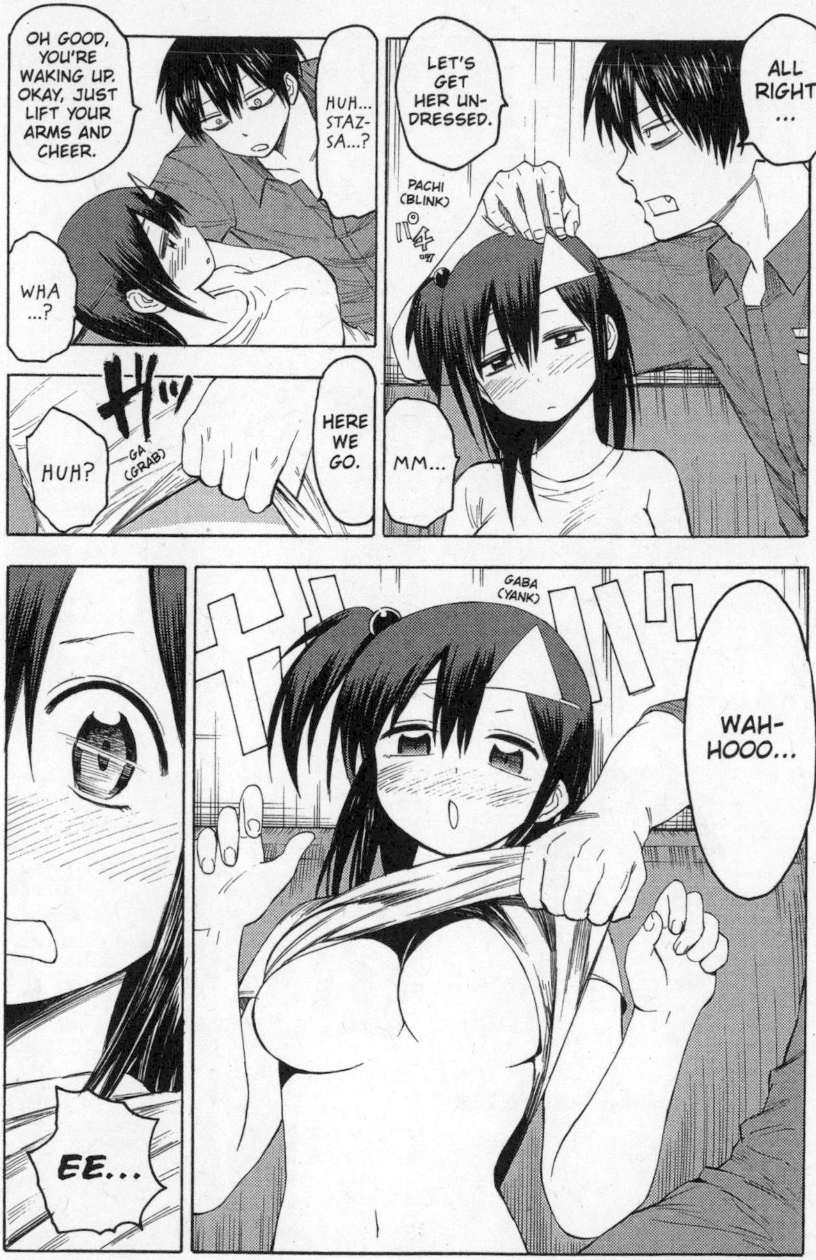
ALL RIGHT ...
LET'S GET HER UN-DRESSED.
PACHI (BLINK)
MM...
HUH... STAZ-SA...?
OH GOOD, YOU'RE WAKING UP. OKAY, JUST LIFT YOUR ARMS AND CHEER.
WHA ...?
HERE WE GO.
GA (GRAB)
HUH?
WAH-HOOO...
GABA (YANK)
EE...

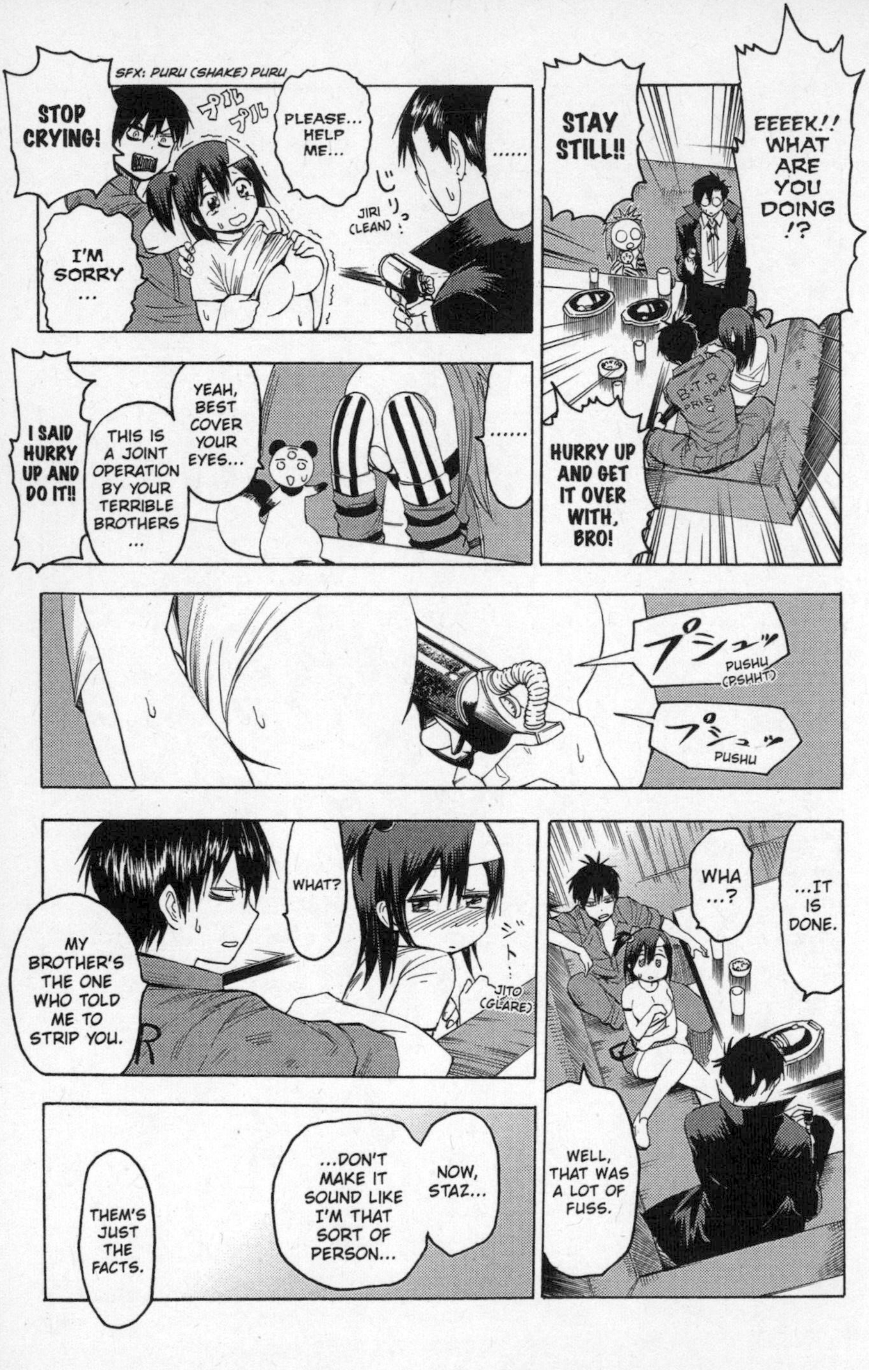
EEEEK!! WHAT ARE YOU DOING!?
STAY STILL!!
HURRY UP AND GET IT OVER WITH, BRO!
......
ジリッ
JIRI (LEAN)
PLEASE... HELP ME...
STOP CRYING!
SFX: PURU (SHAKE) PURU
プルプル
I'M SORRY...
......
YEAH, BEST COVER YOUR EYES...
THIS IS A JOINT OPERATION BY YOUR TERRIBLE BROTHERS...
I SAID HURRY UP AND DO IT!!
プシュッ
PUSHU (PSHHT)
プシュッ
PUSHU
...IT IS DONE.
WHA...?
WELL, THAT WAS A LOT OF FUSS.
WHAT?
ジトー
JITO (GLARE)
MY BROTHER'S THE ONE WHO TOLD ME TO STRIP YOU.
NOW, STAZ...
...DON'T MAKE IT SOUND LIKE I'M THAT SORT OF PERSON...
THEM'S JUST THE FACTS.

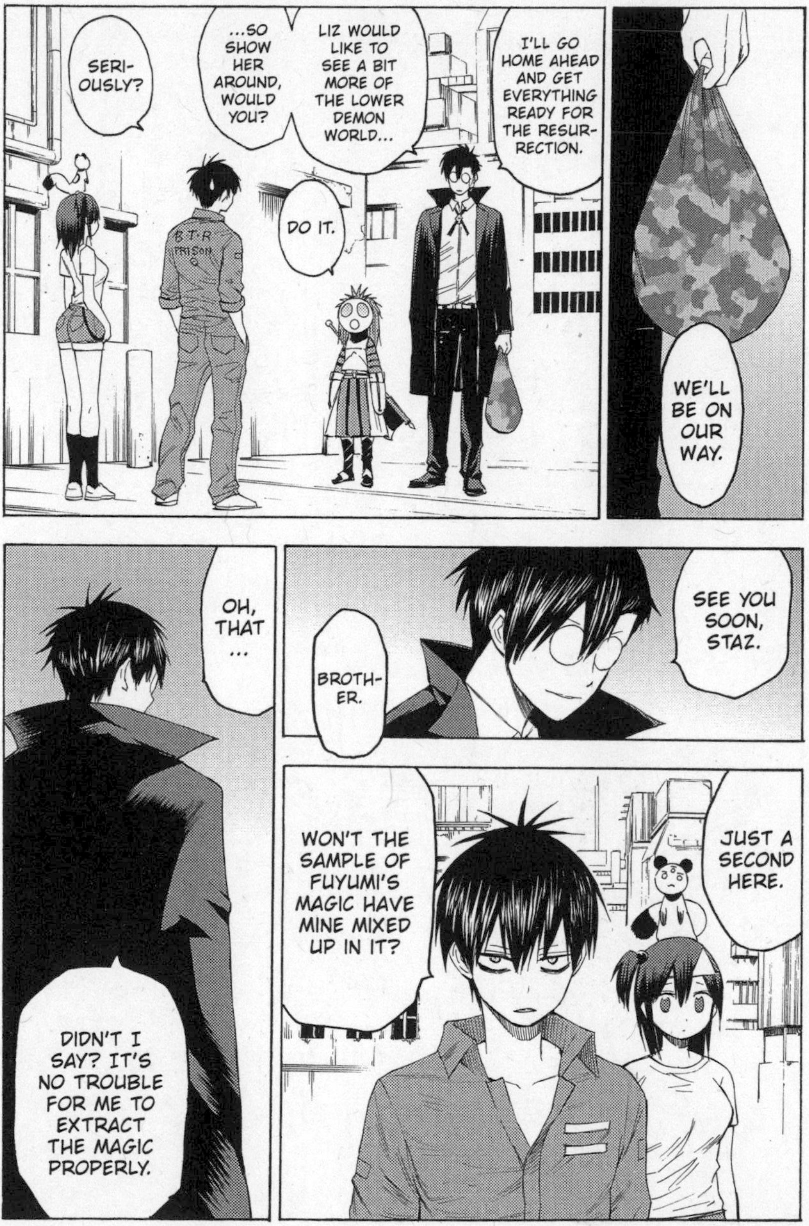
WE'LL BE ON OUR WAY.
I'LL GO HOME AHEAD AND GET EVERYTHING READY FOR THE RESUR-RECTION.
LIZ WOULD LIKE TO SEE A BIT MORE OF THE LOWER DEMON WORLD...
...SO SHOW HER AROUND, WOULD YOU?
SERI-OUSLY?
DO IT.
B.T.R PRISON
SEE YOU SOON, STAZ.
BROTH-ER.
JUST A SECOND HERE.
WON'T THE SAMPLE OF FUYUMI'S MAGIC HAVE MINE MIXED UP IN IT?
OH, THAT ...
DIDN'T I SAY? IT'S NO TROUBLE FOR ME TO EXTRACT THE MAGIC PROPERLY.

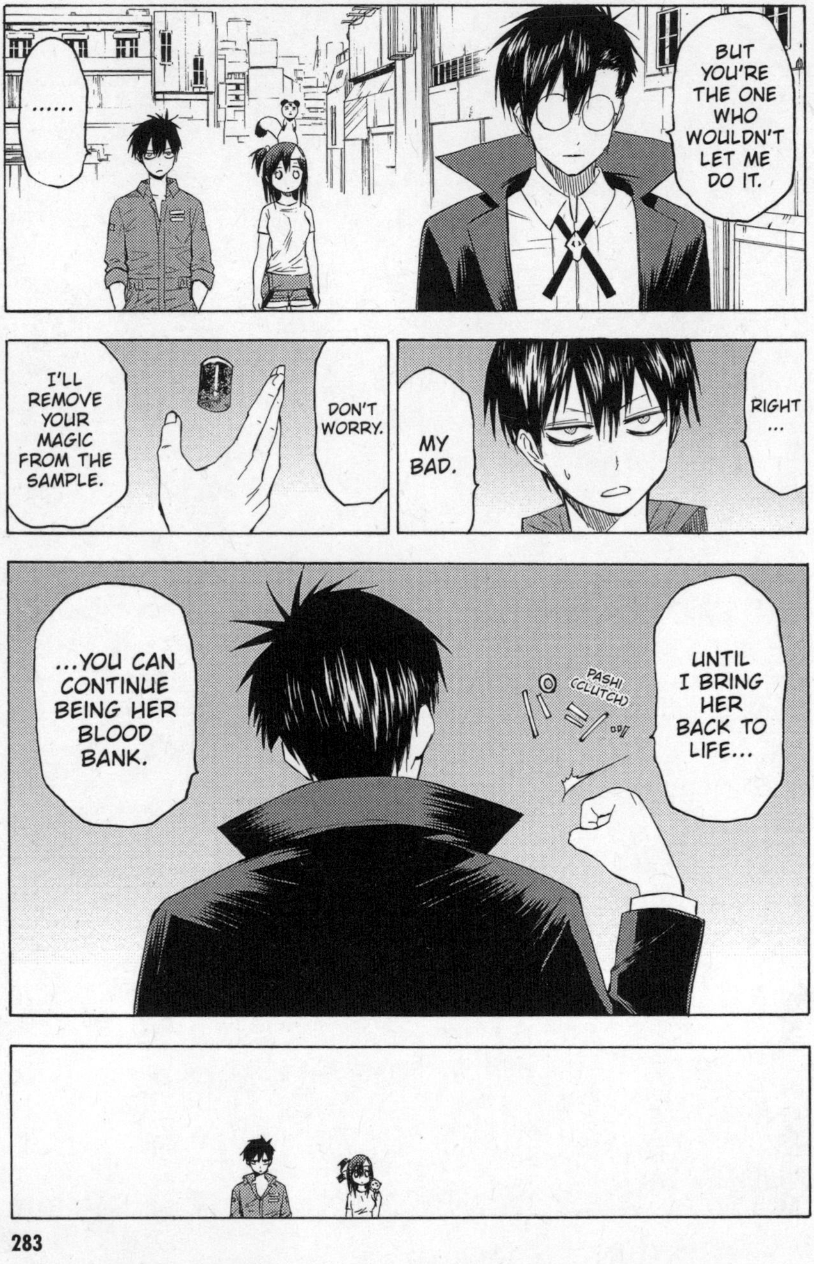
BUT YOU'RE THE ONE WHO WOULDN'T LET ME DO IT.
......
RIGHT ...
MY BAD.
DON'T WORRY.
I'LL REMOVE YOUR MAGIC FROM THE SAMPLE.
UNTIL I BRING HER BACK TO LIFE...
PASHI (CLUTCH)
...YOU CAN CONTINUE BEING HER BLOOD BANK.

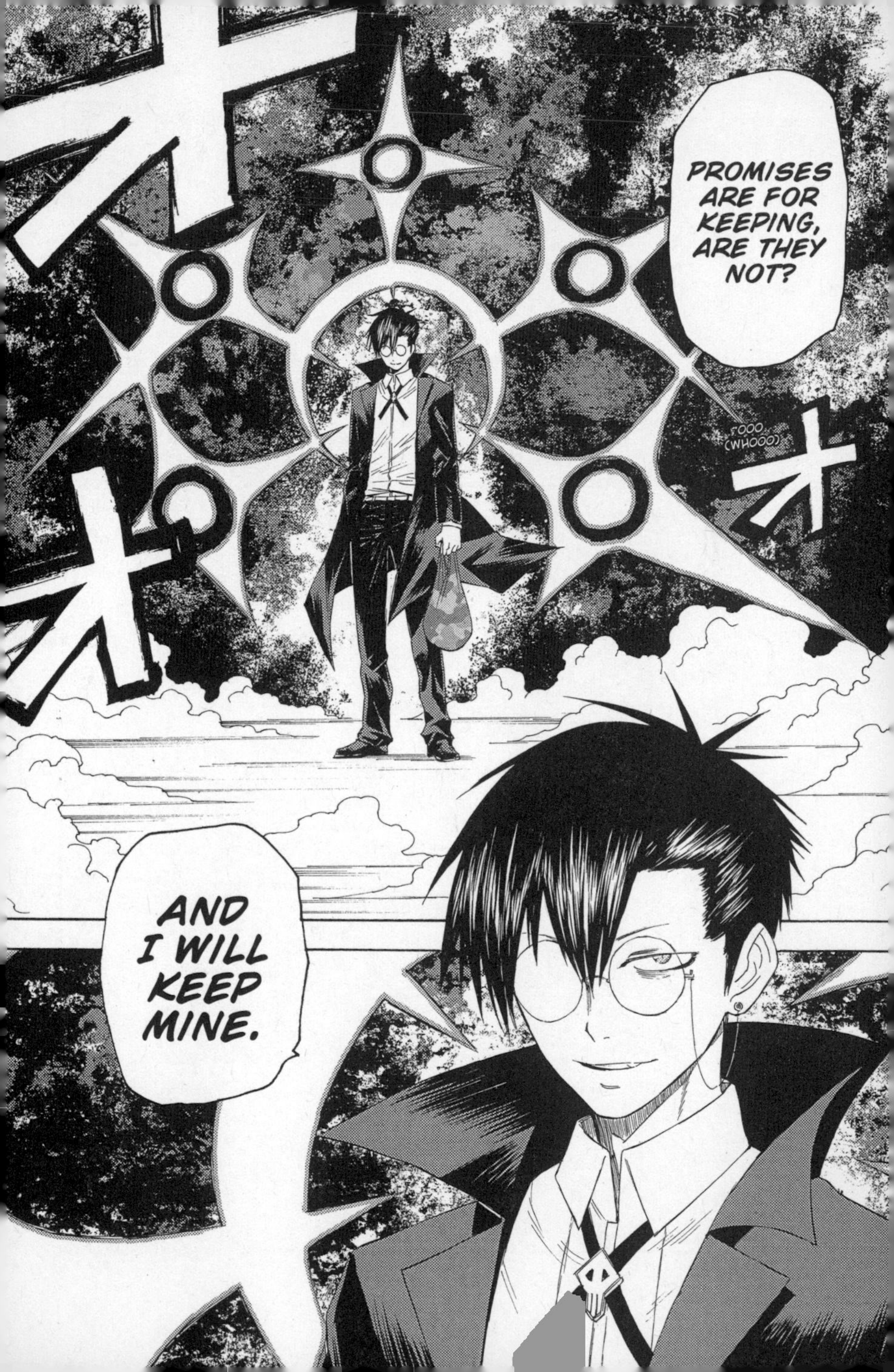
PROMISES ARE FOR KEEPING, ARE THEY NOT?
OOO (WHOOO)
AND I WILL KEEP MINE.

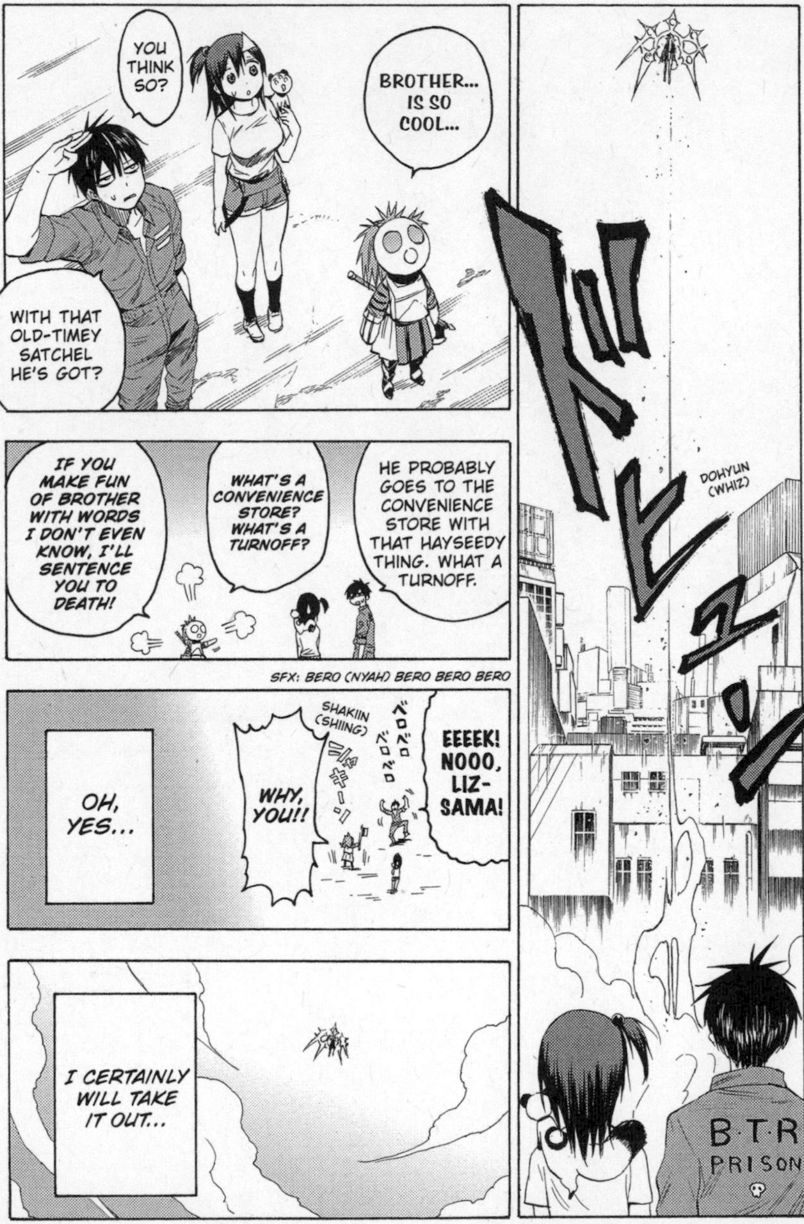
ドヒュン
DOHYUN (WHIZ)
B·T·R PRISON
BROTHER... IS SO COOL...
YOU THINK SO?
WITH THAT OLD-TIMEY SATCHEL HE'S GOT?
HE PROBABLY GOES TO THE CONVENIENCE STORE WITH THAT HAYSEEDY THING. WHAT A TURNOFF.
WHAT'S A CONVENIENCE STORE? WHAT'S A TURNOFF?
IF YOU MAKE FUN OF BROTHER WITH WORDS I DON'T EVEN KNOW, I'LL SENTENCE YOU TO DEATH!
SFX: BERO (NYAH) BERO BERO BERO
EEEEK! NOOO, LIZ-SAMA!
SHAKIIN (SHIING)
WHY, YOU!!
OH, YES...
I CERTAINLY WILL TAKE IT OUT...

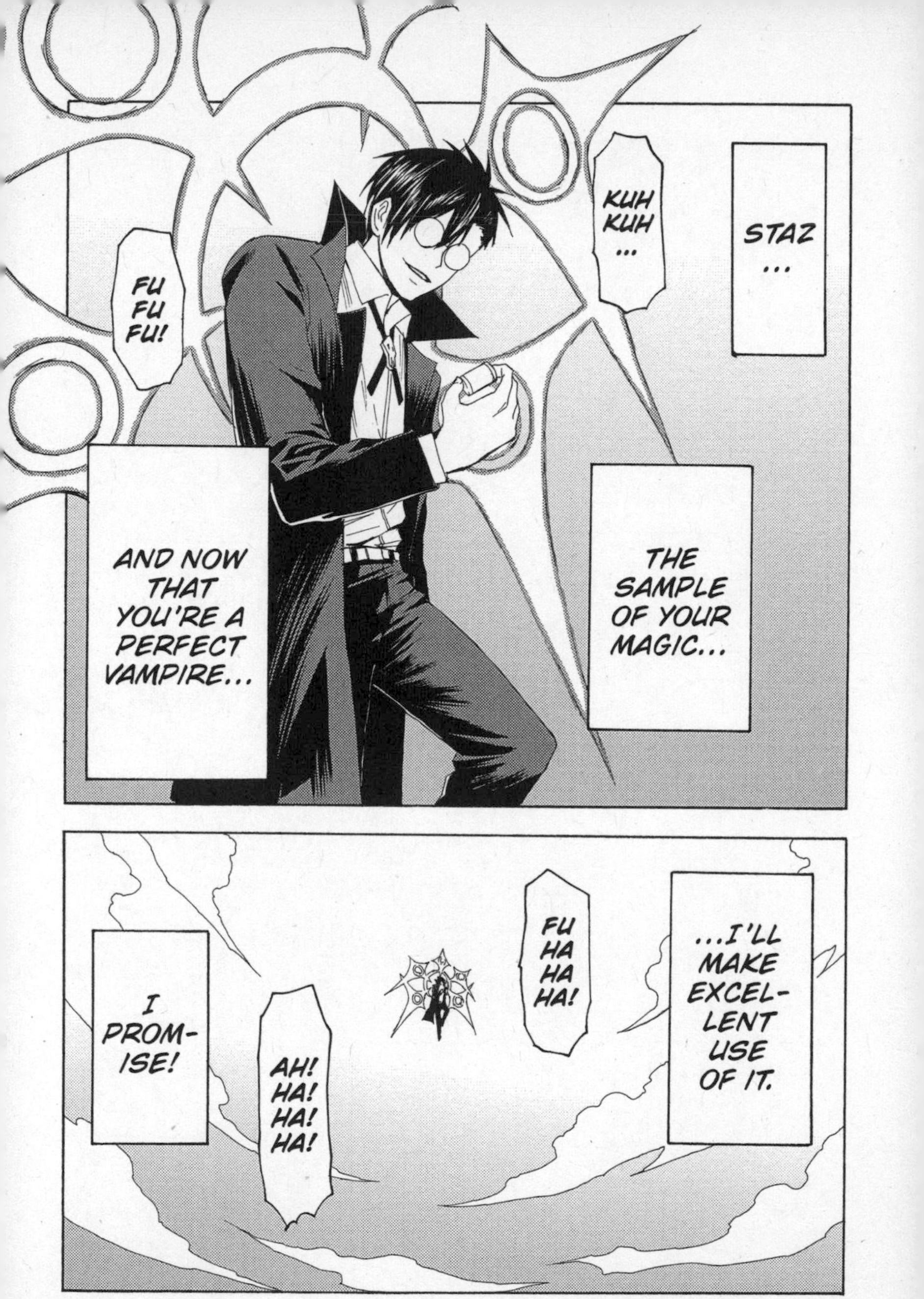
STAZ…
KUH KUH…
FU FU FU!
THE SAMPLE OF YOUR MAGIC…
AND NOW THAT YOU'RE A PERFECT VAMPIRE…
…I'LL MAKE EXCEL-LENT USE OF IT.
FU HA HA HA!
AH! HA! HA! HA!
I PROMISE!

♠ To Be Continued ♠

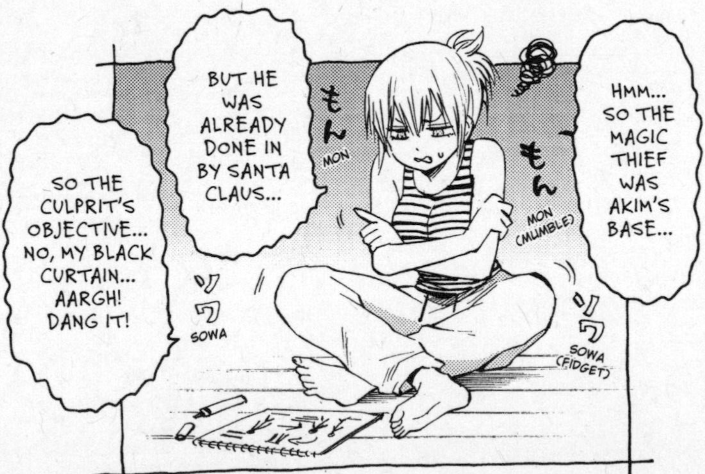
HMM... SO THE MAGIC THIEF WAS AKIM'S BASE...
もん
MON (MUMBLE)
もん
MON
BUT HE WAS ALREADY DONE IN BY SANTA CLAUS...
ソワ
SOWA (FIDGET)
SO THE CULPRIT'S OBJECTIVE... NO, MY BLACK CURTAIN... AARGH! DANG IT!
ソワ
SOWA

BLOOD LAD

CHAPTER 19 ♠ LIZ, FOR THE FIRST TIME

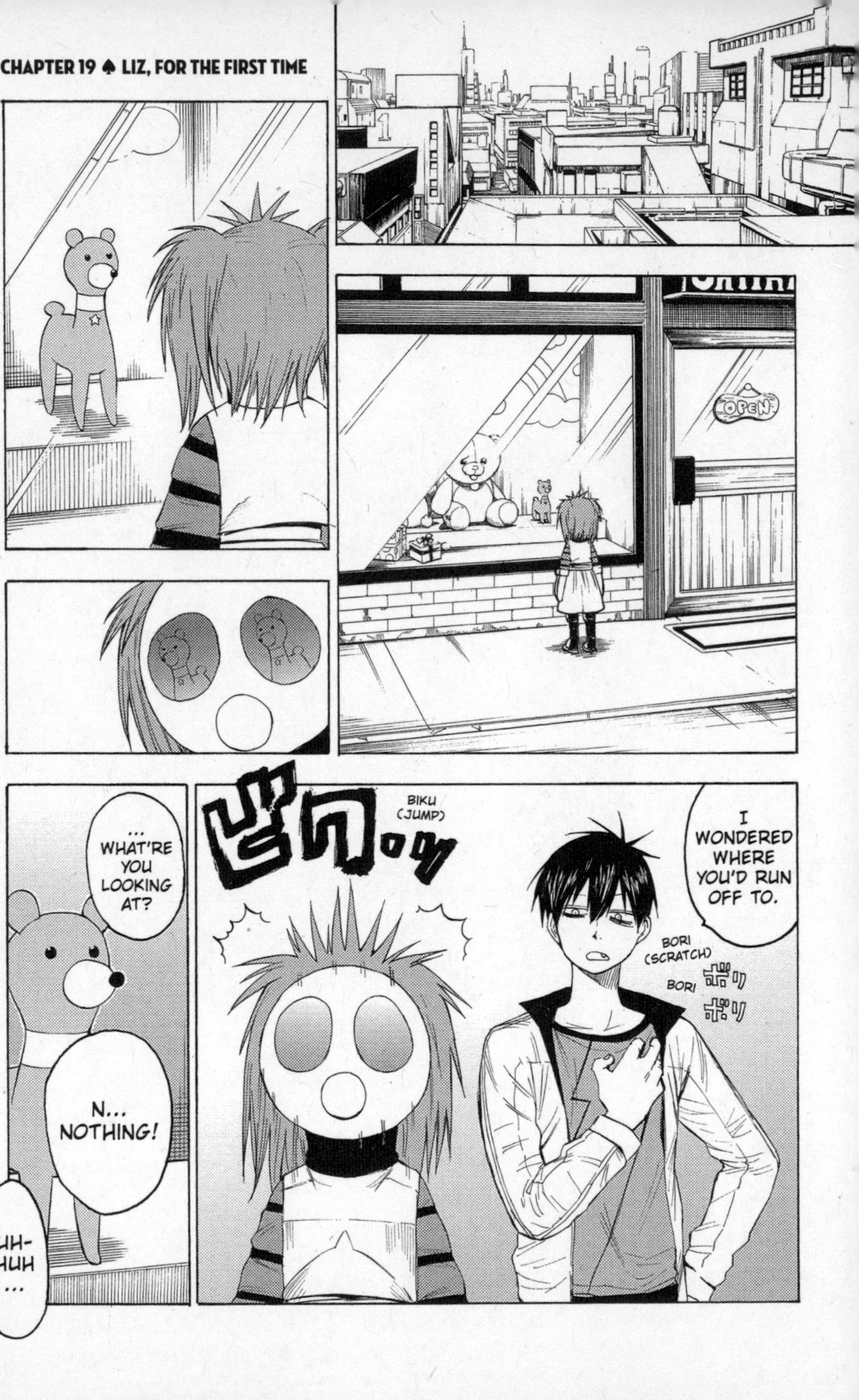
OPEN
I WONDERED WHERE YOU'D RUN OFF TO.
BIKU (JUMP)
ビクッ
BORI (SCRATCH) BORI
ボリ ボリ
... WHAT'RE YOU LOOKING AT?
N... NOTHING!
UH-HUH ...

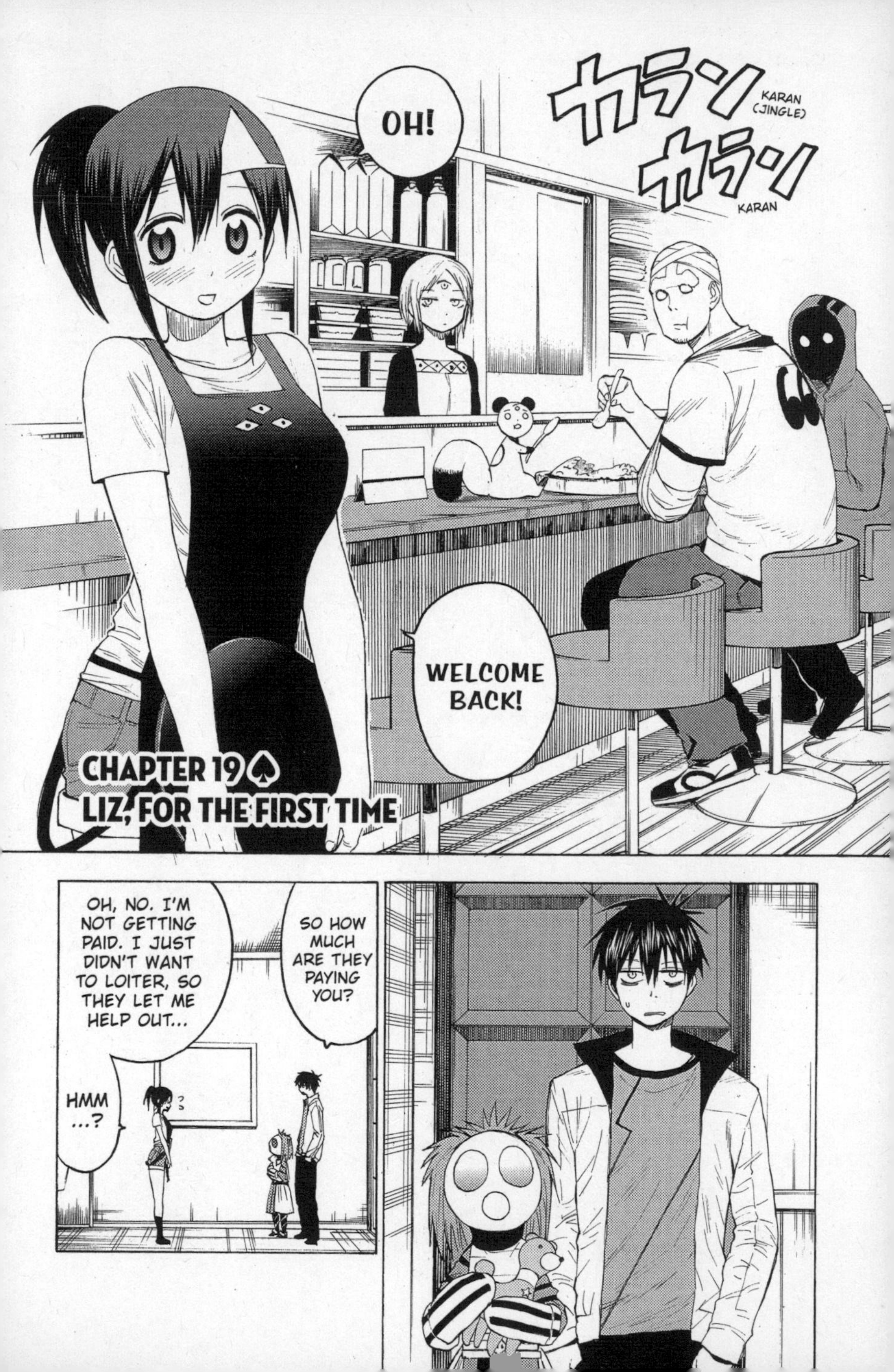
KARAN (JINGLE)
KARAN
OH!
WELCOME BACK!
CHAPTER 19 ♠ LIZ, FOR THE FIRST TIME
SO HOW MUCH ARE THEY PAYING YOU?
OH, NO. I'M NOT GETTING PAID. I JUST DIDN'T WANT TO LOITER, SO THEY LET ME HELP OUT...
HMM ...?

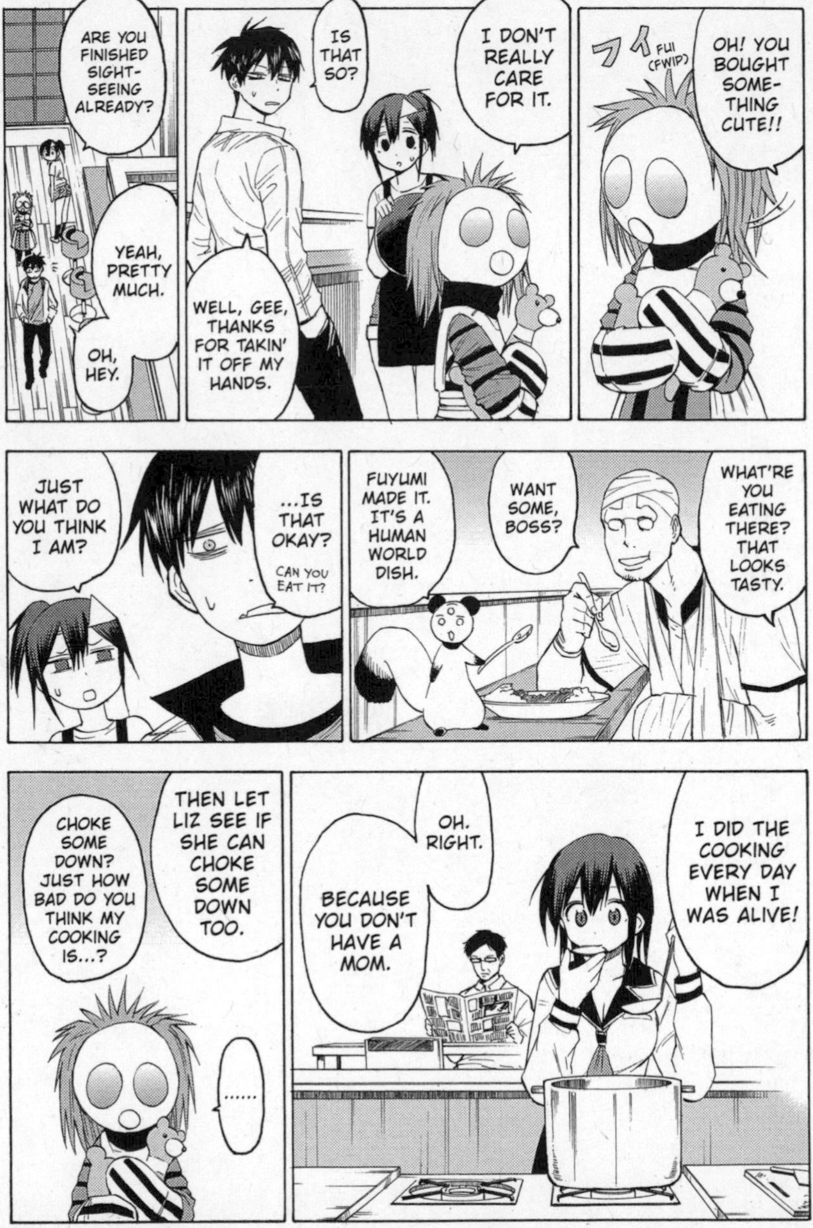
OH! YOU BOUGHT SOMETHING CUTE!!
FUI (FWIP)
I DON'T REALLY CARE FOR IT.
IS THAT SO?
WELL, GEE, THANKS FOR TAKIN' IT OFF MY HANDS.
ARE YOU FINISHED SIGHT-SEEING ALREADY?
YEAH, PRETTY MUCH.
OH, HEY.
WHAT'RE YOU EATING THERE? THAT LOOKS TASTY.
WANT SOME, BOSS?
FUYUMI MADE IT. IT'S A HUMAN WORLD DISH.
...IS THAT OKAY?
CAN YOU EAT IT?
JUST WHAT DO YOU THINK I AM?
I DID THE COOKING EVERY DAY WHEN I WAS ALIVE!
OH. RIGHT.
BECAUSE YOU DON'T HAVE A MOM.
THEN LET LIZ SEE IF SHE CAN CHOKE SOME DOWN TOO.
CHOKE SOME DOWN? JUST HOW BAD DO YOU THINK MY COOKING IS...?
......

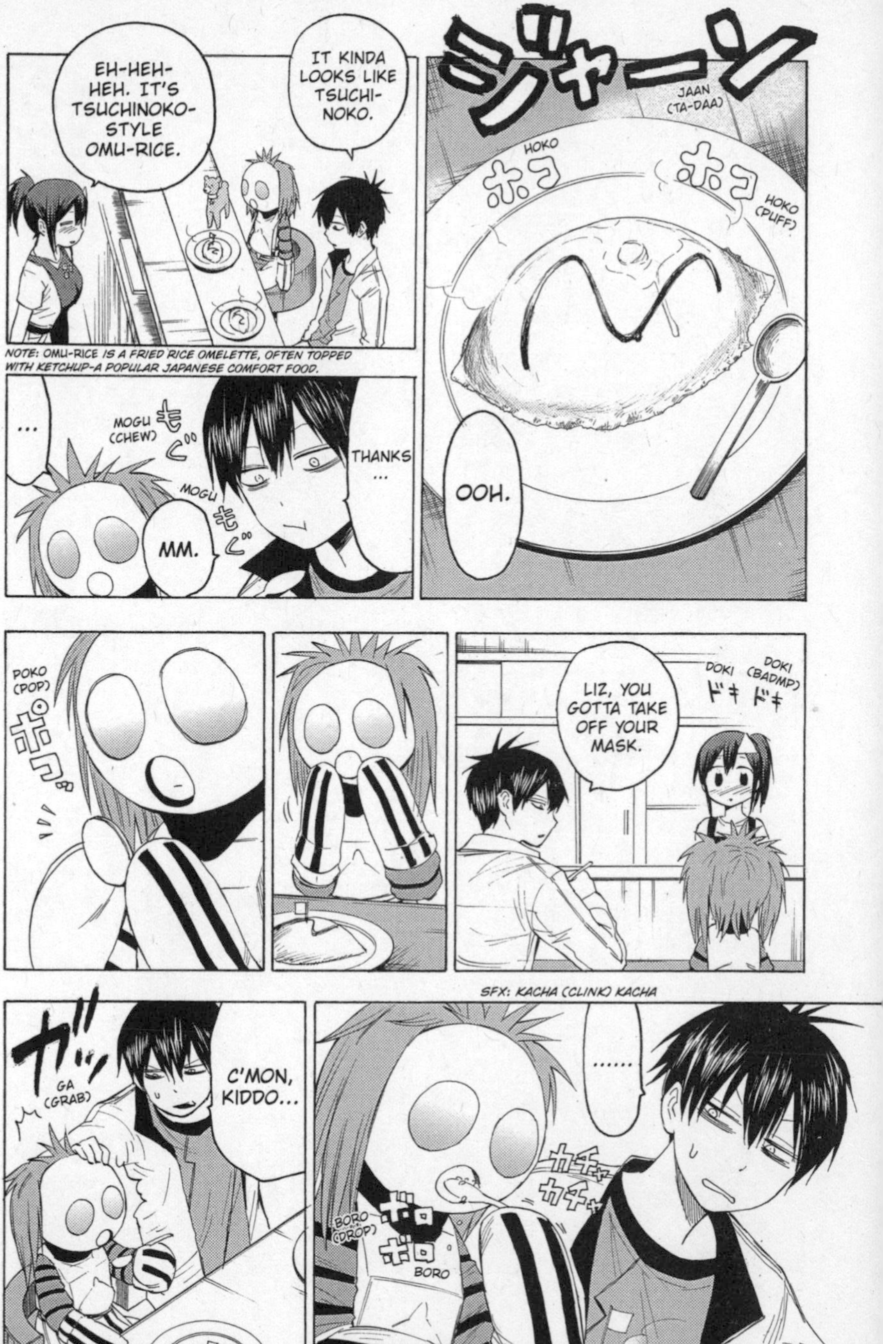
ジャーン
JAAN (TA-DAA)
HOKO
ホコ
ホコ
HOKO (PUFF)
OOH.
IT KINDA LOOKS LIKE TSUCHI-NOKO.
EH-HEH-HEH. IT'S TSUCHINOKO-STYLE OMU-RICE.
THANKS ...
MOGU (CHEW)
MOGU
...
MM.
DOKI (BADMP)
DOKI
ドキドキ
LIZ, YOU GOTTA TAKE OFF YOUR MASK.
POKO (POP)
ポコ
......
カチャ カチャ
ボロ ボロ
BORO (DROP)
BORO
C'MON, KIDDO...
ガッ
GA (GRAB)

NOTE: OMU-RICE IS A FRIED RICE OMELETTE, OFTEN TOPPED WITH KETCHUP–A POPULAR JAPANESE COMFORT FOOD.

SFX: KACHA (CLINK) KACHA

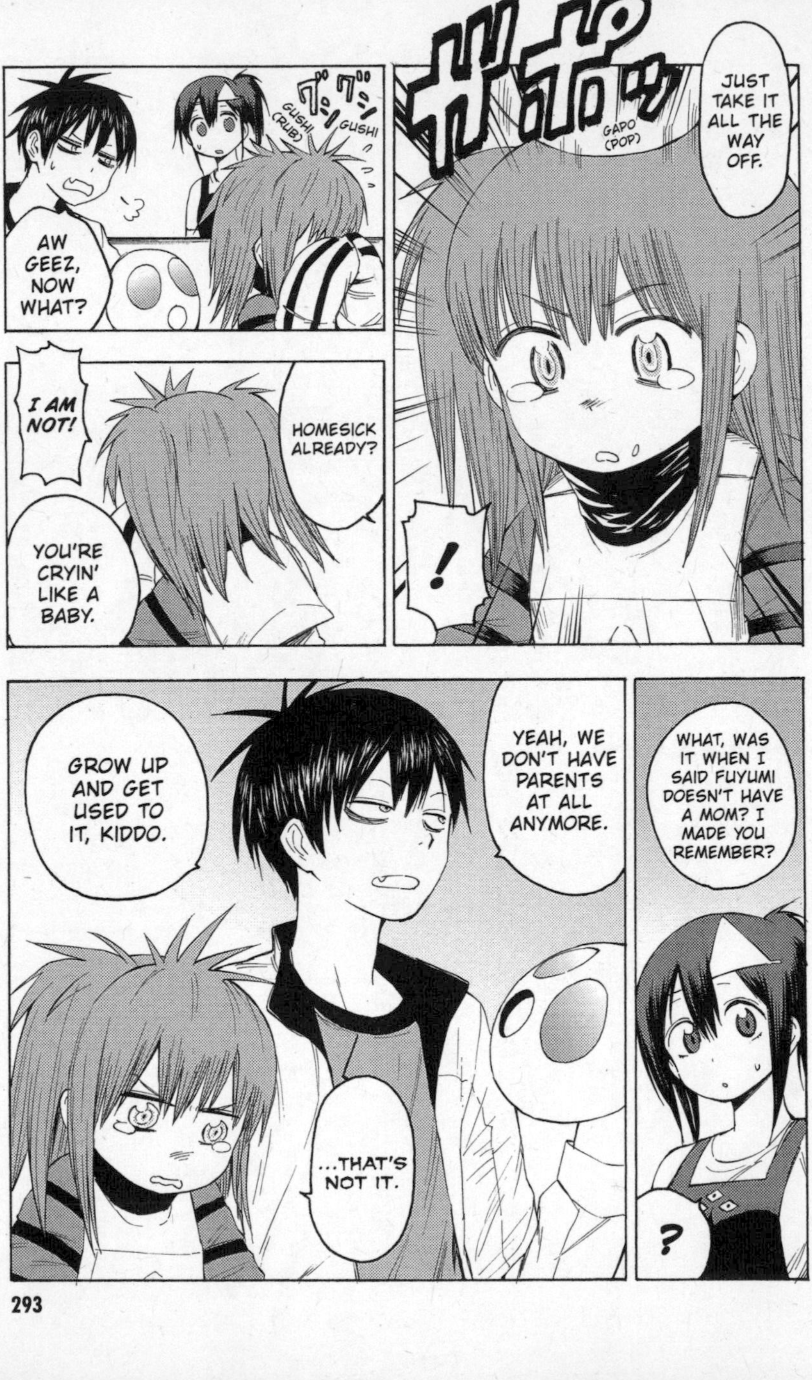
JUST TAKE IT ALL THE WAY OFF.
GAPO (POP)
!
GUSHI
GUSHI (RUB)
AW GEEZ, NOW WHAT?
HOMESICK ALREADY?
I AM NOT!
YOU'RE CRYIN' LIKE A BABY.
WHAT, WAS IT WHEN I SAID FUYUMI DOESN'T HAVE A MOM? I MADE YOU REMEMBER?
?
YEAH, WE DON'T HAVE PARENTS AT ALL ANYMORE.
GROW UP AND GET USED TO IT, KIDDO.
...THAT'S NOT IT.

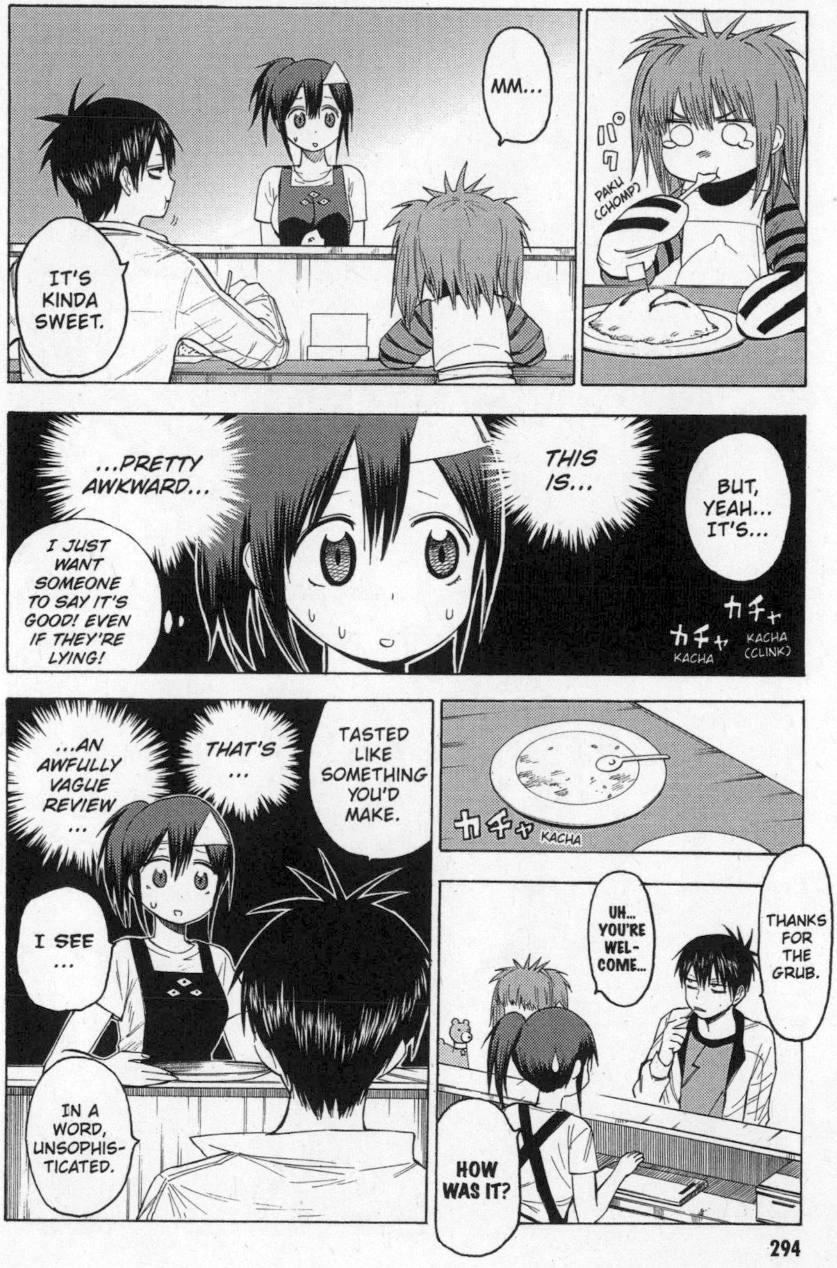
パク
PAKU (CHOMP)
MM...
IT'S KINDA SWEET.
BUT, YEAH... IT'S...
THIS IS...
...PRETTY AWKWARD...
カチャ
KACHA (CLINK)
カチャ
KACHA
I JUST WANT SOMEONE TO SAY IT'S GOOD! EVEN IF THEY'RE LYING!
カチャ
KACHA
THANKS FOR THE GRUB.
UH... YOU'RE WEL-COME...
HOW WAS IT?
TASTED LIKE SOMETHING YOU'D MAKE.
THAT'S...
...AN AWFULLY VAGUE REVIEW...
I SEE...
IN A WORD, UNSOPHIS-TICATED.

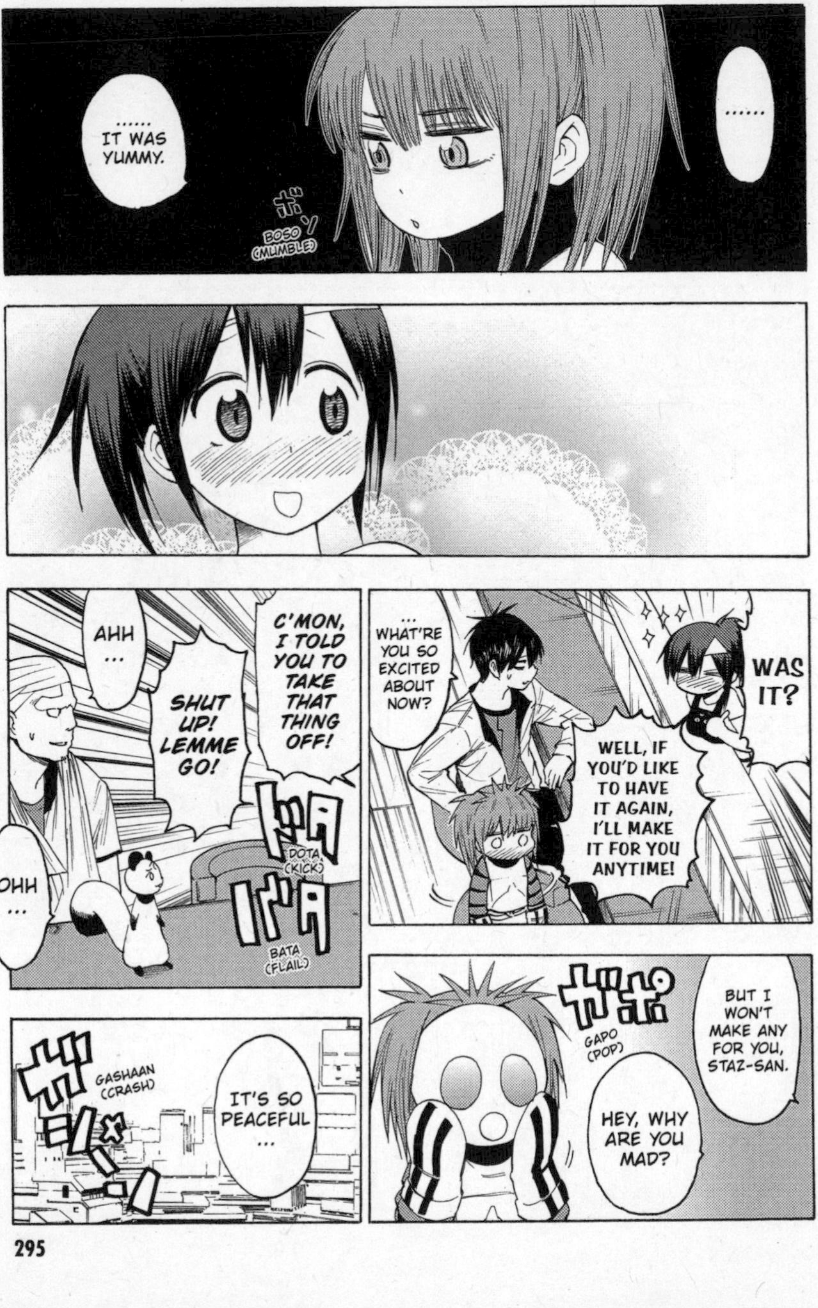
......
...... IT WAS YUMMY.
BOSO (MUMBLE)
WAS IT?
... WHAT'RE YOU SO EXCITED ABOUT NOW?
WELL, IF YOU'D LIKE TO HAVE IT AGAIN, I'LL MAKE IT FOR YOU ANYTIME!
C'MON, I TOLD YOU TO TAKE THAT THING OFF!
AHH ...
SHUT UP! LEMME GO!
DOTA (KICK)
BATA (FLAIL)
OHH ...
BUT I WON'T MAKE ANY FOR YOU, STAZ-SAN.
GAPO (POP)
HEY, WHY ARE YOU MAD?
IT'S SO PEACEFUL ...
GASHAAN (CRASH)

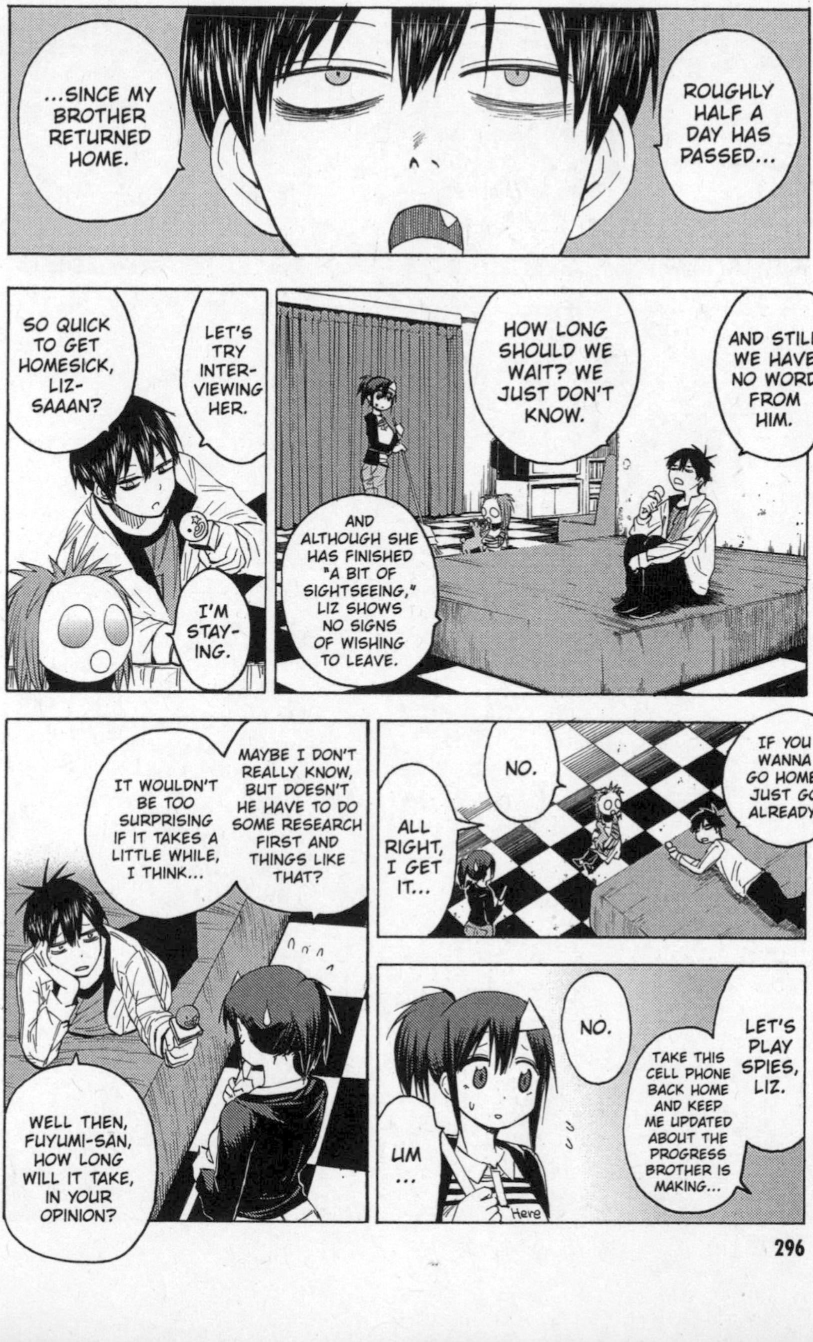

ROUGHLY HALF A DAY HAS PASSED...
...SINCE MY BROTHER RETURNED HOME.
AND STILL WE HAVE NO WORD FROM HIM.
HOW LONG SHOULD WE WAIT? WE JUST DON'T KNOW.
AND ALTHOUGH SHE HAS FINISHED "A BIT OF SIGHTSEEING," LIZ SHOWS NO SIGNS OF WISHING TO LEAVE.
LET'S TRY INTER-VIEWING HER.
SO QUICK TO GET HOMESICK, LIZ-SAAAN?
I'M STAY-ING.
IF YOU WANNA GO HOME, JUST GO ALREADY.
NO.
ALL RIGHT, I GET IT...
LET'S PLAY SPIES, LIZ.
TAKE THIS CELL PHONE BACK HOME AND KEEP ME UPDATED ABOUT THE PROGRESS BROTHER IS MAKING...
NO.
UM ...
Here
MAYBE I DON'T REALLY KNOW, BUT DOESN'T HE HAVE TO DO SOME RESEARCH FIRST AND THINGS LIKE THAT?
IT WOULDN'T BE TOO SURPRISING IF IT TAKES A LITTLE WHILE, I THINK...
WELL THEN, FUYUMI-SAN, HOW LONG WILL IT TAKE, IN YOUR OPINION?

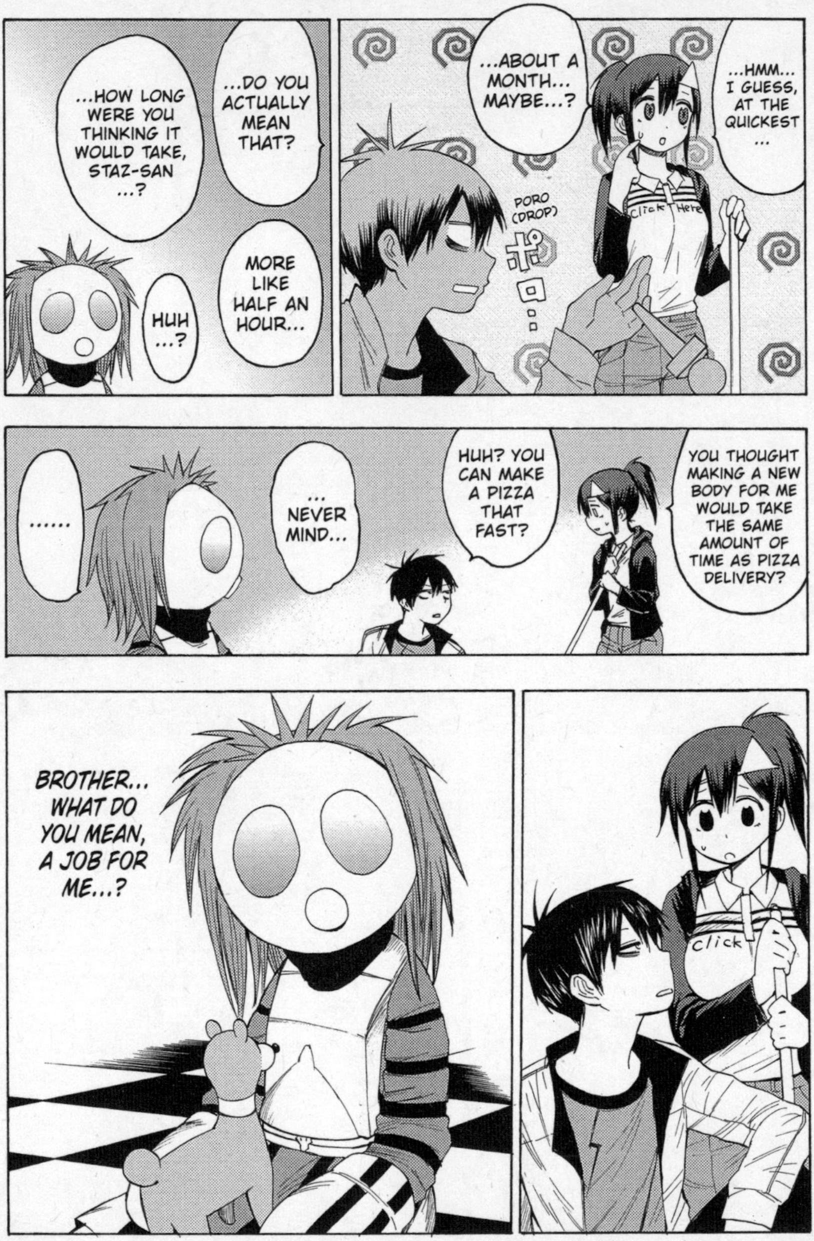
...HMM... I GUESS, AT THE QUICKEST ...
...ABOUT A MONTH... MAYBE...?
Click Here
PORO (DROP)
...DO YOU ACTUALLY MEAN THAT?
...HOW LONG WERE YOU THINKING IT WOULD TAKE, STAZ-SAN ...?
MORE LIKE HALF AN HOUR...
HUH ...?
YOU THOUGHT MAKING A NEW BODY FOR ME WOULD TAKE THE SAME AMOUNT OF TIME AS PIZZA DELIVERY?
HUH? YOU CAN MAKE A PIZZA THAT FAST?
... NEVER MIND...
......
Click
BROTHER... WHAT DO YOU MEAN, A JOB FOR ME...?

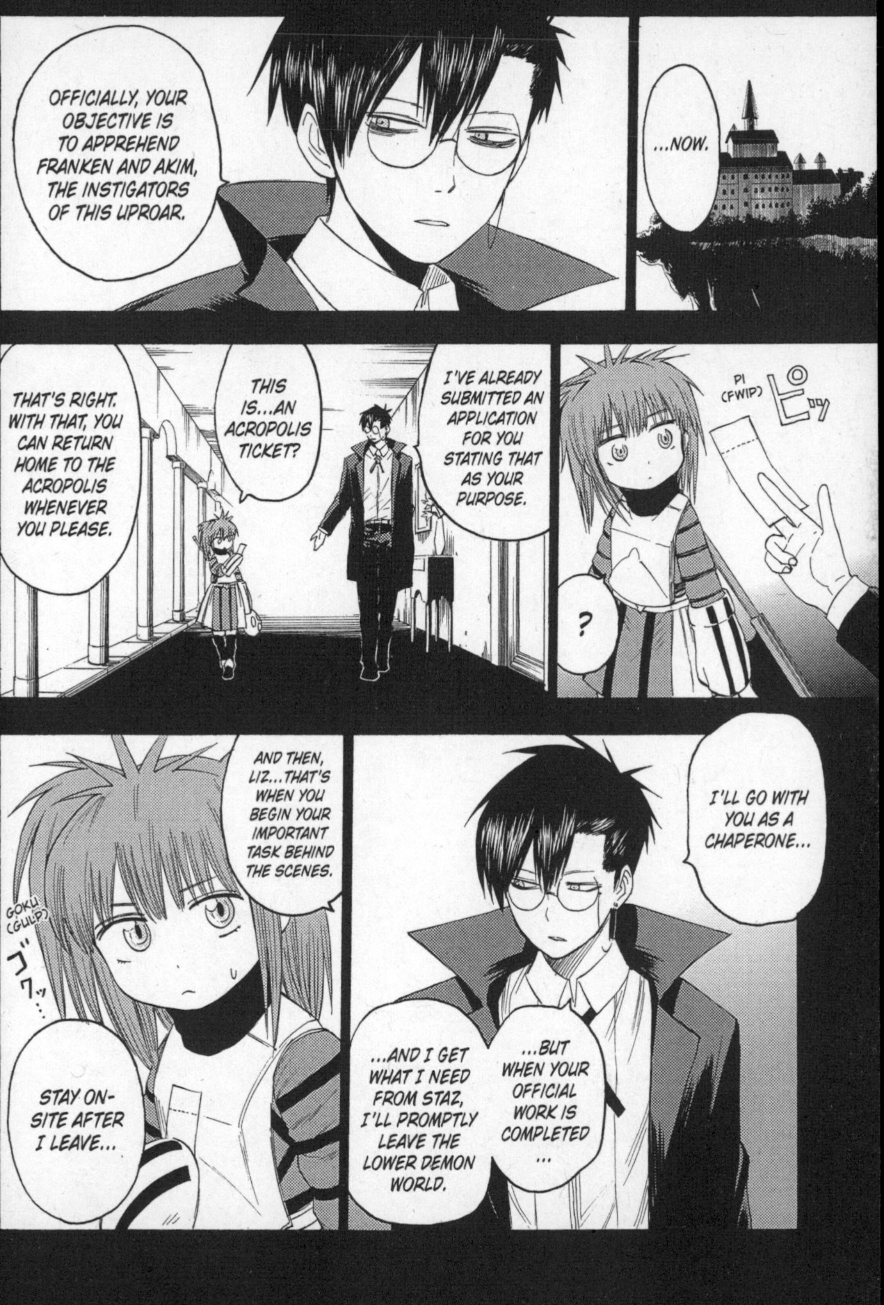
...NOW.
OFFICIALLY, YOUR OBJECTIVE IS TO APPREHEND FRANKEN AND AKIM, THE INSTIGATORS OF THIS UPROAR.
PI (FWIP)
?
I'VE ALREADY SUBMITTED AN APPLICATION FOR YOU STATING THAT AS YOUR PURPOSE.
THIS IS...AN ACROPOLIS TICKET?
THAT'S RIGHT. WITH THAT, YOU CAN RETURN HOME TO THE ACROPOLIS WHENEVER YOU PLEASE.
I'LL GO WITH YOU AS A CHAPERONE...
...BUT WHEN YOUR OFFICIAL WORK IS COMPLETED ...
...AND I GET WHAT I NEED FROM STAZ, I'LL PROMPTLY LEAVE THE LOWER DEMON WORLD.
AND THEN, LIZ...THAT'S WHEN YOU BEGIN YOUR IMPORTANT TASK BEHIND THE SCENES.
GOKU (GULP)
STAY ON-SITE AFTER I LEAVE...

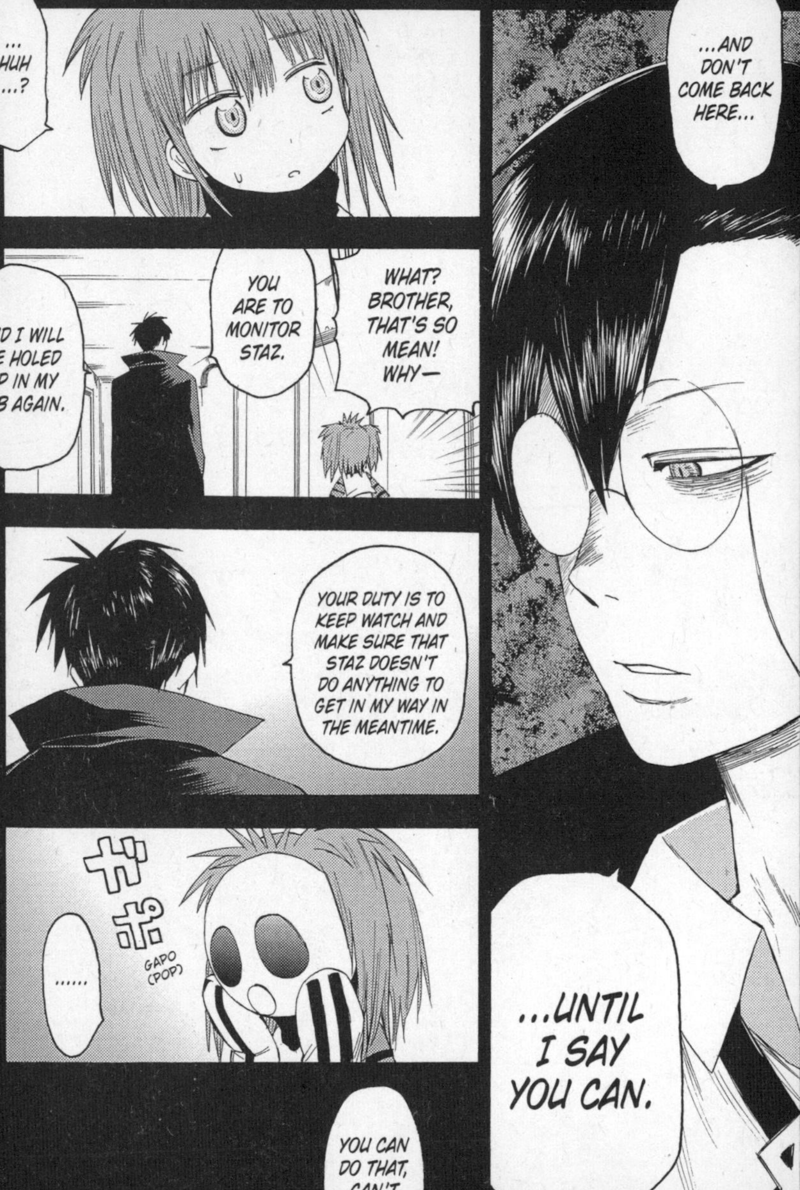
...AND DON'T COME BACK HERE...
...UNTIL I SAY YOU CAN.
YOU CAN DO THAT, CAN'T YOU?
...HUH...?
WHAT? BROTHER, THAT'S SO MEAN! WHY—
YOU ARE TO MONITOR STAZ.
AND I WILL BE HOLED UP IN MY LAB AGAIN.
YOUR DUTY IS TO KEEP WATCH AND MAKE SURE THAT STAZ DOESN'T DO ANYTHING TO GET IN MY WAY IN THE MEANTIME.
ガポ
GAPO (POP)
......

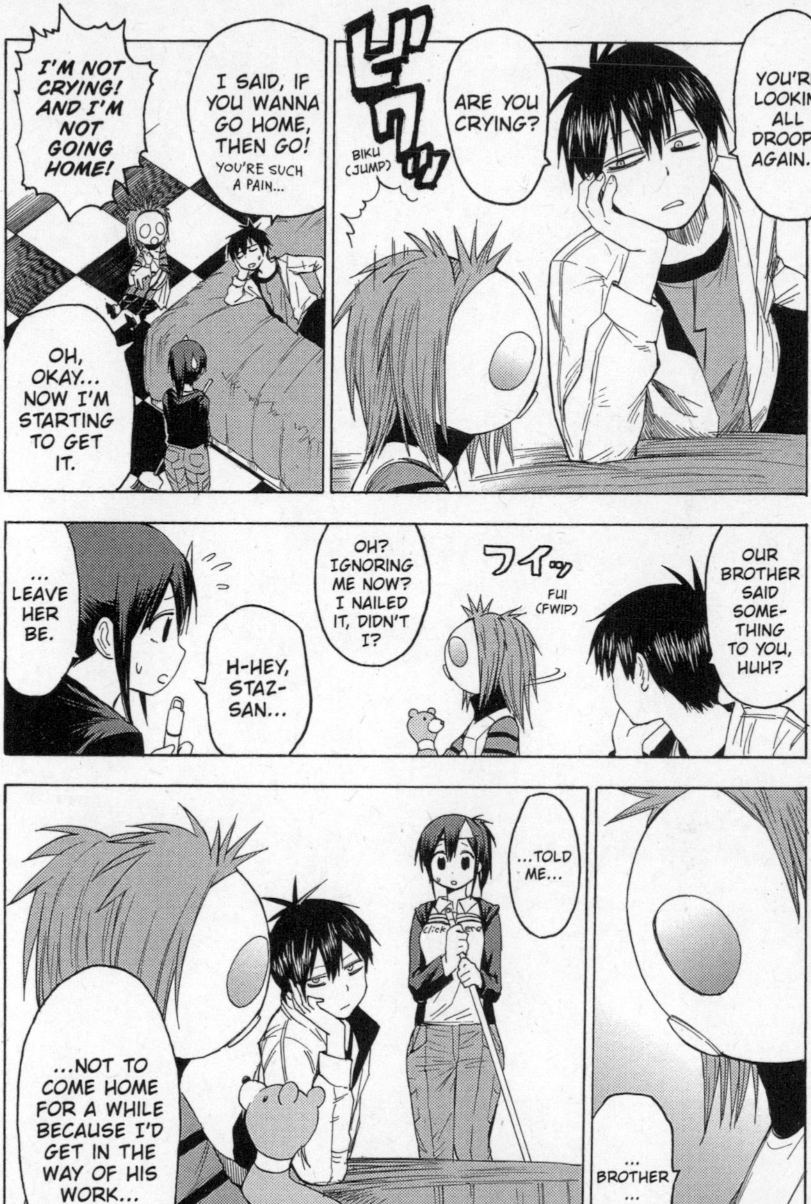
YOU'RE LOOKIN' ALL DROOPY AGAIN...
ARE YOU CRYING?
BIKU (JUMP)
I SAID, IF YOU WANNA GO HOME, THEN GO!
YOU'RE SUCH A PAIN...
I'M NOT CRYING! AND I'M NOT GOING HOME!
OH, OKAY... NOW I'M STARTING TO GET IT.
OUR BROTHER SAID SOME-THING TO YOU, HUH?
FUI (FWIP)
OH? IGNORING ME NOW? I NAILED IT, DIDN'T I?
H-HEY, STAZ-SAN...
... LEAVE HER BE.
... BROTHER ...
...TOLD ME...
...NOT TO COME HOME FOR A WHILE BECAUSE I'D GET IN THE WAY OF HIS WORK...

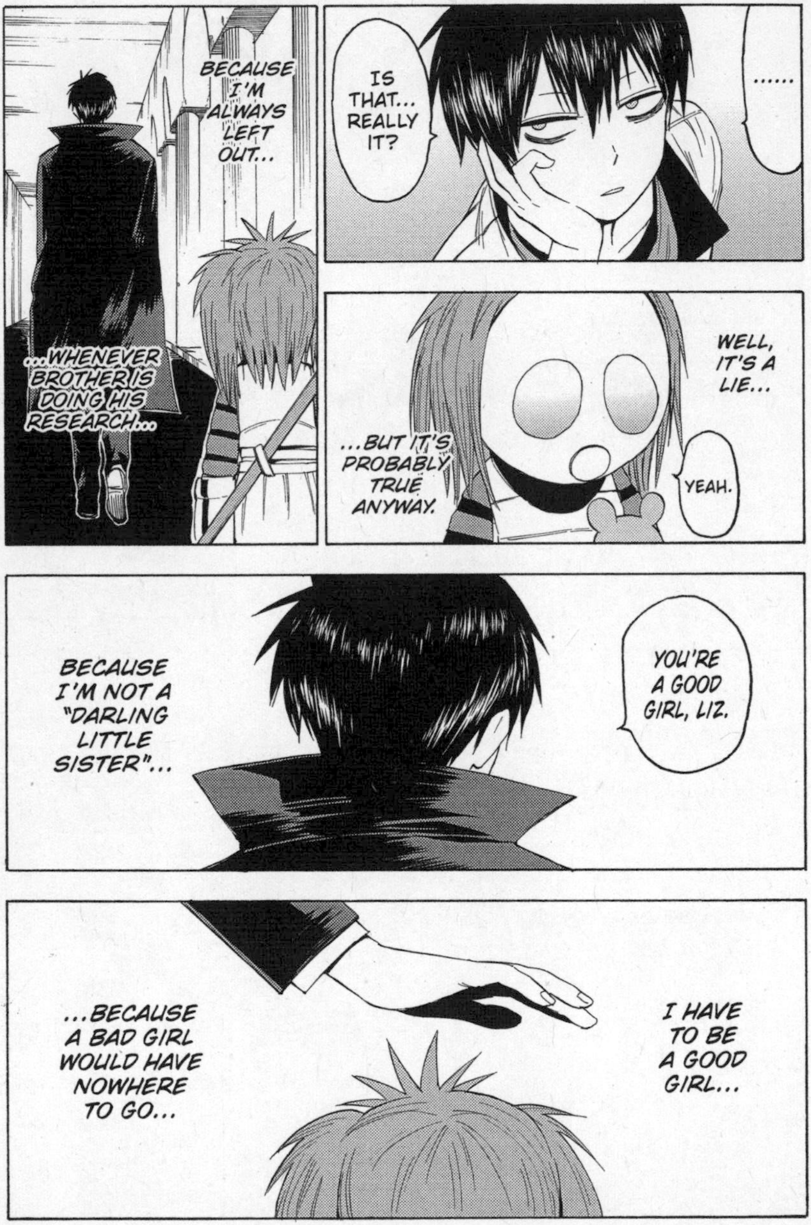
......
IS THAT... REALLY IT?
WELL, IT'S A LIE...
YEAH.
...BUT IT'S PROBABLY TRUE ANYWAY.
BECAUSE I'M ALWAYS LEFT OUT...
...WHENEVER BROTHER IS DOING HIS RESEARCH...
YOU'RE A GOOD GIRL, LIZ.
BECAUSE I'M NOT A "DARLING LITTLE SISTER"...
I HAVE TO BE A GOOD GIRL...
...BECAUSE A BAD GIRL WOULD HAVE NOWHERE TO GO...

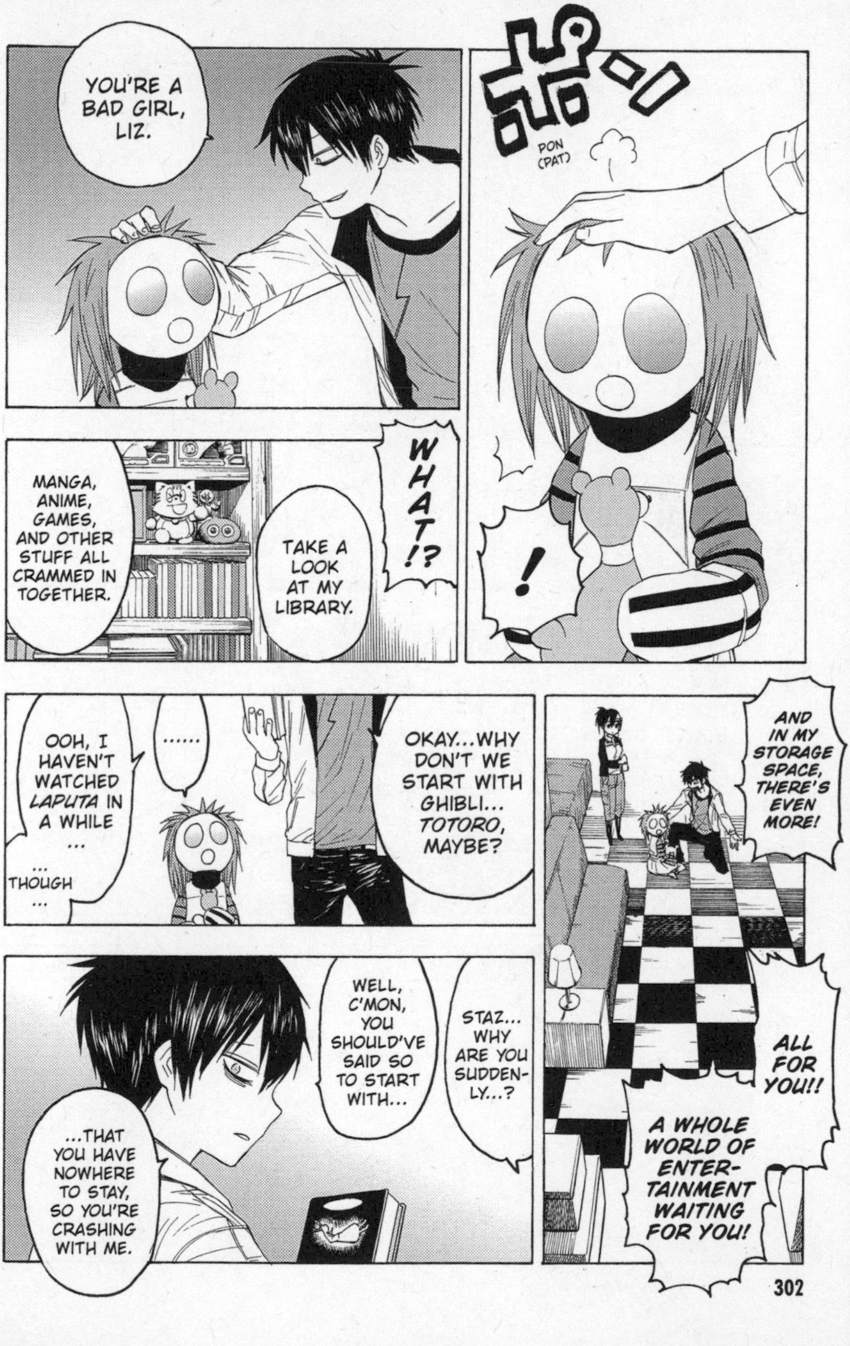
PON (PAT)
!
YOU'RE A BAD GIRL, LIZ.
WHAT!?
TAKE A LOOK AT MY LIBRARY.
MANGA, ANIME, GAMES, AND OTHER STUFF ALL CRAMMED IN TOGETHER.
AND IN MY STORAGE SPACE, THERE'S EVEN MORE!
ALL FOR YOU!!
A WHOLE WORLD OF ENTER-TAINMENT WAITING FOR YOU!
OKAY...WHY DON'T WE START WITH GHIBLI... *TOTORO*, MAYBE?
......
OOH, I HAVEN'T WATCHED *LAPUTA* IN A WHILE ... ... THOUGH ...
STAZ... WHY ARE YOU SUDDEN-LY...?
WELL, C'MON, YOU SHOULD'VE SAID SO TO START WITH...
...THAT YOU HAVE NOWHERE TO STAY, SO YOU'RE CRASHING WITH ME.

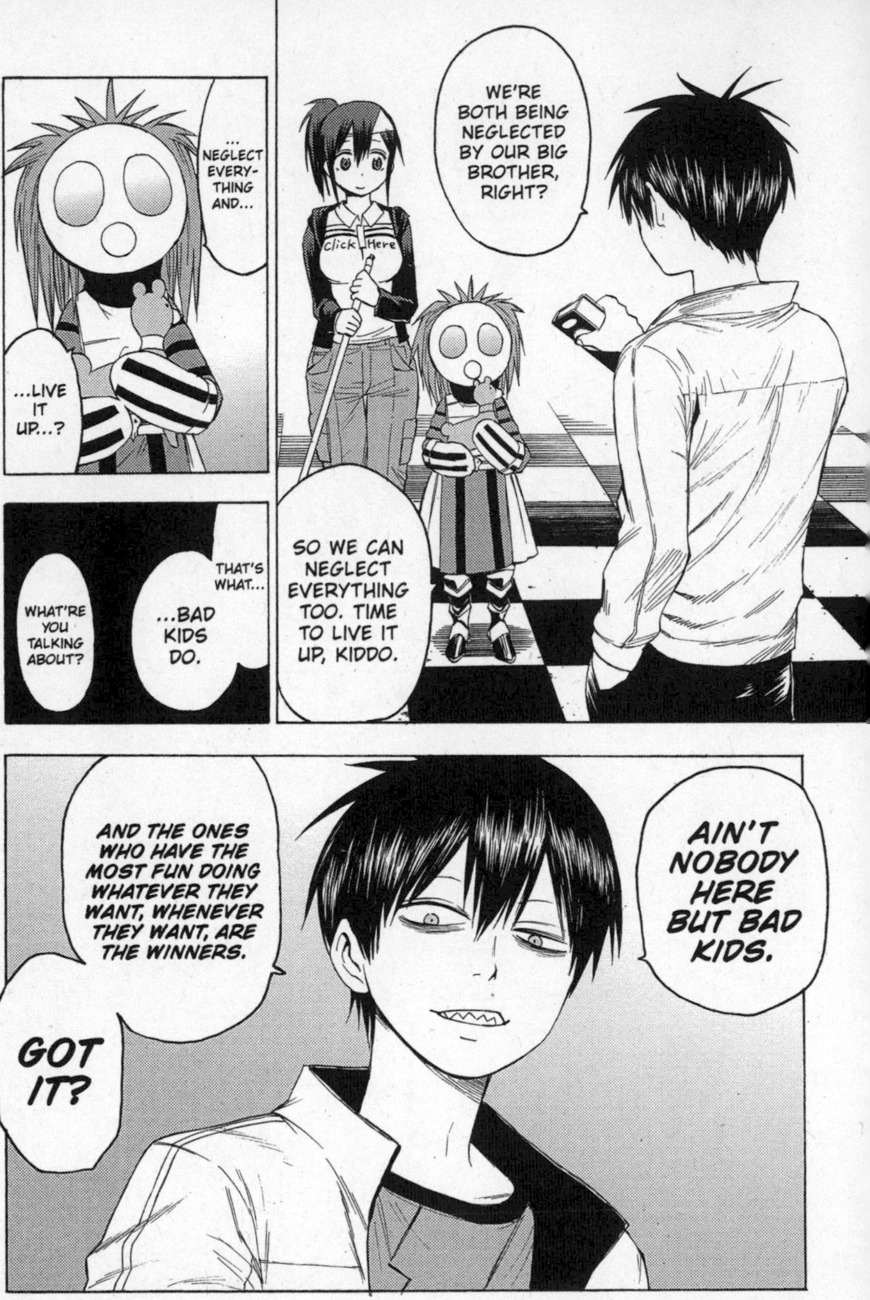
WE'RE BOTH BEING NEGLECTED BY OUR BIG BROTHER, RIGHT?
SO WE CAN NEGLECT EVERYTHING TOO. TIME TO LIVE IT UP, KIDDO.
...NEGLECT EVERYTHING AND...
...LIVE IT UP...?
THAT'S WHAT...
...BAD KIDS DO.
WHAT'RE YOU TALKING ABOUT?
AIN'T NOBODY HERE BUT BAD KIDS.
AND THE ONES WHO HAVE THE MOST FUN DOING WHATEVER THEY WANT, WHENEVER THEY WANT, ARE THE WINNERS.
GOT IT?

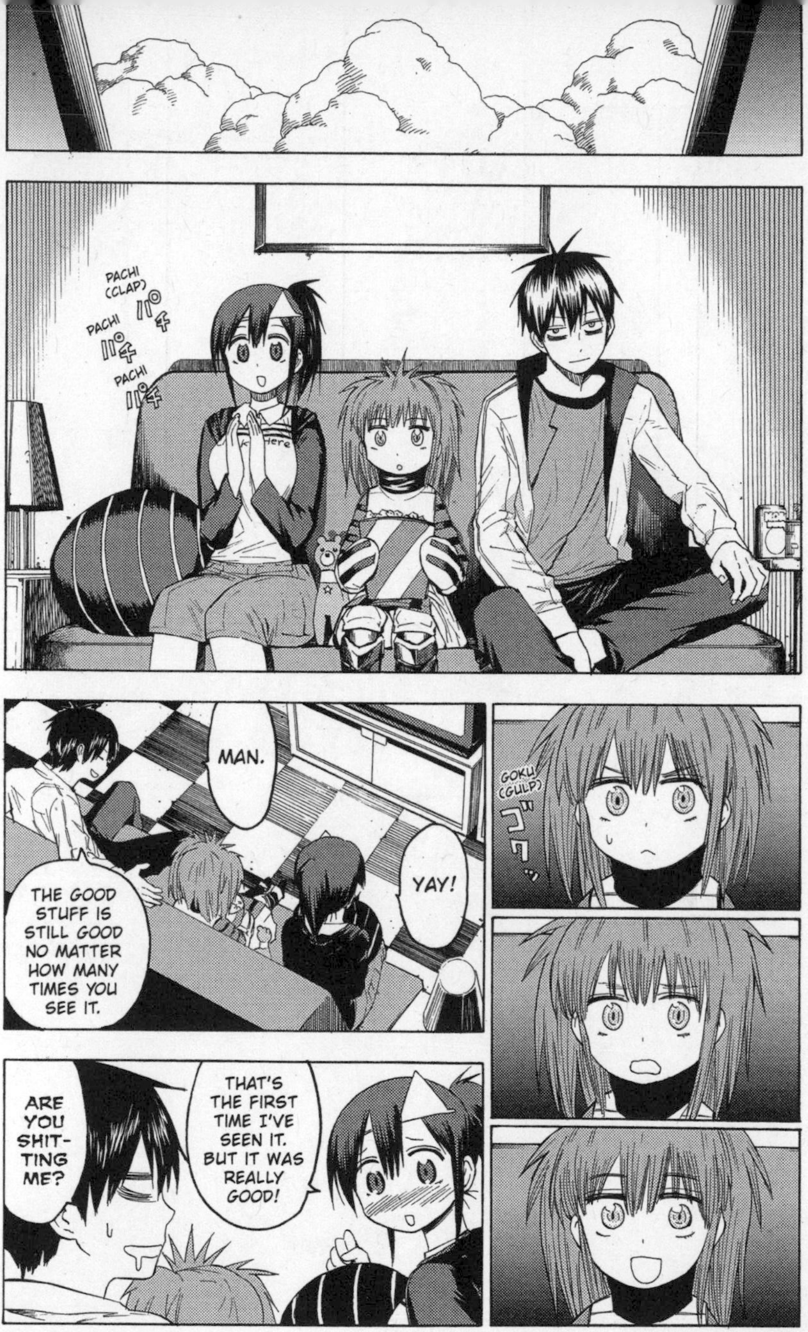
PACHI (CLAP) パチ
PACHI パチ
PACHI パチ
GOKU (GULP) ゴクッ
MAN.
YAY!
THE GOOD STUFF IS STILL GOOD NO MATTER HOW MANY TIMES YOU SEE IT.
THAT'S THE FIRST TIME I'VE SEEN IT. BUT IT WAS REALLY GOOD!
ARE YOU SHITTING ME?

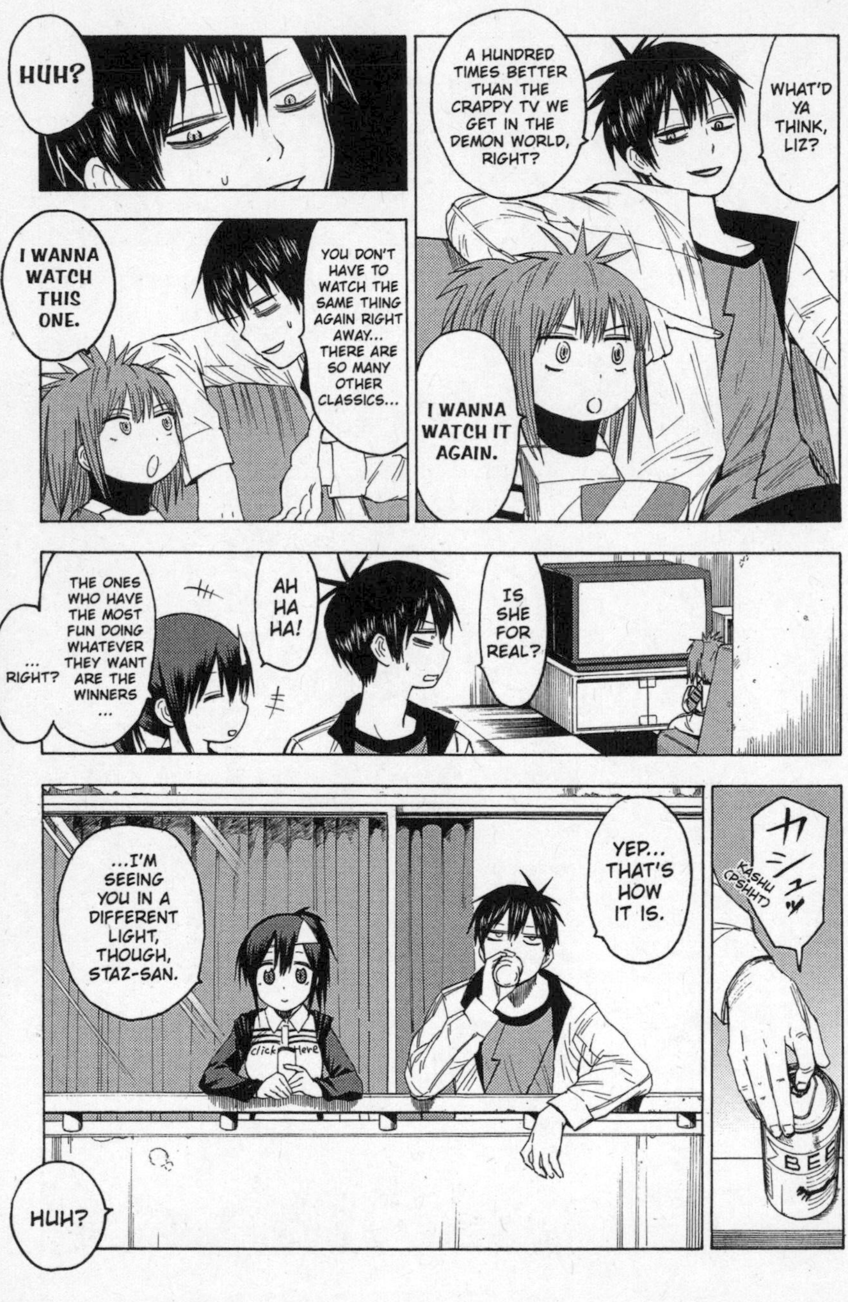
WHAT'D YA THINK, LIZ?
A HUNDRED TIMES BETTER THAN THE CRAPPY TV WE GET IN THE DEMON WORLD, RIGHT?
I WANNA WATCH IT AGAIN.
HUH?
YOU DON'T HAVE TO WATCH THE SAME THING AGAIN RIGHT AWAY... THERE ARE SO MANY OTHER CLASSICS...
I WANNA WATCH THIS ONE.
IS SHE FOR REAL?
AH HA HA!
THE ONES WHO HAVE THE MOST FUN DOING WHATEVER THEY WANT ARE THE WINNERS ...
... RIGHT?
カシュッ
KASHU (PSHHT)
BEE
YEP... THAT'S HOW IT IS.
...I'M SEEING YOU IN A DIFFERENT LIGHT, THOUGH, STAZ-SAN.
click Here
HUH?

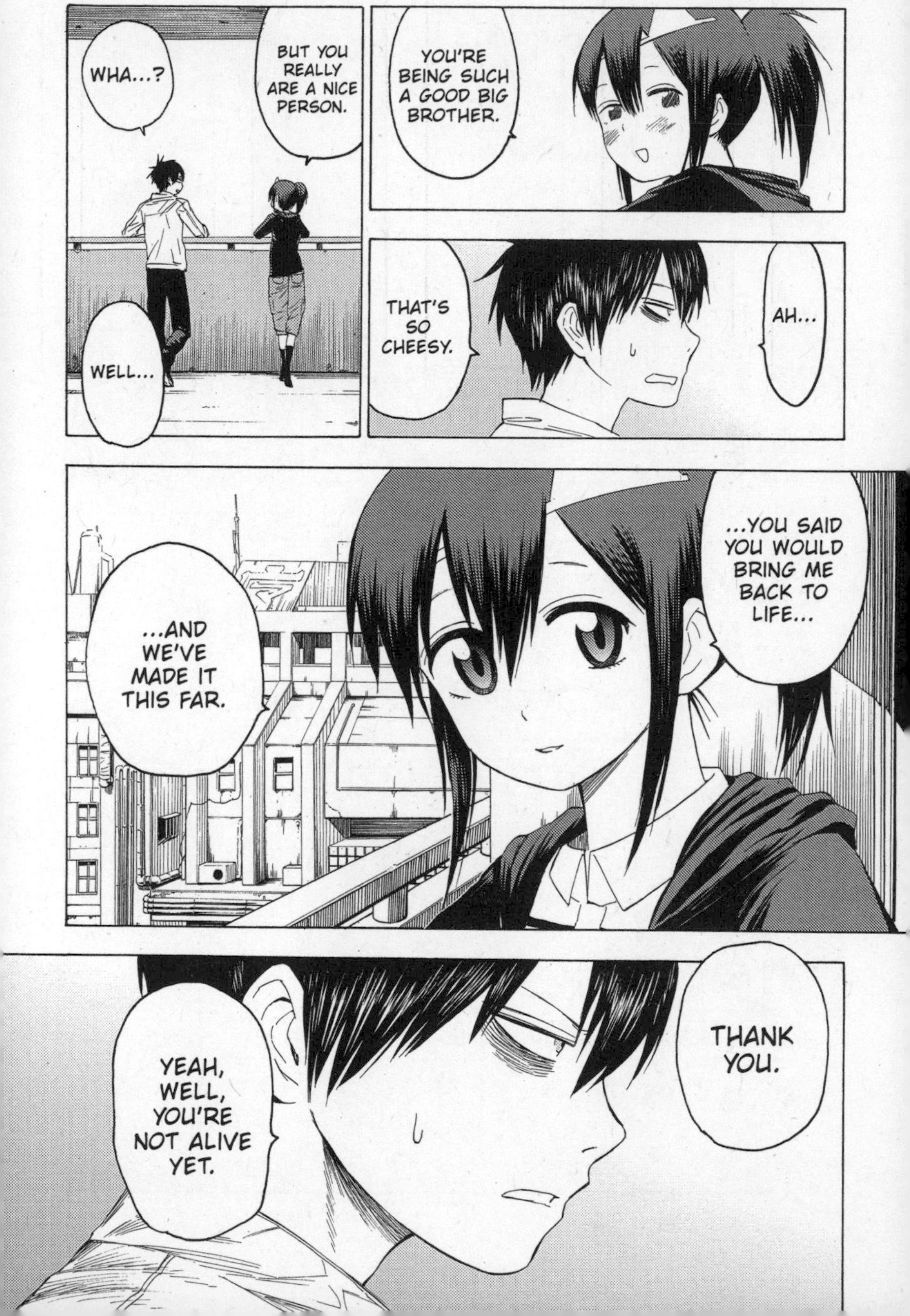
YOU'RE BEING SUCH A GOOD BIG BROTHER.
AH...
THAT'S SO CHEESY.
BUT YOU REALLY ARE A NICE PERSON.
WHA...?
WELL...
...YOU SAID YOU WOULD BRING ME BACK TO LIFE...
...AND WE'VE MADE IT THIS FAR.
THANK YOU.
YEAH, WELL, YOU'RE NOT ALIVE YET.

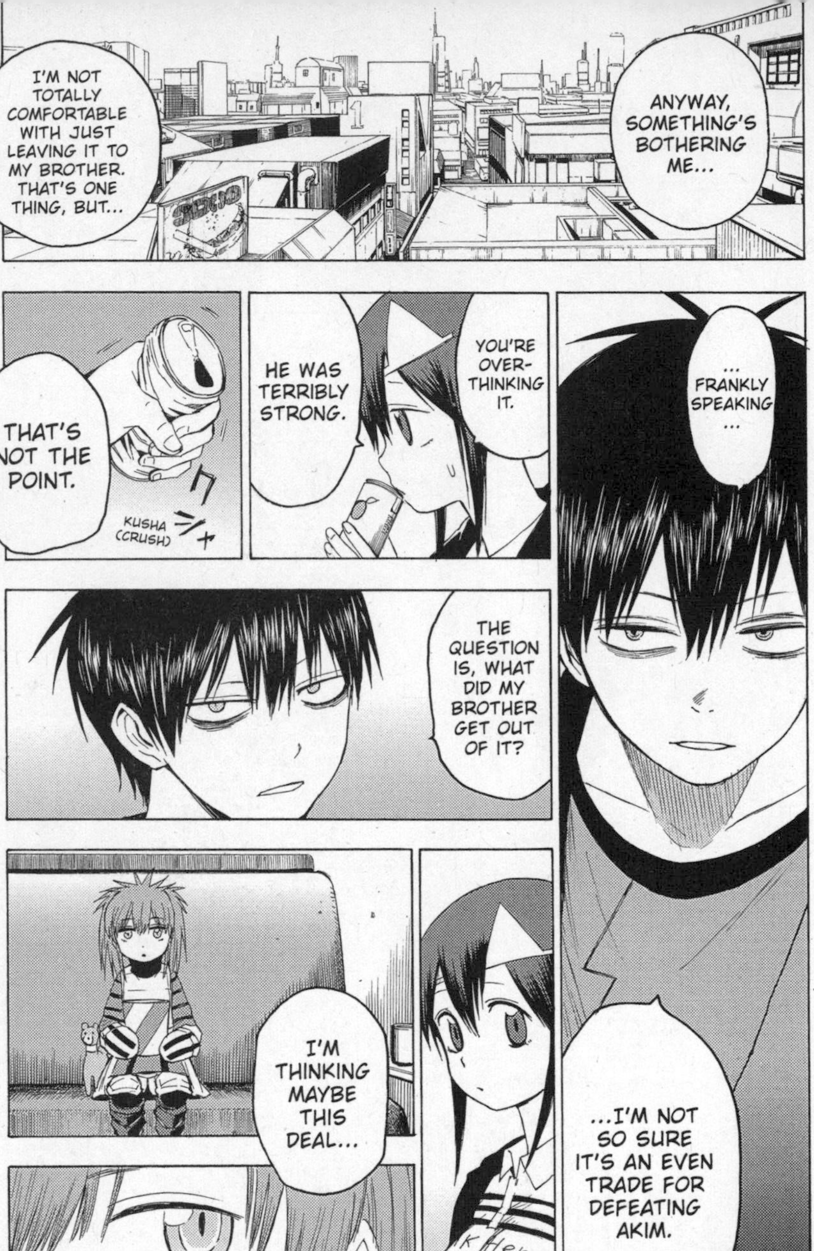
ANYWAY, SOMETHING'S BOTHERING ME...
I'M NOT TOTALLY COMFORTABLE WITH JUST LEAVING IT TO MY BROTHER. THAT'S ONE THING, BUT...
... FRANKLY SPEAKING ...
...I'M NOT SO SURE IT'S AN EVEN TRADE FOR DEFEATING AKIM.
YOU'RE OVER-THINKING IT.
HE WAS TERRIBLY STRONG.
THAT'S NOT THE POINT.
KUSHA (CRUSH)
THE QUESTION IS, WHAT DID MY BROTHER GET OUT OF IT?
I'M THINKING MAYBE THIS DEAL...

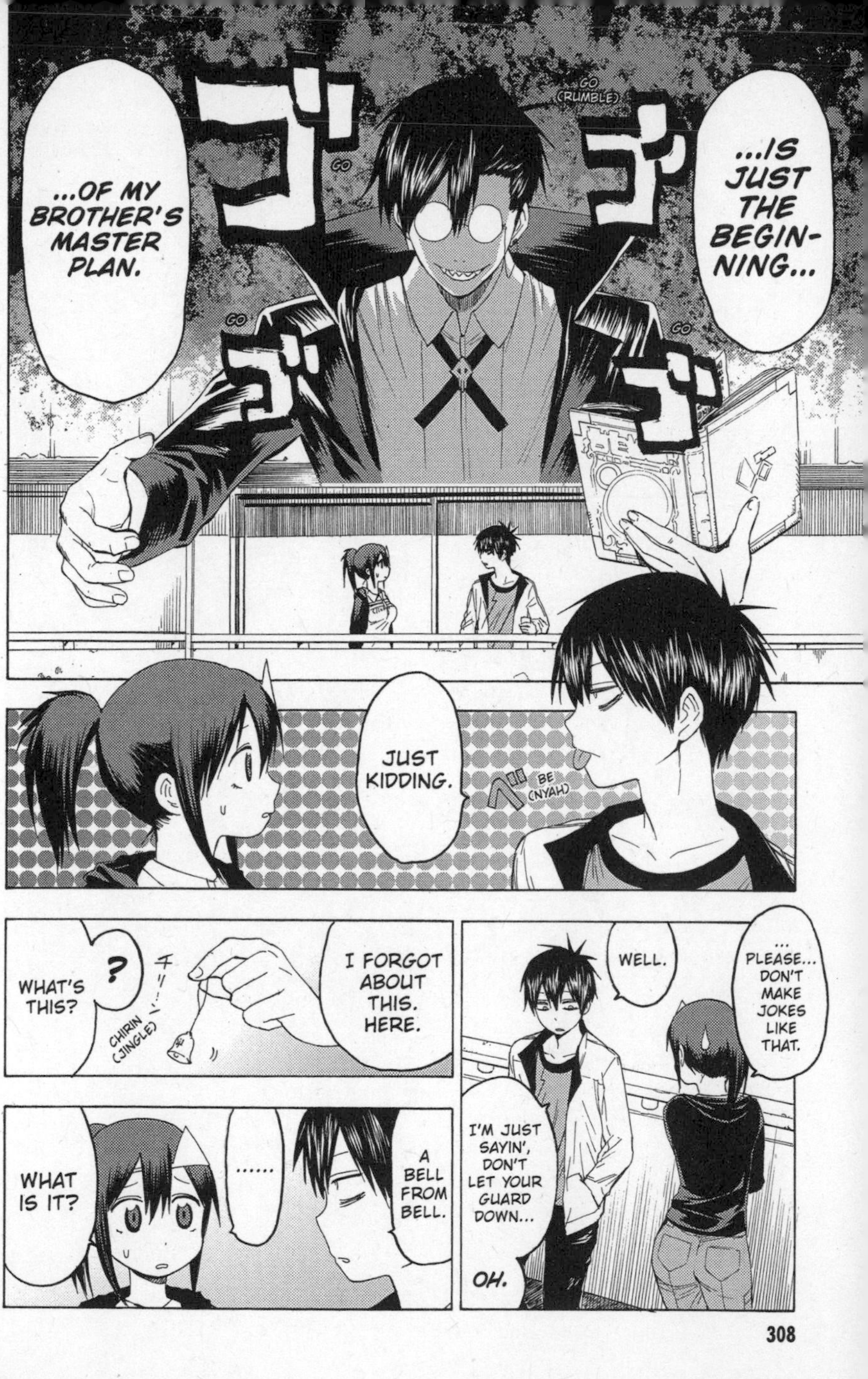
...IS JUST THE BEGIN-NING...
GO (RUMBLE)
GO
GO
GO
...OF MY BROTHER'S MASTER PLAN.
BE (NYAH)
JUST KIDDING.
... PLEASE... DON'T MAKE JOKES LIKE THAT.
WELL.
I'M JUST SAYIN', DON'T LET YOUR GUARD DOWN...
OH.
I FORGOT ABOUT THIS. HERE.
CHIRIN (JINGLE)
?
WHAT'S THIS?
A BELL FROM BELL.
......
WHAT IS IT?

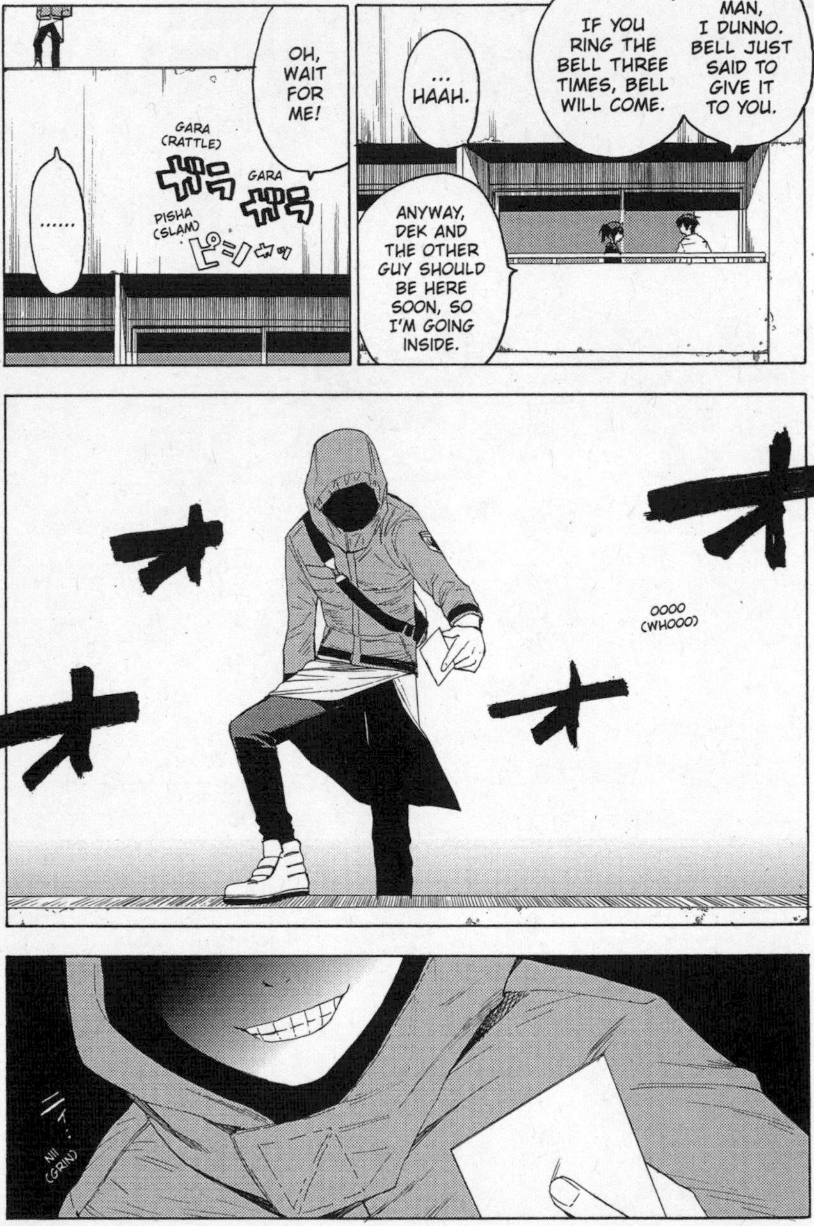
MAN, I DUNNO. BELL JUST SAID TO GIVE IT TO YOU.
IF YOU RING THE BELL THREE TIMES, BELL WILL COME.
... HAAH.
ANYWAY, DEK AND THE OTHER GUY SHOULD BE HERE SOON, SO I'M GOING INSIDE.
OH, WAIT FOR ME!
GARA (RATTLE)
GARA
PISHA (SLAM)
......
OOOO (WHOOO)
NII (GRIN)

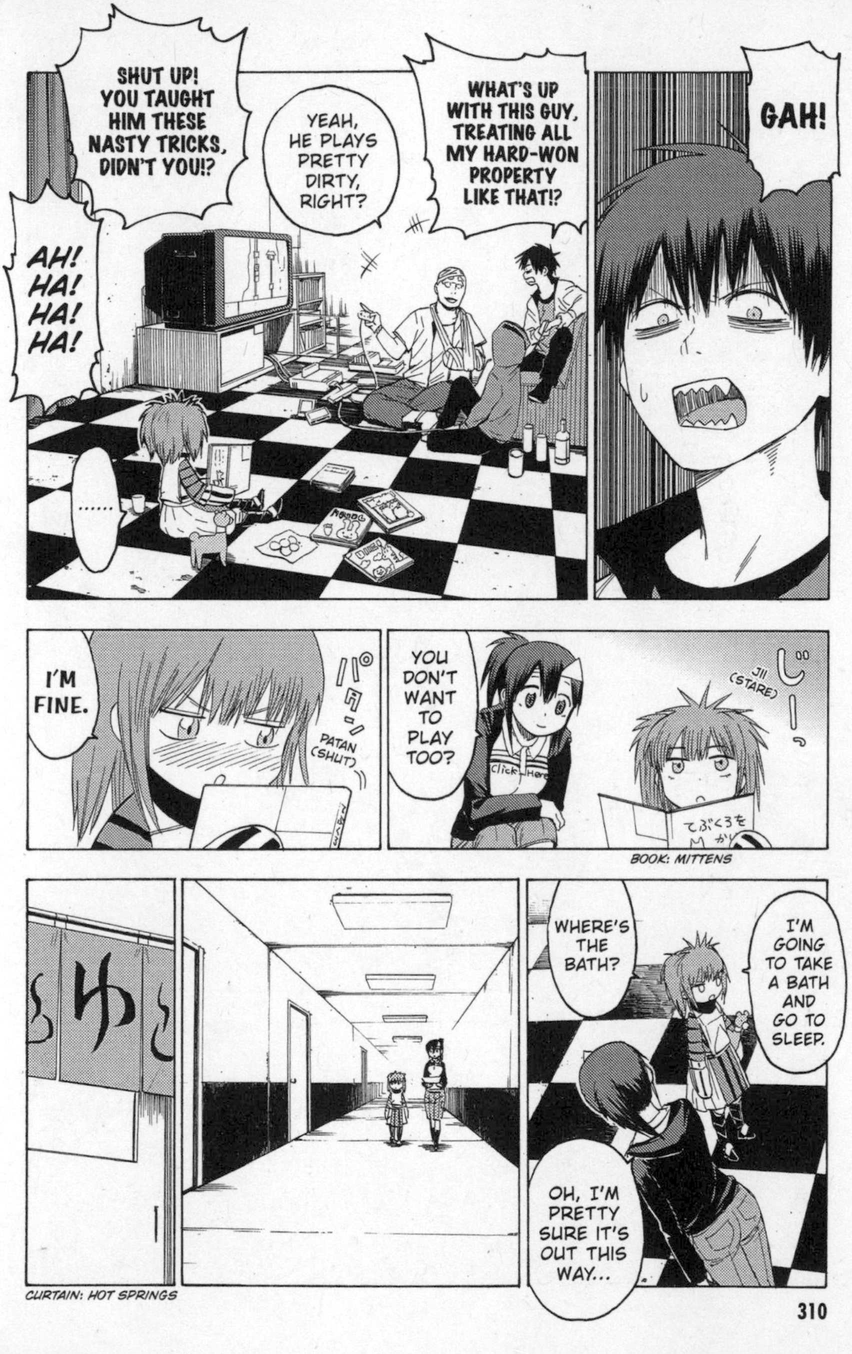
GAH!
WHAT'S UP WITH THIS GUY, TREATING ALL MY HARD-WON PROPERTY LIKE THAT!?
YEAH, HE PLAYS PRETTY DIRTY, RIGHT?
SHUT UP! YOU TAUGHT HIM THESE NASTY TRICKS, DIDN'T YOU!?
AH! HA! HA! HA!
......
じーっ
JII (STARE)
YOU DON'T WANT TO PLAY TOO?
Click Here
パタン
PATAN (SHUT)
I'M FINE.
I'M GOING TO TAKE A BATH AND GO TO SLEEP.
WHERE'S THE BATH?
OH, I'M PRETTY SURE IT'S OUT THIS WAY...
ゆ
BOOK: MITTENS
CURTAIN: HOT SPRINGS

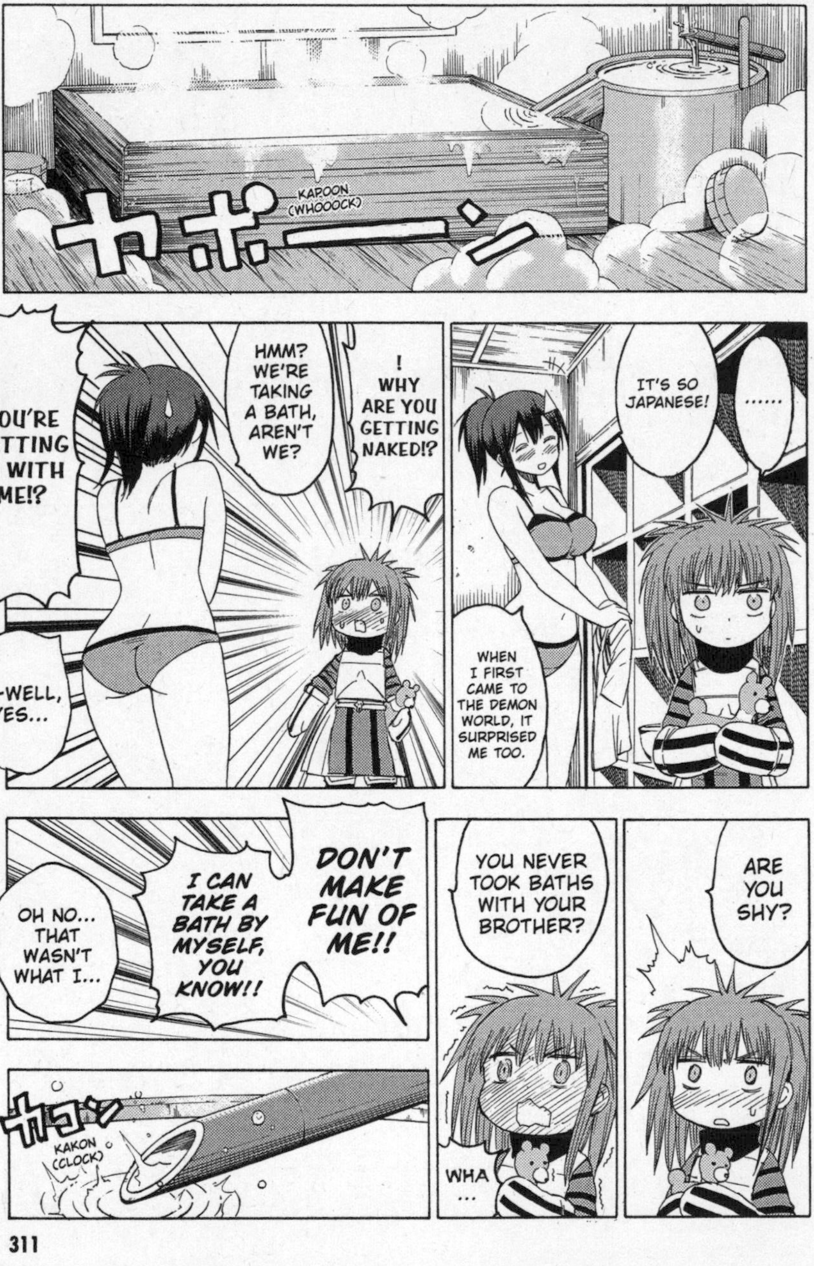
カポーン
KAPOOON (WHOOOCK)
IT'S SO JAPANESE!
......
WHEN I FIRST CAME TO THE DEMON WORLD, IT SURPRISED ME TOO.
! WHY ARE YOU GETTING NAKED!?
HMM? WE'RE TAKING A BATH, AREN'T WE?
YOU'RE GETTING IN WITH ME!?
W-WELL, YES...
ARE YOU SHY?
YOU NEVER TOOK BATHS WITH YOUR BROTHER?
WHA...
DON'T MAKE FUN OF ME!!
I CAN TAKE A BATH BY MYSELF, YOU KNOW!!
OH NO... THAT WASN'T WHAT I...
カコン
KAKON (CLOCK)

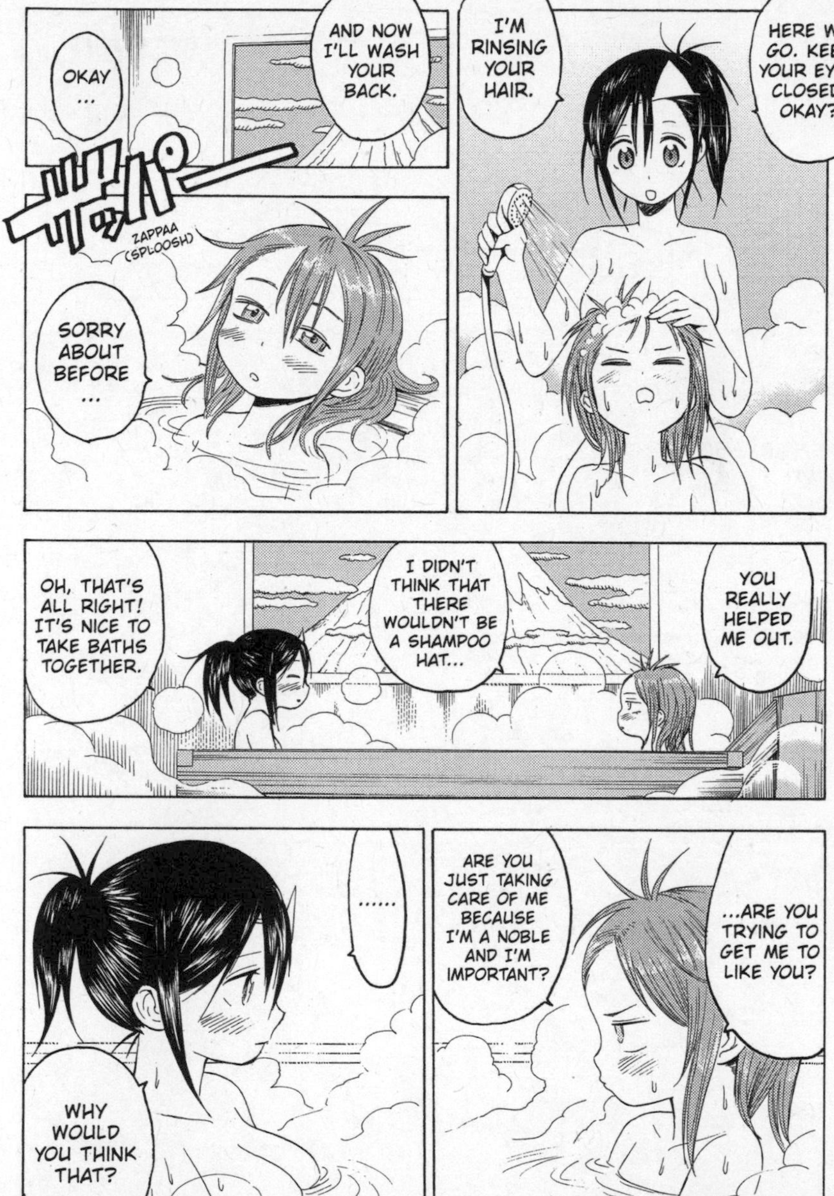
HERE WE GO. KEEP YOUR EYES CLOSED, OKAY?
I'M RINSING YOUR HAIR.
AND NOW I'LL WASH YOUR BACK.
OKAY ...
ザッパー
ZAPPAA (SPLOOSH)
SORRY ABOUT BEFORE ...
YOU REALLY HELPED ME OUT.
I DIDN'T THINK THAT THERE WOULDN'T BE A SHAMPOO HAT...
OH, THAT'S ALL RIGHT! IT'S NICE TO TAKE BATHS TOGETHER.
...ARE YOU TRYING TO GET ME TO LIKE YOU?
ARE YOU JUST TAKING CARE OF ME BECAUSE I'M A NOBLE AND I'M IMPORTANT?
......
WHY WOULD YOU THINK THAT?

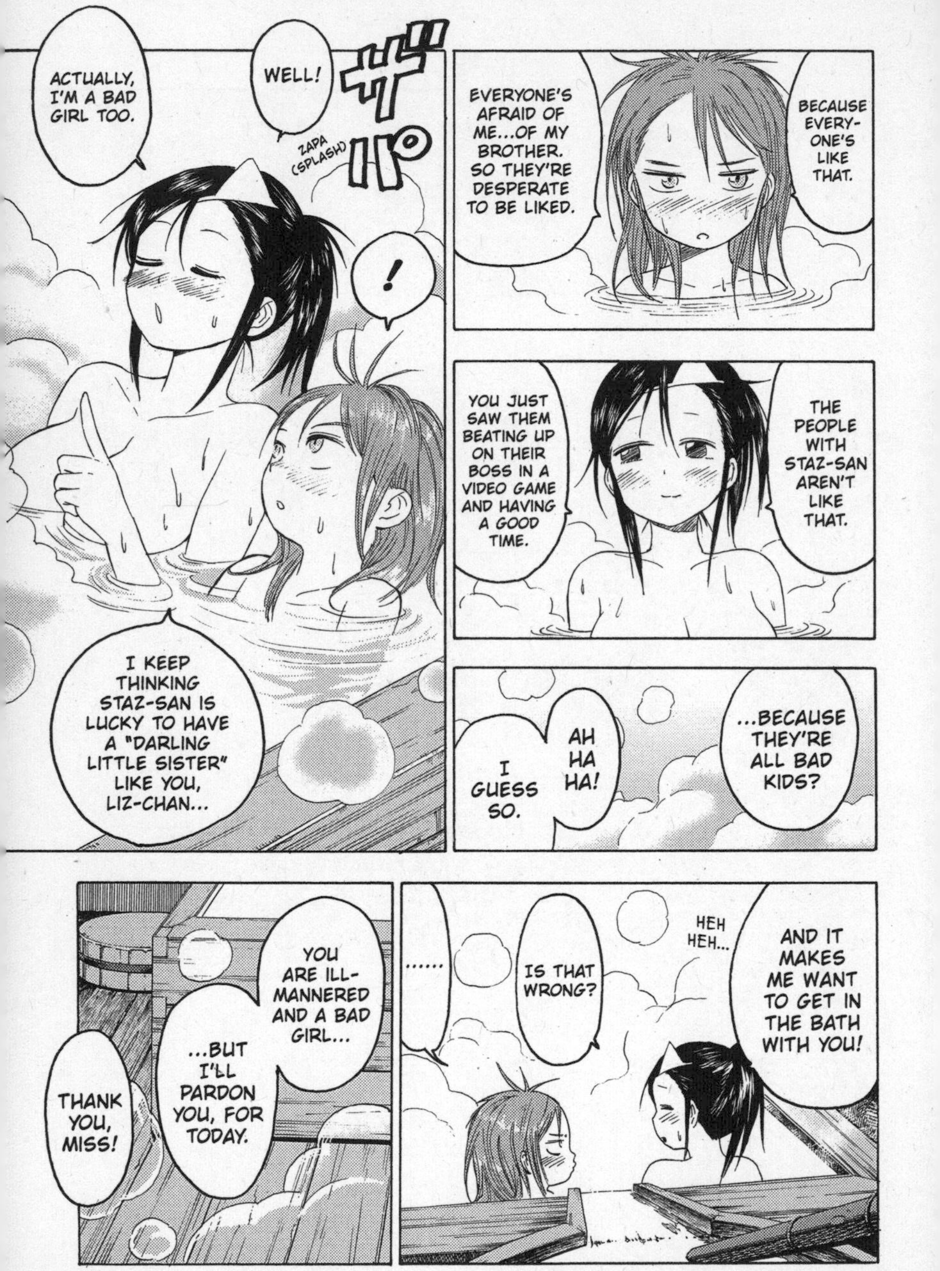
BECAUSE EVERY-ONE'S LIKE THAT.
EVERYONE'S AFRAID OF ME...OF MY BROTHER. SO THEY'RE DESPERATE TO BE LIKED.
THE PEOPLE WITH STAZ-SAN AREN'T LIKE THAT.
YOU JUST SAW THEM BEATING UP ON THEIR BOSS IN A VIDEO GAME AND HAVING A GOOD TIME.
...BECAUSE THEY'RE ALL BAD KIDS?
AH HA HA!
I GUESS SO.
ZAPA (SPLASH)
WELL!
ACTUALLY, I'M A BAD GIRL TOO.
!
I KEEP THINKING STAZ-SAN IS LUCKY TO HAVE A "DARLING LITTLE SISTER" LIKE YOU, LIZ-CHAN...
AND IT MAKES ME WANT TO GET IN THE BATH WITH YOU!
HEH HEH...
IS THAT WRONG?
......
YOU ARE ILL-MANNERED AND A BAD GIRL...
...BUT I'LL PARDON YOU, FOR TODAY.
THANK YOU, MISS!

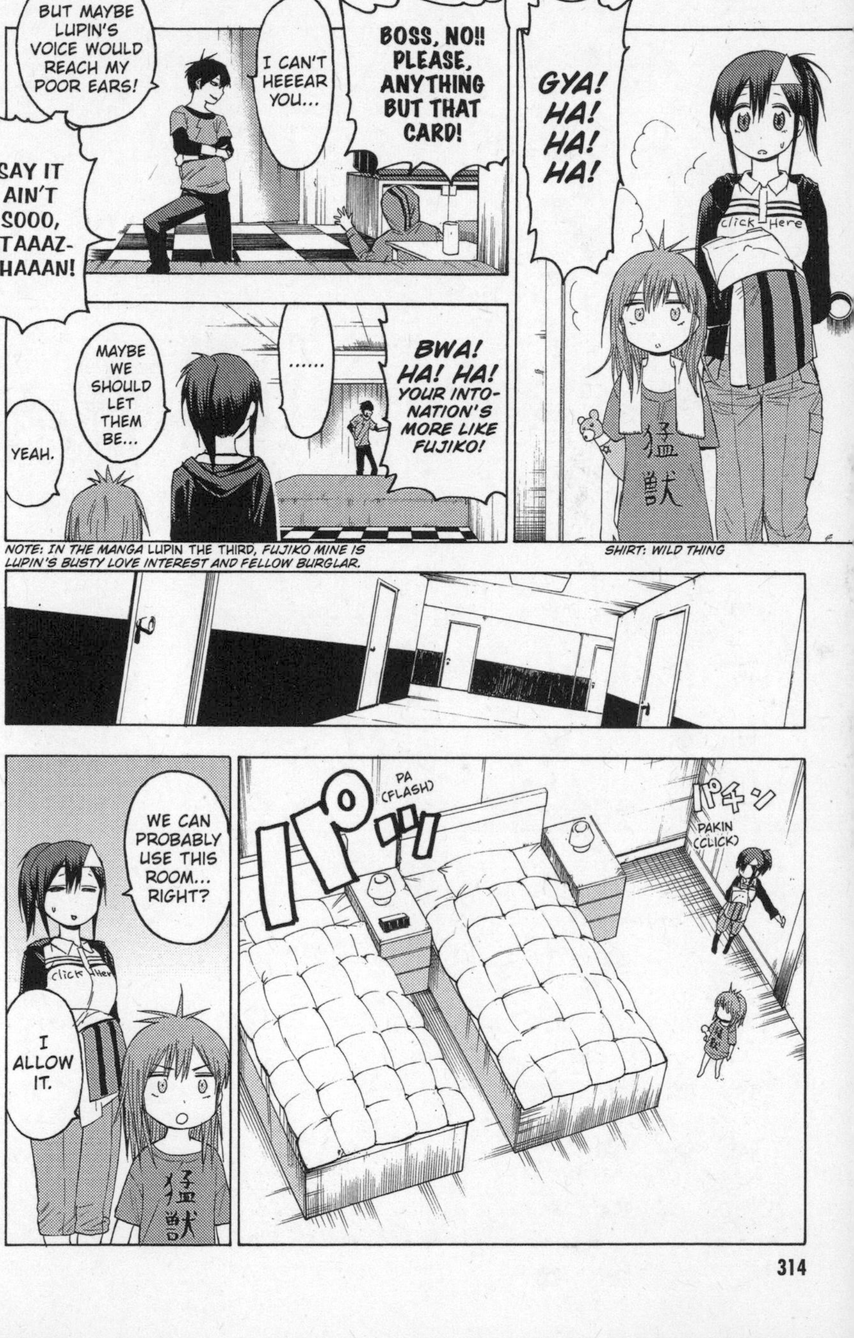
GYA! HA! HA! HA!
Click Here
猛獣
SHIRT: WILD THING
BOSS, NO!! PLEASE, ANYTHING BUT THAT CARD!
I CAN'T HEEEAR YOU...
BUT MAYBE LUPIN'S VOICE WOULD REACH MY POOR EARS!
SAY IT AIN'T SOOO, STAAAZ-CHAAAN!
BWA! HA! HA! YOUR INTONATION'S MORE LIKE FUJIKO!
......
MAYBE WE SHOULD LET THEM BE...
YEAH.
NOTE: IN THE MANGA LUPIN THE THIRD, FUJIKO MINE IS LUPIN'S BUSTY LOVE INTEREST AND FELLOW BURGLAR.
パチン
PAKIN (CLICK)
PA (FLASH)
WE CAN PROBABLY USE THIS ROOM... RIGHT?
I ALLOW IT.
Click Here
猛獣

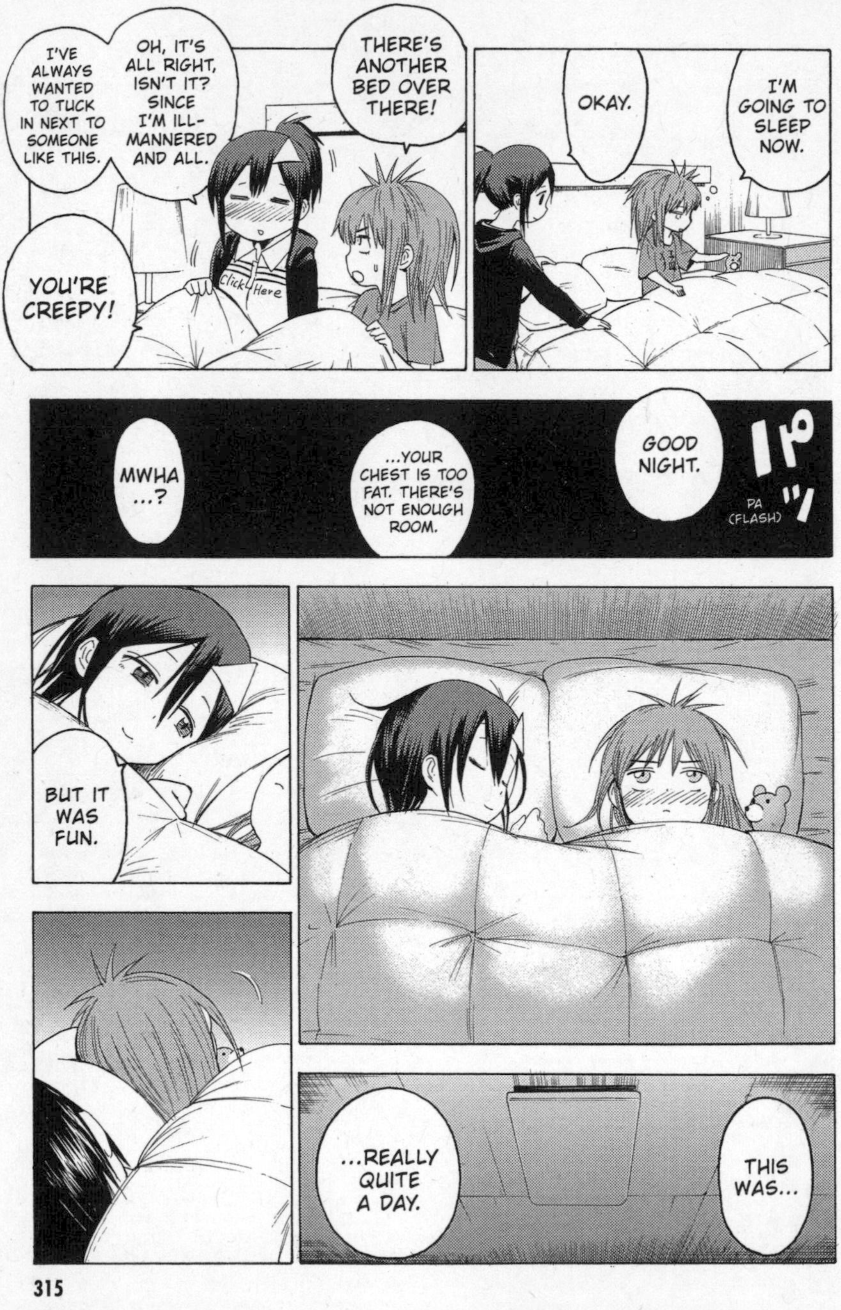
I'M GOING TO SLEEP NOW.
OKAY.
THERE'S ANOTHER BED OVER THERE!
OH, IT'S ALL RIGHT, ISN'T IT? SINCE I'M ILL-MANNERED AND ALL.
I'VE ALWAYS WANTED TO TUCK IN NEXT TO SOMEONE LIKE THIS.
Click Here
YOU'RE CREEPY!
パッ
PA (FLASH)
GOOD NIGHT.
...YOUR CHEST IS TOO FAT. THERE'S NOT ENOUGH ROOM.
MWHA ...?
BUT IT WAS FUN.
THIS WAS...
...REALLY QUITE A DAY.

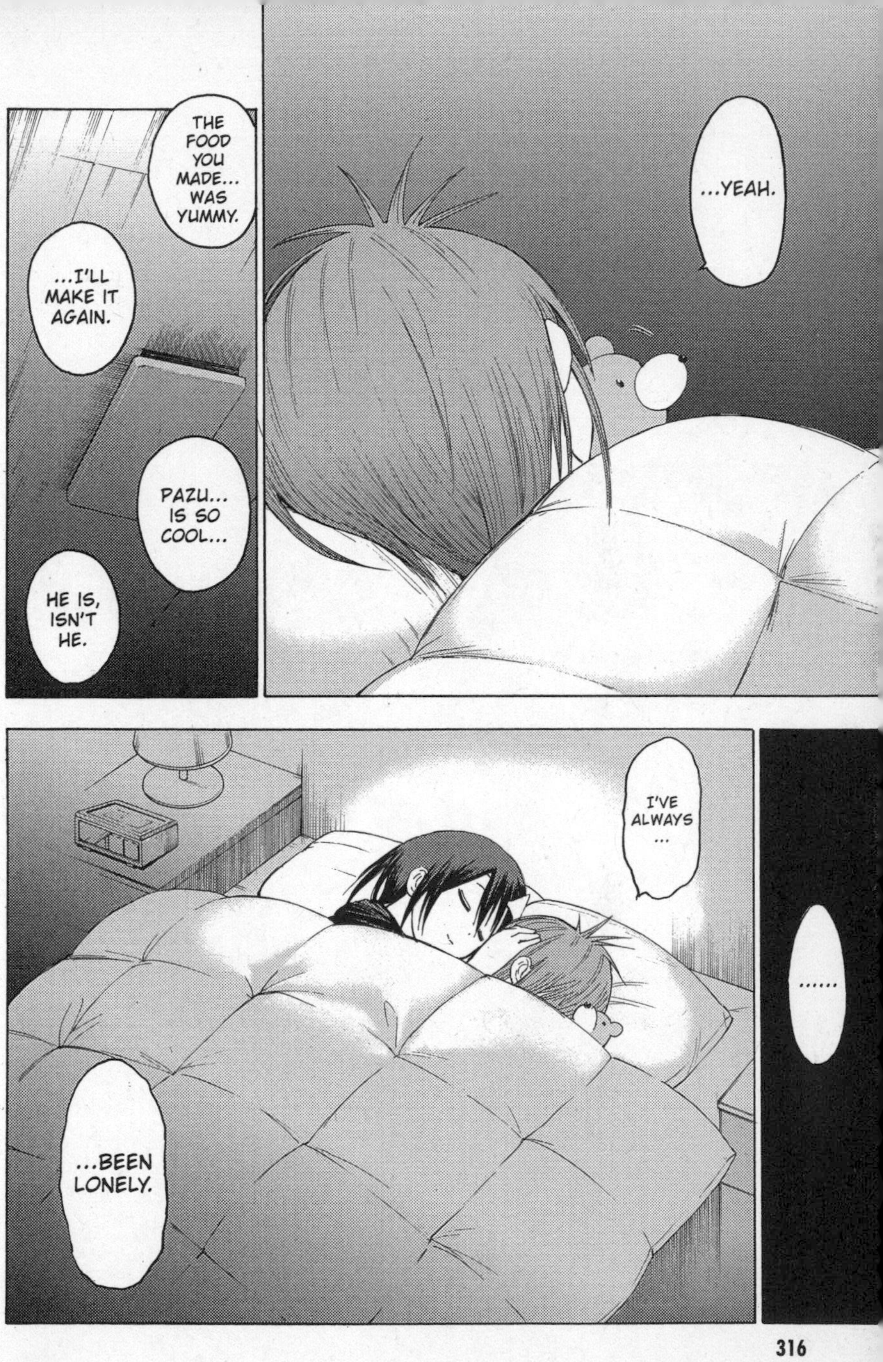
...YEAH.
THE FOOD YOU MADE... WAS YUMMY.
...I'LL MAKE IT AGAIN.
PAZU... IS SO COOL...
HE IS, ISN'T HE.
......
I'VE ALWAYS ...
...BEEN LONELY.

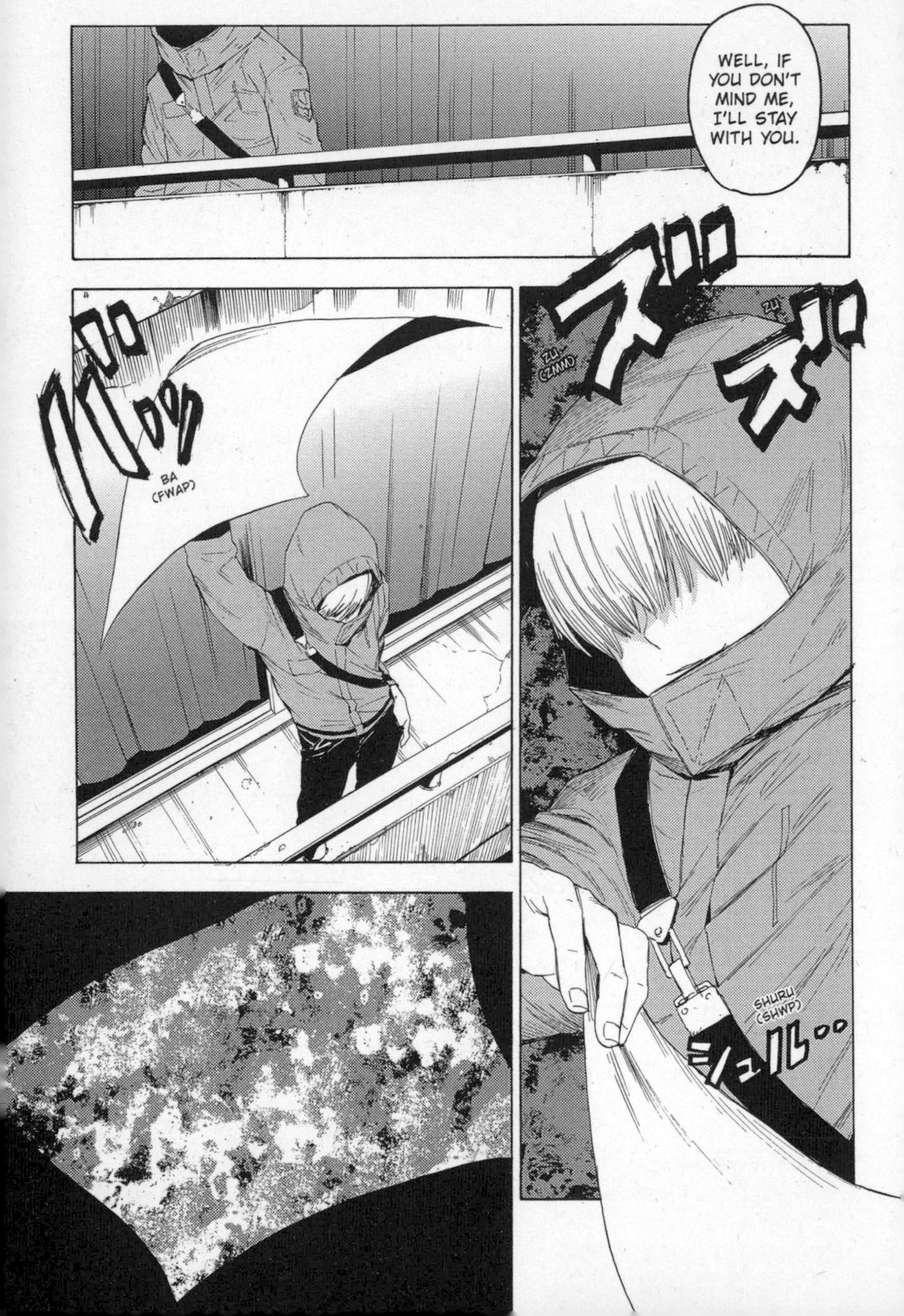
WELL, IF YOU DON'T MIND ME, I'LL STAY WITH YOU.
ZU
ZU (ZMM)
SHURU (SHWP)
BA (FWAP)

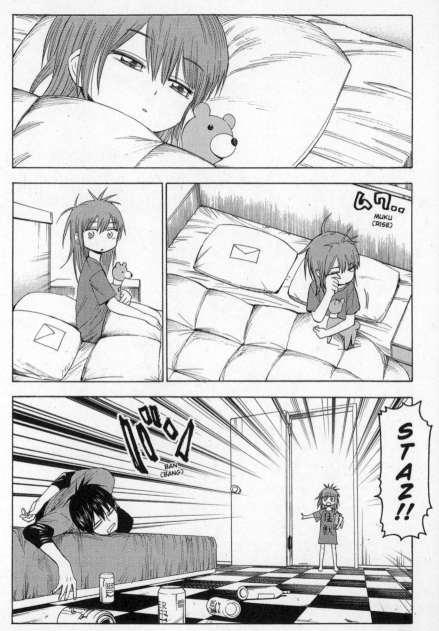

MUKU
(RISE)

BAN
(BANG)

STAZ!!

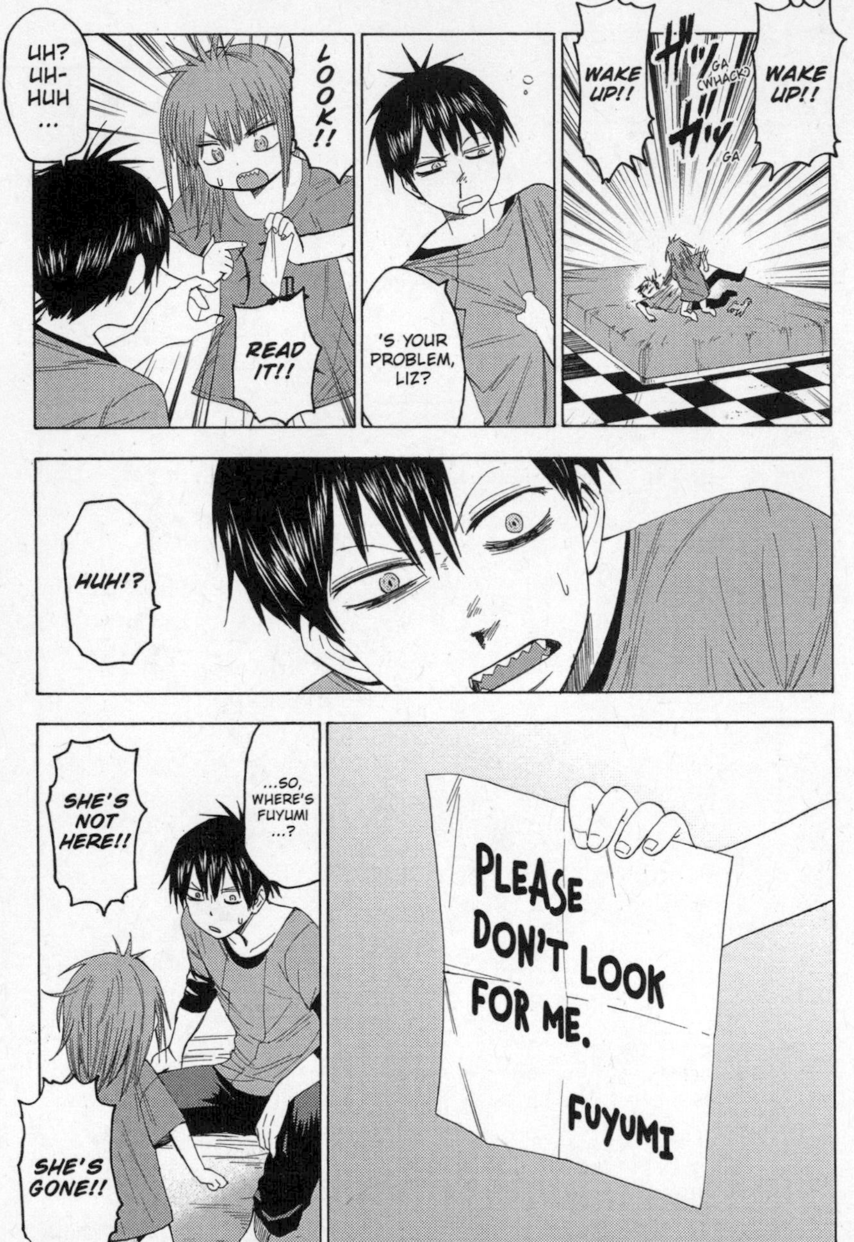
WAKE UP!!
ガッ
GA (WHACK)
WAKE UP!!
ガッ
GA
'S YOUR PROBLEM, LIZ?
LOOK!!
UH? UH-HUH ...
READ IT!!
HUH!?
PLEASE DON'T LOOK FOR ME.
FUYUMI
...SO, WHERE'S FUYUMI ...?
SHE'S NOT HERE!!
SHE'S GONE!!

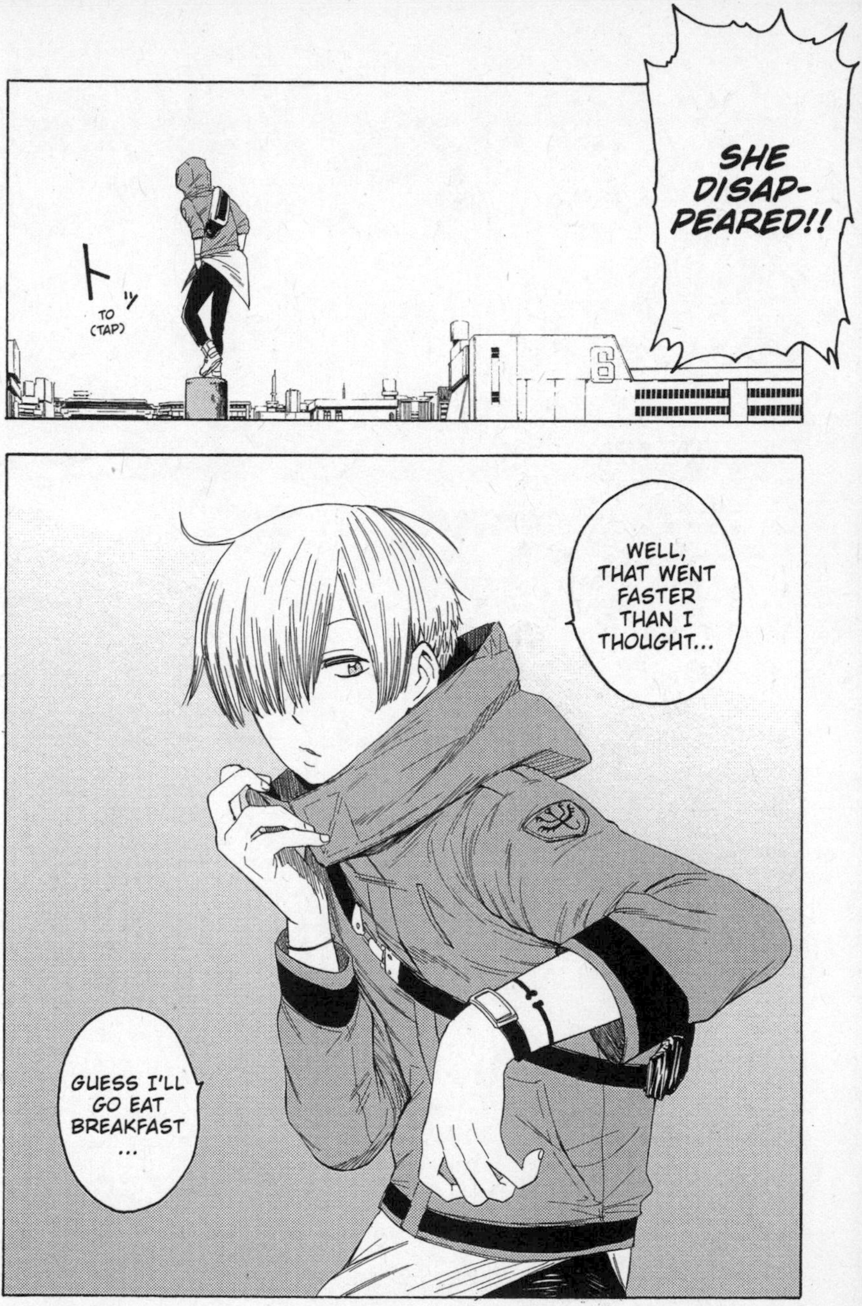
SHE DISAPPEARED!!
トッ
TO (TAP)
WELL, THAT WENT FASTER THAN I THOUGHT...
GUESS I'LL GO EAT BREAKFAST ...

♠ To Be Continued ♠

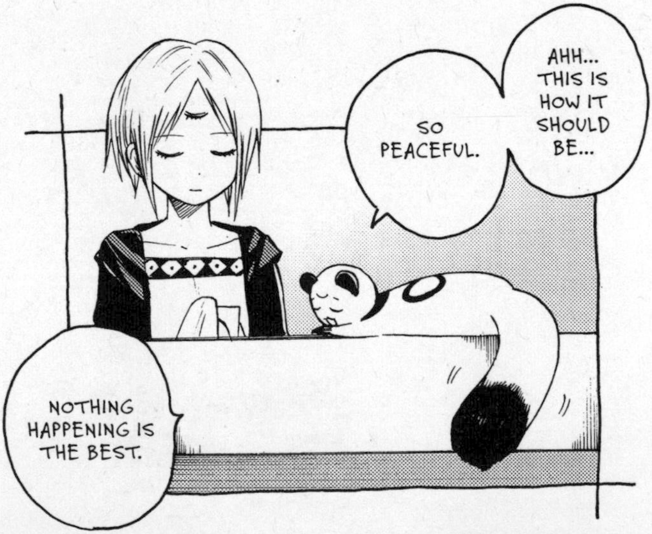
AHH... THIS IS HOW IT SHOULD BE...
SO PEACEFUL.
NOTHING HAPPENING IS THE BEST.

BLOOD LAD

CHAPTER 20 ♠ THE GHOST THIEF AND THE GUARD DOG

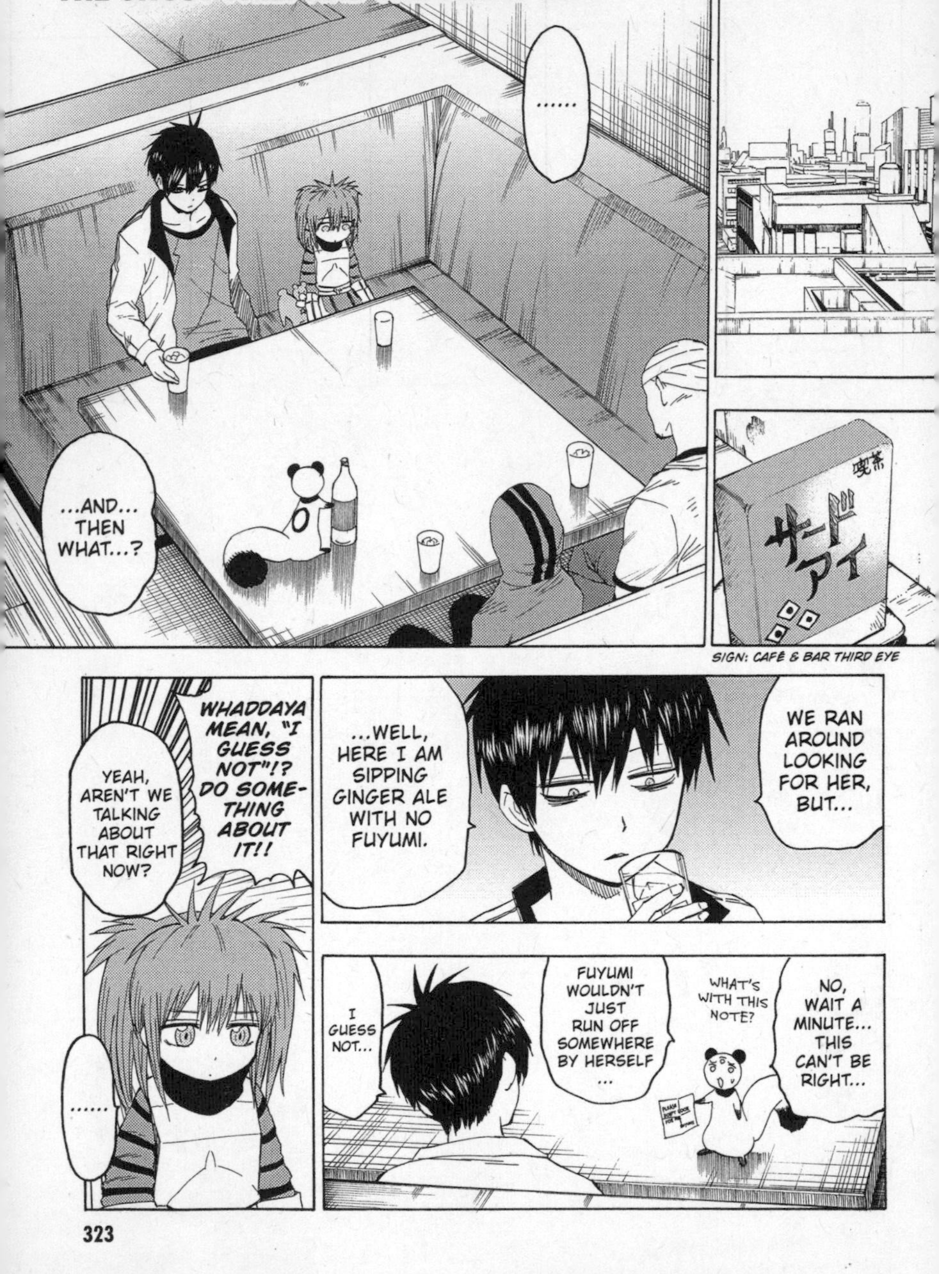
喫茶
サードアイ
......
...AND... THEN WHAT...?
WE RAN AROUND LOOKING FOR HER, BUT...
...WELL, HERE I AM SIPPING GINGER ALE WITH NO FUYUMI.
NO, WAIT A MINUTE... THIS CAN'T BE RIGHT...
WHAT'S WITH THIS NOTE?
FUYUMI WOULDN'T JUST RUN OFF SOMEWHERE BY HERSELF ...
I GUESS NOT...
WHADDAYA MEAN, "I GUESS NOT"!? DO SOME-THING ABOUT IT!!
YEAH, AREN'T WE TALKING ABOUT THAT RIGHT NOW?
......

SIGN: CAFÉ & BAR THIRD EYE

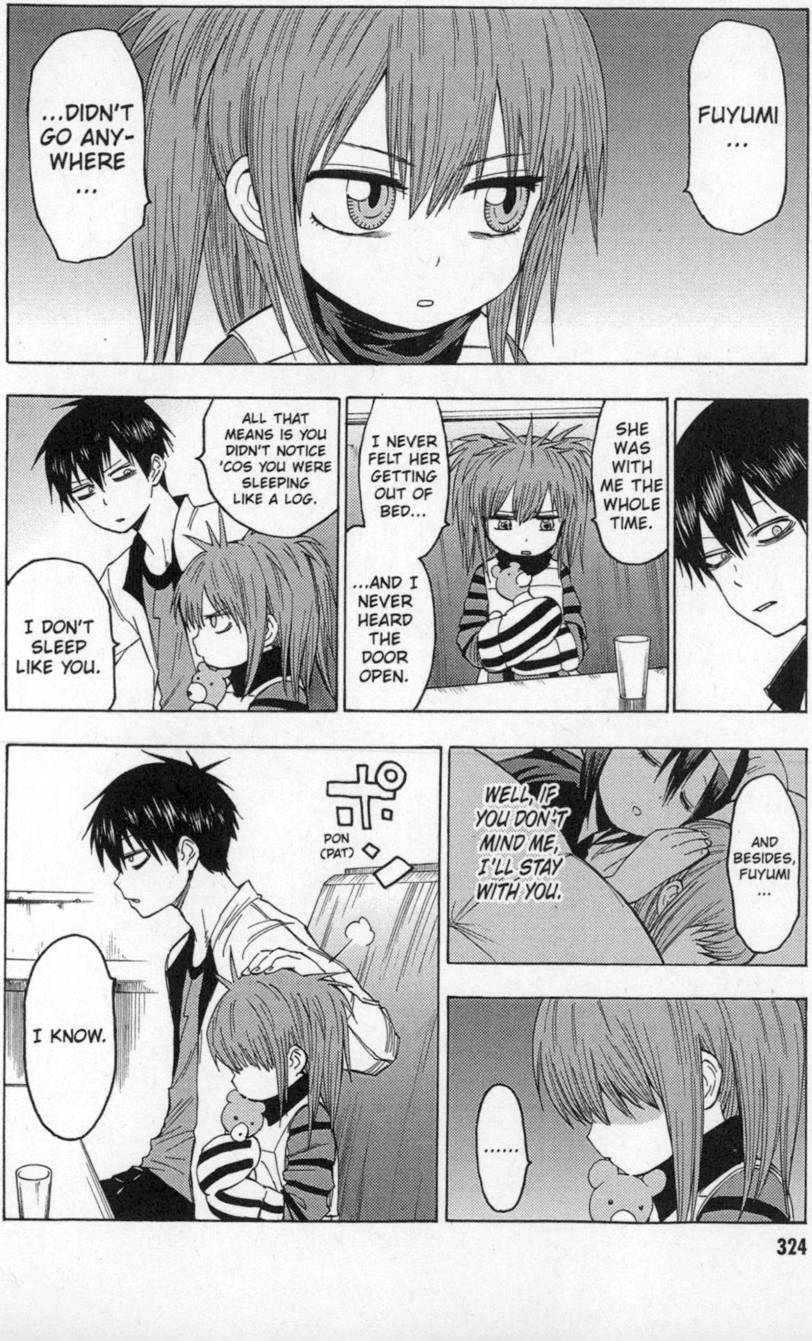
FUYUMI ...
...DIDN'T GO ANY-WHERE ...
SHE WAS WITH ME THE WHOLE TIME.
I NEVER FELT HER GETTING OUT OF BED...
...AND I NEVER HEARD THE DOOR OPEN.
ALL THAT MEANS IS YOU DIDN'T NOTICE 'COS YOU WERE SLEEPING LIKE A LOG.
I DON'T SLEEP LIKE YOU.
AND BESIDES, FUYUMI ...
WELL, IF YOU DON'T MIND ME, I'LL STAY WITH YOU.
......
ポ
PON (PAT)
I KNOW.

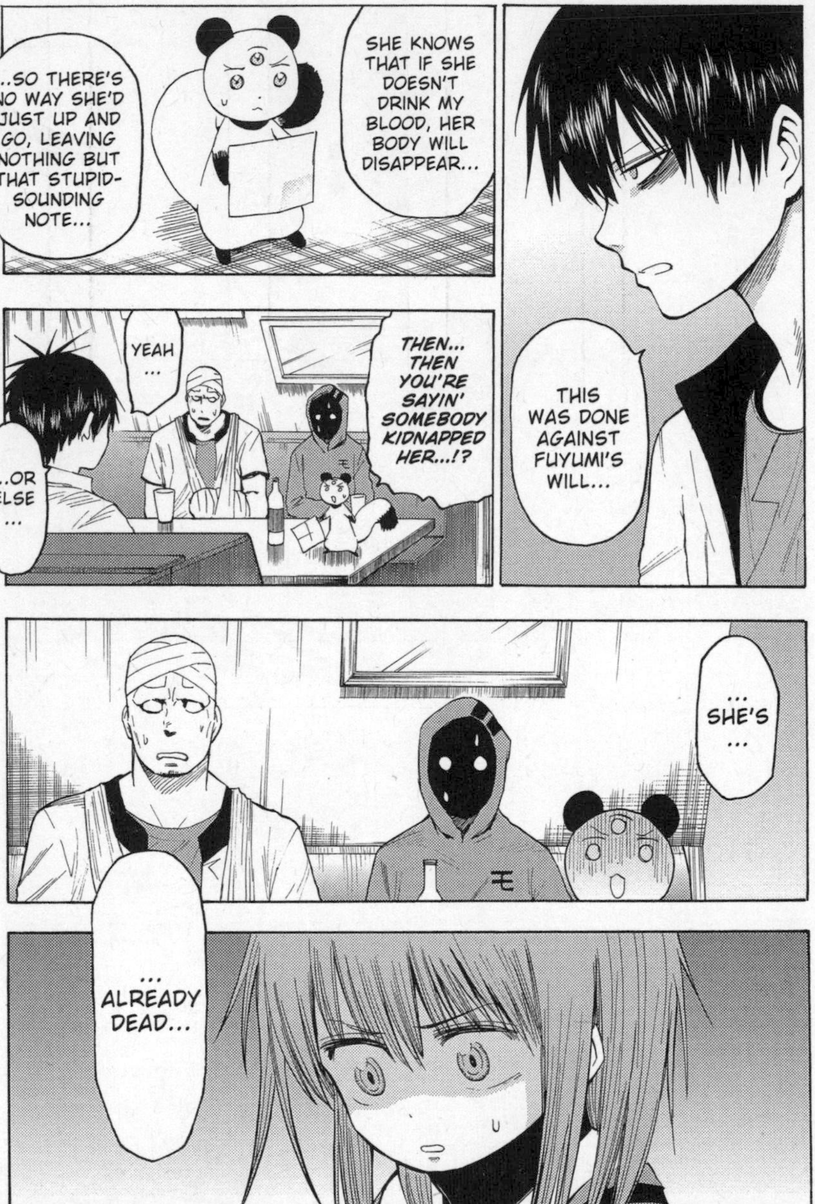
THIS WAS DONE AGAINST FUYUMI'S WILL...
SHE KNOWS THAT IF SHE DOESN'T DRINK MY BLOOD, HER BODY WILL DISAPPEAR...
...SO THERE'S NO WAY SHE'D JUST UP AND GO, LEAVING NOTHING BUT THAT STUPID-SOUNDING NOTE...
THEN... THEN YOU'RE SAYIN' SOMEBODY KIDNAPPED HER...!?
YEAH ...
...OR ELSE ...
... SHE'S ...
... ALREADY DEAD...

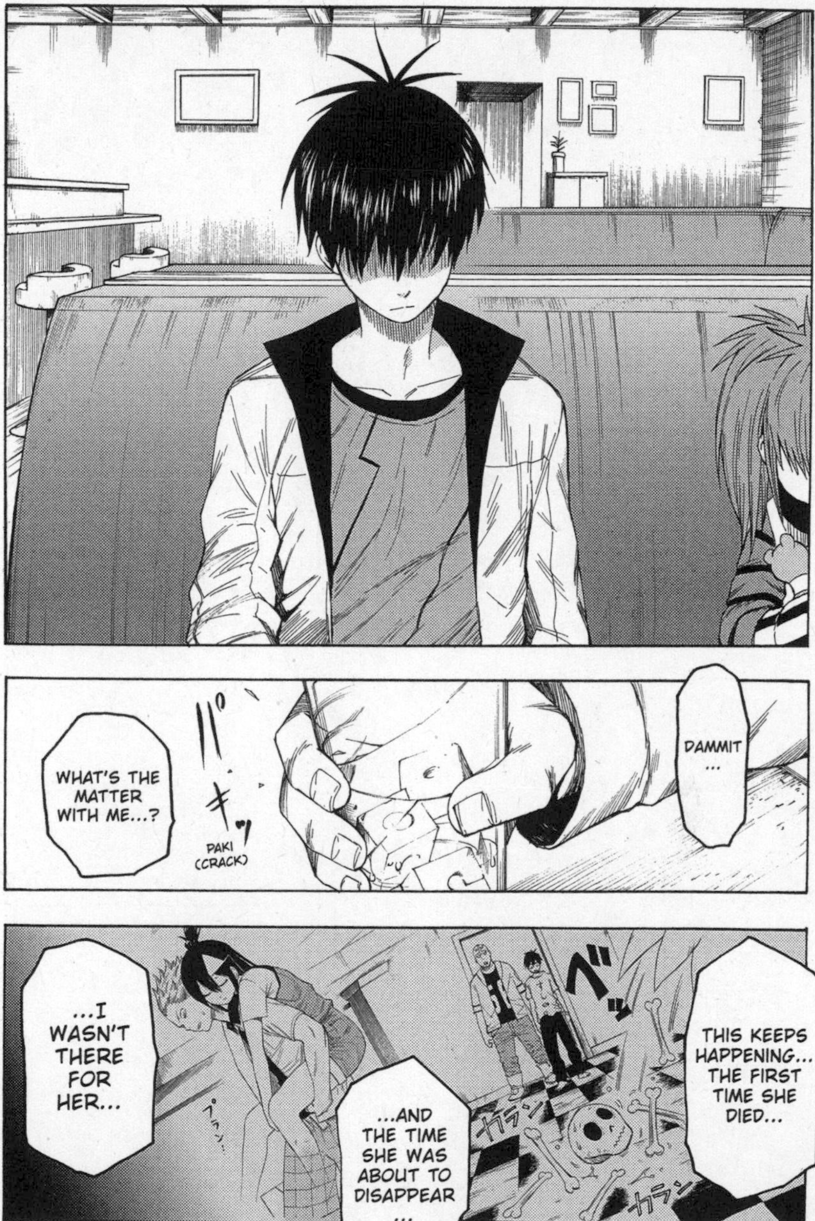
DAMMIT ...
PAKI (CRACK)
WHAT'S THE MATTER WITH ME...?
THIS KEEPS HAPPENING... THE FIRST TIME SHE DIED...
...AND THE TIME SHE WAS ABOUT TO DISAPPEAR ...
...I WASN'T THERE FOR HER...

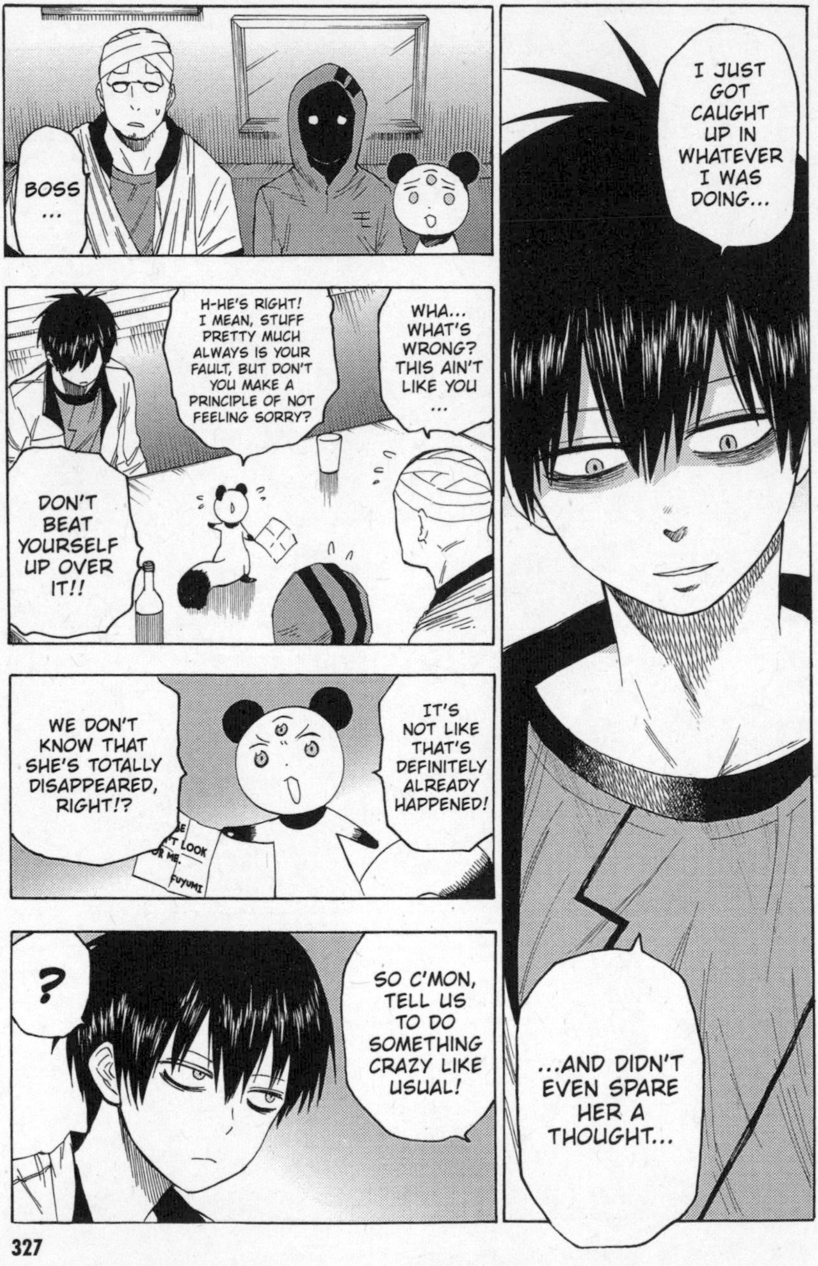
I JUST GOT CAUGHT UP IN WHATEVER I WAS DOING...
...AND DIDN'T EVEN SPARE HER A THOUGHT...
BOSS ...
WHA... WHAT'S WRONG? THIS AIN'T LIKE YOU ...
H-HE'S RIGHT! I MEAN, STUFF PRETTY MUCH ALWAYS IS YOUR FAULT, BUT DON'T YOU MAKE A PRINCIPLE OF NOT FEELING SORRY?
DON'T BEAT YOURSELF UP OVER IT!!
IT'S NOT LIKE THAT'S DEFINITELY ALREADY HAPPENED!
WE DON'T KNOW THAT SHE'S TOTALLY DISAPPEARED, RIGHT!?
FUYUMI
SO C'MON, TELL US TO DO SOMETHING CRAZY LIKE USUAL!
?

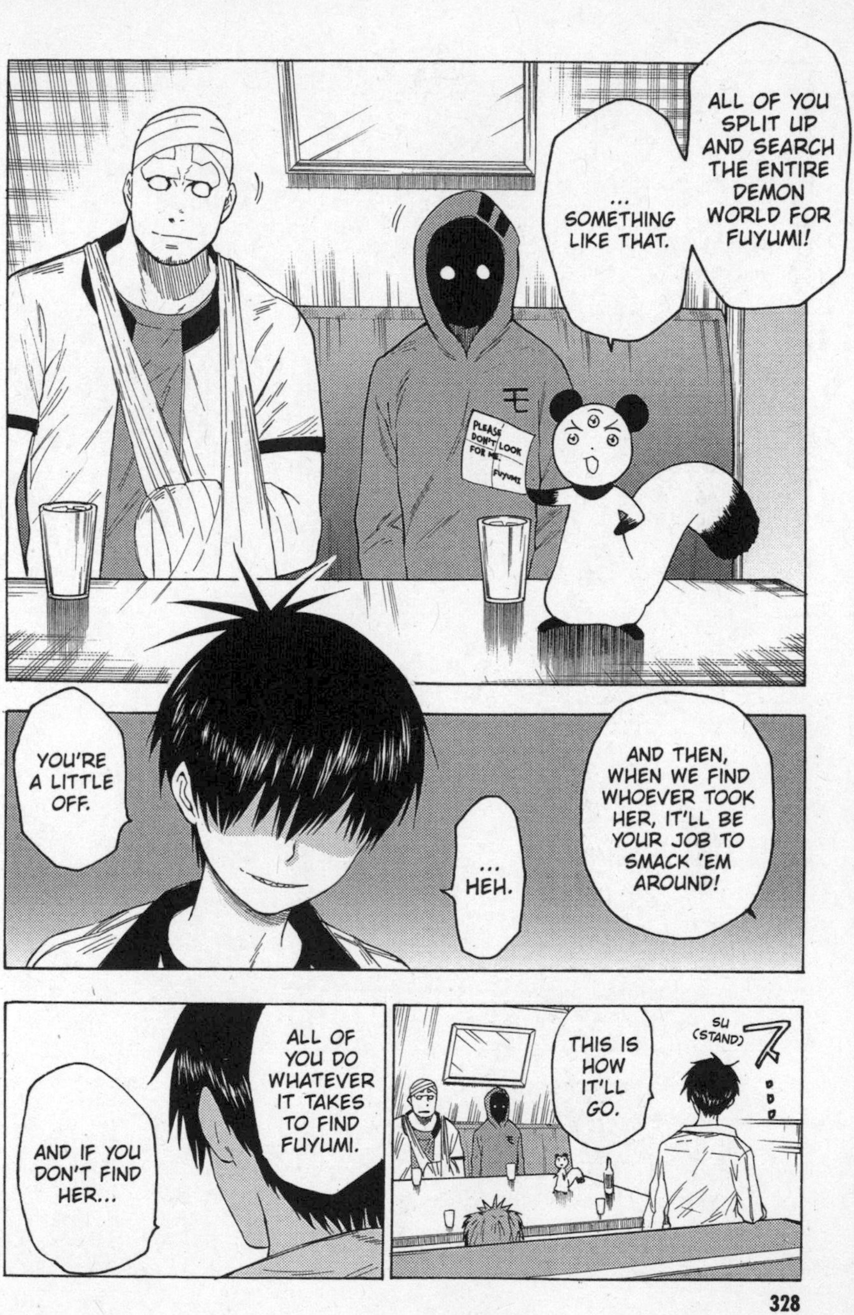
ALL OF YOU SPLIT UP AND SEARCH THE ENTIRE DEMON WORLD FOR FUYUMI!
... SOMETHING LIKE THAT.
PLEASE DON'T LOOK FOR ME. FUYUMI
AND THEN, WHEN WE FIND WHOEVER TOOK HER, IT'LL BE YOUR JOB TO SMACK 'EM AROUND!
... HEH.
YOU'RE A LITTLE OFF.
SU (STAND)
THIS IS HOW IT'LL GO.
ALL OF YOU DO WHATEVER IT TAKES TO FIND FUYUMI.
AND IF YOU DON'T FIND HER...

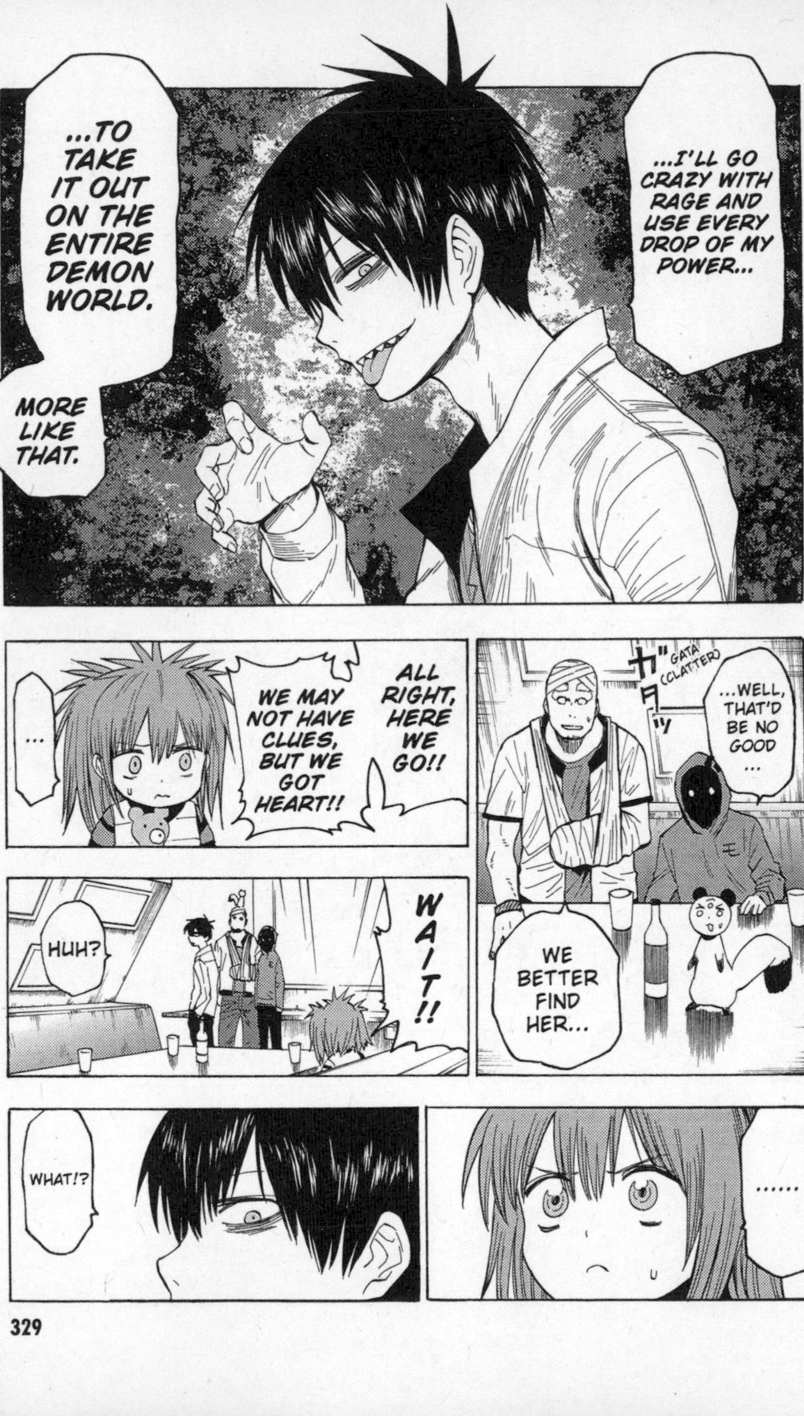
...I'LL GO CRAZY WITH RAGE AND USE EVERY DROP OF MY POWER...
...TO TAKE IT OUT ON THE ENTIRE DEMON WORLD.
MORE LIKE THAT.
GATA (CLATTER)
...WELL, THAT'D BE NO GOOD...
WE BETTER FIND HER...
ALL RIGHT, HERE WE GO!!
WE MAY NOT HAVE CLUES, BUT WE GOT HEART!!
...
WAIT!!
HUH?
......
WHAT!?

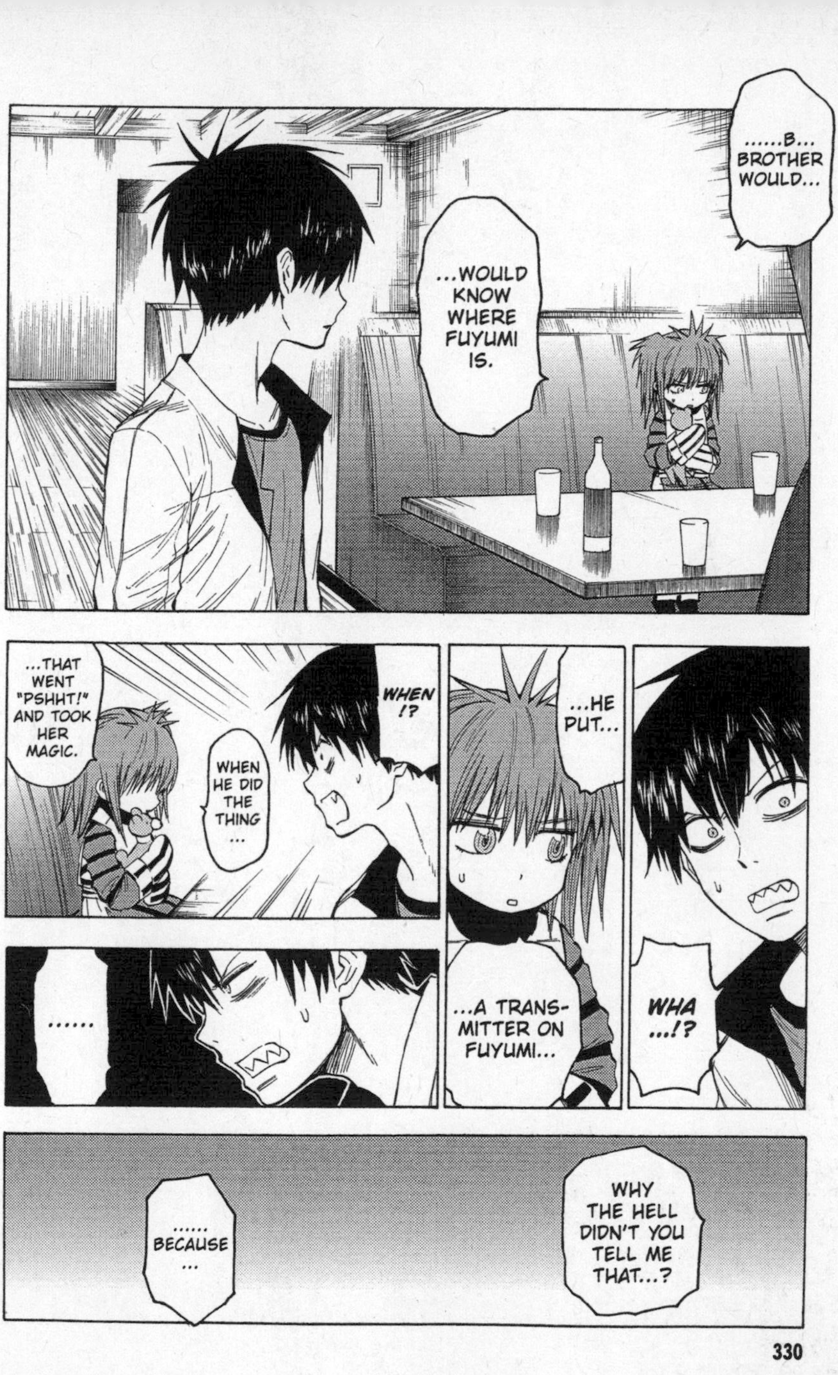
......B... BROTHER WOULD...
...WOULD KNOW WHERE FUYUMI IS.
...HE PUT...
...A TRANS-MITTER ON FUYUMI...
WHA ...!?
WHEN !?
WHEN HE DID THE THING ...
...THAT WENT "PSHHT!" AND TOOK HER MAGIC.
......
WHY THE HELL DIDN'T YOU TELL ME THAT...?
...... BECAUSE ...

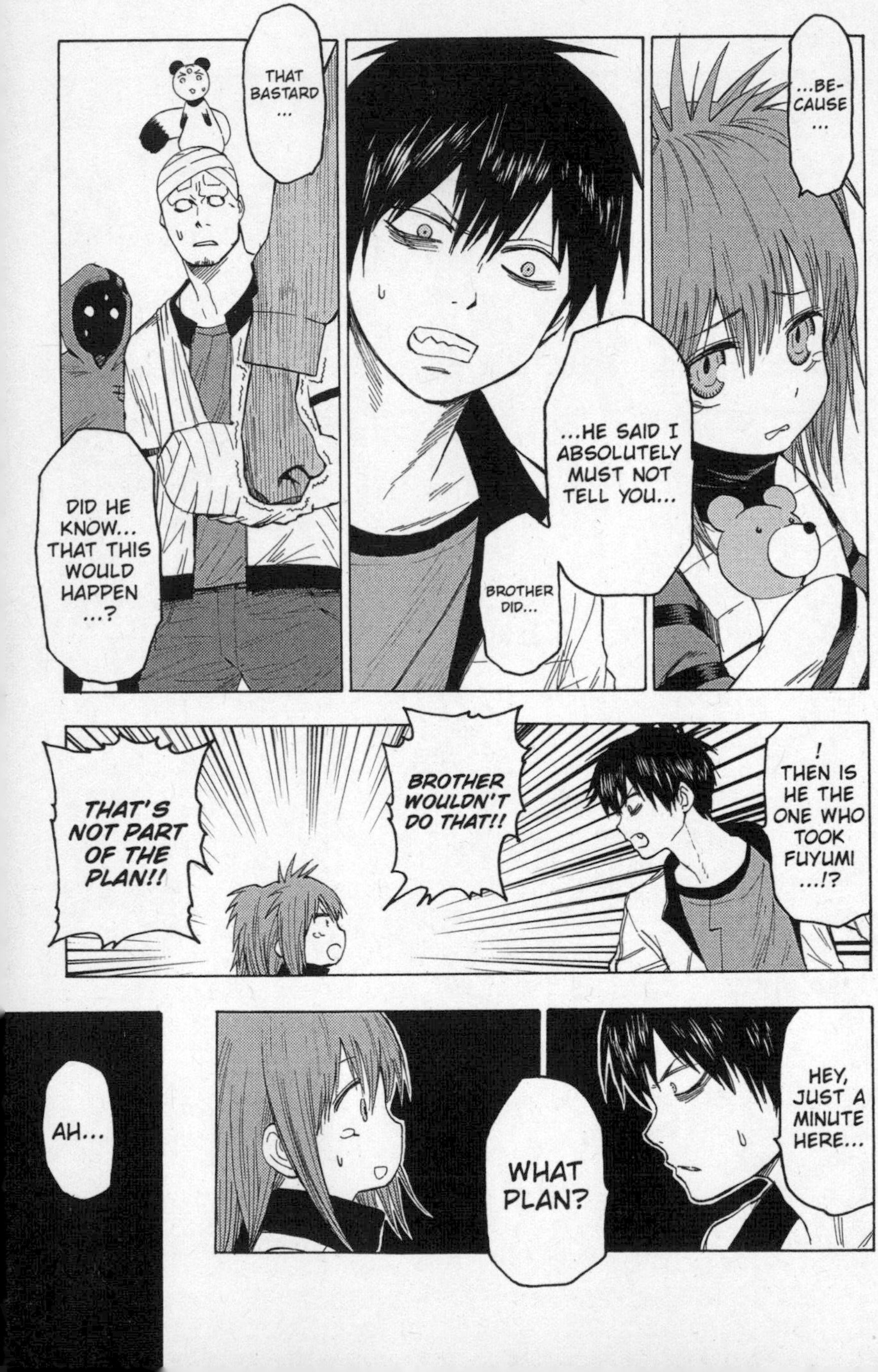
...BE-CAUSE ...
...HE SAID I ABSOLUTELY MUST NOT TELL YOU...
BROTHER DID...
THAT BASTARD ...
DID HE KNOW... THAT THIS WOULD HAPPEN ...?
! THEN IS HE THE ONE WHO TOOK FUYUMI ...!?
BROTHER WOULDN'T DO THAT!!
THAT'S NOT PART OF THE PLAN!!
HEY, JUST A MINUTE HERE...
WHAT PLAN?
AH...

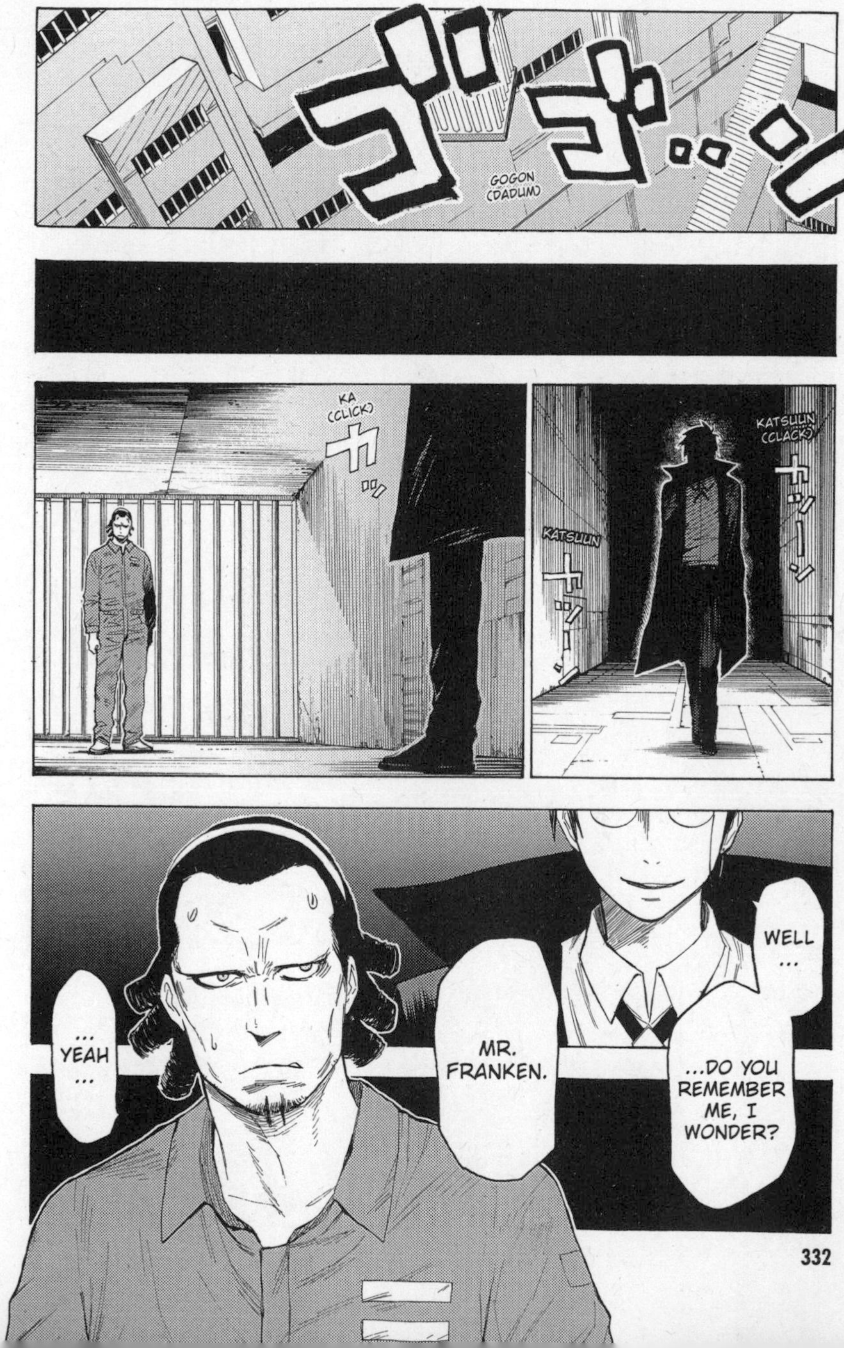
GOGON (DADUM)
KATSUUN (CLACK)
KATSUUN
KA (CLICK)
WELL ...
...DO YOU REMEMBER ME, I WONDER?
MR. FRANKEN.
... YEAH ...

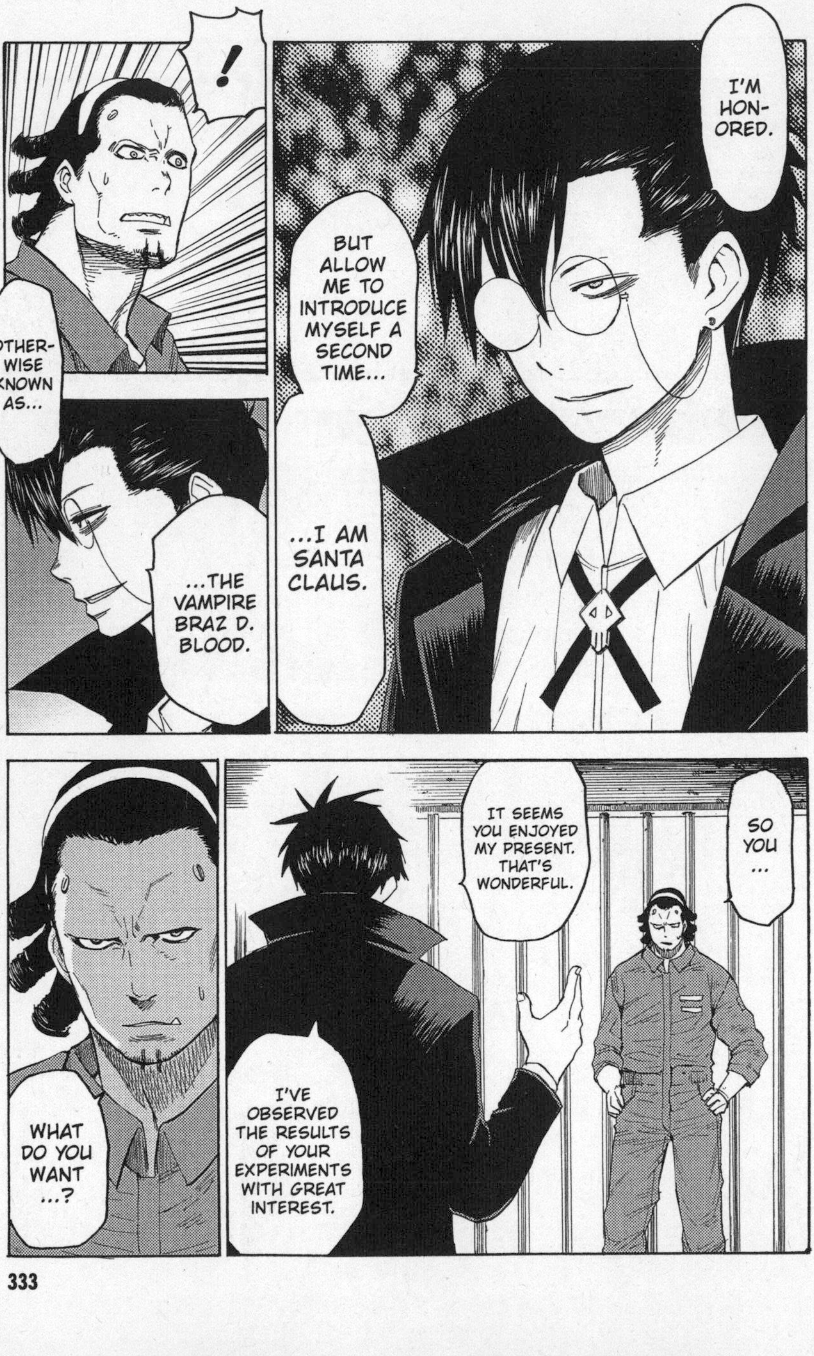
I'M HONORED.
BUT ALLOW ME TO INTRODUCE MYSELF A SECOND TIME...
...I AM SANTA CLAUS.
!
OTHERWISE KNOWN AS...
...THE VAMPIRE BRAZ D. BLOOD.
SO YOU ...
IT SEEMS YOU ENJOYED MY PRESENT. THAT'S WONDERFUL.
I'VE OBSERVED THE RESULTS OF YOUR EXPERIMENTS WITH GREAT INTEREST.
WHAT DO YOU WANT ...?

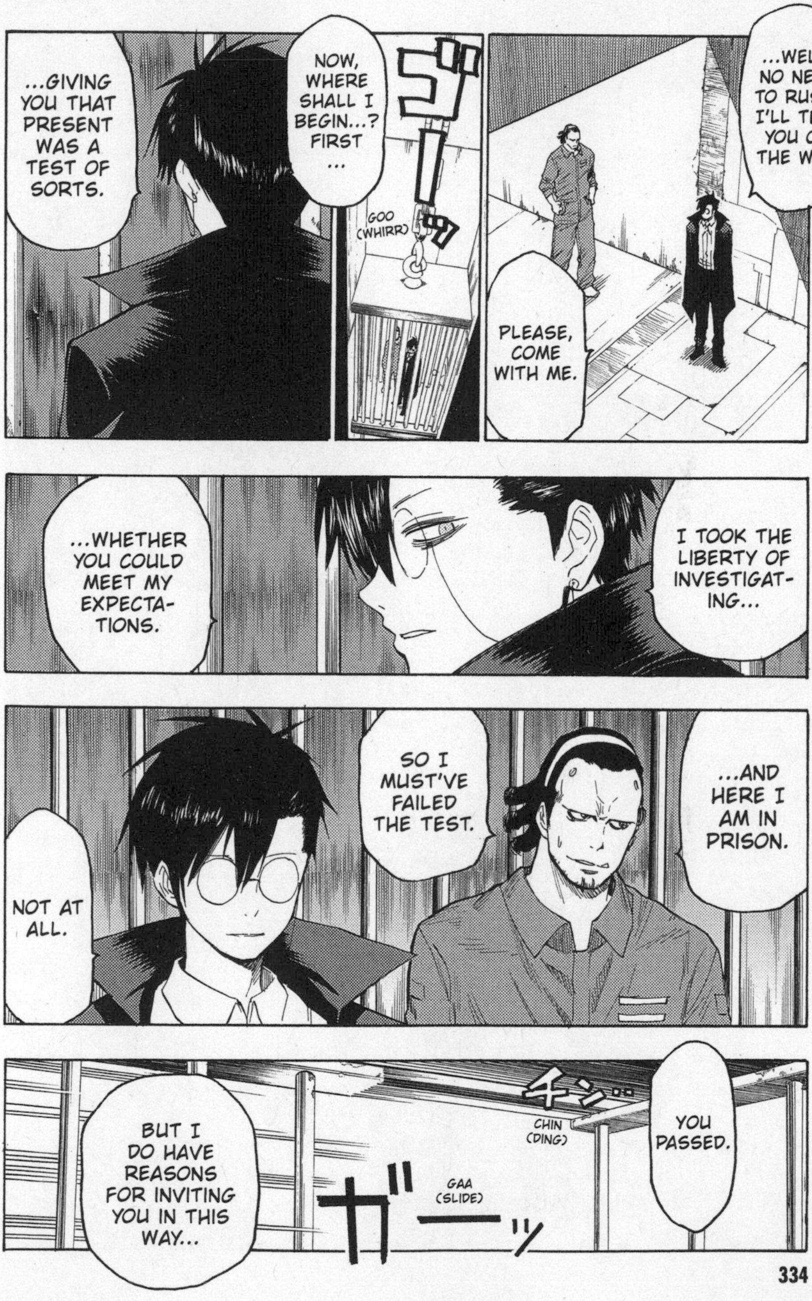
...WELL, NO NEED TO RUSH. I'LL TELL YOU ON THE WAY.
PLEASE, COME WITH ME.
NOW, WHERE SHALL I BEGIN...? FIRST ...
GOO (WHIRR)
...GIVING YOU THAT PRESENT WAS A TEST OF SORTS.
I TOOK THE LIBERTY OF INVESTIGAT-ING...
...WHETHER YOU COULD MEET MY EXPECTA-TIONS.
...AND HERE I AM IN PRISON.
SO I MUST'VE FAILED THE TEST.
NOT AT ALL.
YOU PASSED.
CHIN (DING)
GAA (SLIDE)
BUT I DO HAVE REASONS FOR INVITING YOU IN THIS WAY...

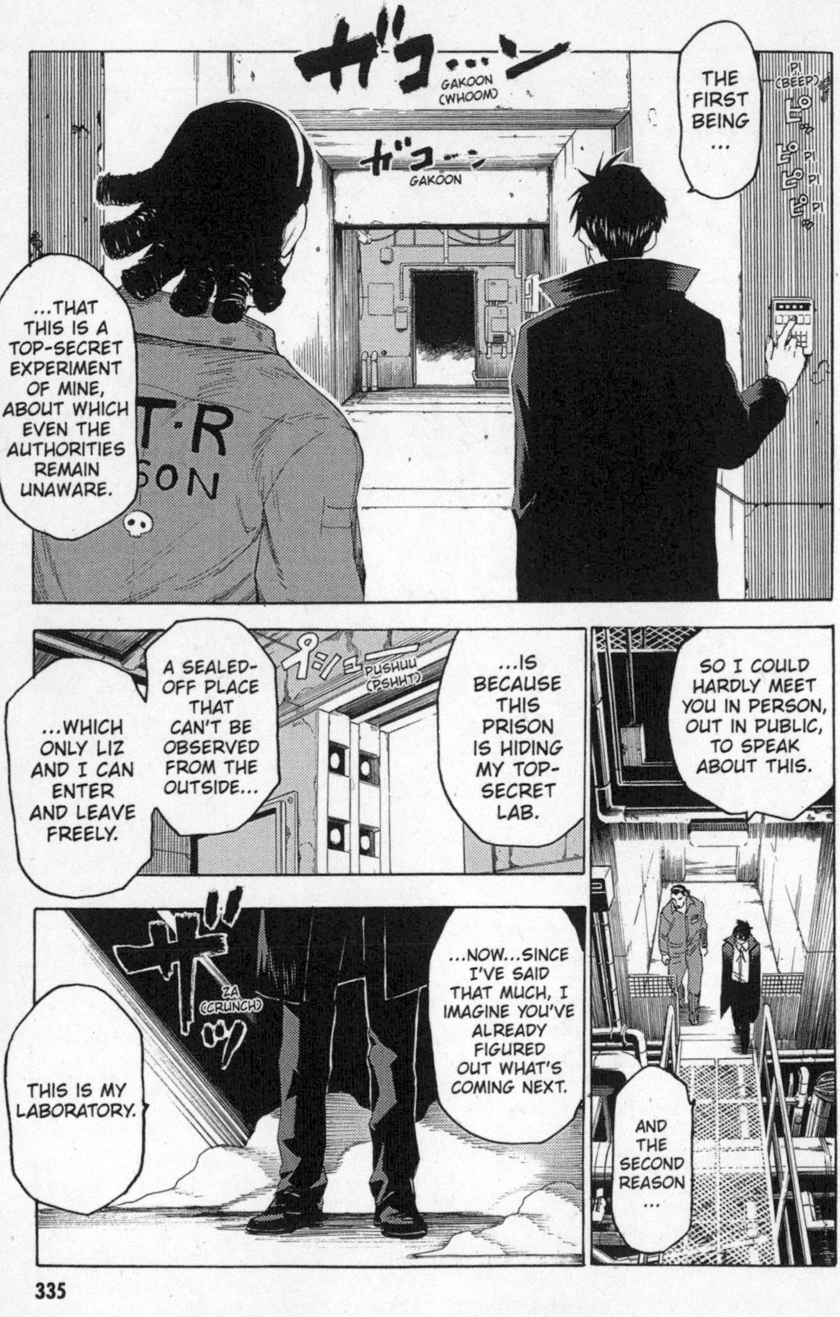
THE FIRST BEING ...
GAKOON (WHOOM)
GAKOON
PI (BEEP) PI PI PI
...THAT THIS IS A TOP-SECRET EXPERIMENT OF MINE, ABOUT WHICH EVEN THE AUTHORITIES REMAIN UNAWARE.
SO I COULD HARDLY MEET YOU IN PERSON, OUT IN PUBLIC, TO SPEAK ABOUT THIS.
AND THE SECOND REASON ...
...IS BECAUSE THIS PRISON IS HIDING MY TOP-SECRET LAB.
PUSHUU (PSHHT)
A SEALED-OFF PLACE THAT CAN'T BE OBSERVED FROM THE OUTSIDE...
...WHICH ONLY LIZ AND I CAN ENTER AND LEAVE FREELY.
...NOW...SINCE I'VE SAID THAT MUCH, I IMAGINE YOU'VE ALREADY FIGURED OUT WHAT'S COMING NEXT.
ZA (CRUNCH)
THIS IS MY LABORATORY.

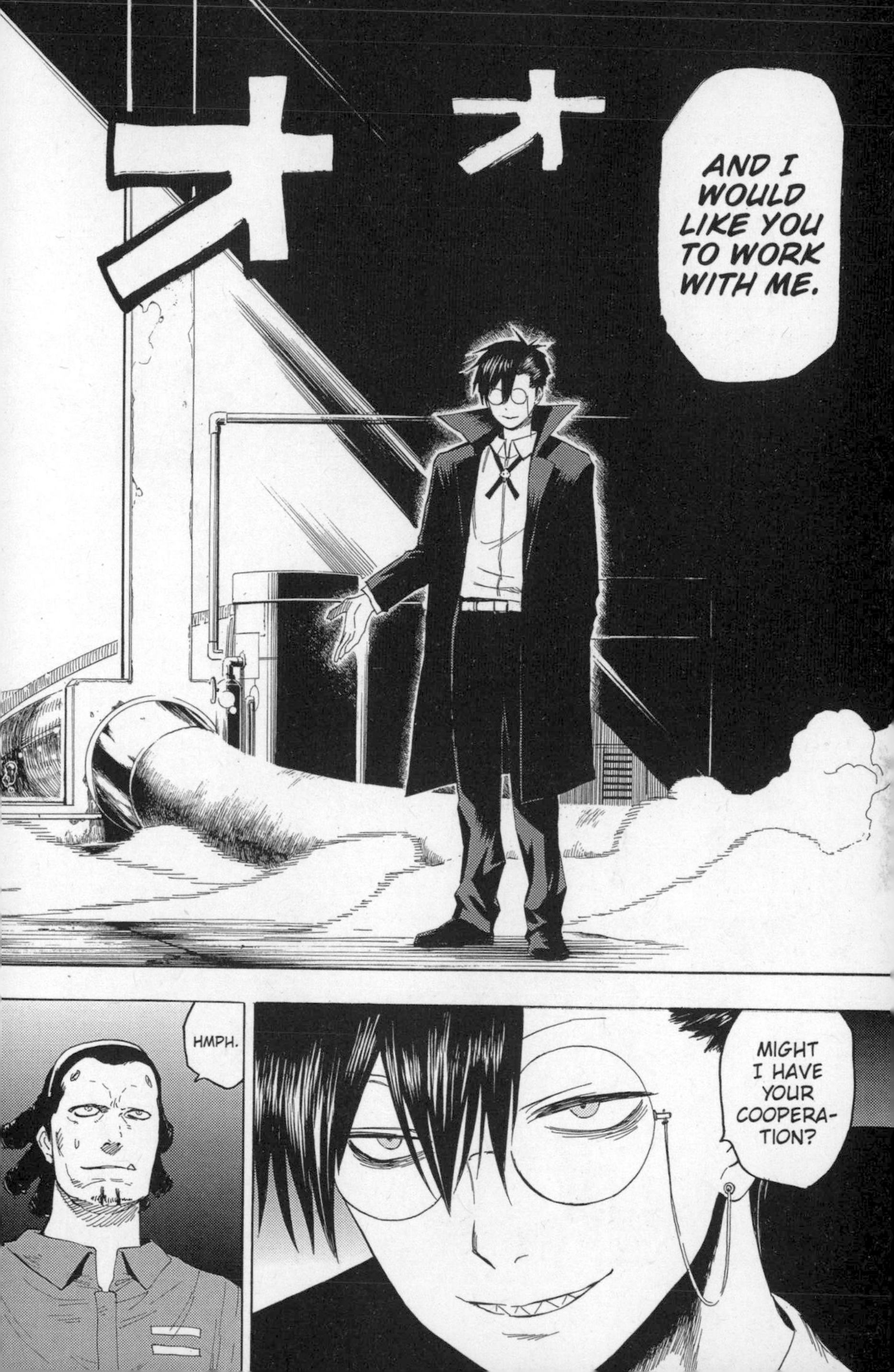
AND I WOULD LIKE YOU TO WORK WITH ME.
オオ
MIGHT I HAVE YOUR COOPERATION?
HMPH.

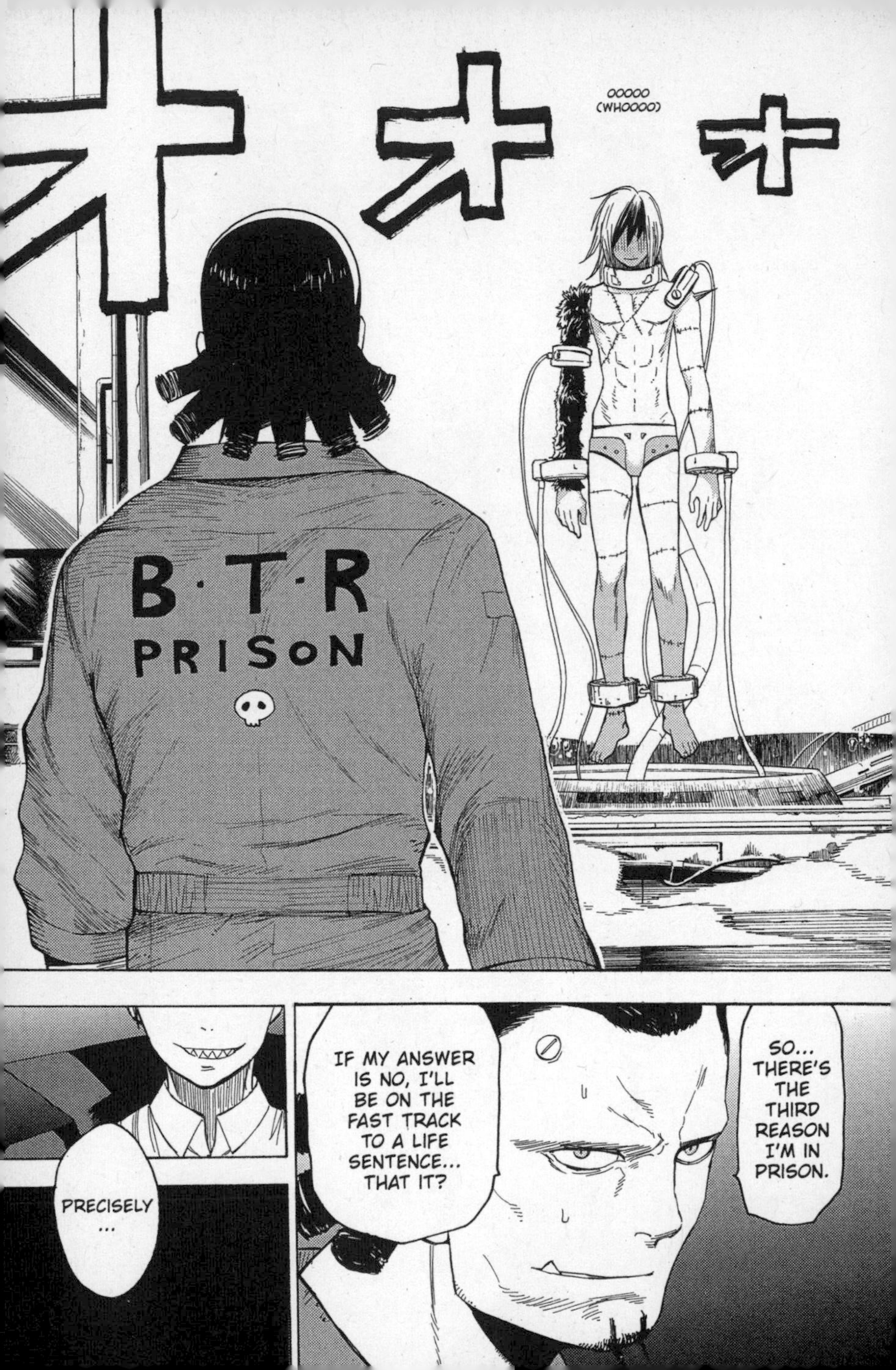
OOOOO (WHOOOO)
B·T·R PRISON
SO... THERE'S THE THIRD REASON I'M IN PRISON.
IF MY ANSWER IS NO, I'LL BE ON THE FAST TRACK TO A LIFE SENTENCE... THAT IT?
PRECISELY...

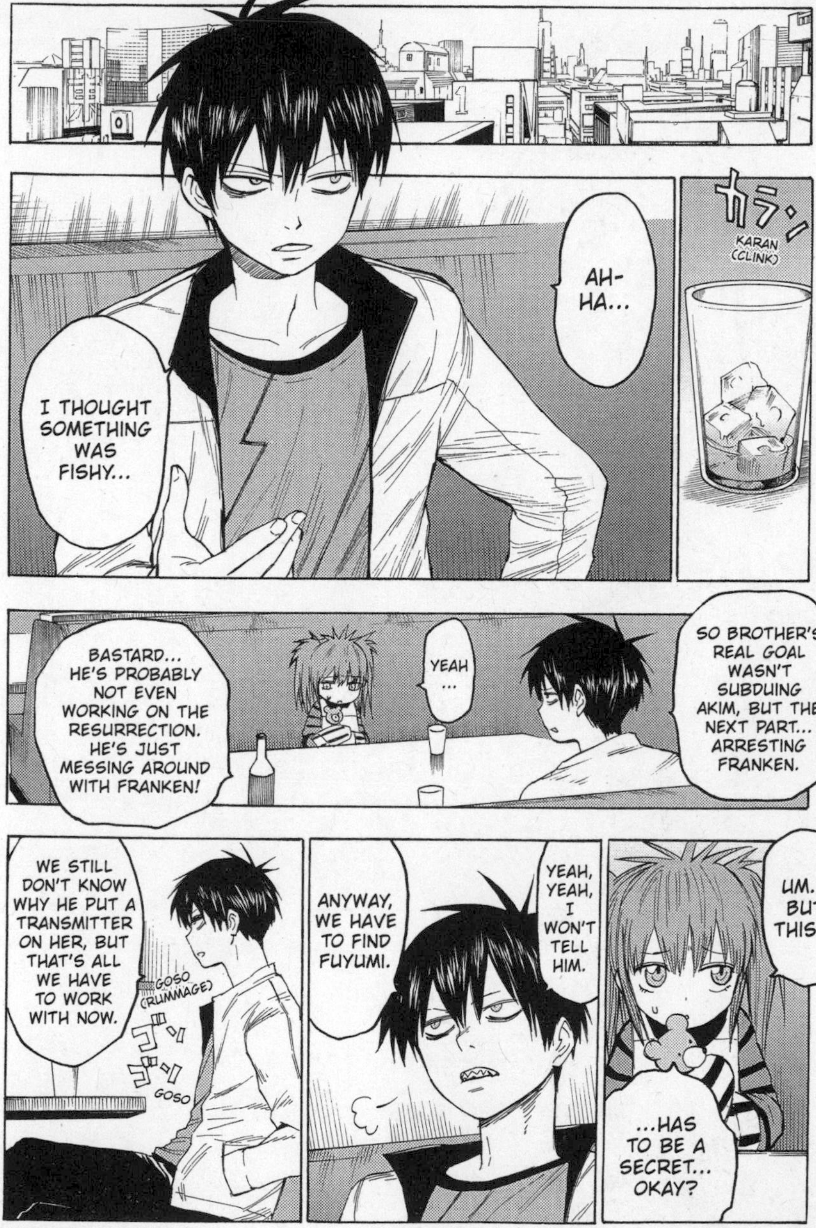

カラン
KARAN (CLINK)
AH-HA...
I THOUGHT SOMETHING WAS FISHY...
SO BROTHER'S REAL GOAL WASN'T SUBDUING AKIM, BUT THE NEXT PART... ARRESTING FRANKEN.
YEAH ...
BASTARD... HE'S PROBABLY NOT EVEN WORKING ON THE RESURRECTION. HE'S JUST MESSING AROUND WITH FRANKEN!
UM... BUT THIS...
...HAS TO BE A SECRET... OKAY?
YEAH, YEAH, I WON'T TELL HIM.
ANYWAY, WE HAVE TO FIND FUYUMI.
WE STILL DON'T KNOW WHY HE PUT A TRANSMITTER ON HER, BUT THAT'S ALL WE HAVE TO WORK WITH NOW.
GOSO (RUMMAGE)
GOSO

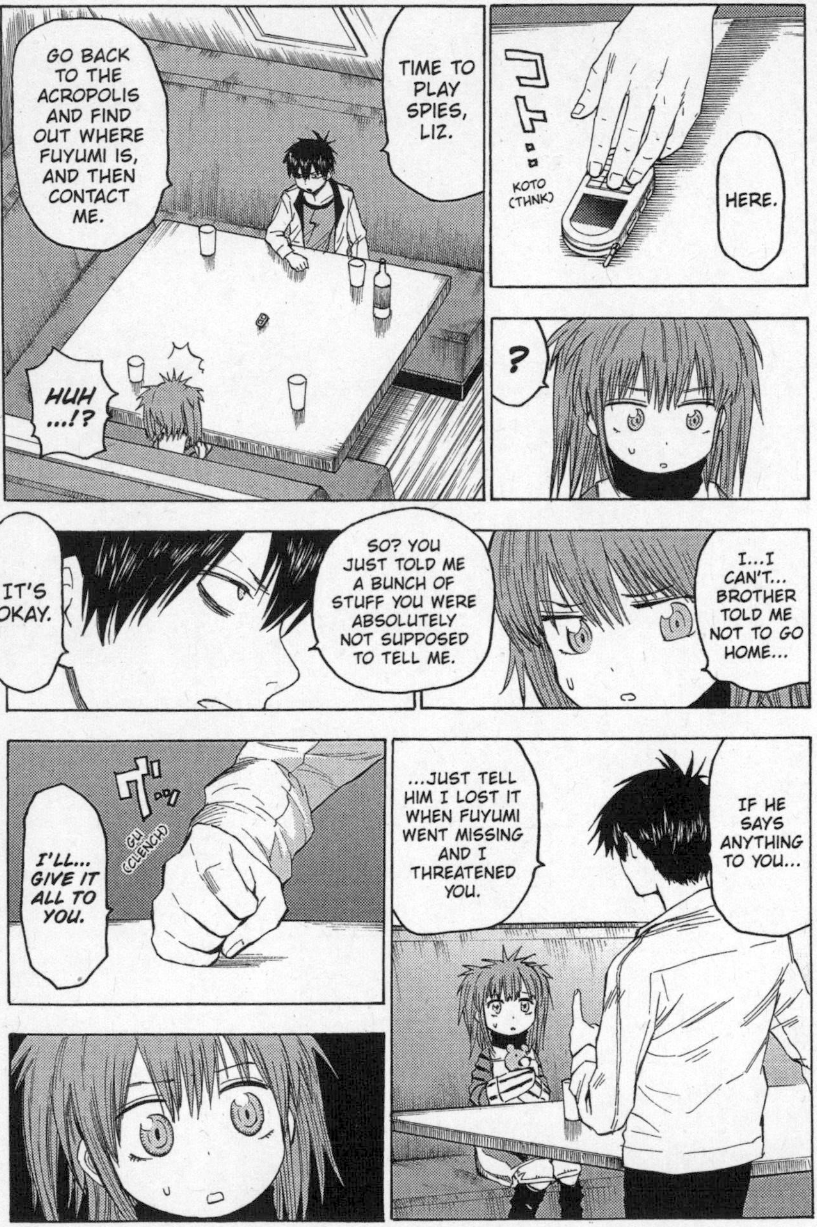
HERE.
KOTO (THNK)
?
TIME TO PLAY SPIES, LIZ.
GO BACK TO THE ACROPOLIS AND FIND OUT WHERE FUYUMI IS, AND THEN CONTACT ME.
HUH ...!?
I...I CAN'T... BROTHER TOLD ME NOT TO GO HOME...
SO? YOU JUST TOLD ME A BUNCH OF STUFF YOU WERE ABSOLUTELY NOT SUPPOSED TO TELL ME.
IT'S OKAY.
IF HE SAYS ANYTHING TO YOU...
...JUST TELL HIM I LOST IT WHEN FUYUMI WENT MISSING AND I THREATENED YOU.
GU (CLENCH)
I'LL... GIVE IT ALL TO YOU.

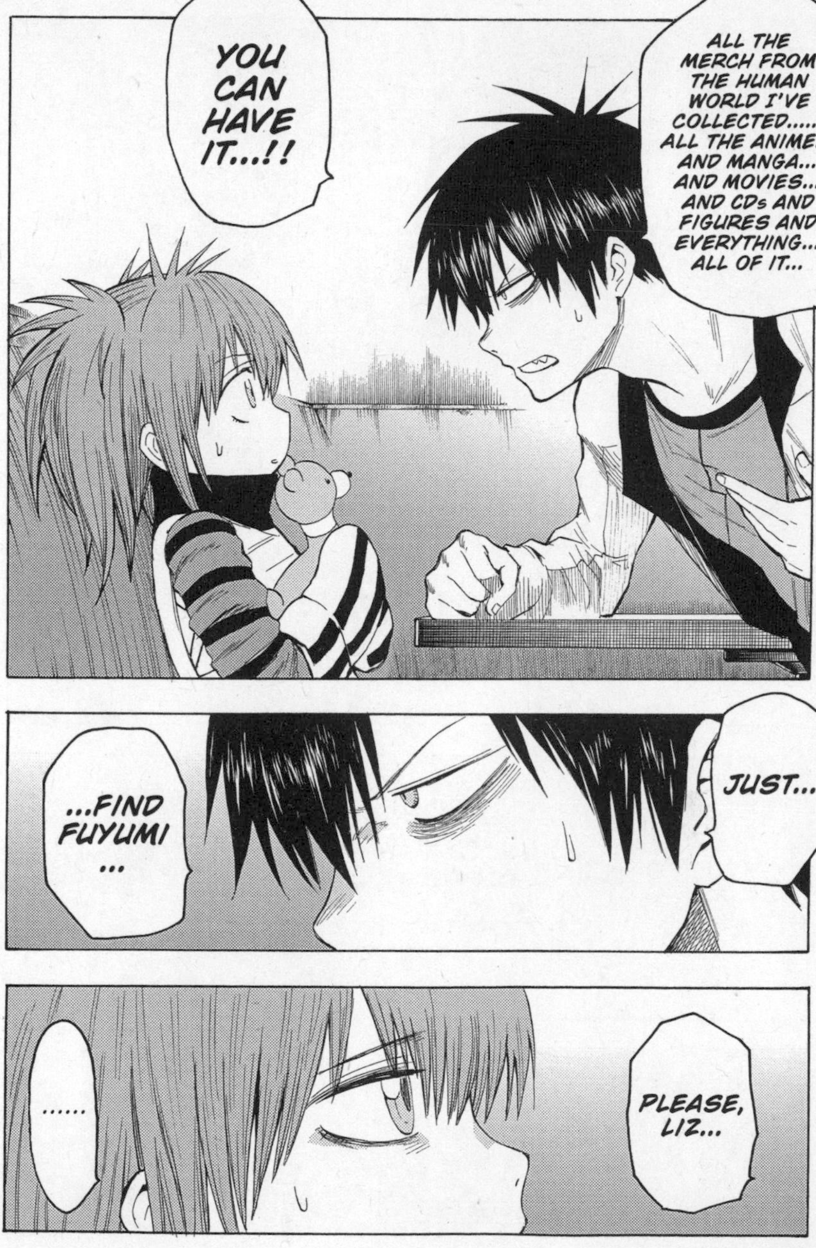
ALL THE MERCH FROM THE HUMAN WORLD I'VE COLLECTED...... ALL THE ANIME... AND MANGA... AND MOVIES... AND CDs AND FIGURES AND EVERYTHING... ALL OF IT...
YOU CAN HAVE IT...!!
JUST...
...FIND FUYUMI...
PLEASE, LIZ...
......

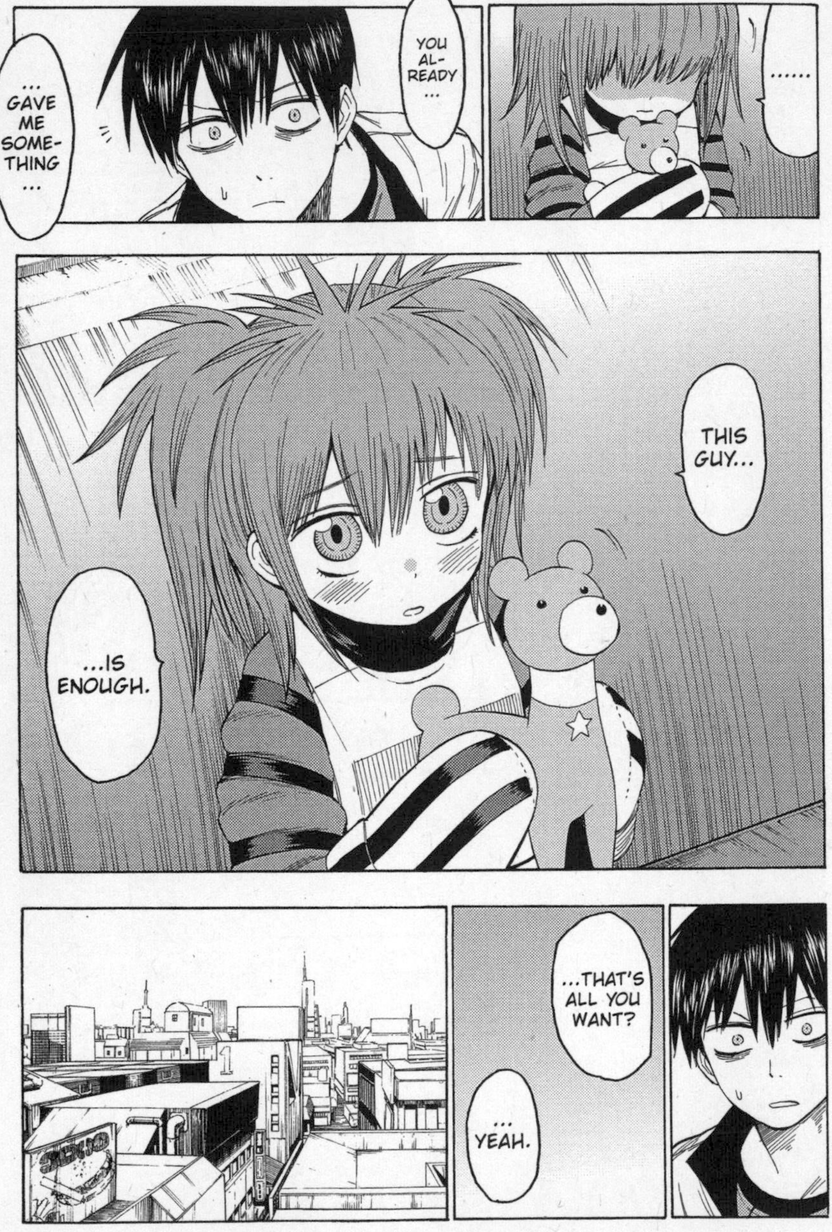
......
YOU AL-READY ...
... GAVE ME SOME-THING ...
THIS GUY...
...IS ENOUGH.
...THAT'S ALL YOU WANT?
... YEAH.

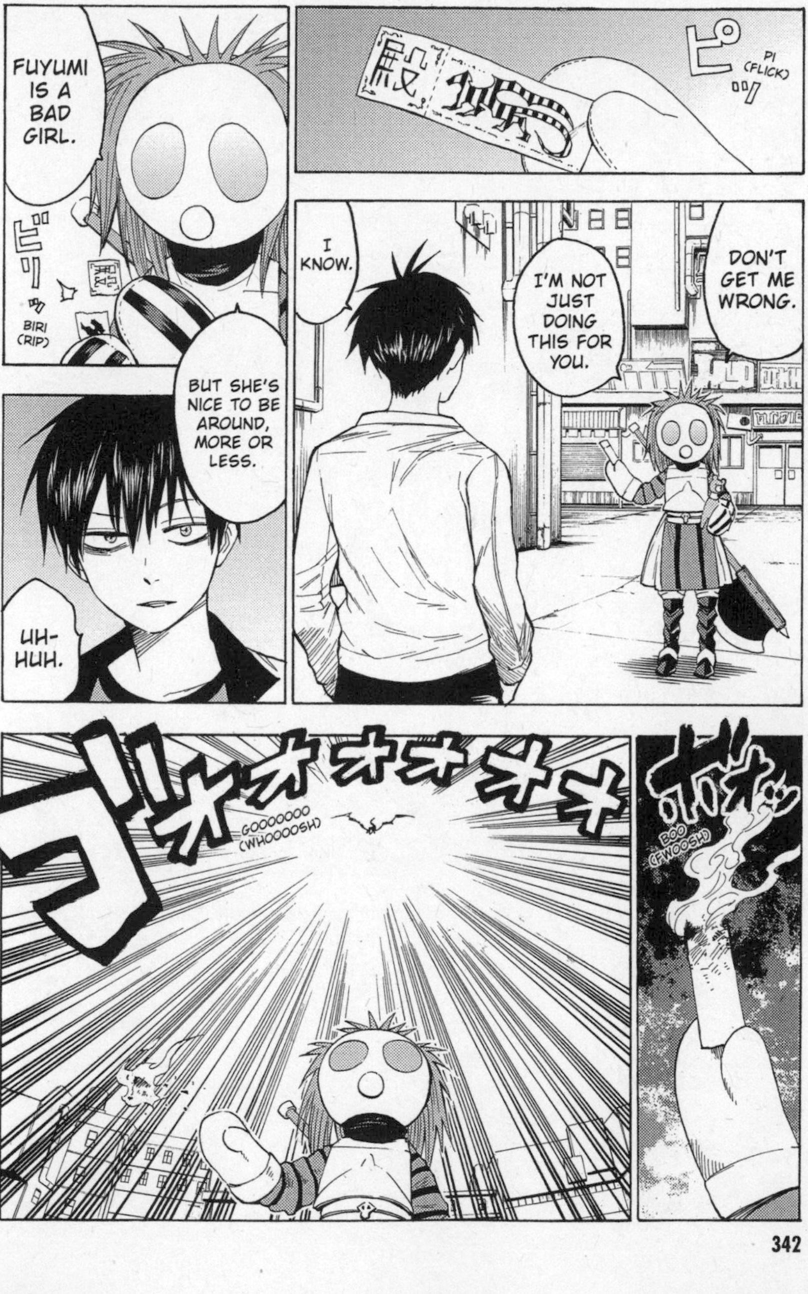

ピッ
PI (FLICK)
FUYUMI IS A BAD GIRL.
ビリッ
BIRI (RIP)
DON'T GET ME WRONG.
I'M NOT JUST DOING THIS FOR YOU.
I KNOW.
BUT SHE'S NICE TO BE AROUND, MORE OR LESS.
UH-HUH.
ボォッ
BOO (FWOOSH)
ゴォォォォォォ
GOOOOOOO (WHOOOOSH)

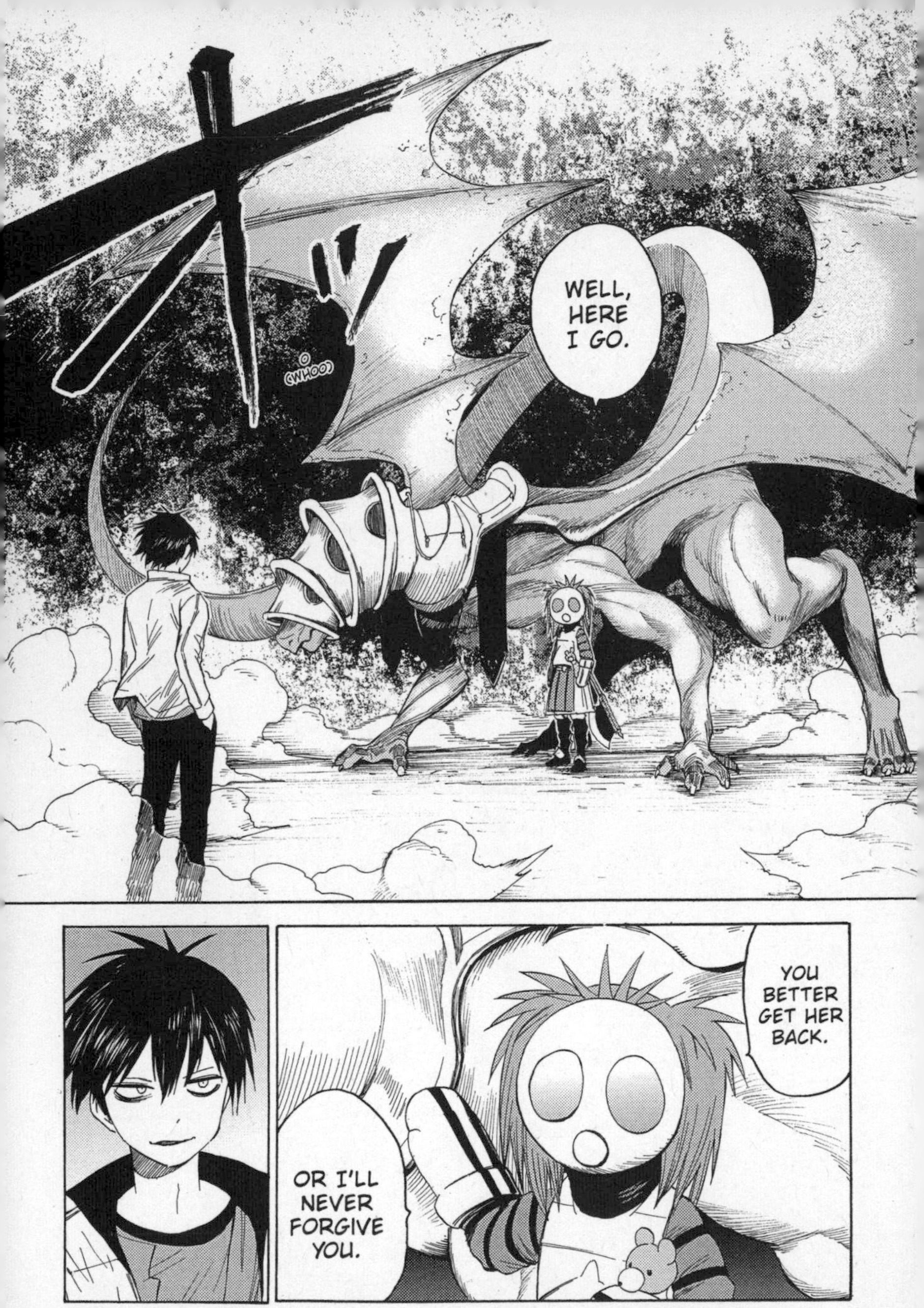
WELL, HERE I GO.
(WHOO)
YOU BETTER GET HER BACK.
OR I'LL NEVER FORGIVE YOU.

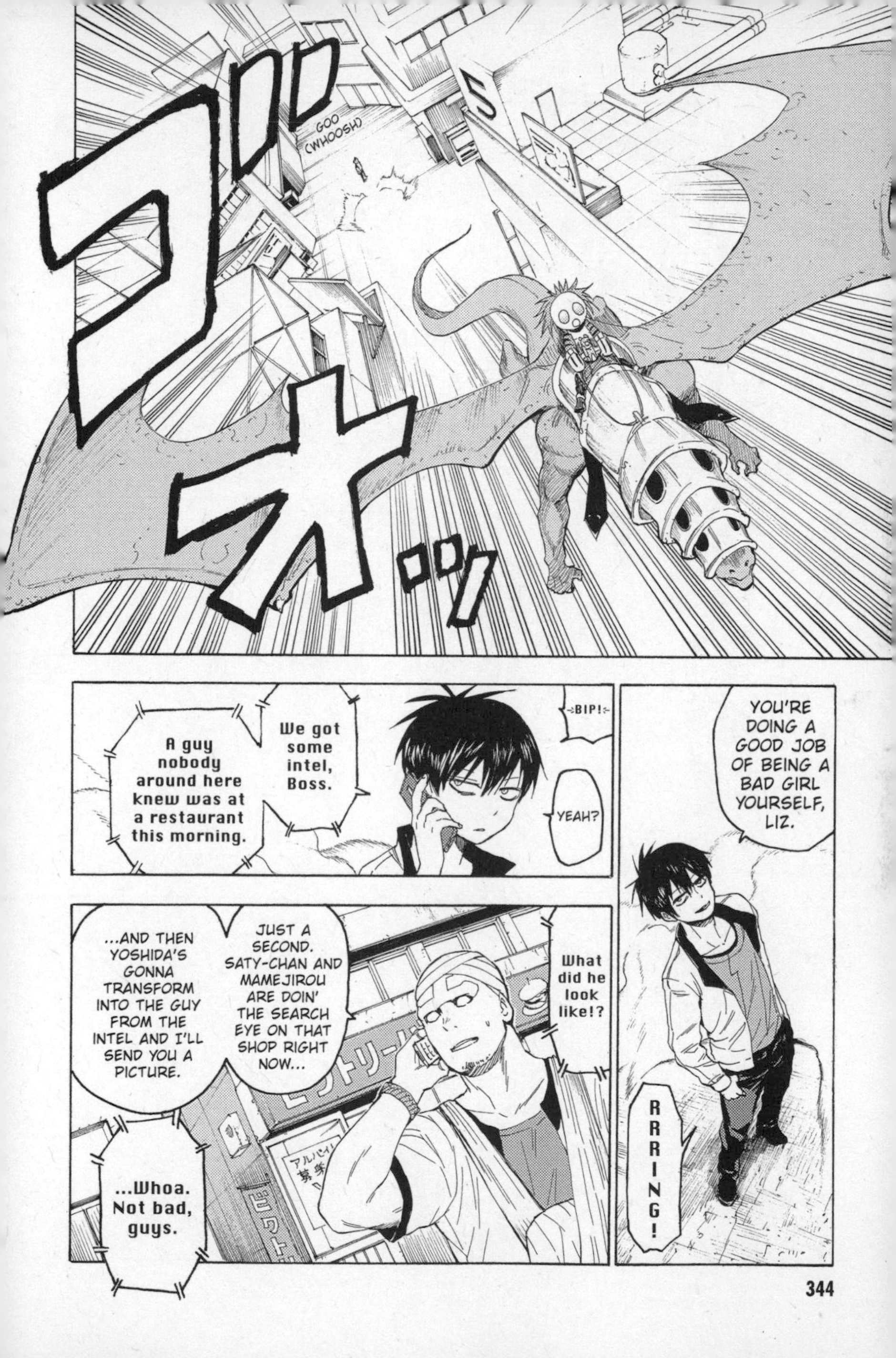
GOO (WHOOSH)
YOU'RE DOING A GOOD JOB OF BEING A BAD GIRL YOURSELF, LIZ.
RRRING!
BIP!
We got some intel, Boss.
YEAH?
A guy nobody around here knew was at a restaurant this morning.
What did he look like!?
JUST A SECOND. SATY-CHAN AND MAMEJIROU ARE DOIN' THE SEARCH EYE ON THAT SHOP RIGHT NOW...
...AND THEN YOSHIDA'S GONNA TRANSFORM INTO THE GUY FROM THE INTEL AND I'LL SEND YOU A PICTURE.
...Whoa. Not bad, guys.

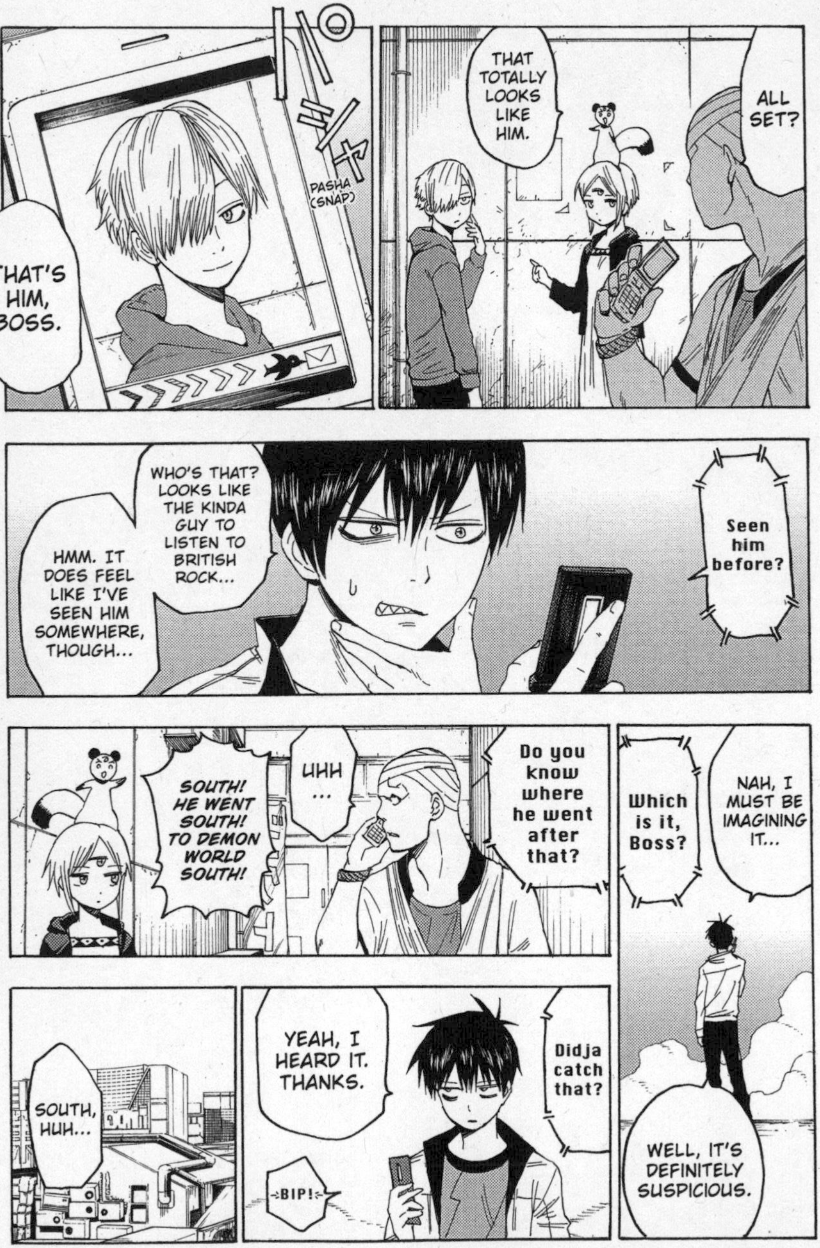
ALL SET?
THAT TOTALLY LOOKS LIKE HIM.
パシャ
PASHA (SNAP)
THAT'S HIM, BOSS.
Seen him before?
WHO'S THAT? LOOKS LIKE THE KINDA GUY TO LISTEN TO BRITISH ROCK...
HMM. IT DOES FEEL LIKE I'VE SEEN HIM SOMEWHERE, THOUGH...
NAH, I MUST BE IMAGINING IT...
Which is it, Boss?
WELL, IT'S DEFINITELY SUSPICIOUS.
Do you know where he went after that?
UHH ...
SOUTH! HE WENT SOUTH! TO DEMON WORLD SOUTH!
Didja catch that?
YEAH, I HEARD IT. THANKS.
BIP!
SOUTH, HUH...

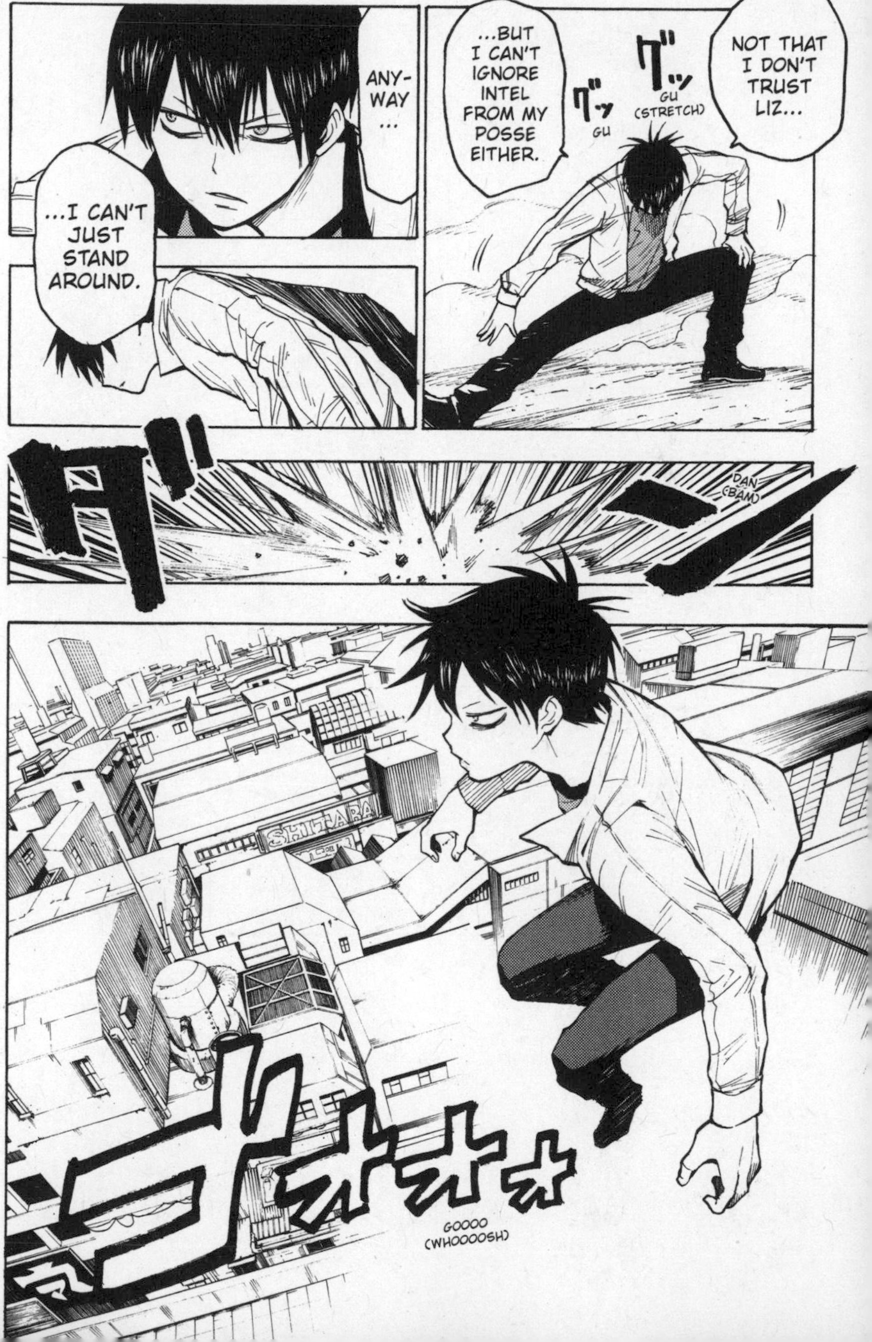
NOT THAT I DON'T TRUST LIZ...
GU (STRETCH)
...BUT I CAN'T IGNORE INTEL FROM MY POSSE EITHER.
GU
ANY-WAY ...
...I CAN'T JUST STAND AROUND.
DAN (BAM)
GOOOO (WHOOOOSH)

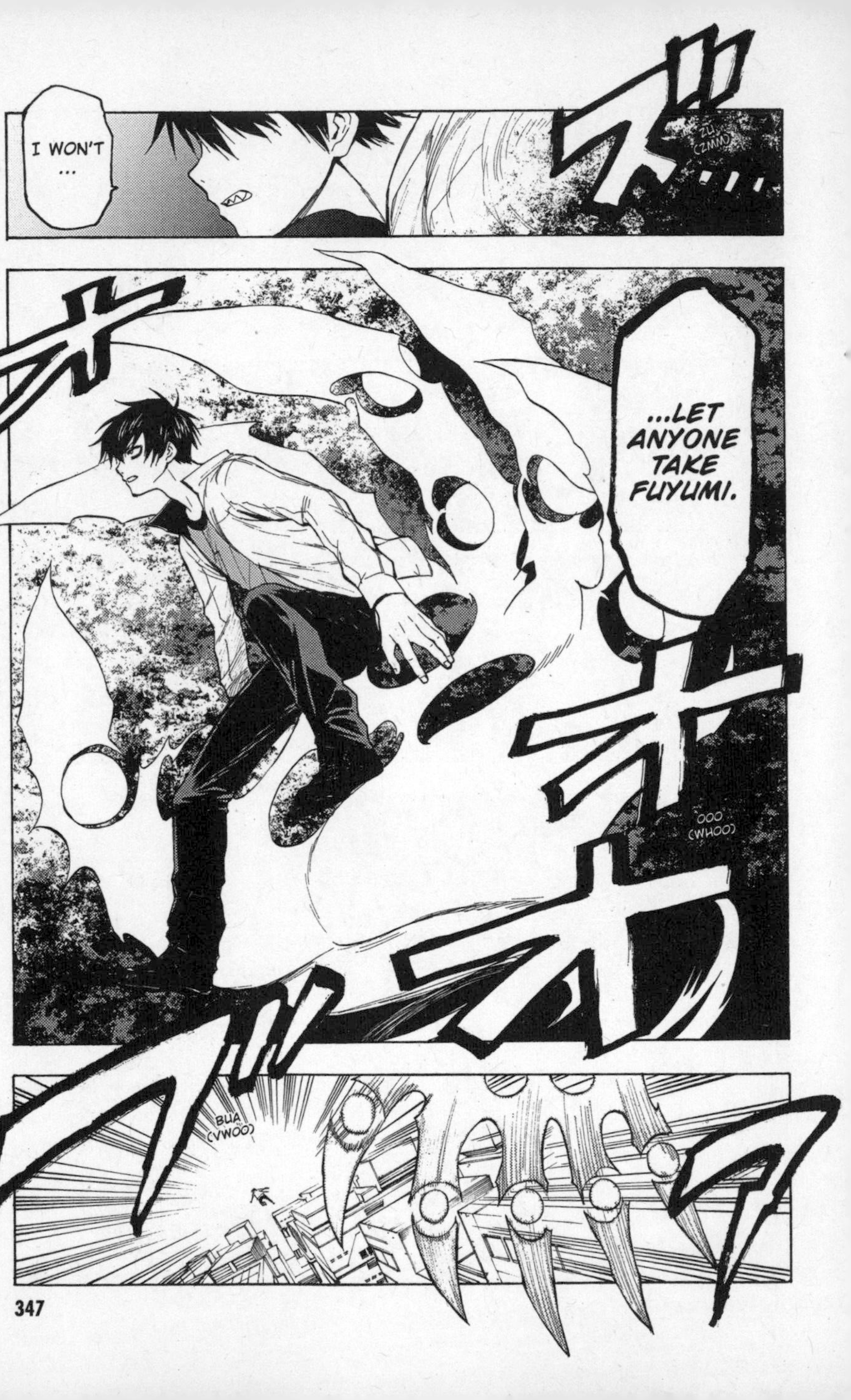
ZU... (ZMM)
I WON'T ...
...LET ANYONE TAKE FUYUMI.
OOO (WHOO)
BUA (VWOO)

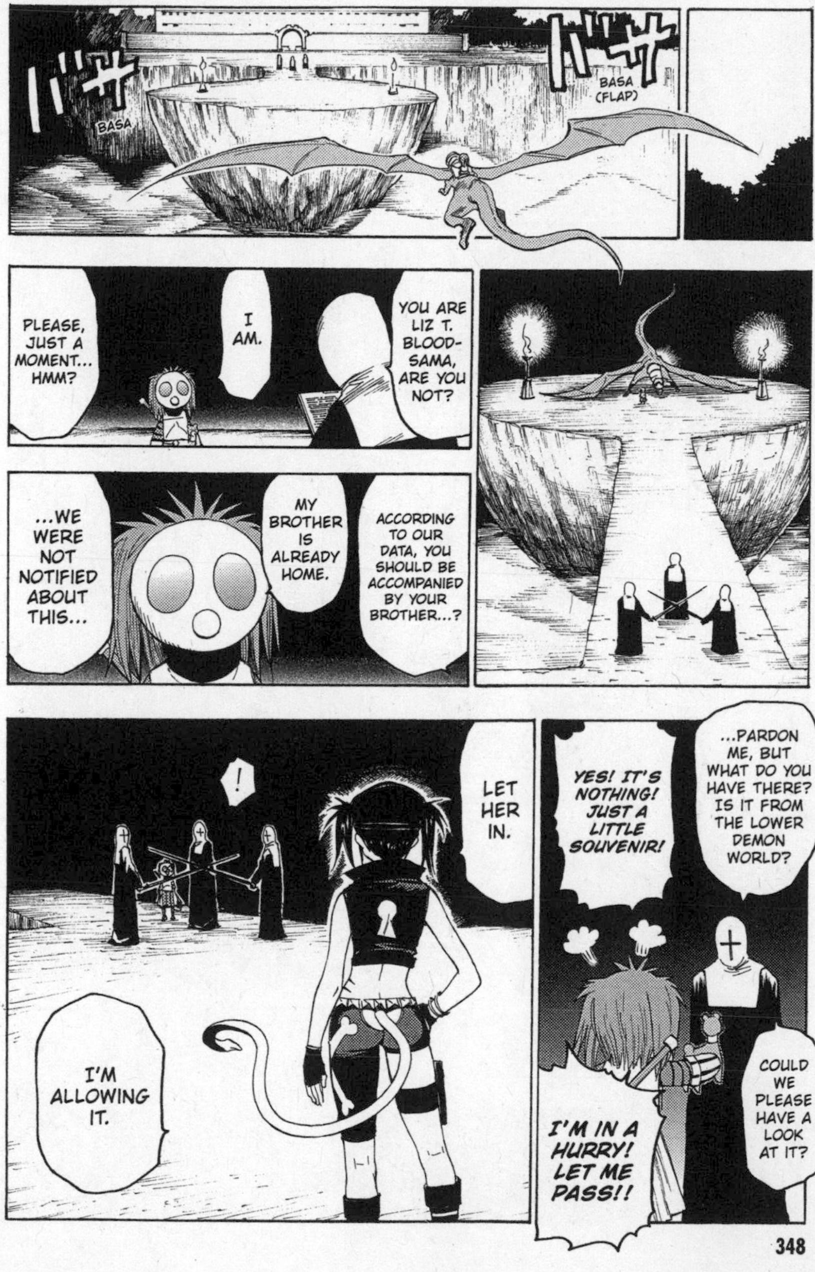
BASA (FLAP)
BASA
YOU ARE LIZ T. BLOOD-SAMA, ARE YOU NOT?
I AM.
PLEASE, JUST A MOMENT... HMM?
ACCORDING TO OUR DATA, YOU SHOULD BE ACCOMPANIED BY YOUR BROTHER...?
MY BROTHER IS ALREADY HOME.
...WE WERE NOT NOTIFIED ABOUT THIS...
...PARDON ME, BUT WHAT DO YOU HAVE THERE? IS IT FROM THE LOWER DEMON WORLD?
YES! IT'S NOTHING! JUST A LITTLE SOUVENIR!
COULD WE PLEASE HAVE A LOOK AT IT?
I'M IN A HURRY! LET ME PASS!!
LET HER IN.
!
I'M ALLOWING IT.

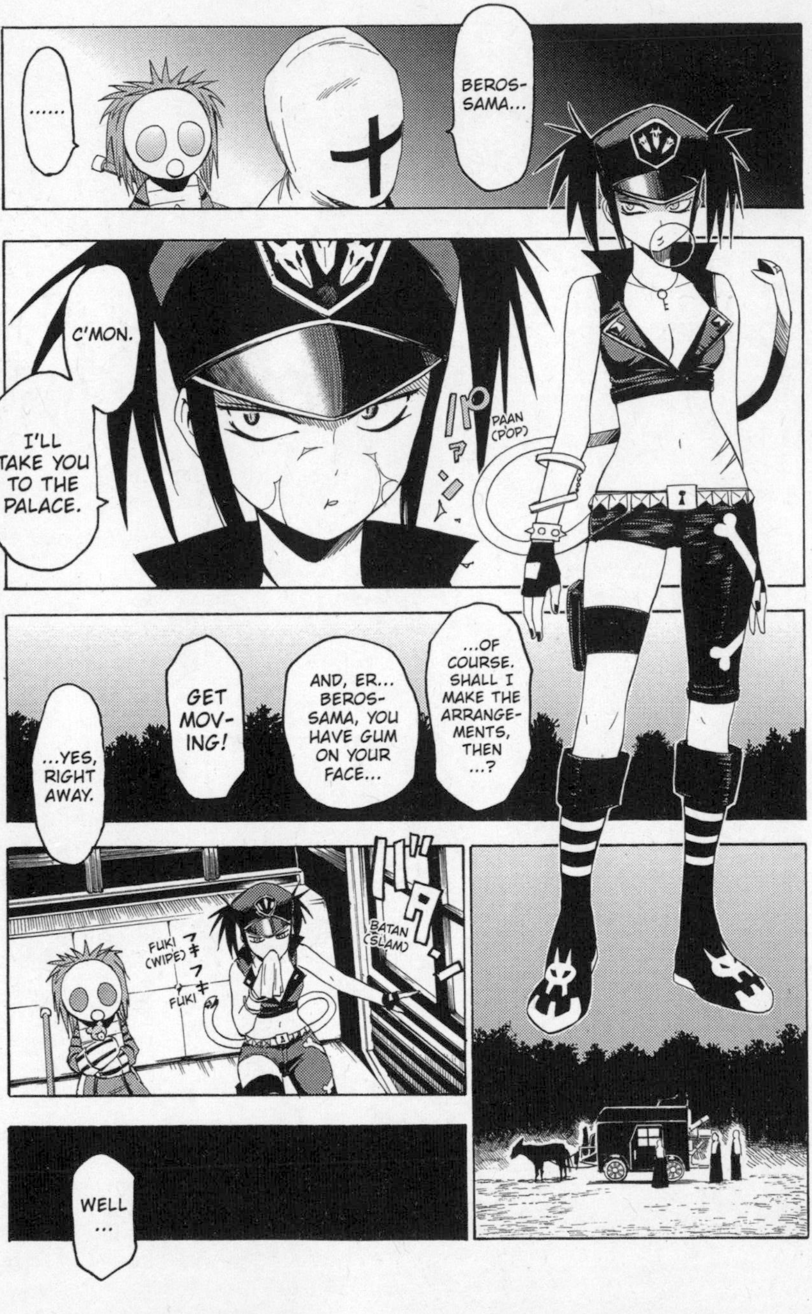
BEROS-SAMA...
......
C'MON.
I'LL TAKE YOU TO THE PALACE.
PAAN (POP)
...OF COURSE. SHALL I MAKE THE ARRANGEMENTS, THEN ...?
AND, ER... BEROS-SAMA, YOU HAVE GUM ON YOUR FACE...
GET MOVING!
...YES, RIGHT AWAY.
BATAN (SLAM)
FUKI (WIPE) フキ
フキ FUKI
WELL ...

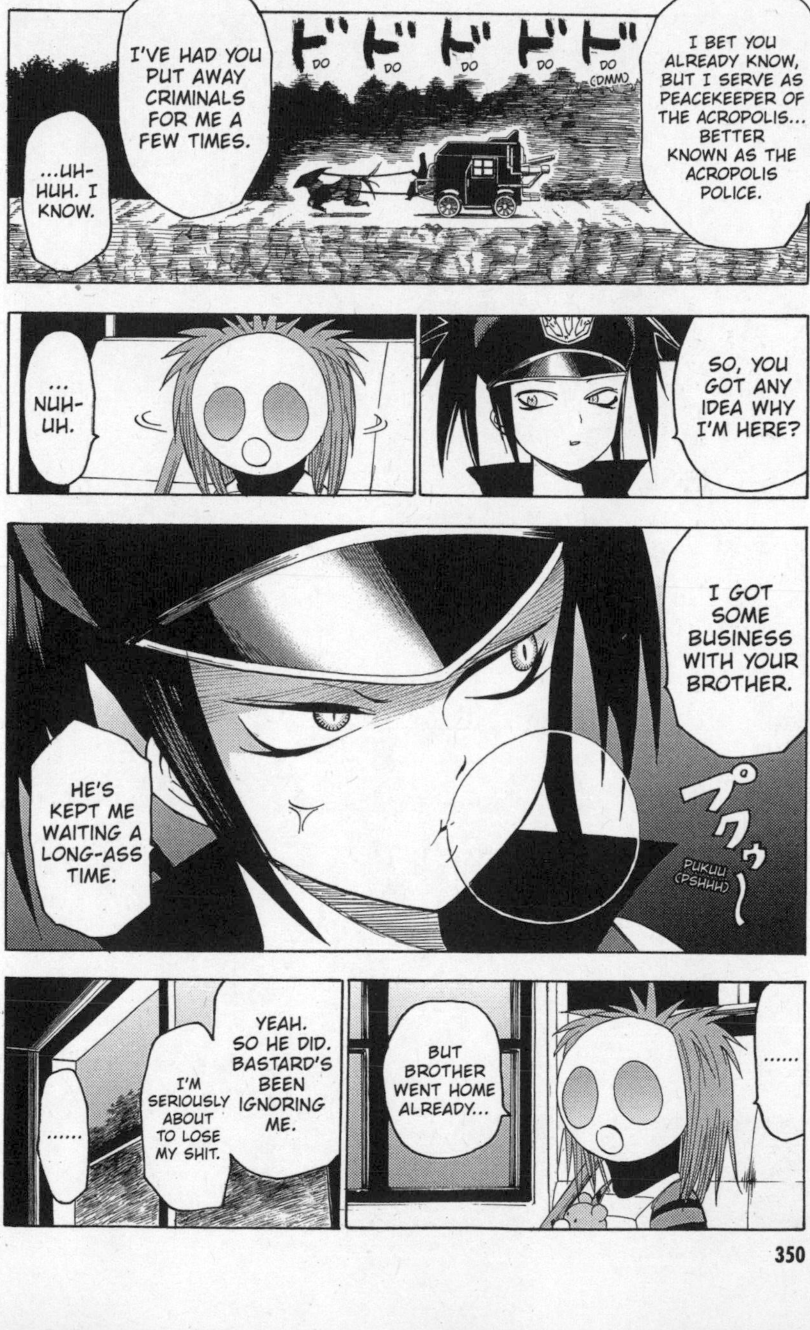
I BET YOU ALREADY KNOW, BUT I SERVE AS PEACEKEEPER OF THE ACROPOLIS... BETTER KNOWN AS THE ACROPOLIS POLICE.
ドドドドド
DO DO DO DO DO (DMM)
I'VE HAD YOU PUT AWAY CRIMINALS FOR ME A FEW TIMES.
...UH-HUH. I KNOW.
SO, YOU GOT ANY IDEA WHY I'M HERE?
... NUH-UH.
I GOT SOME BUSINESS WITH YOUR BROTHER.
プクゥ〜
PUKUU (PSHHH)
HE'S KEPT ME WAITING A LONG-ASS TIME.
......
BUT BROTHER WENT HOME ALREADY...
YEAH. SO HE DID. BASTARD'S BEEN IGNORING ME.
I'M SERIOUSLY ABOUT TO LOSE MY SHIT.
......

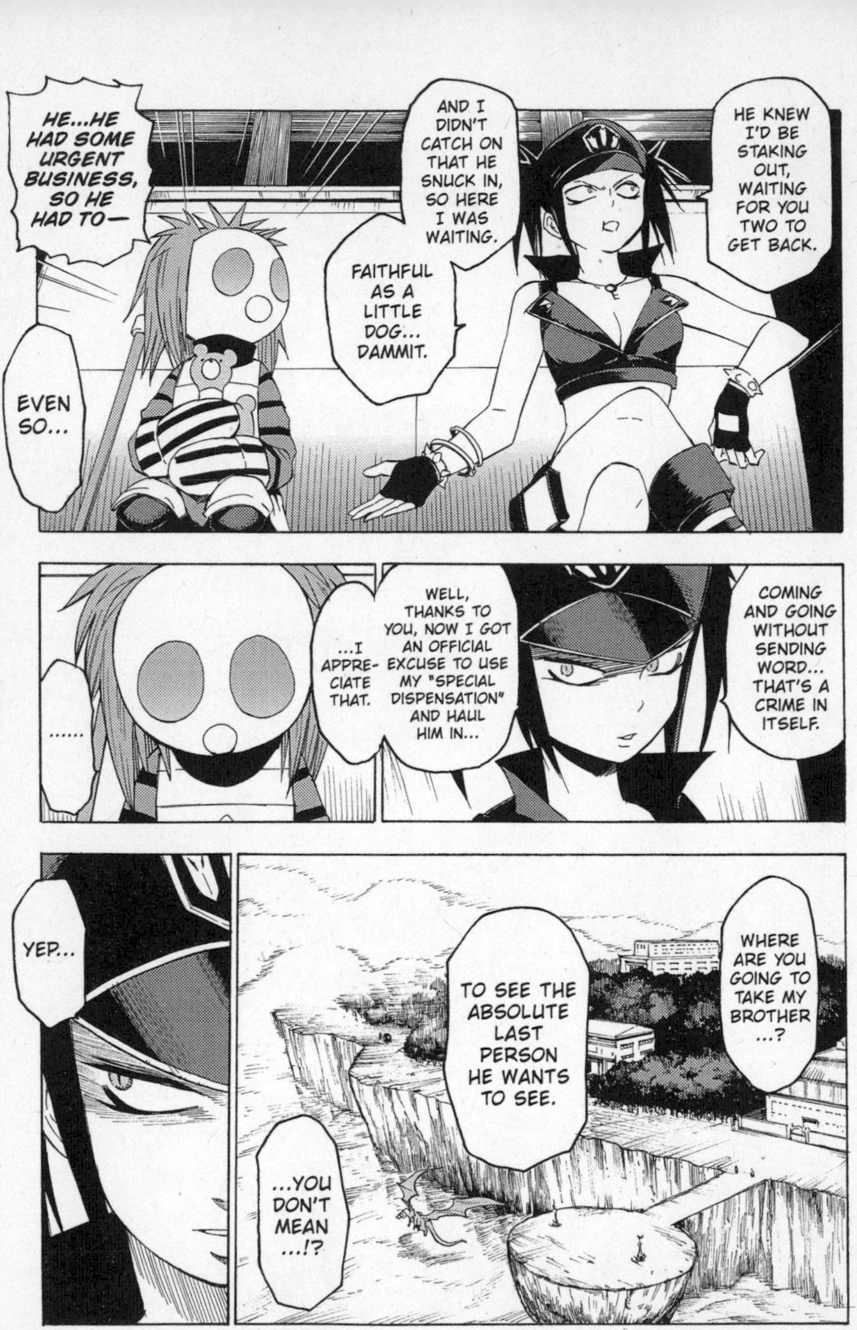
HE KNEW I'D BE STAKING OUT, WAITING FOR YOU TWO TO GET BACK.
AND I DIDN'T CATCH ON THAT HE SNUCK IN, SO HERE I WAS WAITING.
FAITHFUL AS A LITTLE DOG... DAMMIT.
HE...HE HAD SOME URGENT BUSINESS, SO HE HAD TO—
EVEN SO...
COMING AND GOING WITHOUT SENDING WORD... THAT'S A CRIME IN ITSELF.
WELL, THANKS TO YOU, NOW I GOT AN OFFICIAL EXCUSE TO USE MY "SPECIAL DISPENSATION" AND HAUL HIM IN...
...I APPRECIATE THAT.
......
WHERE ARE YOU GOING TO TAKE MY BROTHER ...?
TO SEE THE ABSOLUTE LAST PERSON HE WANTS TO SEE.
...YOU DON'T MEAN ...!?
YEP...

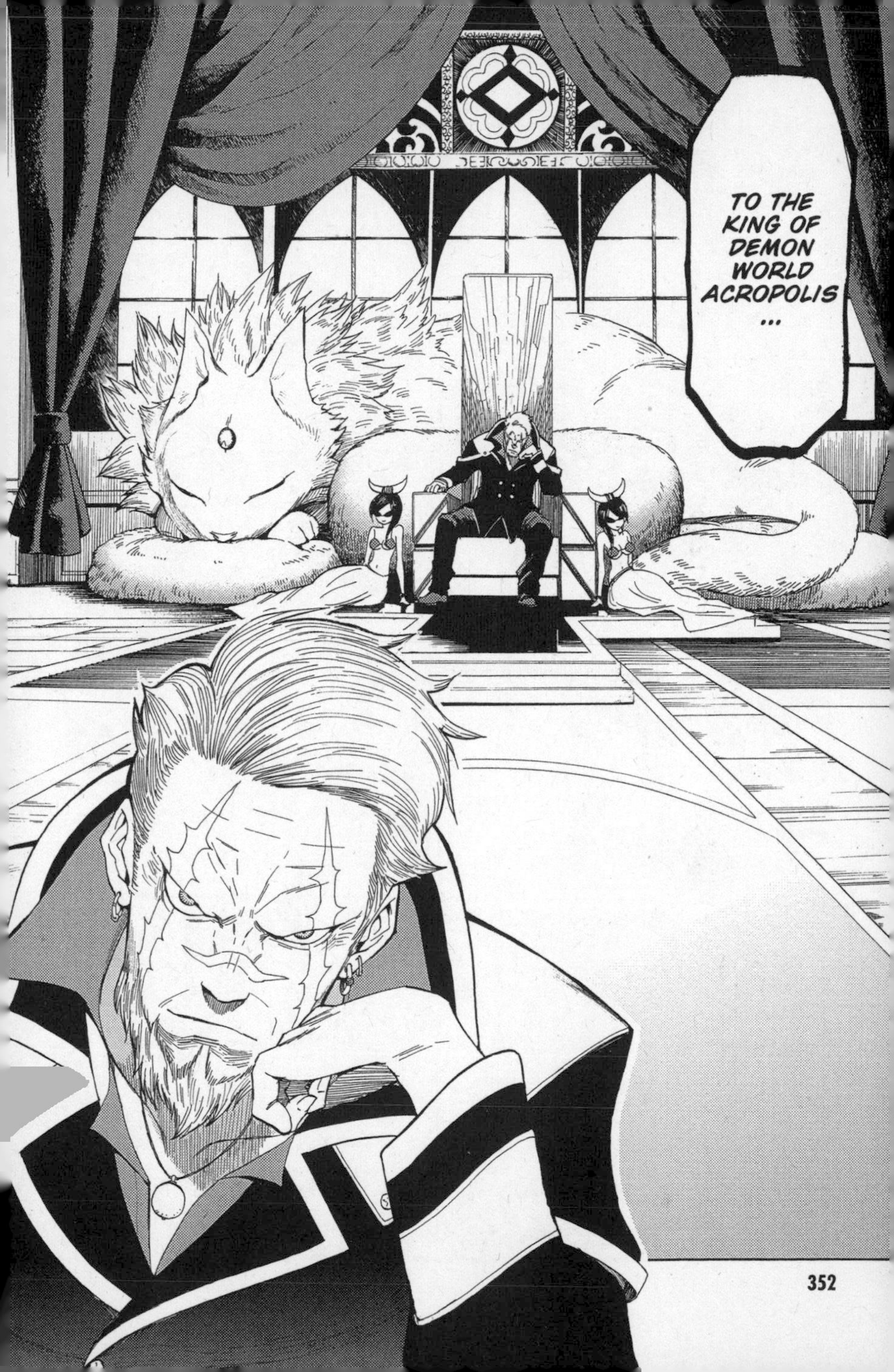
TO THE KING OF DEMON WORLD ACROPOLIS ...

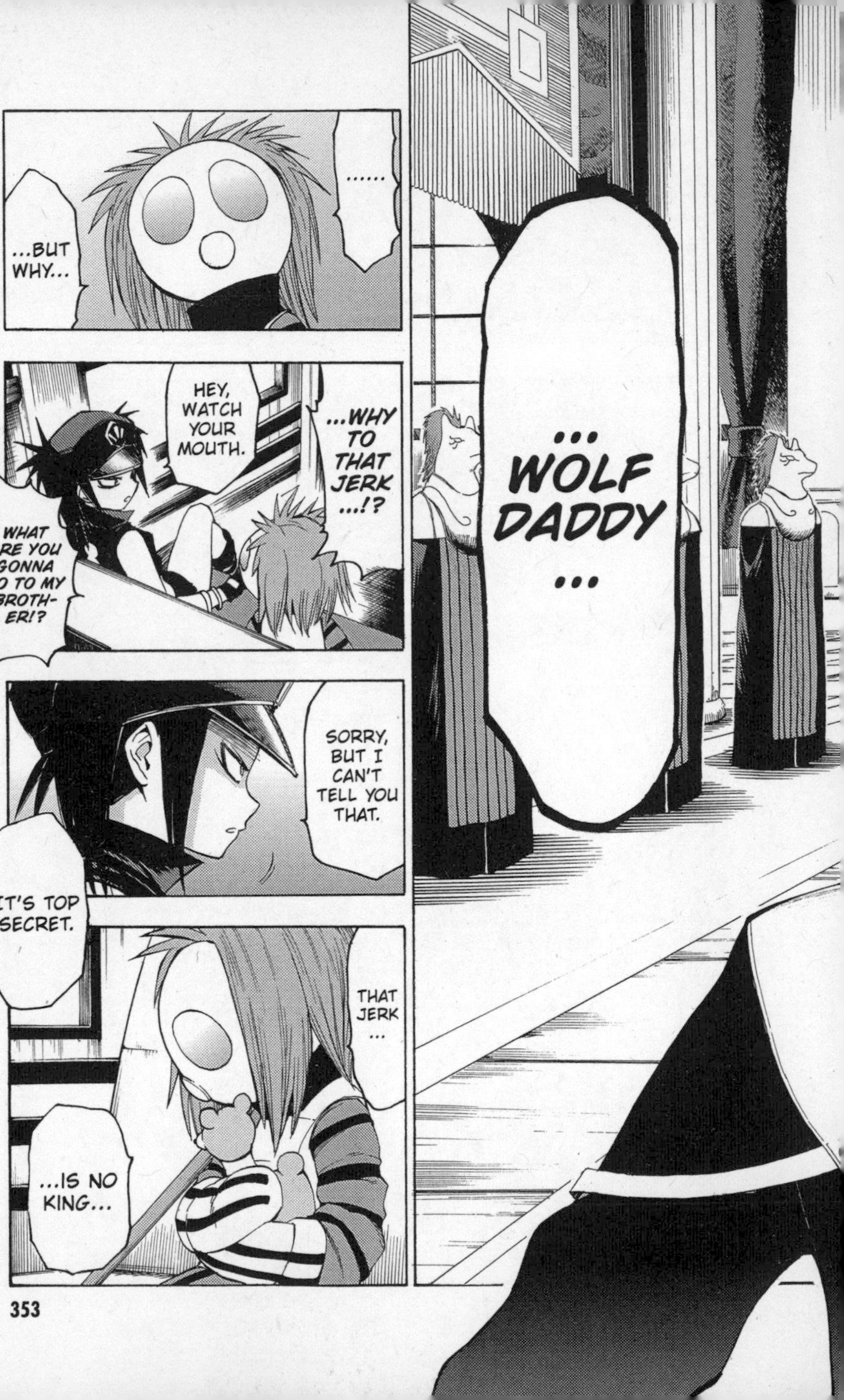
...WOLF DADDY...
......
...BUT WHY...
...WHY TO THAT JERK...!?
HEY, WATCH YOUR MOUTH.
WHAT ARE YOU GONNA DO TO MY BROTHER!?
SORRY, BUT I CAN'T TELL YOU THAT.
IT'S TOP SECRET.
THAT JERK...
...IS NO KING...

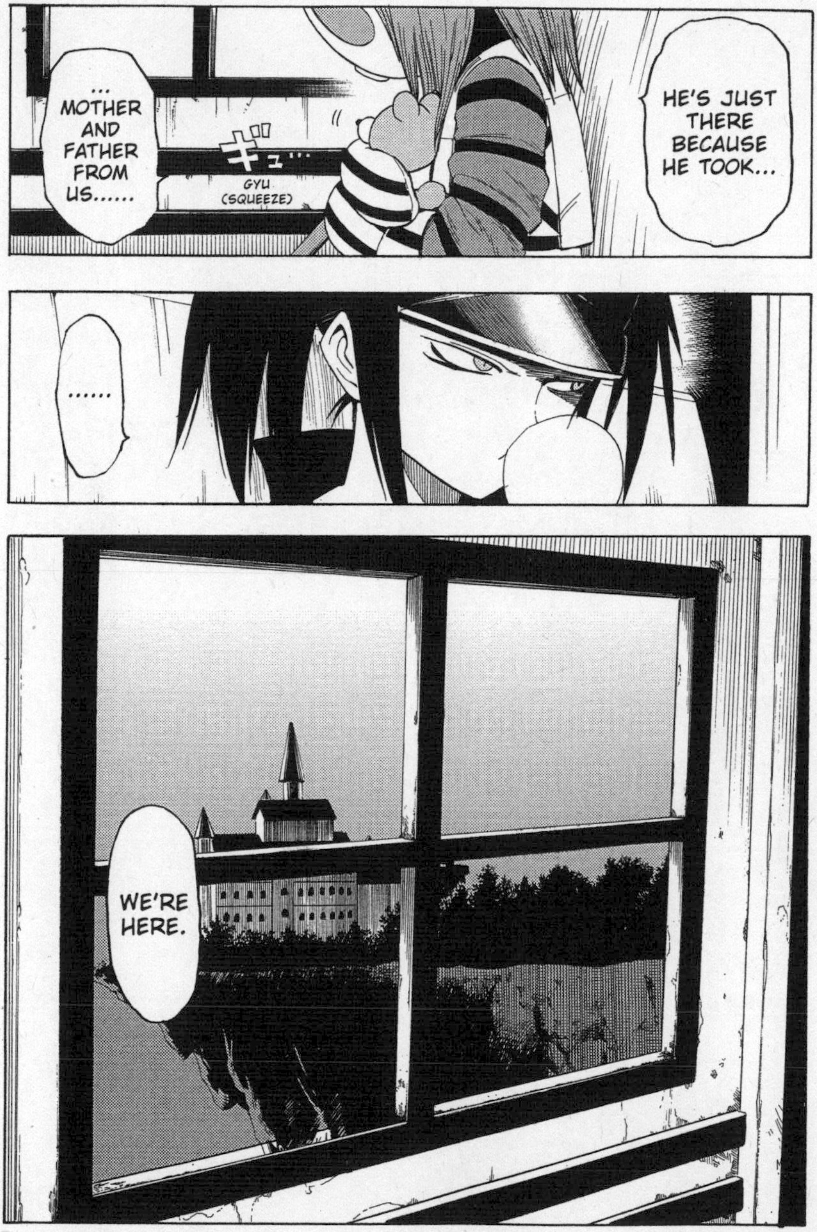
HE'S JUST THERE BECAUSE HE TOOK...
ギュ
GYU (SQUEEZE)
... MOTHER AND FATHER FROM US......
......
WE'RE HERE.

♠ To Be Continued ♠

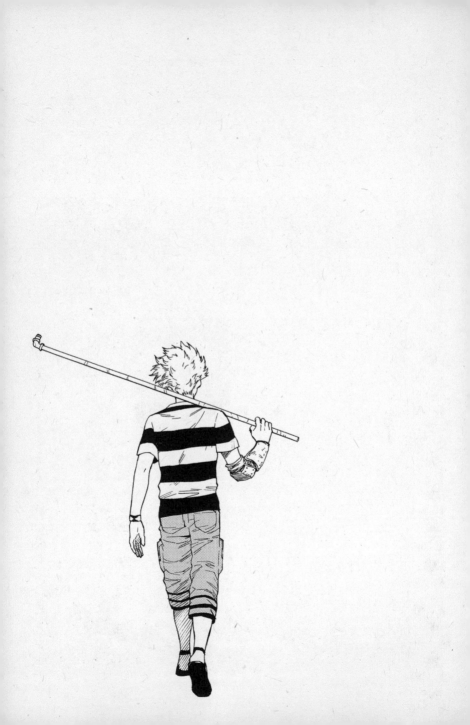

BLOOD LAD

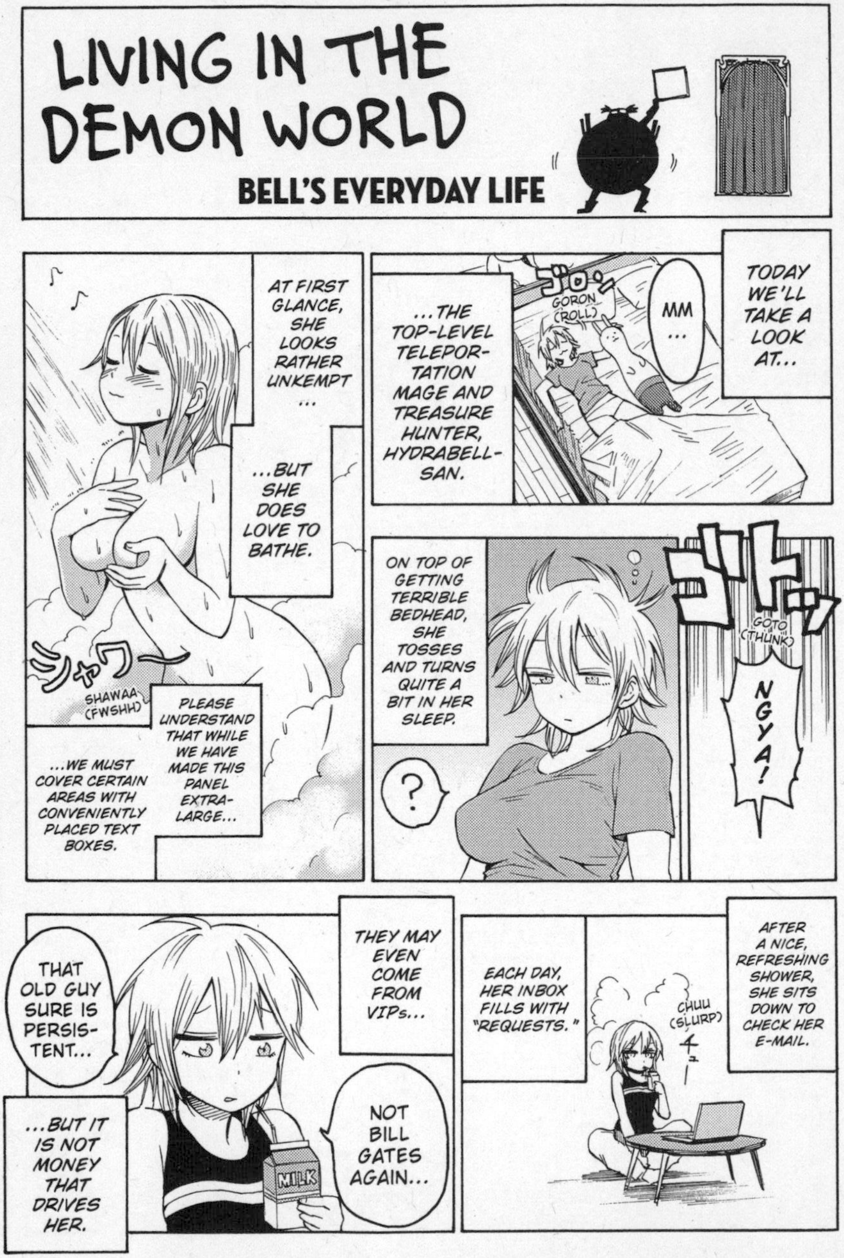
LIVING IN THE DEMON WORLD
BELL'S EVERYDAY LIFE
TODAY WE'LL TAKE A LOOK AT...
MM...
GORON (ROLL)
...THE TOP-LEVEL TELEPORTATION MAGE AND TREASURE HUNTER, HYDRABELL-SAN.
GOTO (THUNK)
NGYA!
ON TOP OF GETTING TERRIBLE BEDHEAD, SHE TOSSES AND TURNS QUITE A BIT IN HER SLEEP.
?
AT FIRST GLANCE, SHE LOOKS RATHER UNKEMPT...
...BUT SHE DOES LOVE TO BATHE.
SHAWAA (FWSHH)
PLEASE UNDERSTAND THAT WHILE WE HAVE MADE THIS PANEL EXTRA-LARGE...
...WE MUST COVER CERTAIN AREAS WITH CONVENIENTLY PLACED TEXT BOXES.
AFTER A NICE, REFRESHING SHOWER, SHE SITS DOWN TO CHECK HER E-MAIL.
CHUU (SLURP)
EACH DAY, HER INBOX FILLS WITH "REQUESTS."
THEY MAY EVEN COME FROM VIPs...
THAT OLD GUY SURE IS PERSISTENT...
NOT BILL GATES AGAIN...
MILK
...BUT IT IS NOT MONEY THAT DRIVES HER.

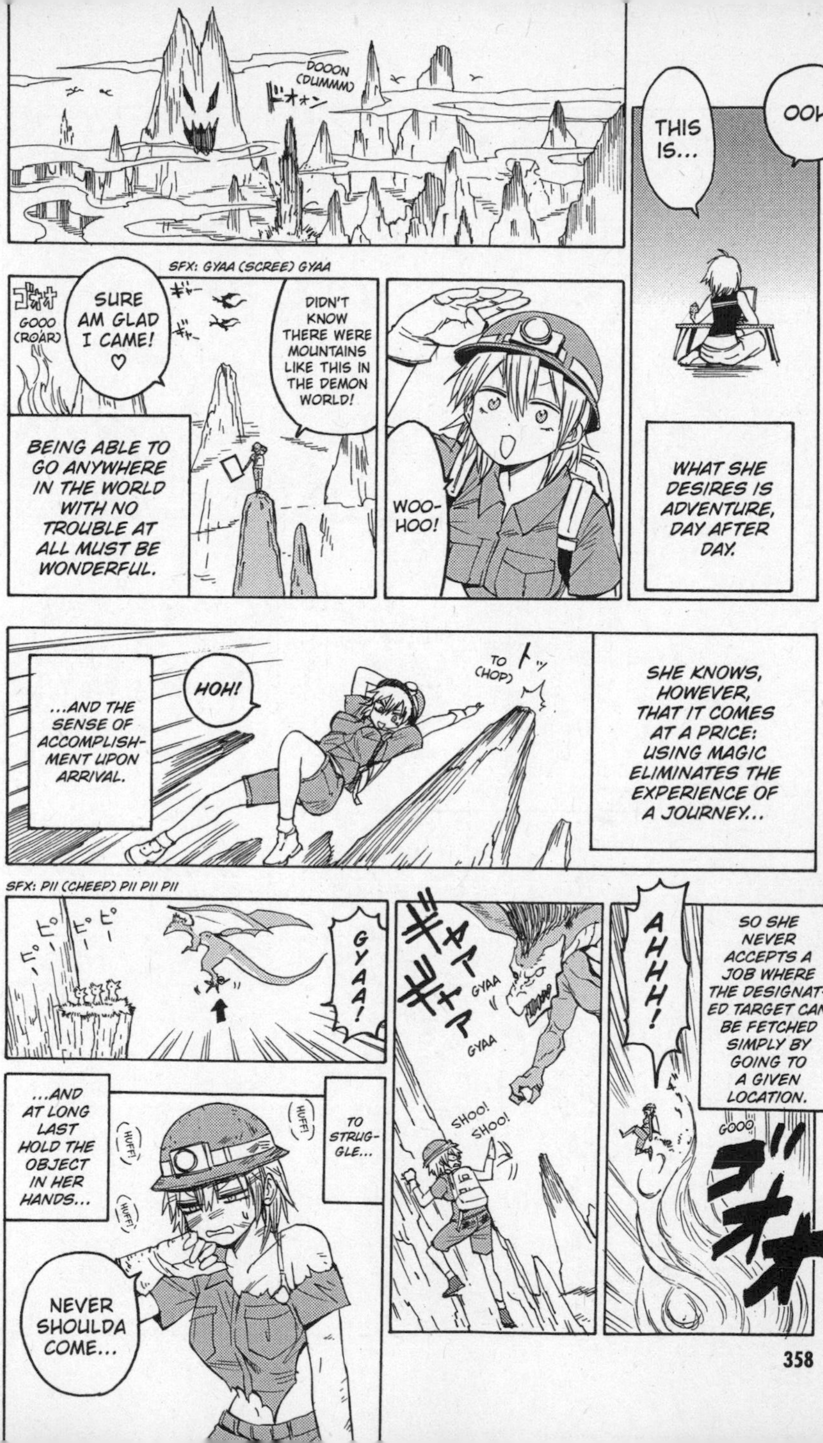
OOH.
THIS IS...
WHAT SHE DESIRES IS ADVENTURE, DAY AFTER DAY.
DOOON (DUMMM)
ドオォン
DIDN'T KNOW THERE WERE MOUNTAINS LIKE THIS IN THE DEMON WORLD!
WOO-HOO!
SFX: GYAA (SCREE) GYAA
ギャー
ギャー
SURE AM GLAD I CAME! ♡
ゴォオ
GOOO (ROAR)
BEING ABLE TO GO ANYWHERE IN THE WORLD WITH NO TROUBLE AT ALL MUST BE WONDERFUL.
SHE KNOWS, HOWEVER, THAT IT COMES AT A PRICE: USING MAGIC ELIMINATES THE EXPERIENCE OF A JOURNEY...
トッ
TO (HOP)
HOH!
...AND THE SENSE OF ACCOMPLISHMENT UPON ARRIVAL.
SO SHE NEVER ACCEPTS A JOB WHERE THE DESIGNATED TARGET CAN BE FETCHED SIMPLY BY GOING TO A GIVEN LOCATION.
AHHH!
GOOO
ゴオオ
ギャアギャア
GYAA
GYAA
SHOO! SHOO!
TO STRUGGLE...
SFX: PII (CHEEP) PII PII PII
ピ ピ ピ ピ
GYAA!
...AND AT LONG LAST HOLD THE OBJECT IN HER HANDS...
HUFF!
HUFF!
HUFF!
NEVER SHOULDA COME...

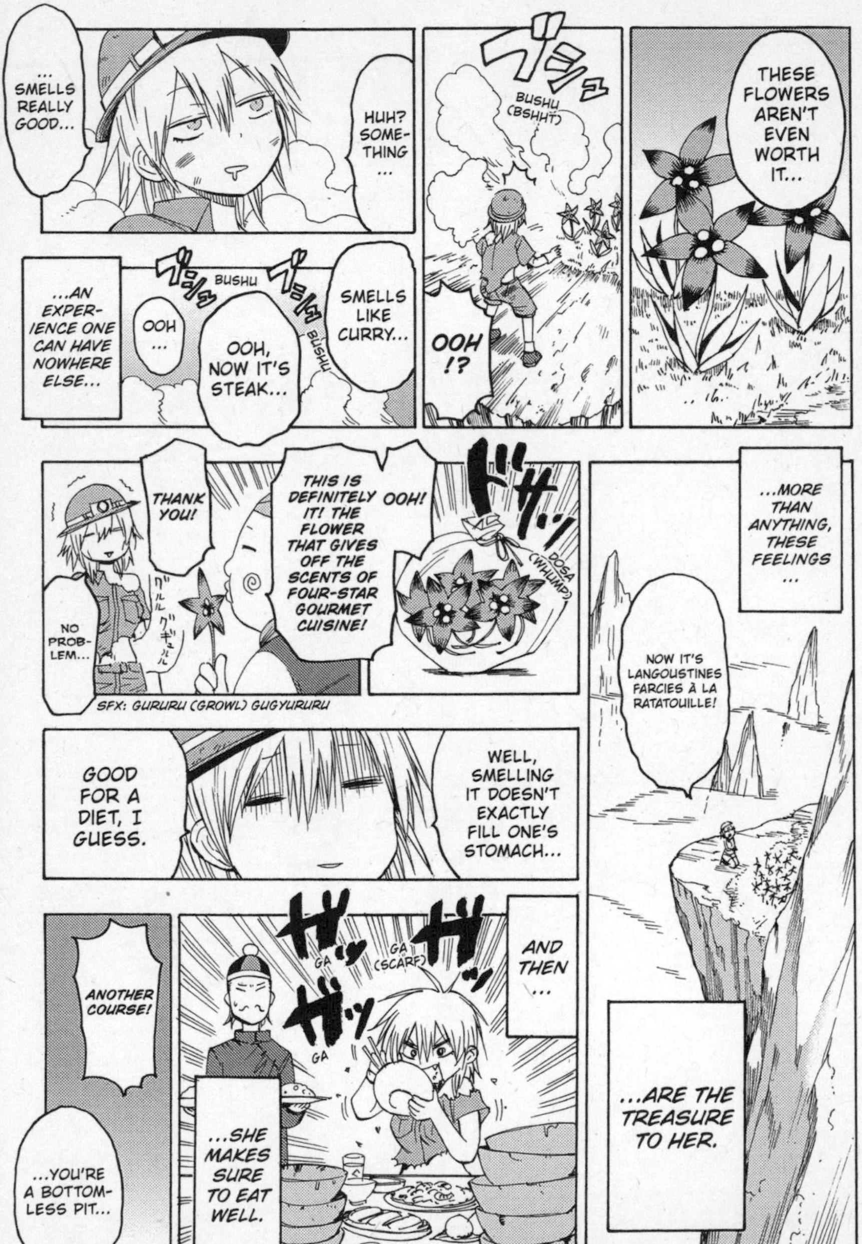
THESE FLOWERS AREN'T EVEN WORTH IT...
BUSHU (BSHHT)
OOH!?
HUH? SOME-THING...
...SMELLS REALLY GOOD...
SMELLS LIKE CURRY...
BUSHU
OOH, NOW IT'S STEAK...
BUSHU
OOH...
...AN EXPER-IENCE ONE CAN HAVE NOWHERE ELSE...
...MORE THAN ANYTHING, THESE FEELINGS...
NOW IT'S LANGOUSTINES FARCIES À LA RATATOUILLE!
...ARE THE TREASURE TO HER.
DOSA (WHUMP)
OOH!
THIS IS DEFINITELY IT! THE FLOWER THAT GIVES OFF THE SCENTS OF FOUR-STAR GOURMET CUISINE!
THANK YOU!
NO PROB-LEM...
SFX: GURURU (GROWL) GUGYURURU
WELL, SMELLING IT DOESN'T EXACTLY FILL ONE'S STOMACH...
GOOD FOR A DIET, I GUESS.
AND THEN...
GA (SCARF)
GA
GA
...SHE MAKES SURE TO EAT WELL.
ANOTHER COURSE!
...YOU'RE A BOTTOM-LESS PIT...

END

BLOOD LAD 3

These images appeared under the jackets of the original editions of *Blood Lad*!

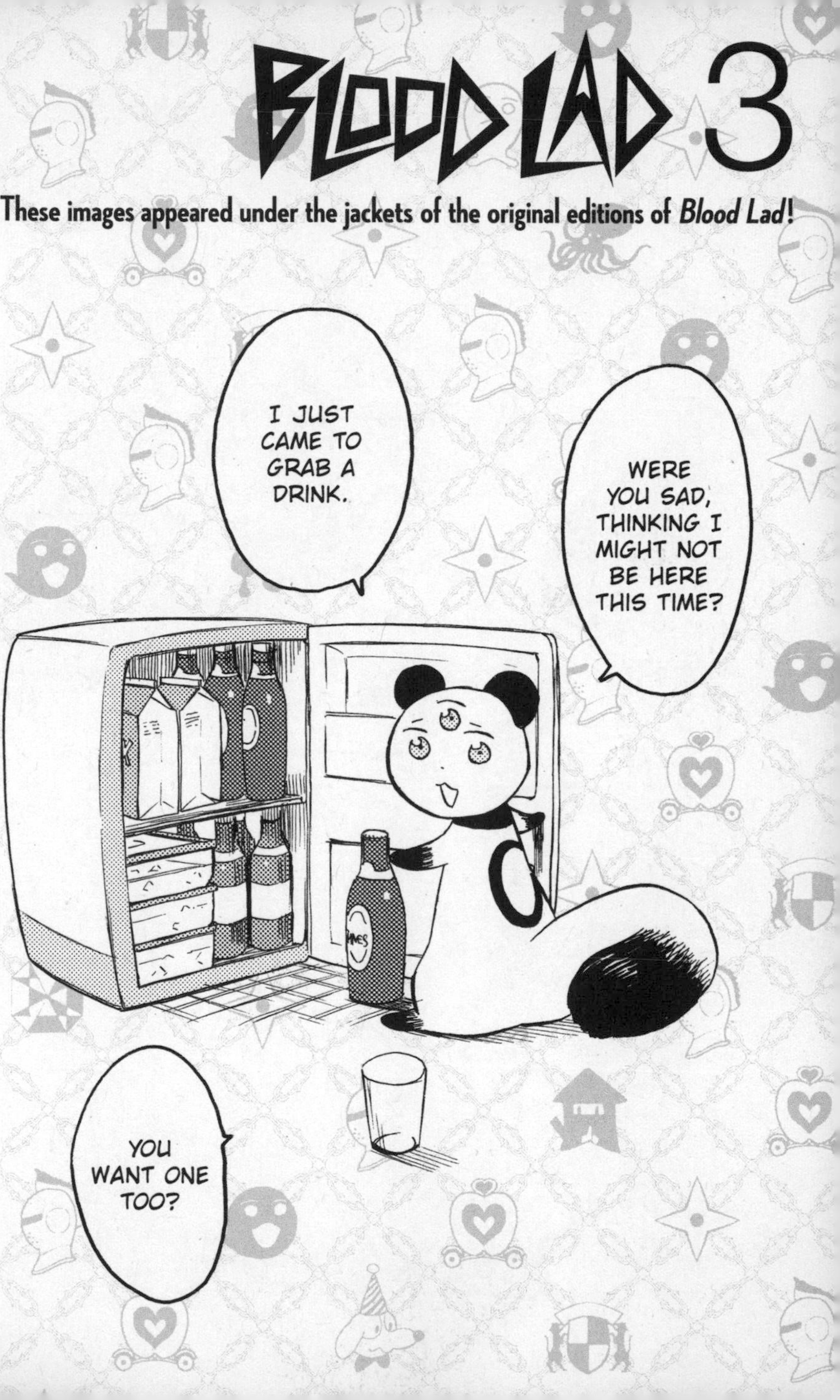
WERE YOU SAD, THINKING I MIGHT NOT BE HERE THIS TIME?
I JUST CAME TO GRAB A DRINK.
YOU WANT ONE TOO?

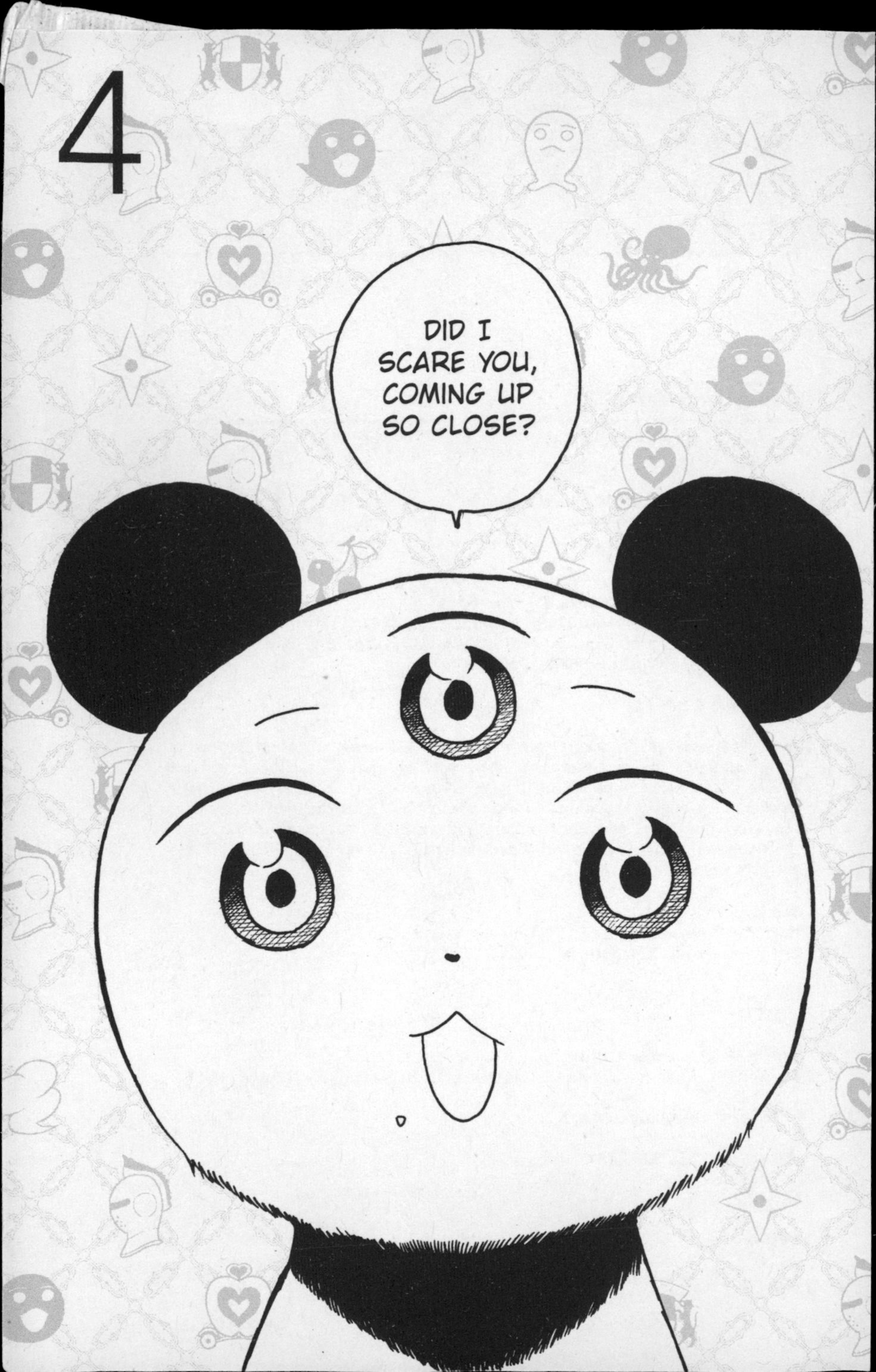
4
DID I SCARE YOU, COMING UP SO CLOSE?

BLOOD LAD 2

YUUKI KODAMA

Translation: Melissa Tanaka

Lettering: Alexis Eckerman

BLOOD LAD Volumes 3 and 4 © Yuuki KODAMA 2011.
Edited by KADOKAWA SHOTEN
First published in Japan in 2010 by KADOKAWA CORPORATION, Tokyo. English translation rights arranged with KADOKAWA CORPORATION, Tokyo, through TUTTLE-MORI AGENCY, INC., Tokyo.

Translation © 2013 by Hachette Book Group, Inc.

Yen Press
Hachette Book Group
237 Park Avenue, New York, NY 10017

www.HachetteBookGroup.com
www.YenPress.com

Yen Press is an imprint of Hachette Book Group, Inc.
The Yen Press name and logo are trademarks of Hachette Book Group, Inc.

First Yen Press Edition: March 2013

ISBN: 978-0-316-22898-5

10 9 8 7 6 5 4

BVG

Printed in the United States of America